Development in Infancy

This topically organized text provides a comprehensive overview of infant development with a strong theoretical and research base. Readers gain a clear understanding of infant development and issues that will be the focus of significant advances in infancy studies in the future. The new fifth edition reflects the enormous changes in the field that have occurred over the past decade. The thoroughly revised chapters emphasize work from the 21st century, although classic references are retained, and explore contextual, methodological, neurological, physical, perceptual, cognitive, communicative, emotional, and social facets of infant development. The fifth edition features a more accessible style and an enhanced pedagogical and teaching resource program.

This extensively revised edition features a number of changes:

- An enhanced pedagogical program features orienting questions at the beginning of each chapter and bold face key terms listed at the end of the chapter and defined in the glossary to help facilitate understanding and learning.
- Two new boxes in each chapter—*Science in Translation* illustrates applied issues and *Set for Life* highlights the significance of infancy for later development.
- Increased emphasis on practical applications and social policy.
- More graphs, tables, and photos that explain important concepts and findings.
- Literature reviews are thoroughly updated and reflect contemporary research.
- All new teaching web resources—Instructors will find PowerPoints, electronic versions of the text figures, and a test bank, and students will find hyperlinked references and electronic versions of the key concepts and the definitions.

Intended for advanced undergraduate or beginning graduate courses on infant (and toddler) development, or infancy or early child development taught in departments of psychology, human development and family studies, education, nursing, social work, and anthropology, this book also appeals to social service providers, policy makers, and clergy who work with community institutions. Prerequisites include introductory courses on child development and general psychology.

service providers, policy makers, and clergy who work with community institutions. Prerequisites include introductory courses on child development and general psychology.

Marc H. Bornstein is Senior Investigator and Head of Child and Family Research at the Eunice Kennedy Shriver National Institute of Child Health and Human Development and Editor of *Parenting: Science and Practice*.

Martha E. Arterberry is Professor of Psychology at Colby College, Maine.

Michael E. Lamb is Professor of Psychology at the University of Cambridge, UK.

Development in Infancy

A Contemporary Introduction
Fifth edition

Marc H. Bornstein
Martha E. Arterberry
Michael E. Lamb

Psychology Press
Taylor & Francis Group

NEW YORK AND LONDON

Please visit the eResources site at www.psypress.com/9780805863635

First published 2014
by Psychology Press
711 Third Avenue
New York, NY 10017

Simultaneously published in the UK
by Psychology Press
27 Church Road
Hove, East Sussex BN3 2FA

Library of Congress Cataloging in Publication Data
  Bornstein, Marc H. Development in infancy : a contemporary introduction.—
  Fifth edition / Marc H. Bornstein, Martha E. Arterberry, Michael E. Lamb.
  pages cm
  1. Infants—Development. 2. Infant psychology.
  I. Arterberry, Martha E. II. Lamb, Michael E., 1953–
  III. Title.
  RJ134.B67
  2014305.232—dc23
  2013000894

ISBN: 978–1–84872–658–1 (hbk)
ISBN: 978–0–8058–6363–5 (pbk)
ISBN: 978–0–203–75847–2 (ebk)

Typeset in Times New Roman
by Swales & Willis Ltd, Exeter, Devon

Printed and bound in the United States of America
by Edwards Brothers, Inc.

To those who kindled our scholarly interests:
Mary Ainsworth, William Kessen, Philip Kellman,
Hanuš Papoušek, and Albert Yonas

Brief Contents

Detailed Contents

Boxes

Figures

Tables

About the Authors

Marc H. Bornstein is Senior Investigator and Head of Child and Family Research at the Eunice Kennedy Shriver National Institute of Child Health and Human Development. He holds a B.A. from Columbia College, M.S. and Ph.D. degrees from Yale University, and an honorary doctorate from the University of Padua. Bornstein was a J. S. Guggenheim Foundation Fellow and a recipient of a Research Career Development Award from the National Institute of Child Health and Human Development. He also has received a number of awards including the B. R. McCandless Young Scientist Award and the G. Stanley Hall Award from the American Psychological Association, and the Distinguished International Contributions to Child Development Award from the Society for Research in Child Development. Bornstein has held faculty positions at Princeton University and New York University. He has published in experimental, methodological, comparative, developmental, and cultural science as well as neuroscience, pediatrics, and aesthetics. Bornstein is Editor Emeritus of *Child Development* and founding Editor of *Parenting: Science and Practice*, and he is co-author of *Development: Infancy through Adolescence, Lifespan Development, Developmental Science: An Advanced Textbook, 6th Edition*, and *Perceiving Similarity and Comprehending Metaphor*. For more information about Dr. Bornstein visit www.cfr.nichd.nih.gov and www.tandfonline.com/HPAR.

Martha E. Arterberry is Professor of Psychology at Colby College, Maine. She received her B.A. from Pomona College and her Ph.D. from the University of Minnesota. She previously was Professor of Psychology at Gettysburg College, Pennsylvania, and she is a collaborative investigator at the Child and Family Research Section of the Eunice Kennedy Shriver National Institute of Child Health and Human Development. Arterberry currently serves as a consulting editor for *Developmental Psychology,* and she is a co-author of *The Cradle of Knowledge: Development of Perception in Infancy*. Her research interests in perceptual and cognitive development include the study of depth perception, three-dimensional object perception, categorization, and memory.

Michael E. Lamb is Professor of Psychology at the University of Cambridge. He received his Ph.D. from Yale University and honorary doctorates from the Universities of Goteborg Sweden and East Anglia. Lamb has written many professional articles on social and emotional development, especially in infancy and early childhood; the development and importance of mother– and father–child relationships; the determinants and consequences of adaptive and maladaptive parental behavior; children's testimony; and applied developmental psychology. He is the co-author of several books, including *Infant–Mother Attachment*, *Investigative Interviews of Children*, and *Tell Me What Happened: Structured Investigative Interviews of Child Victims and Witnesses*. He has also edited several books on fathers and father–child relationships, including *The Role of the Father in Child Development*. His most recent books include *Developmental Science: An Advanced Textbook, 6th edition*, *The Handbook of Lifespan Development*, *Children's Testimony*, and *Children and Cross-Examination: Time to Change the Rules?* He currently edits the American Psychological Association journal, *Psychology, Public Policy, and Law*. The Association for Psychological Science awarded Lamb the James McKeen Cattell Award for Lifetime Contributions to Applied Psychological Research. For more information, visit http://www.psychol.cam.ac.uk/people/mel37@cam.ac.uk.

Preface

Philosophers beginning before Plato speculated about the significance of infancy, but it was not until the late 19th and early 20th centuries that scientific observations of infants and theoretical speculations about infants began in earnest. Charles Darwin and Sigmund Freud were largely responsible for these initiatives. In the middle of the 20th century the scientific study of infancy elicited widespread attention, and infancy has since become one of the most stimulating areas of research in the biological, behavioral, and social sciences. Many investigators now appreciate how much the study of infancy contributes to our knowledge of developmental processes and the balance of the life cycle. Scientific interest in infant development also expanded, in part because of the emergence of some remarkably influential theories, and in part because technological advances have made concentrated and revealing research with infants possible. As a result of this intensified scrutiny, our understanding of infancy itself has increased dramatically.

This fifth edition of *Development in Infancy* reflects changes that have transformed our understanding of infants and their place in human development. Since the publication of the fourth edition, researchers of infancy have continued to exploit creatively many methodological techniques and, as a result, have made new discoveries. We have rewritten each chapter to take into account new research emphasizing work from the 21st century. We have reorganized chapters, restructured contents, and revised our discussions where necessary to reflect current thinking and fresh findings in the field.

This edition of *Development in Infancy* is yet more comprehensive and current than previous ones, paying thorough attention to all major aspects of infant development—contextual, methodological, neurological, physical, perceptual, cognitive, communicative, emotional, and social. Older citations have been replaced by references to recent studies that subsume and extend early reports. With the exception of classic references, we have concentrated on the latest articles and books and, as a result, emphasize new works. In this new edition, we have also endeavored to improve accessibility that has marked *Development in Infancy* in the past. This edition is designed for use as a textbook in classes at all levels, undergraduate and graduate, as well as in various disciplinary contexts—psychology, education, child development, nursing, and social work, for example.

Our goal in revising *Development in Infancy* is to provide a coherent overview of infant development with a strong theoretical and research base. We are selective rather than encyclopedic in our discussions of the literature. Throughout, our strategy is to integrate research and theory so as to introduce readers to conceptually important and descriptively valuable information. Our hope is that readers will gain a clear understanding of infant development and of key issues and problems likely to be the focus of significant advances in the years ahead. This new edition of *Development in Infancy* features:

- A new co-author, Martha Arterberry, who brings additional teaching and research skills to the existing author team.
- Literature reviews that are thoroughly updated to reflect contemporary research.
- More graphs, tables, and artwork that explain important concepts and findings.
- Increased emphasis on practical applications and social policy.
- A writing style that makes the book attractive to students from diverse academic backgrounds.
- Orienting questions at the beginning of each chapter that facilitate understanding and learning.
- Bolded key terms in each chapter, a list of key terms at the end of each chapter, and a complete glossary to help students learn and remember new terms.
- Two new types of boxes in each chapter—one entitled "Science in Translation" illustrating applied issues and the other entitled "Set for Life?" illustrating the significance of infancy for later functioning.
- All new teaching web resources including PowerPoint, electronic versions of slides/text figures, a test bank for the instructors, and hyperlinked references and electronic versions of the key concepts selected, and definitions for students. These resources can be found at www.psypress.com/9780805863635.

Acknowledgments

We would like to thank the following reviewers for their valuable input regarding recommended changes for the Fifth Edition: Sybil Hart, Texas Tech University, Judi Bradetich, University of North Texas, Harriet Darling, The Pennsylvania State University, York Campus, Leslie Ponciano, Loyola Marymount University, Elizabeth M. McCarroll, Texas Women's University, Kristine A. Kovack-Lesh, Ripon College, and one anonymous reviewer. We also thank the editorial and production team at Psychology Press.

Many researchers and theorists have shaped our understanding and contributed to our own fascination with infancy. We are indebted to them, hopeful that our integrative efforts will serve them as well as their students.

Marc H. Bornstein
Martha E. Arterberry
Michael E. Lamb

Chapter 1
Introduction

- *Why do scientists and professional people study infants?*
- *How do biology and experience jointly shape infant development?*
- *What are main effects, interactional, and transactional developmental processes, and how do they differ?*
- *Does understanding typical development help us understand individual differences better?*
- *What are the main differences between stability and continuity?*
- *What are developmental stages, and how do they help us understand infancy?*
- *What are the social, political, and economic implications of understanding development in infancy?*
- *What is a systems approach to understanding development?*
- *What are the four chief questions we ask about a behavior?*

By definition, infancy is the period of life between birth and the emergence of language roughly 1½ to 2 years later. Infancy thus encompasses only a small fraction of the average person's life expectancy, and readers may wonder why we have written a whole book about so brief a period of the life span, and why philosophers, psychologists, and physicians have paid so much attention to infancy.

There are three broad reasons for studying infancy scientifically: philosophical and scientific questions, parental investment, and applied concerns. Infancy has long fascinated philosophers and scientists because it offers the opportunity for human beings to study themselves and to do so from very early in life. Motivations for studying infants are simultaneously routine and complex. Our capacities vary so much it is difficult *not* to wonder how people can be so similar and yet so different. How much do we reflect our genetic endowment, and how are we shaped by our experiences? How much of what we experience as infants has lifelong implications? Questions of these sorts about infancy have motivated philosophers and scientists for centuries.

Whereas philosophers and scientists have been attracted by the opportunity to understand the origins of adult life, parents are heavily invested in infants, their survival, and their socialization and education. Likewise, parents are fascinated by the dramatic ways in which the helpless and apparently disorganized newborn baby is transformed, as if overnight, into the remarkably competent and curious, frustrating and frustrated, child. For everyone who comes into contact with them, infants instill endless curiosity. How

1

much do babies see, hear, feel, and understand? What can they do? What accounts for the striking changes that occur in infancy? How do infants in the same culture differ, and do infants in different cultures vary?

Some professionals have studied infancy in response to urgent social, medical, and biological problems. In the middle of the 20th century, for example, the development of obstetric technologies led to dramatic increases in the survival of preterm infants. What quality of life could they expect? Some babies developed extremely well, whereas others had persisting problems. What accounted for the differences in outcome? Similar reasoning impels infancy researchers eager to address today's applied problems. For example, large numbers of infants are being born to mothers who have used illicit substances, such as crack cocaine, alcohol, and ecstasy. Are these infants neurologically compromised by damage done to their brains in the months before they are born? Do they have the capacity to adapt successfully? Surely, if infancy were better understood, we would be in a position to promote the development of infants whose potential may have been jeopardized. More broadly, what can professionals and policymakers do to enhance the chances that infants will live and thrive, actualizing their fullest potential?

Reflecting these three broad reasons for studying babies, *Development in Infancy* examines the scientific progress being made in the study of infants. The goal of this chapter is to introduce the major theoretical and practical reasons why infancy is so fascinating a focus of research. We first address a core issue for developmentalists, the nature (heredity) versus nurture (experience) debate, beginning with a discussion of long-established philosophical viewpoints on this issue and moving to various models of nature-nurture effects that have historically guided thinking and research about development in infancy. We next turn our attention to the developmental significance of infancy, and more specifically to relations between infancy and later phases of the lifespan, focusing on the debate between those who believe that infancy is part of a seamless or continuous lifeline and those who describe major discontinuities between infancy and later childhood or adolescence. Related to this debate are questions about whether or not infant development proceeds in clear-cut stages. Next, we describe some of the applied issues and questions that make the study of infancy important to those whose chief interests lie in the psychological, educational, public policy, and medical implications of variations in modern life. We discuss interrelations among multiple aspects of development and the questions they provoke. We conclude the chapter with an outline of the contents of this book.

HEREDITY AND EXPERIENCE

Traditionally, theory and research in infancy focus on how structures or physical features (such as specialized areas of the brain for language) or functions or behaviors (such as spoken words) work, their **developmental course** (that is, when they emerge and whether and how they change with age), and what factors influence their development (biology and experience). Thus, the key research questions turn on status, function, origins, and determinants in development. Questions of status are concerned with how far along in development a structure or function is, and typically (but not always) mature adult functioning is the end comparison point. Questions of function address what use a structure or ability provides and why we might be designed to behave in such a manner or develop the particular structure or ability. Questions of origins pertain to how structures and abilities arise, and questions of determinants pertain to which factors influence their development. Certain overriding philosophical issues concerning origins and the course of development recur, and we now turn to discuss them.

Past, Present, and Future

Historically, the study of development in infancy was occupied with the relative roles of heredity and experience. This debate first arose between two groups of philosophers who were interested in **epistemol-**

ogy, understanding where knowledge comes from and how it changes. Extreme views were put forward by nativists on the one hand and by empiricists on the other. These two positions define the classic confrontation between advocates of nature and promoters of nurture.

Empiricists assert that there is no endowed knowledge at birth. Instead, all knowledge comes through the senses, and mental development reflects learned associations. They argue that external stimuli naturally provoke sensations and that through association separate raw sensations fuse into meaningful perceptions. The empiricists' view of the mind early in life was fostered by two separate but coordinated schools of thought. One derived from Locke (1689/1959), who is reputed to have described the infant mind as a **tabula rasa**, or "blank slate." A slightly different empiricist view is attributed to James (1890), who wrote that the world of the infant is a "blooming, buzzing confusion" out of which, presumably, infants' experiences help them to organize and to create mental order. Empiricism is an inherently developmental point of view because it contrasts the innocence and naiveté of infancy with the cognitive and social sophistication of maturity.

The empiricist belief that human beings begin life empty headed was considered both philosophically intolerable and logically indefensible by **nativists**, who argued that God would not create mindless creatures "in His image" and that an awareness of good and evil must be inherent in human beings because it could not be learned in so short a span of time as childhood. As a consequence, nativist philosophers such as Descartes (1638/1824) proposed that humans were endowed at birth with ideas which help even young infants understand the world. Against the empiricists, nativists asserted that the mind naturally, and from the beginning of life, imposes order on sensory input, automatically transforming raw sensations into meaningful perceptions. According to nativists, infants and adults share the same perceptual capacities and therefore perceive the world in much the same way. Because nativist theory postulates that many abilities are present at birth, it is not particularly developmental, although it does acknowledge that certain abilities take time to mature.

The nature-nurture debate is centuries old, but its central issues have remained basic to the study of infancy into our own time. Observing the status and origins of behavior and the dramatic developmental processes that occur in infancy motivates scholars to ask about the sources of change, and attempts at answers inevitably lead to speculations about heredity and experience or nature and nurture. Thus, Gesell (1954, p. 354), the intellectual founder of **maturationism**, the nativist movement in the U.S., wrote that:

> the original impulse to growth … is endogenous rather than exogenous. The so-called environment, whether internal or external, does not generate the progression of development. Environmental factors support, inflect, and specify, but they do not engender the basic forms and sequences of ontogenesis.

Interest in innate biological motives and constraints on infant development continues today in many quarters (Emde & Hewitt, 2001; Harris, 2007; Price et al., 2000; Spelke, 2003).

By contrast, America's premier environmentalist, Watson (1924, p. 104), emphasized the infinite malleability of human beings from infancy:

> Give me a dozen healthy infants, well-formed, and my own specified world to bring them up in, and I'll guarantee to take any one at random and train him to become any type of specialist I might select—doctor, lawyer, artist, merchant-chief and yes, even beggarman and thief, regardless of his talents, penchants, tendencies, abilities, vocations, race of his ancestors.

Many scientists still believe that the environment is the principal determinant of development from infancy (Gewirtz & Peláez-Nogueras, 2000; Riviere, Darcheville, & Clement, 2000; Weir, Soule, Bacchus, Rael, & Schneider, 2000). As a result, the nature-nurture controversy remains very much alive and appears repeatedly in this book.

In the debates among the early philosophers and developmental scientists, a main effects model applied: *Either* heredity *or* experience was considered to be central. In other words, according to the nativist view, if the heredity of the organism was good then the outcome would be good, regardless of whether the environment (or experience) was good or bad. Similarly, if the heredity of the organism was bad, the outcome would be bad, regardless of the environment. By contrast, the nurture main effects model predicts that, if the environment is good, the outcome will be good, regardless of heredity.

By the mid 20th century, the extreme positions of the nativists and empiricists were replaced by an **interactional model** of development (Anastasi, 1958; Piaget & Inhelder, 1967). Unlike main effects proponents, interactionists offered an additive view, in which nature and nurture were believed to shape development jointly. Thus, in simple terms good heredity and a good environment combine to yield a good outcome, and a bad heredity and a bad environment combine to yield a bad outcome. However, good heredity in combination with a bad environment or a bad heredity in combination with a good environment yield medium outcomes.

Despite their differences, Gesell and Watson conceived of development as a static interaction between two life forces—heredity and experience. The **transactional model** of development subsequently provided a more dynamic take on the interaction between constitution and experience—one that was inherently developmental in nature because it added time and a dynamic component to the equation (Sameroff, 2009). Many early developmental scientists (particularly those in psychobiology and ethology) argued that inherited constitution and experienced environment mutually influence one another during the course of development (Gottlieb, Wahlsten, & Lickliter, 2006). Sameroff and Chandler (1975) recognized that inherent characteristics are shaped by experience and vice versa, and that the mutual influence of heredity and experience continues throughout life.

Consider the concrete example that Sameroff and Chandler (1975) articulated when proposing their transactional model. Years of research on prematurity showed that only a minority of preterm babies develop abnormally even when they are initially indistinguishable from preterm babies who later develop quite adequately. Prematurity per se does not necessarily have ill effects, Sameroff and Chandler argued, but parents cope with atypical babies in different ways. Some fail to provide the types of experiences that preterm children need to offset their potential for developmental delay, and preterm infants are at risk over the long term when they are reared in such environments. Because early models typically focused on main effects or individual factors (such as prematurity), it is not surprising that their predictive power was poor. For this reason, it is unlikely that researchers can often identify specific early experiences that directly shape later characteristics. In making predictions about long-term development, the strategy must be to identify immediate effects and then determine how they directly and indirectly influence the child's later experiences.

Figure 1.1 portrays this transaction between the child and the environment through time. This idea of ongoing mutual influence of heredity and environment was a very important advance because it opened up the probability of **epigenesis**, the hypothesis that new phenomena not present in the original fertilized egg can emerge over the course of development through the interaction of preexisting elements with environmental influences.

The transactional view is now widely adopted in infancy research. It holds that, at any point in infancy, the effects of an experience depend on the nature of the specific experience and the heredity of the infant. Moreover, it has been used to explain a variety of developmental phenomena: early behavioral adjustment, the role of culture in shaping the parent–infant context, and child maltreatment, among other things (Bornstein, 2009; Bugental, 2009; Olson & Lunkenheimer, 2009). Similarly, the individual's contribution to his or her own development at any point reflects inherited characteristics in combination with

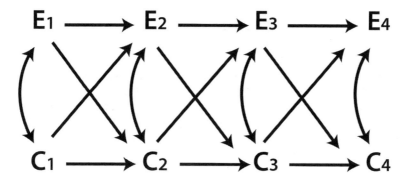

Fig. 1.1 In the transactional model, child and environment are believed to influence each other in a continual process of development and change. (From Sameroff, 2009. Copyright © 2009 by the American Psychological Association. Reproduced with permission. The use of APA information does not imply endorsement by APA.)

that individual's life history. If a particular child's early experiences were harmful, positive new experiences might be able to reverse some adverse effects, but the child could still be worse off than another child whose early experiences were not harmful and who later encountered the same positive new experiences. Infancy is therefore important to those interested in long-term prediction, even if the long-term effects of experiences in infancy are neither obvious nor direct (Box 1.1).

Box 1.1   Set for Life? The Child Is Father to the Man

Bornstein, Hahn, and Wolke (2013) showed that early measures of habituation efficiency (essentially, the speed with which babies come to understand something) are remarkably informative. Their analyses drew on a longitudinal study involving a subset of all the babies born in a region of west-central England between April 1991 and December 1992. Habituation efficiency was measured when the infants were 4 months old by seeing how quickly they got bored (i.e., how efficiently they habituated) looking at a black-and-white checkerboard pattern. Later, the babies were tested using standardized measures of cognitive development such as the Griffiths Mental Development Scales at 18 months, the Wechsler Intelligence Scales for Children at 8 years, and standardized tests of English, mathematics, and science used in the United Kingdom at 14 years. Babies who habituated more efficiently scored higher on the Griffiths at 18 months, had higher IQs at 8 years, and higher academic achievement scores at 14 years.

Like most contemporary researchers of development, we emphasize the ways in which heredity and experience *co*determine the development of the individual. This leads us to stress repeatedly that biologically based propensities—nature—and individual experiences—nurture—mutually influence infancy and the life course afterward. Infants are born with simple yet important behavioral tendencies. These innate tendencies help to direct early development by delimiting the potential for behavior change through experience. Babies who are highly distractible, for example, are likely to learn slowly about objects they see or hear because they are less able to attend to or to concentrate on them for long periods. Patient parenting may help offset this tendency.

With advances in mapping of the human genome, researchers are able to look even more closely at the interaction between genetic makeup and environmental experiences and the effect on development (Pluess & Belsky, 2012). For example, the gene DRD4 plays a role in dopamine signaling. Dopamine is involved in the system that governs attention and reward. Variants of DRD4 are correlated with levels of ADHD and high novelty seeking behavior (Faraone, Doyle, Mick, & Biederman, 2001; Kluger, Sieg-fried, & Ebstein, 2002). Pluess and Belsky (2012) argue that variants of this gene also prepare children to respond differentially to parenting quality. They showed that children carrying a 7-repeat allele (the repetition varies from 2 to 11) responded more strongly to both low and high quality parenting. Children experiencing low quality parenting showed less optimal development and children experiencing high quality parenting showed more optimal development. Thus, Pluess and Belsky suggested that this genetic variation prepared the children to be more responsive to the environment into which they were born. In contrast, children without the 7-repeat profile were not similarly prepared.

Neither biological predispositions nor environmental experiences alone determine the course, direction, termination, or final resting level of development. Rather, these life forces influence one another as development proceeds. As will become clear in this text, infant specialists are interested in learning which experiences affect what aspects of development when and how, the ways in which individual children are so affected, as well as the ways in which individual children affect their own development.

SOME SPECIFIC MECHANISMS OF HEREDITY AND EXPERIENCE

Scientists regularly distinguish between two kinds of biologically based tendencies: species-typical tendencies and heritable influences. **Species-typical tendencies** are those that all humans share. These include, for example, predispositions to cry when distressed, to attend to novel stimuli, and to ignore stimuli that have become boringly familiar. By contrast, **heritable influences** are those that distinguish one person's tendencies from another's, and they are the basis of genetically rooted individual differences. Just as some of us have blue eyes and others have brown eyes, so some infants seem to be inherently more irritable (i.e., cranky or easily distressed) or more distractible (i.e., less able to concentrate on one thing for long) than others. Both species-typical and heritable tendencies exert important influences on development.

The fact that infants are genetically biased to behave in certain ways means that the paths along which they develop are not exclusively determined by the experiences others provide for them. Indeed, infants actively contribute to their own development. Their characteristics and propensities can influence the experiences they will be exposed to and the ways in which those experiences affect them. This view is an essential component of the transactional approach. In addition, most developmental scientists believe that different individuals understand the world in unique ways that reflect their unique interactions and experiences. This approach stresses the individual's tendencies and capacities. For example, researchers of cognitive development propose that infants develop an understanding of the world by interpreting their perceptions and the effects of their own actions.

Unfortunately, confusion often surrounds biological influences. Three false beliefs are especially common. One is the notion that behaviors with a biological origin are fixed and thus cannot be affected by experience. This notion runs counter to all major theories of development and is contradicted by many everyday observations. The ability to cry, for example, is biologically determined, yet the amount an infant cries may vary depending on the environmental stimulants or consequences of the infant's cries, such as the way others around the infant respond to the cries. The second issue is the belief that biologically determined propensities must be present at birth. To discount this belief we need simply point to biologically determined events that directly and indirectly affect psychological development, yet do not occur until many years after birth. Puberty, for example, is a major milestone in biological and psychosocial development, yet it typically begins a decade or more after birth. The third myth is that biologically based behaviors remain stable over time and are not susceptible to change. In fact, some biological proclivities or tendencies change in childhood, either in response to particular experiences or as a result of genetically preprogrammed variations. Thus, both heritable and species-typical traits can be shaped by experience.

As far as experiential or environmental influences are concerned, there are several key facets to which developmentalists must attend. They include source, action, and timing. First, behavioral geneticists distinguish between the shared and nonshared environmental sources of experience. The **shared environment** consists of the environment that affects individuals similarly, such as nutrition, household, and neighborhood. The **nonshared environment** consists of environmental differences that act on individuals in the same situation or setting differently. The nonshared environment may be nonsystematic, or it may be systematic. Nonsystematic events include accidents, illnesses, or other chance circumstances that influence individual development and that contribute to individual differences. By contrast, systematic nonshared influences include gender differences, birth order, differential treatment by parents, and similar family or social factors.

Second, Gottlieb and his colleagues (2006) suggested a useful distinction among several different actions of experience on each aspect of development. Figure 1.2 illustrates them using perceptual development as a model. **Induction** is the most dramatic form of experiential influence. It occurs when a particular experience or set of experiences completely determines whether some aspect of development (a structure or function) emerges. Without the experience, there will be no emergence or development of the structure or function. **Attunement** and **facilitation** occur when certain experiences speed up or slow down the development of a structure or function. Finally, **maintenance** describes a situation in which experi-

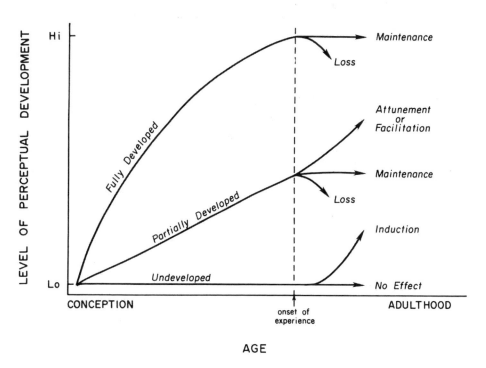

Fig. 1.2 Possible developmental outcomes given different levels of perceptual development before the onset of experience and for different experiences afterward. (From Aslin, 1981; reproduced with permission.)

ence preserves an already partially or fully developed structure or function and the absence of experience will result in loss of the structure or function.

In addition to source and action, the timing of experience is important. By way of example consider two models of how caregiving may affect development. In one model, an experience provided by the caregiver uniquely affects the infant at a particular time point, with effects that endure independent of later experiences or events. This model accords with a sensitive-period interpretation of experience effects (Bornstein, 1989; Dawson, Ashman, & Carver, 2000). A given experience might exert no influence on development at one time; at another it might exert a profound effect; and at a third time again no effect. Alternatively, the caregiving experience might influence development only because it is consistent and thus has a cumulative impact (Sroufe, Egeland, Carlson, & Collins, 2005; Thompson, 2006). Of course, there is nothing to prevent both sensitive period and cumulative impact from operating in different spheres of infant development.

There are several strategies and techniques used by developmental scientists to understand and differentiate hereditary and experiential influences on development in infancy. One such strategy pits infants born at term with those born preterm, because it allows researchers to compare differential development in the context of equivalent postnatal experiences. That is, babies can be matched for **conceptional age** (the time from conception) but contrasted in terms of **postnatal** experience (the time from birth), as we illustrate in Chapter 3.

A second strategy involves identifying variation in specific genes and correlating this variation with development. We already saw one example of this work earlier in this chapter focusing on variation of the DRD4 gene that plays a role in dopamine regulation. Another gene of interest is 5-HTTLPR. This gene is involved in the serotonin system which plays a role in emotionality. There is variation in the length of the allele, and this variation appears to be related to distress reactivity and attachment security (Raby et al., 2012).

A third strategy involves cross-cultural comparison. There are many reasons to conduct cross-cultural developmental research with infants. People are perennially curious about infant development across cultures. Because cross-cultural descriptions of infancy attempt to encompass the widest spectrum of human variation, they tell us about the full range of human experience. Moreover, they facilitate the establishment of valid developmental norms and the identification of human universals. Cross-cultural research also helps us understand life forces at work in development, because this perspective can be exploited to expose important variables that are not highlighted when a single culture is studied. In particular, this approach helps us understand the parts played by culture-dependent and culture-independent forces in development (Bornstein, 2010; Cole & Packer, 2011). Clearly, many of the reasons that motivate cross-cultural developmental research with infants are descriptive, but cross-cultural studies also inform theory.

THE LASTING SIGNIFICANCE OF INFANCY

There has been considerable debate about the long-term significance of development in infancy. Two extreme points of view have competed. Some believe that infancy is not particularly important because the status of the infant or experiences in infancy have little (if any) long-term predictive significance. That is, whatever early development may be, it is replaced later in life. Others argue that behavior patterns and experiences in infancy are important in themselves and are of crucial importance to later life. To these theorists, social orientations, motivations, and intellectual predilections established in infancy set lifelong patterns.

Proponents of the Importance of Early Experience

Since the time of Plato (*ca.* 350BC), philosophers as well as scientists have considered infancy to be uniquely significant. Their rationales are many and straightforward. First, the immature nervous system appears to be especially plastic; it can be shaped by experience (we will use the term **plasticity** to refer to this concept). Second, **neoteny** (the prolongation of infancy, especially in human beings) may have tremendous adaptive significance. Third, what is experienced or learned first has lasting influences, and, finally, infants seem to have an extraordinary facility for learning. All of these factors imply that early experiences disproportionately affect the course of subsequent development. Indeed, even folk wisdom and poetry express the conviction that early life experiences are singularly important. We provide two examples: (1) *The child is father to the man* or (2) *As the twig is bent, so grows the tree.*

Arguments for the special importance of early experiences and early development were popular throughout the first half of the 20th century and derived from a diverse array of theoretical starting points. Freud (1949) was by far the most prominent and vocal advocate of this position. He was also the first major modern psychological theorist to focus attention on infancy, and he justified this focus by suggesting that the ways babies are treated establish lifelong personality traits. Freud proposed that there are critical phases in development during which certain sorts of experience—affecting specific types of traits—are of special significance. He wrote that infancy fell within the **oral phase** of development, during which feeding experiences and other activities that centered on the mouth were particularly prominent. If the baby's needs for oral gratification were overindulged or underindulged in the oral phase, Freud believed, the baby grew into an adult who continually sought oral gratification—through overeating, talkativeness, smoking, chewing gum, and so on. Toward the end of infancy, Freud continued, the oral phase yielded to the **anal phase**. During this period parent–infant interactions centered on toilet training, and long-term personality consequences associated with this phase were likely to involve stubbornness and obsessiveness.

Erikson (1950), one of Freud's followers, portrayed early experiences and their effects differently, but he too believed that early experience is extremely influential. From early feeding experiences, Erikson suggested, children develop **trust or mistrust** in their caregiver rather than concrete oral traits. He also believed that the harmoniousness of early interactions (i.e., whether the infant develops "basic trust") has implications for the way the infant negotiates the next stage of development, in which the key issue is establishing **autonomy or shame**. With respect to toilet training, therefore, Erikson emphasized not the anal organs, but the status of toilet training as a battleground of wills between parent and child as the child tries to exert initial control (by determining when to give the parent the prize he or she seeks). Erikson described eight developmental stages, each marked by a crucial issue. With respect to infancy, basic trust or mistrust is at issue in the first stage, whereas autonomy or shame is at issue in the second.

Erikson's view of how early experiences affect the child's later personality substantially improved on Freud's view in two major respects. First, Erikson portrayed the lessons learned in each phase in more abstract, general terms (e.g., trust and autonomy) than did Freud (e.g., orality and anality), and the psychological issues he described seem pertinent to the stages concerned. Second, Erikson explicitly proposed that the ways in which different stages are resolved are somewhat interrelated. From Erikson's perspective, how much the infant trusts the caregiver may affect the infant's willingness to cooperate in toilet training and other matters. Thus, initial mistrust foretells the child developing into a mistrustful adult and a person plagued by unsuccessful resolution of later developmental issues.

Unfortunately, the ideas of Freud and his followers, including Erikson, were phrased in terms that did not lend themselves to empirical evaluation. Behaviorists and learning theorists such as Watson (1924) and Dollard and Miller (1950) dominated developmental science from the second to the sixth decade of the 20th century. Like the psychoanalysts, these learning theorists stressed the importance of infant experiences and even attempted to recast many of Freud's ideas in terms compatible with behaviorism

(Dollard & Miller, 1950). Unlike Freud and Erikson, behaviorists avoided talking about stages and phases of development. For learning theorists, early experiences are important because they occur first, have no competing propensities to replace, and thus yield to rapid learning. Moreover, early behavior patterns are believed to underlie more complex behavior patterns such as personality traits.

A third group of theorists, **ethologists** (researchers of animal behavior) and **embryologists** (researchers of prenatal physiology), also emphasized the special role of early experiences (Lorenz, 1935/1970; Tinbergen, 1951, 1963). Ethologists and embryologists argue that there are predetermined periods in the maturation of organisms during which time development is maximally susceptible to influence by specific types of experiences (Gottlieb et al., 2006). Just as Freud spoke of an oral phase during which feeding experiences have the greatest impact on the developing personality, the ethologists spoke of a **critical** or **sensitive period** for neural and anatomical structures and various behavioral functions (Bornstein, 1989; Dawson et al., 2000). During such periods, lessons are learned more easily and endure longer than any that follow. Likewise, studies of embryological development have shown that some experiences will have no impact at one point, but devastating impact at another time. Such demonstrations of sensitive periods accord biological and scientific credibility to Freud's model generally, and this notion was later integrated into theories of attachment and language development. The sensitive period concept assigns great importance to infancy and early experiences because sensitive periods tend to occur in infancy and experiences that occur in infancy are likely to have long-lasting influence.

Although psychoanalysts, behaviorists, ethologists, and embryologists similarly but separately asserted the importance of infant experiences for later development, popular acceptance of this view was influenced by dramatic empirical observations published between 1930 and 1950. At that time, reports that children who were reared in impersonal institutions emerged psychologically stunted led to the widespread belief that children needed close relationships in infancy and that the denial of such relationships would jeopardize their mental health (Bowlby, 1951; McCall, van IJzendoorn, Juffer, Groark, & Groza, 2011). An additional perspective on the continuing importance of infancy was offered by the Swiss epistemologist, Piaget (Chapter 7), who theorized that all intellectual capacities are built on simpler developments that take place very early in life, and thus that early experiences are of fundamental importance. It was, however, an incorrect assertion that won more popular support for the importance of early experience than Piaget's theory. In the domain of intelligence, researchers found a high degree of association between IQ scores obtained at 5 years of age and scores attained in adulthood. Because those results implied that a significant proportion of mature intelligence may be predictable from early measures of intelligence, Bloom (1964) made the widely publicized claim that about half of an individual's intelligence is established in the first years of life. This claim is incorrect for a number of reasons, including the fact that correlations quantify the accuracy of prediction, not the amount of intelligence that has developed. Nevertheless, the claim that experiences in infancy have a major impact on functioning in adulthood was widely influential.

By the early 1960s, hardly anyone doubted that early experiences hold a special place in human development. Two trends resulted. One was an increase in the amount of research on infancy, and the other was attempts to engineer enriching experiences for deprived children. With respect to the first, this book is in many ways the result of the cumulative efforts of the science of infancy which was instigated around this time. With respect to the second, by capitalizing on the special sensitivity of the very young, politicians proposed to inoculate children against the debilitating effects of later deprivation. These interventions were not always successful, and they resulted in a decline of confidence in the notion that early experiences were especially influential. Many researchers reported that initial rises in the IQ scores of children in social programs were followed by declines once an intervention program ended. Critics such as Jensen (1969) used such findings to argue that intervention programs had no sustainable benefits. We return to this point later in the chapter.

Stability and Continuity

Central to questions of the long-term significance of infancy is the extent to which development is consistent over time. The term **stability** is used to describe consistency over time in the relative standing of individuals in a group on some aspect of development. Activity level in infants would be stable, for example, if some infants are more active than others when they are young and continue to be more active than others as children and adults when they are older. Stability is concerned with individual differences. A related but separate concept is continuity. The term **continuity** is used to describe consistency in average group scores on some aspect of development over time. Continuity is concerned with the group mean. Thus, for example, activity level would be deemed to show continuity if a group of infants were as active when they were young as when they were older. Strictly speaking, therefore, stability refers to individual levels whereas continuity refers to group levels, and the two are independent of one another (Bornstein & Bornstein, 2008). So a structure or function can be developmentally stable and continuous, stable and discontinuous, unstable and continuous, or unstable and discontinuous.

A concrete example might help to illustrate these points. Bornstein and Tamis-LeMonda (1990) examined stability and continuity in the activities of mothers toward their firstborn infants between the time their babies were 2 months and 5 months of age. Their study focused on two ways in which mothers encouraged infant attention, two kinds of maternal speech, and maternal bids for social play in relation to the infants' exploration and vocalization. A majority of maternal activities were stable, some maternal activities showed continuity, but some increased and others decreased over time. Some maternal activities, like speech, proved stable and continuous. Between the times their infants were 2 and 5 months of age, their mothers spoke to them approximately the same amount overall. Also, those mothers who spoke more when their infants were 2 months old spoke more when their infants were 5 months old, just as those mothers who spoke less when their infants were 2 months old spoke less when their infants were 5 months old. Other maternal activities were stable and discontinuous, showing either general developmental increases (e.g., engaging the infant with objects—called extradyadic stimulation) or decreases (e.g., maternal speech used specifically to babies that has a high pitch and is slower than speech to adults). Some maternal activities were unstable and continuous (e.g., social play), whereas others were unstable and discontinuous, showing either general developmental increases (e.g., maternal speech in adult conversational tones) or decreases (e.g., social stimulation).

Development often makes it difficult to tell whether fundamental change has occurred in an underlying construct (such as attachment, imitation, or fear), or whether there is simply some superficial change in the ways an otherwise unchanging construct is expressed. Again, the distinction is best illustrated by example. Nine-month-olds may express attachment to their parents by clinging, crying, and seeking to be held. One year later, however, signals like talking and smiling have become more common ways to express attachment. And 15 years later, use of electronic communication, like texting, may be used. These developmental changes do not necessarily mean that attachments have changed in strength. Instead, they might simply indicate that different means have been found to express them.

Developmentalists distinguish among types of stability more formally by describing three models of the possible temporal association between variables. One model describes **homotypic stability** of the same aspect of development across time. Child performance on behavior A (e.g., vocabulary size) at Time 1 is related to the performance on the identical behavior A at Time 2 (Figure 1.3A). Another model describes **heterotypic stability** as expressed in physically different but conceptually similar aspects of development. Behavior A (e.g., vocabulary size) at Time 1 relates to behavior B (e.g., symbolic play) at Time 2. Models of heterotypic association typically postulate that a shared construct C in the child underlies the association between behaviors A and B. Perhaps vocabulary size and symbolic play both reflect children's capacity for symbolic understanding (Figure 1.3B). We call this model Heterotypic Stability

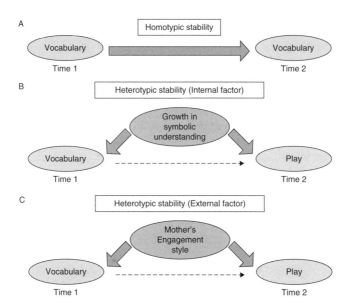

Fig. 1.3 Three models of homotypic and heterotypic stability.

(Internal Factor). A third model, which we call Heterotypic Stability (External Factor), shows that the stability in A or the association between A and B is explained by a mediating variable X that is not in the child but remote from the observed variables (Figure 1.3C). For example, behavior A (e.g., vocabulary size) at Time 1 relates to behavior B (e.g., symbolic play) at Time 2 because of some maternal characteristic X (e.g., style of engagement). This model predicts that once the contribution of X is removed within-infant stability will be reduced or eliminated.

Normative Development and Individual Variation

Two broad classes of questions recur in connection with issues of stability and continuity in infancy. One, concerned with aspects of development in all babies at specific ages or in specific circumstances, asks about **normative development**, whereas the other focuses on **individual variation**. Normative development is characterized by a developmental function (one such function is shown in Figure 1.4). The developmental function reflects the changing status of infants on some aspect of development at different ages. Individual functions focus on differences among infants at any age.

The general developmental function and individual functions are normally related to one another, but they are not necessarily related, as illustrated in Figure 1.4. Figure 1.4 (A) shows when six individual infants, each followed longitudinally, began to speak. Evidently, each infant followed a stepwise developmental path, not speaking up to a certain point and speaking afterward. Averaging across the six infants at each age generated the smooth developmental curve for language shown in Figure 1.4 (B). Notice that this group curve portrays a growth pattern quite *unlike* any of the individual growth functions. Summary portrayals of development like this can thus be misleading.

Questions about the developmental function and questions about individual variation are both important when trying to understand development in infancy. In each of the chapters in this book we discuss normative development, but each child is different from every other from conception and each of us remains an individual throughout development. Most parents are interested in knowing how their own

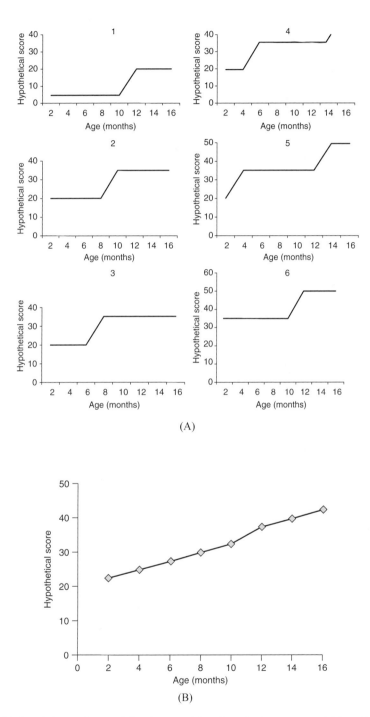

Fig. 1.4 Individual variation and general developmental functions for language acquisition. (A) Developmental functions for six individual infants; as can be seen, each infant develops in a stepwise fashion. (B) A smooth function is created by averaging the six individual functions. Often, such smooth developmental functions accurately represent the group as well as individuals in the group. Here, however, averaging across individuals yields a false smooth group function that is not representative of individuals in the group.

children develop their individual personalities and intellectual capacities. Researchers, too, find questions concerning the origins and growth of individual differences especially appealing in their own right as well as for the light they throw on general developmental trends.

Proponents of Discontinuity

With equally compelling arguments, other theorists have suggested an opposite view to stability, namely that experiences in infancy are peripheral or ephemeral, in the sense that they have little or no enduring effect on development. Instead, these individuals attribute the engine and controls of early development to biology and maturation. Gesell (1954), for example, concluded that, like anatomy, the psychology of the individual unfolds on the basis of a maturing biological program that is unaffected by experience.

One of the most vocal opponents of the overemphasis of early experiences is Kagan (2010), who had earlier studied the impact of social experiences in infancy and early childhood. Kagan came to argue that maturation—the unfolding of genetically determined capacities and individual differences—had been undervalued, pointing to research indicating that major differences in rearing environments had little apparent effect on the way children develop. For example, he argued that daycare and home care have remarkably similar effects on developing infants and that even extreme impoverishment (of, say, a rural Guatemalan environment of the 1970s) does not retard intellectual development in infants (Kagan & Klein, 1973).

Claims that there is little continuity from early development, and that the behavior patterns developed in infancy are unlikely to have predictable long-term consequences, have attracted a great deal of attention. In our view, such conclusions were inevitable and reasonable responses to earlier simplistic notions about the direct, long-range impact of infant experiences. One major difficulty lies in over-reliance on linear, or **main effects**, models of development that hold that early experiences have obvious and direct short- and long-term effects. Freud's psychoanalytic model, for example, assessed linear associations between early experiences and later outcomes, with breastfeeding expected to affect oral personality characteristics directly. However, simple linear relations between early experiences and later development are seldom documented empirically (Sroufe et al., 2005). This does not mean that early experiences are ineffective, however. Instead, the story may be more complicated. For mediated, distal, developmental processes between a predictor and an outcome, indirect paths constitute more sensitive, powerful, and theoretically appropriate relations (Shrout & Bolger, 2002).

This is not at all to say that there are no direct predictions. Researchers initially studied cognitive stability from infancy by examining infants' scores on standardized tests of development (mostly comprising sensorimotor items such as finding a hidden object) and standardized tests of cognitive performance when the infants grew into children. No stability was found, and it was often concluded that one could not predict later performance from measures of cognitive functioning in infancy. As Bornstein and Colombo (2012) describe, however, measures of both infant attention habituation (the rate of decrement in looking at a stimulus following repeated presentations) and recovery of attention to a new stimulus predict scores on intelligence tests in childhood in small to moderate degrees, even after controlling statistically for the possible effects of intervening experiences. Specifically, infants who process information efficiently in the first six months of life perform better between 2 and 21 years of age on traditional assessments of cognitive competence, including measures of language ability, standardized tests of intelligence, and academic achievement.

Stages

The concept of stages invariably arises whenever stability and continuity are considered. A stage is thought to represent a complex pattern of interrelated aspects of development. Dividing the life cycle into stages (or ages or phases) is challenging and subtle, with both theoretical and historical currents tugging at professional and popular opinion. Biology certainly exerts a considerable influence. Self-evident physical, motor, and cognitive components of development have led to the universal recognition of "infancy" as a separate stage of life. Infants creep and crawl, whereas children walk and run; infants do not speak, whereas children do (Figure 1.4 (A)). Social convention also has had important things to say about the distinctiveness of infancy. Infancy is a definable stage of life, based on biological, cognitive, and social data. As Harkness and Super (1983, p. 223) wrote:

> [A] primary function of culture in shaping human experience is the division of the continuum of human development into meaningful segments, or "stages." ... All cultures, so far as we know, recognize infancy as a stage of human development.

The question of stages also speaks to the existence and sources of continuity versus discontinuity in development. As Cole and Packer (2011, p. 90) pointed out:

> A stage is a more or less stable, patterned, and enduring system of interactions between the organism and the environment; a transition is a period of flux, when the "ensemble of the whole" that makes up one stage has disintegrated and a new stage is not firmly in place.

Theoretical positions in the natural and social sciences have legitimately questioned whether the life trajectory is marked by stages. These alternative views assert that development unfolds as a series of gradual transitions. Do human beings develop in the way an acorn becomes an oak (a continuous change), or as a caterpillar becomes a butterfly (a discontinuous change)? For most developmentalists the answer is a question of emphasis. Certainly, some structures and functions in infants undergo discrete changes, but even in them the new absorbs the old, and so human development seems much less dramatic than, say, the larval metamorphosis characteristic of the butterfly. Nonetheless, the concept of life stages constitutes a kind of organizing principle that is used conventionally to compare and contrast assorted aspects of development, at one period or between periods. Stages help make sense of life. They indicate that there are developments and experiences that merit attention in their own right and in terms of their contributions to subsequent development. Many famous developmental theorists—Freud, Piaget, Erikson, and Werner—have championed stage theories of development.

Is development within infancy stage-like? Development involves parallel biological, psychological, and sociological events. The characteristics of one stage distinguish it from preceding and succeeding stages, yet the accomplishments of earlier stages are carried into and mesh with new elements that are indigenous to later ones. The American philosopher and psychologist James (1890, p. 237) wrote that development is "without break, crack, or division." Yet infancy itself has been divided and subdivided into stages. Perhaps the best known are those Piaget described (Chapter 7), but many other scientists have hypothesized bio-behavioral shifts, psychic organizations, developmental crises, and the like, in infancy (Erikson, 1950; Kagan, 2010; Spitz, 1965; Trevarthen, 1988).

Theorists vary in their opinions about the usefulness of the stage concept for studying development. Critics note that stage theories are descriptive rather than explanatory. Stages also downplay differences among people and might not contribute to understanding individual development. In other words, stages are often general and idealistic, but life is filled with variation and inconsistency. Thus, a stage view oversimplifies the true state of development.

Typically, stage theories of development also have a maturationist flavor to them as well as several other distinctive characteristics. For example, stage theories are focused on internal change, and they are unidirectional in time, irreversible in sequence, universal, and goal directed. However, development need not (necessarily) entail progression toward a given end. Contrasting environmentalist perspectives do not include comparable assumptions about the fixed direction of development. Moreover, development may be nonlinear in nature, stalling and even regressing at times (Stern, 1998; Vaal, van Soest, & Hopkins, 2000). When we discuss reflexes in Chapter 4, we suggest that neonates may be capable of certain rudimentary types of walking, but that capacity appears to go away temporarily, only to reemerge as a much more robust dynamic capacity later in infancy and toddlerhood. In short, it might not always be correct to conceive of infancy (as theorists typically do) in terms only of positive changes toward a more mature endpoint.

In summary, by studying infancy we learn about processes and experiences that can have long-term implications for development. Infancy is the first phase of our lives outside the womb, and the characteristics we develop and acquire are fundamental. They are characteristics that endure and are certainly those that later experiences build on or modify. Infancy is only one phase in the lifespan, however, and so our cognitive competencies, social styles, and individual personalities are also shaped by experiences and development after infancy. The start does not fix the course or outcome of development, but it clearly exerts an impact on both.

PARENTAL CURIOSITY AND APPLICATIONS

Beside these philosophical and theoretical reasons, there are compelling practical causes to study infancy. For many parents and professionals, the pervasiveness, rapidity, and clarity of developmental changes in infancy make this stage of life fascinating. The developmental changes that take place during the thousand days after conception—roughly, the prenatal period and infancy—are more dramatic than any others in the human lifespan. The most remarkable of these involve the shape and capacity of the body and its muscles, the complexity of the nervous system, the growth of sensory and perceptual capacity, the ability to make sense of, understand, and master objects and things in the world, the achievement of communication, the formation of specific social bonds, and the emergence of characteristic personal styles. At no other time do such developments occur in so many different aspects of life so quickly. Though many of these developmental changes begin during the nine prenatal months, most continue through, or occur during, the first two postnatal years.

By studying infants we are often reminded of just how complicated some seemingly simple behaviors are. As adults, we sit up and walk without a second thought, but watching a young baby's repeated failures to accomplish such simple feats forces us to reconsider just how much sensorimotor coordination is involved. Many of the behavioral skills we employ in our daily lives are automatic. We gain a new appreciation of their complexity and the processes through which they develop by studying their emergence in infancy.

The desire to improve the lives of infants whose development may be compromised has also motivated a great deal of interest in infancy. The challenges posed by infants born preterm are exemplary in this regard. The ability to intervene medically during perinatal and neonatal development improved dramatically when advances in the design of incubators and respirators made it possible to keep alive preterm babies who formerly would have died at birth. Unfortunately, technical advances sometimes have unexpected consequences. For example, preterm babies are born with underdeveloped lungs and so require oxygen supplementation. Oxygen levels for preterm babies need to be monitored closely. When levels exceed that of the normal environment, damage to the retina can result in permanent blindness (Deuber & Terhaar, 2011).

Political and social motives also focus interest on infancy. The 1960s saw the beginning of the "War on Poverty" in the United States and the introduction of interventions designed to provide children from deprived and underprivileged backgrounds with a "Head Start" during the preschool years so as to prevent later school failure (Lamb & Ahnert, 2006). By 1968 it was widely believed that these programs had failed, and in response to this apparent failure, attempts were made to initiate educational interventions at earlier ages. Early enrichment programs were not failures, however. Rather, it seems that the timing of intervention, the nature of intervention, and the selection of outcome variables are all important (Heckman, 2007; Lamb & Ahnert, 2006). Moreover, interventions must take a multi-pronged approach by recognizing "the importance of the family, the mechanisms through which families create child skills and the stress under which many families operate" (Heckman, 2011, p. 6). This conclusion emerges from long-term prospective studies of children who had either been enrolled in special enrichment programs or assigned to control groups as infants or preschoolers. The outcomes measured in these studies included later school competence, and the results were quite impressive. Children in the experimental groups were less likely to be held back in school than controls, and they were less likely to need special education classes. What exact factors may have mediated these long-term effects are not fully understood, but developmental scientists pointed to the impact of experimental enrichment programs on both the children and their families. Once they are sensitized to the importance of helping their children succeed in preschool, for example, parents might maintain the impetus through the grade school and high school years.

Thus, there is now a proliferation of books and pamphlets designed to help parents enrich their infants' cognitive and social development. Where young infants formerly would have played contentedly with rattles, mirrors, or even scraps of paper, their parents now shower them with toys intended to stimulate their development, such as mobiles, *Baby Einstein* videos, and even electronic media (Figure 1.5).

Finally, there are startling economic implications for understanding the factors that influence development in infancy (and beforehand, Box 1.2). Here we consider one example: cocaine and other opiate use by pregnant mothers (Patrick et al., 2012). Rates of opiate use in pregnancy by mothers in the United States increased five-fold between 2000 and 2009, and many infants born to mothers who used opiates are dependent on the drug. These infants must undergo medically supervised withdrawal, and they are at higher risk for a number of problems, such as respiratory distress, seizures, irritability, and feeding intolerance. Not only is this a difficult way to start life, treatment of these infants is very expensive—averaging around $53,000 per baby in 2009.

Applied and theoretical concerns articulate with one another. The proliferation of successful intervention studies with infants born preterm undermines strict biological determinism in development and shows how experience can affect outcomes. For example, the Infant Health and Development Program

(A)   (B)

Fig. 1.5 (A) A baby enjoying time in a baby gym (Courtesy of Shutterstock, copyright: StockLite). (B) A toddler using a computer (Courtesy of Shutterstock, copyright: Aphichart).

Box 1.2   Science in Translation: The Economics of Infancy

At the family level, babies are expensive. Estimates from a 2012 Department of Agriculture report reveals that a middle-income family with a child born in 2010 can expect to spend roughly US$227,000 for food, shelter, and other expenses necessary to rear that child (not adjusting for inflation). Just to bring a new baby home from the hospital a family is faced with a large number of expenses:

- Car seat—$100
- Clothing—$50
- Diapers—$72 (one-month supply)
- Wipes—$20 (one-month supply)
- Crib with mattress & sheets—$230
- Bottles (unless breastfeeding)—$60
- Formula (unless breastfeeding)—$105 (one-month supply)
- Hospital bill—$15,000 (uncomplicated vaginal delivery, no insurance)

Yet investing in children is cost-effective. Heckman, a U.S. economist and Nobel laureate, conducted an analysis of the relative cost-benefit of early programming for pregnant mothers and young children compared to other social programs, such as increasing student–teacher ratios and adult job training (Heckman, 2006, 2007, 2011). His work is based on several facts of human development, including later abilities build on earlier abilities, critical and sensitive periods in development, ongoing interactions between heredity and environment, and on the observation that children from lower-income families do not do as well in school, perform less well on achievement tests, and experience more difficulties in adulthood (joblessness, crime, and lower home ownership). Interventions that start early and target both cognitive skill building and provide family support have shown positive results, including higher graduation rates, higher salaries, lower rates of teen pregnancy, and lower rates of use of public assistance. In terms of the return on investment, Heckman found that investing in early intervention programs provide a better rate of return than programs targeting older children and adults. This finding has significant implications for social policy decisions.

involved an early intervention in the lives of 985 preterm infants born in 1985 in eight geographical and demographic sites around the United States. The infants' average **conceptional age** was less than 37 weeks (38 weeks is considered full term) and they weighed less than 5.5 pounds at birth (Bradley, Burchinal, & Casey, 2001). The sample was divided into an intervention group and a control group. Infants in the intervention group were given high quality pediatric care, and their homes were visited weekly by trained caseworkers in the first year and biweekly in the second and third years. Their parents were given instructions in how to care for and enhance the development of their babies, and they also had the opportunity to attend professionally led support groups. During their second year of life, the children attended child development centers whose staff was specially trained. Children in the control group received only pediatric care during the same period. Normally, infants born preterm show a variety of neurological, sensorimotor, feeding, and sleep dysfunctions, and they experience numerous problems that make their day-to-day care more difficult. In this study, however, infants in the intervention group had significantly higher mean IQ scores than the control group at 3 years, and their mothers reported significantly fewer behavioral problems than did the mothers of control infants. Thus, environmental supports were shown to mitigate biological vulnerabilities and disadvantages.

The 1960s also saw the emergence of the women's liberation movement. Many popular writers encouraged women to actualize their full intellectual, social, and economic potential, and these developments led to a reevaluation of the former equation of femininity with motherhood. In prior decades, many people believed that only full-time mothers could provide young children with the care they needed to thrive, beliefs that were fostered by an extensive literature on the adverse effects of maternal deprivation (Bowlby, 1951). Since the 1960s, however, social critics have argued that fathers and high quality daycare centers can provide good quality care and thus relieve employed mothers of full-time childcare responsibilities (Lamb, 2013; Lamb & Ahnert, 2006). For example, the quality of children's emotional attachments appears to depend not on the absolute amount of time that parents spend with their infants, but on the quality of parents' interactions with them (Lamb & Lewis, 2011). These developments in turn raise several questions: What constitutes quality interaction between parents and infants? What are the long-term effects of daycare? What difference would it make if fathers rather than mothers took primary responsibility for childcare? The political and social climate for research in infancy thus became highly supportive as parents and policymakers turned to researchers for answers to such questions.

SCIENTIFIC INFANCY STUDIES

Systems

Despite the keen observations of both parents and scientists, and although today more than enough is known to permit the compilation of books on infancy much lengthier than ours, we remain grossly ignorant about many aspects of development in infancy. Our goal in this book is not to review every study and every theory about infants, but to summarize the most salient information available and to provide a coherent picture of development in infancy. To this end, theoretical perspectives and themes will be emphasized and described in each chapter, along with the results of both classic and modern relevant research.

The organization of our book is topical, with each chapter focused on a different aspect or outcome in infant development. This organization has the distinct benefit of permitting a clear focus on the status, origins, and determinants of each aspect of development. When information is organized in this way, however, it is easy to lose sight of the fact that all facets of development are intimately interrelated—that they are different aspects of the same single coherent organism (we return to this theme in Chapter 12). Before examining separate structures and functions, therefore, we first illustrate how they are interrelated.

In recent years developmentalists, particularly those who study infancy, have begun to explore **systems models** of early development (Thelen & Smith, 2006). Development in the systems perspective is dynamic in the sense that the organization of the system as a whole changes as the infant matures and acquires new experiences. As one subsystem emerges, that change brings with it a host of new experiences that influence and are influenced by changes in related component systems. Thus, change is not only dynamic but also thoroughgoing, taking place at many levels in the system at the same time.

These are abstract and difficult-to-grasp principles in and of themselves. Campos and colleagues (2000) provided an extended discussion of the systems approach using the infant's development of self-produced locomotion as a concrete example. Several component processes are involved in, and affected by, the onsets of crawling and walking, structures and functions as far flung as visual-vestibular adaptation (e.g., adjusting body posture and position in light of changing visual information), visual attention to changes in the environment, social referencing (e.g., monitoring the emotions of others to interpret ambiguous situations), and the differentiation of emotions. Higher-level behavioral organization in the infant emerges from the coordination of these component processes, and the emergence of self-produced locomotion (a change in a single process) affects a diverse set of psychological skills including perception of heights, the spatial localization of hidden objects, concept formation, and emotional expression.

Indeed, we can see reverberations in development beyond even these functions. Most babies learn to pull themselves to a standing position and to walk at around 11 to 15 months of age. Diverse aspects of cognitive or social development appear to underlie this change in motor ability, and in turn learning to walk has major implications for both cognitive and social development. As we will discuss in more detail in Chapter 5, infants' interactions with both people and objects change once they can move without the use of their hands (Karasik, Adolph, Tamis-LeMonda, & Zuckerman, 2012; Karasik, Tamis-LeMonda, & Adolph, 2011). Moreover, there is a dramatic change in perspective. Before standing upright, the infant viewed the world from a lying down position or from 6 to 8 inches above the ground while sitting or crawling. The baby can view the world from a height of 2 feet, and a whole new array of objects can be approached, explored, manipulated, and mastered. These new experiences in turn push cognitive development ahead. After being totally dependent on adults for stimulation, the newly walking infant now rapidly acquires the abilities to explore and to find stimulation independently. As far as social development is concerned, the ability to stand, like the ability to crawl, signals significant changes of a different sort in the infant's role vis-à-vis adults. Standing infants seem more grown-up to adults, who in turn treat them differently. Consider the effects that the infant's new ability to walk have on parents. They must now be vigilant about the possibility that the child could fall down steps, accidentally knock over something heavy, or munch on a dangerous house plant. Much more than before, parents must communicate to infants, primarily through their faces, voices, and gestures, messages that help children to regulate their own behavior and to learn—not through potentially dangerous accidents but through the parents' emotional messages—what to approach and what to avoid. Moreover, there are important changes for infants. In addition to exploring their environment, they now have control over their proximity to other people. They can approach and withdraw at will.

Alternatively, consider how a variety of independent developments converge to make verbal communication possible. In infancy, the anatomical structures that speech requires must mature, as must the advanced cognitive capacity to use symbols (words) to refer to things, and the social awareness and emotional relationships that provide the motivation to engage in more sophisticated interaction and verbally communicate with others. Thus, language development depends on anatomical and physiological as well as on cognitive, social, and emotional advances. All of these are crucial, for without them the capacity to speak would not develop. Moreover, the acquisition of speech has profound and obvious ramifications for all other aspects of development.

As we will see in Chapter 2, many spheres of infant life are embedded in one another. For example, inner-biological factors are embedded in the individual, which is embedded in a family, which is embedded in a neighborhood, which is embedded in a community, which is embedded in a culture (Lerner, Lewin-Bizan, & Warren, 2011). At a given point in development, variables from any and all of these levels contribute to the status of a structure or function in infancy. In turn, these multiple levels do not function independently of one another; rather, they mutually influence one another.

Challenges

As the Nobel laureate Tinbergen (1963) once pointed out, there are four chief questions about why a certain behavior occurs. First, there is the question about function: What survival value (if any) does the behavior have? Second, there is the question about causation: What internal and external stimuli or cues elicit or control the behavior? Third, there is the question about ontogenetic development: Why did this child come to behave in this fashion? Last, there is the question about evolutionary history: What aspects of the species' history led members of the species to behave in this way? Answers to all four of these questions are informative. They lead toward complementary rather than competing sorts of information that advance our understanding of each developmental phenomenon. In *Development in Infancy*, accordingly, we try to address all four questions, although much of our emphasis is on causation and development because these considerations have been of greatest interest to developmental scientists.

To address these questions about infant development is not easy, and what we know now has been learned slowly. In large part, this halting progress can be attributed to the enormous practical and logistical problems encountered in studying young infants. Perhaps the major problem faced by researchers is that, at base, they are trying to determine what infants know and feel about the people and things around them, and whether infants understand the effects of those people and things. As we discuss in Chapter 3, researchers must often make inferences about those capacities from apparently unrelated behaviors due to the physical and psychological immaturity of infants. First and foremost, those who study older children or adults can question their research participants verbally, but young infants can neither understand verbal questions nor respond verbally. In addition, infants are notoriously uncooperative; unlike adults they are not motivated to perform for researchers. Other problems that vex investigators are infants' short attention spans, their limited response repertoires, and the variability inherent in most infant behaviors. Finally, measurement of any aspect of infancy depends on infant state.

To assess the capacities of infants in any given domain of development, researchers are forced to design ingenious procedures to elicit a response that is within the infant's capability. When infants do not respond as expected, substantial problems remain. Researchers have to decide whether the infants did not respond because they: (1) did not understand the question, (2) are incapable of performing the task, (3) are incapable of emitting the response, (4) are not paying attention, or (5) are not motivated to respond. Although these problems are not unique to studies of infancy, they are pervasive in this field. Most important, researchers must guard against reaching conclusions about the lack of certain capabilities in infancy based only on the failure of infants to behave in an expected way. Reciprocally, we must not over interpret infants' responses. It is tempting to explain a behavior in terms of mature adult functioning, such as an infant possessing an advanced cognitive understanding, when in actuality they might be responding based on some other lower level process (Keen, 2003; Rakoczy, 2012).

OUTLINE OF THIS BOOK

The major aspects of development in infancy—physical, neurological, perceptual, cognitive, linguistic, emotional, and social—are considered serially in the chapters that follow this introduction. To place our study of infancy in context, we step back in Chapter 2 from the scientific study of different domains of infancy and attempt to describe the several real-world contexts in which babies grow. Infants do not develop in a vacuum; rather, their arrival and presence profoundly shape and are in turn influenced by family members and other people and institutions with whom their families come into contact. Infancy is a phase of the life cycle when adult caregiving could exert extremely salient influences. Not only is caregiving most intense in this period, but infants are thought to be particularly susceptible and responsive to external experiences for reasons described earlier. In Chapter 2, we discuss parenting and family relationships, with particular focus on the ways in which mothers and fathers influence interactions with infants. We then consider the development of infants' relationships with siblings and peers—the other children who bridge the gap between the intra- and extrafamilial social worlds. Many infants today spend time in nonparental care facilities, and we also describe the ways in which early development is affected by various patterns of nonparental nonfamilial care. We end the chapter with a consideration of ethnic, social class, and cultural variations in the contexts of parenting and infant development.

In Chapter 3, we review research methods, describing in some detail the ways investigators today obtain information from young infants. We start by discussing the logic of empirical investigation, including the strengths and limitations of the various types of designs that are used to study status, origins, and developmental processes associated with different structures and functions. We then turn from logic to techniques, and the characteristics of procedures ranging from biographical descriptions and case studies, through naturalistic observations and observations in structured settings, to the recording of psychophysiological and behavioral activities in increasingly structured ways. The chapter concludes with discussions of the scientific method and the ethics of research with infants. Experimental and naturalistic studies carried out in homes and in laboratories underpin our growing understanding of infant development, and it is to these substantive aspects of development that our attention then turns.

Infancy is characterized by remarkable physical and physiological changes, many of which are evident even on casual observation because of their magnitude and scope. In Chapters 4 and 5, we describe early physical, motor, neural, and psychophysiological development beginning from conception. Growth of the central nervous system relates to changes noted in many of these spheres of development. Even when explicit references of this kind are absent, it is important to bear in mind the patterns of physiological and neural development that parallel cognitive and social development. We review aspects of both pre- and postnatal growth in these chapters, for there is good reason to view development across these early months as an unfolding process on which birth has only a rather modest impact.

Perceptual development is discussed in Chapter 6, where we review the major issues that have dominated theorizing on this topic. The best-studied perceptual modality is vision, and our chapter addresses such questions as: what babies are capable of seeing, how they behave when shown visual stimuli, and how they integrate visual information into a coherent view of the world. Unfortunately, less is known about infant hearing and their other senses than about vision, with the exception of research on infant speech perception. It is in the study of visual perception, however, that the age-old battle between nativists and empiricists has been joined with greatest gusto, as we recount in our introduction to the chapter.

In Chapter 7, we describe the growth of cognitive and intellectual abilities in infancy. A qualitative approach, pioneered by Piaget, emphasizes the changing ways in which infants actively attempt to interpret or make sense of their experiences, whereas a quantitative approach addresses what infants know and how they get to know it. The former approach promotes a stage-based view of development in which discrete phases can be discerned, whereas the latter approach places greater stress on measuring individual competencies to permit assessment of developmental change as well as comparisons among individuals. Cognition involves understanding the laws that govern relations among objects in the environment—particularly laws that relate one's own actions to objects and their resulting behavior (e.g., "When I push something, it moves"). In Chapter 7, we also describe various attempts to develop standardized measures of cognitive development and the generally disappointing status of longitudinal research with those measures. However, researchers have found that newer measures of very basic cognitive processes in infancy do predict individual differences in cognitive performance in later childhood. In addition, we discuss research on how the social contexts in which infants develop influence their thinking.

More specialized aspects of infant cognition are the focus of Chapter 8. Here we describe the infant's changing ability to represent events and experiences, to remember them, and to use them in ever more sophisticated ways. Because we now know that infants can learn, researchers have turned their attention to understanding how infants categorize stimuli and events so as to abstract memorable lessons from them. Categorization and representation are essential to the organization of learning and memory, and also play a crucial role in permitting the use of symbols—a basic prerequisite for language development. As we show in Chapter 8, categorization and representation are also central aspects of both social and object-mediated play. Representation thus serves as an important bridge permitting babies to communicate with increasing precision about their thoughts, intentions, and feelings.

Socioemotional and cognitive development are integrally related, even though scholars tend to specialize in the study of one or the other. Communication and interaction are two concepts that help to explain their overlap. Communication refers to the exchange of information between individuals. Early in life, infants communicate with others by means of emotional expressions that function as potent signals. An example is nonverbal distress, like crying. The baby also has the capacity to organize speech sounds, and in remarkably short order the baby's own repertoire of communicative tokens expands to include various gestures and a growing range of social signals, culminating in language. The comprehension of speech combined with the generation of unique utterances rank among the major cognitive goals of the infancy period—perhaps its crowning achievement—but the motivation to acquire language is social. Language is probably the most important medium of social interaction from infancy onward; as such, it stands squarely at the interface of cognitive and social development.

By definition, infancy ends when language begins, but it is increasingly evident that language does not suddenly emerge in the second year of life. Rather, the use of language depends on the ability to segment and process visual and auditory information (Chapter 6), the ability to develop concepts and to represent them symbolically (Chapters 7 and 8), the formation of social relationships and motivations and recognition of the reciprocal basis of social interaction and internalization of the elementary rules of turn taking and communication (Chapter 9). Language development, our topic in Chapter 9, is driven by all of these features of infant life. In addition, the input necessary to learn language is itself a component of social interaction. Language development is also predicated on the child's innate ability and urge to make sense of linguistic experience—itself a complex cognitive task. The relative roles of interactional experience and native competency in language acquisition remain unclear, and as a result language acquisition constitutes a second continuing battleground in the nature–nurture debate.

In Chapter 10, we turn our attention to the development of emotions and temperament. Here we describe the communicative functions of emotions and explore both the origins and developmental significance of individual differences in emotionality and temperament. Emotions and affect permit infants to read others' appraisals and intentions, and they enable infants to (nonverbally) communicate their own appraisals and intentions to others. Emotions also play a major role in organizing behavior within an individual. In turn, emotionality constitutes the core of temperament, commonly defined as a constitutionally based source of individual differences in personality. Temperamental variation is already evident early in infancy, and individual differences in temperament are significant because of their potential to influence infants' cognitive and social interactions. Their unique appeal and broad implications make emotions and temperament in infancy of continuing interest.

We discuss social development within the nuclear family in Chapter 11. A major step in socioemotional development is the formation of attachments, that is, enduring relationships with specific individuals, especially parents. In Chapter 11, we discuss the cognitive prerequisites for forming attachments, the people to whom babies become attached and why, and how adult activities affect the types of relationships established between infants and adults. Throughout these chapters on social and emotional development, our emphasis is on the manner in which interactions with others affect the development of a baby's characteristic social style and how that style influences later interactions and experiences.

Throughout this book we try to stress interrelations among various aspects of development. Chapter 12 is designed to underscore the importance of this perspective by discussing the early development of social cognition—infants' learning about specific people and the way they tend to behave, and how infants come to see the world differently because of their unique experiences and perspectives. Our goal is to illustrate that the development of social understanding depends on the elaboration of several basic cognitive capacities (attention and memory, for example) as well as more complex cognitive competencies (e.g., the development of intentionality and the object concept), all of which relate to physiological development and perceptual accomplishments. Social experiences also play crucial roles in these developmental processes, and social cognition applies to understanding people and their behavior. Moreover, phases of emotional or affective development are integrally related to stages of social and cognitive development as well as to social cognition. Social cognition thus illustrates interdependencies among lines of development that, for purposes of examination, are artificially separated in Chapters 4 through 11.

SUMMARY

Because of the range, the magnitude, and the implications of the developmental changes that occur early in life, infancy is a fascinating and appealing phase of the life cycle. Some of the key issues in developmental study—those having to do with the relative importance of nature and nurture or with interrelations among diverse aspects of development—are rendered in sharpest relief when the focus is infancy. Thus, studying babies tells us about general developmental phenomena as well as infancy as a unique stage of the life cycle.

Patterns of development are inherently complex. Infants' experiences appear to be important, but later experiences often interact with earlier ones to shape developmental outcomes. In addition, not all infant experiences are equivalently meaningful, and certain aspects of development are more susceptible to experience than others. The stability and continuity of developmental domains are significant issues as well. Many theorists have asserted—and many have questioned—the status of infancy as a separate stage in the life cycle as well as the possibility of stages of development within infancy itself.

In the remaining chapters of the book, we review our current understanding of each of the major domains of development in infancy and discuss these issues in detail, for they continue to frame contemporary theorizing about and research on infant development. Focusing on each aspect in turn, we describe significant findings and interpret their meaning. Our review is selective rather than exhaustive, for we want our readers to know and understand meaningful perspectives and facts. In addition, we attempt to highlight the basic findings and key issues with which investigators in each area must grapple, and we relate these issues and findings to the broader questions that guide research on infant development more generally. Whenever possible, we point to connections among different facets of development.

KEY TERMS

Anal phase
Attunement
Autonomy or shame
Conceptional age
Continuity
Critical or sensitive period
Developmental course
Embryologists
Empiricists
Epigenesis
Epistemology
Ethologists
Facilitation
Heritable influences
Heterotypic stability
Homotypic stability
Individual variation
Induction

Interactional model
Main effects
Maintenance
Nativists
Neoteny
Nonshared environment
Normative development
Oral phase
Plasticity
Postnatal
Shared environment
Species-typical tendencies
Stability
Systems models
Tabula rasa
Transactional model
Trust or mistrust

Chapter 2
The Many Ecologies of Infancy

- *In what direct and indirect ways do parents influence infant development?*
- *How do siblings and other family characteristics affect infants?*
- *How do infant–parent, infant–sibling, and infant–peer relationships differ?*
- *In what ways does regular nonparental care—daycare—affect infant development?*
- *Compare the ways in which the quality of parenting and the quality of day care have been conceptualized and measured.*
- *In what ways do early social experiences vary across economic strata, ethnic groups, and cultures? How do these variations shape infant development?*

This book is about infants and the processes that define development in infancy. Infants do not grow up in isolation. Human beings are intensely social creatures, and researchers who ignore the multiple social contexts of infant development risk failing to understand infancy completely and accurately. Different ecologies or contexts provide infants with different cognitive and social experiences and thus contribute significantly to development in infancy. In this chapter, we explore the many "ecologies" in which infants develop.

In Western industrialized cultures, parents typically play the major role in providing infants' experiences, and consequently infant–parent relationships constitute the first focus in this chapter. However, highlighting relationships involving infants and their parents can disguise the extent to which infant–parent relationships are embedded in a broader social context such as the family. The family, in turn, shapes and is shaped by component relationships within it (for example, the relationship between the parents) as well as by the community in which the family is embedded. In the first two parts of this chapter, we discuss the nuclear family, focusing on the ways in which mothers, fathers, siblings, and infants interrelate and influence one another. The evidence we present amply demonstrates that families provide a richly textured array of relationships to infants from the beginning of life. The influence of different individuals in the family on infants is complex because changing family dynamics shape the style and significance of each relationship (Bornstein & Sawyer, 2006; Dunn, 2007a; Lamb, 2012a). Families also take different forms, and in this chapter we address infant development in two-parent families with some discussion of same-sex parent and single-parent families.

Nuclear families represent only one of a variety of contexts that infants experience. Infants in many places are tended by a variety of nonparental care providers, whether in family daycare, daycare centers, villages, or fields. We discuss nonparental care in infant development in the third section of the chapter.

Situations like daycare represent one of the ways in which people outside the family affect infant development in meaningful ways. The society in which the family is embedded is also influential in more indirect ways. Social classes and cultures vary with respect to the patterns of development they expect, encourage, and support. Some ensure that infants are reared in intimate extended families and cared for by many relatives; others isolate mothers and babies. Some treat fathers as irrelevant social objects; others assign complex and intimate responsibilities to fathers. Cultural prescriptions determine, to a great extent, the immediate social contexts experienced by infants, the short- and long-term goals parents have for their children, and the practices used by parents in attempting to meet those goals. The childrearing practices of one's own culture might seem "natural," but some practices are actually rather unusual in a relative sense. Furthermore, few nations in the world are characterized by cultural homogeneity; rather, ethnic and social class differences within cultures color childrearing practices just as surely as cultural differences do. In short, social class and culture play major roles in shaping development in infancy. We explore some effects of social class and culture in the fourth section of this chapter.

INFANT, MOTHER, AND FATHER

It has been said that parents largely "create" persons because mothers and fathers influence the development of their infants in many ways (Sroufe, Egeland, Carlson, & Collins, 2005). Direct effects are most obvious. Parents contribute directly to the genetic makeup of their children and shape their children's experiences; parents also serve as their infants' most immediate social partners. In the natural course of things, the two main sorts of direct effects are confounded: The parents who endow their infant with their genetics also structure their infant's world and experiences. Can we disentangle heritable from experiential influences on the status, origins, and determinants of development of structures and function in infants? Can we tell how the two are mutually influential in development? To study heritable and experiential direct effects, we can appeal to so-called natural experiments where these two effects on the individual can be distinguished, at least to a degree (Chapter 3).

Direct Effects—Heritability

Mothers and fathers directly contribute to the development of their infants by passing on their genes, and behavior geneticists attempt to assess the contributions of genetics and environment to many individual infant characteristics, such as physical growth, intelligence, and personality. Two research paradigms—involving twins and adoptees, respectively—are commonly used to study heredity. Twins born from the same egg and fertilized by a single sperm are **monozygotic**, and they share 100% of their genetic inheritance; twins born from different eggs fertilized by different sperm are **dizygotic**, and they share approximately 50% of genetic inheritance, just as other siblings do. Typical twin studies involve comparing the extent to which certain characteristics are shared by (1) monozygotic twins reared together or apart or (2) monozygotic and dizygotic twins (Saudino, Carter, Purper-Ouakil, & Gorwood, 2008; Segal, 2010). If a characteristic is inherited, identical twins even if reared apart should be more alike, just as identical twins should be more alike than fraternal twins. Behavior geneticists also use adoption designs to examine the degree to which adopted children share traits with their adoptive and biological parents, respectively (Petrill, Deater-Deckard, Schatsschneider, & Davis, 2007). If a characteristic is inherited, biological parents and children should be more alike than adoptive parents and children. Behavioral genetics studies report a high degree of genetic heritability for a surprising range of individual characteristics (Bishop et al., 2003; Knafo & Plomin, 2006). Clearly, parents significantly affect their infants' development and outcomes by endowing them genetically. However, parents and others in the infants' environment also shape infant development by providing formative experiences.

Behavioral patterns that appear inborn and genetically pre-programmed can be a function of complex interactions between the developing organism and its physical and social environment. **Epigenesis** is the developmental process whereby each successive stage of development builds on foundations laid down by preceding stages. Thus, if Gene A is statistically associated with Behavior B in a population, the gene does not necessarily lead directly to the behavior. Rather, Gene A is proximally associated with Behavior B1, which in turn gives rise to B2, which gives rise to B3, and so forth, until the adult phenotypic behavioral profile is attained. A simple example of probabilistic epigenesis can be seen in the barnyard chicken's characteristic pecking at the earth for worms and grubs. This chicken behavior is so universal that the pecking seems innate, genetically programmed to appear shortly after hatching. Wallman (1979) housed newly hatched chicks individually inside plain white cardboard cylinders (actually, ice cream containers) for the first few days of life. Just after they had hatched, he placed white taffeta booties on half the chicks so that they could walk but could not see their toes; the rest went barefoot as chickens normally do. After 2 days, both groups were presented with mealworms, standard chicken fare. Remarkably, the chicks shod in booties were baffled by the worms; many initially ran away, and few ate them. The chicks that had seen their toes, however, as if by instinct, immediately began pecking at the worms. Similar effects were seen when the toes were painted black. So, it turned out that pecking at worms is not as instinctive for chickens as it appears, but requires early visual experience to simulate the behavior. Visual exposure to a stimulus as minimal (but evolutionarily guaranteed to be there) as their own toes, was sufficient to enable pecking behavior, essential to their survival, to emerge. Since most chickens are not reared in ice cream containers wearing taffeta booties, this learning process—the probabilistic epigenesis—is typically masked, and the behavior appears instinctive.

Thus, even in birds, whose behavior superficially appears hard-wired, the individual organism *constructs* behaviors as a process of interaction with expectable experience, and subtle variations emerge as a result of these interactions.

Direct Effects—Parenting

Evidence for heritability does not negate or even diminish equally compelling evidence for direct (and indirect) effects of parenting on infants (Collins, Maccoby, Steinberg, Hetherington, & Bornstein, 2000). To cite an obvious example, genes help make siblings very much alike, but (as we all know) siblings are still very different, and siblings' different experiences contribute to making them distinctive individuals. Thus, even within the same family, parents (and others) create different environments for different children (in Chapter 1, we referred to this as **nonshared environments**). For example, warm, attentive, stimulating, responsive, and nonrestrictive parental activities promote intellectual and social competencies in infants, and infancy is the period during which, in the opinion of most developmentalists, parents exert their most important influences on development (Lamb & Lewis, 2011). Although infancy is a comparatively brief period in the lifespan, no other period of life demands more parental time and investment. Infants are wholly dependent on others' care to survive. Furthermore, adults find infants especially appealing. Adults "melt" in response to an infant smile, find babies fun to play with and talk to, and are fascinated by how rapidly babies grow from being totally helpless at birth to developing unique competencies and personalities. It is no surprise, given how dependent infants are on adults and how much energy parents devote to infants, that infants are considered more responsive to parental input than children in any other developmental period. As a result, developmental scientists have devoted themselves to documenting how parents shape the physical, cognitive, verbal, and social development of infants.

Bornstein (2002, 2006a) distinguished among four major domains of parenting: (1) **Nurturant caregiving** aims at promoting infants' basic survival (providing protection, supervision, and sustenance); (2) **material caregiving** involves the manner in which parents structure infants' physical environments (provision of toys and books and restrictions on physical freedom); (3) **social caregiving** has to do with parental efforts to involve infants in interpersonal exchanges (soothing, touching, smiling, and vocalizing); and (4) **extradyadic caregiving** pertains to how parents facilitate infants' understanding of the world around them (directing babies' attention to and interpreting external events, and providing opportunities to learn). These domains are not mutually exclusive, and it is quite typical for two or more parenting domains to occur simultaneously as, for example, when a parent attempts to read to an infant (extradyadic caregiving) by placing her on her lap and stroking her (social caregiving).

Parents also affect infants directly through two basic interactional mechanisms (Bornstein, 2002, 2006a). One of these, the **specificity principle**, states that specific forms of parenting at specific times shape specific infant abilities in specific ways. For example, Bornstein et al. (1999) found that increases in mothers' verbal responsiveness to infant vocal or exploratory behavior when infants were 13 to 20 months of age (how prompt, appropriate, and contingent mothers were verbally to their infants) predicted infants' vocabulary size at 20 months. By contrast, maternal vocabulary used when speaking to infants did not predict infant vocabulary size. These results support the specificity principle because infant vocabulary level was specifically sensitive to maternal verbal responsiveness and not to how many different words mothers used during mother–infant exchanges. The second interactional mechanism is the **transactional principle**, which states that infants shape their experiences with parents just as they are shaped by those experiences (Bornstein, 2009; Sameroff, 2009). Researchers of infant temperament, for example, propose that the extent to which infants are perceived as "easy" or "difficult" may influence how parents respond to them (Bridgett et al., 2009). The quality of the parents' response, in turn, further shapes infant development. Thus, parenting cuts across several functional domains and influences infant development through specific parent-to-child pathways as well as through reciprocal transactional mechanisms.

Because mothers have traditionally assumed primary, if not exclusive, responsibility for infant care, theorists and researchers have been much more concerned with the mothering rather than the fathering of infants (Figure 2.1). Research and theory about infancy are influenced by cultural assumptions about the centrality of the mother–infant relationship and the impact of mother-provided early experiences on later development. Indeed, to this day, many societies place a very strong emphasis on the mother–infant relationship (Bornstein, 2006a). However, fathers interact with and care for their children as well, sometimes in ways that are quite distinctive (Lamb, 2013; Lamb & Lewis, 2010). In many cultures, for example, play is the dominant characteristic of father–infant interaction. The rising scientific and popular interest in fathers reflects social changes in family structure and functioning that have led fathers to become more involved in the care and nurturance of their infants (Lamb, 2012a; Figure 2.2). The nature of mother– and father–infant relationships and the unique influences of mothers and fathers on infant development are further explored in Chapter 11.

Parents' direct influences on infants reflect genetic inheritance and parental behavior. Importantly, maternal and paternal caregiving is not static. They are constantly changing and, as we explore in this chapter, reflect many sources of influence. Some arise from within individual parents or their context, whereas others are elicited and shaped by the infant. Both the most obvious and the most subtle infant characteristics can affect parents' behavior toward their infants, as we see in the next section.

Indirect Effects

Infants are born into a social environment filled with other people. Gaining a full awareness of other individuals follows a series of stages through which relationships—often called **attachments**—are estab-

Fig. 2.1 Nurturant, responsive parent–infant interaction is critically important for promoting social, emotional, and intellectual development in infancy. (Courtesy of C. J. Soto.)

Fig. 2.2 A father feeding his 2-month-old infant. (Courtesy of M. Arterberry.)

lished with their parents. The formation of attachment reflects the convergence of built-in tendencies on the parts of both infants and parents, and the ways in which individual adults respond varies depending on infant gender, personality, current social, emotional, and economic circumstances, and the parents' own life histories and beliefs. Perhaps as much as any of these factors, however, parental behavior depends on the current status of other relationships within the family. Not only do infants experience multiple relationships, but so too do their mothers, fathers, and siblings. As a result, parents and siblings influence infants not only through interactions with them—direct effects—but also by parents' and siblings' influences on each other—indirect effects. These many influences run indirectly through complex paths and networks (Bornstein & Sawyer, 2006; Fouts, Roopnarine, Lamb, & Evans, 2012). For example, many paternal influences on infant development are indirectly mediated through the father's impact on the mother. In other words, even if the mother has the major direct influence on infant development in a "traditional family" (in which the mother stays at home to care for and socialize her children while the father works outside the home), the father may have important indirect influences (Coley & Schindler, 2008).

One way in which fathers may indirectly affect their children's development, even when their responsibilities limit their opportunities for interaction, was long ago described by Bowlby (1951, p. 13):

> Fathers … provide for their wives to enable them to devote themselves unrestrictedly to the care of the infant and toddler [and] by providing love and companionship, they support her emotionally and help her maintain that harmonious contented mood in the aura of which the infant thrives.

Contemporary research confirms Bowlby's early observation: Parents are more attentive and sensitive to their infants when the relationship between the parents is warm and supportive (Carlson, Pilkauskas, McLanahan, & Brooks-Gunn, 2011; Jessee et al., 2010). Maternal supportiveness has a greater effect on paternal behavior than paternal supportiveness has on maternal behavior, suggesting that fathers are even more susceptible than mothers to indirect influences on their interactions with infants (Sobelweski & King, 2005). It might be that conventional social expectations give fathers greater leeway to choose whether and how to be involved in their children's lives (Shannon, Cabrera, Tamis-LaMonda, & Lamb, 2009). By contrast, mothers are expected to be committed and involved, regardless of their psychological state (Barnard & Solchany, 2002).

Research has broadly questioned the quality of childrearing in older and younger mothers. Taking care of infants is physically challenging and it is thought that older first-time mothers might not be up to the demands (Mirowsky, 2002). Younger mothers are known to have less knowledge about parenting, to have less desirable childrearing attitudes, to have less realistic expectations about infant development than older mothers; and they are less sensitive, appropriate, and responsive to their infants (Bornstein & Putnick, 2007; Bornstein, Putnick, & Suwalsky 2006; Bornstein, Putnick, et al., 2012). Parenting differences between younger and older mothers in Western cultures could be due, in part, to educational differences. Older mothers often have delayed childbearing to pursue advanced education. By contrast, early parenthood is associated with attending low-quality schools, having parents with little education, school failure, early withdrawal from school, and low educational aspirations (Coley & Chase-Lansdale, 1998).

Families today are diverse: Some have two parents—one of each sex; some have two parents—both of the same sex; some have only a mother or only a father (by choice or circumstance). Much of the research on families and their effects on infant development focuses on two-parent heterosexual couples, and recent research is revealing that many of the conclusions about parenting and infant outcomes extend to same-sex couples (Goldberg & Sayer, 2006: Tasker, 2010). Single parenting is different.

There are multiple paths to single parenting, the most common one being an unmarried woman giving birth to an infant conceived either in a romantic relationship or by donor insemination (Tyano & Keren, 2010). According to the U.S. Census Bureau, the number of single women in the United States giving birth has increased by 45% from 1980 to 2008. This increase is due, in part, to changing perceptions and greater acceptance of single-parenthood, and as a result, women, particularly affluent and well-educated ones, are choosing to parent outside of a relationship. Single parenting is not limited only to women. Men, too, are single parents, many of whom have custody after a divorce or out of wedlock birth, but adoption is also an option for some. Single parents confront a number of obstacles, including financial hardship and lack of social support. Both of these factors are stressors that affect parenting, as we will see below, and they can be particularly acute for single parents (Tyano & Keren, 2010).

The quality of mothering and fathering is affected by partner supportiveness, but support appears to be especially important when families are under stress (Leerkes & Cockenberg, 2006). Stress accompanies the transition to the new role of being a parent, and infant characteristics (such as fussiness) also play a role (Guedeney & Tereno, 2010). In addition to the infant's characteristics, the family's economic circumstances can be a source of stress. Economic circumstances have a major impact on the quality of relationships between parents and on the quality of their parenting, and poverty and economic failure are associated with punitive parenting and increased child abuse and neglect (Berger et al., 2011). Poverty and economic hardship are often the focus of arguments between parents that set the wrong tone and detract from each parent's ability to care for an infant optimally (Box 2.1). Stress, therefore, not only affects each parent's behavior directly, it also reduces mutual supportiveness which can adversely affect the quality of the partner's behavior toward the infant.

Box 2.1   Set For Life? Exposure to Domestic Violence Alters Infants' Reaction to Conflict

Dejonghe and her colleagues (2005) investigated whether experience with domestic violence influences the way infants respond to conflict. In their study, 12-month-olds were exposed to an adult having a scripted 30-second telephone argument. After the argument, the adult played with the infant for 5 minutes, during which time infants were rated for their degree of distress using facial, vocal, and postural expressions. Mothers also completed a temperament questionnaire. Thirty of the 89 infants had mothers who reported experiencing domestic violence within the infants' lifetime. Infants exposed to domestic violence showed significantly higher levels of distress compared to infants who did not have experience with domestic violence. Infants without a history of domestic violence showed different levels of distress depending on their temperament. Infants who were judged to be temperamentally more active, less adaptable, and more likely to express negative mood showed greater distress than calmer, more adaptable, and easygoing infants. Exposure to domestic violence seems to elevate a child's later distress response to conflict, and this effect is above and beyond different temperamental styles.

Indirect influences such as the quality of social support from other significant adults is as important to infants and mothers in low-income, single-parent households as to their counterparts in middle-income, two-parent households (Borkowski, Farris, Whitman, Weed, & Keogh 2007; Weinraub, Horvath, & Gringlas, 2002). For example, father support is positively associated with adolescent mothers' self-esteem and efficacy and negatively associated with life stress (Shapiro & Mangelsdorf, 1994). Many infants of adolescent mothers, for example, are part of three-generation families (infant–mother–grandmother) in which parental responsibilities are shared by the mother and grandmother. When adolescent mothers establish some independence from, and good communication with, the grandmothers, the adolescent mothers' parenting is better, and she is at less risk for post-partum depression than when the adolescent mother–grandmother relationships are characterized by confusion and conflict (Shanok & Miller, 2007).

Full understanding of the effects of family climate on infant–parent relationships and other aspects of infant development requires multiple types of data representing multiple levels of analysis. Information about parents' attitudes, values, perceptions, and beliefs helps to explain when and why parents behave as they do. Likewise, observations of parenting in multiple caregiving situations are required to tell the full scope of how parents behave. Parents affect infant development directly through parent–infant interaction. In addition, infant development is affected indirectly by social-environmental supports and stressors that influence parent behavior. Concern with the impact of supportiveness, stress, and other relationships is intrinsic to ecological approaches to the study of infant development (Lerner et al., 2011). Advocates of the contextual approach caution that relationships, like individuals, change over time. As the dynamics of the family change, changes in relationships between parents, and between each of the parents and the infant, can be expected to change.

Some of the most dramatic changes in family dynamics occur when another baby is born into the family. The birth of a sibling alters the roles of each family member and consequently affects the ways in which each interacts with all other family members. Indeed, much interesting work on the dynamics of family relationships focuses on sibling relationships. Zukow-Goldring (2002), for example, described the ways in which Mexican siblings not only care for those younger than them, but, through play, teach younger siblings many of the skills (such as how to make tortillas) they will need to succeed as adults.

INFANTS, SIBLINGS, AND PEERS

Parents play an especially important role in infant development. Through interaction with their parents, babies develop confidence in their own abilities, trust in others, and an awareness of the reciprocal nature of social interaction. Meanwhile, experiences with a variety of other children and adults foster the development of an even more sophisticated and flexible repertoire of social skills by providing exposure to different individuals who have different behavioral styles and provide contrasting patterns of interaction.

Interaction with other children during childhood is an important component of development. In rhesus monkeys, Harlow (1960) found that peer interactions were critical to many aspects of normal development (Figure 2.3). By interacting with their peers, infant monkeys learn how to play, how to fight, how to relate to members of the opposite sex, and how to communicate with other monkeys. When deprived of these interactions with peers, monkeys become socially incompetent adults even when they have experi-

Fig. 2.3 Rhesus monkey peers in play. Such interactions are important in the social development of monkeys. Peers are important to human infants as well. (Courtesy of S. J. Suomi.)

enced good quality care from their mothers. These findings led developmental scientists to pay attention to sibling and peer relationships in infancy. These relationships constitute a bridge between within-family relationships and relationships beyond the home.

Sibling Relationships

As mentioned earlier, siblings in many non-Western, non-industrialized countries assume a major responsibility for childcare (Zukow-Goldring, 2002; Figure 2.4). In some cultures, siblings spend relatively little time playing with infants; most of their interactions, like those of Western parents, involve protection or caregiving. In Western industrialized societies, by contrast, siblings seldom assume any responsibility for infant caregiving, and sibling relationships appear to incorporate features of both the infant–adult and infant–peer systems. On the one hand, infants and siblings share common interests and have more similar behavioral repertoires than do infant–adult dyads. On the other hand, sibling pairs resemble infant–adult pairs to the extent that partners differ in experience and levels of both cognitive and social ability.

These discrepancies often lead to differences in the ways younger and older siblings relate to each other and distinguish them from infant–peer pairs. For example, consistent asymmetries emerge between the roles assumed by preschoolers and their 1-year-old siblings (Abramovitch, Corter, & Lando, 1979; Lamb, 1978a, 1978b). Older siblings tend to "lead" interactions: They engage in more dominant, assertive, and directing behaviors than their younger siblings. Infants, meanwhile, appear inordinately interested in what their siblings are doing; they follow them around and attempt to imitate and/or explore the toys just abandoned by the older children. This strategy maximizes the amount the baby can learn about the environment from the older child. Older siblings spend at least some time teaching object-related and social skills to their younger siblings (including infants), and the amount of teaching increases with the age of the older child. These observations, along with the fact that infants monitor and imitate their older siblings, corroborate the assertion that older siblings may influence the cognitive and social skills

Fig. 2.4 She is only 7 years old herself, but this young Kenyan girl is responsible each day for the care of her infant brother and often for her cousins as well. (Courtesy of T. S. Weisner.)

of infants through combinations of teaching and modeling (Zukow-Goldring, 2002). In our current age of assisted reproduction and delayed childbearing (i.e., older mothers having children), the number of multiple births has increased. In the United States, there were 32 twin deliveries per 1,000 live births in 2006 as compared to 7–10 twin deliveries per 1,000 live births in 1970. Consequently, a number of "first born" children also have same-aged siblings because they are a twin or triplet. Multiple babies of the same age present unique challenges to parents, and the situation provides a unique social context for infant development (Feldman & Eidelman, 2004; Friedman, 2008).

Most researchers concerned with sibling interaction have aimed to describe the relationship and assess its impact on social development (Figure 2.5). In an early short-term longitudinal study, Lamb (1978a) found stability across time in the amount of interaction engaged in by infants and their preschool-age siblings. The sociability of the younger babies determined the amount of attention they received from their siblings; it was not that attention from older siblings helped babies become more sociable. Sex of siblings also influences the sibling relationship: Same-sex siblings typically get along better than different-sex siblings (Martin & Ross, 2005). In addition, maternal management style may also influence cooperation among preschool and infant siblings (Howe, Aquan-Assee, & Bukowski, 2001).

Parent–child and parent–parent relationships also influence sibling relationships. Infants who have secure attachments—close, trusting, and well-meshed relationships—with their mothers protest less and are less aggressive when their mothers play only with their older siblings. For their part, preschoolers who are securely attached to their mothers are more likely to respond to the distress of their infant siblings

Fig. 2.5 Nurturance is an important (and often overlooked) dimension of infant–sibling relationships and appears to be linked to the quality of children's relationships with parents.

nurturantly than less securely attached older siblings (Volling, 2001). Furthermore, siblings are more positive toward each other when they had nurturant relationships with their fathers. In addition, Yu and Gamble (2008) found that the quality of the marriage also affects sibling relationship quality. In their study, Mexican American, European American, and Taiwanese mothers who reported higher levels of marital satisfaction also reported positive sibling relationships among their children. Moreover, this study showed a mutual influence of parenting styles and sibling relationships, such that it was not merely the mother's parenting behavior that influenced siblings. Instead, high-quality sibling relationships also impacted the approaches mothers took toward parenting.

These findings indicate that qualitative aspects of sibling relationships must be considered in the context of children's relationships with parents and the broader family constellation. Indeed, sibling relationships are more prosocial and less aggressive when parent–child relationships and parents' marriages are good, and when parents avoid treating siblings differently and allow (within reason) siblings to settle their disputes themselves. Although studies of differential parental treatment of siblings typically target older children, the differential treatment of infants by their mothers can occur as early as 2 months of age (Kowal, Krull, & Kramer, 2007).

In summary, we know that different-aged siblings play a significant role in infants' social worlds from early in life. They offer degrees of stimulation and entertainment that vary depending on age, gender, age gap, the quality of the children's relationships with parents, and family functioning as a whole. In addition, studies of older children suggest that siblings may be important socialization agents in their own right, shaping both prosocial and aggressive behavior in younger siblings.

Developing Relationships with Other Children

For babies who do not have older siblings, interaction with other children usually does not begin until the child is enrolled in an alternative care setting, an informal play group, or a preschool program. Research on relationships that develop among unrelated children has blossomed in large part because changes in the rates of maternal employment have led increasing numbers of infants to spend extended periods of time with other children.

The development of infant–peer relationships goes through a series of stages (Rubin, Coplan, Chen, Bowker, & McDonald, 2011). In the first year, social interaction between infants is not frequent, and when it does occur it is not sustained for very long. Very young infants show an interest in peers; there seems to be something very interesting about another baby. By 6 months, infants interact in more complex ways—initiating exchanges and responding to one another's social overtures with combinations of looks, smiles, and vocalizations. Their sensitivity to social cues from peers leads infants to continue interacting when their partners are responsive, whereas they cease social bids when their partners are unresponsive. From 6 to 12 months, infant–peer interaction increases, responsiveness to peer overtures and imitation becoming increasingly common, and interaction involving physical contact occurs less frequently.

Empathic and prosocial behaviors first appear between 12 and 18 months of age when infants become aware of their feelings and begin to realize that others have feelings as well (Saarni, Campos, Camras, & Witherington, 2006). By 2 years of age, infants no longer respond contagiously to their peers' emotions, crying and wanting to be soothed when their peers cry. Instead, they observe their peers' negative emotions carefully and attempt to respond appropriately (Bischof-Koehler, 1991), such as offering a toy to a distressed child or alerting an adult that a child is upset ("baby crying" is a typical report). In addition, prosocial (helping, giving, or sharing) responses become increasingly appropriate in the second year (Roth-Hanania, Davidov, & Zahn-Waxler, 2011; Svetlova, Nichols, & Brownell, 2010).

The criteria used for evaluating the quality of peer relationships in infants differ from those for older children (Williams, Ontai, & Mastergeorge, 2007). Older children who engage in more prosocial (as compared to aggressive) behaviors are described as more socially competent. Infants do not engage in many prosocial behaviors and their interactions, on the surface, appear to consist of a lot of conflict. To further understand the interactions among young infants and toddlers, Williams and her colleagues (2007) observed peer interactions of children between 12 and 17 months of age. All children were observed in a child-care setting, and thus had plenty of opportunities to engage with same-aged peers. The researchers found three measures of social competence: peer sociability, active peer refusal, and passive peer avoidance. Peer sociability included smiling at peers, initiating play, imitating, and taking toys from peers. Active peer refusal included refusing peers' attempts to play, turning back to peers, and moving away from peers. Passive peer avoidance included watching rather than participating, and acting as if he/she does not notice peers' attempts to initiate play. The authors noted that negative behavior was not necessarily a sign of poor social competence. For example, taking a toy away from another child was an indicator of social interaction, rather than the hostile act it would be among older children. Hitting or biting, different type of hostile acts, were interpreted as a way for infants to actively avoid interactions. Individual differences in infants' interest in engaging with others were also found. Williams et al. (2007) noted that some infants prefer to play by themselves, a preference the authors attributed to differences in temperament (Chapter 10).

The development of relationships with peers is affected not only by infants' social, cognitive, and emotional attainments, but also by socialization practices within the family (NICHD Early Child Care Research Network, 2005). Infants who experience warm, sensitive parenting and grow up in harmonious families tend to be well adjusted socially, unaggressive, and popular (Ladd & Pettit, 2002). Attachment theorists argue that children who have secure relationships with their parents should be sociable and socially competent (Sroufe, Egeland, Carlson, & Collins, 2005) although the empirical evidence is not very strong or consistent (NICHD Early Child Care Research Network, 2005), suggesting that parent–child relationships are not the only family factors that affect infants' peer relationships.

Childcare providers can play a significant role in facilitating infants' peer relationships. According to Williams, Mastergeorge, and Ontai (2010), providers accomplish this in several ways including distracting children from other children or objects, encouraging children to join a peer group, giving directives ("wave hello"), and talking about another child's presence, objects, clothing, feelings, and intentions. In addition, helpful caregivers respond to actions initiated by the infant but not fully completed. For example, if a child is standing near a peer group looking on, the caregiver may assist the child with joining the group.

In summary, infants develop relationships with peers, but their interactions are different from those seen in later childhood. Infants are curious about each other, and they engage in ways that both facilitate and discourage interactions with others. Adults, both parents and childcare providers, facilitate infants' interactions with peers in many ways.

NONPARENTAL CARE OF INFANTS

So far, we have seen how a greater understanding of infants must acknowledge the richness, diversity, and complexity of their early experiences, including those involving all family members. The majority of infants in the United States are now cared for by someone in addition to a parent, and this situation may have a variety of effects on infant development (Lamb, 2012b). A number of terms are used for nonparental care, including daycare, child care, early childhood education programs, and babysitting. For our discussion, we use the term **daycare** to refer to all nonparental care. Because infant daycare practices contrast with popular beliefs in the unique importance of maternal care, there has been heated controversy about how various forms of daycare affect children's development. Families of all kinds need and use supplementary care for their infants, and these needs are most often driven by economic concerns and motives. Put simply, the rise in the use of out-of-home care in the United States and elsewhere can be attributed to the need and/or desire for women to be a part of the workforce to help support their families and pursue a career (Lamb & Ahnert, 2006).

Commentators and politicians commonly oversimplify the wide variety of nonparental care arrangements on which parents rely. In 2010, of the children of working parents between the ages of 0 to 4 years in the United States, 24% had been placed in center-based care, 14% in non-relative home-based care, and 48% with another relative, such as a father, grandparent, or sibling (www.childstats.gov). Also, the number of hours of nonmaternal care varies considerably by child age (Figure 2.6). Studying the effects of differing types of care on child development is difficult because none of these types of care should be viewed as similar, as the nature and quality of care varies widely across centers, homes, and babysitters. Also, unfortunately, the quality of care often remains unmeasured, even though the quality, rather than the type, of care appears to have a greater impact on children's development (Lamb, 2012b). Furthermore, generalizations about daycare are hampered by the fact that infants are not randomly assigned to daycare and exclusive parental care. The values, practices, and economic profile of parents who do or do not enroll their infants in daycare can differ, and so group differences that might be attributed to daycare may instead be due (at least in part) to variation in the values and behaviors of parents and the communities in which they live. In the U.S., families of higher income are likely to enroll their infants in daycare centers that are of high quality and families in the lowest income brackets are likely to enroll their infants in high-quality federally funded programs like Head Start. Working poor- and middle-income families are most likely to have other relatives care for their infant or place infants in low-quality programs (NICHD Early Child Care Resource Network, 2005). To ensure that later differences can be viewed solely as the effects of daycare, the comparability of infants and families prior to their assignment to various care arrangements must be assured. In all, a thorough understanding of the effects of daycare on infants requires attention both to the background and needs of parents and infants as well as the characteristics of their care arrangements (e.g., quality, extent, and type).

Because so many infants and young children have been placed in out-of-home care, extensive efforts have been made to conceptualize and measure the quality of infant care (Lamb & Ahnert, 2006). Measures of quality typically fall into two types: **Structural measures of child care context** (group size, teacher–

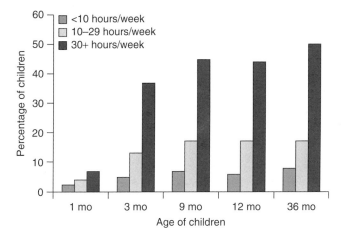

Fig. 2.6 Percentage of children in part-time and full-time nonmaternal care as a function of age. (Created from data in NICHD Early Child Care Research Network, 2005.)

child ratios, and teacher training) assess broad markers of the social and physical environment that bear a straightforward relation to a child's interactions in the setting. **Process measures of child care context** (language-reasoning experiences, caregivers' interactional competence with the children, and the breadth and diversity of the learning curriculum) assess the actual quality of care experienced by children. Table 2.1 shows an example of one measure, the Infant/Toddler Environment Rating Scale (ITERS; Harms, Cryer, & Clifford, 2003). Even though structural measures of quality tend to focus on gross environmental markers, they appear to be associated with process measures. For example, higher staff-to-child ratios and better training correlate positively with caregiver–child interaction and the frequency of parent–caregiver communication (NICHD Early Child Care Research Network, 2005).

Parents' perceptions of quality of childcare do not always match researchers' or those of accrediting organizations such as the National Association for Education of Young Children (NAEYC; Cryer, Tietze, & Wessels, 2002). The areas where there is agreement are those that are easily observable (e.g., appropriate furnishings). Parents tend to give higher ratings than trained observers to those features they value most, and discrepancy increases as the value parents place on the feature increases. In addition, parental income and parental education articulate differently with perceived quality. For the most part, centers with families of higher income tend to be rated as higher in quality by parents and observers. Yet parents with higher education tend to rate quality lower than trained observers, suggesting that parents with higher educational levels are more discerning in their evaluation of daycare programs (Torquati, Raikes, Huddleston-Casas, Bovaird, & Harris, 2011).

Full-day placement in daycare is emotionally and physiologically stressful for many, if not most, infants and toddlers (Ahnert, Gunnar, Lamb, & Barthel, 2004). Other things being equal, the seriousness of the challenge increases as the length of time spent in care increases. Ahnert and her colleagues (2004)

Table 2.1 Components of the Infant/Toddler Environment Rating Scale—Revised (ITERS-R; used to assess quality of daycare settings (Harms, Cryer, & Clifford, 2003))

Space and Furnishings	Indoor space Furniture for routine care and play Provision for relaxation and comfort	Room arrangement Display for children
Personal Care Routines	Greeting/departing Meals/snacks Nap	Diapering/toileting Health practices Safety practices
Listening and Talking	Helping children understand language Helping children use language	Using books
Activities	Fine motor Art Blocks Dramatic play Use of TV, video, and/or computers	Active physical play Music and movement Sand and water play Nature/science Promoting acceptance of diversity
Interaction	Supervision of play and learning Peer interaction	Staff–child interaction Discipline
Program Structure	Schedule Free play	Group play activities Provisions for children with disabilities
Parents and Staff	Provisions for parents Provisions for: • personal needs of staff • professional needs of staff	Staff interaction and cooperation Staff continuity Supervision and evaluation of staff Opportunities for professional growth

used cortisol measures (Chapter 3) to track the adaptation to daycare (an indicator of the child experiencing less stress) and reported that child adjustment in part depends on the quality of prior child–mother attachment relationships. Although child–mother attachment security was unrelated to cortisol levels at home, securely attached toddlers had markedly lower cortisol levels in the centers than insecurely attached toddlers as long as the mothers were also present, suggesting that secure child–mother relationships buffered the stressfulness of entry into daycare. When daily mother–child separations began, however, cortisol levels were similarly elevated in securely and insecurely attached toddlers. The importance of parental support in managing toddlers' stress levels was also evident in the fact that child–mother attachments remained secure or shifted from insecure to secure when mothers spent more days adapting their children to daycare.

Why are care providers often unable to reduce levels of stress effectively, particularly as most children develop meaningful relationships with their care providers? Early studies emphasized that enrollment in daycare allowed children to form significant relationships with providers but did not lead care providers to displace mothers as primary attachment figures (Lamb & Ahnert, 2006). In more recent studies, focus has switched from whether or not children form attachments to the quality or security of the relationships formed. In a synthesis of a number of studies involving nearly 3,000 toddlers, Ahnert, Pinquart, and Lamb (2006) found that secure relationships to care providers were less common than secure relationships to mothers or fathers: 60–70% of parent–infant attachments were secure, whereas only 42% of attachments to nonparental care providers were secure. As with parents, the security of infant–care provider attachment is associated with the sensitivity, involvement, and quality of the care experienced. Children's relationships with care providers, especially in centers, are predominantly shaped by behavior toward the group as a whole (Ahnert et al., 2006). Only in small groups was the security of relationships with care providers predicted by measures of dyadic responsiveness similar to those that predict the security of children's attachments to their parents (Howes & Guerra, 2009).

To help children adjust, many European daycare centers have implemented adaptation programs in which mothers are allowed to accompany their children during the transitional period of enrollment. When mothers familiarize their children to daycare in a more leisurely manner and accompany their children in the center, adjustment is easier, especially when children are securely attached to their mothers (Ahnert et al., 2004; Rauh, Ziegenhain, Müller, & Wijnroks, 2000).

Of course, infants in daycare facilities are not only exposed regularly to an additional set of experiences, but they also have experiences at home that differ from those experienced by peers who do not receive regular nonparental care. For example, parents interact more intensely during shorter time intervals with children who attend daycare (Ahnert, Rickert, & Lamb, 2000; Booth, Clarke-Stewart, Vandell, McCartney, & Owen, 2002). As a result, the total amount of attention children receive from adults is the same, whether or not they are enrolled in out-of-home care. For example, during morning hours, parents focus on communication and basic care, whereas in evening hours parents focus on stimulation and soothing, and bedtime routines are characterized by high levels of intimate emotional exchange (Ahnert et al., 2000).

Changes in parental behavior accompany enrollment in daycare, but adverse effects on child–parent relationships are avoidable, especially when parents and children have established harmonious relationships. The NICHD Study of Early Child Care (2005) found no differences in the proportion of secure attachments whether or not infants had experienced nonmaternal care. Greater maternal sensitivity was associated with increases in the probability that infants would be classified as securely attached to their mothers, and infants whose mothers were less sensitive were more likely to be insecurely attached, especially when the infants spent long hours in care and the daycare was of poor quality. Evidently, parenting continues to shape the quality of child–parent relationships even when children experience daycare (Box 2.2).

Box 2.2   Science in Translation: Teachers? Mother Substitutes? A Bit of Both?

More than half the infants in the United States now spend a considerable proportion of their lives in the care of people other than their parents, and the proportion has been rising dramatically in other developed countries, too (Lamb & Ahnert, 2006). These changing patterns of care have created a situation in which many, if not most, children have opportunities to form significant relationships outside their families, and there is now ample evidence that almost all infants and toddlers form attachments to their nonparental care providers. What are the features of these relationships? Do these attachments tend to be secure? And do they provide the same kinds of support that relationships with parents do?

Ahnert et al. (2006) undertook a meta-analytic study in which they re-examined the results of 40 studies involving nearly 3000 children averaging 2½ years of age. The relationships formed between children in childcare and the adults responsible for their care in childcare facilities were assessed using the same types of measures that have been used to assess children's relationships with their parents. The results showed that child–parent and child–care provider relationships shared some important features. However, the characteristics of interaction with the care providers (not the quality of the children's relationships with their parents) largely shaped the quality of children's relationships with specific care providers. Furthermore, children's relationships with care providers, especially in childcare centers, were associated with measures of the care providers' behavior toward the group as a whole, rather than towards individual children. Clearly, group interaction dominates in childcare centers. Even when care providers are engaged in one-on-one interaction with individual children, they have to pay attention to the rest of the group, too. Only in small groups was the security of relationships with care providers predicted by measures of responsiveness similar to those associated with differences in the security of children's attachments to their parents. These findings made clear that children's relationships with their care providers and parents were different in character, with the "teacher-like" character of the relationships especially prominent in larger groups, and the "mother-like" features also prominent in smaller groups.

The researchers also found that secure attachments to nonparental care providers were less likely than secure attachments to parents. In addition, children were more likely to have secure relationships with care providers the longer they remained in the same facilities with the same providers, thus underscoring the importance of stability of care. The child's age at the time of his or her enrolment in childcare had no effect.

There is growing evidence that relationships with care providers have an important impact on children's development, and this study's findings help to pin-point the features of those relationships that are most likely to affect children's later behavioral and socioemotional functioning in the most positive ways.

Many parents choose daycare arrangements in the belief that peer interactions play an important role in social development, especially by fostering the development of empathy and the acquisition of social skills. Thus, it was surprising when some reports suggested that infant daycare was associated with increased aggressiveness towards peers. The NICHD Early Child Care Research Network (2005) found that the amount of nonmaternal care in the first 4½ years of life predicted behavior problems (including assertiveness, disobedience, and aggression) displayed at home or in kindergarten. The elevated risk of behavior problems on the part of children with extensive daycare histories was evident in reports by mothers, care providers, and teachers. Similar associations, however, were not evident in three other large multisite studies (Love et al., 2003), perhaps because the NICHD researchers studied centers that tended to provide care of mediocre quality, whereas the centers Love and his co-authors studied provided care of higher quality. Quality of care also proved to be important in other large-scale studies (Loeb, Fuller, Kagan, & Carroll, 2004; Votruba-Drzal, Coley, & Chase-Lansdale, 2004). Lamb (2005a, 2012b; Lamb & Ahnert, 2006) has argued that these effects might best be seen not as the direct effects of nonparental care, but as the effects of adult (especially parent, but also caregiver) failures to provide infants with sufficient amounts of emotional support in coping with the stressful challenges of daycare situations.

Researchers who have studied the effects of daycare on cognitive development have found that infants from low-income families tend to benefit when they attend stimulating daycare centers (Lamb & Ahnert, 2006; NICHD Early Child Care Research Network, 2005; Sylva, Stein, Leach, Barnes, & Malberg, 2011). Children from more advantaged backgrounds do not consistently profit from daycare in this way, presumably because they enjoy stimulating environments at home. Indeed, early and extensive daycare can even have negative effects, especially on language development, when the benefits attributable to growing up in advantaged families are attenuated by daycare (Burchinal, Peisner-Feinberg, Bryant, & Clifford, 2000). Positive family factors (such as greater family income, more sensitive mothering, and less authoritarian childrearing attitudes) are associated with more positive child functioning and continue to affect children positively even when they spend much time in daycare settings (Belsky et al., 2007). Indeed, family factors are more reliable predictors of children's cognitive competencies than the quality or type of nonparental daycare (NICHD Early Child Care Research Network, 2005). However, the effects diminish over time, presumably because the beneficial effects of high-quality care are undercut by increasing exposure to less stimulating environments, both at home and at school, as children get older.

SOCIOECONOMIC CLASS, CULTURE, AND INFANCY

Because most social scientists come from, or were trained in, middle-class Western backgrounds, it is not surprising that they have focused their attention on the childrearing practices of people like themselves. Unfortunately, this focus can lead to a tendency to view as deficient, rather than just different, the beliefs, practices, and experiences of those from other backgrounds. Such an emphasis can also lead to the design of interventions to alleviate deficiencies without first understanding the unique strengths of individuals from different backgrounds. The shortsightedness of an ethnocentric perspective was illustrated long ago by analysis of social class differences. As Bronfenbrenner (1961) pointed out, middle-class researchers consistently find ways to portray middle-class values and practices as more desirable and appropriate than those of the lower class, even though the values of both the middle-class and lower-class parents change over time. Thus, when the same values were held at different times by middle- and lower-class parents— say, a preference for bottle or breastfeeding—they were positively evaluated when held by middle-class parents and negatively evaluated when adopted by lower-class parents! In this instance, the positive and negative evaluations clearly said more about researchers and theorists than about the effects on children.

Social Class

In general, social status in the United States is indexed by quantitative factors having to do with parents (Bornstein & Bradley, 2003). A socioeconomic status index is computed using measures of the parents' educational achievement, income, and occupational status. A fruitful framework for understanding social-status differences in early development was advanced by Kohn (1987), who suggested that parents try to instill values that will maximize their children's chances of success in the social stratum in which they are likely to find themselves as mature adults. For example, middle- and upper-class parents in Western industrialized societies expect that their children will hold positions of leadership and professional responsibility; they are thus prone to emphasize self-reliance, independence, autonomy, creativity, and curiosity. Hoff, Laursen, and Tardif (2002) noted that middle-class parents expect their children to show an early mastery of academic-related skills. By contrast, lower-class parents expect their children to have as little opportunity for self-actualization and leadership as they themselves had, and hence tend to emphasize obedience and conformity, values that will maximize their children's chances of success in the roles they are expected to fill in society.

The few published studies addressing differences among social classes report results consistent with these predictions. Middle-class U.S. mothers talk to their babies more than lower-class mothers, even though infants are not yet talking themselves. Hoff et al. (2002) observed social status differences in the functional, discourse, and lexical properties of maternal language. Functionally, lower-class mothers limit their utterances to directions and corrections, instead of acknowledging their infants' actions or attempting to engage them in conversation. As far as discourse is concerned, lower-class infants were less likely than middle-class infants to receive topic-continuing replies to their utterances. Differences in lexical properties of language included middle-class mothers talking more in total, talking more per unit of time, and sustaining longer bouts of verbal interactions than lower-class mothers. Thus, in a variety of ways, middle-class mothers encourage their infants to converse and to expand their communicative abilities.

Of course, extreme economic disadvantage affects infant development in ways that go beyond maternal speech patterns, values, and expectations. Because a large and growing number of U.S. children live in poverty (46% in 2009), there has been a dramatic increase in research devoted to understanding the extent to which living in poverty influences early child development (McLoyd, Aikens, & Burton, 2006). When compared to infants in middle-class environments, infants living in poverty experience lower levels of emotional and verbal responsiveness, fewer opportunities for variety in daily stimulation, fewer appropriate play materials, and more chaotic, disorganized, and unstructured environments (Magnusson & Duncan, 2002). In a study of European American families living in the Appalachia region of West Virginia (known for high rates of rural poverty), Bornstein, Putnick and Suwalsky (2012) found that both younger and older mothers' parenting was enhanced by being married and having the father present in the home. It is possible that marital status and father presence legitimized the mother's status as a parent in her own or others' eyes, and thus contributed to positive parenting. Consequently, father involvement can serve as a buffer against life stresses and other difficulties common to communities where financial and other resource strains are common, such as Appalachia.

Many studies on African American families in the United States confound social class and ethnicity, comparing poor or lower-class African American infants with upper-class European American infants. Recent studies have shown social class differences in parental behavior and patterns of parent–infant interaction in low-, middle-, and upper-class African American homes, similar to what is found in European American homes (Fouts, Roopnarine, & Lamb, 2007). In one study, Fouts, Roopnarine, Lamb, and Evans (2012) observed low- and middle-class African American and European American families with 3- to 4-month-old infants for 12 hours across 4 days. Observations centered in and around the home focused on parental and nonparental caregivers engaging in emotional availability, affection, caregiving, and stimulation. Fouts et al. found differences across socioeconomic status in maternal and paternal holding, maternal carrying, and paternal caregiving (Figure 2.7). In contrast, they found ethnic differences in maternal availability, affection, caregiving, and stimulation. Such findings indicate that some of the differences previously attributed to ethnic differences should instead be attributed to social status and, moreover, that socioeconomic status and ethnicity have independent effects on the social experiences of young infants.

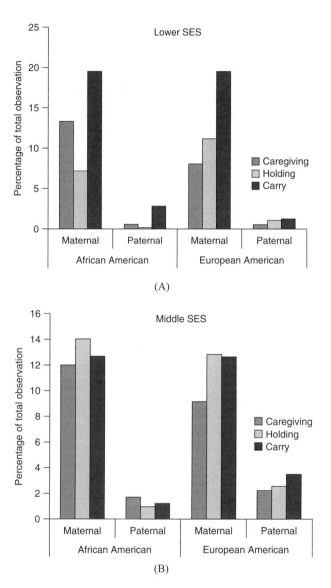

Fig. 2.7 Percentage of time lower SES (A) and middle SES (B) African American mothers and fathers engaged in caregiving activities, holding, and carrying their 3- to 4-month-old infants. Note the differences between mothers and fathers varies more as a function of SES than ethnicity. (Created from data in Fouts, Roopnarine, Lamb, & Evans, 2012.)

In summary, social status exerts direct and indirect influences on infant development. Mothers from different economic classes engage with their infants differently, and the undue hardships and stress created by extreme economic disadvantage are likely to diminish parents' ability to respond effectively to their infants, structure and organize their environment, and provide them with even the minimal levels of stimulation needed to support development. Social status, however, needs to be studied alongside ethnicity so that the independent effects of each factor can be clearly indentified.

Culture

As we wrote in Chapter 1, many reasons have been offered to justify cross-cultural developmental research (Bornstein, 2012). First, people are always curious about development in foreign cultures, and anthropologists have often reported about childhood and childcare in the cultures they study. Awareness of alternative modes of development sharpens perceptions and enhances understanding of our own culture. Second, to the extent that cross-cultural developmentalists attempt to describe the widest spectrum of human variation, their accounts are the most comprehensive available. They play an essential role in documenting the full range of human experience and in establishing valid developmental norms. Third, the examination of other cultures facilitates the quest to understand forces at work in development by exposing variables that are highly influential but may be "invisible" from a monocultural perspective. Fourth, cross-cultural research permits natural tests of the universality of psychological constructs (Chapter 3).

Clearly, many of the reasons motivating cross-cultural developmental research are descriptive, but some salient ones concern developmental processes. According to Werner (1988, p. 97):

> The yeoman's service that a cross-cultural perspective can provide for … researchers is to encourage them to take a systematic look at contextual parameters that vary across and within cultures and that are often restricted and/or confounded in the settings and samples they choose to study. Investigators who observe [child] behaviors in [other countries] find there is a wider range of biological and psychological factors that influence the development of infants than in industrialized countries.

Take daycare as an example. One of the reasons why the effects of daycare have constituted such a controversial and heavily researched topic is that nonparental care was (incorrectly) believed by influential Europeans and North Americans in the mid-20th century to be unnatural, representing a break with traditional daycare practices (Lamb, 2012b). However, historically, aristocratic and affluent Europeans and North Americans have long depended on wet nurses, nannies, and governesses to care for their children. In his biography of Charles Darwin, Stone (1980) recounts that Charles and his siblings were reared by a nanny, slept in a separate house from their parents, and were allowed to dine with adults in the family only when their feet could touch the floor while sitting at the dining room table. The existence of such powerful ideological beliefs underscores the importance of social and cultural factors in shaping the social ecology of infancy. There are many societies in which both nonmaternal care practices and maternal employment are normative; citizens of these societies might be amazed to find cultures in which mothers are expected to devote themselves extensively to childcare and risk criticism for deviating from this pattern. Cultures help to "construct" children by influencing parental beliefs about childrearing and attributions about the developmental capacities of infants, which in turn influence parents' practices (Cole & Packer, 2011).

Parents' ideas about child development and childrearing are thought to serve many functions. They may determine parental behavior; they may help to organize the world of parenting because ideas affect parents' sense of self and competence in their role; and, in a larger sense, they may contribute to the "continuity of culture" by helping to define culture and the transmission of cultural information across generations (Bornstein, 2009). This notion is illustrated in the following study that investigated mothers from both collectivist and individualist cultures. In collectivist cultures, such as Argentina, Japan, and Korea, the group tends to be valued over the individual, and thus there is an emphasis on the interconnectedness of the members of the community. Individualist cultures, such as Belgium, Israel, Italy, and the United States, tend to value independence of the self more. In a study of mothers of 20-month-olds in seven countries (Argentina, Belgium, Israel, Italy, Korea, Japan, and the United States), mothers were assessed for their competence and satisfaction in parenting, their knowledge of infant development, and their personality (Bornstein et al., 2007). Systematic differences between collectivist and individualist cultures were found. For example, mothers from individualist cultures who scored higher on neuroticism (i.e., the tendency to worry a lot, be nervous, emotional, and insecure) reported less competence and satisfaction in parenting, but mothers from collectivist cultures who scored higher on neuroticism reported more satisfaction with parenting. Bornstein et al. suggest that neuroticism undermines feelings of competence and satisfaction in individualist cultures where independence is valued, but it does not in collectivist cultures because such social sensitivity is a valued trait and thus does not undermine mothers' satisfaction with parenting.

Recognizing the pervasiveness of cultural influences on infant development, Harkness and Super (2002) argued that the development of every infant must be viewed in the context of the **niche** in which the infant is reared. There are three ways in which niches vary: physically, ideologically, and in custom. Variations in **physical circumstances** are readily apparent. Consider two infants: One is born into a group of nomadic hunter-gatherers, living in temporary homes, and spending much of each day in large multiage groups obtaining food (Jung & Fouts, 2011). The other is born into a modern Western culture, isolated at home with a single adult, whose food is purchased, and who comes into contact with a smorgasbord of individuals, few of whom are seen frequently or show much interest in the child's welfare. Cultural differences in **ideology**, or worldview, influence such factors as the frequency with which the infant is cared for by other children or unrelated adults, the extent to which the infant is allowed to explore, and whether the infant's experiences are nurturing or restrictive (Hewlett & Lamb, 2005). Illustrating **customary**, or typical, dimensions are infant–mother sleeping arrangements that result in very different expectations about "norms" such as sleeping through the night (Harkness & Super, 2002). Sleeping through the night without waking is a developmental milestone anxiously awaited by Western parents eager to avoid the disrupted sleep patterns brought about by the need to retrieve, feed, change, and put their infants back to bed. Persistent night waking is also a source of great anxiety for parents. This is not the case, however, in cultures in which infants and young children routinely sleep with their parents (Figure 2.8).

Fig. 2.8 Like many infants around the world, this infant remains strapped to her mother's back except at night, when she sleeps in her mother's bed. (Courtesy of C. Super.)

An informative example of the pitfalls attending an ethnocentric view of development is provided by examining the literature on motor development in infancy. A pioneer in this area was Gesell (1945), who set himself the goal of documenting early physical (and psychological) development in infants. On the basis of extensive and careful research conducted with infants and families in the United States, Gesell constructed detailed "cinematic atlases" of "normal development" and confidently offered "developmental diagnoses" of the progress and prognosis of normal and abnormal infant development. Gesell assumed that he had discovered universal developmental sequences, for he worked with such young infants and on behaviors thought to be almost wholly under biological control (Bornstein, 2001). The regularity of motor development that he observed in babies no doubt reinforced this belief. Only later in the 20th century did infant testing reach beyond such middle- and upper-SES European American families. The results of cross-cultural comparisons, first among American Hopi Indians and later among peoples in Bali and Africa, undermined many of Gesell's assumptions. These studies showed that babies often deviate from the accepted norms for European Americans with respect to both the stages and the timing of motor development in the first two years. Hopi infants begin to walk alone late (Dennis & Dennis, 1940); Balinese infants follow a different set of stages on their way to walking (Mead & MacGregor, 1951); and African Ganda and Wolof infants tend to be more advanced in sensory, psychological, and motor development than European American age norms would predict (Ainsworth, 1967).

What is the source of these developmental differences? As we read in Chapter 1, Gesell (Gesell & Amatruda, 1945) believed that early development largely unfolds under genetic control. Some data on motor development support a hypothesis of genetic differences among babies. Nine-hour-old neonates in Uganda are advanced in neuromuscular status (Geber & Dean, 1957a, 1957b), and native Africans are advanced beyond European Americans in skeletal maturation and bone growth at birth (Tanner, 1970). However, the majority of investigators have come to favor an environmentalist position on psychomotor development. Dennis and Dennis (1940) suggested that Hopi locomotor retardation reflected Hopi babies' traditional early constriction on the cradle board; Mead and McGregor (1951) proposed that the manner in which Balinese mothers habitually carried their infants promoted the babies' unique motor performance; and Ainsworth (1967) attributed advanced Ugandan motor abilities to a nurturing climate of physical freedom.

The environmentalist interpretation gains more credence when one examines the evidence and the babies closely. First, there is significant variability in the order that U.S. infants achieve different motor milestones, and, second, infants across cultures have different motor experiences before they make coordinated movements (Adolph & Berger, 2011). Takada (2005) describes the "gymnastic" routines that African mothers perform to stimulate the motor development of their infants. In the same vein, Hopkins and Westra (1988, 1990) surveyed English, Jamaican, and Indian mothers living in the same English city and found that Jamaican mothers expected their infants to sit and to walk much earlier, whereas Indian mothers expected their infants to crawl later. In each case, the infants performed in accordance with their mothers' expectations. The researchers were able to trace the precocity of Jamaican infants to a pattern of care termed "formal handling," which involved passive stretching movements and massage from birth, and to the introduction of practice stepping from about the third month.

Of course, innate differences in infant psychomotor abilities still may exist, and prenatal factors, such as maternal nutrition, activity, or anxiety level, could (and do) influence fetal development (Chapter 4). However, the cross-cultural data show that psychomotor differences among infants reflect the influence of childrearing practices.

The research on cultural differences in psychomotor development illustrates problems that arise when researchers attempt to discern the origins of cultural differences. Other, more subtle problems also bedevil meaningful cross-cultural comparisons. For example, the distinction between private and public life, rules regarding the treatment of visitors, varying sizes of homes, or differences within culture often severely limit the ability of investigators to obtain representative, valid, naturalistic accounts of infant life that can be compared cross-culturally. Social scientists and psychiatrists have long argued about the potential effects of the communal childrearing practices once employed on **Israeli kibbutzim**. When Maital and Bornstein (2003) compared caregiving activities of kibbutz mothers and professional caregivers on kibbutzim (**metaplot**), with whom mothers shared responsibilities for childrearing according to formalized social norms, they found that kibbutz mothers and metaplot engaged in different levels of caregiving with the same baby. Kibbutz mothers provided more social stimulation than did the metaplot, and the metaplot provided infants more learning than social experiences, a task that is in line with their "job descriptions." Mothers and their babies' daycare providers appear to provide infants with different and complementary kinds of experiences, which may in turn promote different infant competencies.

Differences in cultural ideology also make for subtle, but potentially meaningful, differences in patterns of infant–parent interaction. European American mothers of 12- to 15-month-old infants emphasized the development of individual autonomy, whereas Puerto Rican mothers focused on maternal–infant interdependence and connectedness (Harwood & Feng, 2006). These differences relate to the mothers' actual behavior, with European American mothers using suggestions (rather than commands) and other indirect means of structuring their infants' behavior, whereas Puerto Rican mothers use more direct means of structuring, such as commands, physical positioning, and restraints to get their infants' attention. These observations are consistent with a variety of reports emphasizing the collectivist orientation of Latin American families as opposed to the individualist orientation of European American families. The distinction between interdependent/sociocentric versus individual/independent childrearing ideologies is also illustrated in the work of Bornstein and his colleagues in studies of Japanese and American mothers and their 5-month-olds (Bornstein, Cote, Haynes, & Bakeman, in press). American mothers respond more to their infants' orienting to the environment relative to their infants' social orientation, whereas Japanese mothers respond more to their infants' social orientation. When responding to their infants, Japanese mothers tend to direct their infants' attention to themselves, whereas American mothers tend to direct their infants' attention away from themselves and to the environment. Viewing their own findings in the context of earlier research Bornstein and his colleagues (in press, p. 4) concluded:

> In a nutshell, U.S. American parents typically wish to promote autonomy in their children, and they organize parent-child interactions to foster child autonomy in consonance with individualism and self-actualization generally associated with and appreciated by U.S. American culture. U.S. American mothers respond to their infants' initiations. Japanese mothers want to see their children as an extension of themselves and work with their children to consolidate and strengthen *amae* (mother-child mutual dependence) in accord with collectivity, and an emphasis on interpersonal sensitivity deemed critical in Japanese society. Japanese mothers encourage and lead their infants in interactions.

Parents face a particular challenge when they migrate to a new culture. For example, African immigrants to Australia encounter a different set of beliefs regarding appropriate parenting practices, such as use of corporal punishment (Renzaho & Vignjevic, 2011). Whether a community values spanking as a method of parenting is an obvious example of a cultural difference. Some differences in parenting practices, however, are less obvious to observers and to the parents themselves. In studies of Japanese American and South American families who had moved to and been living in the United States for approximately eight years, Bornstein and Cote (2001; Cote & Bornstein, 2000, 2001, 2003) reported that South American mothers engaged in more social behavior, talked to their infants more, and provided more auditory stimulation in their infants' environment than did Japanese American mothers. Like their mothers, South American infants engaged in more social behaviors than did Japanese American infants. These differences reflected South American mothers' higher levels of collectivism and Japanese American mothers' emphasis on nonverbal rather than verbal interaction. Mothers reported that they engaged in more social behavior than teaching behavior with their infants (consistent with prescriptions of both South American and Japanese cultures), but when actually observed, mothers engaged in more teaching than social behavior (consistent with U.S.-based parenting norms). This contradiction between what mothers believed they did and what they actually did suggests that parenting behaviors may acculturate more quickly or readily than parenting beliefs.

Distinctive childrearing cognitions and practices are not limited to comparisons between European American and non-European American families. Tamis-LeMonda and Kahana-Kalman (2009) documented differences in parenting expectations among African American, Mexican immigrant, Dominican immigrant, and Chinese immigrant mothers in the United States within hours of the birth of their babies. In their study, new mothers were asked three questions: (1) How do you think things will change in your life and your family now that you have a baby? (2) What are your hopes and plans for your child and family over the next year? (3) Do you have any concerns right now about your child or family? Mothers' responses to these open-ended questions were coded as addressing four general categories—child development, parenting, family, and resources—that have been documented as areas of concern for middle-income European American mothers. Tamis-LeMonda and Kahana-Kalman found that mothers' concerns focused most on resources and least on child development. African American and Dominican immigrant mothers were the most concerned with the issue of resources, and many comments pertained to raising their children in a better environment. Chinese immigrant mothers focused the most on child development, especially in the context of the child's future education, and Mexican immigrant mothers spoke most about family.

Also, differences in parenting practices toward infants can be found across preindustrial, non-Western "small-scale" cultures. For example, Fouts, Hewlett, and Lamb (2005, 2012) compared nursing and weaning practices of the Bofi farmers and foragers of central Africa. These two groups live in close proximity but have different work and family lives, as a result of being farmers or foragers (foragers spend part of the year in the forest hunting and gathering their food). Differences in the age of weaning and in child distress were observed among these two groups, with maternal work, supplementation of breast milk by other foods, and sharing of childcare serving as influencing factors.

In summary, considerable overlap exists in parenting practices among families in different cultures, and one of the challenges facing infancy research is determining which aspects of infant development and parenting are culture specific and which may be culturally universal. It is also important to acknowledge that considerable variation in parenting exists within every culture and between cultures. Cultural ideology shapes infant development and infant care patterns in profound ways. It is important also to keep the cultural relativity of much of our thinking and knowledge about infants in mind, because it may set limits on the generalizability of our findings.

SUMMARY

We cannot understand infant development fully unless we know more about the ecologies in which infants develop. Within-family experiences may have the major impact during the first years of an infant's life. In this chapter, we addressed four general questions: To what extent do members of the family and characteristics of its social and economic ecology influence infant development? What are the characteristics of peer interactions in infancy? What are the effects of nonparental care arrangements? How do social status and cultural factors affect the ways in which infants are reared?

The family network is the primary context within which infants establish relationships with their parents and siblings. However, today, increasing numbers of infants have significant experiences outside the family, often through enrollment in alternative care settings such as daycare centers. The effects of out-of-home care vary depending on its type and quality as well as on characteristics of infants and their families. Social status and cultural variations in patterns of childrearing also exert pervasive influences on the ways in which infants are reared and what might be expected of them as they grow up. These variations deserve study because they illustrate the limits on much of what we know about development in infancy by highlighting the narrow perspective researchers often bring to infancy studies, and because they identify important factors in infant development that are often discounted or overlooked completely.

KEY TERMS

Attachments	Monozygotic
Collectivist	Niche
Customary	Nonshared environments
Daycare	Nurturant caregiving
Dizygotic	Physical circumstances
Epigenesis	Process
Extradyadic	Process measures of child care context
Ideology	Social caregiving
Individualist cultures	Specificity principle
Israeli kibbutzim	Structural
Material caregiving	Structural measures of child care context
Metaplot	Transactional principle

Chapter 3
Methods of Research in Infancy

- *What are the strengths and weaknesses of longitudinal and cross-sectional designs in infant research?*
- *In what ways do biographies and case studies, systematic observations in naturalistic and standardized situations, interviews and questionnaires, structured tests, and experiments contribute to our understanding of infancy?*
- *What are the weaknesses of each research strategy?*
- *What information can be gained from measures of the autonomic and central nervous systems?*
- *Describe the ways in which reliability, validity, causality, and correlation affect the value of a study of infants.*
- *What ethical considerations are needed when conducting research with infants?*

Most of the chapters in this book concentrate on the "whats" and the "whys" of infant development. The story would be far from complete, however, without describing "how" we have reached a growing understanding of infancy. The chief purpose of this chapter is to introduce (1) the main procedural issues encountered by developmentalists asking "questions" of and interpreting "answers" from infants and (2) the ethical questions which must be addressed by those who seek to study individuals too young to give informed consent. Here we explore key aspects of infant research with this purpose in mind. Some topics echo general developmental considerations; others are uniquely relevant to research on infancy because infants are unusual research participants.

Infants are, by definition, nonverbal and they are also, especially in the earliest months of life, motorically incompetent and subject to rapid changes in emotional and behavioral state. Strategies geared to overcoming these limitations are the focus of this chapter. How much we have learned about infant behavior and development, mostly in the last 30 years, is testimony to the ingenuity and persistence of researchers in meeting and overcoming the challenges posed by infants themselves.

We begin this chapter with a discussion of the central goals of most infancy research because research questions guide investigators to adopt specific research approaches. We describe the designs, controls, and methodologies associated with different general research aims. Then, we turn our attention to the observational, experimental, and psychophysiological techniques used to expand our knowledge of physical, perceptual, cognitive, communicative, emotional, and social development in the first years of life. Next, we elaborate on questions of interpretation and measurement. At the same time, we address some overarching methodological considerations such as context, state, point of view, age, and performance versus competence. We conclude with a discussion of research ethics.

LOGIC AND DESIGN IN INFANCY RESEARCH

Why study infants? Infancy research is largely concerned with understanding the status of different structures (e.g., physical features of the brain, such as the visual or auditory cortex) at different points early in life and with their functions (e.g., visual or auditory perception). Focusing on status and function so close to the beginning of life, investigators of development in infancy are also naturally concerned with the origins of those phenomena as well as the biological and experiential forces that influence the course of their development. Each of these concerns has called for specific methods which must be understood clearly to grasp the nature, as well as the limits, of the contribution of research to our knowledge of infancy. Here, we consider the logic and design of studies organized to address questions of status, function, origins, and determinants of development.

Longitudinal and Cross-Sectional Designs

Several research strategies have been adopted to examine the nature of different structures or functions at different ages. Researchers typically adopt either longitudinal or cross-sectional designs (Hartmann, Pelzel, & Abbott, 2011). Each has advantages and disadvantages.

Longitudinal designs involve repeated measurement of the same infants over time and constitute a principal method of assessing development. The longitudinal design provides the only means of evaluating stability or change in the same infants over time. Thus, developmental sequences or stages in infancy can only be studied longitudinally; dynamic relations across different domains in development and cause–effect relations between early experiences and later outcomes must be studied in this way as well.

To illustrate a longitudinal design, we first must describe a common procedure used in the study of infant perception and cognition—**habituation**. (Later in this chapter we discuss habituation more.) In this procedure, infants are shown the same stimulus over repeated trials and their looking at the stimulus is monitored. Typically, infants become bored with the stimulus, suggesting they recognize it as the same one seen previously, and their level of attention declines across repetitions. It is commonly believed that habituation can be an index of information processing. Colombo and his colleagues (Colombo, Shaddy, Richman, Maikranz, & Blaga, 2004) studied habituation in the same infants from 3 to 9 months and measured infant cognitive development and language at 12, 18, and 24 months. On the basis of their habituation performance across ages, infants distributed themselves in two main clusters: One group of infants' attention levels decreased sharply (as expected), and another group of infants showed different patterns of change that were not consistent with this normative trend. When assessed later on, performance by the infants who habituated sharply was much more predictable and consistent from 12 to 24 months than was the performance of infants in the other group.

Longitudinal designs make it possible to study **stability** and **continuity** over time (Bornstein & Bornstein, 2008; Hartmann et al., 2011). Stability refers to consistency over time in the relative ranking of individuals in a group on any particular measure. Continuity, by contrast, refers to consistency over time in the group mean level. For example, Bornstein and his colleagues (Bornstein et al., 2010) observed mothers and their infants naturally interacting in their homes when the infants were 5 and 20 months old. The researchers assessed interaction in each mother–infant dyad on measures of infant responsiveness and maternal sensitivity. By looking at the mean level of interaction across time, they explored continuity whereas by looking at individual scores on such measures, they were able to address questions about the stability within individuals and dyads. Stability and continuity are independent of each other: Individuals in a group may maintain their rank order on a particular ability (for example, an infant might show sharp declines in habituation across multiple assessments) but the group mean scores might increase or decrease over time (so infants might habituate more quickly as they get older).

Although longitudinal designs have advantages that make developmental conclusions about stability and continuity possible, they have a number of prominent and troubling disadvantages as well. First, it is often difficult to guarantee the cooperation of babies over long periods of time, so attrition (i.e., drop out) is a common problem in longitudinal designs. Second, where attrition is systematic (for example, stressed families are more likely to drop out of a study over time than less stressed families), there is a threat of systematic bias in the findings: The families who remain in the study might not be representative of all those who began it weeks, months, or years earlier. Third, repeated testing can affect behavior: Performance normally improves with practice, and earlier performance can affect later performance. Fourth, the duration of longitudinal studies (even in infancy) makes them extremely expensive in terms of time and resources. They require extended commitment from investigators as well as from their participants. Finally, the slow course of human development sometimes poses additional problems: An investigator studying infant attachment before and after the onset of stranger wariness, for example, must wait a year before the 6-month-olds who participated in the first phase of a study reach the follow-up phase at 18 months of age.

For these reasons, most developmental studies involve **cross-sectional designs**, in which investigators compare different groups of participants of different ages. This strategy has a number of advantages. First, a researcher can obtain "developmental" answers relatively quickly: She can determine whether stranger wariness changes between 6 and 18 months by comparing wariness in 6- and 18-month-old infants without waiting a year for the 6-month-olds to grow up. Second, repetition effects (such as adjustment to a strange experimenter) can be avoided because each infant is tested only once. Third, no infants are lost because they do not attend testing sessions at every age.

However, cross-sectional designs are not without their own shortcomings. First, the origins and consequences of individual differences and their stability over time cannot be investigated. For example, in the study of infants' responsiveness and maternal sensitivity discussed previously, Bornstein et al. (2010) could have identified levels of emotional relationships at 5 and 20 months, but the investigators could not have determined that these patterns were stable over time had they adopted a cross-sectional methodology. Cross-sectional studies only reveal age differences and do not help identify developmental processes, fluctuations in development, or individual differences in development. Second, when children of different ages respond differently in a given situation, investigators usually infer that time or development is the cause of the difference without relying on longitudinal evidence. That is, in adopting the cross-sectional approach, investigators assume that their younger infants are essentially like older infants, except that they are younger. **Cohort effects** threaten this assumption, as when children in the different age groups have experiences that render the two groups different. Suppose that most of the 18-month-olds in a study of stranger wariness had been cared for at home by a parent, whereas most of the 6-month-olds' mothers and fathers went to work right after the babies were born, placing those babies in the primary care of others. Clearly, the different early experiences of the 6- and 18-month-olds, rather than development, could influence their later responses to strangers. Cohort effects might obscure the developmental phenomena of greatest interest to the researcher and could limit the generalizability of findings.

Although longitudinal and cross-sectional approaches to developmental study have both advantages and disadvantages, researchers usually assume that the two designs will or should yield basically similar results. Very few investigators have tested this assumption directly, but some studies show the expected convergence. For example, Colombo and his associates (Colombo et al., 2004) studied the development of habituation using a design that allowed for the simultaneous comparison of longitudinal and cross-sectional strategies of data collection. One group of infants was tested longitudinally at 3 to 9 months of age, and other independent samples of infants were tested cross-sectionally at 4 to 9 months. In each test, babies were shown color photographs of faces, and the researchers measured the amount of time infants looked at the stimuli until they habituated. The two experimental approaches yielded basically similar results—and support similar developmental conclusions—about habituation. Figure 3.1 plots peak look duration by age for infants in each of the experimental designs. In both designs, babies of a given age habituated in approximately the same amount of time, older babies habituated more quickly than younger babies, and the greatest decline in accumulated looking time occurred between 4 and 6 months of age.

Regardless of the study design, researchers who measure some structure or function at two or more time points confront a fundamental measurement problem. Change occurs rapidly during infancy, and the same structure or function can take different forms at different ages. For example, fear might look different in 6-month-olds (e.g., crying) and in 18-month-olds (e.g., behavioral inhibition), but the underlying source (i.e., fear) may be the same. As a consequence, no matter what developmental design a researcher adopts, he or she must be acutely aware of this issue. Researchers can choose between two strategies for dealing with the issue: Using the same items at different ages or using different age-appropriate items at different ages. Six- and 18-month-olds are sufficiently different that different behaviors might be needed to measure the same underlying construct, namely fear.

Natural Experiments, Twin, and Adoption Designs

Beyond characterizing developmental status and function, infancy researchers are interested in identifying (at least to some degree) genetic and environmental influences to address questions of origin and forces that affect development. To do this, investigators have often appealed to different kinds of **natural experiments**. For example, comparisons can be made between infants who are not assigned randomly to different groups (as is the case in true experiments) but still experience different "treatments" (such as different cultures) in the course of growing up. It is obviously not possible or ethical to assign children randomly to deprived versus normal experiences, so the long-term effects of institutionalization in early infancy must be studied by comparing naturally occurring instances of deprivation. To assess influences of social deprivation on emotional development, therefore, the happiness and sadness of infants reared in

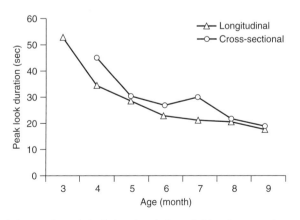

Fig. 3.1 Developmental changes in peak look duration during a habituation procedure. The cross-sectional curve represents independent samples for each age group; the longitudinal curve represents the same sample of infants tested at each age. (From Colombo et al., 2004; reproduced with permission.)

intact families might be compared with those of infants reared in socially depriving institutions. Results of such a natural experiment involving Romanian children adopted in the United Kingdom (UK) prior to 2 years of age showed that infants were severely developmentally delayed when they first entered the UK, with half of infants falling below the third percentile in weight, height, and performance on standardized tests of intelligence (McCall et al., 2011). By the age of 4 years, however, Romanian children adopted in the UK before 6 months of age caught up when compared to a group of 4-year-old UK children who were adopted from UK mothers before 6 months of age. Furthermore, some catch-up was evident among Romanian children placed into adoptive homes after 6 months. Thus, although early global deprivation in infancy retards development, deprivation effects can be tempered by placement in more enriched environments.

The shortcomings of natural experiments are many, such as the possibility that children in the groups being compared were not the same to begin with. For example, infants from disadvantaged backgrounds might be more likely than infants from advantaged backgrounds to be placed in institutions. As a result, differences between infants in the two groups might be accounted for by institutionalization, different prenatal experiences, or the combined influence of the two factors.

The study of the relative importance of nature and nurture has been significantly advanced through the introduction of twin studies (Galton, 1876). These studies compare *monozygotic* twins, who develop from one fertilized egg that has split, with *dizygotic* twins, who develop from two separate fertilized eggs. Monozygotic twins share 100% of their DNA; dizygotic twins share only 50% of their DNA, like other sibling pairs. Comparisons of monozygotes reared apart or treated differently from infancy and comparisons of monozygotes with dizygotes reared from infancy under identical circumstances has lent much power to a psychological understanding of the origins of behavior. In McGraw's (1933, 1939) classic studies, the weaker of two monozygotic twins received special training from infancy, and his performance relative to his brother improved as a result of the selective training.

If a trait such as dyslexia has a genetic basis, the concordance, or co-occurrence, of the trait will be significantly higher in monozygotic than in dizygotic twins. In 1987 researchers from the Colorado Twin Study reported that this is indeed the case. The concordance for dyslexia was 68% for monozygotic twins, but only 38% for dizygotic twins (DeFries, Fulker, & LaBuda, 1987). It is worth noting, however, that among monozygotic twins who share *all* their DNA, co-occurrence of dyslexia fell well short of 100%. This indicates that other factors must be highly relevant as well. Monozygotic twins who are discordant for reading ability can thus be of great clinical and theoretical interest, since they highlight potential environmental influences.

Comparisons between infants whose biological backgrounds differ from those of their adopting families provide a powerful means of evaluating the impact of heredity and experience on infant development (Leve et al., 2007). In these comparisons, researchers ask whether an adopted infant is more like the biological parent, with whom the infant shares genes but not environment, or more like the adoptive parent, with whom the infant shares a home environment but no genes. In a number of domains, including imitation, physical development, problem behaviors, and language development, twin and adoption studies have provided information about the interaction between genes and the environment in shaping development across childhood (McEwen et al., 2007; Moulson, Fox, Zeanah, & Nelson, 2009; Oliver, Dale, & Plomin, 2004).

Specialized Developmental Designs

Additional specialized designs are often used to address other questions about status, function, and origins in infancy. The **age-held-constant paradigm**, for example, is used to assess the influence of variables other than age on the development of a structure or function, because all infants are tested at the same age. For example, in a study on the transition from crawling to walking, Karasik, Tamis-LeMonda, and Adolph (2011) recruited infants who, at 11 months, were crawling. By 13 months, half of the infants were walking, and the researchers compared the crawlers' and walkers' interactions with objects. They found that the walkers accessed distant objects, carried objects, and approached their mothers to share objects, whereas crawlers accessed objects close at hand and shared objects while remaining stationary.

Understanding and differentiating the relative contributions of hereditary and experiential influences on development in infancy can be accomplished by comparing structure or function in groups of infants matched for either **maturational age** or **experiential age**. The first comparison group uses infants who were conceived at the same time and so are of the same **conceptional age**; the second comparison group uses infants who are all tested the same amount of time after birth and thus have the same **postnatal age**. One strategy pits infants born at term with those born preterm. By providing a peek at the growth and development of the individual sometime in advance of that which is otherwise possible, the study of preterm infants helps to fix and elucidate the earliest behavioral capacities. The study of **preterm** infants thus helps us to understand to what degree full gestation is necessary and what exactly about the last phases of growth and development in utero better prepare the infant for extrauterine life. Shirley (1938) administered 215 developmental tests to 63 infants born weighing less than 5 lb (2.27 kg). Those weighing less than 4 lb consistently showed one-month retardation between birth and 18 months, while those who weighed 4–5 lb showed normal behavior by 9 months of age. In Chapter 4, we discuss the outcomes of preterm birth in more detail.

Another reason for studying preterm compared to full term infants is that it allows researchers to compare differential development in the context of equivalent postnatal experiences. That is, babies can be matched for conceptional age but contrasted in terms of postnatal experience or they can be matched for postnatal experience (e.g., 2 weeks after birth) but contrasted in terms of conceptional age. For an example of the latter we turn to a study that took advantage of the fact that not all babies are born on or near their due date (approximately 38 weeks after conception). To investigate the effects of experience on the blink response to impending collision (referred to as looming, see Chapter 6), Pettersen, Yonas, and Fisch (1980) assessed preterm (born 3 to 4 weeks before their due date), full term (born within 1 week of their due date) and postterm infants (at least 3 weeks after their due date) at 10 weeks of age. Thus, all of the infants were the same postnatal age (10 weeks), and all three groups had about the same amount of experience perceiving the world. They differed, however, in terms of biological age. The preterm babies were biologically 3 to 4 weeks younger than the full term babies, and the postterm babies were biologically at least 3 weeks older than the full term babies and 6 to 7 weeks older than the preterm babies. The researchers found that blink rates varied as a function of term status. Preterm babies blinked less often to an approaching object than full term babies and postterm infants blinked more frequently, allowing Pettersen et al. to conclude that rate of blinking is governed by maturational rather than experiential factors. (Obstetric practice today rarely allows pregnancies to extend much beyond the due date so studies with postterm babies are no longer possible, at least in the United States.)

In summary, researchers of infant development have adopted a variety of strategies to identify and describe the status, function, and origins of diverse aspects of development. These strategies all have advantages and disadvantages associated with them. The choice of strategy depends on the specific question being asked.

PROCEDURES AND TECHNIQUES IN INFANCY RESEARCH

Infancy studies had their formal beginnings in attempts by researchers to do systematically what parents around the world do naturally—observe their babies. The first psychological studies of children were descriptions of infants in their natural settings by their own parents. Over time, observation systems have become much more sophisticated and informative, and today systematic and programmatic experimentation is the norm. In this section of the chapter, we lay out a taxonomy of procedures and techniques, discussing general approaches to observation and experimentation with infants. Our methodological taxonomy is organized to reflect strategies for asking questions of infants and to underscore the fact that methodologies require different degrees of inference on the part of investigators. To bring the discussion to life, we draw on examples from studies of perceptual, cognitive, communicative, emotional, and social development.

How a baby perceives, feels, and thinks is basically private. The absence of language and the motoric incompetence of infants force us to gain an understanding of infant experiences by **inference** from immature behaviors. How accurate, reliable, and credible our understanding is, therefore, depends on many factors.

Some of the methods adopted by developmental scientists to overcome the difficulties of studying infants—whether observing them or testing them—yield only very weak inferences; other methods yield stronger ones. For example, if a sound produces a regular pattern of electrical responses in the brain, we can be certain that at least some internal connections between the ear and the brain are present. Unfortunately, even regularity of brain response tells us nothing about how or even whether the infant actually "perceives" the sound. It could be that the brain registers a stimulus, but the infant is not conscious of it. Even if two different sounds, such as a high-pitched tone and a low-pitched tone, gave rise to two different patterns of electrical activity in the brain, we still would not know whether the infant perceived either or both of the two sounds, or whether the infant perceived the two sounds to be the same or different. However, if we were able to instruct or train the infant to respond in one way to one sound and in another way to another sound, we would have clear evidence of auditory perception and discrimination. In this section of the chapter, we discuss some standard observational and experimental techniques used historically and today to understand infancy.

Baby Biographies and Case Studies

Jean-Jacques Rousseau (1781) was among the first to write about the integrity of childhood as a separate stage of life. About the same time, Count Philippe de Montbeillard made a close analysis of the physical growth in his own son between 1759 and 1777; it exemplifies a database valuable both for the historical record and as a model for early child study (Chapter 5). Not long after, Tiedemann (1787) wrote a psychological diary of the growth of a young child, in other words a **baby biography**.

Three types of baby biographies have been produced throughout history (Wallace, Franklin, & Keegan, 1994). **Domestic diaries**, which are the oldest of the three types, were typically written by mothers for their personal satisfaction, and they provide insights into parental philosophies about the nature of childhood and childrearing. **Educational diaries** were written to explore the impact of teaching or childrearing practices on children's behavior and development. Finally, **scientific diaries** were written to yield empirical knowledge about infant behavior and development.

Both educational and scientific diaries came into their own in the second half of the 19th century, which witnessed an intense focus on evolution and development (Lerner et al., 2011). At that time Charles Darwin assembled for publication his observations, made in the early 1840s, of his firstborn son William Erasmus, nicknamed Doddy (Conrad, 1998; see Figure 3.2). Darwin's publication of "A Biographical Sketch of an Infant" simultaneously in the German journal *Kosmos* and the influential English journal *Mind* in 1877 founded the study of infancy. Darwin, already famous for the *Origin of Species*, published in 1859, specifically recounted sensory, intellectual, and emotional development in Doddy's first year (Box 3.1). Perhaps the greatest of the modern baby biographers was Jean Piaget, most of whose writing and theorizing about development in infancy refers to observations of his own three young children, Jacqueline, Lucienne, and Laurent. In part because of Darwin, scholars came to believe that adult human beings could be better understood with reference to their origins—in nature, in the species, and in childhood.

Fig. 3.2 Charles Darwin, age 33, with his eldest child, William (*aka* Doddy).

Box 3.1   Excerpts from *A Biographical Sketch of an Infant* by Charles Darwin

During the first seven days various reflex actions, namely sneezing, hickuping, yawning, stretching, and of course sucking and screaming, were well performed by my infant. On the seventh day, I touched the naked sole of his foot with a bit of paper, and he jerked it away, curling at the same time his toes, like a much older child when tickled. The perfection of these reflex movements shows that the extreme imperfection of the voluntary ones is not due to the state of the muscles or of the coordinating centers, but to that of the seat of the will. At this time, though so early, it seemed clear to me that a warm soft hand applied to his face excited a wish to suck. This must be considered as a reflex or an instinctive action, for it is impossible to believe that experience and association with the touch of his mother's breast could so soon have come into play. During the first fortnight he often started on hearing any sudden sound, and blinked his eyes. ... At the age of 32 days he perceived his mother's bosom when three or four inches from it, as was shown by the protrusion of his lips and his eyes becoming fixed; but I much doubt whether this had any connection with vision; he certainly had not touched the bosom. Whether he was guided through smell or the sensation of warmth or through association with the position in which he was held, I do not at all know.

   Anger. It was difficult to decide at how early an age anger was felt; on his eighth day he frowned and wrinkled the skin round his eyes before a crying fit, but this may have been due to pain or distress, and not to anger. When about ten weeks old, he was given some rather cold milk and he kept a slight frown on his forehead all the time that he was sucking, so that he looked like a grown-up person made cross from being compelled to do something which he did not like. When nearly four months old, and perhaps much earlier, there could be no doubt, from the manner in which the blood rushed into his whole face and scalp, that he easily got into a violent passion. ...

Fear. This feeling probably is one of the earliest which is experienced by infants, as shown by their starting at any sudden sound when only a few weeks old, followed by crying. [... When he was 4½ months old] I one day made a loud snoring noise which I had never done before; he instantly looked grave and then burst out crying. Two or three days afterwards, I made through forgetfulness the same noise with the same result. May we not suspect that the vague but very real fears of children, which are quite independent of experience, are the inherited effects of real dangers and abject superstitions during ancient savage times? ...

Pleasurable Sensations. It may be presumed that infants feel pleasure while sucking, and the expression of their swimming eyes seems to show that this is the case. This infant smiled when 45 days, a second infant when 46 days old; and these were true smiles, indicative of pleasure, for their eyes brightened and eyelids slightly closed. The smiles arose chiefly when looking at their mother, and were therefore probably of mental origin. ...

Affection. This probably arose very early in life, if we may judge by his smiling at those who had charge of him when under two months old; though I had no distinct evidence of his distinguishing and recognizing anyone, until he was nearly four months old. When nearly five months old, he plainly showed his wish to go to his nurse. With respect to the allied feeling of sympathy, this was clearly shown at 6 months and 11 days by his melancholy face, with the corners of his mouth well depressed, when his nurse pretended to cry. Jealousy was plainly exhibited when I fondled a large doll, and when I weighed his infant sister, he being then 15½ months old.

Association of Ideas, Reason, etc. When four and a half months old, he repeatedly smiled at my image and his own in a mirror, and no doubt mistook them for real objects; but he showed sense in being evidently surprised at my voice coming from behind him. Like all infants he much enjoyed thus looking at himself, and in less than two months perfectly understood that it was an image; for if I made quite silently an odd grimace, he would suddenly turn round to look at me. ... When five months old, associated ideas arising independently of any instruction became fixed in his mind; thus as soon as his hat and cloak were put on, he was very cross if he was not immediately taken out of doors. ...

Means of Communication. The noise of crying ... is of course uttered in an instinctive manner, but serves to show that there is suffering. After a time the sound differs according to the cause, such as hunger or pain. ... When 46 days old, he first made little noises without any meaning to please himself, and these soon became varied. An incipient laugh was observed on the 113th day. When five and half months old, he uttered an articulate sound "da" but without any meaning attached to it. When a little over a year old, he used gestures to explain his wishes: ... At exactly the age of a year, he made the great step of inventing a word for food, namely, mum, but what led him to it I did not discover. ... Before he was a year old, he understood intonations and gestures, as well as several words and short sentences. He understood one word, namely, his nurse's name, exactly five months before he invented his first mum; and this is what might have been expected, as we know that the lower animals easily learn to understand spoken words.

The strengths and weaknesses of baby biographies are worth considering. On the positive side, attention paid by important figures such as Darwin clearly excited more general interest in children and in the study of children. Succeeding talented authors also made exceptional and intuitive observers. The first baby biographers documented basic information about development, and on the basis of their observations they generated numerous novel and important hypotheses about infant development. On the negative side, baby biographies are limited for a variety of reasons. In methodological terms, baby biographers most frequently observed only single children, usually their own. These children could hardly have been representative of the population at large and, perhaps like their parents, they were exceptional. Biographers were not concerned with comparison groups, and their observations were not always systematic. Furthermore, some baby biographers recorded their observations as they observed them, but many employed a retrospective methodology, trying to recall what the infant's early life was like at a later time. Baby biographers were also subject to bias in their observations. Frequently, these diarists were women and men with strong theoretical points of view who tended to report anecdotes and data that supported their theories. On balance, however, baby biographies initiated child study in spirit and in fact, and for this reason they constitute an important historical source.

Consider, too, insights obtained from a related source—**case study**. The close focus on single individuals helps to document events that are otherwise hard to observe, and they are especially valuable theoretically when they reveal capacities that are supposed to be absent at the age in question. One recent case study observed parents reading to their infant from before birth to when she turned 6 months old. In an attempt to explore the effects of reading aloud on developing literacy skills, Holland (2008) observed Maggie and her parents daily in her home and/or in her childcare setting. Holland quantified the amount of literary stimulation (e.g., number of books read per day, play songs) and observed Maggie's reactions, such as signs of comfort and levels of attention. Holland concluded that reading aloud is beneficial to infants' language development as well as their interactions with parents and caregivers.

Case studies can be informative, but we never know about the generalizability of what is observed. Also, we often cannot determine the extent to which an observed behavior or capacity is limited to a specific situational circumstance or a specific infant. In addition, as we have seen, baby biographies are limited by uncertainties concerning the objectivity of the reporter.

Systematic Observations

As child study developed into a scientific discipline, researchers came to rely less on baby biographies and case studies, instead embracing systematic observation and experimentation as the principal means of learning about children. For example, researchers today aim to conduct studies in which systematic observational techniques are used to gather information about infants. In conducting such observations, researchers must first address some basic strategic questions. Should children be observed in naturalistic or standardized contexts? Should the researcher aim to observe and record whatever children choose to do during the observation, or should the researcher make an effort to ensure that each child is observed in a context that places similar demands on all the children? Who should do the observing: mother, father, care provider, or researcher? When should the observations take place: at random times, on a schedule, any time of the day or at an optimal time of the day? Answers to these questions have implications for the results obtained. Although naturalistic sampling would appear to be ideal because it provides a picture of infants' typical behavior or capacity, it could be problematic if, for example, various infants in the study are observed in very different situations, making comparison among them difficult. In addition, because researchers can usually sample only a very small slice of an infant's everyday life, snapshots of infants' lives based on naturalistic sampling can be misleading, particularly when they exclude behaviors in situations that are deemed to be of special significance. In one study, for example, infants' budding language was studied in three conditions in the home: The children were observed playing by themselves with their mother nearby, the children and mothers were observed playing together, and the children and mother were observed at a time when the mothers expected "optimal" language production (say, in the bath or at bedtime). Children produced more utterances and word roots and expressed themselves in longer sentences when in interaction than when playing "alone," but children's utterances were most sophisticated in the "optimal" language production situation (Bornstein, Painter, & Park, 2002). Consequently, researchers often standardize situations and their psychological demands, choosing to study babies only when they will be awake and alert, at play, or under no stress. Naturalistic and semi-structured observations are common, and more structured or standardized observations are increasingly the rule.

However, sometimes it is important to study infants naturalistically in a variety of situations. This could be especially helpful when studying children from cultures that have not been well studied, or when researchers want to explore how differently children behave in different situations. To understand how infants in different cultures stop breastfeeding, for example, Fouts, Hewlett, and Lamb (2012) observed children from dawn to dusk. Similarly, differences in infant social interactions with adults in low- and middle-income African American and European American families can only be illuminated by observing infants and adults at all hours of the day, regardless of the situation (Fouts, Roopnarine, Lamb, & Evans, 2012). Again, how the researcher structures the observation needs to reflect the question the research is addressing.

Having decided on the situation in which to observe children, researchers must determine whether to obtain a description of events (either by using a checklist, event recorder, or notebook) in real time or to use some kind of electronic device (e.g., video recorder or computer) to record behavior so that it can be reviewed and analyzed in greater detail at a later time. Video records have an important history in infancy studies. Between 1910 and 1940, Gesell developed his photographic technique to provide a permanent and detailed record of infants' developing psychological capacities (Bornstein, 2001). Digital video technology has become extremely common because it permits researchers to gather behavior that can be then reviewed to obtain a finer-grained understanding and to assess agreement in the accounts provided by different observers viewing the same sequences of behaviors. Moreover, it allows for the study of contingencies between behaviors, such as the infant's smile and the parent's touch (Figure 3.3).

Such **time-based records** allow researchers to construct two sorts of measures: Simple indices of the frequency and duration with which particular behaviors occur and indices of the likelihood that specific behaviors precede or follow one another. For example, as we mentioned earlier, Bornstein and his colleagues (2010) observed mothers and their infants at age 5 and 20 months while interacting in their homes. The researchers coded emotional relationships in each mother–infant dyad, including the amount of infant responsiveness to mother and maternal sensitivity. Time-based recordings of interaction also enable researchers to examine the degree to which one individual's behavior is contingent on the behavior of another. For example, Goldstein and Schwade (2008) studied the role of feedback from mothers on their 9½-month-old infants' vocalizations. Half of the mothers were instructed to provide contingent responses to their infants' babbling, and the other half of the mothers gave noncontingent responses (that is, they spoke to the infants whether or not the infants had babbled). Infants receiving contingent responses restructured their babbling, incorporating the patterns from their mothers' speech. For some research questions, frequency counts are more useful than estimates of the likelihood of certain contingencies. For other questions, contingencies are more appropriate. Researchers must choose their measures depending on the specific questions of interest.

In more standardized situations, babies are filmed as they respond to one or several stimuli or probe events. For example, in a deferred imitation task in which infants are shown someone doing something with a novel object and are later given the opportunity to act similarly, Dixon and his colleagues (2012) filmed infants as they tried to remember tasks ("make a rattle" or "feed a bear") demonstrated 6 months earlier. From the video record, the researchers coded for whether three key actions previously modeled were reproduced by the infants.

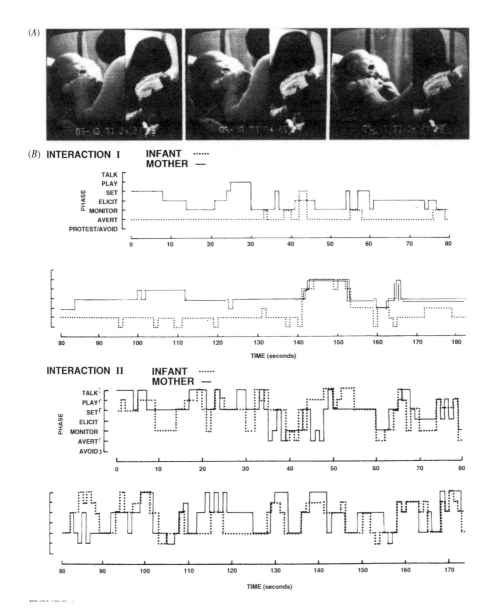

Fig. 3.3 (A) Split-screen technology is used to obtain video records that can be recoded time and again at slow speed to describe the synchronization of infant and parental behavior. (B) To perform sequential analyses, it is necessary to examine relations between the timing of the participants' behaviors. In this figure, the infant's and mother's behaviors are both displayed, so that their synchrony and asynchrony are clear.

Interviews and Questionnaires

The advantage of observations that use systematic techniques in naturalistic, semi-standardized, or standardized situations is that researchers can obtain objective accounts of behavior. To find out about babies, researchers also ask questions of those who know them best. Interviews and questionnaires can provide rich information not readily obtained by observation. For example, in a study designed to evaluate whether flexible work hours translate into more parental time with children, Baxter (2011) asked Australian work-ing parents to keep work-day and weekend diaries describing the activities of their infant and with whom they interacted. The results showed that more flexible work hours allowed parents to distribute work and family activities, but it did not translate into more parental time with children. Time diaries of this type provide contextual information about infants' daily lives that would have been more difficult, and more costly, to obtain from direct observation.

Interview and questionnaire techniques suffer from some of the same distorting influences that beset baby biographies, but they play a valuable role in helping researchers make their studies more repre-sentative of infants' daily lives. As observational techniques have become more popular, developmental scientists have sometimes come to question the representativeness of what they observe, especially of brief observations conducted in selected, standardized situations. Representativeness might not be impor-tant when researchers are simply trying to define infant capacities, such as the ability to find a hidden object. However, it is sometimes important to establish representativeness. As a result, many researchers use questionnaires and interviews to gain information about the representativeness of what they have observed and to supplement their observations.

Interview protocols and questionnaires can be helpful in getting information from individuals who are much more familiar with their own tendencies or those of their children than even professional observers are. However, because parental reports can be distorted, they are best used in combination with objective reports and descriptions by disinterested observers to construct coherent and presum-ably valid accounts of infant development. In this regard, the Q-sort technique pioneered by Block and Block (1980) has been helpful. In the Q-sort, observers (such as parents) classify equal proportions of some items as "very descriptive," "somewhat descriptive," "not characteristic," and "extremely unchar-acteristic" "of my infant." Respondents cannot just give socially desirable responses (because they are forced to conform to a pre-specified distribution), and this requirement enhances the reliability and validity of reports. Q-sorts have been used effectively in studies of parental sensitivity. For example, after observing a mother and child interact in a natural setting that had competing demands for the mother (such as caring for an infant and being interviewed by an experimenter), observers sorted 90 maternal actions into categories ranging from least like the mother to most like the mother (Bigelow, Littlejohn, Bergman, & McDonald, 2010).

In summary, researchers use interviews and questionnaires in their own right to obtain more repre-sentative data about infants, and researchers use these techniques to supplement more objective strategies to obtain more comprehensive data about infants from multiple sources.

Neurological Assessments

Neurological assessments have been used to evaluate structure or function in both the autonomic nervous system (ANS) and central nervous system (CNS) in infants.

Autonomic Nervous System A widely applied neurological approach involves monitoring the responses of the **autonomic nervous system** (the parts of the nervous system concerned with the involun-tary control of internal organs, including the heart, lungs, and digestive tract). Orienting reflexes, respira-tion, and heart rate can be measured even in the youngest infants. Heart rate has proved to be an especially sensitive and revealing index of infant capacity (Diaz & Bell, 2011; Porges, 2011; Richards, 2010). For example, heart rate indicates whether an infant is simply staring blankly at a stimulus (heart rate is stable) or is actually attending to and processing the stimulus (heart rate slows during periods of concentration). Heart rate does not depend on infant motor skills such as reaching or crawling, and because it reflects infant state, researchers can tell whether infants are about to become drowsy or fussy. It is also remarkably sensitive, with changes of up to 25 beats per minute occurring even when behavioral changes are not observable. Researchers have used heart rate changes to explore the development of complex affective reactions in babies. For example, Moore (2009) studied 6-month-old infants' responses to anger, excitement, or neutral affect displayed by an experimenter. In addition, parents completed a questionnaire about parental conflict, allowing the researchers to group the children as experiencing "anger" or "non-anger" in their home life. Moore found no group difference in heart rate changes triggered by the emotional stimuli.

One aspect of heart rate that has served researchers well is its variability. Heart variability is indexed by **vagal tone**, a reflection of heart rate changes mediated by the vagus nerve and controlled by the para-sympathetic branch of the ANS (Porges, 2011). Respiratory control centers in the brainstem modulate vagal nerve influences on the heart, producing rhythmic increases and decreases in heart rate, and in this way it is possible to identify a respiratory rhythm in the heart rate pattern. This heart rate oscillation is called **respiratory sinus arrhythmia**, and the amplitude of this rhythm is a measure of cardiac vagal tone (Porges, 2011). This measure is useful in infant research because it is sensitive to changes in attentional state. Also, it is an important index of individual differences in infants' capacity to regulate state of arousal and respond appropriately to environmental demand. An example comes from a study comparing memory recall in preterm and full term infants. Haley, Grunau, Weinberg, Keidar, and Oberlander (2010) tested babies at 6 months of age in a deferred imitation task that involved a puppet wearing a mitten with a bell inside and then tested after a delay for their memory of the puppet and its action. Haley et al. found that infants who suppressed vagal tone during the demonstration later showed better memory.

Neuroscientists also measure **neuroendocrines** and **hormones** in an attempt to map development in infancy. Neuroendocrines are cells that are stimulated neuronally, and they release hormones into the blood. Hormones are chemicals released by a cell or a gland in one part of the body that sends out messages affecting cells in other parts of the organism. We focus on two examples—cortisol and oxytocin—both of which are easily measured by collecting a saliva sample using a cotton swab. The development of procedures for measuring levels of cortisol has been especially fruitful among those interested in understanding infants' responses to stress (Laurent, Ablow, & Measelle, 2011). **Cortisol** is a substance secreted by the body at times of stress, such as when infants are frightened or separated from their parents (Ahnert, Gunnar, Lamb, & Barthel, 2004). Whereas heart rate responds almost immediately to such incidents, accelerated cortisol secretion is measurable in saliva 15 to 45 minutes afterward. Measures of cortisol and heart rate thus provide different information about infants' responses to stimuli and events.

Another biochemical marker that can be correlated with behavior is oxytocin. **Oxytocin** is a peptide that plays a role in regulation of social behavior (MacDonald & MacDonald, 2010), and among its functions is directing attention to the eye region of faces (Guastella, Mitchell, & Dadds, 2008). In infancy, oxytocin levels increase during feeding, and more so for breastfed than bottle-fed infants (Grewen, Davenport, & Light, 2010). Feeding is a context that often involves face-to-face contact, so it might also play a role in making the caregiver's face appear familiar (deHaan & Carver, 2013).

Central Nervous System   Most research tapping the **central nervous system** (brain and spinal cord) to index infant development has been directed at understanding neurological anatomy or gross cortical electrical activity. Studies focused on neuroanatomical development usually ask questions about the early ontogeny of physical structures and then proceed to make inferences about function. This research strategy thus involves the presumption that structure (e.g., the anatomy of the visual system) naturally comes before function (e.g., visual perception). Infants must have eyes before they can see. Using this approach, however, our understanding of function is inevitably constrained by knowledge of the development and status of the underlying structure. Structure is a necessary but not a sufficient condition for function: Newborns have legs but do not walk. Therefore, so far as inferences about function are concerned, evidence based on structure alone is very weak.

The second kind of research into central nervous system activity assesses functional development in the intact human infant through the use of electrophysiological or neuro-imaging techniques. The principal electrophysiological technique has involved the cortical **event-related potential** (ERP). By placing electrodes on the scalp (Figure 3.4), researchers record brain responses to brief events, such as a face appearing on a screen for half a second. A strength of this technique is studying the time course of information processing, and researchers are particularly interested in the location of the response (such as what part of the cortex—occipital, temporal, parietal, or frontal/prefrontal, Figure 3.5), the magnitude of the response (amplitude), and how long it takes to reach the peak amplitude or the timing of the response (latency). The study of memory is commonly assessed using such procedures. For example, in one study on working memory described in Chapter 5, infants were shown an object being hidden and electrical activity was recorded (Bell, 2012). Bell found that infants who remembered the location of the object showed a different pattern of electrical activity than infants who did not remember the object's location. Moreover, ERP can be used to predict later cognitive functioning. Newborn speech perception, as detected by ERPs, it turns out, predicted oral language function at 3 and 5 years of age and ultimately single-word reading at 8 years of age (Molfese, Fonaryova-Key, Maguire, Dove, & Molfese, 2008). In another study, 6-month-olds with a family history of language learning impairment showed a poorer ERP response to rapidly presented nonlinguistic auditory stimuli (Benasich et al., 2006). There are challenges to using this methodology. The responses are individually weak and rapid. Moreover, many presentations of the same stimulus must be administered, and the responses averaged, before the ERP can be distinguished from the background of ongoing spontaneous brain waves (Nelson, de Haan, & Thomas, 2006). Requiring infants to endure a large number of trials is difficult, and as a result, ERP studies are plagued by a high participant drop-out rate (Stets, Stahl, & Reid, 2012).

Magnetoencephalography (MEG) is another technique that allows researchers to measure cortical functioning, but it allows for higher density of recording and greater temporal and spatial sensitivity than EEG recordings. Using MEG, Imada and his colleagues (2006) investigated the link between speech perception and speech production. By presenting newborns, 6-month-olds, and 12-month-olds with speech and non-

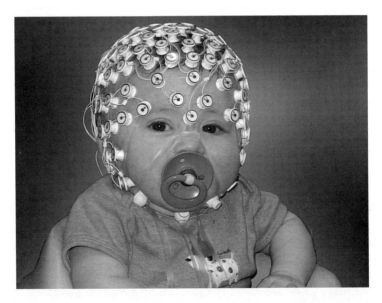

Fig. 3.4 An infant wearing a high-density EEG sensor array (the Geodesic Sensor Net). The elastic net contains 128 individual sensors for recording scalp EEG and ERP signals. (Courtesy of Electrical Geodesics, Inc.)

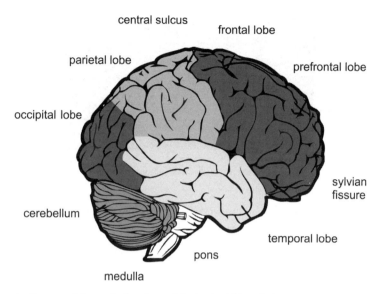

Fig. 3.5 Schematic diagram of the cortical regions of the brain. Although there are connections amongst all of the regions, generally the occipital region, at the back of the head, receives information from the visual system, the parietal region, towards the top of the head, receives information from the somatosensory (touch) system, and the temporal lobe, towards the side of the head, receives information from the auditory system. The frontal and prefrontal lobes, at the front of the head, control motor movements and higher order cognitive functions. The cerebellum, although not a cortical region, also plays an important role in movement. (Courtesy of Shutterstock. Copyright: MikiR.)

speech sounds, they showed that the same brain regions used for speech production were activated as early as 6 months of age when speech was presented, but the same was not true for nonspeech sounds. The authors concluded that the speech production areas of the brain require experience with speech for development.

Whereas electrophysiological measures such as the ERP can be used to document *when* brain activity takes place, neuroimaging techniques are especially useful in documenting *where* brain activity occurs. Neuroimaging makes use of changes in metabolism to pinpoint specific central nervous system regions that underlie specific motor (such as moving a limb) or mental (such as attending to a visual display) activity. Researchers use **positron emission tomography** (PET), for example, to measure the release of positrons that results from the decay of radioactive glucose previously injected into the bloodstream. Higher levels of positron emission take place in brain regions where higher levels of brain activity are occurring. Shi and colleagues (2009) used PET to explore differences in cortical functioning between preterm and full term newborns, and they found that there was less glucose utilization by preterms compared to full terms, suggesting that some of the differences in cognitive functioning that are found between these two groups of infants may be present at birth and not solely the result of experiences in neonatal intensive care units (Chapter 4). PET depends on very expensive equipment (e.g., a cyclotron is needed to make the radioactive agents) and on radioactive injections, raising ethical considerations especially when infants are involved.

Functional magnetic resonance imaging (fMRI) and **near infra-red spectroscopy** (NIRS) avoid some of the ethical problems and also provide excellent spatial resolution and a more accurate localization of specific brain activity than does PET. fMRI and NIRS identify regions of brain activity by electronically scanning slices of the brain in different orientations and measuring subtle, ongoing changes in oxygen usage. These techniques are extremely useful in identifying specific areas of the brain underlying behaviors (Figure 3.6; Carlsson, Lagercrantz, Olson, Printz, & Bartocci, 2008). Because clear imaging is

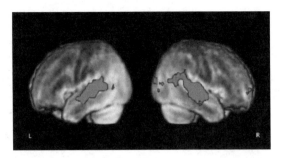

Fig. 3.6 Example of an fMRI image showing areas of activation during a voice perception task (From Blasi et al., 2011; reproduced with permission.)

not possible when participants move their heads, fMRI and NIRS techniques have not yet been used much in studies involving infants; however, some questions can be asked when infants are sleeping. For example, Blasi and colleagues (2011) presented sleeping 3- to 7-month-old infants with emotionally neutral, positive, and negative speech sounds as well as nonvocal environmental sounds. They found increased responding to vocalizations, particularly sad ones, suggesting an early specialization for the human voice and negative emotions. Functional neuroimaging studies of typically developing children document the gradual shift from diffuse to focal organization in response to specific tasks (Durston & Casey, 2006).

In young infants, psychophysiological indices can be more objective and sensitive than behavioral measures. Neurological approaches also are valuable in studies of atypical development. For example, the ERP can help in the diagnosis of infant deafness: If the infant does not or cannot respond behaviorally to sound, the evoked potential can at least help to tell whether or not basic brain pathways are intact. However, a word of caution regarding the use of neurological measures is in order. A basic principle of neuroscience is that many factors determine a response, and thus there is never an exact one-to-one correspondence between a physiological index (such as heart rate acceleration or cortisol level) and a psychological state (such as fear). For example, a sigh, momentarily dozing off, or a bodily movement can also produce changes in heart rate. It is thus incorrect to assume, without corroborating behavioral evidence, that a particular physiological index conclusively demonstrates the existence of a particular psychological state. Despite many virtues, the contributions of neuroscience to our understanding of infancy are limited by the large amount of inference involved in interpreting physiological responses and because many factors other than those of interest to researchers may influence psychophysiological responses. The fact that a stimulus creates an identifiable pattern of activity in the brain does not mean that the stimulus is registered in perceptually meaningful and functional ways. To study conscious function, behavioral data provide stronger inferences.

Testing in Structured Test Situations

For many questions, useful data for understanding infancy can only be obtained if infants are tested in structured settings. In response, researchers have developed an impressive array of behavioral techniques to assess diverse aspects of developmental structure and function. In doing so, investigators try to capitalize as much as possible on the most developed response capacities of infants, presumably responses over which infants have the most control. Many behavioral response procedures used in infancy measure looking, orienting, head turning, or sucking because these are responses that babies can easily make early in life. Among these procedures, the most prominent kinds yield evidence of infants' natural preferences and different kinds of learning. Again, we have ordered the discussion that follows according to the approximate strength of inference that each paradigm commands.

Natural Preference.   Babies do not hide their likes and dislikes, so to assess early sensitivity and capacity, researchers have often simply recorded infants' expressed **natural preferences**. In the late 1950s, Robert Fantz argued that if babies look preferentially at one of two stimuli regardless of the spatial location of the two, their preference reveals a capacity to discriminate the two stimuli. A number of studies on face perception have shown that within the first few months of life infants show strong preferences for certain types of faces, including attractive over unattractive faces, faces of their own race, and faces of females (Balas, Westerlund, Hung, & Nelson, 2011; Slater et al., 2010).

Infants also indicate preferences outside of the visual domain. Steiner (1977, 1979) used facial reactions indicative of natural preferences to investigate infant taste and smell. He gave newborns sweet, sour, or bitter substances to taste, and vanilla or raw fish to smell, while he photographed their "gustofacial" and "nasofacial" expressions—all prior to the first time these neonates had ever eaten. Figure 3.7 shows his results. By their preference reactions, newborns made clear that they had impressive senses of taste and smell.

Demonstrable preference offers good evidence for function, but the preference paradigm suffers from a major shortcoming: The failure to demonstrate a preference is fundamentally ambiguous. For example, an infant might look to mother and stranger equally (showing no preference) but still be able to tell them

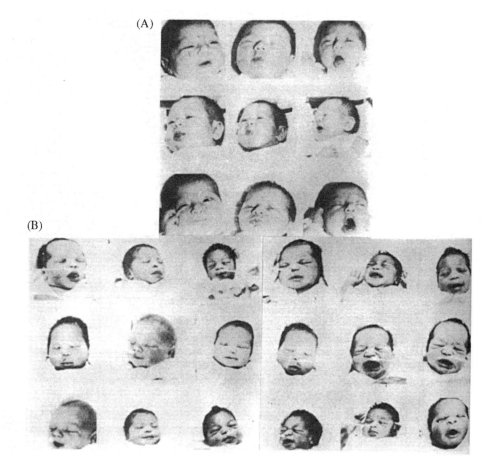

Fig. 3.7 (A) Infants' "gustofacial" response to the taste of sweet (left column), sour (middle column), and bitter (right column). (B) Infants' "nasofacial" response to the smell of vanilla (left panel) and raw fish (right panel).

apart (and may very well prefer one to the other). Consequently, many investigators have turned to paradigms that depend on more active infant behaviors. Among the most prominent today are conditioning and habituation.

Conditioning. Like all living organisms, infants learn and so develop control over some of their behaviors. Researchers can use those behaviors to answer questions. In **operant conditioning**, a naturally occurring behavior is rewarded so that it will occur more frequently. A wide variety of simple and complex infant behaviors have been conditioned, including sucking (Eimas, 1975), eye movements (Schaller, 1975), head rotations (Papoušek & Papoušek, 2002a), vocalizations (Bloom, 1979), and foot kicks (Rovee-Collier & Cuevas, 2009a; Figure 3.8). The **conditioned head-turn procedure** is an example. Here, the baby sits on a parent's lap with a loudspeaker to one side. When a sound (a tone or speech syllable) is played through the loudspeaker and the baby responds by orienting to it, the baby is rewarded by the activation of a colorful mechanical toy just above the speaker. Infants quickly learn to orient to the sound, and experimenters then manipulate the sound to answer their scientific questions. By varying the physical intensity and frequency of test tones, researchers have learned about infant hearing, such as how loud sounds have to be for infants to hear them (Saffran, Werker, & Werner, 2006).

Habituation and Novelty Responsiveness. Conditioning techniques provide reasonably clear data about infant capacities because babies respond actively, voluntarily, and definitively—"communicating" about their functional abilities. However, some forms of conditioning take time and can be dif-

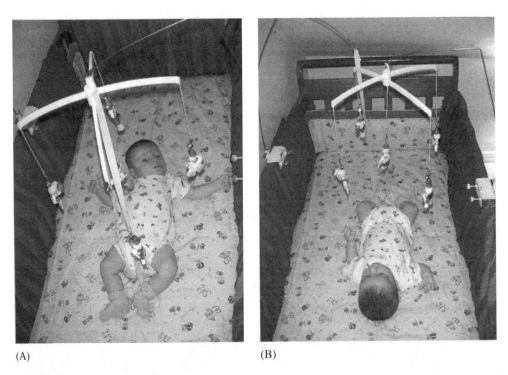

(A)   (B)

Fig. 3.8 An example of the set up for conditioning foot kicking with 2- and 3-month-olds. A ribbon connects the mobile to the infant's foot (A) and the infant quickly learns that by kicking, the mobile will move. Test for memory of the mobile (either immediately or after some delay) is done without the ribbon attached to the foot (B), but the rate of foot kicking indicates whether or not the infant remembered he/she used to be able to make the mobile move. (Courtesy of C. Rovee-Collier.)

ficult for babies; moreover, only a limited number of responses can be studied using operant techniques. Habituation and novelty responsiveness represent alternative, equally informative, and often more easily implemented research strategies.

As we explained earlier in the chapter, when placed in an otherwise homogeneous environment, an infant will typically orient and look at a stimulus, but if the stimulus remains visible or is presented repeatedly, the infant's attention to it will diminish or **habituate** (Figures 3.1 and 3.9). After habituation, the infant can be tested with the familiar stimulus and a new (novel) stimulus. If infants recognize the familiar stimulus as being old and the novel stimulus as being new, they should look more at the novel than at the familiar stimulus. **Novelty responsiveness** is calculated as the amount the infant looks at the novel stimulus relative to the familiar following habituation (Figure 3.9).

Habituation and novelty responsiveness have proved to be easy, versatile, and fruitful research techniques, allowing investigators to assess many aspects of perception and cognition such as detection, discrimination, categorization, recognition memory, and conceptual abilities (Bornstein, Mash, & Arterberry, 2011; Flom, Gentile, & Pick, 2008; Kavsek, 2009; Soska & Johnson, 2008). But habituation has its drawbacks as well: A habituated baby is often temporarily unhappy with the boredom of the stimulus, and looking at a stimulus does not necessarily mean that it is perceived.

Preference, conditioning, habituation, and novelty responsiveness are discrimination methods. Other procedures use **adaptive responses** in infants. Adaptive responses include blinking, reaching, and crawling. Uses of these behaviors will be described in Chapter 6. One other active behavior that merits mention here is where infants look. To a certain extent this has been harnessed in looking preference studies in which infants' looking at one stimulus are compared to their looking at another. Pioneered by Salapatek and Kessen (1966) and renewed by recent technological advances, precise eye movements can be monitored (Haith, 2004; Oakes, 2012). Thus, **eye tracking** is another powerful method for understanding infants' perception. Recording pupil dilation or the location of infants' eye movements, their number, and their duration allows us to make inferences about attention allocation and information processing that are difficult to make with other common methodologies, such as habituation or preferential looking in infancy (Aslin, 2012; Sirois & Jackson, 2012). In Figure 3.10, you can see the location of fixations made by one

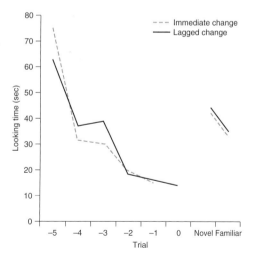

Fig. 3.9 Schematic representation of infant habituation and novelty responsiveness. One group of infants received stimulus change immediately on attainment of habituation criterion (dotted line), and the other received one additional trial with the habituated-to stimulus (solid line). Both groups attained the habituation criterion within five trials (looking was 50% below initial levels). Comparison of groups on the test trials yields evidence that infants looked more to the novel test stimulus than at the familiar one.

(A)

(B)

Fig. 3.10 The location of infants' fixations when attending to an image of an animal in a congruent context (A—the tiger is in a field) and an incongruent context (B—the tiger is in front of a store). (After Bornstein, Mash, & Arterberry, 2011).

infant while inspecting complex visual scenes. However, there are challenges when working with infants. Notably, head movements disrupt data collection, so it is difficult to use eye tracking in tasks involving infant action, such as reaching or crawling/walking (Corbettta, Guan, & Williams, 2012). However, new developments in technology are allowing the collecting of eye gaze data on mobile infants (Franchak, Kretch, Soska, & Adolph, 2011).

Norm- and Criterion-Referenced Tests. A final class of highly structured settings uses norm-referenced or criterion-referenced tests. These tests include large numbers of related items, and the infant is awarded a score based on the number of items completed successfully. **Norm-referenced tests** are so named because they have undergone standardization on a carefully chosen, typically large, reference group that represents the population of infants to be assessed by the test. An example of a norm-referenced infant assessment is the **Bayley Scales of Infant Development-II** (Black, Hess, & Berenson-Howard, 2000). This test has age-based norms. An infant's raw score (number of items successfully completed) is compared to a distribution of raw scores obtained from their same-age standardization group, and a standardized score is then derived depending on where the raw scores fall in the standardized distribution. By contrast, **criterion-referenced assessments** provide information about how an infant performs on a logically ordered series of items without reference to a standardization group. An example of a criterion-referenced infant assessment is the **Užgiris-Hunt Ordinal Scales of Psychological Development** which assess infant performance on a variety of Piagetian-based tasks (Chapter 7; Užgiris & Hunt, 1975). Here, the infant's performance reflects her or his relative level of functioning.

Schedules, assessments, and stages in infant physical and psychological growth brings order out of chaos for parents and the ideas of normalcy and range to professionals involved in psychological assessment. A recently developed assessment aimed at the early identification of autism is a checklist designed to assess communication development every 3 months from 6 months to 24 months (Pierce et al., 2011). The assessment, the Communication and Symbolic Behavior Scales Developmental Profile Infant-Toddler Checklist, is shown in Table 3.1. In one study, 10,479 infants were screened by pediatricians and 184 were followed due to poor performance on the assessment. Of the 184 children, 72% were later diagnosed as having autism spectrum disorder (ASD) or some other type of atypical development, such as a learning disability or developmental delay. Ideally, such a tool can be used to ensure that infants at risk for atypical development and their parents receive early intervention.

Table 3.1 Sample items from the *CSBS DP™ Infant–Toddler Checklist* used by pediatricians to screen for autism and other developmental delays (full scale is available at www.brookespublishing.com)

Does your child pick up objects and give them to you?	Does your child use sounds or words to get attention or help?
Do you know when your child is happy and when your child is upset?	Does your child let you know that he/she needs help or wants an object out of reach?
About how many different words does your child use meaningfully that you recognize (such as baba for bottle; gaggie for doggie)?	When you call your child's name, does he/she respond by looking or turning toward you?
Does your child show interest in playing with a variety of objects?	About how many blocks (or rings) does your child stack?

In summary, investigators have developed a variety of creative techniques to overcome the major impediment infants present to research—their inability to speak. Some researchers have relied on observations, some on neurological measurements of the autonomic and central nervous systems, and others on behavioral measures of preference and learning. In doing so, modern investigations have unearthed important information about structure, function, and development in infancy.

INTERPRETATION AND MEASUREMENT ISSUES IN INFANT RESEARCH

Having discussed issues of logic and design as well as the chief procedures and techniques of infant study, we briefly review in this section some more general issues having to do with measurement and interpretation of research results. We focus on correlation and causality, reliability and validity, and multiple assessment and converging operations.

Correlation and Causality

The study of infant development implies the evaluation of stability and change over time. Two general approaches have evolved to address these questions. One is descriptive and looks for lawful relations between the growth of a structure or function and the infant's age. This approach is **correlational**. A high positive correlation indicates that a high score on one variable is associated with a high score on the other variable. Figure 3.11 shows, for example, that the weight and length of the fetus increase regularly over the course of prenatal development. This simple relation between growth and age yields direct information about normative development. Deviation from this course would alert parents and health providers about potential fetal compromise.

The fact that growth and time are correlated, however, does not mean that growth is a function of time or that growth is "caused" by time. Correlational studies can yield important information about associations between two variables in development, but they provide no evidence of **causal** relations between the two. To evaluate causality, experiments are needed. In the traditional experiment, participants are randomly assigned to treatment and control (no-treatment) groups, and any differences between groups can, therefore, be attributed to the differing experiences of the groups (see, for example, our discussion of interventions for preterm infants in Chapter 1).

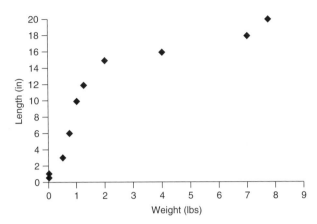

Fig. 3.11 Relation between weight and length during prenatal development. Generally, as length increases so does weight, but it is not a perfect linear function, as earlier in development (left side of the plot) length increases faster than weight.

Sometimes, experiments on particularly important phenomena are not possible. For example, if researchers limited some rat pups to an inadequate and impoverished diet, they would soon find these pups becoming lighter and smaller than rat pups offered unlimited quantities of nutritionally balanced food. Such an experiment using human infants would not be permissible, of course, although comparable data might be obtained in a **natural experiment** or **quasi-experiment**. For example, children in orphanages awaiting adoption have different nutritional experiences, and the children, once adopted, arrive with varying degrees of stunted growth, as measured by height, weight, and head circumference. Taking advantage of this unfortunate situation, Pomerleau and colleagues (Pomerleau et al., 2005) explored the relation between malnutrition and cognitive and motor development. They found differences among children from China, other parts of East Asia, and Russia in terms of their status on arrival at their new home and in terms of change in these domains after 3 and 6 months with their adoptive families.

Correlational studies are often used in an exploratory fashion to identify variables that might affect development. Subsequently, those variables can be manipulated experimentally to confirm their role in development. For example, Belsky, Goode, and Most (1980) hypothesized that parents influence the extent to which their infants explore the environment, and so they conducted two studies, the first correlational and the second experimental. In Study 1, the investigators saw separate groups of mothers and infants at each of four infant ages—9, 12, 15, and 18 months. Mothers and infants were observed at home twice. During those observations, the investigators systematically counted how frequently mothers stimulated their infants either by physically pointing to or highlighting objects, or by verbally instructing or naming. On the basis of their observations, the investigators assigned mothers scores for "stimulation." The researchers also observed infants' manipulation and play, and on this basis independently assigned infants scores for "exploratory competence." In accord with their hypothesis, measures of maternal stimulation and infant exploratory competence correlated with one another at each age and across all four ages; that is, mothers who stimulated their babies more had babies who explored their environments more competently. However, these results were only correlational and so are subject to various interpretations. For example, it could be that stimulating mothers provoke their infants to explore the environment more competently *or* that more competent infants elicit more stimulation from their mothers.

To determine which interpretation was correct, Belsky and his colleagues designed Study 2, an experiment in which a sample of 1-year-olds was divided randomly into experimental and control groups. The investigators visited each mother–infant dyad in the two groups weekly. The first visit involved a maternal interview. The second and third visits involved observations of mother–infant interaction like those conducted in Study 1. The fourth, fifth, and sixth visits involved interventions for dyads in the experimental group and continued observations for those in the control group. Finally, the seventh visit comprised observations of interaction within mother–child dyads in both groups, as did the eighth (and last) visit, which took place two months later. In the intervention, the investigators rewarded mothers who stimulated their babies. These rewards worked, and, as a consequence, mothers in the experimental group were stimulating their babies more by the seventh visit than were mothers in the control group. Importantly, in the seventh and eighth visits, infants in the experimental (mother-rewarded) group received higher scores for exploratory competence than did infants in the control (mother-not-rewarded) group.

By following the exploratory correlational study with an experimental manipulation, these investigators were able to identify maternal activities that influenced the development of infant exploratory competence and to specify causal relations between mothers and infants. Belsky and his coworkers showed that maternal stimulation could facilitate at least one aspect of infant cognitive development.

Reliability and Validity, Multiple Assessment, and Converging Operations

No matter what the experimental design, both logic and practice dictate adherence to certain general step-by-step requirements in studying development in infancy. These steps include evaluations of the reliability and validity of measures and the need for multiple assessments and converging operations. These criteria are especially important in studies of infants, where alternative explanations can compromise the quality of data.

Reliability and Validity. Infancy is a fast-developing and highly variable point in the life cycle and, as a result, infants frequently prove to be rather poor study participants, especially as far as their consistency is concerned. Thus, **reliability** of measurement is a particularly important issue. To be valuable and meaningful, a behavior observed in an infant one day ought to be similar to that observed in the same infant a short time later, or the behavior would not be a reliable index of the infant. For example, Bornstein and his colleagues (Bornstein, Gini, et al., 2006) evaluated the reliability of infants' and mothers' emotional relationships with one another through observations and coding of their interactions. Video recordings of infants and mothers were made at home one week and at the laboratory the next week, and their behaviors were coded along a series of dimensions, such as responsiveness in infants and sensitivity in mothers. The babies and mothers showed individual variation in the different scales, but they also showed short-term reliability across time and context. In other words, those mothers who were more sensitive in week one were more sensitive the next week as well. Note, however, that the inherently changeable nature of infancy can undermine reliability. Rapid development in infancy interferes with the researcher's ability to distinguish reliable from unreliable phenomena. Rapid development also makes it difficult to determine which performance is representative of the baby: the baby's optimal performance, the baby's average performance, or the baby's minimal performance.

In addition, measurements need to have **validity** in the sense that they measure what they are supposed to measure. Assessments must contain items, tasks, or tests that themselves bear at least some

face validity; that is, measures should have an obvious, common sense association with what they are supposed to measure. Measures of perception should measure baby's perception and not baby's motor ability. Researchers have to be aware of both **internal validity** (the ability to make causal statements about whether one variable caused another to change) and **external validity** (constructs investigated in one situation relate in a theoretically meaningful way to constructs assessed in another situation and perhaps at another age). For example, measures of the security of infant–parent attachment might be validated by studies showing associations between attachment security and measures of infant–parent interaction (Sroufe et al., 2005; van den Dries, Juffer, van IJzendoorn, & Bakersman-Kranenburg, 2009). **Predictive validity** occurs when a measure in one domain (infant information processing) predicts later performance in another domain (childhood IQ; Fagan, 2011). The construct of attachment security gains importance from the demonstration that individual differences in the security of infant–parent attachment predict infants' friendliness with strange adults, their persistence in problem-solving situations, and their social competence with peers (Thompson, 2006). Face validity comes into play regarding decisions about the way to measure attachment security and infant–parent interactions. Predictive and external validity are illustrated by associations with other behaviors: Infant attachment security predicts interactions with strangers and can be extended to interactions with peers. What is difficult to demonstrate in this example is internal validity. Without an experimental design in which infants are assigned to sensitive or insensitive parents, we cannot conclusively assert that parental behavior is causing attachment security.

Reliability and validity are typically measured in terms of correlations. If Infant A does well, Infant B moderately, and Infant C poorly in some assessment on one day, and each infant scores similarly on the next day, the assessments of these children would have good reliability. If their scores on those assessments were correlated with their scores on some other measure of the same or a related construct, the original assessment would show good validity.

Multiple Assessment and Converging Research Strategies.

Despite widespread fascination and decades of intensive research, what we know about infants has been learned only slowly and with difficulty. Infants are notoriously uncooperative, are not motivated to perform for researchers, may be unable either to understand or to answer questions unambiguously and reliably, have limited attention spans and response repertoires, and show variability in most measures of performance. To assess infants in any given domain, researchers must design clever procedures to elicit responses that are within the infants' capabilities. When infants do not respond as expected, researchers have to decide whether the infants did not "understand" the question, were incapable of performing the task or of emitting the response, were not paying attention, or were not motivated to respond. When infants do respond, we need to be careful to not over-interpret the meaning of that response because although it might look like functioning that is on par with older children or adults, it might not be (Keen, 2003; Rakoczy, 2012).

Indirect measures often provide only uncertain information. Therefore, in studying infancy it is wise to use several different items (**multiple assessments**) and to employ several different strategies to assess the same phenomenon (**converging operations**). For example, math ability is too complex and multi-dimensional to be represented by one or two math questions. Hence the need for multiple assessments. Moreover, multiple assessments, especially in diverse contexts, represent individuals better than single, brief assessments (Hartmann et al., 2011; Box 3.2). For example, in a study of infant temperament, Bornstein, Gaughran, and Seguí (1991) measured and compared infant activity level in terms of reaching, kicking, and other motor behaviors and they did so with infants when alone, when with their mothers, and when with an observer on two different days.

Box 3.2   Set For Life? Assessing the Impact of Regulatory Problems on Cognitive Development

Wolke and his colleagues (2009) investigated whether regulatory problems experienced by infants at 5 months affected cognitive development at 20 months and 56 months. Regulatory problems include difficulty with feeding, sleeping, and self-calming. Because a number of other factors, such as parent–child relationship, breastfeeding, and neonatal status, may also affect later cognitive development, the researchers evaluated the respective contributions of a number of variables. Regulatory problems at an early age make a significant contribution to cognitive development in later years even when other factors have been accounted for.

Sometimes infants fail to exhibit some capacity when tested one way, yet reveal that capacity when tested in a different way. On other occasions, alternative explanations of the observed behavior are equally plausible. Converging operations consist of two or more experimental strategies that permit the investigator to select or eliminate alternative hypotheses as explanations for an experimental result. Converging operations are often necessary to show that the infants' responses actually reveal the inferred capacity, and that infants' apparent successes are not simply artifacts of a given testing procedure. In the temperament study mentioned earlier, mothers and observers were both asked to rate infant activity on different occasions and in different situations. Mothers and observers assessed the infants' temperament similarly, showing a convergence of measures.

There are no rigid guidelines about how to do research with infants, and results obtained with any one method should not be considered definitive. A method that is suitable for asking one type of question at a given age may be inappropriate for the same or other questions at other ages. Conversely, methods that are not appropriate in one situation can yield valuable information in another. Without careful thought, even well-established methods can yield misleading conclusions.

SPECIAL RESEARCH ISSUES WITH INFANTS

Research with infants is special in many ways. In the final section of this chapter on research methods, we discuss issues concerning context, state, point of view, age comparisons, performance versus competence, and ethics. Each is especially important in research with young infants.

Context

Urie Bronfenbrenner (1979) once wrote "it can be said that much of developmental psychology, as it now exists, is *the science of the strange behavior of children in strange situations with strange adults for the briefest periods of time*" (pp. 18–19). Because traditional research often lacked **ecological validity** (ability to generalize to everyday contexts and behavior), he wrote that researchers needed to pay greater attention to the context in which children were studied. Methods have changed since then, and the developmental science of infancy has come of age.

As we discussed in Chapter 2, social and cultural context determine infants' experiences. They also define the limits of generalizability of findings about infants. Infancy research is conducted in laboratories as well as in homes, and location of a study is an important variable. Laboratory studies are valuable because the testing context can be controlled. However, questions often arise concerning how well laboratory-based findings and principles apply outside the laboratory in real life. Laboratory studies can show that some infants are capable of some capacity or performance, but they do not show whether that capacity or performance is typical of the infant. Furthermore, infancy is a highly reactive stage of life, and infants may perform differently in the familiarity of their home as opposed to strange laboratory situations. Because the home is comfortable and secure, a researcher might tap the infant's naturalistic performance there, but the research also risks uncontrolled factors (such as the unexpected ring of a doorbell) that could undermine the quality or goal of an observation.

Of course, the significance of the home-versus-laboratory distinction will depend on the methods, strategies, and purposes of the particular research. The distinction is presumably less important in studies that attempt to demonstrate the existence of specific capacities, such as maternal behavior or infants' communication. Mothers show no home–laboratory differences in levels of emotional sensitivity (Bornstein, Gini, et al., 2006) nor do infants show a difference in the frequency and duration of their vocalizations at home and in the laboratory (Bornstein, Haynes, Painter, & Genevro, 2000). One might need to conduct observations in both contexts, perhaps assessing parental behaviors in the laboratory first and then conducting naturalistic observations in the home, or vice versa. Clearly, the interchange (or not) between laboratory and field helps us to further understand the phenomenon under investigation.

State

One of the most important and ever-present influences on infant performance is behavioral state of arousal. Newborns and infants often shift rapidly and unpredictably from one state to another and may remain in a state of attentive alertness only for brief periods of time (Chapter 5). Even when the infant capacities are present and a task is well designed, state may facilitate or interfere with infant performance. If state is not accounted for when assessing infants, then the baby's opportunities to perform might be unfairly or incorrectly evaluated. A baby who is awake, content, and attentive ought to have a better chance to perform well or participate more sensitively than one who is drowsy, hungry, and inattentive. Infant state also plays a central role in understanding the reliability or predictive validity of infant performance. Unless the infant's state is the same in both the test and retest assessments, high reliability should not be expected. Failures to find reliability in infant behavior do not tell us which testing session truly represents the infant's capacities.

Point of View

We see the world—literally and figuratively—through adult eyes. Infants do not. They see the world through infant eyes. What looks like one thing to us might look quite differently to a baby, and it can be a serious mistake to misattribute our adult perspective to the baby (Franchak, Kretch, Soska, & Adolph, 2011; Figure 3.12). As a consequence, research in infancy needs to be sensitive to the infant's point of view.

Performance versus Competence

In considering infancy studies and their findings, it is critical to distinguish between performance and competence. **Performance** concerns what infants do under certain conditions in certain contexts. Clearly, it is important to know what infants will do in different circumstances. However, such information does not tell us what infants *can* do in optimal circumstances. **Competence** defines the infant's potential ability. Competence is often inferred from performance, but it is not necessarily the case that performance

 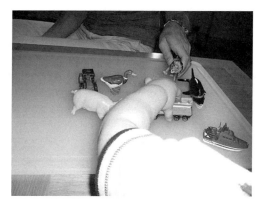

Fig. 3.12 Images of an array of toys from an adult's view (A) and an 18-month-old child's view (B). (Courtesy of M. Arterberry.)

accurately indexes competence. Competence might far exceed performance. Obviously, all of the different methods that we have discussed in this chapter need to be qualified by whether they reveal information about infant performance or infant competence.

Ethics

The last, but by no means least, important consideration of infancy research is the ethics of enlisting babies so young and helpless that they cannot understand what is happening to them, much less render their own (informed) consent to participate in research. Any discussion of research methods with infants would be incomplete without formally considering issues related to harm, deception, confidentiality, and consent (Sales & Folkman, 2000). Human beings who participate in research are not "guinea pigs" with whom experimenters can do what they want. Dennis and Dennis (1940) reported a "study" conducted in the 1930s in which twin infant girls were reared in a single room--rarely spoken to or played with--to see if the girls would develop normally despite these deprivations. Such a study is totally unethical by any standard and today would not be permitted.

Much developmental research is worthwhile, and places research participants—even infants—at little or no risk. Still, the benefits of research always have to be weighed against the potential risks to the individual. Society at large benefits from the knowledge provided by developmental science, but it must judge that benefit against the cost to the individuals who participate. When children, especially infants, participate in research, special ethical problems arise. Infants can be particularly vulnerable, and in some situations they might be harmed more extensively than children or adults by any negative effects of experimentation. At-risk and typically developing infants might be differently affected by the same research situations. Of course, infants are also unable to judge the risks and benefits flowing from their participation in a study. Because there are no easy answers to these problems, all research conducted today must be approved by special institutional ethics committees.

To offset potential risks to infant participants or to their families, researchers must satisfy certain criteria, as outlined by the Society for Research in Child Development (SRCD, 2007). These include the following:

1   Avoid procedures that could harm the child either physically or psychologically and use procedures that create the least amount of stress possible.

2   Consent must be obtained from the parent and assent from the child, if possible. Parental consent practices include providing full information about what will be happening to them and their child. In some cases, withholding information from the parent is appropriate, especially if it could influence the parent's behavior, which is also under study. Nonverbal signs of willingness can be taken as assent from very young children, and as procedures progress, babies and toddlers are not shy about communicating their discomfort. Researchers have an obligation to be sensitive to these signs of discomfort and to discontinue the study. Also, the responsible individual (or the parent) normally has the right to withdraw the child from participation in a study at any time.

3   Incentives to participate in the research project must be fair and appropriate (e.g., a sticker for a toddler; mileage reimbursement for a parent).

4   Correct actions in light of unforeseen consequences. When procedures result in undesirable outcomes (such as undue stress), researchers are obligated to redesign their protocols.

In addition to protection from physical and psychological harm, researchers are obliged to protect privacy. Research findings are confidential, and researchers take care to protect the identity of participants in research reports, as well as in discussions with students or colleagues. Finally, researchers are obliged to share the general findings with participants, and in the case of children, with the parents. Immediately after testing, the investigator should clarify for the participant or parent any misconceptions that might have arisen. At the conclusion of the project, which could be years later, researchers should provide a summary of the general findings to parents.

SUMMARY

Babies are particularly challenging research participants. They are mute, motorically inept, and subject to state fluctuations. Yet they are also important and attractive to study, however, for a host of reasons. Our goal in this chapter has been to introduce the "hows" of infancy research; in succeeding chapters, we turn attention to the "whats" and "whys" of infant development.

Most infancy studies are concerned with the status, function, and/or origins and trajectory of different aspects of development. In this chapter we have discussed general design issues in studies of infants. Investigators usually employ longitudinal or cross-sectional designs in efforts to describe and understand structure, function, origins, and development in infancy. We also described techniques used in different kinds of studies, noting the shift from reliance on baby biographies—a research strategy initiated more than a century ago—long before the systematic study of infant (or, for that matter adult) psychology led to reliance on systematic observation and experimental research. Many different approaches have been used to record and to quantify structure and function in infancy—observational, physiological, and behavioral—and each raises important issues about interpretation and measurement in infancy studies. Correlational studies abound in infancy research, and they help to reveal associations among variables, but causality is usually identified by experimentation. Furthermore, research in infancy (as in any science) needs to meet canons of reliability and validity, and with infants, multiple assessments and converging operations are required. Infant performance and competence reflect context, state, and point of view of the infant. Finally, all research must be conducted with ethical considerations in mind to prevent any harm to infant participants.

KEY TERMS

Adaptive responses
Age-held-constant paradigm
Assessments
Autonomic nervous system
Baby biography
Bayley Scales of Infant Development-II
Case study
Causal
Central nervous system
Cohort effects
Competence
Conceptional age
Concordance
Conditioned head-turn procedure
Continuity
Converging operations
Correlational
Cortical event-related potential
Cortisol
Criterion-referenced assessments
Cross-sectional designs
Domestic diaries
Ecological validity
Educational diaries
Experiential age
External validity
Eye tracking
Face validity
Functional magnetic resonance imaging
Habituate

Habituation
Hormones
Internal validity
Longitudinal designs
Magnetoencephalography
Maturational age
Multiple assessments
Natural experiment
Natural preferences
Near infra-red spectroscopy
Neuroendocrines
Norm-referenced tests
Novelty responsiveness
Operant conditioning
Oxytocin
Performance
Positron emission tomography
Postnatal age
Predictive validity
Preterm
Quasi-experiment
Reliability
Respiratory sinus arrhythmia
Scientific diaries
Stability
Time-based records
Užgiris-Hunt Ordinal Scales of Psychological Development
Vagal tone
Validity

Chapter 4
Prenatal Development, Birth, and the Newborn

- *How are the stages of prenatal development defined?*
- *What principal prenatal factors shape infant development?*
- *What factors occurring between fertilization and birth influence sexual differentiation?*
- *What principal prenatal factors shape infant development?*
- *How does preterm birth affect development?*
- *How are the newborn baby's characteristics assessed?*
- *What is the purpose of infant reflexes?*
- *Describe the structural and functional development of the sensory systems.*

Infancy is a time of rapid physical and nervous system growth and development. The study of these aspects of infancy is important for many reasons. First, principles of physical and nervous system development provide models for other aspects of psychological development. For example, the distinction between innate and congenital is important in infancy studies. The term **innate** applies to structures or functions that are attributed to heredity even though they might not appear full-blown at birth; they may also be influenced by prenatal experience. By contrast, **congenital** applies to structures or functions that are present at the time of birth but are not acquired by heredity. Many characteristics related to sexual differentiation are innate but not congenital because they emerge years later, at the time of puberty. By analogy, it could be that certain cognitive abilities and socioemotional propensities are also innate but not congenital. In contrast, as we will discuss later in this chapter, a child born with a facial malformation, such as a flat nose and widely spaced eyes, has experienced a congenital defect, often associated with the mother's consumption of alcohol during pregnancy.

The study of physical and nervous system development has a second set of implications for understanding infancy as well: Development in these very basic spheres of life often influences development in other spheres of life. Consider two examples. The young infant cannot pinch (use the thumb and forefinger together) to hold an object, but must instead grasp (using the palm and whole hand). It takes about 14 months until the average infant can hold an object in the more mature fashion, and this transition marks a major change in the infant's tactile and visual inspection of objects. Improvements in holding should enhance cognitive development, as suggested by influential theorists such as Piaget (Chapter 7).

This chapter and the next address physical and nervous system development in infancy. Birth occurs during an ongoing developmental process—it neither initiates nor terminates development. Consequently, postnatal development is best considered against the backdrop of prenatal development. Our goal in this chapter is to focus attention on those issues that might help us understand infancy after birth, and thus we discuss genetics, anatomical changes before and just after birth, the birth process, and the early capacities of the newborn. In Chapter 5 we discuss sleep cycles, states of arousal, and the autonomic and central nervous systems as well as motor development. Each of these topics could warrant individual chapters, so our treatment is necessarily selective. We highlight research findings and central principles while discussing each topic.

GENETICS, GENETIC TESTING, AND PRENATAL DEVELOPMENT

Development begins long before birth, so here we consider prenatal influences on the growth of both structure and function. Long ago it was believed that the organism-to-be was "preformed" in the mother's egg waiting to be released, or in the father's sperm waiting for a medium in which to grow. Modern biology tells a different story.

Genetic Endowment

Figure 4.1 shows the process of **meiosis**, which involves complex changes in the reproductive cells (**gametes**) of each parent that split so as to retain half the number of chromosomes present in the original cell. An unfertilized egg (**ovum**) is released by the ovaries and descends the fallopian tube. Membranes of the fallopian tube secrete enzymes that loosen the shell surrounding the ovum, and this permits a single sperm to meet and fertilize the egg. The resulting 23 pairs of **chromosomes** compose the genetic makeup of the individual, with one member of each pair contributed by each parent. Chromosomes contain genes that themselves are composed of chemical codes of DNA that guide the development of all structure and function.

The endowment of parental chromosomes is the first critically important event in the life of a child. However, no one today argues that the **genotype** (the genetic makeup of the individual) exactly predicts the **phenotype** (the observed characteristics of the individual). Clearly, different people with different genetic endowments sometimes can look alike or act similarly, just as identical twins with exactly the same genetic endowment might look or act differently. There are clear genetic contributions to many aspects of development. The phenotypic variability we see in the different people around us, however, springs from several sources because genetic endowment and lifelong experiences *together* shape the characteristics and behaviors of individuals.

Some birth disorders are inherited. For example, in the case of hemophilia, a blood-clotting disorder, a gene on the X chromosome disrupts the normal process of blood clotting. For most cases of hemophilia, mothers (who are asymptomatic) pass the gene on to their sons. Other disorders are caused by malformations in the genes. The latter are typically attributable to spontaneous mutations or to incompatibility of the parents' genes. These disorders can be caused by a single gene or by many genes, and they can be transmitted by one parent or by both. Here we consider several examples of birth disorders caused by malformations in the genes. In 1959, Lejeune discovered that children with Down syndrome have 47 chromosomes rather than the normal 46 (23 from each parent). Having an extra chromosome is one of the most common chromosomal disorders. **Trisomy-21**, or **Down syndrome** (shown in Figure 4.2), occurs in slightly less than 1 out of every 1,000 live births. Its prevalence has decreased by about 60% since the 1970s, the likely result of increased availability and use of prenatal testing (Cheffins et al., 2000; also see below). Down syndrome birth rates vary with the age of the parents, with a 1 in 2,000 rate among 20-year-old women but a 1 in 30 rate among 45-year-old women (Table 4.1). Paternal age is also associated

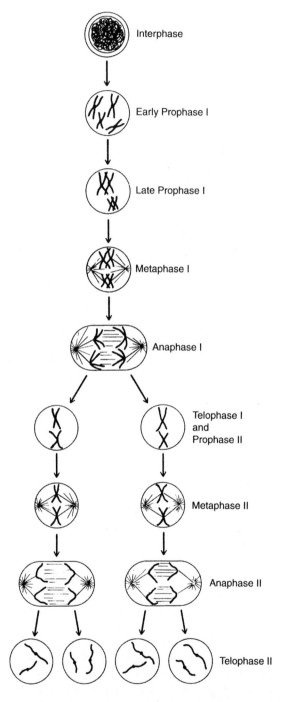

Fig. 4.1 Each parent cell splits and contributes to the genetic makeup of the child through a process of reduction called meiosis. In meiosis, the original parent cell duplicates the chromosomes in the cell and then the cell splits, eventually creating four daughter cells. Through fusion of the ovum and sperm, a full complement of chromosomes is again present.

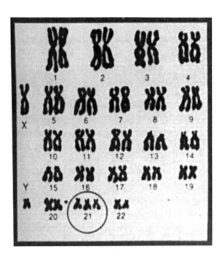 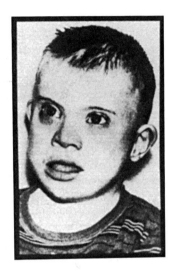

Fig. 4.2 (A) The chromosomal makeup of a Down syndrome child. Down syndrome is also known as trisomy-21 after the triplet of chromosomes that appears in position 21. (B) Down syndrome is associated with a variety of identifiable physical characteristics, and with mental retardation.

Table 4.1 Incidence rates for Down syndrome as a function of maternal age. (From the National Down Syndrome Society, 2011)

Maternal age	Incidence of Down syndrome
20	1 in 2,000
25	1 in 1,200
30	1 in 900
35	1 in 350
40	1 in 100
45	1 in 30

with increasing mutations, potentially contributing to risk for autism and/or schizophrenia (Kong et al., 2012). Men with **Klinefelter syndrome** have two or more X chromosomes and a Y chromosome (XXY instead of the normal XY); this problem occurs in about 1 male out of every 500 live births, but not all show symptoms. Males with Klinefelter syndrome have genitalia and secondary sexual characteristics that are underdeveloped and average to low-average IQs. One in every 2,500 female births has **Turner syndrome**, an X chromosome with no second X (unlike the usual XX). As with Klinefelter syndrome, the symptoms can vary: Turner syndrome females are short, with thick short necks, broad chests, and nonfunctional ovaries; yet they have typical intelligence and social skills (Suzigan, Silva, Guerra-Junior, Marini, & Maciel-Guerra, 2011).

The chromosomal structure of a fetus can be evaluated using procedures such as **amniocentesis**. In this technique, amniotic fluid is drawn off through the abdominal wall of the mother. Fetal cells are then cultivated and swelled chemically so that they can be observed individually by light microscopy. Amniocentesis is often used in genetic testing when a pregnancy is considered to be "at risk," for example, when there is a family history of genetic anomaly or the mother is over the age of 35. The procedure is typically done around the fourth month after conception. Earlier chromosomal assessment is possible through **chorionic villus sampling** (CVS). Villi, which also contain fetal tissue, are protrusions of the chorion membrane which surrounds the fetus and later becomes the placenta. CVS can be done as early as 8 to 10 weeks. Both amniocentesis and CVS can be used to diagnose congenital defects such as muscular dystrophy, spina bifida, Down syndrome, and to screen fetal DNA for inherited disorders such as sickle cell anemia and hemophilia (Chen et al., 2004; Cotter, 2004; Peyvandi, Garagiola, & Mortarino, 2011). Amniocentesis and CVS are associated with some risk, with a 1 in 200 chance for spontaneous abortion with experienced technicians (Evans & Wapner, 2005). In addition, CVS has been linked to slightly elevated rates of limb deficiencies before 10 weeks of age (Evans & Wapner, 2005).

Expectant mothers can be tested noninvasively via a blood test that measures **maternal serum alphafetoprotein** (MSAFP). Assessed during 11 and 13 weeks gestation, this measure has an 80–90% success rate for identifying chromosomal disorders such as Down syndrome (Slack, Lurix, Lewis, & Lichten, 2006). Another noninvasive assessment option is **ultrasound imaging** (Figure 4.3). In this common procedure, sounds are sent into the pregnant woman's body from a probe applied to the abdominal skin. A computer analyzes pulses that are reflected back and uses them to map structures within the body (Levi & Chervenak, 1998). Current practice typically begins with MSAFP, followed up by ultrasound and possibly CVS or amniocentesis. Parents undergoing **in vitro fertilization** (the egg and sperm are united outside of the mother's body and then introduced into the uterus after fertilization) have the option of a single cell being tested for genetic or chromosomal abnormalities before the embryo is transferred (Slack et al., 2006). Recent advances have resulted in whole-genome sequencing of a human fetus using noninvasive techniques (Kitzman et al., 2012). Perhaps this advance will someday lead to routine fetal screening for more than 3,000 single-gene disorders.

Early Stages of Development

Developmental scientists often describe growth in terms of stages, distinguishing three main stages of prenatal development: the period of the **zygote** (approximately conception to 2 weeks), the period of the **embryo** (approximately 2 weeks to 8 weeks), and the period of the **fetus** (approximately 8 to 40 weeks). Counting conventionally starts from the mother's last menstrual period rather than the time of concep-

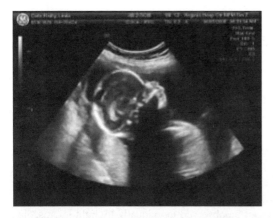 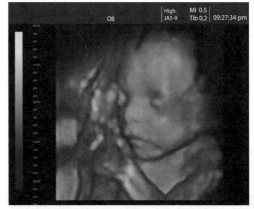

Fig. 4.3 Two ultrasound images. (A) the typical low-resolution ultrasound that can be used to assess the integrity of the fetus, including sex (around 22 weeks gestation), limb length, and structural integrity of the heart. (Courtesy of L. Cote.) (B) a high-resolution ultrasound that can be used to identify more specific structural abnormalities, such as facial features if one suspects the fetus might have Down syndrome. (Copyright: Valentina R. Courtesy of Shutterstock, Inc.)

tion, about 2 weeks later. Note that pregnancy from the mother's perspective is divided into three equally spaced trimesters that do not map onto these periods of prenatal development.

The **zygote** is the initial union of ovum and sperm, the fertilized egg. This first stage lasts from the moment of conception through the time that the new organism (sometimes referred to as a **blastocyst**) travels toward the uterus, where it implants itself (within weeks) in the **endometrium** or nutrient-rich lining of the uterus. Multiplication of cells proceeds rapidly during this period. By the end of this very brief zygotic phase, human cells have already begun to differentiate, that is, to assume specialized roles depending on their location. Even more differentiation emerges during the period of the embryo. Simultaneously, other parts of the blastocyst develop into support systems for the fetus, most notably the placenta. The **placenta** connects the body of the developing organism to the body of the mother and permits the exchange of nutrients and waste via channels in the thick, tough, tubular **umbilical cord**.

The period of the **embryo**, the second stage of conceptional life, begins when hairlike structures, the villi, anchor the blastocyst to the uterine wall. The embryonic period is critically important for the differentiation of organs, limbs, and physiological systems. Even by the time of uterine implantation, it is possible to distinguish three layers: the **ectoderm** (from the outer layer of the blastocyst), which will form skin, sense organs, and central nervous system structures of the brain and spinal cord; the **mesoderm** (from the middle layer), which will form muscles, blood, and the circulatory system; and the **endoderm** (from the inner layer), which will form digestive, respiratory, and internal organs. Particularly notable by the fourteenth day is the appearance of the **primitive streak**, which is the first overt stage in the development of the central nervous system.

By 3 months after conception, the human embryo is little more than 1 inch (2.5 cm) long but has many physical characteristics similar to those recognizable in the mature organism. Many organs are distinguishable from one another although they are not fully developed. The embryo is strangely proportioned: The head, for example, constitutes a much larger portion of total body size than it will at any other time in

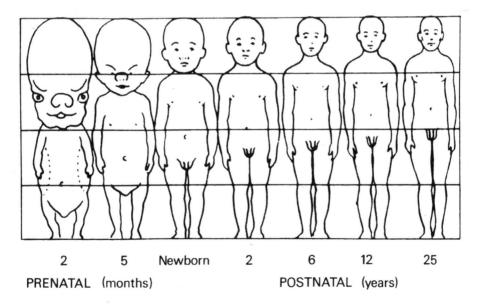

| 2 | 5 | Newborn | 2 | 6 | 12 | 25 |

PRENATAL (months)   POSTNATAL (years)

Fig. 4.4 Proportional growth of the human between the second prenatal month and maturity. This figure shows the principle of cephalocaudal ("head to tail") development: One-half of the 2-month fetus is represented by the head, but this proportion shrinks to one-eighth by maturity.

life, between one-third and one-half of the entire length of the embryo (Figure 4.4). Large eyes are obvious. Less clearly visible, but no less remarkable, are the tongue and teeth buds. Arms and legs, although tiny, are recognizable as well; there are even fingers and toes. The embryonic stomach produces digestive juices, the kidneys filter blood, and the heart beats. Perhaps the least developed organs are those that constitute the respiratory system, probably because they are not functional so long as the embryo remains in the fluid environment of the womb.

The period of the **fetus** begins when the differentiation of major organs is complete, around 2 months after conception, and is marked by the first appearance of bone cells. This is a time of increasing function and great change in bodily proportions (Figure 4.4). The organs existing at the beginning of the fetal stage only crudely resemble the forms they will later take. On a structural level, cellular differentiation and organization dramatically alter the functional capacity of the organs. In addition, the connections among different organs take shape during the fetal period, so a more integrated and coherent functional organism emerges. We can see arm buds in the embryo, for example, but during the fetal period the arms lengthen, joints develop, fingers separate and grow nails, and a complex network of veins develops to nourish the cells while a network of muscle connections lays the groundwork for the finely coordinated movements that the arm will make later.

Functional capacity increases steadily during the fetal stage as well. After 3 months, the fetus begins to swallow and urinate, and various reflex behaviors emerge (see below). By 4 months, fetuses are felt to move *in utero* (referred to as **quickening**); by 6 months, fetuses are capable of breathing and crying; and by 7 months, fetuses may survive in the extrauterine environment (called **the age of viability**), although with recent medical advances, even younger premature infants have a chance of survival (Tyson et al., 2008).

So many critically important events occur during pregnancy that volumes have been devoted to the study of prenatal development (Nelson, 2000). It is not possible for us to review all of this material, and so we have selected two illustrative issues to explore in some detail. Both **prenatal experiences** and **sexual differentiation**, or the biological processes that result in the developing organism becoming a girl or a boy, represent events before birth that can have far-reaching consequences for psychological growth in the human infant after birth, although we hasten to note that the impact of discrete events at any point in development can be modified by later events, in keeping with a transactional perspective on development (Chapter 1).

Prenatal Experience

The time before birth is a period of rapid and extensive development, as well as one of enhanced tenuousness and susceptibility. Some developmental theorists, such as Gesell, argued that biology and maturation are the prime movers of development, but we now know that experiences from outside the organism as well as experiences produced by the organism itself even during early gestation influence prenatal development. Indeed, an important foci of developmental psychobiology are the study of fetal motor, sensory, perceptual, and learning capabilities, how the development of specific systems in the fetus are affected by intra- and extrauterine experiences, and how fetal activity contributes to the development of the central nervous system (Marin-Padilla, 2010).

What experiences are important in prenatal development? How do they exert their effects and when? In Chapter 1, we discussed several roles of experience in development, including induction, facilitation or attunement, and maintenance. Even embryonic behavior appears to play an important role in development: Chick embryos that are immobilized suffer muscle and joint abnormalities, perhaps because their own movements normally help to determine which neuronal connections will grow and which will not in the course of prenatal development. Human fetuses are extremely active. Spontaneous motor activity occurs in cycles of about 1 to 4 minutes, begins early in the second trimester of pregnancy, remains stable up to and shortly after birth, and predicts state and emotional regulation in early infancy (DiPietro, Costigan, & Pressman, 2002; DiPietro, Ghera, & Costigan, 2008).

A host of external factors influences the course and character of prenatal development; their effects may be positive or negative, depending on the nature of the experience. They include maternal characteristics (e.g., age, diet, and stress) as well as the contraction of diseases, ingestion of drugs, and exposure to environmental toxins. During intrauterine life, the fetus is protected from many insults because the placenta filters harmful factors, called **teratogens**, and prevents some, but not all, from harming the fetus. However, others pass the placenta: Diseases, drugs, and environmental toxins pose particular threats to the integrity of the fetus (Rassmussen, 2011).

Maternal Characteristics.   Maternal age is one important characteristic that affects fetal development: Younger and older women are at increased risk for birth complications. Mothers 17 years and younger are at risk for higher rates of preterm births and other complications (Keskinoglu et al., 2007). In a study of over eight million live births to women aged 30–54, women who were 35 years of age or older were at higher risk for early birth (less than 32 weeks), prolonged labor, excessive bleeding, diabetes, and pregnancy hypertension than younger women (Luke & Brown, 2007).

Diet is another maternal characteristic that affects the developing fetus. Women whose diets are well balanced experience fewer complications during pregnancy, have shorter labors, and bear healthier babies. In particular, malnutrition during pregnancy, especially deficiencies in protein, zinc, and folic acid, have been linked to central nervous system dysfunction, including neural tube defects, prematurity, and birth defects (DeMarco, Merello, Cama, Kibar, & Capra, 2011). The timing of malnutrition during pregnancy also appears to affect the type and degree of ill effects obtained. More severe consequences (e.g., neural tube defects and hydrocephalus—a buildup of fluid in the brain) are associated with severe malnutrition that begins early in pregnancy, whereas prenatal malnutrition that begins later is associated with low birth weight (American Dietetic Association, 2002). In Box 4.1, we discuss maternal dietary recommendations and the benefits of exercise.

Box 4.1   Science in Translation: Maternal Diet and Exercise

The health of the mother before, during, and after pregnancy has significant impact on child outcome. In this chapter, we discuss a number of ways things can go wrong with a pregnancy and how the developing person can be harmed during the 9-month journey from conception to birth. A number of these potential problems can be ameliorated if mothers, and expectant mothers, take care of themselves. Nutrition is an important component to providing an optimal prenatal environment. Mothers who are of a healthy weight before conception, eat a balanced diet, and exercise regularly have fewer complications with their pregnancies, and they have healthier babies. Once pregnant, mothers need to be mindful of weight gain—not too much and not too little. According to the American Dietetic Association (2002), mothers with pre-conception BMI (Body Mass Index) ranging between 19.8 to 26.0, should gain 25–35 lb (11.5–16 kg) during the course of the pregnancy. Mothers who are underweight at conception should be monitored closely for weight gain (28–40 lb, 12.5–18 kg), especially during the second and third trimesters. Mothers who are overweight should gain less (15–25 lb; 7–11.5 kg for mothers with BMI between 26 and 29, and only 15 lb (7 kg) for mothers with BMI over 29). Mothers expecting twins or triplets can be expected to gain up to 45 lb (20.4 kg) or 50 lb (22.7 kg), respectively. Mother's weight gain is correlated with fetus weight and increased weight in the mother is related to increased fat cells in children—which may put them at risk for weight-related diseases later in life. Nutritional content of food is also important. Folic acid, iron, calcium, B vitamins and other minerals such as zinc and copper are especially important during pregnancy. Most pre-natal vitamins have the required nutrient supplements, and women are encouraged to begin vitamin usage when they are planning to become pregnant and continuing while breastfeeding (Chacko, Anding, Kozinetz, Grover, & Smith, 2003).

One way to control weight is to exercise during pregnancy. Moderate exercise of 30 minutes three times a week is appropriate for pregnant mothers. Recommended activities include walk-ing, swimming, running, aerobic dancing, and riding a stationary bicycle. In addition to keeping mothers fit, aerobic exercise also may help the baby's cardiovascular functioning. In a study that monitored fetal heart rate of mothers who exercised and those who did not, it was found that when at rest, fetuses had lower heart rates and greater heart rate variability—both good things (Chapters 3 and 5)—at 36 weeks of the pregnancy compared to fetuses whose mothers did not exercise (May, Glaros, Yeh, Clapp, & Gustafson, 2010). May et al. propose that when mothers exercise, the fetus is exposed to an increase in norepinephrine, a catecholamine known to influ-ence fetal cardiac control.

In short, planning is an important step toward ensuring a successful pregnancy and a healthy child. A healthy lifestyle before getting pregnant—nutrition, exercise, weight control—set the stage for an optimal prenatal experience for both the mother and child.

Several psychological, familial, and sociological factors influence prenatal development. For exam-ple, maternal stress affects maternal hormones that, in turn, affect the fetus. Chronic stress during preg-nancy is associated with premature labor and birthing complications (Paz et al., 2011). Because social status is associated with factors such as poor nutrition, high life stress, and inadequate medical care, the children of impoverished women tend to have poorer outcomes (McLoyd et al., 2006). Pregnancy in itself can be a stress-provoking experience, especially for first-time mothers, even among low-risk women (Lynn, Alderdice, Crealey, & McElnay, 2011; Box 4.2).

Box 4.2   Set for Life? Prenatal Maternal Stress Impacts Intellectual and Language Skills in Toddlers

To see if prenatal maternal stress affects intellectual and language capabilities, Laplante and his colleagues (2004) took advantage of an ice storm in Quebec, Canada in January, 1998. The ice storm caused loss of power to over 1.5 million homes in some cases for more than 5 weeks. This natural disaster provided random exposure to varying degrees of stress to a large number of women at various stages of their pregnancies. Fifty-eight women participated in this study; 21 were in their first trimester, 14 were in their second trimester, and 23 were in their third trimester during the ice storm. Mothers rated the extent to which they were affected by the storm, includ-ing reporting on exposure to lack of heat, lack of water, duration of loss of power, and per-sonal injury. Their infants were assessed at 24 months for cognitive functioning and language development. Toddlers whose mothers experienced higher levels of stress during the pregnancy scored lower on tests of cognitive ability, spoke fewer words, and understood fewer words. Tim-ing of the stress was also an important factor: Toddlers whose mothers experienced moderate to high levels of stress during the first or second trimester fared worse than those whose moth-ers experienced stress in the third trimester. Moderate to high levels of prenatal maternal stress affect toddlers' language development and intellectual development.

Disease.   Sexually transmitted diseases, smallpox, and measles can cross the placental barrier and affect prenatal development. For example, women who contract German measles (rubella) during the first trimester of pregnancy (when central nervous system structures such as the eyes and ears are rapidly developing) have a 50% risk of bearing infants who have cataracts or are deaf. Various other long-term abnormalities attend rubella, such as brain damage and mental retardation. Fortunately, as part of child-hood immunizations in resource-rich countries, infants receive a vaccination for rubella so that most adult women and their embryo or fetus should have protection from this disease. Developing countries are increasingly providing immunization against rubella: In 2009 130 countries provided the vaccine resulting in a world-wide reduction of congenital birth defects due to the disease (Reef, Strebel, Dabbagh, Gacic-Dobo, & Cochi, 2011).

A disease for which there is no vaccine (yet) is HIV/AIDS. The Human Immunodeficiency Virus (HIV), which produces Acquired Immunodeficiency Syndrome (AIDS), passes the placental barrier to infect the developing fetus. The first cases of AIDS in children were reported in 1982. In 2009, 370,000 children worldwide became infected with HIV, and 40,000–60,000 pregnant women died of AIDS (UNAIDS.org). The vast majority of HIV-positive children under 13 years of age acquired the disease from an infected mother during pregnancy, labor, and delivery or through breastfeeding. Although these numbers are alarmingly high, the story changes when you look at resource-rich regions of the world, such as the United States, Canada, and Europe: In 2009, virtually no children became infected with HIV. This low infection rate is the result of widespread public health service efforts since 1994 to obtain routine, voluntary testing of pregnant women for HIV and to provide zidovudine (AZT) and other anti-retroviral drugs to infected women during pregnancy and delivery and to infants of infected women after birth. Without AZT, the mother-to-infant transmission rate of HIV is about 25%. When infected pregnant moth-ers are given AZT, HIV transmission rates drop to less than 2% (Dao et al., 2007).

Pediatric AIDS typically progresses along one of two developmental tracks. About 20% of HIV-infected infants will be seriously symptomatic (e.g., delayed physical growth; opportunistic bacterial infections such as pneumonias, internal organ abscesses, and meningitis; delays in normative develop-mental achievements) by the end of the first year and are not likely to survive past 4 years of age (Newell et al., 2004). For the remaining 80%, the progression of the disease is much slower. Importantly, medical and developmental prognoses for infants with HIV infection can improve dramatically with anti-retroviral therapy, aimed at blocking HIV replication, and restriction of breastfeeding (Dao et al., 2007).

Drugs.   It is estimated that many pregnant women smoke tobacco (18%), drink alcohol (9.8%), and use illicit drugs (4%; Jones, 2006). Nicotine from cigarette smoking is believed to constrict placental blood vessels, temporarily depriving the developing fetal brain of oxygen, stimulating the cardiovascular sys-tem, and depressing the respiratory system. Women who smoke have a higher incidence of spontaneous abortions, preterm deliveries, low birth weight, intrauterine growth retardation, and a number of structural abnormalities (Hackshaw, Rodeck, & Boniface, 2011). Moreover, smoking during pregnancy places a child at risk for poor cognitive functioning later in life (Mezzacappa, Buckner, & Earls, 2011; Motlagh et al., 2011). Similar cognitive deficits are also found for marijuana use during pregnancy (Goldschmidt, Richardson, Willford, & Day, 2008).

A particularly well-studied example of the sensitivity of the fetus to everyday drugs concerns the effects of alcohol. Jones and his colleagues published two papers in 1973 on children with similar patterns of malformation, growth deficiency, central nervous system dysfunction, and mental retardation. They noted that all the children had alcoholic mothers and termed this birth defect **fetal alcohol syndrome** (FAS; Jones & Smith, 1973). These publications stimulated research on the effects of alcohol ingestion during pregnancy. **Fetal alcohol spectrum disorder** (FASD), of which FAS is one type, is now consid-ered to be the leading cause of mental and growth retardation with a known etiology. Like women who smoke, women who drink excessively during pregnancy also experience higher incidences of spontaneous abortions, stillbirths, and preterm deliveries (Patra et al., 2011). Diagnostic criteria for FAS include pre- or postnatal growth retardation, central nervous system abnormalities such as microcephaly (a small head) and seizures, low muscle tone and motor impairments, mental retardation, attention deficits, hyperactivity, and craniofacial abnormalities such as a narrow forehead, small nose and midface, and a low nasal bridge (Vaurio, Crocker, & Mattson, 2010). Figure 4.5 shows photographs of a human child and two mouse fetuses, comparing structural abnormalities. Some children exposed to alcohol prenatally do not have the characteristic structural abnormalities, yet they show deficits in a number of areas, including cognition, social interaction, communication, personal living skills, and adaptive behavior (Jacobson, Jacobson, Stanton, Meintjes, & Molteno, 2011; Jirikowic, Kartin, & Olson, 2008).

Prenatal alcohol exposure may also have insidious long-term effects. In an extensive review of the literature on prenatal alcohol exposure, Kelly, Day, and Streissguth (2000) reported elevated rates of intellectual deficits in individuals who were exposed prenatally to alcohol. They also reported that adults who were exposed to alcohol before birth had higher rates of criminal and sexualized behavior, depression, suicide, and parental neglect of children. Clearly, there is no one-to-one correspondence between prenatal alcohol exposure and these later difficulties. From a transactional perspective, however, it is likely that such exposure predisposes individuals toward early intellectual, attentional, and social behavior deficits that could in turn lead to more seriously maladaptive life outcomes.

Illicit drugs such as cocaine and heroin also affect prenatal development and postnatal functioning. Both substances transfer easily from mother to fetus: Traces of cocaine can be found in the urine of the newborn, and babies can be born addicted to heroin or methadone (Eyler et al., 2001). Epidemiological studies reveal linkages between prenatal cocaine abuse and increased rates of spontaneous abortions, stillbirths, and premature separation of the placenta, as well as reduced gestation lengths by an average of 15 days compared to drug-free controls. In neonates, prenatal cocaine exposure has also been linked to low birth weight, reduced head circumference and body length, high levels of irritability, poor state organization, and increased risk for **Sudden Infant Death Syndrome** (SIDS), an unexpected death within the first year of life. Longer-term effects of cocaine exposure include modest intellectual and language deficits (Bandstra, Morrow, Mansoor, & Accornero, 2010; Bornstein, Mayes, & Park, 1998).

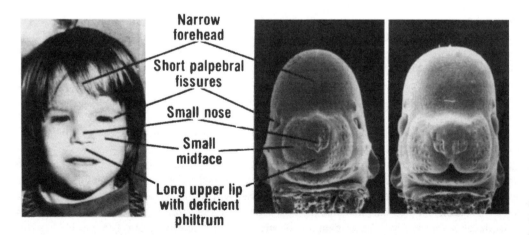

Fig. 4.5 A child with fetal alcohol syndrome and 14-day-old mouse fetuses from ethanol-treated (left) and control (right) mothers. (Courtesy of K. K. Sulik.)

Babies born to heroin addicts are themselves addicted at birth, and such babies begin withdrawal from their addiction within 1 to 3 days after birth. Withdrawal symptoms can be severe and include tremors, irritability, vomiting, diarrhea, and sleep disturbances (Keegan, Parva, Finnegan, Gerson, & Belden, 2010; Patrick et al., 2012). Heroin-addicted mothers are frequently weaned onto methadone, a drug whose effects are less severe. Unfortunately, infants become addicted to methadone as well and go through a similar period of early postnatal withdrawal. Prenatal heroin or methadone exposure has been linked to low birth weight, and in one study 45% of infants with heroin-abusing mothers were born too small in comparison to 15% of infants of non-drug abusing mothers (Keegan et al., 2010). Infants prenatally exposed to heroin are also at serious risk for HIV infection because their mothers frequently share needles with other addicts. Like prenatal cocaine exposure, long-range effects of heroin may include lower IQ, and attentional and behavioral problems (Ornoy et al., 2010).

Fortunately, discontinuing drug use may lead to improvements in infant development. Scherling (1994) reported that 40% of children whose mothers used cocaine pre- and postnatally had IQ scores of 85 or lower. By contrast, only 15% of children scored at this level when mothers stopped using cocaine postnatally. It is likely that mothers who discontinue drug use postnatally parent better and rear their children in safer environments than mothers who remain on drugs. Such improvements might, in turn, improve child development (Jones, 2006).

Tragically, seemingly harmless drugs can also have simple to catastrophic consequences for babies, even when parents and physicians are acting in the best interests of the mother and fetus and the drugs have no observable effects on the mothers. In the late 1950s and 1960s, European physicians sometimes prescribed the sedative thalidomide for pregnant women suffering from morning sickness. Those women who took thalidomide during the period when fetal limbs were differentiating (the first trimester) subsequently gave birth to babies with limb buds rather than full limbs. Ingestion of thalidomide at other times did not have such tragic consequences (Newman, 1985). Until 1971, a laboratory-produced female hormone, diethylstilbestrol (DES), was sometimes prescribed for women who had difficulty bringing their pregnancies to term. The insidious effects of DES took about 30 years to make themselves known. The effects included a substantially increased risk of rare cervical and vaginal cancers in grown women who were DES exposed before birth. Less frequently, DES led to the formation of cysts in the ducts where sperm are stored, low sperm counts, or abnormally shaped sperm in grown men who were so exposed *in utero*. These effects are thought to be attributable to high levels of circulating estrogen at the time when fetal sex organs were differentiating (see the next section). DES daughters also have an increased risk of problem pregnancies and infertility, and even their daughters are thought to be at higher risk for cancers—so, exposure in the grandmother may affect the granddaughter!

Clearly, prenatal exposure to drugs has both short- and long-term consequences for developing human beings. Consequently, today, medical practitioners are especially cautious about giving medications to pregnant women. In addition, women are advised to consult with their physicians before taking over-the-counter medications. Caution also applies to herbal and botanical treatments. Not much is known about the potential effects on prenatal development, yet, their use as part of alternative or complementary medical approaches to managing pregnancy are on the rise (Table 4.2; Adams, Sibbritt, & Lui, 2011; American Dietetic Association, 2002).

Environmental Toxins.   The physical environment also poses toxic hazards for fetuses. Those that have been identified as teratogens include PCBs (polychlorinated biphenyls), DDT, mercury, and lead, and each has adverse implications for development (Brubaker et al., 2009; Pathak et al., 2011). PCBs are synthetic hydrocarbons that were used widely in industry before being banned in the United States in the 1970s. Residues of PCBs are still present in the soil, water, and air, and can be ingested by eating fish from contaminated lakes. Prenatal PCB exposure is linked to lower birth weight, smaller head circumference,

Table 4.2 Herbal and botanical supplements that may not be safe for use during pregnancy. (From ADA, 2002)

Angus castus	Cottonroot	Horsetail	Pulsatilla
Aloes	Cornsilk	Horseradish	Queen's Delight
Angelica	Crotalaria	Hydorcotyle	Ragwort
Apricot Kernal	Daminana	Jamaica Dogwood	Raspberry
Asafoetida	Devil's Claw	Juniper	Red Clover
Aristolchia	Dong Quai	Liferoot	Rhubarb
Avens	Dogbane	Licorice	Rue
Blue Flag	Ephedra	Lobelia	Sassafras
Bogbean	Eucalyptus	Mandrake	Scullcap
Boldo	Eupatorium	Mate	Senna
Boneset	Euphorbia	Male Fern	Shephard's Purse
Borage	Fenugreek	Meadow-sweet	Skunk Cabbage
Broom	Feverfew	Melliot	Stephania
Buchu	Foxglove	Mistletoe	Squill
Buckhorn	Frangula	Mothenwort	St. John's Wort
Burdock	Fucus	Myrrh	Tansy
Calamus	Gentian	Nettle	Tonka Bean
Calendula	Germander	Osha	Uva-Ursi
Cascara	Ginseng	Passion-flower	Vervain
German Charmomile	Golden Seal	Pennyroyal	Wild Carrot
Roman Charmomile	Ground Ivy	Petasites	Willow
Chaparral	Grounsel	Plantain	Wormwood
Black Cohosh	Guarana	Pleurisy Root	Yarrow
Blue Cohosh	Hawthorne	Podophyllium	Yellow Dock
Cola	Heliotropium	Pokeroot	Yohimbe
Colstfoot	Hops	Poplar	
Comtrey	Horehound	Prickly Ash	

shorter gestation, poorer autonomic and reflex functioning, and long-term deficits in memory (Jacobson & Jacobson, 1994). DDT and other organochlorines (as these types of chemicals are called) have been most commonly used as pesticides in farming and for mosquito control in neighborhoods. Although now outlawed in a number of industrial countries, DDT is still being used in the developing world, such as India, and exposure has been linked to growth retardation (Pathak et al., 2011).

Another environmental toxin is BPA (bisphenol A), a chemical found in a number of consumer plastics including food and beverage containers. In one study, fetal exposure to BPA was measured at about 16 and 26 weeks gestation and child behavior was measured at 3 years of age. Braun and his colleagues (2011) found that BPA exposure was correlated with higher levels of childhood anxiety and hyperactivity and lower levels of emotional control and inhibition, particularly for girls. This finding suggests that girls may be differentially sensitive to the effects of BPA exposure prenatally.

BPA may also affect the development of children postnatally (a topic we explore further in Chapter 5). For example, babies are fed from plastic bottles, but those bottles are made of synthetic chemical resins such as BPA which can leach into the contents. BPA is associated with brain damage in mice (Kabuto, Amakawa, & Shishibori, 2004). Although there is controversy about its long-term effects, Canada banned the sale of baby bottles made with BPA in 2008.

Teratogens are altogether insidious. The selectivity and time boundedness of their consequences combine to make them difficult to discover because they sometimes do not have easily detectable, systematic, or pervasive effects. Other factors further complicate this story; the **dose-effect relation** is one. Usually, mechanisms of action are straightforward, such that greater amounts (in dosages or exposures) are associated with greater effects, making the effects of the toxin clear (Needleman & Bellinger, 1994).

Sometimes, however, the probability of structural (anatomical) malformation in the organism follows one dose-effect curve, whereas the probability of functional (behavioral) deficit in the same organism follows different curves. In addition, structural and functional effects may show a threshold growth curve (i.e., toxic effects do not emerge until some fixed dose level is exceeded), as is the case with alcohol consumption. Patra, Bakker, Irving, Jaddoe, Malini, and Rehm (2011) reviewed a number of studies comparing pregnant mothers who did and did not drink. They found that the dose-response relationship for low birth weight and small for gestational age showed no effect up to 10 g pure alcohol (equivalent to an average of 1 drink/day). Preterm birth showed no effect up to 18 g pure alcohol (about 1.5 drinks/day). After those thresholds, there was a linear increase in risk of birth complications as consumption increased.

Timing and Comorbidity.   Studying the effects of diet, drugs, and other environmental influences (such as lead exposure) on the developing embryo or fetus is complicated by several other factors. First, the impact of such toxins will vary as a function of when in development they are introduced (e.g., drinking in the first trimester of pregnancy vs. the last trimester). A **sensitive period** is defined as a time during which the organism is especially vulnerable to external influences that alter or modify its structures or functions, often, though not always, in an irreversible fashion (Bailey & Bruer, 2001; Bornstein, 1989). As explained in Chapter 1, sensitive periods are programmed organism–environment interactions that occur between the time a structure or function emerges and the time it reaches its mature state. Typically, they encompass the epoch during which the system is undergoing its most rapid growth. The development of each organ, limb, or sensory system is most rapid during a distinct period, and each is most vulnerable to insult or damage during this period. For example, the eyes develop most rapidly in the second month of pregnancy, and so the visual system is especially vulnerable during this period. All of the major organ systems differentiate early in gestation, and therefore as organ development slows toward the end of gestation, the likelihood of gross structural malformation as a result of external factors declines. With respect to many teratogens, older fetuses are at much less risk than younger ones (although oxygen deprivation, for example, might be more important to the older fetus). Even if they are present for only a short time, toxins alter normal structure or function, or prevent it from emerging at all, whereas those structures or functions that differentiate earlier or later will remain largely unaffected. Consequently, the effects of a toxin depend as much, or more, on timing than on the nature of the toxin itself: Two different toxins could have very similar effects at the same phase of prenatal life, yet neither might affect development at other stages.

Prenatal experiences might also have immediate effects, as indicated by research on the effects of prenatal exposure to cocaine and heroin on neonatal functioning, and they might show long-term "sleeper" effects and produce IQ deficits and behavior problems later in life. Finally, if exposure to teratogens continues beyond the prenatal period, risk to the child might not decline: Parents who smoke place their infants at risk for bronchitis, pneumonia, and asthma due to the effects of second-hand smoke. Exposure to lead at different times in early childhood (before or after the child's second birthday) has different consequences for the child's cognitive functioning. Findings such as these make it difficult to pinpoint specific effects of prenatal exposure to teratogens.

Finally, it is often difficult to study the effects of a single toxin or teratogen because one, such as alcohol use, is **comorbid** (occurs simultaneously) with another risk factor such as smoking, poor diet, and substandard housing with lead exposure. Animal studies, in which there is a high level of control and fewer ethical concerns, can identify the impact of one toxin, such as the way nicotine induces DNA damage or how caffeine impacts cardiac development in mice, but in studies with humans, researchers must rely on statistical techniques to try to isolate the effects of one teratogen from another (LaMaestra et al., 2011; Mezzacappa et al., 2011; Wendler et al., 2009). Moreover, it is likely that a child exposed prenatally to a nonoptimal environment will continue to experience a nonoptimal environment after birth. Abuse is likely to co-occur with other factors that place infants at developmental risk, including mothers' abuse of other drugs, continued abuse of the drug after the infant's birth, poverty, unhealthy lifestyles, poor prenatal care, parental psychopathology, and parental neglect (Mayes & Truman, 2002). Furthermore, in the postnatal period, the drug culture has pervasive confounding negative effects on the child's family and community, exposing the child to such well-recognized environmental hazards as poverty, violence, abandonment, homelessness, inadequate health care, and inadequate parenting. Because addiction prevents many mothers from caring for their children adequately, infants born to addicts frequently experience multiple short-term foster placements, separations, and/or repeated moves (Mayes & Truman, 2002). As a consequence, it is difficult to determine whether developmental delays are a product of drug use, poverty, parents' mental illness, and/or problems in parenting.

It is possible that nonoptimal prenatal experiences might not be all that bad. Pluess and Belsky (2011) suggest prenatal experiences and fetal response prepares the child to respond flexibly to his or her postnatal environment. Using maternal stress and postnatal child temperament as measures, they argue that more flexible or malleable individuals—those that show **plasticity**—are more responsive to their current environmental situation. Consider a child whose mother experienced a lot of prenatal stress. This child is likely to be of low birth weight and described as a "difficult" child temperamentally, in that he or she is difficult to soothe, fearful, and/or perceived as demanding by the parent. The child, however, might not always continue to be difficult. The way the parent responds dictates child outcome. A harsh parenting environment will lead to continued negative behaviors whereas a supportive and sensitive parenting environment predicts a more positive developmental trajectory. Pluess and Belsky claim that the child is prepared prenatally to move along one or the other trajectory, thus demonstrating a gene–environment interaction.

Sexual Differentiation

To illustrate the sequences of prenatal development and to relate processes of biological and psychological development to one another, we next examine sexual differentiation. Hormones determine sexual differentiation—whether an embryo/fetus becomes a boy or a girl. The child's sex obviously affects the way parents and adults treat the child from the start. The sex-differentiated treatment of girls and boys, in turn, influences acquisition of gender identity and development of behavioral gender differences. Although many of these influences may be indirect, prenatal factors contribute to this important aspect of personality development.

The process of sex determination begins at conception. The ovum always contains one X chromosome, because the XX pair characteristic of female cells can only split into two X-bearing gametes, whereas the XY pair characteristic of male cells splits into one X-bearing and one Y-bearing gamete. If the father's X-bearing sperm fertilizes the ovum, it will link with the mother's X to yield a female XX constellation. If the Y-bearing sperm unites with the X-bearing ovum, it yields a male XY pair. A single gene located on the Y chromosome appears to deliver the trigger that activates male development.

Whether or not the blastocyst has XX or XY sex chromosomes has very little direct impact on the course of early development. In the first 1½ months after conception, all embryos (regardless of sex) have similar gonadal structures. If the embryo has XX chromosomes, this streak develops into ovaries, whereas if there are XY chromosomes, testes will develop. This development represents the first step in the process of sexual differentiation. Thereafter, as far as we know, the sex chromosomes have no direct influence on morphological, physiological, or behavioral development.

Nevertheless, several further stages occur in the development of anatomical sex differences. During the second stage, the recently differentiated gonads assume the formative role. Approximately 1½ to 2 months after conception the testes begin to secrete the hormone testosterone. Testosterone stimulates the development of the **Wolffian duct system** (the precursor to male internal reproductive organs). Another hormone secreted by the testes at this time, **Mullerian Inhibiting Substance** (MIS), discourages the **Mullerian duct system** (the precursor of the internal female reproductive organs) from developing. Both the Wolffian and the Mullerian ducts are present during the first "genderless" month after conception. The presence or absence of MIS and testosterone determines which of the systems will develop and which will shrivel away. In the "natural" course—that is, without testosterone—the Mullerian duct system would develop, female organs would differentiate, and the Wolffian ducts would atrophy.

The external genitalia are formed in the next stage. The presence of testosterone determines that testicles and a penis will develop. In the absence of testosterone, the undifferentiated genitalia will develop into a vulva and clitoris (Figure 4.6). Finally, in the fourth stage, the testosterone secreted by the male testes suppresses the natural rhythmic function in the hypothalamus and the pituitary—the two "master glands" in the hormonal system. If testosterone is not secreted during the second and third trimesters of pregnancy, the pituitary establishes a cyclic pattern of hormone secretion, which is characteristic of females.

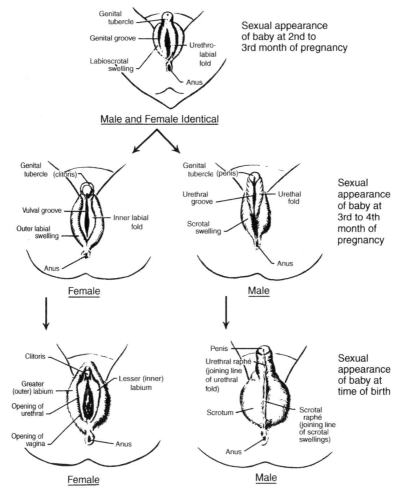

Fig. 4.6 There are several discrete stages in the development of anatomical sex, each sharply distinguished from the adjacent ones by a series of critical events.

It is important to note that each stage of sexual development is independent of other stages. As in the case of toxic substances, any interference with the normal course of development will have a very specific effect on the fetus and the nature of the effect will differ depending on its timing. We can view each of the stages of anatomical sex differentiation as a gate: Whatever developments have already taken place are immune to disruption by later deviations in the developmental process. At each gate, male or female development is equally likely to occur regardless of the path followed up until that point. (For example, when, as a result of a rare genetic defect, the fetal tissues cannot absorb the hormones released by the new testes, the 2-month-old fetus will develop a female Mullerian duct system exactly as if it had ovaries rather than testes.) The key to each gate is not directly related to the previous phase—the presence or absence of testosterone and tissues sensitive to it are critical. Furthermore, once a gate is passed it cannot be reopened.

What implications does this developmental course have for our understanding of psychological sex differences (Hines, 2004, 2010)? We could speculate that the postnatal determinants of sexual differentiation are analogous to prenatal influences. Perhaps the social experiences that shape the sex-typed behaviors of girls and boys act on an organism that can readily learn to behave in either a masculine or feminine manner. The birth process might close the gates on the anatomical and physiological changes that take place in the intrauterine period, but the path to masculine- and feminine-type behavior may remain open, to be shaped by parental treatment in the first years of life. Alternatively, it could be the case that prenatal sexual differentiation "organizes" the brain in either a feminine or masculine direction, predisposing the child to be more receptive to and perhaps seek out socialization experiences in accord with her or his prenatal sexual differentiation. We return to this discussion in Chapter 11.

BIRTH AND THE NEONATE

Birth

After approximately 280 days of gestation (at least for first-time, European American middle-income mothers with uncomplicated, spontaneous labor deliveries), some unknown factor causes the mother's pituitary gland to release a hormone (**oxytocin**) that in turn instigates muscular contraction and expulsion of the fetus from the uterus. The uterus is actually a muscle that expands during pregnancy. **Labor** involves involuntary uterine contractions, beginning at the top of the muscle, that literally force the fetus out. The duration of labor is influenced by a variety of factors, but contractions last 16 to 17 hours on average for firstborns. Even the birth process appears to reflect cultural context, however. Shostak (1981) wrote a biography of a !Kung woman living in the Kalahari desert of Africa in the middle of the 20th century. At the time of delivery Shostak observed the mother simply walking a short way out of the village, squat against a tree, and give birth.

Various dangers must be negotiated during the birth process. The narrowness of the birth canal leaves most newborns looking red and battered with misshapen heads, but these effects are temporary. More significant are dangers associated with oxygen deprivation (**anoxia**). The fetus can experience anoxia for many reasons:

1   The umbilical cord (through which the mother supplies the baby with oxygen) is pinched during a contraction.
2   The cord has wrapped around the baby.
3   The baby is holding on to and squeezing the cord.
4   The baby's orientation in the birth canal is unusual. Babies are normally born head-first, but sometimes they present feet or buttocks first (**breech**) or in a hammock position.

Whatever the cause of a deficiency, a baby who is deprived of oxygen for a very short amount of time is in little danger; however, deprivation for just a few minutes or more is thought to risk some brain damage because brain cells require continuous oxygenation to survive and function. Anoxia has two major effects on the brain. First, unlike other living cells, brain cells are not usually replaced when they die. Thus, damage to or loss of brain cells is permanent (although there are compensations of different kinds; see Chapter 5). Second, anoxia leads to a buildup of pressure in the blood system and, because the brain is especially vulnerable, this pressure can lead to bleeding in the brain (**intraventricular hemorrhage**). Fortunately, the probability of anoxia is limited because birth is a time of great stress and the infant's metabolic rate and temperature fall during delivery, reducing the need for oxygen. Moreover, minor and even moderate degrees of anoxia typically do not have long-term effects because the brain may develop alternative pathways to overcome early localized handicaps. Severe anoxia, however, places the infant at risk for brain damage and associated adverse consequences including seizures, cerebral palsy, and impaired cognition. Gray skin color is an immediate indication of anoxia, and this is recorded in the Apgar assessment of the newborn (discussed below).

The pain of childbirth prompts some women to make use of anesthesia at some point during labor and delivery. Local anesthetic methods such as the epidural block are common (60% in one study; Capogna, Camorcia, & Stirparo, 2007), and they are effective in reducing labor pain without adverse effects on the infant. The epidural block is administered at the spine and reduces sensation in the lower extremities, allowing the mother to remain conscious but alleviating some or most of the pain. A downside of the epidural block is the possible loss of mobility, which makes it difficult for mothers to move around or to push during the final stages of delivery (Collis & Davis, 2010). Many fathers or other supportive partners are present during delivery, and their presence helps the mother cope with the pain. A happy side effect of mother's receipt of an epidural: reduction in father's anxiety and stress during the labor and delivery (Capogna et al., 2007)! Babies are not all born naturally, for a number of reasons, including health of the mother, health of the fetus, and fetal position. Instead, they are delivered by **Cesarean section**, which is a surgical procedure that involves cutting into the uterus to remove the baby. C-sections, as they are called, accounted for approximately 33% of all births in the United States in 2010, up from 21% in 1997 (Menacker & Hamilton, 2010). Reasons for C-sections vary but include maternal age (older women are more likely to have C-sections), better prenatal diagnosis of factors that could affect the success of a vaginal birth, and mothers preferring the predictability of a planned birth rather than waiting for labor to start naturally. C-sections, however, are not without risk of complications, and it takes the mother longer to recover. Moreover, reasons for the first C-section may persist in subsequent pregnancies, making it likely a woman will have multiple C-sections during her child-bearing years.

On average, the newborn measures 20 inches (51 cm) and weighs 6 to 9 lb (2,700 to 4,100 g). At conception, the zygote is the size of two microscopic germ cells; by the end of the first postnatal year the child has tripled in birth weight and added 10 inches (25.4 cm) in height. The rapid rate of growth and differentiation achieved in this short period will never recur at any other point in the life cycle.

An argument can be made that birth represents a transition in a process of continuing development. The organism before and after birth does not usually deviate from the normal, genetically maturing schedule; central nervous system function and motor behavior are not discretely altered by the birth process, and at a more molecular level physiological characteristics, such as the infant's unique blood chemistry, emerge slowly over the entire course of gestation. Like the fetus, the newborn is dependent on others. For example, newborn infants are unable even to maintain their own body temperature, lacking both the insulating material (subcutaneous fat) and the functional neural capacity. Newborns depend on caregivers to keep the temperature of their environments relatively constant so that their own limited capacities to adjust body temperature are not taxed. But birth is also a monumental event. With incredible suddenness, and for the first time, the child is responsible for circulation and respiration, and the newborn, unlike the fetus, is subject to previously unknown imbalance, deprivation, discomfort, and stimulus variety.

Birth is also a monumental event for parents, and hormones play a role in facilitating caregiving behavior in mothers and fathers. For mothers, hormones activate key brain regions to increase mothers' attraction to infant cues, influence her affective state, and render her attentive and sensitive to her baby's needs so that she learns from her experiences and behaves appropriately (Numan, 2006). The neuropeptide oxytocin (Chapter 3) has been associated with cognitive, emotional, and behavioral aspects of bonding-related factors, such as empathy, closeness, and trust (Grewen, Girdler, Amico, & Light, 2005). Moreover, oxytocin enhances memory for familiar faces. In one study, adults were given oxytocin or a placebo and then familiarized with a set of faces and a set of non-social images (landscapes, sculptures, and houses) in a task where they had to judge how approachable each image was (Rimmele, Hediger, Heinrichs, & Klaver, 2009). In a surprise recognition test 24 hours later, the group that received oxytocin showed better face recognition than those in the placebo group, whereas both groups showed similar levels of recognition for non-social stimuli. The effects of oxytocin are not limited only to mothers: Higher levels of oxytocin are associated with sensitive parental behaviors in fathers as well (Feldman, Weller, Zagoory-Sharon, & Levine, 2007).

Fathers also show changes in testosterone levels after the birth of a child. Testosterone stimulates the development and maintenance of traits and behaviors that contribute to mating, including musculature, libido, aggressiveness, and courtship (Archer, 2006; Bribiescas, 2001). Following the birth of a child, a sign of successful mating, fathers engaged in daily child care have lower testosterone levels than fathers not involved in care (Gettler, McDade, Agustin, & Kuzawa, 2011). Men with greater testosterone also reported feeling less sympathy or need to respond to infant cries than men with lower testosterone (Fleming, Corter, Stallings, & Steiner, 2002).

Preterm Birth

The typical or term infant is delivered about 40 weeks after the mother's last menstrual period. However, among the 4 million new births each year in the United States, approximately 12% are born too early (Figure 4.7; Martin, Osterman, & Sutton, 2010). An infant is considered preterm if born before 37 weeks gestational age, and of low birth weight if born under 2,500 g (about 5.5 lb). Gestational age and birth weight are highly correlated as fetuses gain most of their weight during the last two months of pregnancy (Figure 4.8).

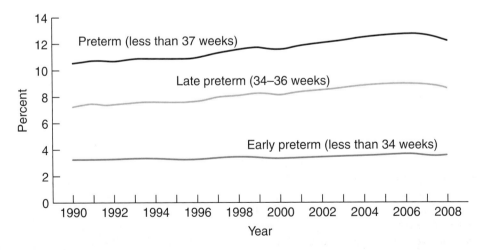

Fig. 4.7 Trends in premature births across 18 years. (From the Center for Disease Control, http://www.cdc.gov/nchs/data/databriefs/db39.htm; reproduced with permission.)

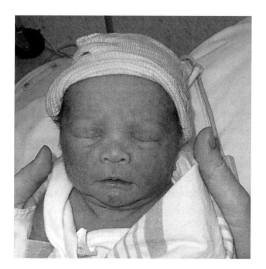 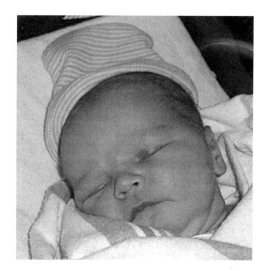

Fig. 4.8 Newborn pictures of two brothers, one born at 34 weeks (A) and one born at 40 weeks (B) gestation. Despite his preterm birth and low birth weight, baby A was otherwise healthy and showed no long-term effects of prematurity. (Courtesy of L. Cote.)

Babies may be born preterm for a number of reasons. First, abnormalities in the mother's reproductive system or general health might prevent her from carrying the pregnancy to term. Multiple births (e.g., twins) also place excessive demands on the mother, and thus many multiple births are preterm. Second, the mother's reproductive system might be immature or may not have had sufficient time to recover from a previous pregnancy; young teen mothers are at greater risk of delivering preterm babies (Cooper, Leland, & Alexander, 1995). Third, as discussed earlier, conditions that adversely affect general health—including drug use, poverty, malnutrition, inadequate medical care, and unhealthy lifestyles—are associated with preterm delivery.

Many more preterm babies survive today than they did formerly as a direct result of ongoing technological advances in neonatal care that promote the viability of very small infants, although over half of infants born at 22 to 25 weeks gestation still die before they reach 22 months of age (Tyson et al., 2008) and preterm birth often has adverse consequences for survivors, too. Serious health problems and developmental delays are more pronounced among very preterm (less than 32 weeks gestational age) and very low birth weight babies (less than 1,500 g or 3 lb 5 oz at birth). It is likely the problems these infants face are the result of factors leading to preterm birth (such as maternal diet, health, drug abuse) and of postbirth experiences in the hospital.

Babies who are marginally preterm often face little danger. They might be hospitalized briefly for observation or to gain weight and are then discharged. A variety of medical complications can arise when the degree of prematurity is more marked. Preterm low birth weight babies have average hospital stays of 45–50 days and between one-third and one-half experience one or more hospitalizations during the first three years of life (Behrman & Butler, 2006). **Respiratory distress syndrome** (RDS) is associated with infants born at less than 32 weeks of gestational age (Mosca, Colnaghi, & Fumagalli, 2011). These babies often lack **surfactin**—a soapy substance that coats the lungs and facilitates the exchange of oxygen from the air. To assist them in breathing, preterm babies are placed in incubators where the concentration of oxygen is much higher than in the normal environment. The actual concentration has to be titrated carefully to avoid producing **retinopathy of prematurity**, a disorder produced by excess oxygen that involves damage to the retinas, causing permanent blindness (Deuber & Terhaar, 2011). Very young preterm babies can also develop a condition known as **bronchopulmonary dysplasia**, or chronic lung disease, identified by the thickening and inflammation of the walls of the lung and a reduced airway, resulting in a significant decrease in the amount of oxygen the infant can inhale (Mosca et al., 2011). Very preterm, very low-birth weight babies are also at significant risk for brain complications, such as **intraventricular hemorrhage** (IVH). IVH is bleeding in the brain areas surrounding the ventricles and it can injure the hippocampus, a site for recognition memory (Aylward, 2005). For a number of reasons, therefore, the immature preterm infant may need close supervision in a hospital for the first weeks or months of life.

In addition to health risks, there are also psychological risks. Very preterm, very low birth weight infants are more likely than term infants to have lower IQs and developmental and learning disabilities (Kavsek & Bornstein, 2010; Rose, Feldman, Jankowski, & Van Rossem, 2011). In the United States, prematurity and low birth weight are linked to socioeconomic disadvantage (Alexander & Slay, 2002), and thus many preterm low birth weight infants are at medical *and* environmental risk. It is important that, in the absence of clear organic bases for abnormal development (e.g., blindness and brain damage), the degree to which preterm babies develop well or poorly reflects the caregiving environment the baby encounters after hospital discharge. Preterm babies who grow up in enriching, supportive homes do better, whereas those in more deprived environments develop more poorly (Goldberg & DiVitto, 2002).

The smallest of preterm infants who have survived are approximately 0.5 lb (280 g) and are born around 25 weeks gestation. In a case study of two such infants, Muraskas, Rau, Castillo, Gianopoulos, and Boyd (2012) reported that between 2 to 3 years of age these children (both females) had normal language development, the need for corrective lenses, and depressed mental functioning. One showed delays in motor development whereas the other did not. By 5 years of age, one was in a kindergarten classroom for typically developing children while receiving some additional educational support.

Infant Examinations

At about 1 minute and 5 minutes after birth, newborns in most U.S. hospitals are given their first tests, administered to determine the need for intervention and to document normal functioning. The **Apgar**, named after its originator Virginia Apgar (1953), rates babies as 0, 1, or 2 on each of five dimensions, easy to remember because of the anagram: Appearance, Pulse, Grimace, Activity, and Respiration. The criteria for each score are listed in Table 4.3. Total scores of 3 and below are critically low and require medical attention, whereas total scores between 7 and 10 give evidence of a generally healthy baby.

The Apgar is only one of several tests designed for very young babies. It is probably the best known because it is administered right in the delivery room, but it is obviously only a gross screening instrument. Other tests have been developed to evaluate the status of newborns more thoroughly and systematically. The **Dubowitz Test** (Dubowitz & Dubowitz, 1981) is used to estimate the infant's gestational age. It

Table 4.3 Criteria and scoring of the Apgar Test

	A	P	G	A	R
Score	Appearance (color)	Pulse (heart rate)	Grimace (reflex irritability)	Activity (muscle tone)	Respiration (respiratory effort)
0	Blue, pale	Absent	No response	Limp	Absent
1	Body pink, extremities blue	Slow (below 100)	Grimace	Some flexion of extremities	Slow, irregular
2	Completely pink	Rapid (over 100)	Cry	Active motion	Good, strong cry

scores babies on a variety of neurological items (including posture and reflexes) and external characteristics (including skin quality and gross morphology). The **Neonatal Behavioral Assessment Scale** (NBAS; Brazelton & Nugent, 1995) evaluates the baby's neurological intactness on 18 reflex items and the baby's interactional repertoire on 27 indices of information processing, motoric capacities, ability to control state, and response to stress.

Reflexes

Although human neonates appear helpless, they are capable of a small number of integrated and organized—if limited—behaviors. Many of these **reflexes** are biologically meaningful in that they suggest survival value or adaptive significance. Reflexes are simple, unlearned stimulus-response sequences common to all members of a species. A general characteristic of reflexes is their all-or-nothing quality; if elicited, they occur in full-blown form.

Reflexes are traditionally divided into three groups. The **approach reflexes**, concerned with intake, include breathing, rooting, sucking, and swallowing. **Rooting** (shown in Figure 4.9A) occurs in response to stimulation around the mouth; it involves tracking, searching, and head redirection toward the source of stimulation, and it typically concludes with sucking. Rooting is of major significance to newborns because it allows them to locate and ingest food. The second major class of reflexes is concerned with **avoidance**. This group includes coughing, sneezing, and blinking, as well as muscle withdrawal (Figure 4.9B). These reflexes keep foreign substances or stimulation away from the baby (sneezing to expel irritants, for example). The third class of reflexes, categorized under the nondescript term "other," does not have obvious functions. Phenomena such as the **palmar grasp** (babies close their fingers when something touches their palm), **Babinski reflex** (when the bottom of the foot is stroked, the toes fan out), and **Moro response** (described below) were important at an earlier point in human history but continue now without obvious meaning. For example, the Moro reflex (Figure 4.9C) is the tendency to swing the arms wide and bring them together again in the midline (as if around the body of a caregiver). This reflex is elicited by a loud sound or when the baby suddenly loses support. Similarly, the palmar grasp (Figure 4.9D1) tightens when whatever the baby is holding is suddenly raised; this grasp allows babies to briefly support their own weight. These reflexes are still present in many nonhuman primate newborns (Figure 4.9D2), helping such creatures maintain proximity to their mothers by clinging to body hair. Moreover, responding to a loss of support, as infants do with the Moro reflex shows that the vestibular system, which controls our balance, is working.

The regularity of reflex function in human infants provides pediatricians and neurologists with a means of assessing normal development; reflexes are involved in every major neonatal examination and screening test. Figure 4.10 shows the time course of the emergence and disappearance of a variety of reflexes before and after birth. Evidently, most reflexes develop before birth and are only present for 4 to 8 months postnatally. Peiper (1963), among others (including innumerable pediatrics texts), discusses at length the reflexes and their potential utility in psychological research. Not only do reflexes give evidence of sensory process function (e.g., pupillary constriction has been used as an index of visual sensitivity from Baldwin (1895), down to Banks & Munsinger (1974)), the reflexes also index normal maturation and their appearance is as important as their disappearance in showing the development of underlying neurology (Nagy, 2011).

One question is: Why do some reflexes disappear? One possibility is that most reflexes have their origins in the deepest and most primitive parts of the central nervous system. So long as these neurological structures dominate function, the reflexes endure. As higher cortical processes come into play, however, they inhibit subcortical structures and so prevent the expression of reflexes. An alternative possibility is that the reflex never really goes away; it is merely hidden. As the infant gains body weight, the limb gets

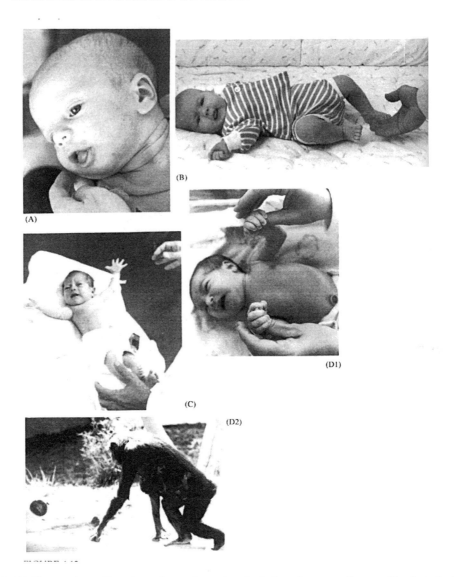

Fig. 4.9 (A) The rooting reflex: A gentle touch on the cheek from breast or finger will orient the baby, mouth open and lips pursed, ready to suck. (B) An avoidance reflex. (C) The Moro reflex: When they are dropped suddenly, babies throw their arms upward and then together. (Courtesy of T. B. Brazelton.) (D) The palmar grasp: When an object is placed in the baby's palm, the hand reacts by gripping (D1), sometimes so powerfully in the first hours that the baby can temporarily support his or her entire weight. Nonhuman babies, here a pygmy chimpanzee (D2), hold on to their mothers by grasping and clinging to ventral hair. (Courtesy of H. Papouśek.)

heavier but muscle strength does not increase at the same rate. Thelen, Fisher, and Ridley-Johnson (1984; see also Adolph & Berger, 2011) tested 4-week-old infants for the stepping reflex while in water (someone supported the child in an upright position). Infants, who on land did not show the stepping reflex, did so while in the water, presumably because the buoyancy of the leg in water made the leg lighter which allowed the weaker muscle to move it.

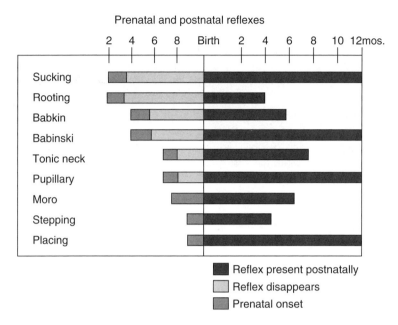

Fig. 4.10 The variable appearance and disappearance of prenatal and postnatal reflexes. Some reflexes, such as sucking and rooting, appear very early in prenatal development, whereas others, for example, stepping and placing, appear much later. Some reflexes, such as rooting and stepping, disappear early in postnatal development, whereas others, like sucking and placing, persist well past the first year of life.

Reflexes are a child's first movements. Consciously controlled movements emerge across the first year of life, and refinement of movement continues well into childhood. We continue our discussion of motor development in Chapter 5.

Development of the Sensory Systems

The sensory systems are the principal way we get information from the environment: sight, hearing, smell, taste, and touch. The senses begin to function before birth and determining approximately when they begin to function normally is important for several reasons. First, knowing about the development of the sensory systems advances our understanding of the general relation between structure and function. Just because we have a structure does not mean it functions. Second, it is theoretically and practically important to learn how early brain development may be influenced by sensory stimulation. Preterm babies are often born as many as 2½ to 3½ months before their expected due date and are therefore exposed to environmental stimulation from which they would normally be shielded. When sensory systems are not functional at this stage, preterm infants are "protected." When specific sensory systems do function, however, preterm babies may be adversely affected by stimulation in the environment, such as the neonatal intensive care unit.

Two generalizations about the development of the sensory systems are well established. First, maturation within systems tends to occur peripherally (at the sense organ) before it occurs centrally (in the brain). For example, the eye differentiates structurally and reaches functional maturity before the visual cortex does (Johnson, 2011a), although the retina is not fully developed at birth and development of the fovea (the part of retina where vision is most precise) continues up to 4 years of age (Kellman &

Arterberry, 2006). Second, across systems different senses achieve structural and functional maturity at different times. Figure 4.11 shows the development of four sensory systems—touch (cutaneous), position (vestibular), hearing (auditory), and vision (visual). This "staggered" developmental schedule is thought to have several biopsychological advantages, notably that developmental focus on one system at a time permits the organism to "concentrate on" reaching high levels of functional maturity in each (Turkewitz & Kenny, 1982).

Babies are reasonably well prepared to perceive the world almost as soon as extrauterine life begins: Indeed, newborns in the first hours appear to be in a state of heightened sensory awareness, perhaps because of the rigors of the birth experience. By the second trimester of gestation, the eye and visual system, the ear and auditory system, the nose and olfactory system, the tongue and gustatory system, and the skin and somatosensory system are essentially mature structurally, although their levels of functional competence lag behind (Menacker & Batshaw, 1997; Mennella & Beauchamp, 1997; Steinberg & Knightly, 1997).

How early can the embryo—fetus—neonate sense stimulation? How good are those sensations? These two developmental questions translate into "psychophysical" ones having to do with, first, the strength of a physical stimulus that is necessary to elicit a sensation of some sort (**absolute threshold**) and, second, the amount a physical stimulus must change to yield a new sensation (**discrimination threshold**). These two "threshold" questions—absolute vs. discrimination thresholds—define the basics of the study of sensation. In general, a systematic sensory psychophysics of infancy is still lacking, but we possess some basic information about elementary sensory sensitivities.

Touch, Taste, and Smell

The **somesthetic** system regulates temperature, tactile, and positional information. Nervous tissue grows out centrally to reach the skin by the middle of the first trimester, and maturation of relevant parts in the

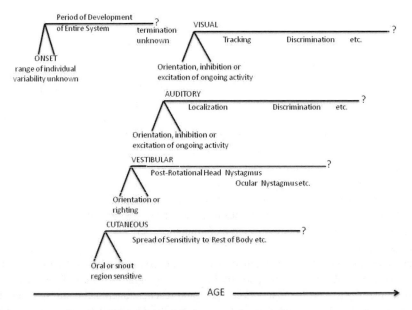

Fig. 4.11 The order in which the sensory systems begin to function is similar in many species: cutaneous, vestibular, auditory, visual. (From Gottlieb, 1971; reproduced with permission.)

spinal cord has begun by the second trimester of gestation. Touch reflexes and vestibular circuitry (responsible for balance) develop early, and neuromotor organization in the brain stem and spinal cord produce fetal face and hand movements that suggest preadaptation for manual and oral grasp. In an early study, Spelt (1948) investigated tactile sensitivity *in utero* with fetuses ranging from 7 to 9 months of gestational age. He used a loud clapper to elicit fetal movement, pairing clapping with vibrotactile stimulation. Spelt reported that, after as few as 15 paired stimulations, fetuses moved regularly when the tactile stimulus was presented alone. Although the fetus is known to move about spontaneously in the second trimester and later orient itself (presumably using gravity), very little is understood about prenatal development of the complex somatosensory system. Infants appear to be highly responsive to tactile stimulation, and attachment theorists have long emphasized the salience of touch "contact comfort" for the establishment and maintenance of emotional intimacy and infant–parent attachment (Bowlby, 1969; Harlow, 1958). Also, systematically administered tactile stimulation appears to foster weight gain and growth in high-risk preterms and to minimize distress responses to painful procedures (Ferber, & Makhoul, 2008; Goldberg & DiVitto, 2002).

Newborn babies appear to discriminate among sensory qualities that signify different tastes and smells, and they even prefer certain tastes and smells to others. Taste buds form and are connected to taste nerves by about the twelfth week of gestation (Mennella & Beauchamp, 1996), and the ability to taste develops before birth. Replicating long-forgotten findings reported in the last century by Preyer (1881, 1888), Steiner and his colleagues (Steiner, 1977; Steiner, Glaser, Hawilo, & Berridge, 2001; see also Oster, 2005) found that neonates display characteristic facial expressions when sweet, sour, and bitter substances are placed on their tongues (Figure 3.7A). A sweet stimulus evoked an expression of satisfaction, often accompanied by a slight smile and by sucking movements. A sour stimulus evoked lip pursing, often accompanied or followed by wrinkling the nose and blinking the eyes. A bitter fluid evoked an expression of dislike and disgust or rejection, often followed by spitting or even by the preparatory movements of vomiting. These taste discriminations are organized at a primitive level of the brain, because Steiner also observed them in babies who had no cortex and in nonhuman primates. The magnitude of the newborn's reaction to sweet and bitter stimuli also varies with the intensity of the stimulus. Flavors of the foods that the mother eats are present in the amniotic fluid surrounding the fetus, and fetuses develop flavor preferences that last into childhood and adulthood (Trout & Effinger, 2012). A similar mechanism is likely at work regarding alcohol preferences following prenatal exposure to alcohol (Youngentob & Glendinning, 2009).

The sense of smell is less important to humans than to many other species, and this sensory modality has elicited less attention from infancy researchers than have vision, audition, and even taste. In early studies that paralleled his work on taste, Steiner (1977, 1979) observed neonates' facial expressions and reactions to odors placed on cotton swabs held beneath the baby's nose. Steiner found that newborns responded in qualitatively different ways to different food odors (Figure 3.7B). Butter and banana odors elicited positive expressions; vanilla, either positive or indifferent expressions; a fishy odor, some rejection; and the odor of rotten eggs, unanimous rejection. Indeed, soon after birth, infants discriminate among a wide variety of odors and can use their sense of smell in association-learning tasks (Goubet et al., 2002; Goubet, Strasbaugh, & Chesney, 2007). Moreover, the presence of familiar odors can alleviate distress in newborns. Goubet, Strasbaugh, and Chesney (2007) exposed newborns to a vanilla scent, either on a scarf worn by their mothers or placed in their crib. Following this exposure, infants experienced a heel stick (a procedure for drawing blood) with the familiar odor, a new odor, or no odor present. Infants showed less distress after the heel stick when the familiar odor was present compared to the infants in the new odor and no odor groups.

One odor appears to be particularly appealing to young infants and learned very quickly: that of their mother. Porter (Cernoch & Porter, 1985; Porter, Bologh, & Makin, 1988) systematically compared olfactory recognition of mother, father, and stranger by breastfed and bottle-fed infants only 12 to 18 days after birth. Babies were exposed to pairs of gauze pads worn by an adult in the underarm area on the previous night, and babies' duration of orienting was recorded. Only breastfeeding infants oriented preferentially and only to their own mother's scent, thereby giving evidence that they discriminate their mother from others. Infants did not recognize their fathers preferentially, and bottle-fed infants did not recognize their mothers, suggesting that breastfeeding infants are exposed to and learn unique olfactory signatures. Mothers also recognize the scent of their babies after only 1 or 2 days (Mennella & Beauchamp, 1996). Olfactory exchange in mother–infant dyads thus appears to be mutual. The chemical composition of breast fluids is similar to the chemical composition of amniotic fluid, and infants may be pre-attuned to respond selectively to their mothers' unique olfactory cues (Porter & Winberg, 1999). But learning may also be a part of the process. In naturally occurring circumstances (namely, breastfeeding) the odor is, of course, that of their mother, but young babies can learn to prefer other odors during feeding (Allam, Marlier, & Schaal, 2006). The ability to recognize mothers very early in life by olfactory information alone might play an important role in the early mother–infant relationship (Chapter 11).

Like touch, taste and smell may reach structural maturity and functional competence early in infant development. For these systems, however, birth is a significant event. Taste stimuli are homogeneous prenatally (the fetus is immersed in amniotic fluid) and heterogeneous postnatally. Odor stimuli become gaseous and are carried by air rather than liquid and carried by amniotic fluid. Touch, taste, and smell have received less attention than vision and audition, but these sensory systems play key roles in the first year of life, including all-important decisions about what is nourishing and what is not. The olfactory system is highly developed at birth, and preferences for pleasant (e.g., bananas or chocolate) over unpleasant odors (e.g., rotten eggs) appear to mirror adult preferences (Steiner, 1979). The gustatory and olfactory sensory systems thus have a primitive history, advanced developmental status, and extraordinary sensitivity.

Audition

The ear develops very early in gestation, and by the end of the first month after conception the **cochlea** (part of the inner ear responsible for perceiving sound) is anatomically distinct. At birth, the peripheral sensory system is essentially mature (Saffran et al., 2006), as is the auditory nerve. During the last trimester of pregnancy, the fetus can hear and habituate to sounds outside of the uterus, including mother's heart beat, her voice, and loud sounds such as a car horn honking. Mature function is still inhibited, however, until amniotic fluid has drained from the middle ear.

Newborn infants can discriminate sounds of different intensities and frequencies, and after about 5 months of age infants can reliably identify the location of a sound (Neil, Chee-Ruiter, Scheier, Lewkowicz, & Shimojo, 2006). Newborns also appear to respond selectively to sound frequencies that occur within the range of the human voice (Saffran et al., 2006). We discuss audition in more detail in Chapter 6.

Vision

The early ontogenesis of vision has been studied most thoroughly. The eye and the retina develop rapidly in the first and second trimesters of gestation, although the development of fine retinal structures such as the fovea may not be complete until four years of age (Kellman & Arterberry, 2006). Similarly, the neural pathways supporting vision continue to develop well into postnatal life (Johnson, 2011a). At birth, vision is poorer than the other sensory systems. Infants' ability to see fine detail (**acuity**) is limited, and thus they cannot see most objects or people beyond 18 inches (45 cm) away (Kellman & Arterberry, 2006). Even at distances of less than 18 inches, newborns only see regions of high contrast. As such, newborns are often described as legally blind. They can, however, still perceive, and in Chapter 6 we describe numerous visual accomplishments of very young babies.

When considering the different developmental trajectories of vision and the other senses, it is important to keep in mind that somesthesis, audition, olfaction, and gustation can be stimulated and exercised before birth, whereas naturalistic, complex, patterned, and colorful visual stimulation can only be experienced after birth. To the extent that experience influences development, vision is at an ecological disadvantage.

All of the senses develop during the prenatal period. One of the principal ways in which fetuses are prepared for their future extrauterine life is by substantial prenatal investment in the development of the central and peripheral sensory systems. In Chapter 6, we show how infants make use of sensory information for perceiving their world.

SUMMARY

Physical and motor growth in pre- and postnatal infancy are impressive because they are such obvious developments and because change in each is extremely rapid at this point in the life cycle. Developments in these spheres also have important implications for other spheres of psychological development. In this chapter, we discussed genetic contributions to early growth and how we know about them. Researchers of prenatal development distinguish stages of growth and recognize distinct sensitive periods during which different prenatal experiences are especially influential. We discussed birth and preterm birth. Examinations are used to assess the status of the newborn and the degree to which newborns are prepared for extrauterine life. All infant evaluations emphasize important reflexes and their neurological indications. The sensory capacities to touch, taste, smell, hear, and see all progress in the fetal period so that the infant is born in a state of high sensory preparedness.

KEY TERMS

Absolute threshold	Ectoderm
Acuity	Embryo
Amniocentesis	Endoderm
Anoxia	Endometrium
Apgar	Fetal alcohol spectrum disorder
Approach reflexes	Fetal alcohol syndrome
Avoidance	Fetus
Babinski reflex	Gametes
Blastocyst	Genotype
Breech	Gonadal streak
Bronchopulmonary dysplasia	In vitro fertilization
Cesarean section	Innate
Chorionic villus sampling	Intraventricular hemorrhage
Chromosomes	Klinefelter syndrome
Cochlea	Labor
Comorbid	Maternal serum alphafetoprotein
Congenital	Meiosis
Discrimination threshold	Mesoderm
Dose-effect relation	Moro response
Down syndrome	Mullerian duct system
Dubowitz Test	Mullerian Inhibiting Substance

Neonatal Behavioral Assessment Scale
Ovum
Palmar grasp
Phenotype
Placenta
Plasticity
Prenatal experiences
Primitive streak
Quickening
Reflexes
Respiratory distress syndrome
Retinopathy of prematurity
Rooting
Sensitive period

Sexual differentiation
Somesthetic
Sudden Infant Death Syndrome
Surfactin
Teratogens
The age of viability
Trisomy-21
Turner syndrome
Ultrasound imaging
Umbilical cord
Uterus
Wolffian duct system
Zygote

Chapter 5

Physical and Motor Development in Infancy

- *What basic principles describe physical and motor development in infancy?*
- *What are states of arousal, and how does their organization change in infancy?*
- *Why does heart rate vary, and how does its study inform our understanding of infancy?*
- *How and why do neurons, dendrites, axons, synapses, and neural networks develop pre- and postnatally?*
- *What can we learn about infants by monitoring electrical activity in their brains?*
- *Define heart rate, vagal tone, EEG, and ERP and illustrate what each tells us about infant development.*
- *Are neural cells specialized in function?*
- *How is the brain susceptible to experience?*
- *What is the progression of motor development?*

Anatomical, physiological, and psychological growth are all dramatic in infancy, but because of its infinite complexities and astonishing ability to regulate and integrate information, the development of the nervous system is especially noteworthy. The adult human brain contains approximately 100 billion **neurons**. Because relatively few new neurons are generated after birth, an average of 250,000 new cells must be generated every minute prenatally. In the space of approximately 9 months, a single fertilized egg evolves into a complex, self-regulating, differentiated nervous system, and in an additional 9 to 12 months after birth develops into a conscious child capable of intelligent feelings, thoughts, and actions. In this chapter, we consider several aspects of physical development including development of the autonomic and central nervous systems and motor development. In addition, we consider the roles of biology and experience in shaping infant growth.

Perhaps because physical growth is so easy to observe and quantify, it was a very early subject of study among people interested in human development. Figure 5.1 shows Count Phillippe de Montbeillard's observations of his own son's physical development; these data were gathered in the mid-18th century, but they are still relatively accurate. For example, de Montbeillard's insightful decision to plot height gain (and not simply height) over age, shows just how great growth is during infancy relative to all other times (including puberty).

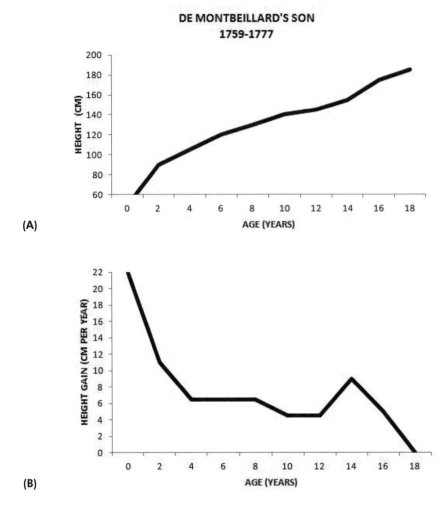

Fig. 5.1 The growth of the son of Count Philippe de Montbeillard from birth to the age of 18 years. (A) shows the height he reached at each age and (B) shows annual increments in height. (From Tanner, 1962; reproduced with permission.)

Principles of physical growth are sometimes considered topics of lesser psychological importance because growth data are merely "descriptive." However, the story of physical growth is significant because growth data provide vital normative guidelines for human development, and the physical characteristics of the child have implications for the child's development in many other psychological domains.

Four general principles of development are exemplified in the study of physical growth. The first general principle is **directionality**. Whether the subject of study is anatomical growth, complexity of function, or voluntary control, development seems to follow several characteristic directions. The first is that development proceeds **cephalocaudally**, that is from "head to tail." The visual system reaches anatomical maturity earlier than do the legs, and infants have voluntary visual control much earlier in life than they begin to walk. Body proportions change in this way too (Figure 4.4). Second, development proceeds **proximodistally**, that is from the center of the body outward. Infants acquire control over their neck and torso before their fingers. Third, development typically proceeds in a **mass-to-specific** fashion, that is from large muscle groups to fine ones. Infants move their arms before they are able to flutter their fingers. Fourth, development frequently involves a **hierarchical integration**, that is simple skills develop separately and then become organized into more complex ones. For example, when reaching for an object, younger infants will move their arm toward the object and grasp it once the object touches the palm, whereas older infants will anticipate the grasp by modifying the shape of their hand during the arm movement.

A second general principle of psychological development that derives from studies of physical growth is the **independence of systems**. Figure 5.2 plots the rates of growth for three major systems, illustrating the point that components of the human being are differentially developed at, or soon after, birth and grow along very different courses through the first year or two of life. By 2 years, for example, the nervous system has achieved more than one-half of its adult status, whereas physical characteristics of the body have developed to less than one-third of their eventual goal, and, of course, secondary sexual characteristics have hardly developed at all.

A third general principle of physical growth and development is **canalization**, or robustness which refers toward the persistence of a developmental outcome despite less than optimal circumstances. The evolutionary biologist Waddington (1962) observed that life often involves the narrowing or restricting of alternatives so that one is selected in preference to others. In this view, corrective processes can adjust or allow for catching up in the face of non-optimal conditions. We can observe this phenomenon in the domain of physical development, although, again, it applies in other realms too. By age 8, preterm infants have typically caught up to the general population in terms of weight and head circumference. Moreover, preterm infants who show rapid weight gain within the first year have higher IQ scores at age 8 (Belfort et al., 2010). In this realm there is good predictability and, psychologically speaking, extraordinary stability despite the fact that children grow up in different circumstances.

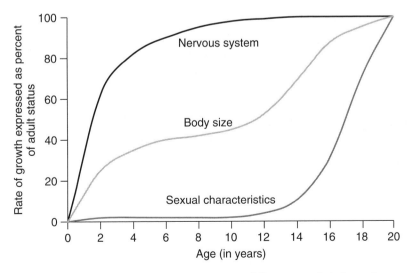

Fig. 5.2 Different bodily systems grow toward mature status at different rates. In infancy, the nervous system is highly developed, body size is less developed, and secondary sexual characteristics are least developed of all.

A fourth general principle concerns the interplay between norms and individual differences. Many physical, biological, and psychological characteristics are typically distributed in a **statistically normal** fashion, that is, the distribution in the population forms a bell-shaped curve. Consider physical height. Very few adults are either 4 or 7 feet tall; many more are 5 and 6 feet tall, and most are in between. The average might represent the distribution of some structure or function, but the range and form of the distribution are critically informative about the structure or function as well. For example, the age at which infants first walk or talk has enormous psychological importance, but the true range is extraordinary, especially when considered as a proportion of the child's age. Some children first walk at 10 months, others at 18 months; some children say their first word at 9 months, others at 29 months. Timing may be meaningful only for the extreme cases. All adults can generally walk and talk sufficiently, suggesting that the exact onset of walking or talking might be less meaningful in the long run than anxious parents and relatives often think. **Norms** are the averages for a population and their distribution, but they are descriptions rather than explanations; they represent likely outcomes rather than actual or even ideal outcomes.

Individual differences arise out of the continuing interaction of nature and nurture (Chapter 1), the child's unique combination of biology and experience. In addition, individual differences can follow many different courses in development. Consider three examples: Different individuals might follow different developmental rates but eventually reach the same mature level of structure or function; different individuals may follow the same rate of development but stop growing at different final resting levels of structure or function; and different individuals might follow different rates and reach different final developmental levels. These diverse developmental trajectories can have many causes.

At birth as well as through the course of the first years, infants in resource-rich countries tend to be healthier, heavier, and longer than infants in resource-poor countries. These differences presumably reflect the effects of prenatal and postnatal nutrition and care, maternal health and education, and genetic variation. By the end of the first year of postnatal life, the average American infant weighs about 20 pounds (9 kg) and is about 30 inches long (76 cm). However, even within affluent countries such as the United States, children born into low socioeconomic statuses have lower birth weight and they are at a higher risk for obesity (Moss & Yeaton, 2011; Paul, Lehman, Suliman, & Hillemeier, 2008). Clearly, adequate nutrition is critical for healthy physical development.

THE NERVOUS SYSTEM

In large measure, the diverse and remarkable accomplishments of infancy reflect impressive developments in the nervous system. However, it is difficult to establish causal relations between brain and behavior for several reasons. First, brain–behavior relations are bidirectional. Genetically predetermined brain development may permit new behaviors that generate new interactions with the environment which then feed back to influence brain development. Consequently, neurological growth always reflects the dynamic interplay of genetic influences and selected (including self-generated) experiences. Second, much of our knowledge in this field derives from studies of nonhuman organisms, and we need to be cautious about applying them to human beings. All systems do not work the same way in different species. Third, behavior typically has multiple causes. Although brain–behavior interactions are complex, it would be surprising if development was not reflected by parallel changes in the "software" (functions) and "hardware" (structure) of the brain.

The nervous system, comprising all the neural tissues in the human body, can be considered from both a structural and a functional perspective. From the structural point of view, the nervous system may be divided into central and peripheral components. The major **central** components are the brain and spinal cord, and the **peripheral** components include the nerve fibers that connect **receptors** (such as the eye) and **effectors** (for example, the muscles) to the brain. From the functional point of view, the nervous system may be divided into somatic and autonomic components: The **somatic** division is comprised of voluntary conscious functions, and the **autonomic** division is concerned with automatic and non-voluntary processes.

In this section, we review major developments in the autonomic and central nervous systems from structural and functional points of view. When considering **autonomic nervous system (ANS)** development in the first section of the chapter, we focus particularly on states of arousal and heart rate as key indicators of function. When discussing **central nervous system (CNS)** development in the second section, we focus on different levels of neural and brain development and on aspects of motor development. As in Chapter 4, our goal is not to be comprehensive but to introduce select and meaningful biological events that underpin or accompany important psychological events.

AUTONOMIC NERVOUS SYSTEM DEVELOPMENT

The fetus and the newborn are biological organisms. Much of their functioning, as we have already learned, is survival oriented but not yet under conscious or voluntary control. Moreover, we have referred to continuities as well as discontinuities between the pre- and postnatal periods of infant development. In considering ANS function in the infant, we first consider the cycles and states that overtly characterize infants, and we next discuss the development of heart rate and its applications for understanding infancy. The first topic underscores the growth of self-regulation; the second highlights an important "window to the infant mind."

Cycles and States

On first observation, newborn activity appears to be spontaneous, disorganized, and sporadic. Babies seem to be constantly moving their eyes, hands, and feet without apparent purpose. Over longer periods they appear to shift randomly and unpredictably from sleep to alertness (Rivkees & Hao, 2000). Newborns, however, are not quite so unpredictable. Close and consistent inspection reveals that fetuses and infants are more or less regular in many ways and that their systems cycle in detectable patterns or rhythms. Many rhythms seem to be natural or **endogenous**, perhaps because of molecular "pacemaker cells" in the brain. In short, apparent irregularity is only just that, apparent. The question we explore here is "How" do these regulatory systems mature and thus appear more regular?

Naturally occurring or spontaneous behaviors in infants are organized at fast, medium, and slow rhythms (Rivkees, 2003). Some activities occur regularly at high frequencies and cycle (appear and disappear, or increase and decrease) perhaps once or more every second. Heartbeats, breathing, and sucking exemplify fast biological rhythms that maintain life, and kicking and rocking illustrate fast cycling behaviors. Other general movements of the body cycle at intermediate rates, such as involuntary body movements, on the order of once every minute or two; they emerge before birth and continue to cycle at the same rate postnatally (Groome et al., 1999). As an example, consider sleep states. During the night we pass through five different states (labeled 1–4 and REM, the latter a period of dreaming that includes **rapid eye movements**—hence the label REM). The full cycle takes about 90 to 110 minutes and then it repeats throughout the night. Sleep is an example of a low frequency cycle. Other biological functions have an even lower frequency, cycling in periods of up to 24 hours, and are governed by the **circadian clock** (Rivkees, 2003). The circadian clock is an internally driven biochemical, physiological, and behavioral process that adjusts to environmental cues, such as day–night light cycles.

The coordination and integration of different cycles has long been recognized as a major accomplishment of neurological organization. Degree of stability over time differs among infants, and these differences are important: The amount of time infants spend in different states has implications for development in other domains, such as language and social interaction (Chapters 9 and 11), because rhythmic pauses in babies' sucking and stages of the sleep–wake cycle cue adults to initiate play and caregiving. Thus, many sophisticated infant activities could have their roots in cyclic behaviors of the prenatal and early postnatal periods. The circadian timing system, for example, develops prenatally, and the neurological site of a circadian clock is identifiable by mid-gestation in primates (Rivkees, 2003).

State of arousal is a significant infant characteristic, too, because newborns shift frequently among states of sleep, drowsiness, alertness, distress, and activity. Thoman (1990) quantified 10 behavioral states of arousal in infants (Table 5.1) that reflect reliable or stable dimensions of individuality. The percentages of time in a day babies spend in the different states are presented in the last column of Table 5.1. The distribution of time among states differs depending on whether infants are alone or with their mothers. Babies in Western industrialized countries are usually with their mothers when awake and alone when asleep (although sleeping trends are changing, as we explain later in this chapter). In many countries around the world infants sleep bundled on their mothers' backs and share a bed at night (Rogoff, 2003).

Table 5.1 Primary behavioral states in young infants. Adapted from the descriptions and data provided by Thoman and Whitney (1990).

State	Characteristics	Percent of time in this state when alone
Awake		
Alert	Eyes open, bright, and attentively scanning.	6.7
Non-alert waking	Eyes open but dull and unfocused Motor activity often high; isolated fussing is possible.	2.8
Fuss	Continuous or intermittent low-intensity fussing.	1.8
Cry	Intense vocalizations, singly or in succession.	1.7
Transition states between sleep and waking		
Drowse	Eyes either open or opening and closing slowly; usually little motor activity.	4.4
Daze	Eyes glassy and immobile; usually little motor activity. This state usually occurs between episodes of Drowse and Alert.	1.0
Sleep–wake transition	Usually generalized motor activity; eyes may be closed or open and close rapidly. Isolated fusses may occur. This state usually occurs when the baby is awakening.	1.3
Sleep states		
Active sleep	Eyes closed, uneven respiration, and low muscle tone despite sporadic movement. Rapid eye movements (REMs) occur intermittently, as do smiles, frowns, grimaces, sighs, grunts, cries, mouthing, and sucking.	50.3
Quiet sleep	Eyes closed, respiration slow, regular, and deep. Tonic motor tone but limited motor activity, especially in preterm infants.	28.1
Transition sleep state		
Active–quiet transition sleep	Typically occurs between periods of active and quiet sleep; eyes closed and little motor activity. Respiration pattern is intermediate between that of quiet and active sleep.	1.9

Figure 5.3 shows how sleep–wake patterns change over the course of the life cycle. It can take months for the infant to establish a predictable schedule of behavioral states. It appears that some states, such as fussing and crying, show greater individual stability than do other states, such as waking (St. James-Roberts, 2007). In addition, the degree to which infant states are regulated has important implications for infant care and parental well-being.

Infant state is significant for many key reasons. First, state determines how infants present themselves, and whether and how infants respond to tactile, visual, and auditory stimuli often depends on their state. In quiet alertness, for example, an infant may attend to a voice that has no effect on the same baby when he or she is crying. Second, infant states influence adult behavior. Adults rock and soothe distressed babies instead of trying to show them toys. Infants who are temperamentally fretful elicit different patterns of care than do infants who cry only infrequently (Chapters 10 and 11). In this way, infants affect their own development. Third, state regularity serves as a marker of nervous system integrity. Poor state regulation is common among infants born preterm, infants who have suffered significant perinatal complications (such as intraventricular hemorrhage or anoxia, see Chapter 4) and infants with **congenital** brain malformations. Also, poor state regulation in early infancy can indicate higher risk for **SIDS** (sudden infant death syndrome; Cornwell & Feigenbaum, 2006). Finally, abnormal sleep state patterns in neonates can also cue medical problems, such as epilepsy (Nunes & Costa da Costa, 2010).

Regularity of states in very young babies thus provides a window on the maturity and integrity of the nervous system. However, it does not solely reflect infant biology. The way a baby is cared for can influence state as well. For example, in a study of preterm infants in neonatal intensive care nurseries, Scher et al. (2009) found that newborns who received extensive skin-to-skin contact showed more quiet sleep than those who did not receive such contact. This type of care is sometimes called "Kangaroo Care" because after infant kangaroos are born, they spend an additional 9 months in close contact with their mothers in her pouch, and it has been found to be effective in promoting development in preterm infants as well as reducing pain (Ferber & Makhoul, 2008; Scher et al., 2009). The organization of sleep states and sleep disturbances is also responsive to broad cultural differences in caregiving practices. For example, differences exist across cultures in terms of average bedtimes and amount of nighttime sleep (Wada et al., 2009).

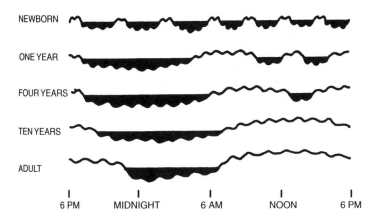

Fig. 5.3 The black areas represent sleep in this schematic representation of the basic sleep–wake cycle. (After Kleitman, 1963.)

States of quiet alertness in infants are initially both rare and brief, but this changes noticeably over the first months of life. However infrequent and short they may be at first, periods of quiet alertness are extremely important because they allow infants to extract information from and adjust to their new and complex social and physical environment. During these moments, infants can look around and become familiar with the features of parents' faces, or study a mobile hanging over the crib, gradually learning how to produce interesting movements. Much of what infants learn about objects, people, and their own abilities appears to be acquired during periods of quiet alertness and attentiveness.

In adults, sleep and wakefulness are accompanied by recordable psychophysiological indices, such as REMs that occur during dreaming and specific patterns of brain or electroencephalographic (EEG) activity. The same is true of infants, and most infant states can be reliably identified on the basis of EEG criteria by approximately 4 months of age (Rozhkov & Soroko, 2000). As we have suggested, the organization of the sleep–wake cycle reflects neurological maturation, the developing ability of babies to regulate their own states, and experience.

The organization of sleep cycles is affected by many experiential factors, such as stress around birth, parental caregiving, exposure to day–night lighting conditions, and cultural beliefs. Among the Kipsigis in East Africa, infants sleep with their mothers and are permitted to nurse on demand. During the day they are strapped to their mothers' backs, accompanying them on their daily rounds of farming, household chores, and social activities (Super & Harkness, 1997). Kipsigis infants often nap while their mothers go about their work, and so they do not begin to sleep through the night until many months later than infants in the United States.

In Japan, it is traditionally believed that infants and mothers need to establish *amae*—an indigenous Japanese concept of relatedness, one special meaning of which denotes empathic closeness and interdependence of the infant with the mother (Behrens, 2004, 2010). *Amae* is an everyday Japanese word and prominent construct used to characterize family relationships. Doi (1973, p. 75) referred to *amae* as "an attempt psychologically to deny the fact of separation from the mother." Modern authorities have observed that Japanese mothers tend to maintain close physical proximity to their infants, who rarely experience separations from them (e.g., Behrens, 2004; Behrens, Hesse, & Main, 2007). Japanese infants are constantly within their mothers' reach, and co-sleeping and co-bathing from birth are conventional, normative, and virtually universal practices (e.g., Takahashi, 1986).

Research conducted with families in the United States shows that infant–parent co-sleeping alters the infant's sleep experience due to arousal levels, the frequency and duration of nursing, infant sleeping position, and the number of maternal inspections. For example, while sleeping in the same bed (a type of **co-sleeping** called bed-sharing), mothers nurse their infants three times more frequently than they do when their infants sleep in an adjacent room, and mothers who bed-share stop breastfeeding their babies later than mothers who do not (Buswell & Spatz, 2007). The reasons parents may or may not co-sleep are varied and complex, and there is still no agreement over what is best for the baby (McKenna & Volpe, 2007). There are advantages regarding ease of breastfeeding, but there is also concern that infant–parent co-sleeping leads to increased infant death (Cohen, Chen-Yee, Evans, Hinchliffe, & Zapata-Vazquez, 2010). In 2011, a couple in Utah was charged with child-abuse homicide for the death of their 3-month-old, who died while sleeping in her parents' bed. The risk of death aside, bed-sharing may not be the best for infants. Hunsley and Thoman (2002) claim that bed-sharing leads to less quiet sleep in babies, as measured by the amount of quiet sleep engaged when co-sleeping babies slept alone. Infants may experience stress when co-sleeping due to frequent waking or less amount of time in quiet sleep. Sleep is important, not only in the short term but long term, as early disturbed sleep is related to later reports of depression and anxiety (Jansen et al., 2011). In an attempt to balance infant proximity to parent but reduce health risks, **room-sharing** (infant sleeping in her/his own bed in the parent's bedroom) has been suggested as an alternative to bed-sharing (Hunsley & Thoman, 2002; McKenna & McDade, 2005).

In summary, an important task for the young infant is to establish regulation of state. Predictable sleep–wake cycles are important for infant learning and development. In addition, they are important for parents, as they, too, need regularity and predictability in order to parent adequately. Where the baby sleeps varies by culture and there is by no means a universal opinion on what is best. Early growth of self-regulation, as documented by changes in the sleep–wake cycle, provides an indirect way for researchers to map the maturation of the brain, a topic we turn to after considering regulation of heart rate.

Heart Rate

As mentioned in Chapter 4, the human heart begins to beat early in the period of the embryo. At first, heart rate is rather constant, suggesting that strong endogenous or autonomous "pacemakers" are at work. By about 24 weeks, however, heart rate switches from autonomic to neural control. After birth, heart rate is extremely sensitive to psychological state and has been used to help interpret what the infant might be thinking, feeling, or doing (Diaz & Bell, 2011; Peltola, Leppanen, & Hietanen, 2011; see Chapter 3). It is also an important index of individual differences among infants.

Changes in heart rate index both sustained visual attention and reactivity to psychologically meaningful stimulation (Chapters 3 and 6; Porges, 2011; Richards, 2010). The vagus is the 10th cranial nerve and a major component of the parasympathetic nervous system. The vagus serves as an important bidirectional conduit carrying specialized motor and sensory pathways involved in the regulation of visceral state and affect. Vagal motor fibers originate in the brain and regulate muscles of the face, head, and heart and thereby regulate cardiovascular activity, digestion, metabolism, and thermoregulation. Polyvagal theory (Porges, 2011) asserts that the vagal system provides the physiological foundation for regulating arousal, state, and reactivity to stimulation that underlies individual differences in self-regulation, information processing, temperament, and emotion.

Vagal signals to the heart have a characteristic respiratory rhythm ascribable to interneuronal communication between brainstem centers regulating vagal output and respiration (Porges, 2011). Rhythmic change in heart rate variability (**Respiratory Sinus Arrhythmia** (RSA)) can be assessed noninvasively from the **electrocardiogram** (ECG). Estimates of RSA have been used as measures of cardiac vagal tone during resting (baseline) states (i.e., in the relative absence of environmental challenge) and during environmental challenge (i.e., presentation of stimuli). Resting RSA is theorized to measure the structural organization of the vagal system and the capacity to maintain homeostasis in the absence of environmental demand. Vagal regulation during environmental challenge—the capacity to engage and disengage vagal outflow—is an appropriate response to stimulation or stress. Baseline-to-task change in vagal tone therefore serves as an index of vagal regulatory function.

To evaluate and compare the development of the vagal system and its regulatory capacity in a prospective longitudinal study, Bornstein and Suess (2000a) measured vagal tone, at 2 months and at 5 years, in both children and their mothers. Levels of child resting vagal tone (heart rate with no stimulation) changed between 2 months and 5 years with children reaching adult levels of resting vagal tone by 5 years. Moreover, by 5 years, children and their mothers were similar in resting vagal tone. Children and their mothers were also similar in baseline-to-task change in vagal tone at 2 months and at 5 years. Similarly, Alkon and her colleagues (2011) showed development of resting vagal tone and of baseline-to-task change from 6 months to 5 years of age in Latino children, but at the same time there was considerable individual consistency in vagal tone across this time frame. Together, these findings suggest a biological component to regulatory capacity.

In a second study, Bornstein and Suess (2000b) investigated the role of cardiac vagal tone in infant information processing (habituation). Physiological self-regulation was measured by the changes in vagal tone from baseline to habituation. Decreases in vagal tone indicated the mobilization of attention and were related to habituation efficiency at both 2 and 5 months. These findings suggest that physiological self-regulation via the vagal system plays a role in information processing, a conclusion recently supported by Diaz and Bell (2011) in a study that monitored infants' attention, heart rate, and EEG at the same time.

Vagal tone is also an index of infant distress in social situations. Hill-Soderlund et al. (2008) measured heart rate during the **Strange Situation** (as explained in Chapter 11, this procedure evaluates attachment relationships). Children who did not show outward signs of distress when a parent left the room nevertheless showed changes in heart rate measures that suggested they were experiencing internal distress. The fact that there were few behavioral (or external) signs of distress suggests that these children relied on self-regulation to a greater degree than other children of the same age.

In summary, the ANS begins to develop regulatory functions early in prenatal life and involves regular cycles and states of arousal from birth. Both cycles and states have considerable impact on other psychological and behavioral characteristics of the developing infant and their parents. Among the best-studied aspects of ANS functioning is heart rate, which has been used to measure development in many spheres of infant life, from sensation and perception to emotional reactivity and social sensitivity.

CENTRAL NERVOUS SYSTEM DEVELOPMENT

The CNS is largely concerned with information processing and mediating the organism's activity in the environment. To adjust to the complex changes from prenatal to postnatal life, the CNS develops in many ways and at many levels simultaneously. These include the cellular level at one end of the spectrum and the overall structure of the brain at the other. Not only do many structural changes take place prenatally and in infancy, but rapid and complex functional changes of many kinds occur during this period as well. In this section, we discuss the measurement and evaluation of the main features of CNS development before and just after birth. In addition, we review some principles by which experience helps to shape the growth and development of brain function.

The Cellular Level

Figure 5.4 shows a single **neuron**, whose gross structure, including **cell body**, **nucleus**, **dendrites**, and **axon**, is clearly recognizable. Dendrites conduct information to the cell body, whereas axons transmit information away from the cell body by way of the **action potential**, the electrochemical exchange along the axon fiber; this fiber can be infinitesimally short or extremely long (up to 3–4 feet, approximately 1 m). Neurons communicate with each other neurochemically by **neurotransmitters**. The most common neurotransmitters are norepinephrine and acetylcholine, but more than 50 different neurotransmitters have been identified. Undeveloped neurons are nude; developed ones are usually (though not always) wrapped in a sheath of **myelin**—a fatty tissue that surrounds the axon and facilitates the speed of nerve conduction, rendering information transmission more efficient (Klingberg, 2008).

We have already commented on the astounding proliferation of cells in the human brain. Moreover, the brain is a highly structured architectural wonder. As it develops, it follows identifiable principles. For example, cells segregate into specialized areas loosely related to function. In humans, genetic pre-programming ensures an abundance of the cells needed to perceive, think, feel, and act. In the following section, we highlight some of the main developments that occur in the CNS.

Several facts about intracellular structure and function are of special interest to researchers of neural development in infancy. These include:

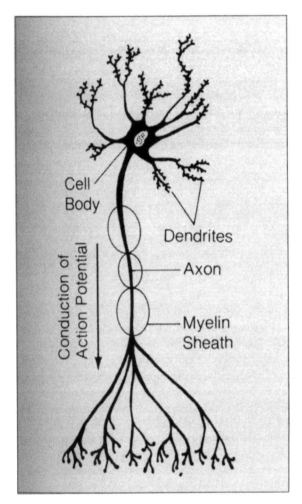

Fig. 5.4 A single neuron showing the cell body and nucleus, dendritic fibers, and the axon, surrounded by a myelin sheath, and flow of the action potential.

1   The birth and maturation of individual cells;
2   The development of interconnections among cells, including dendritic branching, synaptogenesis, neurochemical transmission, and organizational networking;
3   The specialization of cellular function, including interconnectivity, synaptic elimination, and cell death.

Development of the CNS is a highly complex process the intricacies of which are not fully understood (Johnson, 2011a; Stiles, 2008, for detailed discussions of the topic). The CNS originates as a cell layer on the outer surface of the embryo and is already visible 1 month after conception. Neurons continue to appear throughout the period of the embryo and well into that of the fetus. After cells are born (a process called **neurogenesis**), they grow, migrate, and eventually associate with one another to form relatively stable interconnected patterns.

The layers of the brain are generated from the inside out so that cells constantly migrate, sending their axons from one location to a distant location. A fascinating aspect of neural development is that migration routes seem to be predetermined. Migrating cells appear to "know" their addresses, although it is not understood exactly how. After their generation and migration, individual cells grow **dendritic** connections and **myelinate**. Dendrites and axons continue to grow, and dendrites continue to branch out through adulthood. The process of myelination loosely correlates with the development of function and provides a general index of maturation, although functional activity occurs in the absence of myelination. With myelination, the velocity of neurotransmission within a cell more than triples, from a rate of less than 20 ft (6 m) per second to more than 60 ft (18 m) per second. The visual, auditory, and somesthetic cortex myelinates before birth, whereas higher brain centers, such as the prefrontal cortex, that integrate information are not completely myelinated until puberty (Shaw et al., 2006).

Chronic alcohol intake during the prenatal period appears to inhibit the formation of axons and dendrites and the processes involved in cell migration, all of which may contribute to overall lower levels of brain volume (Lebel, Roussotte, & Sowell, 2011). Lead damages tissue by destroying nerve cells and myelin (Brubaker et al., 2009). These facts help to explain why prenatal alcohol ingestion and lead exposure have such profoundly adverse effects on postnatal development (Chapter 4; Box 5.1).

Box 5.1 Set For Life? Isolating the Effects of Cocaine on Development

It is difficult to isolate the effects of one illicit substance, such as cocaine, on development because pregnant women who use such substances also engage in other harmful behaviors, such as drinking alcohol, smoking tobacco, and/or using marijuana. Rivkin and his colleagues (2008) conducted a study to try to isolate the effects of cocaine from other substances on infant neural development. They recruited a sample of 35 newborn infants who had experienced prenatal exposure to one or more substances. Fourteen infants had intrauterine exposure to cocaine whereas the rest did not. In addition to biomedical markers for exposure, mothers were interviewed to obtain estimates of the amount of prenatal exposure to cocaine, alcohol, tobacco, and/or marijuana. When the children were 10 to 14 years of age, an MRI was conducted to assess their neurological status. The MRI showed that prenatal exposure to cocaine resulted in significantly less cortical gray matter, less total brain volume, and smaller head circumference. There was no significant effect for marijuana. However, as the number of exposed substances increased, so did the neurological impairment.

Perhaps the two most important developments in the communication between cells involve biochemical neurotransmission and the restructuring of neural organization. During early maturation, increasing dendritic complexity is reflected in the growth of spines or trees connected to neighboring cells, a process called **arborization**. Conel (1939–1959) illustrated this feature of growth in human brains (Figure 5.5). In the first two years of life, circuitry between neurons proceeds to the point where there are up to 10,000 connections per cell. Likewise, the number of **synapses**, connections between axons and dendrites which are necessary for communication between neurons, regularly increases in early life (a process called **synaptogenesis**), another indication of enhanced capacity for information transmission. During early development, synapses are overproduced in many parts of the brain, with no part appearing to develop faster or slower than any other. Synaptogenesis in the human brain occurs at different times, accounting for changes in function with age (Shonkoff, & Phillips, 2000). Progressive changes in the biochemistry of synaptic neurotransmission influence behavioral development in combination with structural changes, because functionally related systems come to share the same neurotransmitters.

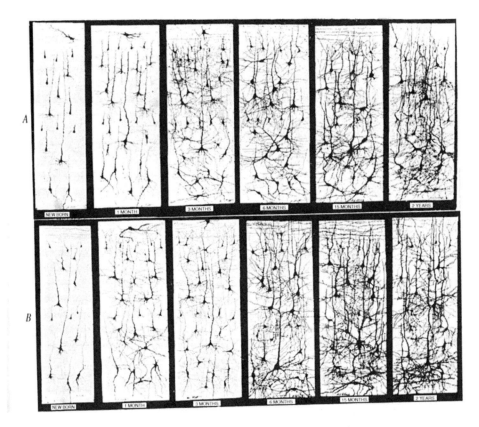

Fig. 5.5 A schematic illustration demonstrating how dendritic arborization and the myelination of neurons increase from birth to 2 years of age (depicted from left to right). (Courtesy of J. L. Conel.)

In human beings, neurons and neural connections in most areas of the brain are initially overproduced and then diminish in number even before birth. Figure 5.6 shows data from humans of different ages regarding the elimination of synapses, a process called **pruning**, in an illustrative region of the brain. Many explanations for this process of cellular overproduction and subsequent elimination have been offered:

1 perhaps not all neurons connect successfully to their appropriate targets;
2 perhaps neurons have an intrinsic tendency to reduce the number of their connections or to support only a limited number of synapses;
3 perhaps activity itself helps to establish and maintain neural circuits, with different activities determining which synapses are retained and which eliminated; and/or
4 perhaps simple space considerations in the skull force the elimination of connections.

Regardless of the reason for overproduction and then pruning, in time, the "chaotic" immature pattern of multiple intercellular connections is replaced by an "efficient" and streamlined information transmission system. Bergström (1969) formally modeled the structural development of neuronal interactions in a clear, though highly simplified, geometry. She suggested that interneural transmission is originally net-like in structure, with more or less random connections among communicating neurons. A discrete stimulus that excites this system is likely to result in a diffuse or global response. In the more developed

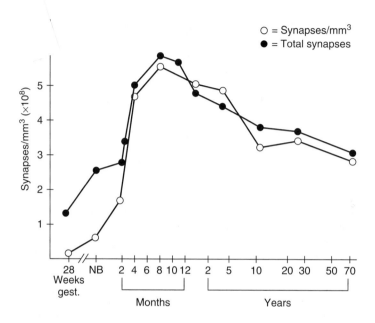

Fig. 5.6 Synapse counts in layer 3 of the middle frontal **gyrus** of the human brain as a function of age. Note the rapid increase in synapses through the first year of life and the decrease by puberty and into old age. (From Huttenlocher, 1990; reproduced with permission.)

state, interconnections are more orderly and tract-like, rather than net-like. These are often called **white-matter fiber tracts**, as they are made up of bundles of myelinated axons. A discrete stimulus now produces a precise response that is exact in time and parallel in space with the stimulus. By way of illustration, consider how younger and older babies might respond to a loud clap. Early in life, such a sudden auditory stimulus elicits a gross response, like a whole-body shudder and perhaps even crying. Sometime later, the same clap leads to a discrete turn of the head.

These startling developments at the intercellular level do not mean that maturation alone accounts for cellular communication and interconnectivity. Hebb (1949) proposed a **motor-neurological theory** of perceptual development, reasoning that a few rudimentary perceptual abilities—such as the capacity to distinguish an object from the background—might be inborn. Beyond highly limited innate capacities like these, however, Hebb theorized that the bulk of perceptual development ought to be based on motor behavior and experience. Imagine what might happen when we see a form, such as a cube. As we scan it, we develop an internal representation of it that is related to the movements of our eyes as well as to the activity of cortical neurons repeatedly excited by the form. The pathways in the brain activated by scanning the form eventually aggregate into units Hebb called **cell assemblies** that help construct familiar perceptions. Experience thus promotes the organization of cell assemblies, and metabolic changes (presumably via neurotransmitters) facilitate connections among these cells to promote perceptual pathways. With repeated experience, Hebb contended, particular stimuli persistently excite specific pathways along which synaptic resistance is reduced and cross talk between cells is promoted.

To illustrate, consider the following: Imagine two villages that are separated by some fields and hills. At first, villagers who want to travel from one or the other make their own way across the fields and hills. Soon, however, some discover the paths of least resistance, and the paths that are more difficult (those over higher hills, or across always marshy fields) become used less and those that are shorter and easier to navigate become used more. Travel across some paths eventually disappears altogether, and the used paths first become walkways then streets then highways. You might have noticed a similar process on your campus. Despite the fact that there are sidewalks, perhaps planned by landscape architects, from one building to another, students often take the most direct and easiest path, even if it means cutting across the grass. The same process, essentially, is happening neurologically: Some pathways are being used and others are not.

Thus, the infant brain has multiple potential pathways, whose functional specialization emerges from subtle intrinsic differences in their initial connectivity (i.e., what connects most efficiently to what), the density of synaptic connections, and the speed of processing information. Equally important is the infant's adaptive need as an organism to accomplish basic goals (e.g., eating, sleeping, speaking, playing, and loving). As the infant interacts with the environment in service of these goals, certain pathways become preferentially activated by different types of activity and experience for which they have a structural advantage. These pathways will be more routinely activated and will similarly recruit other pathways in service of the function, whereas less efficient or less appropriate pathways will be decreasingly involved.

Johnson and colleagues (2005) have explored these developmental processes in the context of the social brain network, primarily in relation to face processing and eye gaze in infants. Both are fundamental to successful social development. Typical adults respond to faces in characteristic ways. For example, most adults recognize faces more quickly and accurately when the faces are upright than when they are upside down. This preferential response suggests that in the adult, the face-processing network is finely tuned to upright faces. Because infants cannot report what they see, Johnson measures ERPs to find out how they perceive faces. Between 4 and 12 months of age, infants come to respond differently to upright verses inverted faces. Significantly, regions that are activated by faces in adults are only partially activated by faces in the infant brain. Thus, Johnson argues, adult behavioral competence does not appear because new brain regions mature and come online. Rather, relevant regions are active and available from the outset. They become more finely tuned and integrated for processing faces as a function of interactive specialization. This occurs in the matrix of daily, repeated experience looking at faces and the neural architectural constraints that support this skill.

Brain Structure

The human brain grows at a phenomenal rate as developing neurons aggregate into cell masses that soon give the brain its characteristic structure. As can be seen in Figure 5.7, the cortex of a human fetus in the second trimester already reveals **sulci** (indentations) and **gyri** (lobes) of its eventual adult form. These structural features are thought to develop because inner and outer cortical layers grow at different rates, but the result is being able to fit a very large number of neurons into the relatively small space of the skull. Laid out flat the cerebral cortex of the human brain is a sheet about the size of a napkin consisting of about 10 billion neurons divided into discrete subdivisions or areas that process particular aspects of sensation, movement, and cognition.

The two hemispheres and the brain stem contain three major substructures that develop in an orderly fashion (Johnson, 2011a; Stiles, 2008). **Subcortical structures** that control state (such as the hypothalamus) and the arousal system (for example, the reticular formation) emerge first. Indeed, nuclei of the **reticular formation**, which govern sleep/wake cycles, are among the earliest to differentiate in the brain. Components of the **limbic system** and **basal ganglia**, which govern emotion, instinct, and posture, develop next. Then, finally, the **cortex** and **cortical association areas** concerned with awareness, attention, memory, and the integration of information emerge. They are also among the last to myelinate and are influenced most by experience with the outside world. The developmental phases for these three major components of the nervous system overlap, and development in each component continues well past infancy (Shaw et al., 2006).

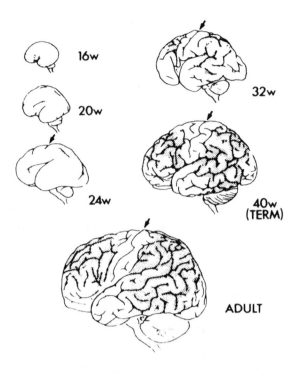

Fig. 5.7 The developing human brain is viewed from the side in this sequence of drawings, all of which are reproduced at the same scale. The characteristic convolutions and invaginations of the brain's surface do not begin to appear until about the middle of gestation. (From Trevarthen, 1974; reproduced with permission.)

The **corpus callosum** is a fiber bundle that connects the two hemispheres of the brain. We know that it is among the last CNS structures to myelinate, and this fact may have startling consequences for the neurology of the newborn infant. Research with adults who have had their hemispheres surgically disconnected by cutting the corpus callosum (to stop the spread of electrical seizures across the brain) indicates that the two hemispheres of the brain share unequally in mental duties, with language processed predominantly in the left hemisphere and spatial information in the right hemisphere for right-handed people (Johnson, 2011a). Normally, the left half of the brain controls the right half of the body, and the right half of the brain controls the left half of the body. Fetuses as young as 12 weeks gestational age show a strong tendency to move their right arms, suggesting dominance of left brain before birth (deVries et al., 2001).

Gazzaniga (1970) once theorized on neuro-maturational grounds that the normal neonate is born, for all practical purposes, with a split-brain. Support for Gazzaniga's statement comes from a study showing that the cortically mediated transfer of visual information between the hemispheres of the brain is not evident before 24 months of age (Liégeois, Bentejac, & de Schonen, 2000). Therefore, during early infancy, input to the right hemisphere comes primarily from the left eye and input to the left hemisphere comes primarily from the right eye. As a consequence of this bias, a congenital cataract that blocks all patterned input to the left eye causes deprivation of input mainly to an infant's right hemisphere, whereas a congenital cataract in the right eye causes deprivation of input mainly to the left hemisphere. After treatment by surgical removal of the cataract and fitting with a new lens, input to both hemispheres can be restored.

Le Grand, Mondloch, Maurer, and Brent (2003) compared visually normal individuals to patients treated for congenital cataracts that blocked all patterned input to either the left eye or the right eye. Despite years of visual input being available to both hemispheres following corrective surgery in infancy, patients showed impaired development of processing faces when early deprivation was to the right hemisphere but not the left hemisphere. Thus, the neural circuitry responsible for adults' face expertise requires early visual experience. However, the two hemispheres are not equipotent: It seems that only the right hemisphere is capable of using early input to develop expertise at face processing.

Electrical Activity in the Brain

Although we are unable to observe or to measure directly the activity of single cells in the brains of human beings, it is possible to assess structural and functional growth indirectly by measuring gross electrical activity of the brain. EEG recordings reflect spontaneous electrical activity over masses of individual cells under the scalp (Luck, 2005). Figure 3.4 shows a baby's EEG being assessed, and Figure 5.8 displays records of scalp EEG activity on five occasions during the first two years of life. In broad outline, neonates have low-voltage, largely undifferentiated, irregular brain activity. Over the course of the first year, the dominant rhythm in the EEG increases from about three to five cycles per second (during the first quarter of the first year of life) to seven to nine cycles per second (by the end of the first year). By the time they are 2 years of age, toddlers have high-amplitude and regular burst-pause patterns of EEG activity. Changes in the EEG signal are believed to reflect the developing excitability and organization of large masses of neurons and so provide clues regarding the online function of different areas of the brain (Thatcher, 1994).

Increases in activity over the frontal areas of the cortex parallel changes in behavior (such as finding hidden objects; see Chapter 7) that demand cognitive and memory skills believed to be mediated by the **frontal cortex** (Nakano, Watanabe, Homae, & Taga, 2009; Reynolds & Courage, 2010; Reynolds & Richards, 2005; Woodward, Edgin, Thompson, & Inder, 2005). In retrieving an object from a box, for example, human infants aged 7 to 9 months will attempt to reach for the object only on the side through which they can see it even when that route is blocked (as would be the case with a transparent box), but by 12 months human infants retrieve objects even when they have to reach around from the open side (such as reaching with the right hand over the box to an opening on the left side, called an "awkward reach"). Infant monkeys show the same pattern of reaches except that the development in infant monkeys is faster. At 2 months they show the awkward reach, but by 4 months infant monkeys perform perfectly. The prefrontal cortex is intimately involved in success on this task. A "prefrontal" adult monkey (one with a lesion in that brain structure) behaves like a young infant. Goldman-Rakic et al. (1997) hypothesized that a proliferation of synapses in the prefrontal cortex governs the ability to represent the location of the object mentally and guide action appropriately.

Search tasks often require infants to keep track of the location of a hidden object across successive trials. In Chapter 7, we will discuss the A-not-B task. In this task, infants are shown an object hidden at a location (A) across successive trials. Then the object is hidden in a new location (B). To successfully find the object, infants need to update their memory regarding the object's location. Eight-month-old infants typically have difficulty with such a task, and it appears that a source of this difficulty is maturation of connections between the frontal and parietal cortices. Bell (2012) compared EEGs of infants who successfully found the object at location B to those who did not. Notably, the successful infants had greater coherence in electro-cortical activity along the frontal-parietal pathways than unsuccessful infants, suggesting the importance of communication among those to areas for updating memory.

Another informative aspect of the EEG signal is the degree of **hemispheric asymmetry**, which has been associated with certain emotions in both infants and adults (Chapter 10). The frontal region of the brain is involved in the expression and regulation of emotion. More specifically, activation of the right

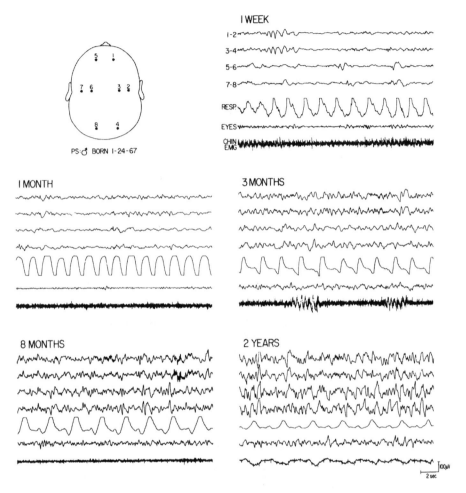

Fig. 5.8 Records of electroencephalographic (EEG) activity, respiration, eye movements, and electromyographic (EMG) activity taken on five occasions during the first two years in one child's life. The first four sets of waves in each panel correspond to leads from electrodes located over different surface positions on the scalp. In broad outline, neonates show low-voltage, largely undifferentiated and irregular EEG patterns, but by the time they are 2 years of age toddlers show high-amplitude and regular burst patterns in their EEGs. (From Sterman & Hoppenbrouwens, 1971; reproduced with permission.)

frontal cortex is typically observed during the experience or expression of negative affect (including anger and distress), whereas activation of the left frontal cortex is associated with the expression or experience of positive affect (such as happiness). Differences in reactivity or temperament at 4 months are correlated with prefrontal structural differences at age 18 (Schwartz et al., 2010). Specifically, 18-year-olds identified as highly reactive at 4 months of age showed greater thickness of the ventromedial prefrontal cortex compared to those identified as low reactive. Another study showed that infants with right frontal EEG asymmetry showed higher levels of anxiety and less ability to regulate their emotions as children (Hannesdottir, Doxie, Bell, Ollendick, & Wolfe, 2010). Thus, differences in neurological structure are correlated with differential responses to stress. Of interest is the direction of these effects. Does differential responding to stress shape neurological development or do differences in neurological structure govern differences in behavior? The role of experience and its impact on development will be discussed in more detail later in this chapter.

Finally, EEG can be used as a measure of the integrity of the CNS. Aydin, Kabakus, Balci, and Ayar (2007) found significant variability in EEG among children with Down syndrome, particularly in the right hemisphere frontal, temporal, and parietal lobe regions, and Pivik, Andres, and Badger (2011) found that ERP depended on infant diet.

ERPs average EEG electrical activity relative to some discrete stimulus, and so describe a specific pattern of brain activity evoked by a specific stimulus, as we discussed in Chapter 3. As shown in the top panel of Figure 5.9, the ERP for a stimulus at first assumes a simple form but is already quite complex by the time of birth (although it still differs from the adult form, which is shown for comparison). As shown in the bottom panel of Figure 5.9, the time between stimulus onset and the appearance of the major component of the ERP (the positive crest at P_2) shows a reasonably orderly decrease with age until it reaches adult values. The amplitude of the ERP (Figure 5.9) follows a more complex developmental course: It diminishes with age up to the normal time of birth, then increases to 3 years (not shown), then decreases again so that, in essence, adults and newborns have similar amplitudes.

ERPs provide valuable information about the normal maturation of the brain, and ERPs can be used to determine whether and when sensory pathways function. Consider the difficulty we would encounter in trying to determine whether an infant who does not respond behaviorally to a sound (by blinking or startling) has a functioning auditory system. By recording the infant's ERPs, we can determine at least whether the infant's brain responds to sound, although of course we would still not know whether the sound was "perceived." For example, in a study on speech perception, infants heard /pa/ on 80% of trials and /ba/ on the remaining 20% of trials (Pivik, Andres, & Badger, 2011). In this type of "odd ball" paradigm, of interest is whether infants notice the change in sound and respond with a larger electrical response on the more novel, less frequent /ba/ trials. Such a response indicates that the infant's brain discriminates the two sounds.

Brain Plasticity

The preceding description of cellular and structural development in the brain suggests that, perhaps because the brain is so crucial to survival, CNS development in prenatal and early postnatal life is preprogrammed and specialized. As it turns out, neural development is far from fixed. For example, experimental work with animals such as monkeys indicates that disrupting the amount of neural input from one brain area (the thalamus) to another area (the cortex) reduces the size of that target area. In addition, if a section of cortex is moved to a different part of the brain, the transplanted part adapts structurally and functionally to its new location (e.g., if moved to the visual cortex, cells from the auditory cortex become responsive to visual stimuli; Johnson, 2011a). In this final section on CNS development, we discuss two perspectives on the effects of experience on brain development: experience-dependent and experience-expectant.

Greenough, Black, and Wallace (2002) distinguished experience-expectant and experience-dependent processes. **Experience-expectant processes** are common to all members of the species and evolved as a neural preparation for incorporating general information from the environment efficiently and satisfactorily. The overproduction and later trimming of synaptic connections between nerve cells illustrates experience-expectant information storage. A psychological example comes from learning language. All babies, regardless of whether they can hear or not, begin to babble in the middle of the first year of life. Hearing babies continue to babble, and these early sounds emerge into words. Deaf babies stop babbling. Thus, for both hearing and deaf babies, the system is prepared for language development, but without the expected experience—exposure to language—the developmental process is stalled. By contrast, **experience-dependent processes** of information storage reflect learning and brain change unique to individual

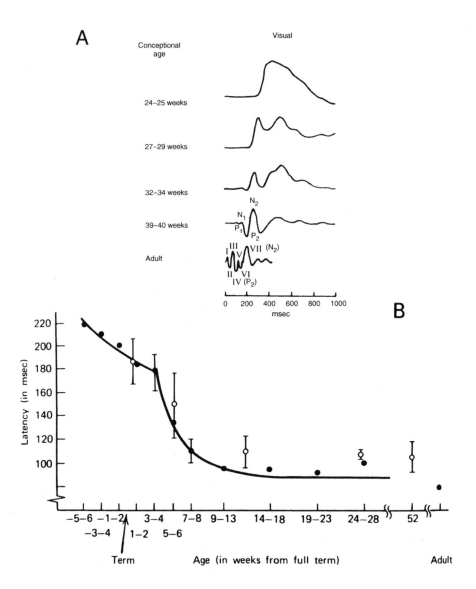

Fig. 5.9 (A) Cortical responses evoked by visual stimuli in preterm infants, term newborns, and adults. (Derivations are bipolar: Oz-Pz for the visual response. Surface negativity is plotted upwards.) (B) Latency of the major positive component of the visual-evoked response as a function of age in weeks from term. (The solid and open symbols represent data from two different experiments. The vertical lines passing through the open symbols signify ± 1 *SD* for the group.) (From Berg & Berg, 1987; reproduced with permission.)

experience. The neural basis of experience-dependent processes appears to involve the active formation of new synaptic connections that are a product of experience with particular individual events and thereby contribute to individuality. An example refers us back to infants born with cataracts. As noted earlier, visual input is critical for full development of the visual cortex (LeGrand et al., 2003).

Both external experience and self-produced experience can modify brain structure and influence brain function. External experience, via enrichment or deprivation, affects the fine and gross structure of the nervous system as well as functional properties of cortical neurons. Such effects are evidenced by changes in the size of individual neurons and of brain structures as well as by the number and structure of synapses, enhanced neural connectivity, and strengthened neural circuitry. For example, rats raised in complex environments (i.e., supplied with toys and opportunities for play and exploration) develop visual cortices that are heavier and thicker than those of litter mates raised in barren, standard laboratory cages; they also show improved performance on problem-solving tasks (Greenough et al., 2002).

An example of enrichment in humans is bilingualism. Children exposed to more than one language from birth have a different linguistic experience than those exposed to only one language. Bilingual children are exposed to more than one language in different ways in different families. One pattern involves one parent speaking both languages. Another pattern is "one parent one language" in which one parent speaks one language and the other parent speaks another language. A third pattern is children are exposed to one language in the home and another through child care. One study on the brain development of toddlers exposed to Spanish and English measured ERP responses to known and unknown vocabulary words in both languages (Conboy & Mills, 2006). Between 19 and 22 months, toddlers were assessed for which language was their dominant language, primarily based on vocabulary size, and their brain maturation was measured using ERP. The researchers found different ERP profiles between the two languages. Specifically, the two languages were processed by different brain systems. Moreover, they found hemispheric differences for the dominant language, as is found in children exposed to only one language, but equal amounts of activity across both hemispheres for the non-dominant language. Thus, the exposure to more than one language early in life influences neural development.

An example of the effects of deprivation on neural development comes from studies of Romanian children (Moulson, Fox et al., 2009; Moulson, Westerlund, Fox, Zeanah, & Nelson, 2009). Three groups of children were compared in their processing of faces: children who had lived their whole lives in an orphanage (institutional care group), those who had experienced an orphanage but were placed in foster care between 5 and 31 months of age (previously institutionalized group), and children who never experienced institutional care (never-institutionalized group). Children in institutionalized care have fewer opportunities to engage with people and to see a variety of different faces. In some orphanages, the infant–caregiver ratio was 20 to 1 (regulations for child care certification in the United States is typically three or four infants to one care giver). Moulson and her colleagues were interested in whether the opportunity to see different faces impacted face recognition and the processing of emotional expressions. To assess face recognition, children were shown images of familiar and unfamiliar faces and their brain responses were measured at several time points during the first 3½ years of life (Moulson, Westerlund et al., 2009). Institutionalized children showed low amplitudes in ERP response overall compared to children who were not institutionalized. In addition, children who were placed in foster care showed an increase in ERP amplitude after placement, suggesting that the earlier effects of social deprivation can be reversed. Similar results were found for the processing of emotional expressions (angry, happy, fearful, sad): Lower amplitude was found for institutionalized children compared to never-institutionalized children, and children placed in foster care showed increases in amplitude at later assessments (Moulson, Fox et al., 2009). Interestingly, the researchers found no difference between the groups in responsiveness to different facial expressions. Highest amplitudes were for fearful facial expressions and smallest amplitudes were for happy faces, a finding that is consistent with children's greater facility in processing negative as opposed to positive emotions (Batty & Taylor, 2006).

Research on face processing in typically developing babies and those who have atypical experiences, such as institutionalization, has potential relevance to autism, a developmental disorder that primarily affects social development. Johnson and colleagues (2005) have speculated that in children with autism, for whatever reason, the expected process of specialization and tuning of the social brain network is disordered. Whereas typical children develop well-tuned, sensitive, and acute mechanisms for processing faces and other social cues, children with autism appear to process social and nonsocial stimuli in a relatively undifferentiated manner.

Retrospective analysis of home movies indicates that children do not suddenly become autistic at age 2 or 3; subtler behavioral differences can be detected very early in life (Clifford, Young, & Williamson, 2007; Palomo, Belinchon, & Ozonoff, 2006). For example, Clifford and her colleagues looked at home movies taken of infants between 9 and 14 months of age. The children fell into three groups: those who were later diagnosed as autistic, those who were later diagnosed with a developmental or language delay, and typically developing children. The movies were coded for behaviors that reflected social deficits typical of autistic disorder, such as eye contact, pointing, gaze monitoring, and social peer interest. The authors found that the infants who were later identified as autistic showed deficits in a number of those behaviors.

The deficits seen in autism might have a physiological basis, as we now know that patterns of brain development over the first two years of life are different for children who are later diagnosed with autism (Wolff et al., 2012). A study of infant siblings of children with autism tracked the development of white-matter fiber tracts between the various brain areas (there is a higher likelihood of a child developing autism if he/she has an older brother or sister with autism). At 6 months of age, infants who later developed autism had an increase in white-matter fiber tracts compared to those who did not later develop autism. At 12 months and 24 months children who did not develop autism had more intense connections. This interesting pattern of first over-production of tracts and then, perhaps, more pruning, warrants more investigation as researchers try to more fully understand the neurological underpinnings of autism.

In light of the different kinds of information and different sources of experience, it becomes clear that brain structure and function are plastic or moldable. Indeed, two kinds of **plasticity** are common in the nervous system: modifiability and compensation. The **modifiability** of cellular sensitivity by experience is illustrated in Figure 5.10, which shows how individual cells in the cat visual cortex respond to lines in

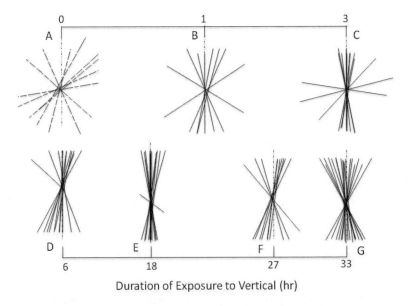

Duration of Exposure to Vertical (hr)

Fig. 5.10 The orientation sensitivity of cells in the cat cortex as a function of experience with the vertical orientation. (A) With no exposure to vertical (zero hours), cells in the cortex are sensitive to all orientations. (B) When exposed to vertical stripes for as little as 1 hour during a sensitive period, cortical neurons begin to demonstrate a bias: Most are sensitive to vertical stimuli. (C–G) Three to 33 hours of exposure further sharpen cortical sensitivities to vertical stimuli, but not by much. (From Blakemore & Mitchell, 1973; reproduced with permission.)

different orientations at 28 days of age. Figure 5.10A demonstrates that, in the absence of specific orientation experiences, the "naive" cortex contains cells sensitive to all orientations (Wiesel & Hubel, 1974). By contrast, the cat in Figure 5.10B was exposed to vertical stripes for 1 hour at a **sensitive period** (Chapters 1 and 4) early in its life. As can be seen, 1 hour of exposure was sufficient to change the sensitivity of cells in its cortex. More cells were devoted to vertical and near vertical orientations, whereas fewer cells were devoted to other orientations. Figures 5.10C–G show that 3 to 33 hours of selective exposure do not sharpen cortical sensitivity to vertical stripes much, illustrating that at 1 hour a threshold was reached for selective sensitivity and that additional exposure did not increase the response. Children who have experienced institutionalization early in life and then placement in foster care before 2 years of age show better psychosocial outcomes at 8 years of age than those placed after 2 years of age (Vanderwert, Marshall, Nelson, Zeanah, & Fox, 2010), suggesting a sensitive period for sociability.

Studies like these demonstrate, first, newborn specificity at the cellular level (e.g., to orientation); second, initial cellular **equipotentiality** of sensitivity (i.e., sensitivity to all orientations); third, cellular susceptibility and **plasticity** (i.e., to specific experience); and, fourth, restriction of this susceptibility (i.e., a sensitive period). In general terms, we are apparently born with a brain ready to respond to critical features of our environment, but our brain can adapt to the environment in which we find ourselves. The window of modifiability is opened early in life so that we can prepare ourselves quickly and efficiently for the particular environment in which we will presumably develop.

Compensation is the second kind of neuronal plasticity. **Compensation** involves the ability of some cells to substitute for others, permitting recovery of function after neuronal loss or damage. Innumerable studies in the neurosciences show that, up to a certain point in development, local cellular defects can be compensated for by neighboring cells; after some sensitive period, however, the defect will be permanent (LeGrand et al., 2003). The same general compensatory mechanisms seem to operate on much larger scales too. A basic principle of brain plasticity has been that when the brain is damaged early in development, subsequent functioning is less impaired than when injury is sustained late in development. Many neurologically minded developmental scientists have theorized about these phenomena. Lashley (1938) suggested that brain systems are largely redundant because capacities are multiply represented; therefore, young still-developing nervous systems may more easily compensate for parts that have been damaged. Alternatively, different parts of the nervous system might be specialized but sufficiently flexible to take over the role of damaged areas, even if at some cost to their own special capacities. It is also possible that young neurons and young brains are less specialized with regard to function and so are able to compensate more flexibly (Johnson, 2011a).

The plasticity of nervous tissue is also illustrated by restoration of function following CNS damage, due to illness, disease, or the normal process of aging (Kolb, 1989). It has long been recognized that cells in the peripheral nervous system regenerate, but the postnatal CNS was believed to be structurally static, such that recovery of function following damage in childhood or maturity could only be mediated by the development of alternative pathways. However, the resilience and adaptability of the infant brain have impressed researchers, and the success of embryonic brain tissue grafts in nonhuman species shows that new cells or new cell processes can develop to repair damaged parts of the CNS or replace cells that have died (Burns, Verfaillie, & Low, 2009; Johnson, 2011a). Moreover, some areas of the CNS continue to produce new neurons. Neurogenesis persists into adulthood in humans and other animals at least in the hippocampus and dentate gyrus, two regions involved in learning and memory (Jabes, Lavenex, Amaral, & Lavenex, 2010; Leuner & Gould, 2010; Seress & Abraham, 2008).

In summary, CNS development in infancy has been studied at the cellular level and in terms of overall brain structure. At each level, important questions arise concerning the interplay between strict maturational progress and the diverse array of experiences that affect the development of single cells and the brain as a whole.

MOTOR DEVELOPMENT

Motor development is as dramatic as physical growth. Table 5.2 shows Bayley's (1993) normative findings of monthly motor accomplishments of infants between birth and 30 months. The infant's ability to coordinate physical movement develops impressively over the first 2½ years. Movements seem uncontrolled for the first few months, but coordination develops rapidly thereafter. From the newborn, unable to roll over from the position in which originally placed, emerges the toddler who is increasingly deft; so much so that parents quickly learn that they must constantly monitor their 2-year-olds.

Table 5.2 Representative items from the Bayley Scales of Infant Development

Age observed (Months)	Mental Development Index	Psychomotor Development Index
1	Habituates to rattle	Thrusts arms in play
2	Follows ring in an arc	Holds head erect and steady for 15 seconds
3	Inspects own hands	Sits with support
4	Picks up cube	Sits alone momentarily
5	Looks for fallen spoon	Uses whole hand to grasp small pellet
6	Cooperates in games	Attempts to raise self to sit
7	Puts cube in cup	Rotates trunk while sitting alone
8	Turns pages of book	Walks with help
9	Pats toy in imitation	Stands alone
10	Puts six beads in box	Throws ball
11	Closes round container	Walks up stairs with help
12	Places one peg in board repeatedly	Walks backward
14	Points to two pictures	Stands on left foot with help
16	Says eight different words	Uses pads of fingertips to grasp pencil
18	Points to five pictures	Uses hand to hold paper in place
20	Uses a three-word sentence	Jumps from bottom step/stair
22	Displays verbal comprehension	Stands alone on right foot
24	Builds tower of eight cubes	Stands alone on left foot
26	Imitates vertical and horizontal strokes on paper	Walks on tiptoe for four steps
28	Discriminates pictures	Laces three beads
30	Understands concept of one	Imitates hand movements

The sequence and coordination of motor development depend on physical maturation and experience. Certainly, this schedule of development depends on the growth of limbs and muscles sufficiently strong and organized to act in a coordinated fashion. We can only presume simultaneous development of neural control over muscle movement. Two related neurological systems direct motor activity (including reflexes): The **pyramidal system** controls precise, rapid, and skilled movements of the extremities (such as walking), and the **extrapyramidal system** controls posture and coordination. As these systems develop, the infant is able to move about and manipulate objects. The neuromuscular systems begin developing early in the second trimester of pregnancy, and the child's own movements, even as a fetus, feed back to enhance development (Box 5.2).

Despite these regularities of motor development, it is not the case that infants can automatically accomplish more mature and complicated motor feats as they mature physically. Experiences also influence the course of development, from being placed to sleep on the back versus the stomach (a change about 10 years ago as a preventative measure against SIDS but one that reduces the chance to strengthen neck, arm, and back muscles), wearing diapers or other constrictive clothing versus going naked, and daily repetitive limb movements (Campos et al., 2000; Cole, Lingeman, & Adolph, 2012).

Box 5.2 Science in Translation: When Should Babies Learn to Swim?

Advocates of infant "swimming" have suggested that swimming is natural because babies make reflexive kicks when placed in water and only need practice to develop purposeful swimming skills from their reflexive kicking. Furthermore, many parents believe that children who learn to swim in infancy will not only become better swimmers, but will also be unafraid of water in childhood. This view suggests that babies would benefit from swimming lessons from the earliest months. But is this really true? Do babies of all ages benefit as much from swimming lessons, or do they need to be "ready" to really benefit?

Zelazo and Weiss (2006) designed a study to answer these questions. Eight 4-, eight 8-, seven 12-, and seven 16-month-old infants who had never swum before were tested in a swimming pool and were then given four months of training in the form of five (4-month-olds) or eight (all other infants) lessons over the next four months. The findings were unequivocal. When first introduced to the pool, the infants behaved similarly, regardless of age. There were few instances of any of the swimming behaviors measured: kicking, arm flexion, righting response, swimming, and turning 180° and grasping the pool wall. All infants benefited from the lessons, however, regardless of age. One behavior in particular was affected differently depending on the infants' ages: turning 180° and grasping the side of the pool. The infants studied from 12 to 16 and from 16 to 20 months learned this more complex combinatorial skill much more rapidly than the other infants, and after they had acquired the skill, they performed it more rapidly too. According to Zelazo and Weiss, these findings suggest that a significant neurological milestone is achieved around 12 months of age.

In answer to our question, then, we can say that infants learn to swim most effectively when they start lessons early in the second year of life. Earlier lessons might help babies to feel at home in water, but they do not really allow them to learn the types of skills that make them competent swimmers.

Two significant events in the development of motor control in infancy are reaching and locomotion. Infants begin reaching between 4- and 5-months of age, but manual coordination is far from fully developed at that stage. Increasing control over the hands and arms provides for the planning of actions and opportunities for tool use. For example, when anticipating contact with an object, infants plan the trajectory of their arm(s) and modify their hand shape depending on the location and/or properties of the object (Chen, Keen, Rosander, & von Hofsten, 2010; Gronqvist, Brodd, & von Hofsten, 2011; Yonas, Granrud, Chov, & Alexander, 2005). Tool use requires control over fine motor movements, and thus emerges later than reaching (Needham, 2009). In addition to controlling their manual actions, infants must also learn the most efficient way to use tools. For example, when feeding using a spoon, there is a correct way to pick up the spoon (Keen, 2011). Holding the spoon such that the food end is toward the center of the body allows for easy access to the mouth. Moreover control of movement is important so that the contents do not spill.

Learning to locomote in infancy involves complex reciprocal relations among maturation, perception, and experience (Adolph & Berger, 2011). Here we consider two examples. The first pertains to the transition from crawling to walking. Kretch and Adolph (2013) investigated infants' judgments of different sized drop-offs as crawlers and walkers. The drop-offs were either small steps or large cliffs. Experienced 12-month-old crawlers refused to go over the cliffs but novice 12-month-old walkers stepped over the cliffs and needed to be rescued from falling by the experimenters. Kretch and Adolph concluded that with the new mode of locomotion, infants needed to re-assess the conditions for safe locomotion, particularly the differences between what can be done by crawling and walking. Another example of the interplay between maturation, perception, and experience comes from infants' carrying objects while locomoting (Karasik et al., 2012). Locomotion by either crawling or walking brings infants into contact with distant objects. Infants also like to share objects with other people, and thus they often carry objects while locomoting. Both crawlers and walkers engage in a number of strategies for carrying objects, as illustrated in Figure 5.11, and the more locomotor experience infants have, the more they carry objects while moving. A surprising finding by Karasik and her colleagues was that walkers fell *less* when carrying objects. Despite engaging in a more attention-demanding task (walking and carrying), balance control appeared to improve compared to when not carrying objects.

Thus, although there are the expected achievements in locomotion with age (i.e., from crawling to walking), infants' ability to negotiate a challenging motor task, such as descending a sloped surface or moving through an opening, is not automatic. Infants take into account properties of the surfaces or openings, such as the degree of slant or width of a doorway, and explore different methods of locomotion before settling on a specific locomotive mode, such as crawling backward or turning the body sideways (Adolph & Berger, 2011; Franchak & Adolph, 2012).

As we mentioned in Chapter 1, systems theory maintains that growth in one sphere of life will have an impact on other domains of development. Consistent with this theory, motor development affects

Fig. 5.11 Different modes of carrying objects by crawlers and walkers. (From Karasik, Adolph, Tamis-LeMonda, & Zuckerman, 2012. Copyright © 2012 by the American Psychological Association. Reproduced with permission. The use of APA information does not imply endorsement by APA.)

multiple aspects of psychological growth (Thelen, 2000, 2001). Consider the development of the capacity to grasp an object with both hands. At the very least, this skill requires the coordination of fine motor movements in the hand as well as two arms, two hands, and two eyes. The development of control over motor behaviors also makes possible the expression of intentional social- and object-related aspects of cognitive and social growth. Reaching increases infants' appreciation of object properties, including faces, and crawling experience is associated with less negative affect and more flexible memory (Herbert, Gross, & Hayne, 2007; Libertus & Needham, 2011; Whitney & Green, 2011). For example, Herbert et al. showed that 9-month-old infants who were crawling were able to recall a novel action when tested in a different context. The same-aged infants who did not crawl were very good at recalling the novel action when tested in the same context but showed no evidence of recall when tested in a novel context. Presumably, experience with self-locomotion provided infants with opportunities to retrieve information in a range of contexts, thus leading to more flexibility in recall. Moreover, there could be a reciprocal relationship between object exploration and locomotion. Crawling infants who showed more interest in objects, carried objects, and shared objects with others over distance at 11 months were more likely to walk by 13 months (Karasik et al., 2011).

An intriguing example of the relation between motor development and later cognitive functioning comes from a study of the precursors of reading that was conducted in Finland (Lyytinen et al., 2001). The Jyvaskyla Longitudinal Study of Dyslexia tracked children at risk for reading impairment and a comparison group of children without known risk from birth through 9 years of age. The researchers initially surveyed all expectant families in the Finnish city of Jyvaskyla and surrounding communities between 1993 and 1996, more than 8,000 in all. They eventually identified 410 parents with suspected dyslexia who were willing to participate in an individual assessment. Those who met the stringent criteria for the study (dyslexia in a parent and a close relative) were recruited. A primary hypothesis was that a speech perception deficit present at birth gives rise to dyslexia later in life. This study, however, also evaluated coexisting developmental issues, such as self-regulation as well as infant motor development, temperament, and environmental factors that could influence the emergence of a reading problem, thereby allowing for a more complex developmental model. As predicted, newborns in the at-risk group responded differently to speech sounds by ERP, and by 6 months, the groups displayed subtle but reliable differences in their ability to categorize speech sounds and a poorer processing of nonlinguistic auditory stimuli (Benasich et al., 2006). A fascinating twist emerged, however, when the researchers considered motor development (Viholainen, Ahonen, Cantell, Lyytinen, & Lyytinen, 2002; Viholainen et al., 2006). At-risk children whose motor development was delayed during the first year of life had more limited vocabularies and shorter sentences at both 18 and 24 months and poorer language competence at 3 and 5 years of age. At age 7, the at-risk children with slow motor development read more poorly than children in the control group, even children in the control group with slow motor development. Children in the genetically at-risk group with good motor development, however, read as well as children in the control group! Because this study is correlational (Chapter 3), we cannot conclude that slow motor development was causing poor reading in 7-year-old children. Instead, it is likely that one or more mechanism underlying good and poor readers also underlies motor development.

In addition to influencing the baby's perception of the world, motor development also influences parent–infant interaction. When a baby first reaches deliberately, rolls over, stands upright, or walks, it is an occasion for joy and for telephone calls to grandparents. These achievements also signal all sorts of cognitive and social changes at home, like "child proofing" the house. Change, as well as rate of change, is impressive. So is the average child's physical energy. It is estimated that each hour the average toddler takes 1,200 steps, falls 16 times, and spends 30 minutes playing with objects (Franchak et al., 2011). A popular—if apocryphal—anecdote that circulates among parents holds that, at the height of his physical prowess, Jim Thorpe (an Olympian and professional football and baseball player who is described as the greatest athlete of the 20th century) was asked to do everything that a toddler did, exactly the way the toddler did it. As the story goes, Thorpe gave up exhausted after a few hours, whereas the toddler continued blithely for the rest of the day.

SUMMARY

The principles of physical and motor development provide models and metaphors for infant development in other spheres. Neurological developments occurring pre- and postnatally correspond to or underpin many of the observable trends that interest developmental scientists. Infants initially lack the capacity to modulate their own states of arousal and thus seem to move erratically from one state to another. However, with development, infants come to show consistent (if gross) cyclic organization of state. In addition, neurological development appears to underlie the emergence of organized sleep patterns resembling those of later life. Reliable individual differences in heart rate soon emerge, and predictable changes in heart rate in response to various types of stimulation provide a powerful tool for assessing infants' states of development and general responsivity. In the CNS, intracellular and intercellular structure and function change dramatically over the first years of life as neurons are born, develop, and connect with one another so as to permit increasingly efficient and complex transmission of information. Alongside remarkable programmed specializations, malleability and compensation attest to the great neural plasticity in infancy. Moreover, with maturity, infants gain increasing control over their own movements, allowing for independent exploration of their world.

KEY TERMS

Action potential
Arborization
Autonomic
Autonomic Nervous System (ANS)
Axon
Basal ganglia
Canalization
Cell assemblies
Cell body
Central
Central Nervous System (CNS)
Cephalocaudally
Circadian clock
Co-sleeping
Compensation
Congenital
Corpus callosum
Cortex
Cortical association areas
Cycle
Dendrites
Dendritic
Directionality

Effectors
Electrocardiogram
Endogenous
Equipotentiality
Experience-dependent processes
Experience-expectant processes
Extrapyramidal system
Frontal cortex
Gyrus (pl. gyri)
Hemispheric asymmetry
Hierarchical integration
Independence of systems
Individual differences
Limbic system
Mass-to-specific
Modifiability
Motor-neurological theory
Myelin
Myelinate
Neurogenesis
Neuron
Neurotransmitters
Norms

Nucleus
Peripheral
Proximodistally
Pruning
Pyramidal system
Rapid eye movements
Receptors
Respiratory Sinus Arrhythmia
Reticular formation
Room-sharing

Sensitive period
Somatic
Statistically normal
Strange Situation
Subcortical structures
Sulci
Synapses
Synaptogenesis
White-matter fiber tracts

Chapter 6

Perceptual Development in Infancy

- *How and why has early perceptual development served as a battleground between nativists and empiricists?*
- *How do infants perceive depth?*
- *What factors influence attention?*
- *When and how do infants perceive forms, orientation, and movement?*
- *Do infants perceive color? Why is it difficult to study infant color perception?*
- *How well do infants hear? In what ways are infants especially sensitive to speech sounds?*
- *How and when do infants develop cross-modal perceptions?*
- *How do perception and action interact?*

Perception constitutes the necessary first step in experiencing and interpreting the world. For this reason, philosophers, psychologists, physiologists, and physicists alike have been attracted to the study of perception. Our everyday experiences raise many intriguing perceptual questions. How do we achieve stable perceptions amidst constant fluctuations in the environment? How do perceptions come to be invested with meaning? How are the individual features of things we perceive synthesized into organized wholes? How do we see a three-dimensional world when visual processing begins with a two-dimensional image in the eye?

The study of perception was initiated by philosophers who were interested in the origins of knowledge. As we read in Chapter 1, extreme views were put forward by empiricists, who asserted that all knowledge comes through the senses and grows by way of experience, and by nativists, who reasoned that human beings must enter the world with rudimentary knowledge and abilities that help to order and organize what they experience. These philosophers mainly engaged in theoretical speculation and argument. It was not until physics and psychology joined forces at the beginning of the 20th century that scientific experimentation was introduced into the study of perception. But philosophy did focus attention on infancy, because the development of perception at or near the beginning of life is necessarily the proper period in which to study the origins and early growth of knowledge.

In addition to this philosophical purpose, studies of perception in infancy address other questions. They provide information about the quality, limits, and capacities of the sensory systems described in

Chapter 4. Determining how the senses function in infancy permits us to glimpse into the infant's world and tells us what aspects of the environment might meaningfully influence early development. Finally, understanding perception in infancy provides a starting point against which maturation and the effects of experience in development can be assessed.

We begin our consideration of perceptual development in infancy with a discussion of philosophical foundations and motivations for studying perceptual development empirically. To illustrate this approach we provide an in-depth example of a classic historical controversy. We next consider the central role of attention and its development. Then, we turn to the heart of the matter and review what is known about perception in infancy. Following the growth of research in this field, we focus on sight and hearing (see Chapter 4 for information about taste, smell, and touch). In the final sections of the chapter, we discuss three overarching issues in infant perception: how perceptions arising from different sensory modalities coordinate, the interplay of perception and action, and how experiences influence the development of perception.

PHILOSOPHICAL QUESTIONS AND DEVELOPMENTAL RESEARCH

Perceptual development has served as a kind of battleground between nativists and empiricists, and by way of illustration we examine one exemplary skirmish in detail. It concerns the ways infants come to perceive depth in space. We selected this example for several reasons. First, depth perception is crucial to determining the spatial layout of the environment, recognizing objects, and guiding motor action. Second, the study of depth perception addresses an interesting psychophysical question, namely how we perceive the three dimensionality of the environment when the flat retina at the back of the eye first codes information in only two dimensions. Third, debate on this question exemplifies the typical historical course: It began with hotly contested philosophical disputes that spanned the 17th to 19th centuries before prompting experimentation in the 20th century. Throughout this time, philosophers and scientists consistently looked to infancy to help decide how depth perception develops.

A Nativist–Empiricist Debate

How do human beings come to perceive depth in visual space? Writing in the treatise *La Dioptrique* in 1638, the French philosopher René Descartes offered an answer to this question that assumed the mind's intuitive grasp of mathematical relations. Descartes believed that knowledge is inborn and that human beings are guided by "natural" laws. He reasoned that our two eyes form the base of a triangle whose apex lies at the target under our gaze. When we look at a target that is far away, our lines of vision are more nearly parallel and the base angles of the triangle approach 90 degrees. When we look at a target that is close, the base angles of the triangle are acute. Therefore, the closer the target is, the more acute the angles are. Descartes (1638/1824, pp. 59–66) concluded that distance is given by "an act of thinking which, being simple imagination, does not entail reasoning." Descartes was correct in observing that our eyes converge more for near than for far points of interest and that degree of convergence is directly related to target distance. But are infants sensitive to the difference in angles for near and far objects?

Later, the empiricist George Berkeley in his *Essay Towards a New Theory of Vision* put forward a different explanation for depth perception. Berkeley (1709/1910) argued that human beings do not intuit distance by "natural geometry." Rather, Berkeley theorized that infants learn object size through feedback from their tactile and motor experience. In essence, Berkeley claimed that infants associate the large apparent size of objects with bringing their two eyes close together in conjunction with the small amount they have to move their arms when reaching for nearby objects. Likewise, infants associate the small apparent size of objects with the parallel position of the two eyes and the large arm movements that need to be made when reaching for faraway objects. Berkeley hypothesized that reaching in association with convergence of the eyes and the appearance of objects leads to visual understanding of depth and distance. In other words, touch teaches vision.

Nativists countered Berkeley's experiential argument with logic. In the *Critique of Pure Reason*, Immanuel Kant (1781/1924) asserted that the human mind does not rely on experience for meaning but innately organizes sensations into meaningful perceptions. Kant's theoretical argument was buttressed with two observations. First, depth perception emerges too early in life to be based on extensive experience and learning, and second, adults with limited experience can still perceive depth. The nativist belief that a capacity to perceive depth must be inborn also motivated some of the first experimenters in the field to seek specific biological substrates that might underlie the ability to perceive depth. Initially, such mechanisms were simply postulated, but in modern times sensory physiologists recording from single cells in the cortex have found hard evidence for them (Chapter 5).

Immediately after Kant, the debate turned back to a defense of empiricism. In his classic *Handbook of Physiological Optics*, Hermann Helmholtz (1885/1965) argued that the nativists' "intuition theory is an unnecessary hypothesis." Helmholtz wrote that it is uneconomical to assume mechanisms of innate perception, especially when "It is not clear how the assumption of these original 'space sensations' can help the explanation of our visual perceptions, when the adherents of this theory ultimately have to assume … that these sensations must be overruled by the better understanding which we get by experience."

Research Resolutions

At this juncture in history, experimental study began to replace philosophical speculation. In fact, experimental psychology, which started only in the 20th century, was at first specifically organized to address just such issues. Three lines of research illustrate how questions about the origins of depth perception have been addressed experimentally. All three are valuable because no one alone provides definitive information, but the three together converge to draw a picture of how depth perception first develops. The starting point for one line of research was the following observation:

> Human infants at the creeping and toddling stage are notoriously prone to falls from more or less high places. They must be kept from going over the brink by side panels on their cribs, gates on their stairways, and vigilance of adults. As their muscular coordination matures, they begin to avoid such accidents on their own. Common sense might suggest that the child learns to recognize falling-off places by experience—that is, by falling and hurting himself. But is experience really the teacher? Or is the ability to perceive and avoid a brink part of the child's original endowment?
>
> (Gibson & Walk, 1960, p. 64)

To address these questions, Gibson and Walk (1960) began experiments to investigate depth perception in infants using a **visual cliff** (Figure 6.1). One side of the cliff shows the baby an illusory drop, but the other side does not. Gibson and Walk found that only a very small minority of infants between 6 and 14 months of age crawled across the "deep" side when their mothers called them. From these results, they concluded that depth perception must be present in infants as young as 6 months of age. By 6 months, however, children may already have had plenty of experience perceiving depth. Schwartz, Campos, and Baisel (1973) studied pre-crawling babies by monitoring heart rate when the babies were exposed to shallow and deep sides of the visual cliff. Babies as young as 2 months of age showed a decrease in heart rate when exposed to the deep side, indicating increased attention or interest. Thus, babies give evidence that they perceive depth long before they locomote but still show little fear of depth. The wariness of drops shown by older infants might result, not from actual experience with falls, but from the anxiety parents

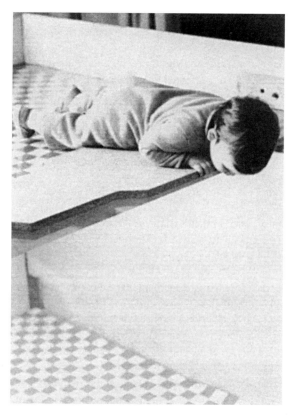

Fig. 6.1 The visual cliff. There is glass on both sides, but on one side there is a deep space between the glass and the checkered floor (the "deep" side). On the other side the checks are right under the glass (the "shallow" side). Infants are placed on the center board and observed regarding whether they are willing to cross the "deep" side. (Courtesy of R. Walk.)

display when their infants approach a drop. Infants look to their parents and use their parents' emotional cues to interpret ambiguous events (Chapter 10).

Visual cliff experiments represent one way that investigators have sought to explore the infant's capacity to perceive depth. In actuality, three types of stimulus information specify depth, and we have organized the following discussion of early depth perception around them: **binocular**, **static monocular (pictorial)**, and **kinetic cues**. As Descartes and Kant argued, we have at least two bases for perceiving depth because we are **binocular** (have two eyes). Our two eyes receive slightly different images of the visual world (to see for yourself, close one eye and look straight ahead; now open that eye and close the other). The convergence angle of the two eyes, and the disparity between the two images they yield, provide some information about depth. **Binocular convergence** may provide functional information about depth as early as 2 months of age (Kellman & Arterberry, 2006).

Purely **static monocular information** helps us to perceive depth as well. Static monocular cues to depth are well known and often referred to as pictorial depth cues because artists as far back as Leonardo da Vinci, Michaelangelo, and others in the Renaissance described many ways of portraying depth in a flat painting. One such pictorial cue is **relative size**. If two objects are known to be similar in size, having one appear smaller than the other in a two-dimensional space makes the smaller appear farther away. Another is **linear perspective**: Two lines known to be parallel in real life (e.g., railroad tracks) are seen as moving away from the viewer if they are drawn to converge. **Texture gradients**, another monocular cue, signal depth when the elements of the textured surface gradually reduce in size. Other monocular cues include **interposition** (when contours of one object partially block another object from view, the first object is perceived to be closer than the second) and **shading** (contours of an object oriented away from a light source will appear darker than contours oriented toward the light, providing the illusion of depth). Granrud, Yonas, and their colleagues (Arteberry 2008; Hemker, Granrud, Yonas, & Kavsek, 2010; Kavsek, Granrud, & Yonas, 2009; Yonas, Arterberry, & Granrud, 1987) have conducted systematic studies organized to explore infants' responsiveness to a variety of (pictorial) depth cues and found that infants become sensitive to these cues between 5 and 7 months of age.

The world and the infant perceiving it are constantly in flux, and movement information from this continuously changing structure provides additional cues to depth. There are several such **kinetic** cues to depth. When an object looms directly toward us on a "hit path," its image on the retina expands and we normally move to avoid the impending collision. Yonas (1981; Náñez & Yonas, 1994) conducted experiments to study object **looming** (also called **optical expansion**). Babies viewed a translucent screen onto which a silhouette of a three-dimensional object was cast. (This technique avoids actually threatening babies with a solid object and cuing them with the air changes that an actual approaching object might cause.) Yonas found that babies as young as 1 month consistently blinked at approaching objects. Sensitivity to approaching patterns develop faster than receding ones, and infants are particularly sensitive to the motion paths of objects when they cross their line of sight (Brosseau-Lachaine, Casanova, & Faubert, 2008; Schmuckler, Collimore, & Dannemiller, 2007). Consider another kinetic cue, **motion parallax**: Objects (or parts of objects) that are closer to you move across your field of vision faster than objects (or parts of objects) that are farther away. The relative motion of the objects gives information for depth. Although infants as young as 2 months of age are sensitive to relative motion for perceiving 3D object shape (Arterberry & Yonas, 2000), they do not appear to use this information to perceive depth until at least 4 months (Nawrot, Mayo, & Nawrot, 2009). Related to motion parallax is the cue **accretion-deletion of texture**: When you move through the environment, closer surfaces are perceived to block more distant ones. Such differences in the covering (deletion) and uncovering (accretion) of object surfaces provides information about the relative depth of objects, and infants respond to this information by 5 months (Craton & Yonas, 1990).

In summary, depth perception experiments have demonstrated that infants are sensitive to binocular and kinetic information by 3 to 5 months of age but might not be sensitive to static monocular information until 5 to 7 months of age. It is important to point out, however, that infants younger than 3 months of age probably perceive depth. Limits to our understanding of infant perception of depth are placed on us by our methods of study (Chapter 3) and by the fact that spatially appropriate actions (like blinking or reaching) are the best measures for determining whether infants perceive a depth difference. Younger infants are limited in their action repertoire, thus making it difficult to determine whether they are perceiving depth. There may never be a final triumph for nativism or for empiricism. No matter how early in life depth perception can be demonstrated, the ability still rests on some experience, and no matter how late depth perception emerges, it can never be proved that only experience has mattered. Nevertheless, the nativism–empiricism debate permeates the developmental study of depth perception and (as we shall see) many other content areas in infant perceptual development.

ATTENTION

Much perceptual research in infancy depends critically on the attention babies pay (Chapter 3). As we just learned in our brief review of depth perception, our understanding of infants' capacity rests on whether infants orient and look. Attention determines which information enters the brain, and attention is the gateway to perception. Attention also underlies awareness, experience, and interpretation of the world

Attention is therefore a significant mechanism by which infants acquire knowledge about the world. To what and to whom infants attend serve as prominent markers of their perceptual and cognitive functioning (Dixon & Smith, 2008). Attention in infancy also has social consequences (Kristen, Sodian, Thoermer, & Perst, 2011). Gaze is the basic unit of social exchange; establishing eye-to-eye contact with a newborn is not only rewarding to a caregiver but also sets in motion the routines and rhythms of social interaction and play. For these important reasons we now examine perceptual attention.

The young infant (like the adult) is bombarded by sensory stimuli. An important general aspect of infant functioning is that, even from birth, babies both actively seek out and attend to certain sources of information in their environment. Patterns of attention demonstrate that infants select and, importantly, filter features of the environment and are not simply passive registrants of experience. Figure 6.2 shows infant heart rate before, during, and after paying attention to a static visual stimulus. Notice the drop in heart rate as infants orient to the stimulus and visually inspect it (sustained attention). Heart rate begins to rise again as infants disengage from the stimulus (pre-attention termination). Researchers have identified a number of factors that influence infants' attention, including stimulus complexity, contrast, and motion.

Additionally, researchers have asked what is happening when infants get bored in a typical habituation procedure that relies on a decrease in attention over time (Chapter 3). In a short-term longitudinal study, Colombo et al. (2010) measured heart rate while infants habituated. Infants tested at 4, 6, and 8 months showed a decline in overall amount of looking: Infants at 4 months exhibited longer durations of looking than they did at 6 and 8 months. Also, regardless of age, infants showed a startle response on the very first trial. When the stimulus was shown for the very first time, its appearance surprised the babies (imagine being in a dimly lit room looking at a blank screen and all of a sudden a brightly lit image of a face appears). Perhaps more interesting was the observation that infants repeatedly showed characteristic heart rate changes (namely, deceleration during sustained attention and acceleration during attention termination) on each habituation trial. In fact, even though overall number of seconds of looking decreased across trials, heart rate patterns showed that infants continued to engage in cognitive activities. In other words, infants showed sustained attention across the testing session, even though the stimulus, presumably, was becoming familiar to them. Thus, as infants become "bored" during habituation they are still cognitively engaged.

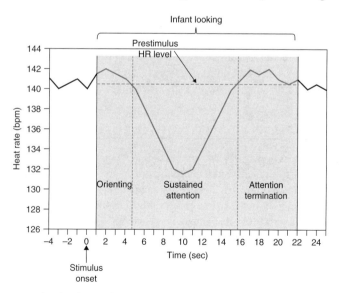

Fig. 6.2 Infant heart rate deceleration and acceleration while attending to a visual image. (From Bornstein & Colombo, 2012; reproduced with permission.)

Related to engagement is the likelihood of being distracted. Key to being an active information processor is the ability to shift attention. On the one hand, remaining attentive to one stimulus is important as that allows for a deeper level of processing and/or familiarity (Oakes, Kannass, & Shaddy, 2002). On the other hand, an inability to disengage from one stimulus may have implications for lost opportunities to learn about new stimuli in the environment. Attentional inertia is a term that has been used to describe infants' continuing engagement with a stimulus (Richards & Anderson, 2004). Specifically, **attentional inertia** pertains to the decrease in likelihood of disengagement as the duration of a look increases, and, notably, infants are less distractible as look duration increases.

Despite the risk of attentional inertia, infants are able to disengage and attend to something new. Moreover, other people help. For example, infants' attention can be directed by an adult waving new objects, pointing, and/or saying "look at this." Even without speaking or touching an object, others can cue infants to look at a new location by moving their eyes (and sometimes their heads), and it is up to the baby to follow the direction of gaze. Whereas **gaze following** in a complex environment (where there may be other objects in the way) might not fully mature until 12 months of age, newborn infants will turn their eyes or head toward a nearby object after seeing an adult shift her eyes in that direction (Farroni, Massaccesi, Pividori, & Johnson, 2004). Moreover, infants at 3 months shift their gaze back and forth from the adult to the object, seemingly as a way to keep the social connection to the person and share the mutual experience of attending to the object (Perra & Gattis, 2010).

Researchers of infant attention could be accused of using particularly "uninspiring" stimuli, such as black-and-white checker boards, basic geometric forms, or static faces. Whereas these stimulus decisions maximize visibility, simplicity, and ease of comparison across studies, they do not always allow for generalization of findings, as many objects in the infant's world move. Therefore, researchers have also focused on infants' attention to complex multimodal stimuli, in part due to technological advances in ease of creating and showing dynamic multimodal stimuli and some bold claims by the American Academy of Pediatrics Committee on Education (2001) recommending that children under 2 years of age should not be exposed to screen media (e.g., TV, movies, computers). Using stimuli such as segments from Sesame Street or Teletubbies, we now know that heart rate patterns are similar for dynamic audio-visual patterns and for professionally produced media, and starting around 12 months of age infants show longer amounts of looking to professionally produced media (Richards & Cronise, 2000). In addition, comprehensibility of the media becomes a factor in guiding attention between 18 to 24 months of age (Pempek et al., 2010).

In summary, attention serves as a principal gateway to cognition in infancy, as well as being among the most conspicuous indexes of infant affect and state of arousal. For these developmental and experimental reasons, attention is critical to substantive studies of infant perception.

VISUAL PERCEPTION

Perception is private. There is no way for one person to know what another person's perceptions are like without making inferences from their reports or behaviors. Moreover, infants are mute and motorically underdeveloped. As a result, our knowledge of infants' perceptions must be inferred from their behaviors, such as those that index attention. In the next sections of this chapter, we discuss studies that have fleshed out our understanding of the infant's visual and auditory worlds. Certainly our knowledge of the infant's perceptual world is still incomplete, but one must be impressed with how far the study of infant perception has progressed toward revealing just what perception in infancy is like.

For adults, perception is complex and normally difficult to fathom. As infants do not yet carry all of the perceptual baggage that adults do, nor do infants have language or much knowledge of the world, we suspect that the most basic and general perceptual mechanisms are likely to be the most salient to guide infants' actions and govern their acquisition of information about the world around them. For this reason, we take a **bottom-up approach**—focusing on the input to the senses and how infants make sense of it—rather than a **top-down approach**—one that relies on higher cognitive processes.

We begin by considering perception in the visual modality. In general, the visual world is specified by dimensions of pattern, viewpoint, movement, and color. To gain a glimpse into the infant's visual world, we review sensitivity to each of these dimensions.

Pattern, Shape, and Form

When and how well do infants first see forms? When do they see forms as a unit—as more than their individual elements? In the 1960s, Kessen, Haith, and Salapatek attempted to assess sight in human newborns (Haith, 1980, 1991; Kessen, Haith, & Salapatek, 1970). They photographed the reflection of a stimulus on the front of a baby's eye, assuming that infants' "fixating" on a stimulus implied their "perceiving." Some of the original findings from this research effort are still among the most provocative, demonstrating basic principles of visual perception in the earliest stages of infancy. First, even newborns actively seek visual stimulation and input, scanning the environment in a controlled and alert fashion to find things to inspect, even in the dark. Second, newborns seem to focus most of their attention on the boundaries of figures, where the greatest amount of information is contained. So, looking strategies adopted by newborns seem to guarantee that they will learn something about figures or objects.

Studies of organized visual scanning indicate that newborns and young infants see something when they look at patterns, but scanning does not tell us how well or what infants see. After all, the fact that an infant scans an angle of a triangle does not mean that the infant resolves the contour perfectly or perceives the triangle (or even an angle of it) as adults do. Many kinds of studies have been developed to address these questions about higher-order perceptions of form and pattern (Kellman & Arterberry, 2006).

Fantz originated a preference technique to study **visual acuity**, or how well infants see fine detail (like going to the optometrist). By capitalizing on the observation that infants prefer to look at heterogeneous rather than homogeneous patterns, Fantz, Ordy, and Udelf (1962) showed babies pairs of patterns to look at. One member of the pair was always gray, and the other a set of black-and-white stripes that varied systematically in width. (The two stimuli were also always matched in overall brightness.) The stripe width that failed to evoke a preference (longer looking) was taken as the boundary of the baby's ability to tell stripes from solid gray. Figure 6.3 shows an infant being tested for visual acuity, and Figure 6.4 provides a concrete idea of just how well newborn babies actually see. By this measure, infants show a remarkable development in acuity between 2 weeks and 5 months.

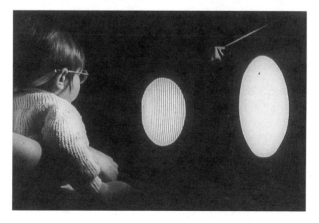

Fig. 6.3 An infant's visual acuity being tested. (Courtesy of J. Atkinson and O. Braddock.)

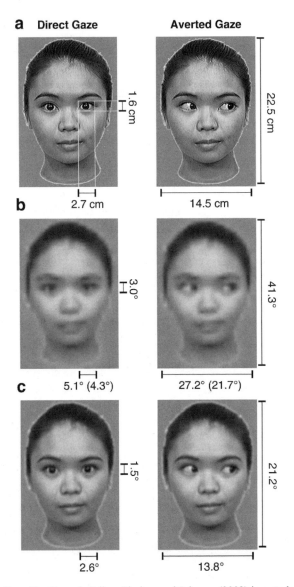

Fig. 6.4 The face stimuli used by Farroni, Csibra, Simion, and Johnson (2002) in a study of infants' perception of faces with direct and averted eye gaze. The three sets of faces show how the stimuli might appear to: (A) adults; (B) a newborn; and (C) a 4-month-old infant. (From Farroni, Csibra, Simion, & Johnson, 2002; copyright (2002) National Academy of Sciences; reproduced with permission).

In the 50 years since Fantz's original study, techniques for measuring infant visual acuity have grown in sophistication, but the results show high agreement with the initial findings (Kellman & Arterberry, 2006). Visual acuity is relatively poor in newborns, but it improves rapidly and, by about 6 months of age, is almost the same as that of normal adults. Moreover, this procedure has been adapted by Teller and her colleagues so that infant acuity can be assessed in a pediatrician's office (Teller, McDonald, Preston, Sebris, & Dobson, 1986) so that, if necessary, babies can be fitted with glasses.

Infants can see detail, but when do they actually perceive forms as whole forms? This question is interesting practically and theoretically because some gestalt theorists (like Köhler (1929) and Koffka (1935), for example) proposed that the perception of whole forms is innate, whereas constructivists (like Hebb (1949) and Piaget (1952)) proposed that perception of whole forms is built up from perceptions of individual elements—lines and angles and surfaces. The question has proven remarkably difficult to answer because almost any discrimination between two forms (say, a triangle and a circle) can be explained as a discrimination on the basis of some simple feature (such as discriminating an angle from an arc or discriminating different amounts of contour) without implicating "whole form" perception. Indeed, forms typically integrate multiple features (for example, color and shape), and proper perception occurs when these individual features are synthesized into a single, unified compound stimulus (e.g., a red triangle).

An important component of form is external edges. Forms viewed in isolation of other objects or surfaces typically have fully visible edges. However, when forms are in a cluttered environment, it is possible that parts of the edges are not visible. **Subjective contours** involve extrapolating edges where none are present. For example, consider Figure 6.5A and B. The black elements help the perceiver to complete the edges of the illusory square in A but not in B. When infants are able to perceive static subjective figures as complete forms, such as in Figure 6.5A, has been controversial, with some suggesting as early as 3–4 months and others suggesting as late as 7 months (Kavsek, 2002). We do know, however, that when the form moves, subjective contours are perceived earlier. In Figure 6.5C and D, the black elements are rotated, creating the impression of a square moving across the screen in C but not in D. Using both habituation and preferential looking techniques, Valenza and Bulf (2007) showed that newborns perceived subjective contours in moving displays but not in static displays.

As a special visual pattern, the face has engendered a large perceptual literature. Infants are very attracted to faces, although it has long been unclear whether this attraction is founded on an innate, species-specific predisposition to attend to faces (Johnson & Morton, 1993) or based on the fact that faces contain features that infants find intrinsically interesting (i.e., faces are three-dimensional, move, produce sounds, and have areas of high contrast; Slater, 1993).

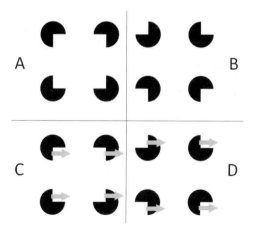

Fig. 6.5 Four stimulus patterns used in Valenza and Bulf (2007) experiments. Pattern A is a static image that produces subjective contours forming a square. Pattern B does not produce a static subject contour. The inducing elements in C and D move. C produces a kinetic subject contour, that is a square that moves across the black elements, whereas in D, despite movement of the inducing elements, a subjective contour is not created. (From Valenza, & Bulf, 2007; reproduced with permission.)

Early work with two-dimensional stimuli (photographs of faces) suggested that the basis for infants' attraction was the presence of contrasts in facial configurations. These findings, involving two-dimensional, nonmoving stimuli, were replicated in a number of different laboratories (Bushnell, 1982; Kleiner, 1987). However, when two-dimensional stimuli in a normal face pattern, a scrambled face pattern, and a blank stimulus are moved slowly in an arc-like path (Figure 6.6), newborns look at and track the normal face pattern significantly more than the scrambled face pattern, and in turn show a preference for the scrambled face pattern over the blank stimulus (Johnson, Dziurawiec, Ellis, & Morton, 1991). Viewed in the context of other studies demonstrating that newborns can imitate facial expressions (happiness, sadness, surprise), prefer attractive over unattractive faces, and show a preference for their mother's face over another female face, these results suggest that newborn infants possess some innate knowledge of faces and possess a specialized mechanism for processing facial configurations (Bushnell, Sai, & Mullin, 1989; Field, Woodson, Greenberg, & Cohen, 1982; Quinn, Kelly, Lee, Pascalis, & Slater, 2008; Slater et al., 2000).

This does not mean that infants' knowledge of faces is complete at birth. As human babies grow (and improve in their acuity), the internal features of faces become more prominent (Turati, Macchi Cassia, Simion, & Leo, 2006). Five-month-old infants can discriminate between a face with typical spacing of the eyes and mouth from a face with exaggerated spacing between features, and they recognize faces across different emotional expressions (Bhatt, Bertin, Hayden, & Reed, 2005; Bornstein & Arterberry, 2003). Even later in the first year of life, infants come to "specialize" in recognizing faces like those in their environment, showing better recognition skills among faces of their own race compared to faces of other races (Kelly et al., 2009).

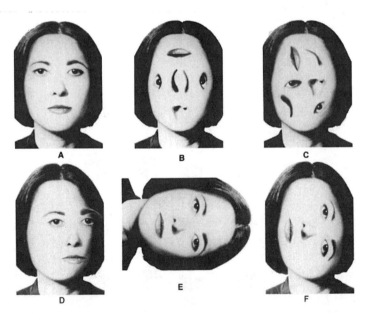

Fig. 6.6 Experimental facial stimuli used in studies with infants. (A) The photograph of a normal face in the prototypical vertical symmetry. (B) The same face with internal features rearranged, but still symmetrical. (C) Internal facial features rearranged asymmetrically. (D) Internal facial features symmetrical, but off center. (E) The normal face turned on the horizontal. (F) The normal face, but with internal features turned on the horizontal. Such stimuli are used to assess infant sensitivity to the internal versus overall configuration of facial features and the face as a whole.

Viewpoint

Objects in the world are also specified by their coordination in space, including their orientation, location, and movement. Consider your coffee mug. If you place it on the table and move to the other side of the table, it may look different. For example, the handle might not be visible, or if it is visible the handle's shape might appear to be different from when you saw it earlier. Also, the logo on the front of the cup might not match the logo on the back of the cup. However, you have no trouble still recognizing it as your cup. You might use top-down knowledge to help you with this recognition task (you remember what the back of the cup looks like from previous experience, and you know you just walked to the other side of the table), but you could also be relying on principles of perception. Solid objects do not change but our viewpoints of them do. Being able to recognize an object from different perspectives is an important step toward experiencing a stable perceptual environment. This process is termed **viewpoint invariance**—the understanding that an object viewed from different viewpoints is still the same object.

The notion of viewpoint invariance is related to **shape constancy** and **size constancy**. When viewing an object, such as a square, at different distances, the image on the retina changes in size. A closer object will project a larger image than a farther object. If the perceiver is sensitive to the distance of the square, he/she will see the square as the same size. Similarly, with shape constancy, as a square is tilted in depth, the projection on the retina changes from a square to trapezoidal shape. Again, distance information provides the perceiver with the information that the square is not deforming, but instead is tilting in depth. There is evidence that size and shape constancy function early in life (Arterberry & Kellman, 2006). Viewpoint invariance is considered in light of more complex objects (such as multi-part objects) and across more complex transformations (complete rotation or changes in orientation; Figure 6.7). In one study, 5-month-olds were familiarized to a simple, novel object either by a series of images depicting a single view of the object, or a series depicting different views around its vertical axis (Mash, Arterberry, & Bornstein, 2007). Infants in the single view group failed to recognize the same object when inverted, but infants in the group seeing multiple views successfully recognized the object when inverted. A control experiment confirmed that infants were capable of discriminating subtle shape differences in the stimulus objects. Because such performance requires an initial extraction of 3D form, these findings suggest that infants are capable of combining discrepant static views into a cohesive representation of an object's 3D visual form. Kraebel and Gerhardstein (2006) showed evidence of viewpoint invariance in 3-month-olds. These lines of research provide converging evidence that babies, still only in the first year of life, can perceive form *qua* whole form.

Habituation   Test

Fig. 6.7 Stimuli used by Mash, Arterberry, and Bornstein (2007) to test infants' recognition of an object across multiple viewpoints. Infants in SV saw the same view of the object during the habituation phase. In contrast, MV infants saw multiple views. At test, the same object was presented in a different orientation.

Movement

Movement is an inherent feature of the world around us, and of ourselves. Movement detection is present from early infancy, although precision in perceiving motion increases across the first 2 years of life (Farzin, Rivera, & Whitney, 2011; Mason, Braddick, & Wattam-Bell, 2003). For example, **directional sensitivity** emerges between 6 and 13 weeks, and it may be dependent on cortical maturation (Birtles, Braddick, Wattam-Bell, Wilkinson, & Atkinson, 2007; Braddick, Birtles, Wattam-Bell, & Atkinson, 2005). The visual system may be pre-adapted to perceive movement because doing so carries distinct advantages: Things that move bring protection, nutrition, danger, and opportunities for exploration and play. Furthermore, motion provides information that is essential for developing stable perceptions of objects and spatial layouts (Kellman & Arterberry, 1998, 2006).

Infant's perception of motion is actually quite sophisticated. Ruff (1982, 1985) tested the abilities of infants in the first 6 months to recognize and discriminate among different motions of rigid objects. For example, she first habituated babies to a series of objects, each of which moved the same way (say, from side-to-side). Ruff then tested the same infants with a novel object moving in the now familiar side-to-side motion and with a novel object moving in a novel way (say, from side-to-side and rotating). Both 3½- and 5-month-olds discriminated the two directions of motion, and 5-month-olds also discriminated rotation from oscillation around the vertical as well as left versus right rotation. Ruff used different objects to ensure that the babies did not rely on specific shape cues to achieve these discriminations of movement, and others have shown that 2- and 4-month-old babies see form across different axes of motion when viewing wire figures and moving random dot displays, which when in motion create the perception of surfaces of a three-dimensional object (Arterberry & Yonas, 2000; Kellman & Short, 1987).

Motion also provides us with information about object properties. Consider the rod/block figure in the top half of Figure 6.8. Most adults who view a stationary display like this readily perceive it as a single rod that is partially hidden by a box (called an "occluder") because mature perceivers make use of edge-sensitive processes to perceive object unity. This follows the Gestalt principle of good continuation (unconnected edges will be perceived as connected if the edges are relatable in some way; Kellman, Yin, & Shipley, 1995) and the pictorial depth cue of interposition discussed earlier in this chapter. Kellman and Spelke (1983) found that 4-month-olds do not perceive the rod as complete when it does not move. When habituated to a stationary version of Figure 6.8, they looked longer to the complete rod display (bottom left of Figure 6.8), suggesting that they found the complete rod novel. In contrast, when the rod moved behind the occluder (either translated left to right, moved up and down, or moved forward and back in depth), 4-month-olds looked longer to the broken rod display (bottom right of Figure 6.8), thus treating it as novel. They treated the complete display as familiar by continuing to show a low level of looking (bottom left of Figure 6.8). Newborns consistently show the reverse pattern of looking (Slater, Johnson, Brown, & Badenoch, 1996). Following habituation to the moving rod behind the block, they look longer to the complete rod display, indicating that they are unable to use the motion information to determine the unity of the rod behind the occluder. Two months of age appears to be a transition period for perceiving object unity from motion, with studies showing inconsistent results on whether 2-month-olds see a complete rod or a broken rod behind the occluder (Johnson, 2004). Various explanations have been suggested, including size of the occluder (Arterberry, 2001); however, it might be the case that some infants fixate on only one part of the display (e.g., the top part of the rod) rather than on the whole display (e.g., both ends of the rod), and these attention biases might limit infants' interpretation of the continuation of the rod behind the occluder (Johnson, Davidow, Hall-Haro, & Frank, 2008).

Motion also helps reveal **figural coherence**. This is the perceptual grouping of elements having an invariant set of spatial relations. For example, when you fan your fingers, the relative position of the

HABITUATION DISPLAY

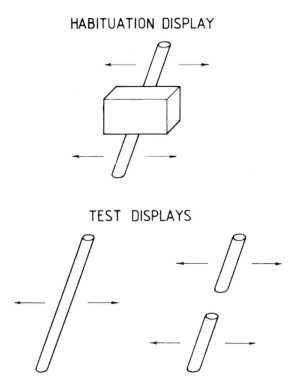

TEST DISPLAYS

Fig. 6.8 Habituation and test displays used to investigate infants' understanding of partly occluded objects. (Courtesy of A. Slater.)

knuckle and finger nail of each finger remains constant despite the fact that your fingers are now farther away from each other. Coherence may be extracted from relative motions that are coordinated among the elements. A compelling example of figural coherence is the so-called point-light walker display, which specifies motions typical of human beings (Figure 6.9). When adults observe such a dynamic light display, they can identify the motion and the object in less than 200 milliseconds, whereas static displays of the same information are essentially non-interpretable. Similar sensitivity to structural invariance in dynamic displays is evident in infants as young as 5 months of age (Booth, Pinto, & Bertenthal, 2002). Infants apparently do not perceive these displays as unrelated "swarms" of randomly moving dots, nor do they focus on the motion paths of individual lights. Rather, infants are sensitive to the overall coherence of the figure based on its biomechanical motion, and it is likely that different brain areas are recruited for processing biological motion (Lloyd-Fox, Blasi, Everdell, Elwell, & Johnson, 2011; Marshall & Shipley, 2009). Whether infants "see" a solid person in a human point-light display has been debated, but by 6 months of age they perceive these displays as depicting a solid object (Moore, Goodwin, George, Axelsson, & Braddick, 2007).

In summary, infants in the first year of life see elements of patterns as well as pattern wholes, show developing sensitivity to several dimensions of spatial information, including depth, invariant viewpoint, and movement, and even use movement to perceive object form. We now turn to consider infants' perception of another visual dimension, color.

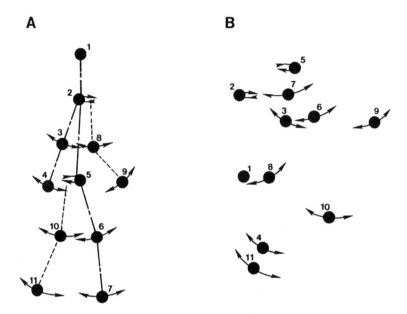

Fig. 6.9 (A) An array of 11 point lights attached to the head and joints of a walking person: The head and right side of the body are numbered 1 through 7, and the numbers 8 through 11 mark those of the body's left side. The motion vectors drawn through each point light represent the perceived relative motions within the figure. (B) An anomalous walker identical to A except that the relative locations of the point lights have been scrambled as shown. (Correspondingly numbered point lights have the same absolute motions.) (From Bertenthal, Proffit, & Cutting, 1984; reproduced with permission.)

Color

Patterns and objects in the environment not only vary in terms of spatial dimensions that help specify, identify, and distinguish them, but they are also perceived as having color. Indeed, color is an intellectually impressive and aesthetically attractive kind of information. Infants see colors and seem to do so pretty well.

Darwin speculated about the development of color vision in his son Doddy and his other children as far back as the 1870s, but real progress toward understanding the development of color vision only began a century later. Formidable problems challenge those who attempt to study color vision. For example, **hue** and **brightness**, the two major components of color, vary together, so that whenever the color of a stimulus changes both its hue and brightness are changing. To compare two stimuli on the basis of what we usually think of as color (hue) alone, we must first equalize or otherwise account for the brightnesses (luminance) of both. With adults, this is relatively easy to do because adults can be asked to match colored stimuli for brightness. In babies, however, the precise relation between brightness and color was not known for a long time, and babies certainly cannot be asked to match brightnesses. There are also clear functional differences between infant and adult vision (Sireteanu, 1996). In short, if we show babies a red and a green circle, and they distinguish between the two, they might be doing so on the basis of brightness differences or on the basis of hue differences. We would not know which. As a consequence, understanding infant color vision needs to begin with studies of brightness perception and, on the basis of proper brightness controls, may proceed to test infant discrimination, preference, and organization of color.

By approximately 3 months of age, babies are nearly as efficient as adults when the task is to compare brightness differences between visual stimuli (Kellman & Arterberry, 2006). It has been somewhat more challenging, however, to demonstrate that infants younger than 8 weeks can discriminate differences in hue alone, although experiments comparing chromatic (color) sensitivity using electrophysiological and behavioral techniques agree that, across a broad range of conditions and most of the visible spectrum, the infant's sensitivity to color differences is reasonably similar to that of adults (Bornstein, 2006b, 2007; Franklin, Bevis, Ling, & Hurlbert, 2010).

When researchers wish to assess infant hue discrimination per se, it is possible to adopt several different strategies to un-confound brightness. For example, it is possible to match brightness using an adult standard in specific regions where infants and adults are known to be comparable, or to vary brightness systematically or unsystematically so that brightness is not an influential factor in hue discrimination. Peeples and Teller (1975) capitalized on the baby's preference for heterogeneity, showing 2- and 3-month-olds two screens, one white and the second white with either a white or a red shape projected onto it. They then systematically varied the brightness of the shape around the adult match to the brightness of the background screen. When the white shape was darker or brighter than the screen it created a pattern that babies favored (relative to the homogeneous white comparison). At the brightness match point, however, the babies did not prefer either screen. Just a shade of brightness difference between the colored shape and the screen engaged the babies to look. The investigators concluded that babies' brightness sensitivity is acute. However, babies always preferred the red shape–white screen combination, independent of whether the red shape was dimmer, equal to, or brighter than the white screen, demonstrating that even when the red shape matched the white screen in brightness, they still saw the hue difference. This was one of the first studies to surmount the brightness problem and to show (at least some) color vision in infants.

Adams, Courage, and Mercer (1994) used a similar procedure to demonstrate that neonates discriminate red from gray, but not blue, green, or yellow from gray. Thus, neonates can detect some color, although their color vision may be limited by the absence and immaturity of cone receptors in the retina and of post-receptor pathways in the brain for processing color information. Color vision develops very rapidly, however, and Adams et al. demonstrated that infants could successfully discriminate blue, green, yellow, and red by 3 months of age.

Adults do not merely see colors; they perceive the color spectrum as organized qualitatively into **categories of hue** (Bornstein, 2006b, 2007). Although we certainly recognize blends in between, we distinguish blue, green, yellow, and red as qualitatively distinct. The infant's color space is similarly organized. It could be that the way in which the visual system functions lends vision such organization, or it could be that infants learn to organize the visual world, say, when they acquire language. Bornstein, Kessen, and Weiskopf (1976a, 1976b) studied this question using a habituation-dishabituation strategy with 4-month-olds. They found that babies who were habituated to a light of one color readily noticed when a light of a different color was shown on a test trial even when the two lights were matched in brightness. These investigators then proceeded to determine whether babies perceived color categorically—that is, whether babies regard two different blues, for example, as more similar than a blue and a green. Bornstein and his coworkers habituated babies to a blue near the boundary between blue and green. On test trials following habituation, the babies were shown a blue light, a blue near the boundary between blue and green, and a green light all matched for brightness. One test stimulus was the familiar one, and two differed from the familiar stimulus by identical physical amounts; however, one new test light fell into the blue range (like the familiar stimulus), whereas the other was green. Babies shown the new blue stimulus treated it and the familiar blue as the same, whereas they treated the green stimulus differently. As shown in Figure 6.10, the overall pattern of results showed that infants categorize the visible spectrum into relatively discrete hues of blue, green, yellow, and red, and in ways similar to that of adults even though infants, like adults,

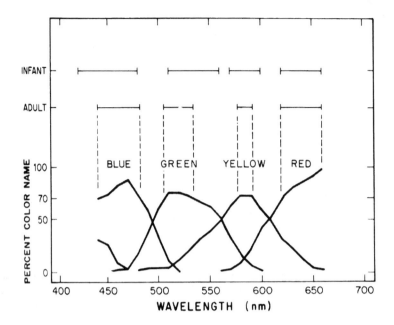

Fig. 6.10 This figure shows how closely infants' categorical perceptions of color resemble those of adults. The lower panel indicates the likelihood that adults label light of a given wavelength using one of four basic color names (after Boynton & Gordon, 1965). The upper panel summarizes the results of hue category studies of 4-month-old infants by Bornstein, Kessen, and Weiskopf (1976a). (From Teller & Bornstein, 1987; reproduced with permission.)

can still discriminate among colors within a given category (Bornstein, 1981). Franklin and Davies (2004) further documented the categorical perception of color in infancy.

Color controls attention, pleases, and informs. Perceiving color and doing so categorically combines with seeing pattern, locating objects in space, and tracking movement to aid babies in organizing and making sense of what they see.

AUDITORY PERCEPTION

Much less is known about audition than about vision in early life, even though audition is of major importance to infants (Saffran et al., 2006). It is an everyday observation that newborns hear sounds: Make a sudden loud noise and a neonate will startle. We also know that fetuses hear *in utero*, as discussed in Chapter 4, and that the auditory system is very developed if not yet fully mature at the time of birth.

Sound is specified principally by two characteristics, **frequency** and **amplitude**. Frequency is the rate at which sound waves vibrate, and encodes pitch (bass to treble), whereas amplitude is the intensity of sound waves, indicating how loud a sound is (volume). Human beings hear sounds in the frequency range of approximately 20 to 20,000 hertz (Hz). Human speech is a complex interplay of different sound frequencies at different intensities distributed over time. In recent years, infancy researchers have focused principally on four basic issues; the first three concern the infant's abilities to detect sounds of different frequencies, to discriminate among frequencies, and to localize sounds in space. Research into these basic abilities has not captured the interest of investigators in the field of infant audition nearly as much as the fourth, namely the way babies respond to more complex sounds that specify human speech.

Basic Auditory Processes

How loud does a sound have to be for the infant to hear it? For adults, the amount of energy that defines the **auditory threshold** varies with the frequency of the sound: Both low (below 1,000 Hz) and high (above 10,000 Hz) frequencies require more energy to register than middle frequencies. Using behavioral and psychophysiological techniques (Chapter 3), infancy investigators have sought to determine how the infant's threshold for intensity perception varies across the frequency spectrum. Infants appear to hear low-pitch sounds worse and high-pitch sounds better than adults do, and there are nearly continuous developmental improvements in hearing at low and high frequencies during the first 2 years of life (Saffran et al., 2006).

Infants clearly discriminate among sounds of different frequencies, qualities, and patterns. For example, newborn infants respond to a 20% change in frequency but not a 5% change (Novitski, Huotilainen, Tervaniemi, Näätänen, & Fellman, 2007), and 5- to 8-month-olds discriminate tones differing by only about 2% change in frequency (adult frequency discrimination is about 1%; Olsho, Schoon, Sakai, Turpin, & Sperduto, 1982). Newborns also prefer human speech and rhesus monkey vocalizations over nonsense speech, and a preference for human speech over primate vocalizations emerges by 3 months (Newman & Hussain, 2006; Vouloumanos, Hauser, Werker, & Martin, 2010). Furthermore, infants are sensitive to various features of music, including preferences for different pitches for different types of songs (e.g., lullabies and play songs) by 6- to 7-months (Box 6.1). By 11 months, infants perceive both phonetic and pitch information in songs (Lebedeva & Kuhl, 2010; Tsang & Conrad, 2010).

Box 6.1   Science in Translation: Chilling Out to the Music

As we show in the text, an army of researchers has demonstrated over the last 40 years that very young infants have remarkable perceptual capacities. In the case of auditory perception, infants seem capable of perceiving features of their mothers' speech patterns sufficiently well that newborn infants can distinguish their mothers' voices from the voices of other new mothers speaking to their newborn infants. In addition, as Trehub (2003) has observed, young infants are sensitive to many fundamental features of music and are capable of discriminating pitch and differences in timing as well as listeners who have had many years to listen to and learn about music.

Evidently, young infants not only enjoy listening to music but are affected by the experience. Arnon and his colleagues (2006) compared the differential effects of live music, recorded music, and no music on the psychophysiology and behavior of preterm infants in a neonatal intensive care nursery. All 31 participants were healthy, but weighed less than 1,500 grams and were born at 32 or fewer weeks post-conception. During three daily 30-minute sessions of "music therapy," the infants in three music groups did not differ in heart rate or behavioral state or any of the other measures. In the 30 minutes immediately following the sessions, however, heart rate declined and behavioral state improved (they calmed, moved into deeper sleep, or became more alert) when the infants had listened to live music, but not when they listened to recorded music or no music at all. This suggests that music therapy might have meaningful benefits for preterm babies, especially when the music is live.

Sensitivity to sound and the direction from which it is coming enables perceivers to find people and objects in space. Consider what you do when you hear a noise behind you. Most likely, you turn your head and/or body to look at it. Thus, our auditory system plays an essential role in localization, and this is accomplished by using information provided by the amount of time it takes for a sound to reach each ear. Because our ears are located on either side of our head, most sounds arrive to the two ears at different times (an exception would be if the sound source were directly in front of or behind us). We use this difference in timing to locate the sound, and thus make an appropriate eye, head, or bodily movement to learn more about its source. One of the earliest studies on **auditory localization** involved making a clicking sound to one side of the head of a newborn baby who was less than 10 minutes old. When the infant made a response (on half of the trials she did not do anything), she almost always moved her eyes in the direction of the sound (Wertheimer, 1961). With age, infants are quicker to respond and more accurate in locating targets (Neil et al., 2006). Moreover, as their motor abilities mature, infants reach for sounding objects in the dark (Berthier & Carrico, 2010).

In summary, infants are equipped with quite good hearing. The infant's auditory abilities highlighted here, along with other studies showing that infants may be especially sensitive to sounds in the frequency ranges of human speech (see next section), illustrate the biological preparedness of the infant's auditory system. Like the visual system, infants apply these basic abilities almost immediately to the highly complex tasks of perceiving, deciphering, and making sense of their world.

Speech Perception

In general, human speech is centered at relatively low frequencies, and certain characteristics of human speech may be special for babies. On the most basic level, speech is characterized by great rates of acoustic change and by complex structures, both of which are preferred by infants (Saffran et al., 2006).

Very young human infants seem to attend selectively to and imitate human over nonhuman sounds, and parents adjust to their infants' sensitivity and capacity by using speech characteristics to which babies are especially attuned (Chapter 9). **Child-directed speech** differs from and simplifies normal adult-directed speech in sound patterns, words used, grammar, and gesture. For example, it is higher in pitch, exaggerated in intonation, follows a sing-song rhythm, abbreviates utterances, and repeats. Child-directed speech is also nearly universal across cultures (Schachner & Hannon, 2011). Furthermore, very young infants prefer to listen to child-directed speech over adult-directed speech, even when the language they are hearing differs from their native tongue (Saffran et al., 2006).

Human speech consists of several features, including **prosody** (rhythm) and the units of sound (**phonemes**). Moreover, perceivers must be able to recognize the same sounds (such as "papa") across various speakers, who may have different pitch ranges, different accents, and different affective states (happy vs. angry). Extracting the meaningful units from speech might be the most important task initially for the young infant (and future language learner). Eimas, Siqueland, Jusczyk, and Vigorito (1971) found that babies not only distinguished between speech and nonspeech sounds but also among different speech sounds in an adult-like manner. We discuss research on this topic at some length because it tests several basic issues in the nature–nurture debate and is relevant to infants' perception of speech.

From all of the possible speech sounds that can be produced (phonetics), each language uses only a subset (phonemics), and one dimension along which meaningful phonemes are distinguished is their voicing. Variations in **voicing** are heard when a speaker produces different frequencies of sound waves at slightly different times. In voicing, a sound like /b/ (pronounced "ba") is produced by vibrating the vocal cords and producing higher frequencies at or before the time the lips are opened and low-frequency energy is released—/b/ is a voiced phoneme. By contrast, for sounds like /p/ (pronounced "pa"), the vocal cords do not begin to vibrate at higher frequencies until sometime after the lips release lower frequencies. Thus, the high-frequency components of a sound may precede the low-frequency components, the two components may begin at about the same time, or the high-frequency components may come after the low-frequency. The relative onset times of low and high frequencies cue phonemic perception. It is a well-established fact that adults perceive differences in voicing more or less categorically: Although we can distinguish fine differences in the onset times of low- and high-frequency sounds, we tend to classify different examples of voiced (/b/) or voiceless (/p/) sounds, respectively, as similar, but easily discriminate between the two classes. In English, we distinguish voiced and voiceless sounds—/b/-/p/, /d/-/t/, and /g/-/k/. Thus, different people say /b/ and /p/ in different ways, yet we seldom misidentify these speech sounds. As we explained when describing Bornstein's research on the perception of colors, **categorical perception** involves the propensity to treat as similar otherwise discriminable stimuli and to respond differently to another (even physically close) range of stimuli.

Many people have assumed that phenomena so consistent and significant as the categorical perception of speech sounds might have a biological foundation. To test this assumption, Eimas and his coworkers (1971) asked whether preverbal infants perceive voicing categorically. Using an apparatus in which infants' sucking above a certain amplitude turned on a sound, these investigators presented infants with a voiced phoneme (/b/) until the infants habituated to it. Afterward, they divided infants into three groups: One group heard the related voiceless phoneme (/p/), a second group heard a physically different voiced phoneme from the same category (/b'/), and a third group continued to hear the habituation stimulus (/b/). The two new test stimuli (/p/ and /b'/) were equally different from the habituation stimulus (/b/) in terms of the relative onset times of low- and high-frequency components, but the two presumably differed unequally in psychological terms (because adults categorize the two /b/ sounds together and distinguish them from /p/). In fact, 1- and 4-month-olds behaved as though they perceived speech sounds categorically: Babies distinguished between /b/ and /p/, but not between the two /b/s. In other words, babies categorized sounds as either voiced or voiceless long before they themselves used language or even had extensive experience hearing language. This experiment showed that infants not only discriminated speech contrasts involving voicing, but did so categorically. Because 1-month-olds responded so, the results also suggest that categorical perception of some sounds could be innate.

However, Eimas' experiment did not rule out a role for experience. In Chapter 1, we discussed several roles that experience might play including facilitation, attunement, and induction. The babies who participated in the Eimas experiment were born into monolingual English-speaking families in which the voiced–voiceless distinction is common, as in "ba-by" versus "pa-pa." It turns out that categorical perception is partially developed at birth (fetuses can hear and have experience with speech in the womb) and that its further development is facilitated or attuned over the first months of life through postnatal experience. A number of studies have shown that within the first 6 months of life, infants distinguished many phonetic contrasts, even those that do not characterize the language to which the infants are exposed (Saffran et al., 2006). With continuous exposure to one language, the ability to distinguish phonetic or tonal contrasts outside the native language decreases, especially when non-native contrasts do not readily conform to those found in the infant's own language (Mattock & Burnham, 2006; Werker, Maurer, & Yoshida, 2010). Infants reared in bilingual environments show a specialization to the contrasts present in both languages at the same age as monolingual infants do, indicating that the linguistic specialization process is not delayed by exposure to more than one language (Burns, Yoshida, Hill, & Werker, 2007).

One lesson from the research on categorical speech perception in infants is that certain perceptual discriminations which seem to be universal and developed at birth actually need to be maintained by linguistic experiences. If not, they may be (partially) lost if absent from the language heard by the child. Other discriminations are possible at birth, but they can be altered by experience. Still others can be induced in infants and children by exposing them to certain speech sounds. Categorical perception of speech is one of the ways in which infants are prepared to learn language, a topic we return to in Chapter 9. Box 6.2 describes another link between auditory processing and language.

Box 6.2   Set For Life? Auditory Processing Problems Predict Later Language Impairment

Specific language impairment (SLI) is diagnosed when children suffer a language processing error that does not relate to any neurological disorder. SLI is evidenced by children using incorrect verb tense, incorrect order of verb and subject within a sentence, and a limited vocabulary. Benasich and Tallal (2002) investigated the link between auditory processing in infancy and later development of SRI. At 6 to 9 months infants were assessed for the processing of rapid auditory cues. In this task, infants were trained to look either left or right when they heard a tone. The interval between presentations of the tones was manipulated to determine the rapidity with which infants responded to the different sounds. After this initial assessment, the infants were followed from 12 to 36 months of age to assess their language development. Infants who performed less well on the auditory processing task around 7.5 months of age were the children who also showed less advanced language development at 36 months.

MULTIMODAL PERCEPTION

As mature perceivers, we experience the world multimodally, that is information about objects and events is available to our different sensory modalities simultaneously. When we are at the beach, for example, we see the waves, hear the surf pound, smell the salt air, feel the breeze and sun on our skin, and so forth. These sensory impressions go together naturally to evoke an integrated experience. Furthermore, some information available in only one modality can cross or transfer to another; when we feel a shell, we might expect to see that it is slightly curved with a textured surface. Information obtained by looking, listening, and touching is often coordinated from very early in life.

A compelling difference of opinion exists among researchers of perceptual development concerning infants' **multimodal** sensitivities. This dispute centers on whether sensations are initially integrated and differentiate in development or whether they are initially fragmented and integrate in development. Integrationists propose that the newborn's senses are unified at birth, in that infants detect correspondence across modalities and that perceptual development consists of progressively distinguishing among sources and features of stimulation in the environment (Gibson, 1979). For example, Bower (1977, pp. 68–69) wrote, "A very young baby may not know whether he is hearing something or seeing something. … Very rapidly, [however,] babies develop the ability to register not only the place, but also the modality of an input." In this view, a baby's earliest perceptions are not tied to a particular modality, but rather information is perceived as amodal, that is as belonging to no modality in particular. A contrasting school of thought argues that the processes involved in integrating information across modalities are complicated, that very young babies are unable to integrate information from the different senses, and that the ability to coordinate input across the senses develops over the first year(s) of life through experience (Bryant, 1974).

Much of infant research supports the integrationist view, in that newborns and very young infants have been observed to respond in a similar fashion to events that impinge on multiple sensory modalities. They also recognize what they initially perceived using different sensory modalities. As we described earlier, newborns will orient and look toward the location of a sound. Furthermore, as babies attend to speaking people, they are learning about the auditory features of the language, in addition to the visual features of speech, namely the movement of the mouth (Teinonen, Aslin, Alku, & Csibra, 2008). In fact, infants in the first 6 months of life display sensitivity to a range of **amodal** dimensions, from the temporal synchrony of object trajectory and impact to voice and face coordination (Bahrick, 2004). For example, newborn infants tactually recognized a textured surface seen previously when they were able to hold an object, showing some coordination between manual touch and vision at birth (Sann & Streri, 2008). As we will see in the following section on perception and action, as infants begin to develop reaching skills, they modify their hand movements in response to the visual properties of the objects they hope to grasp, again showing an inter-coordination between touch and vision (Barrett, Traupman, & Needham, 2008).

Young infants are sensitive to multimodal information when different senses are stimulated in distinct ways. It is clear that the basic sensory systems are functioning at birth, and infants then or soon after perceive complex and sophisticated information. Moreover, infants perceive some information arriving via the different senses in a coordinated way, and they make information about stimuli acquired in one modality available to other modalities. The result is a redundancy of perceptual information. Why does a young infant, who does not do much on his or her own, need multiple sources of information about their world? Bahrick and Lickliter (2000; see also Bahrick, 2004) suggest that this redundancy aids learning. Their hypothesis, the **intersensory redundancy hypothesis**, consists of several components, including the importance of multimodal events in capturing infant attention, which then facilitates information processing, learning, and memory of multimodal events over unimodal ones. One outcome of this hypothesis is that multimodal events will have an advantage, especially early in infancy when infants' attentional resources are limited.

Research supports this view. For example, Bahrick, Lickliter, and Flom (2006) showed infants a multimodal event in which a hammer tapped a surface while an auditory track provided a corresponding sound with each surface contact. Two versions of the event were shown (Figure 6.11). In one, the hammer pounded down—an orientation as if one were pounding a nail into the floor. In the other version, the hammer pounded up—as if one were pounding a nail into the ceiling. In addition, some infants saw a unimodal event, one in which the sound track was not present and only the movement of the hammer was available. Following habituation to the hammer in one orientation, infants were presented with the hammer in a different orientation. Infants aged 3 and 5 months responded to the change in orientation in the unimodal event, but not in the multimodal event. Bahrick et al. explain that the multimodal nature of the event—the hammer–surface contact—captured the infants' attention such that a change in orientation of the hammer was not processed (or was not salient enough to warrant a novelty response). Toward the end of the first year of life, infants come to be able to attend to both multimodal and unimodal properties of events, presumably because of increases in attention capacities (Bahrick, Lickliter, Castellanos, & Vaillant-Molina, 2010; Flom & Bahrick, 2010; Lewkowicz, 2004).

A

B

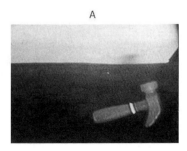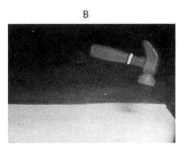

Fig. 6.11 Static images from dynamic events showing a hammer tapping a surface. Note the change in orientation of the hammer: (A) is similar to tapping on the ceiling, and (B) is similar to tapping on the floor. (From Flom & Bahrick, 2010. Copyright © 2010 by the American Psychological Association. Reproduced with permission. The use of APA information does not imply endorsement by APA.)

We have focused thus far on visual-tactile integration and visual-auditory integration. Another form of multimodal integration is visual-proprioceptive. **Proprioception** is the sense of our body in physical space. The information for proprioception comes from our vestibular system (in our inner ear) and receptors in our muscles and joints. Remaining upright and moving smoothly through space requires the coordination of the visual and proprioceptive systems (a topic we will explore more fully in the next section). Infants, even before they are able to walk, have an understanding of the visual consequences of their movements. The first studies to document infants' visual-proprioceptive coordination were conducted by Bahrick and Watson (1985) and Morgan and Rochat (1997). The typical procedure involves showing 3- to 5-month-old infants a video image of their legs moving and an image of another child's legs or the mirror reversal of their own leg movement. This latter condition would be like feeling you are moving your left leg forward but you see your right leg move. The results indicated that infants discern the difference between views of their leg movements that are congruent with their own actual movements from views that are incongruent with their actual movements. Further work showed that infants are still able to recognize their own movements even when the spatial and temporal contingencies are mildly disrupted (Schmuckler & Jewell, 2007).

In summary, not only is each sensory system functioning at or soon after birth, but young infants experience coordination among the senses. It is possible that babies are not aware which sensory modality is providing which type of information. Instead, they are aware of an object, event, or even themselves in the world. We have seen several examples of coordination between touch and vision from the start, suggesting that Berkeley's notion of touch teaching vision might not be accurate. However, in the next section we will see some examples of enhanced visual sensitivity as a result of experiences gained through touch.

PERCEPTION AND ACTION

It is difficult to talk about perception without talking about action. We move in order to perceive—we move our eyes, our head, and our limbs—and as a result of perceiving we might move (reach to grasp an object or run away from something). We have already discussed an example of acting in order to perceive when we covered auditory localization. Very young infants are fairly accurate in detecting the visible location of a target based initially on auditory information. They turn their eyes/head in the direction of the sound source in order to visually inspect the object. Another example of acting in order to perceive comes from research on infants' ability to predict the trajectory of a moving object. Von Hofsten, Kochukhova, and Rosander (2007) found that infants between 16 and 20 weeks were able to visually track an object behind a centrally placed occluder and anticipate its re-emergence. In other words, they moved their eyes to the other side of the occluder *before* the object reappeared. Object tracking extends to reaching behavior: Older infants are able to reach and grasp a moving object (Fagard, Spelke, & von Hofsten, 2009). Moreover, infants anticipate the substance of an object when beginning a reach. Barrett, Traupman, and Needham (2008) presented infants with different balls to grasp. Some of the balls were solid, necessitating a full hand power grasp (imagine grasping a basket ball with one hand); whereas some of the balls were non-rigid, so a precision grip with fingers extending inside the outer edge of the ball was possible (imagine picking up a slightly deflated soccer ball). Infants as young as 5 months made anticipatory hand movements that matched the type of ball they were preparing to grasp. In other words, before the infants even touched the ball, they prepared for the grasp by modifying their hand shape based on visual information.

The coordination of action and perception allows us to more fully explore the world, and in this realm touch plays a key role. From the earliest self-produced movements, touch helps infants acquire knowledge about the world. By the middle of the first year, babies reach for everything in sight and often bring what they touch to their mouths. Gesell (1945) recognized the importance of object manipulation in infancy, but it was really Piaget (1936/1953, 1937/1954) who brought the significance of manipulation to center stage when he proposed that such seemingly simple **sensorimotor** behaviors constitute the very foundations of knowledge. We discuss Piaget's theory in greater depth in Chapter 7; here we simply note that Piaget grasped the fundamental significance of object manipulation when developing an understanding of how the world functions. Piaget observed that over the first 18 months of life, babies repeat their actions, first related to their bodies, then on simple objects, and eventually between objects. Psychologically, infants transition from simple manipulation and exploring object properties before 9 months to relational and functional activities with objects afterward.

Object manipulation has become an important subject of study in its own right, and information processing in infancy is closely tied to tactile exploration. Infants learn about shape, substance, and other object properties through their explorations (Fontenelle, Kahrs, Neal, Newton, & Lockman, 2007; Perone, Madole, Ross-Sheehy, Carey, & Oakes, 2008). Even blind infants engage in manual exploratory behavior: They shake, bang, and finger objects similarly to sighted infants, and both groups show similar amounts of mouthing (Bradley-Johnson, Johnson, Swanson, & Jackson, 2004).

Mature object manipulation does not emerge until babies are able to reach and grasp objects on their own. The development of reaching occurs around 5 months of age, and at that time we see an explosion in their object exploration. As infants interact with objects in this new way, they may acquire new knowledge about them. Needham (2000), for example, found that 3½-month-olds who engaged in more object exploration were better at segregating objects composed of two different looking parts compared to 3½-month-olds who explored less. To further study this phenomenon, Needham and her colleagues (Libertus & Needham, 2010; Needham, Barrett, & Peterman, 2002) gave pre-reaching babies "sticky" mittens to facilitate their own object exploration (active experience) or asked parents to show infants a set of objects (passive experience; Figure 6.12). After approximately 2 weeks of daily experience, infants with active experience showed more mature object exploration than those who had passive experience, and infants'

Fig. 6.12 Infants provided with different object exploration experiences. (A) Infants wear mittens that stick to the objects and thus facilitate self-guided object exploration. (B) The objects do not stick to the mittens, thus the parent must hold the object for the infant to explore it visually (From Libertus & Needham, 2010; reproduced with permission.)

attention to actors and actions differed for the two groups. Apparently, the experience of exploring objects on one's own gave infants a head start in object exploration generally, and it enhanced the infants' understanding of the interactions people have with objects.

Perceptual information also affects locomotion. We monitor our direction of travel and postural stability by information in our peripheral vision. The movement of the visual world as we move through it is called **optic flow**. We have already seen one example of infant sensitivity to optic flow when we discussed infants' responsiveness to looming. With looming, most of the textural changes occur in the central visual field. However, optic flow is also present in our peripheral visual field. To study infants' sensitivity to peripheral optic flow, often they are sitting or standing in a moving room apparatus. During testing the walls or ceiling can be moved. For example, when the walls are moved backward, optic flow cues the perceiver that they are swaying forward. The appropriate response is to adjust one's posture backward to counteract the perceived sway. Sitting infants lean and standing infants step or fall in response to changes in object flow. The precision of the response is correlated with the child's own stage of self-locomotion (pre-crawling, crawling, walking), and infants of the same age but with different locomotor experience show different responses in the moving room. Uchiyama and colleagues (2008) documented the role of locomotor experience by giving pre-locomotor 7-month-old infants experience with self-locomotion using a scooter (a powered-mobility device that infants could control with a joy stick). Infants who experienced mobility using the scooter responded to changes in optic flow like infants who were moving on their own. Thus, sensitivity to optic flow is coordinated with the onset of self-produced locomotion, suggesting that the perceptual system is tuned as a result of newly emerging forms of self-motion, such as crawling and walking.

In addition to maintaining posture, locomoting infants use perceptual information to adapt their movements properly (Adolph & Berger, 2011). If the surface on which infants are moving appears safe, infant locomotion proceeds without modification; if the surface appears to be unsafe in any way, infants pause, look, and sway side-to-side or rock over their feet forward and backward to seek out additional visual and mechanical information about the surface and their ability to maintain their balance when traversing it. Infants use alternative forms of locomotion (e.g., backward rather than forward crawling) or refuse to move at all if surfaces are deemed too risky. They even modify their behavior depending on the amount of friction the surface provides (Adolph, Joh, & Eppler, 2010). This research illustrates the mutually reciprocal influences of perception and movement during infancy.

In summary, perception and action are interrelated. Even with a limited repertoire of actions, infants act in order to perceive and they act as a result of perceiving. Their multimodal world is enriched by their actions, and in several cases their perceptual abilities are enhanced by new actions such as object manipulation and locomotion. These effects of experience are further discussed in the next section.

EXPERIENCE AND EARLY PERCEPTUAL DEVELOPMENT

What are the roles of experience in early perceptual development? Which experiences matter in what spheres of perceiving and how early? As we have seen, perceptual abilities are already remarkably well organized at birth. However, theorists and researchers have long argued that perceptual experience is still critical for normal psychological growth and development. We have encountered examples of the role of experience on perceptual development. Recall that the "sticky" mittens provided infants with early experience with reaching and this experience affected their subsequent object exploration and understanding of actors and actions. Also, the role of self-produced locomotion changed infants' responsiveness to optic flow. Both of these examples bring to mind Held and Hein's (1963) work with kittens on the influence of action on perception. These researchers created an apparatus called the kitten carousel (Figure 6.13).

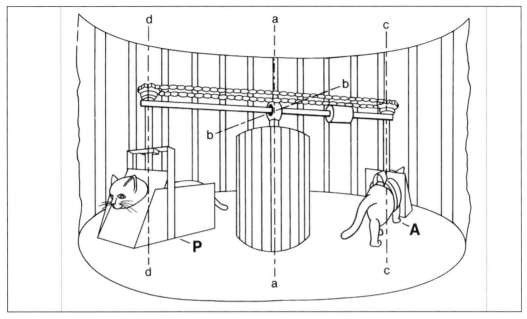

Fig. 6.13 Kitten A roams actively under its own power, moving a second kitten passively. Both receive the same amounts of visual stimulation. Later both were tested on various tasks, like the visual cliff. The active kittens avoided the deep side of the cliff, but the passively moved kittens did not. (From Held & Hein, 1963. Copyright © 1962 by the American Psychological Association. Reproduced with permission. The use of APA information does not imply endorsement by APA.)

This device allowed two animals to obtain essentially the same amounts of experience but in two entirely different ways. One kitten was allowed to move about on its own; a second kitten was moved by the first. Thus, the two kittens' visual experiences were equivalent, but the first obtained its actively and the second passively. The kittens were raised in the dark until they could locomote, and afterward they were allowed 3 hours a day in the carousel. The results of tests given when the kittens reached maturity were compelling: The cats who had been allowed to move about on their own avoided the deep side of a visual cliff, stretched out their paws appropriately in preparation for contact with a solid surface, and blinked at looming objects. By contrast, even after extensive transportation in the carousel, the passively moved cats failed to show such spatially sensitive behavior.

We consider two more examples of how experience impacts perceptual development, one in vision and one in audition. Both examples show, in contrast to the facilitative effects of experience on perception, a deficiency of fine-tuning due to lack of experience. First we consider an example for vision. Taking advantage of a naturally occurring experiment, Maurer, Lewis, Brent, and Levin (1999) were able to examine the impact of experience on the development of visual functioning by studying infants born with a dense cataract in one or both eyes. A cataract is a clouding of the lens; overall presence of light can be perceived but fine patterned stimuli cannot. Some infants are treated for cataracts within 10 days of life. For others the treatment might come later but typically within the first year of life. Tests of visual acuity that were administered within 10 minutes of initial insertion of the new lenses revealed newborn-like acuity among all infants regardless of age. Remarkably, follow-up tests revealed modest but very reliable improvement in visual acuity after just 1 hour of focused visual input, and for those receiving the surgery late in the first year of life the pace of acuity improvement was faster than the pace for normally sighted infants. Years later, those who had two cataracts at birth, thus resulting in binocular deprivation, showed impaired perception (Maurer, Lewis, & Mondloch, 2005). For example, they had difficulty integrating features into a global form, recognizing faces from different points of view, and discriminating individual faces differing in the spacing of the internal features. Yet, other areas of perception were spared: They were able to discriminate large, high contrast shapes, discriminate faces based on overall external contour or a specific internal feature, and recognize eye gaze, emotional expressions, and mouthed vowels. The fact that some abilities are spared and others affected suggests that there are specific brain regions underlying these areas and that there is plasticity in some parts but not others.

In the cataract example, we saw a decrease in function in some areas as a result of visual deprivation. We see a similar decrease in function in auditory perception, but it is interpreted as specialization as the result of specific experiences. When we explored speech perception, we discussed infants' perception of non-native speech contrasts. Early in infancy (6 months and younger) infants perceive distinctions among a number of speech contrasts, and between 6 and 12 months they lose the ability to discriminate contrasts that are not present in their linguistic environment. This specialization also applies to features of music in the infants' environment. Soley and Hannon (2010) tested for US and Turkish infants' preferences for music with either Western (2:1) or Balkan (3:2) meter. Both Western and Balkan meters are found in music in Turkey. They also tested a third, arbitrary meter (8:5, 7:4, and 8:3). Turkish infants showed no preference for Western or Balkan meters, but they preferred these meters over the arbitrary meter. US infants showed a strong preference for the Western meter rather than the Balkan and arbitrary meters. Thus, infants' musical preferences are shaped by the musical experiences in their respective cultures.

The two examples show a tuning of function based on experience. These experiential effects suggest that infants come into the world equipped to perceptually explore their environments, and in addition to learning about objects, people, and events, they are also learning about regularities in their environment, such as which sounds occur more often in language, and their perceptual systems are being refined to respond to these regularities.

SUMMARY

Investigators who study early perceptual capacity have overcome the major impediments infants present—their silence and motoric immaturity—by establishing communication with infants in a variety of ingenious psychophysiological and behavioral ways. In doing so, modern investigators have systematically and forever eradicated the notion that infants are perceptually naive. Research in infant perception addresses many questions concerning the status and natural functions of the senses near the beginning of life, the possible roles of experience, and philosophical issues about the origins of knowledge.

Infants are basically prepared to perceive and acquire information from the world that newly surrounds them. Furthermore, from the very beginning of life, babies actively seek out that information and show distinct preferences for certain kinds of information. Thereafter, their perceptual world becomes increasingly organized. Visual acuity and the ability to detect and discriminate speech develop rapidly. In infancy, visual-auditory and visual-tactual information is integrated into multimodal perceptual wholes. Babies distinguish and attend to properties of objects as well as to relations among properties; these abilities combine to promote the child's cognitive understanding of the object world. Infants seem pre-adapted to perceive in ways that facilitate the organization of incoming information, which in turn advances the development of their perceptual systems.

KEY TERMS

Accretion-deletion of texture
Amodal
Amplitude
Attentional inertia
Auditory localization
Auditory threshold
Binocular
Binocular convergence
Binocular cues
Bottom-up approach
Brightness
Categorical perception
Categories of hue
Child-directed speech
Directional sensitivity
Figural coherence
Frequency
Gaze following
Hue
Interposition
Intersensory redundancy hypothesis
Kinetic cues
Linear perspective

Looming
Monocular cues
Motion parallax
Multimodal
Optic flow
Optical expansion
Phonemes
Proprioception
Prosody
Relative size
Sensorimotor
Shading
Shape constancy
Size constancy
Static cues
Static monocular information
Subjective contours
Texture gradients
Top-down approach
Viewpoint invariance
Visual acuity
Visual cliff
Voicing

Chapter 7
Cognition in Infancy

- *What are distinguishing characteristics of Piaget's theory of cognitive development in infancy?*
- *What features characterize the stage of infant sensorimotor development?*
- *Why and how have developmentalists challenged Piaget's theory?*
- *How do the information processing and early learning perspectives on cognition in infancy differ from Piaget's view?*
- *Distinguish among the three major types of learning.*
- *How well do traditional infant tests predict later intelligence?*
- *How do the processes of habituation and novelty responsiveness illustrate information processing?*
- *How informative and predictive are individual differences in habituation?*
- *How do parents shape infant cognition?*

Although it might not always be apparent, there is no question that even very young infants have an active mental life. They are constantly learning and developing new ideas, and they do so in many different ways. Moreover, what infants learn, and the capacities they demonstrate in doing so, affect virtually all aspects of their later development. The questions that currently motivate thinking and research about infant cognition are these: What is infant cognition? How well can it be measured? What can infants learn about the world around them? How do they learn? How do cognition and learning develop in infancy? How do infants differ from one another in their mental abilities? How can we foster mental development in infancy and later? How do infant mental abilities relate to later cognition, emotion, and social development?

These questions have long puzzled developmentalists, and the answers advanced today form the major topics we cover in this chapter and the next. Specifically, in this chapter we address basic theories and studies of mental life in infancy. The topics include Piaget's views of cognitive development and some of the important contributions of post-Piagetian researchers, learning in infancy, the information-processing approach to infant cognition, and the ways in which the infant's interactions with objects and people influence mental development. In Chapter 8, we follow this introduction to the fundamentals of infant mental life with discussions of some prominent ways infants use their cognitions in categorization, concept formation, memory, and symbolic play.

Cognition in infancy encompasses what is known, what is learned, and how this information guides infants' behavior. There are two main schools of thought about infant cognition, and they relate back to some of the ideas we introduced in Chapter 1. Piaget was a major proponent of one school of thought; he focused on normative developmental functions and qualitative descriptions of infant mental life—what all human babies "know and do." He hypothesized that mental development is discontinuous and characterized by universal stages. The contrasting school of thought includes the learning and information-processing perspectives. These theorists have emphasized the continuous, quantitative nature of growth in infant cognition as well as individual differences in what knowledge they acquire and how and why babies acquire knowledge. In this chapter, we describe these general approaches to assessing mental life in infancy. At the outset, it is important to emphasize that these schools of thought about the infant's mental life do not compete with one another but, rather, represent coexisting and mutually informative perspectives. One day researchers of infant cognition will likely achieve a synthesis of the two.

Before proceeding, consider for a moment what kind of mental life you yourself might engineer for the human infant. Certainly, you would not want to fix the infant's intelligence in advance of any actual experience. It would be shortsighted and counterproductive to disregard the possible effects of experience because intelligence naturally includes the ability to adapt successfully to the environment. By the same token, however, you probably would not want to leave mental development wholly to experience. In fact, both of these criteria appear to have been met in the evolution of the development of infant cognition.

There is another point to consider too: What is cognition for an infant? If we simply consider **face validity**, we can easily agree that when infants do something, such as search for and find a hidden object, their activity "looks" intelligent. We could also assess validity in terms of **prediction**, concluding that some measure of infant mental life must be assessing cognitive functioning when it predicts the child's later intelligence. For example, if efficiency in infant perception predicted intelligence test performance in elementary school, and intelligence test performance was systematically related to school achievement and job performance, we would tend to believe that aspect of infant perception was measuring something about intelligence in infancy.

Keeping these design criteria and validity in mind, we now describe different ways of thinking about mental life in infancy. We begin with Piaget and the qualitative perspective on infant cognitive development.

THE PIAGETIAN VIEW OF COGNITIVE DEVELOPMENT IN INFANCY

Between 1925 and 1932, the Swiss biologist and philosopher Jean Piaget watched closely as his own three children, Jacqueline, Lucienne, and Laurent, grew from infancy, taking note of the enormous intellectual progress each made during the first two years of life. Soon afterward, Piaget (1952) published the *Origins of Intelligence in Children*, a compilation of his observations and informal experiments.

To understand Piaget's theory, we need to appreciate that Piaget saw himself as a philosopher as much as a scientist and that he was formally trained as a biologist. He was initially motivated by a desire to resolve the debate about the origins of knowledge. Piaget was fascinated by the way in which the human mind seems naturally to organize knowledge into categories of, for example, space, time, causality, and substance. However, Piaget did not believe the nativist idea that these universal categories were innate. At the same time, he also disagreed with the empiricist view that all knowledge was derived from experience. (We discussed these contrasting views in Chapters 1 and 6.) Rather, Piaget came up with a radically new solution to the philosophical problem of the origins of knowledge. Piaget suggested that each infant constructs an understanding of the world on the basis of his or her own activity and interactions in the world.

In this part of Chapter 7, we examine several key features of Piaget's theory. They include the elements and dynamics of his theory of knowledge (the scheme, the schema, and adaptation), his view that action is the basis of knowledge, and his notion of development proceeding in a sequence of stages. Despite his advances, there are, as we will see, many unresolved aspects to Piaget's views of cognitive development in infancy.

Piaget's Theory of Knowledge

In contrast to both nativist and empiricist views, Piaget began with the proposal that knowledge is not derived from sensations or perceptions, nor is knowledge gained from information provided by others. Rather, Piaget argued that individuals construct knowledge initially out of their own motor activity. Piaget did not think that sensations and perceptions are unimportant, of course; he emphasized their role in correcting and modifying motor activity. A revolutionary implication of this assumption concerned the nature of **mental representation**. Mental representation refers to the ability to think about people and objects even in their absence, and it is an important foundation of cognition. If sensations and perceptions are not sources of knowledge, then thoughts, images, and ideas in the mind—mental representations—cannot be the residues of sensation, as both nativists and empiricists believed. Piaget held, rather, that such mental materials involve the internalization of motor activity. His theory holds that the process of internalization unfolds very slowly for two reasons: First, motor activity initially does not closely match external reality, but comes to match that reality over time. Second, motor activity might be internalized as thought or image or idea only if it is well rehearsed. Thus, in contrast to both nativism and empiricism, Piagetian theory does not claim any evidence for representation until the age of approximately 18 months.

The Scheme

For the empiricists, the basic elements of knowledge were sensations. For the nativists, the basic elements were innate ideas as well as sensations. For Piaget, the basic element of infant knowledge is the **scheme**. This is a hard concept to define concisely, although its meaning is to some extent captured in the notion that schemes are central nervous system structures that produce motor activities capable of processing information in the environment. Stated simply, schemes are ways of acting on the world. In newborns, schemes are more or less automatic motor activities, although not all reflexes (sneezes and coughs) are schemes. However, many can be used to acquire or process information in the environment; sucking, grasping, looking, hearing, and tasting are examples. Notice that Piaget considered looking and hearing to be actions—not simply the passive registration of sensory information. According to Piaget, knowledge begins to develop as the elaboration of simple reflex schemes present in the newborn.

Piaget's notion of the scheme rests on the claim that knowledge begins with actions rather than sensations. However, Piaget argued that there must be a central mechanism for filtering out sensory inputs (i.e., we do not attend to every stimulus that falls on our sense organs) and for assigning meaning to sensations. Schemes help the infant give meaning to stimulation. Behavioral schemes (physical activities) dominate infancy, but eventually, mental schemes, which are cognitive activities, come into play. Piaget then distinguished between schemes and schemas, the signifiers or symbols that constitute mental life after the advent of representational abilities. In Piaget's system, the child acquires schemas at the end of infancy. Piaget took note of the fact that infant cognition is not static. Rather, infants create, respond to, and adjust to an ever changing world; that is, infant mental development is self-modifying. To explain processes underlying development, he invoked the concept of adaptation.

Adaptation

Adaptation is the fundamental process whereby schemes are altered through experience. Adaptation involves two complementary processes, **assimilation** and **accommodation**. When information can be processed according to an existing scheme, the information is said to be **assimilated**, and meaning is assigned to the sensation. For example, a newborn infant who mouths a finger and starts sucking is said to have assimilated the finger to the sucking scheme. For the moment, the finger has a single meaning or function—it is suckable. The individual sensations—taste, touch, vision, and so forth—that are simultaneously experienced have no meaning in themselves unless or until the infant turns his or her schemes to them. According to Piaget, assimilation is a conservative process because the infant does not change an existing way of acting on the world.

At times, however, an existing scheme cannot successfully assimilate the information in a stimulus. For example, the infant may try to mouth a fist rather than a finger, and of course will not succeed if attempts to do so are the same as attempts to mouth the finger. Two things can happen. One is that the infant can fail to assimilate and simply move on to another activity. Alternatively, the infant can change the scheme so as to permit new information to be processed; for example, the infant might widen the mouth. The modification of an existing scheme to apply to a new situation is termed **accommodation**. Importantly, in Piaget's view, the environment does not simply act on a passive, receptive child. Rather, the child actively changes in order to better respond to the environment.

Although we have described assimilation and accommodation as separate processes, the two always occur together so that the infant's schemes can better match reality and reality can be better understood. Normally, the balance between assimilation and accommodation is shifting, giving temporary pre-eminence to one or the other process. Thus, for example, assimilation predominates during play. In pretend play, reality can be interpreted in any way one wishes. Accommodation predominates during imitation: The actions of the child change to match stimulation as closely as possible.

Cognitive development through accommodation occurs slowly. The child does not suddenly modify all schemes to accord with physical reality. The agreement between existing schemes and the novel demands of the environment must be sufficiently high that the child knows which schemes to modify. When there is agreement between reality and the child's schemes, a state of mental balance or **equilibrium** is said to exist. Piaget supposed that physical and mental activity are geared to maximizing the **equilibration** process, because it represents a crucial aspect of adaptation brought into play to resolve contradictions between the child's comprehension of the world at any given stage and the reality in which the child lives. Piaget was primarily interested in processes whereby mental equilibrium at more and more encompassing levels can be attained.

Action as the Basis of Knowledge

Piaget contended that knowledge begins with action and that acquiring knowledge depends on doing rather than observing passively (although we know that observational learning does often occur). Thus, Piaget was a constructivist in that he believed that individuals actively build their own development. Piaget's influence is evident in our book's frequent stress on the active role infants play in shaping their own development (see also Kellman & Arterberry, 2000).

Stage Theory: The Decline of Egocentrism

Perhaps the best-known feature of Piaget's theory is his doctrine of stages. Piaget hypothesized that mental development unfolds in an invariant sequence of cognitive developmental periods. As a whole, infancy encompasses a sensorimotor period. It is followed, in the Piagetian system, by preoperational, concrete operational, and formal operational periods through childhood and adolescence. Within the sensorimotor period in infancy, Piaget detailed an additional stage-wise sequence of development. Here we illustrate that sequence with respect to the infant's move away from relatively self-focused to relatively world-focused ways of thinking. We call this development the decline of egocentrism.

Stages.   Before discussing this decline, it is useful to review Piaget's conceptualization of stages. In the Piagetian system, observed behaviors are believed to reflect an underlying structure, and behaviors related to each stage are thought to emerge in relative synchrony with one another, thereby giving evidence of the stage as a whole (Chapter 1). Thus, the child's thoughts at any one time are believed to be coherent, making for a particular view of the world. Importantly, the child's current stage defines the way the child views the world and processes information in it.

When formulating his theory of infant cognitive development, Piaget stressed a central aspect—the progress of the infant away from egocentrism. **Egocentrism** for Piaget does not mean selfishness, self-centeredness, or egotism. Rather, it refers to infants' understanding of the world in terms of their own motor activity and their inability to understand it from any other perspective. Piaget described six stages in the decline of egocentrism during infancy. These stages follow a progression, and they are roughly age-related. Piaget's stages also provide evidence of the gradual realization that objects in the outside world are related to one another, at first when they are physically present and subsequently when they are representations in the mind. The notion of declining egocentrism and the associated stage theory are at the heart of Piaget's view of cognition in infancy, and so we describe these stages in some detail.

Stage 1 Reflexive Schemes: Birth to 1 Month.   At this stage, infants accommodate very little to environmental stimuli, and thus mental development is minimal and very slow. Piaget believed that the infant in Stage 1 cannot recognize that stimuli belong to solid objects in the outside world because different schemes appear uncoordinated (i.e., independent of one another). Because the information processed by one scheme cannot be shifted into or processed by another scheme, the infant does not know that a sound and a sight relate to the same object (contrary to recent research discussed in Chapter 6). Furthermore, because reflex schemes are not accommodated to reality, the child is most egocentric at this stage. According to Piaget, stimulation from the outside world merely gives schemes something on which to operate. The infant extracts little or no information about the outside world from this stimulation.

Stage 2 Primary Circular Reactions: 1 to 4 Months.   During the second stage, the infant takes steps toward coordinating schemes, but such inter-coordination still provides little information about the outside world. For example, 3-month-olds can coordinate their hands and mouths and may repetitively grasp and let things go, but they still appear to repeat these actions for their own sake rather than because they are learning about the outside world. Piaget used the term **primary circular reactions** to describe the infant's tendency to repeat chance discoveries involving the coordination of two actions. He called them circular reactions because they are repetitions of chance discoveries, and designated them primary because they are the earliest of a series of circular reactions to emerge in infancy. Another such coordination occurs when infants turn toward the source of sounds. According to Piaget, there is no evidence that infants expect to see something; rather, infants turn to activate looking and hearing schemes simultaneously.

Stage 3 Secondary Circular Reactions: 4 to 8 Months.   For the first time egocentrism declines noticeably, and infants now appear to be aware of relations between their own behavior and the environment. For example, when infants accidentally produce environmental events they may repeat them, suggesting that they want to review their effects on the environment. Because infants produce actions repeatedly (as they did in Stage 2), Piaget still spoke of circular reactions, although he called these **secondary circular reactions**. Now infants begin to notice and focus on events in the outside world. Nevertheless, egocentrism is still prominent: Understanding the world is based on action, rather than on an appreciation of relations among objects. Thus, for example, if an infant discovers that kicking the side of the crib causes a mobile to move, the infant might continue to kick even when too far away to reach the side of the crib. Despite the sensory evidence to the contrary, the baby repeats previously successful actions.

Stage 4 Coordination of Secondary Circular Reactions: 8 to 12 Months.   By Stage 4, infants have the ability to coordinate secondary circular reactions. One circular reaction might be to reach for an object and another might be to pull a placemat closer. Combining these actions would entail pulling a placemat toward the self, and then reaching for an object sitting on the placemat (which is now within reach). Moreover, egocentrism has declined markedly, and the infant has finally constructed some relations among environmental stimuli. Infants now appear to understand that one object can be in front of another. Consequently, the infant is now able to remove a cover hiding an object; this is something that should have been possible (in terms of motor abilities) far earlier if the infant had understood relations between the hidden object and the cover. Egocentrism has still not disappeared, however; we know this because infants still commit the **A-not-B error**. The A-not-B error is a mistake infants make around 8 months or so. By this age, infants can retrieve an object that is fully covered, but if the location of the hidden object is switched across trials, infants search at the first place they found the object (A) rather than at the correct location (B). For Piaget, this shortcoming constituted strong evidence that perceptual information is not sufficient to account for cognitive understanding and behavior. Rather, what infants remember and act on is their success with prior actions.

Stage 5 Tertiary Circular Reactions: 12 to 18 Months.   In this stage, many infant schemes are accommodated to the world outside the infant, and many unexpected relations among objects are discovered. This progress is facilitated by the emergence of **tertiary circular reactions**, in which the child causes something to happen accidentally (as in secondary circular reactions) but then systematically and deliberately varies the manner in which the event is brought about. For example, an infant might attempt to see whether milk leaks out of a bottle at different rates depending on the angle of the bottle and the force with which it is shaken. These tertiary circular reactions help infants understand that their actions can produce novel ends. This achievement anticipates the infant's capacity to engage in insightful problem solving (without relying on trial and error) at a time when novel means must be employed to achieve novel ends.

Remnants of egocentrism remain even at this stage, however. We know this from a major limitation in the infant, namely the inability to conceive **invisible displacements**. If in one continuous movement an object is hidden behind and then re-emerges from screen A, and then hidden behind screen B and then re-emerges from screen B, and finally is left behind screen C, Stage 5 infants can find the object only if they actually see the object being removed from and hidden behind each screen. If an adult's hand conceals the object being hidden, infants appear as if they have no idea where the object is or how to go about searching for it. In short, Stage 5 infants still have an incomplete understanding of the possible relations between objects and screens; thus, they do not appreciate the permanence of objects and so cannot represent their invisible movements. Furthermore, although infants no longer make the A-not-B error when searching for hidden objects, their solution for new problems involves a slow process of trial and error. This result also gives evidence that infants use their knowledge of previous actions and do not rely on perceptual information.

Piaget (1953) provided a dramatic illustration of egocentrism in the Stage 5 child. He described placing his 15-month-old daughter Jacqueline in a playpen with a cardboard rooster just outside it. (Playpens in those days had slats, like a crib, not the mesh screening used today in the typical "Pack and Play.") The rooster had to be tilted away from the child in order to be pulled between the slats of the playpen, and Jacqueline should have been able to see that the slats of the playpen would get in the way if she tried to pull the rooster in sideways. She tried to do this anyway. Moreover, although the rooster kept banging against the slats, Jacqueline did not try to adjust the orientation of the rooster. Only when the rooster fell from her hands accidentally in the right orientation did she succeed in bringing the toy into the pen. However, even this accidental success did not affect her behavior when her father once again placed the rooster outside her playpen. Only after Jacqueline started to drop the rooster deliberately and systematically vary its position was she able to solve the problem.

Note the importance of chance discoveries, the inattention to perceptual evidence, and deliberate variation of means only after chance success in this example. In discussing this stage of development, Piaget seemed to support an empiricist theory of problem solving, but emphasized action rather than perception. He seemed to shift theoretical stance, however, when he discussed problem solving in Stage 6.

Stage 6 Mental Representation: 18 to 24 Months. The hallmark of Stage 6 is the infant's emergent capacity for mental representation. In the case of the object concept, infants can now imagine the whereabouts of an invisible object for the first time. They can also imagine invisible trajectories, so that when a ball rolls under a sofa, for example, the infant will move around the sofa and anticipate the re-emergence of the ball rather than attempting to follow its trajectory directly. This shows successful representation of space. Infants are also now able to imitate people even in their absence or imitate events they witnessed at an earlier point in time (called **deferred imitation**). Now, too, symbolic play becomes possible, and children also become capable of insightful problem solving. As evidence of this newfound ability, Piaget (1953) described the behavior of his other daughter, Lucienne, when she faced a problem similar to Jacqueline's. Lucienne, while in her playpen, at first tried to pull the toy in sideways; however, as soon as she met resistance from the slats, she reoriented the toy so that she could pull it in easily. In demonstrating this sudden, successful solution of a novel problem, Lucienne met all of the criteria for what Piaget called representation; the ability to anticipate the solution to a problem mentally without overt trial and error.

Stage 6, then, culminates the infant's movement away from sensorimotor egocentrism. The child's practical knowledge of the world is now so realistic that solutions to problems can be reached even prior to any direct experience with them. According to Piaget, however, attaining mental representation and insightful problem solving is made possible only by many slow, struggling anticipatory accommodations. Thus, intrinsic tendencies of the organism, experience, and the emergence of new cognitive capacities play intertwined roles in the development of sensorimotor intelligence. The stage-wise decline of egocentrism with development typifies Piaget's approach to the study of cognition.

Décalage

According to Piaget, all aspects of cognitive development undergo such progressions. In Table 7.1, we list the sequences of development in four of the most important cognitive domains as described by Piaget. Normally, a stage theory would suppose that all of the component features of a stage emerge together. However, this is not always the case. **Décalage** refers to an unevenness in development across cognitive domains. Piaget (1952b, 1954) described several décalages in his books on infancy. An especially striking example is the décalage shown by his children, who attained Stage 6 of imitation some weeks before they attained the same stage in object permanence, spatial understanding, or causality. This décalage is somewhat predictable if, as Piaget holds, imitation underlies the ability to represent absent objects. Piaget

Table 7.1 Sequence of some important sensorimotor developments in Piagetian theory

Stage	Means–end behavior	Object permanence	Space	Imitation
1	Reflex schemes	No special behavior toward absent objects	Practical groups. *Separate spaces* for each scheme (buccal space, visual space, tactile space, etc.)	"Reflexive contagion"—stimulus in environment elicits a response in the baby, which happens to match the stimulus that elicited the infant's reaction (e.g., contagion of crying in newborn nursery).
2	Inter-coordination of schemes Primary circular reactions Absence of means–end behavior	No special behavior toward absent objects	Inter-coordination of schemes and of separate *Spaces*. Infant can look at what he/she hears, hear what she/he says, holding what he/she grasps.	"Pseudo-imitation"—only certain types of actions are "imitated": those that continue movement of accommodation even after the stimulus is no longer perceived. Can imitate an action the infant can produce readily and that is directly available to the senses (e.g., cooing). Imitation here "paced" by the parent or model (the parent directly *elicits* the modeled action—e.g., smiling).
3	Primitive, chance, means–end relation Secondary circular reactions	Beginning of search for objects when object is only hidden, or when object is systematically followed until it disappears.	Objects in space understood only in relation to the infant's body and actions, but are not related to one another.	Systematic imitation of models but only with movements the infant has made and noticed self doing. Cannot imitate new, unfamiliar actions or stimuli.
4	Deliberate means–end relation Means, however, must be familiar	Objects searched for successfully after being seen hidden but only in place where previously found.	Relation of objects to one another begin to be understood. Far-space comprehension. Size and shape constancy improve.	Imitation of actions whose performance is not visible to baby. However, the actions must already be within the infant's existing behavioral repertoire, begins new sounds and sights.
5	Use of new means (discovered by chance) to obtain new ends. Tertiary circular reactions. Deliberate variation of means to an end.	Object searched for after being visibly displaced from one hidden place to another, but not when invisibly displaced.	Understanding relation of objects to one another is completed, except for absence of inclusion of self as one of the objects in space, and absence of mental representation of objects in space.	Systematic imitation of new models. Infants can imitate actions even though they cannot see themselves make the action.
6	Insightful problem solving. New means discovered to attain a new end, even in absence of chance discovery. Internalized trial and error.	Correct, systemic search for object after multiple *invisible* displacements.	Infant relates self to other objects in space. Representation and imagination of relative position of objects.	Deferred imitation.

did not explain what he thought produces décalage. He wrote about each cognitive domain separately—there is a chapter on object permanence, one on space, and a book on imitation—and he only rarely discussed the synchrony or asynchrony of development across domains. However, using the term stage to refer to each newly attained sensorimotor level implies that changes in cognitive capacity are consistent and fairly widespread across abilities.

Challenges to Piaget's Theory

In many ways, Piaget's theory of cognitive development is unrivaled in elegance and scope, and there is empirical corroboration for many of his proposed developmental achievements as well as for the sequences in which they occur. His theory has served as the foundation for the study of infant cognition. The topics Piaget identified, including infants' conceptions of objects, number, time, space, and causality, have been principal subjects for research in infant cognition ever since Piaget identified them, and perhaps no other theory in infancy has undergone such intense scrutiny. The inevitable result of such attention, however, is the emergence of a body of work that takes issue with Piaget's formulations, assumptions, and observations.

One of Piaget's basic tenets is that cognition is rooted in action, without which infants would be unable to derive meaning from sensory and perceptual events (which, in Piaget's view, are disconnected and uncoordinated in early infancy). However, in grounding all knowledge in motor activity, Piaget mistakenly ignored the vital contributions of perceptual and sensory activity to representation and knowledge. Décarie (1969), for example, found that limbless children (whose mothers had taken thalidomide during the first trimester of pregnancy—see Chapter 4) develop a normal cognitive life despite the absence of normal sensorimotor experience through their infancy. In addition, Piagetian theory does not give sufficient credit to the remarkable sensory and organizational capacities of newborns and young infants. For example, as we learned in Chapter 6, the newborn's perceptual world appears to be multimodally integrated, rather than composed of disconnected information coming from the different senses.

A second theoretical issue in Piagetian studies is whether the attainment of one stage in a given domain guarantees that the infant is in the same stage of development in another domain: Is mental development synchronous or sequential? Décalage is neither rare nor small in magnitude, and so it is necessary to examine this aspect of Piaget's theory critically. For instance, the Užgiris-Hunt (1975) *Ordinal Scales of Psychological Development* attempt to categorize the infant's overall performance into one of Piaget's six sensorimotor stages. However, Užgiris and Hunt (1975) found so many décalages while constructing the *Ordinal Scales* they were forced to conclude that progress in each area of cognitive development may be independent of progress in the others. For this reason, they opted to publish six scales of sensorimotor intelligence rather than a single scale, and they reported only modest correlations in individual performance across these scales, a point we return to later.

Perhaps the greatest empirical challenges to Piaget's theory of sensorimotor development, however, come from findings indicating that capacities for mental representation of the physical world appear much earlier in development than Piaget supposed. Two lines of research contribute to this conclusion. The first is work showing that infants' capacity for perceiving and representing the physical world is much better developed than Piaget ever thought. He was limited in his conclusions by his methods. The second is work showing that infants can imitate facial expressions of others within minutes after birth, indicating that a rudimentary capacity to represent the external world mightf be present at birth. We discuss each of these lines of research in turn.

According to Piaget, infants' understanding of objects and their permanence develops across the first two years of life. Around 4 months of age, infants can retrieve an object that is partly covered. At 8 months or so, infants can retrieve an object that is fully covered, but if the location of the hidden object is switched across trials, infants search at the first place they found the object (A) rather than at the correct location (B;

the "A-not-B error"). Later, at 12 months, infants can find objects hidden in different locations but they have difficulty with invisible displacements, such as when objects are moved to a new location without the infant seeing the object (for example, when hidden in a hand). In these typical Piagetian tasks, infants show these behaviors very reliably: There is no question that infants respond as *if* they do not completely understand object permanence. However, when infants are tested in a task that does not require active search, they appear to have a greater understanding of the continued existence of objects even when they are out of view. The first study to test infants' object permanence using looking time was conducted by Baillargeon, Spelke, and Wasserman (1985). In their study, infants viewed a screen that rotated towards and away from them (Figure 7.1). Following habituation to the screen, a box was placed in the display area such that, as the screen rotated away from the infant, the box was hidden from view. In one event, the screen stopped at the location of the now-hidden box. This event was called the "possible" event because if you believe the box continues to exist, the screen would have to stop. In a second event, the screen did not stop: It continued to rotate away from the infant, apparently passing through the space occupied by the now-hidden box. This event was called the "impossible" event as two objects cannot occupy the same space at the same time. Baillargeon and her colleagues found that 5-month-old infants looked significantly longer to the impossible than the possible event, suggesting that infants had an expectation that the box continued to exist even though it was out of sight.

Using this variant of the habituation-dishabituation method, called the **Violation of Expectation** paradigm, Baillargeon and others have conducted a number of studies testing infants' understanding of objects and their physical properties (Baillargeon, Li, Gertner, & Wu, 2010). For example, infants respond with more looking when an object passes behind a screen with a window in it but the object does not appear in the window compared to when it does appear there (Aguiar & Baillargeon, 2002). Also, infants anticipate the trajectory of an object when it disappears and then reappears behind a screen by moving their eyes to the point of reappearance before the object arrives there (Bertenthal, Longo, & Kenny, 2007).

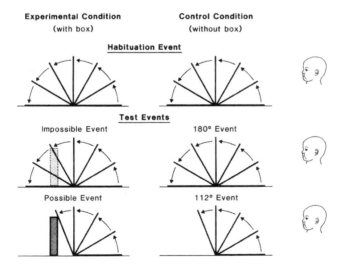

Fig. 7.1 Impossible and possible test events (left) used by Baillargeon et al. to test infants' understanding of object permanence. In the experimental condition (left), the screen appeared to pass through the box in the impossible event but it stops at the location of the box in the possible event. In the control condition (right), the screen moved in a similar manner to the test events but the box was not present. (From Baillargeon, Spelke, & Wasserman, 1985. Copyright © 1987 by the American Psychological Association. Reproduced with permission. The use of APA information does not imply endorsement by APA.)

Moreover, 4-month-old infants also remember the location of a hidden object, such that, if someone goes to retrieve an object from behind one of two screens, infants look at the screen where the object is hidden (Ruffman, Slade, & Redman, 2005). As infants mature, they gain additional understandings about relations among objects, such as that objects provide support, into which containers different sized objects fit, and the interactions between people and objects (Hespos & Baillargeon, 2001; Poulin-Dubois, Sodian, Metz, Tilden, & Schoeppner, 2007; Wang, Baillargeon, & Paterson, 2005).

Baillargeon, Li, et al. (2010) suggest that infants are born with specific learning mechanisms that enable rapid acquisition of knowledge about event categories (events in which an object collides with another object, is hidden by another object, or supports another object) and object categories (animate objects, inanimate objects that move, and inanimate objects that do not move). Infants first learn about the event or object concept as a generalized whole, and with experience gradually accumulate knowledge about variables that are relevant to the concept. For example, at 2½ months of age, infants' understanding of collision is relatively simple. They expect any moving object to displace any stationary object on impact, and they appear surprised when this does not happen. By about 6 months of age, infants can understand that a large moving object will, on impact, displace a stationary object further than a small moving object. By 8 months, infants begin to take the stationary object's shape into account in determining whether it will be displaced by a moving object. Similar knowledge progressions are evident in infants' understanding of occlusion and support events.

This nativistic idea, in addition to the inferences Baillargeon and others draw from their empirical work, are not without controversy. Some critics feel that these types of experiments are not well controlled or that the interpretations extend too far beyond the data (Cohen & Cashon, 2006). A lingering question is why we find different results based on task such as looking versus searching. Other researchers have tried to address this methodological question, and interesting findings have emerged about infant search skills. For example, infants successfully find an object in the dark before finding it hidden under a cloth, suggesting that infants do not forget the object exists but instead they have difficulty integrating the actions involved in removing the cloth to then find the object (Shinskey & Munakata, 2003). Also, if weights are placed on infants' arms, they do not show search errors, suggesting that causing infants to slow the reach planning process (because their arms are heavy they are slower to move) allows infants to plan a reach to the correct location (Riviere & Lecuyer, 2008). Thus, the predominant explanation for search errors might be immaturity of the prefrontal cortex, which governs inhibition and infants' ability to plan a reach (Call, 2001; Lew, Hopkins, Owen, & Green, 2007) rather than an immaturity of motor skills per se.

Infants' imitation of facial expressions within the first days of life also leads to the conclusion that a capacity for representation is present earlier than suggested by Piaget. In their first experiment, Meltzoff and Moore (1977) observed 12- to 21-day-old infants' responses to an adult modeling a mouth movement—tongue protrusion, mouth opening, and lip pursing. The infants imitated the actions (Figure 7.2). To imitate these actions, infants needed to be able to perceive the gesture (remember, their vision is not very clear at this age, see Chapter 4), know how to produce the action, and more importantly match an action they see (the action made by the other person) with one they feel (the action they are making themselves). This requires representational abilities. This study was contested, in part, because Piaget asserted that infants do not imitate until the fourth sub-stage of sensorimotor development (8–12 months of age) and do not develop representational abilities until the sixth sub-stage (18–24 months). However, over 35 years later with 25 replications from 13 independent laboratories, it is generally accepted that imitation and representational abilities *are* possible at birth (Meltzoff, 2011; but see Jones, 2009; Ray & Heyes, 2011).

The presence of imitation at birth, according to Meltzoff (2011), is the starting point for infants to learn about their social worlds. As they develop, infants can remember actions across longer time periods (e.g., 1 week), use imitation to identify people with whom they have previously interacted (are you the person who did "this" before?), and are more interested in people who imitate them, suggesting a

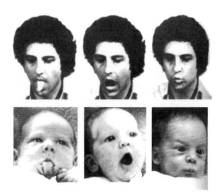

Fig. 7.2 These photographs show 2- to 3-week-old infants imitating. (From Meltzoff & Moore, 1977; reproduced with permission.)

bidirectional process (Meltzoff, 2007). In short, infants come into the world prepared to interact with those around them and these early imitative capacities set the stage for mature social interactions that have a foundation in cognition (Box 7.1).

Box 7.1   Science in Translation: Does a Conscience Develop from Copying Mom Pouring Tea or Feeding a Bear?

As we show in the text, developmental scientists have long argued about the age at which infants are first able to imitate others, not least because the ability to imitate, in the view of some theorists, demands the capacity to represent another's behavior mentally and then attempt to match it with one's own behavior. This debate has kept focus on the cognitive prerequisites for imitation, but imitation has also been of interest to psychologists studying the development of social and moral behavior. Freud was one of the first theorists to propose that children began to behave morally because they emulate respected adults (particularly fathers, in Freud's view).

Forman, Aksan, and Kochanska (2004) showed that there is a link between imitation in infancy and later indices of conscience in 3-year-olds. In the course of teaching their 14- and 22-month-old infants to clean a table, participate in a tea party, and feed a bear, mothers were asked to model actions for their children to imitate. At each age, coders made note of how well the infants imitated their mothers' behavior and how eager they were to do so. Then, when the children were 33 and 45 months old, three aspects of conscience development were measured. Two involved adherence to rules when not under adult surveillance (not touching a prohibited toy when mother left the room; not cheating in a rigged game where it was impossible to win without cheating), and one measured guilt in terms of the amount of distress shown when the toddlers were led to believe that they had damaged valuable objects.

As Forman and his colleagues predicted, the infants who imitated more, later showed more conscience (both internalized conduct and guilt) than preschool-aged peers who had not imitated as much or as eagerly. These associations were not explained by differences in compliance during a clean-up task, suggesting that readiness to imitate was a precursor of later conscience, and that moral development could be promoted if infants are encouraged to imitate others, perhaps especially their parents.

We have seen only two examples—object permanence and imitation—from the tremendous amount of research suggesting that Piaget seriously underestimated infants' perceptual and cognitive capacities. Indeed, Haith and Benson (1998) cite many studies that illustrate that infants' competencies in understanding temporally ordered events, means–ends relations, space, causality, and number are in play much earlier in development than Piaget predicted. In their view, this has led to the emergence of a variety of "mini theories" that purport to explain the developmental course of specific infant competencies in specific domains of development using very specific methodologies. Perhaps this was inevitable in light of the common criticism that Piaget's theory was too general and too all-encompassing to explain the whole of infant cognition. However, Haith and Benson (1998) argued that such specialization and over-focus on specific infant abilities has led post-Piagetian researchers to be more concerned with demonstrating the precocity of young infants at the expense of understanding how particular abilities develop. Today we continue to know more about *what* infants can do *when* and less about *how* these abilities develop.

INFANT LEARNING

In the preceding part of this chapter, we discussed Piaget and post-Piagetian perspectives on normative cognitive development in infancy and the idea of **qualitative** stages that all infants experience. Qualitative explanations of development involve change in structure or organization, such that there is a particular sequence that is followed and it is often difficult to revert back to an earlier stage. Our goal was to describe how infants may come to understand the world on the basis of their biological inheritance and the common experiences they have interacting with the world. In the next parts of the chapter, we introduce more **quantitative** approaches to the study of cognition in infancy. Quantitative explanations focus on changes in amount or degree; for example, a behavior becomes more efficient or refined but is fundamentally the same behavior guided by the same structure. Here we focus on learning and information-processing perspectives, approaches that interpret infant cognitive development in terms of the acquisition of associations and the application of processing mechanisms to bring information from the environment into the cognitive system. When we refer to these processes, we mean the formation and encoding of information. In Chapter 8, we discuss what happens to that information afterward, that is in memory and conceptual representation. Like Piaget's system, these theories propose rules that apply to all infants; for example, the laws of learning (see immediately below) are presumably universal and followed by all individuals and all species. Unlike Piaget's emphasis on normative group-level development, these two approaches concentrate on individual differences in cognitive functioning early in life.

Learning and information processing are believed to underlie the infant's slow but steady acquisition of knowledge about the world. After all, learning reflects underlying brain plasticity and change. In Chapter 3, we introduced the basic concepts and procedures behind learning paradigms (such as operant conditioning) and behind two components of information processing (habituation and novelty responsiveness), also showing how each is applied as a methodological technique to study infancy. Here, we discuss learning and information processing again, this time as functional components of infant mental life. Toward that end, we review research on their early emergence, individual variation and reliability, and patterns of developmental change.

Classical and Operant Learning and Imitation

Recall from Chapter 3 that **classical conditioning** capitalizes on the existence of stimulus–response relations built into the organism, as when a loud sound elicits an eye blink. The loud sound is called the **unconditioned stimulus** (UCS; because it elicits a response in the absence of any learning or conditioning), and the response it gives rise to is called the **unconditioned response** (UCR). In classical conditioning, a **conditioned stimulus** (CS), a stimulus that is initially neutral and does not elicit the response, is paired with a UCS. After repeated pairings of the CS with the UCS, the CS takes on properties of the UCS and elicits a **conditioned response** (CR), like the UCR. That is, learning by association takes place.

Several infant reflexes (UCRs) lend themselves readily to classical conditioning, and even newborns learn to make associations and subsequently make use of what they have learned. Fifer and his colleagues (2010), for example, conditioned eye blink responses (CR) in newborn infants to a tone (CS) that was paired with an air puff (UCS) directed at the infants' eyelid. Infants in the experimental group, in which the tone was a reliable predictor of an air puff, made increasingly more anticipatory eye movements than infants in the control group, in which the tones and puffs were presented at random (Figure 7.3). Most

(A)

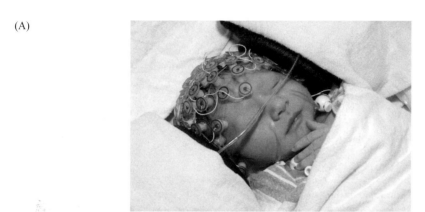

(B)

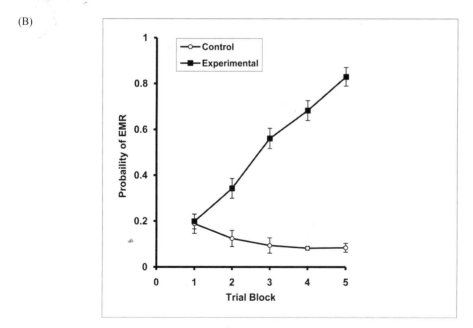

Fig. 7.3 (A) A newborn infant being tested for learning of the contingency between a tone and an air puff. The tube under the infants' eyes delivered puff of air; (B) The resulting eye blink response (labeled EMR) for the group in which the tone predicted the air puff (Experimental) compared to the group in which there was no contingency between the tone and the air puff (Control). (From Fifer et al., 2010; reproduced with permission).

striking about this experiment was that the infants were asleep during the procedure! Fifer et al. (2010) suggest that the ability to learn while asleep is an important component for helping babies adapt to their new and highly stimulating postnatal environment.

Operant conditioning involves associations between one's own action and the consequence of that action. Actions that are **reinforced** (or rewarded) are more likely to be repeated in the future, whereas actions that are **punished** are less likely to be repeated. The major difference between operant conditioning and classical conditioning is that in classical conditioning a previously neutral signal comes to elicit a response through association, whereas in operant conditioning the probability of a naturally occurring response is increased by reinforcement and decreased by punishment, stimuli that happen *after* the response.

In Chapter 3, we discussed several different operant conditioning paradigms that tap different voluntarily controlled motor activities, such as sucking, head turning, or kicking. Like classical conditioning, operant conditioning is a fundamental process of learning that is present from birth. Vouloumanos and Werker (2007) provided an example of operant conditioning in 1- to 4-day-old infants using human speech and complex non-speech stimuli as contingent reinforcers of infant sucking. The experimenters first measured the infants' baseline rates of sucking, and they then determined the average interval between infants' spontaneous sucking bursts. Next, they presented the infants with the speech and non-speech stimuli on alternate trials. Infants could maintain the stimulus if they sucked at a rate that was 80% faster than their baseline. Most infants in the study sucked more to hear real human speech as compared to the complex non-speech stimulus, showing that speech is an effective reward for infant learning. The results also suggest that infants come into the world with a bias for listening to human speech.

Imitation or **observational learning** is a third and particularly efficient way to learn. During infancy, imitation provides a mechanism for acquiring information of all sorts—just by watching or listening. How early infants imitate and what they can imitate are significant research issues, as we learned when discussing the infant's ability to imitate facial movements such as tongue protrusions, mouth openings, and lip pursing (Figure 7.2). However, the reliability and interpretation of early infant imitation have not been without controversy (Jones, 2009; Ray & Heyes, 2011). Developmental studies have shown that imitations of tongue protrusions and mouth openings naturally decrease over the first three months of life and then reappear at 6 months of age along with other types of imitation (Masur, 2006; Ray & Heyes, 2011). Why would imitation of facial gestures decline over time if they reflect a capacity for imitation that is present from birth? Maratos (1998) proposed that infants' early imitation of facial gestures is possible because infants are born with a preconception of the human face (a point we discussed in Chapter 6), an innate capacity for perceiving the equivalence between the facial movements of others and movements of their own face, and the ability to represent the human face at a purely sensory level. Thus, it is possible that early infant imitation could represent an effort to communicate on an emotional level, and the decline in facial imitation takes place because other, more complex effective means of communication (smiling and vocal and gestural imitation) emerge with time. Alternative explanations for the changes in imitation appeal to learning arguments: Infants are more likely to imitate as they experience a range of actions to imitate and as they experience being imitated by another person (Ray & Heyes, 2011). Finally, it is possible that mirror neurons play a role in imitation. **Mirror neurons** are neurons that respond when someone observes another person making an action, typically with an object (Del Giudice, Manera, & Keysers, 2009). The neurons that fire are the same neurons that would fire if the person were actually doing the action. Research with nonhuman primates suggests that mirror neurons help translate observed actions into one's own actions, and watching others' actions, as infants would do in imitation contexts, may help tune the perception–action system to prepare infants to make the actions in the future (Gallese & Rochat, 2013). Regardless of the underlying mechanisms, imitation is an important component in infants' learning and, with development in perceptual skills and motor control, infants' opportunities to learn from imitating expand considerably (Paulus, Hunnius, Vissers, & Bekkering, 2011; Yang, Sidman, & Bushnell, 2010).

Limiting Conditions on Learning

Even when necessary cognitive capacities are present and the learning task is well designed, many factors influence the course of learning in infants. Two conditions that might limit learning are prominent. One is behavioral state (Chapter 5). In the case of visual learning, at least the first steps in learning require that the infant be alert long enough to perceive a signal and to respond to it appropriately (as we discussed earlier, some types of learning can occur while infants are sleeping). Long ago, Papoušek and Bernstein (1969) demonstrated that the extent infants could learn through conditioning depended on infant state. They found that learning took place most readily during periods of quiet alertness; not surprisingly, less learning took place when infants were drowsy or crying.

The association used in learning is another limiting condition. It was once assumed that any stimulus–response association could be learned. We now know that this is not the case. Even with older infants, among whom learning is quicker, it is by no means the rule that classical or operant conditioning can be established with any stimulus, that any behavior can be strengthened through operant reinforcement, or that any act can be imitated. Thus, there are natural constraints on learning, and this means that researchers must carefully design their attempts to evaluate the infant's ability to learn. Failures to establish learning could indicate that a particular association cannot be learned, not that learning itself is impossible. Researchers have to determine whether the infant is physically capable of the response demanded and can perceive the stimulus. Ethologists (Hinde & Stevenson-Hinde, 1973) and learning theorists (Seligman, 1970) have argued that certain associations are "prepared," in that they are biologically more appropriate than others, and so are learned more readily. Blass and his coworkers (1984) claimed that their success in classically conditioning newborns in the first days of life reflected their choice of an association between a natural mode of parent–infant communication (facial touch) and a desirable nutrient reinforcer (sugar). Certain stimuli and responses appear to go together naturally, and it is easier to learn to associate such naturally co-occurring contingencies.

Before concluding this discussion, it is essential to point out that the fact that infants can learn does not guarantee that they always make use of all these learning devices in their daily life. This is a good example of the competence–performance distinction we raised in Chapter 3.

INFANT INFORMATION PROCESSING

Conditioning techniques provide reasonably clear data about learning because babies respond actively and voluntarily and clearly communicate their functional abilities. However, conditioning often takes time and is relatively difficult to implement. We can also learn something about infants' cognition simply by observing them as they regard the world and process information about it. Information processing tells us about the activities infants use in representing and manipulating information mentally; it is not a comprehensive theory of cognition or of development but, rather, an approach to studying mental processes (Bornstein & Colombo, 2012).

Habituation and Novelty Responsiveness

As we described in Chapter 3, an infant will typically orient and attend to a novel stimulus, but if that stimulus remains available to view, the infant's attention to it will usually diminish. **Habituation** is the decline in responding to a stimulus that is available continuously or is presented repeatedly. If the infant is then tested with both familiar and novel stimuli after habituation, the infant will tend to look at the familiar stimulus less than at the novel stimulus. The greater attention to the new stimulus is called **novelty responsiveness**. Habituation and novelty responsiveness must reflect (at least) two component processes: The construction of some sort of central mental representation of the stimulus material, and the continuing comparison between the stimulus being presented and that mental representation. The infant's disinterest in the now familiar stimulus presumably indicates that the infant has learned something about the stimulus, and the infant's novelty response to the new stimulus presumably indicates that the infant can discriminate between the new and the familiar stimulus. If the external stimulus and representation match—giving evidence that the baby has come to "know" the stimulus—there is little reason to continue to look; however, mismatches appear to maintain the infant's attention so that a novel stimulus, introduced after habituation to the (now) familiar stimulus, typically re-excites the infant's attention. Habituation therefore gives a strong face valid indication that it has something to do with information processing (Bornstein & Colombo, 2012).

Three additional points help to confirm an information-processing interpretation of habituation. First, older infants habituate more efficiently than younger infants (Figure 7.4). Second, infants of the same age require more time to encode information from a complex stimulus than from a simple one. Caron and Caron (1969) demonstrated this effect clearly. They showed three groups of 3½-month-olds four different multicolored geometric designs serially on four trials followed by five repeated presentations of either 2 × 2, 12 × 12, or 24 × 24 checkerboards. All three groups maintained a high level of looking on the initial four trials, during which stimulation varied; all three groups looked less on the repetition trials, but the three groups declined differentially, and habituation clearly reflected stimulus complexity. Following habituation, infants showed a novelty response to a new stimulus introduced on the next three trials. Third, habituation appears to be a central process: Slater, Morison, and Rose (1983) showed that newborn babies who habituated to a stimulus while viewing it through only one eye later showed recognition when viewing the same stimulus through the other eye. This interocular transfer indicates that information about the stimulus is processed centrally.

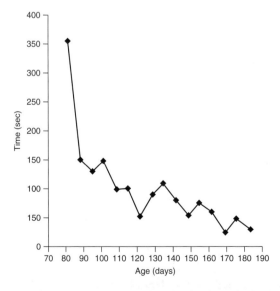

Fig. 7.4 Total accumulated looking time to reach a constant habituation criterion in one infant studied weekly between her second and seventh months. The time required to habituate is long in early infancy and declines steadily and rapidly toward middle infancy. (After Bornstein, Pécheux, & Lécuyer, 1988.)

Individual Variation and Stability in Infant Learning and Information Processing

Learning and information processing give good evidence of mental functioning in infancy. The next logical questions are: Do some infants learn or process stimulus information more quickly, efficiently, or completely than others? Is infant performance reliable? How do learning and information processing change and develop over the course of infancy? Do learning, habituation, or novelty responsiveness inform us about other cognitive differences among infants? Do they tell us anything about future childhood cognitive capacities? It turns out that habituation has been studied most with respect to these questions, novelty responsiveness less, and classical and operant conditioning and imitation least.

Considerable research has been conducted to date on two important measurement concerns with respect to information processing, namely, distinguishing individual variation among infants and determining whether individual differences constitute reliable (replicable) characteristics of infants. As we see later in this chapter, individual variation among infants may say quite a lot about their future mental life.

There is ample evidence, as we have learned, that infants habituate and show novelty responsiveness even in the first days of life, just as they may be conditioned. Importantly, individual infants differ considerably in habituating and reacting to novelty; that is, they show **individual variation** (Arterberry & Bornstein, 2002; Bornstein & Colombo, 2012). Other things being equal, infants vary with respect to the amount of looking or rate of decrement in attention. For example, some 3-month-olds who are shown images of animals or vehicles habituate in seconds, whereas others may take minutes (Arterberry & Bornstein, 2001). Likewise, babies vary in their response to a new stimulus following familiarization. Some show novelty responsiveness (giving more than 50% of their total looking to the novel stimulus relative to the familiar one), some perform at chance levels, and some give a familiarity preference (Arterberry & Bornstein, 2002; see Figure 7.5).

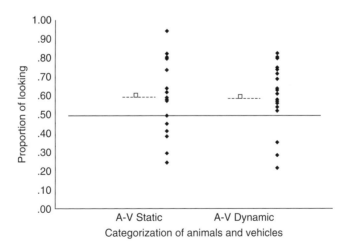

Fig. 7.5 Novelty responsiveness in 3-month-old infants in two experiments in which infants viewed images of animals and vehicles, either in static images or in moving (dynamic) point-light displays. Each diamond represents an individual infants' proportion of looking to the novel stimulus compared to the total amount of looking in the test phase following habituation. The open squares show the group average. Values greater than .50 indicate that infants looked longer to the novel stimulus. (From Arterberry & Bornstein, 2002; reproduced with permission.)

Qualitatively speaking, infants appear to show (at least) three styles in habituating. Bornstein and Benasich (1986) identified linear/exponential decrease, increase-decrease, and fluctuating patterns of habituation among 5-month-olds shown either a single face or a single geometric pattern. Figure 7.6 shows an example of each kind of baby. The baby in the top panel looks a lot at the stimulus at first and then rapidly stops looking; this baby exemplifies a rapid habituator who shows a **linear or exponential decrease** in looking at the stimulus. The baby in the middle panel looks only a little at first, but then

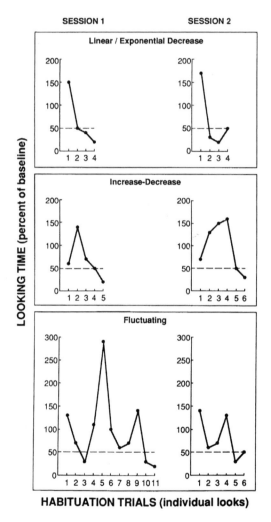

Fig. 7.6 Results of two infant-control habituation sessions for three infants who were shown a single female face wearing an affectively neutral expression. Individual looks are plotted as a percentage of the mean of the first two looks, called the baseline, and set equal to 100%. These infants illustrate three main patterns of habituation and the short-term reliability of habituation patterns. The infant at the top showed a linear or exponential decrease from baseline to a 50% habituation criterion in two sessions; the infant in the middle first looked more, then rapidly habituated to criterion both times. The infant at the bottom showed a fluctuating looking-time function in each session before reaching the habituation criterion. (In these plots, data points are rounded to the nearest 10%.) Exponential decrease habituators require significantly less accumulated looking and fewer exposures to the stimulus than increase-decrease or fluctuating habituators. (From Bornstein & Benasich, 1986; reproduced with permission.)

appears to become interested in the stimulus before finally habituating; this baby illustrates a habituator whose looking **increases then decreases**. The looking curve of the baby in the bottom panel seems to **fluctuate** before looking stabilizes at habituation. Linear/exponential decrease babies constituted about 60% of a sample of 5-month-olds shown a single stimulus; increase-decrease babies about 10% of the sample; and fluctuating babies about 30% of the sample. Importantly, linear/exponential babies required approximately half as much exposure to a stimulus to habituate as increase-decrease or fluctuating babies.

These individual differences in habituation also appear to show moderate **short-term reliability**. That is, given the same testing conditions, a baby is likely to habituate in approximately the same way on different occasions spaced reasonably close together in time (Brian, Landry, Szatmari, Niccols, & Bryson, 2003; Lavoie & Desrochers, 2002). Thus, different infants tend to show considerable variation in how they habituate and recover looking, yet the same infants tend to process information in a reasonably consistent fashion on different occasions. Variation and reliability are important because they say that, to some degree at least, infants differ in response sensitivity and those differences are in the infant rather than the procedure, the stimulus, or the situation. These conclusions, in turn, allow us to have confidence when measures of habituation and novelty responsiveness are used in other ways, as we will see below.

Developmental Changes in Learning and Information Processing

Newborns (and even fetuses) learn, but this does not mean that learning before or after birth is complete; developmental changes in learning continue during and after infancy. The nervous system matures rapidly during the first postnatal months, permitting longer periods of alertness and better organization of infantile state (Chapter 5). By 3 months of age, infants are readily conditioned. By 6 months, almost all the physiological immaturities that might restrict attention, perception, and information processing have disappeared, further facilitating learning. In addition, the child's growing curiosity ensures repeated opportunities to learn.

Indeed, as they age, infants change impressively in how they learn, although longitudinal studies of infant conditioning are rare. Hoffman, Cohen, and de Vido (1985) compared the performance of 8-month-old infants directly with that of adults in classical conditioning of an eye blink (CR), normally elicited by a tap to the flat region of skin between the eyebrows (UCS). A tone was the CS. Infants acquired the conditioned association more slowly than adults, and the latency of their conditioned responses was slower (even though the latency of the unconditioned response was faster in infants).

Habituation also improves with age. One of the first papers on infant habituation ever published documented this increasing efficiency (Fantz, 1964), and, as we saw in Figure 3.1, the duration of infants' peak look decreases as they age. Moreover, the cumulative amount of time needed to habituate to a stimulus decreases dramatically over the first year of life (Figure 7.4). Several mechanisms could account for individual differences in infant habituation rates and for developmental improvements in these rates. Speed of information processing is one such mechanism. Rapid information processing presumably accounts for mental agility and quickness, whereas slow processing is associated with deficits in IQ (Colombo & Mitchell, 2009). Another possible mechanism is short-term memory. Variation in the ability to remember stimuli presented over time might account for variation in habituation and novelty responsiveness. Rose and her colleagues (2011) found that infants' performance on a visual recognition memory task at 7 months predicted their performance on a variety of cognitive tasks at 11 years of age (Box 7.2). It is intuitive that short-term memory capacity would be implicated in Rose's findings that infants who performed well on a memory task at 7 months showed strong cognitive performance at 11 years of age given that habituation cannot take place without memory of the stimulus. A third possible mechanism is the infant's ability to deploy attention efficiently, focusing on relevant stimulus features and inhibiting attention to irrelevant stimuli (Barbaro, Chiba, & Deák, 2011). Finally, neural maturation could play a role. Specifically, during habituation and dishabituation, different areas of the cortex are involved (Nakano, Watanabe, Homae, & Taga, 2009). For example, 3-month-olds habituated to an auditory stimulus initially showed global cortical activation; the temporal and frontal areas both showed high levels of responsiveness. As the habituation phase progressed and the stimulus became familiar, activity was specific to the temporal cortex, the region where auditory information is processed. Following habituation, presentation of a novel stimulus activated the prefrontal cortex in addition to the temporal cortex, suggesting that the prefrontal cortex is involved in perceiving novelty. Of course, any or all of these mechanisms working together may be involved in infants' developmental advances.

Box 7.2   Set For Life? Prematurity and Later Cognitive Functioning

Newborns delivered before their due date are at risk for lower cognitive functioning, including delayed language development, trouble in school, and lower scores on IQ assessments. Rose and her colleagues (2008) investigated the role that early information processing differences between term and preterm infants might play in these later deficits. Infants were assessed on five aspects of infant cognition: recognition memory, recall memory, encoding speed, representational competence (tested in a cross-modal transfer paradigm), and attention. When the children were 2 or 3 years of age, they were assessed for their mental development using the Bayley Scales of Infant Mental Development. Performance on the information processing measures, specifically attention and encoding speed, accounted for the deficits in mental development later in life. Thus, attention and encoding speed are impacted by prematurity, which in turn affects other aspects of cognitive development, such as memory, representation and mental functioning at age 2 and 3 years.

In learning, and especially in information processing, researchers have developed techniques that allow them some access to the mind of the infant. Very young babies learn and imitate, habituate attention to familiar stimuli, and recover attention to novel stimulation. Individual differences are notable in all of these processes, and these processes become more efficient over the course of infancy. We now consider the implications of these mental processes in infancy for cognitive functioning in childhood and beyond.

INFANT MENTAL LIFE AND THE QUESTION OF VALIDITY

To this point, we have reviewed two schools of thought about infant cognition and learning. The school associated with Piaget describes qualitative stages of development in early thinking and stresses universal processes of mental life in infancy. A second school, which is associated with learning and information-processing theories, describes the development of thinking abilities in quantitative terms and emphasizes individual variation. With these views in mind, we now return to the validity questions posed at the outset of the chapter. How do we know what infants know? Does what infants know tell us anything about their later development? We think that we know something about infants' performance on tasks and in situations that seem to require thinking or intelligence.

Recall from our discussion of the first baby biographies (Chapter 3) that in the last quarter of the 19th century, many attentive observers of children documented the basics of infant development. Infant biographies provided a wealth of ideas for items that could be adopted for use in "intelligence" tests for babies. Moreover, the evidence developed from baby biographies had two important implications. First, baby biographies showed that infants of different ages were competent at different tasks. Consequently, the items in infant tests could be graded for difficulty. For example, picking up an object from a table is an easier action to plan and execute than pulling a placemat toward you to bring an object closer so you can pick it up. Second, baby biographies gave evidence of considerable individual variation among infants of the same age. Many early investigators developed standardized tasks for infants that were graded in difficulty by age, and for years their sequences, scales, and schedules of infant behavior proved valuable in defining normal development. The best-known and most widely adopted tests have been the *Bayley Scales of Infant Development*, although the Užgiris-Hunt *Ordinal Scales of Psychological Development* also merit discussion.

Beginning in the 1920s, Nancy Bayley endeavored to measure mental and motor growth from infancy. As part of the Berkeley Growth Study, Bayley (1933) published the *California First Year Mental Scale*. She based this scale on the performance of middle-income children observed monthly from birth through 1½ years of age. In the 1960s, Bayley (1969) published a major revision and restandardization of this effort, called the *Bayley Scales of Infant Development* (BSID), and this assessment has been revised and restandardized to become the BSID-II (Bayley, 1993; Black & Matula, 2000). The BSID are divided into a *Mental Development Index* (the MDI consists of 178 items) and a *Psychomotor Development Index* (the PDI consists of 111 items). The BSID assess motor, sensation, perception, cognition, memory, language, and social behavior in infants over the first 2½ years of life (Table 5.2).

When Piaget was eventually translated into English in the 1950s, his work began to affect research in many areas, including infant intelligence testing. The best-known infant test to have developed from the Piagetian approach is the Užgiris-Hunt (1975) *Ordinal Scales of Psychological Development*. Their scales assume hierarchical relations among infant achievements at different levels, in that they consider later, higher-order accomplishments to encompass and subsume earlier, lower-order ones. Furthermore, their scales are not tied to chronological age, but the succession of tasks within any sequence is believed to follow an intrinsically logical order. The *Ordinal Scales* consist of six sets of distinct sequences appropriate for infants ranging from 1 to about 24 months of age. One scale is concerned with the infant's increasing knowledge of the existence of objects outside the immediate context, based on infant visual pursuit and object permanence. A second assesses means–end relations, such as the use of implements to obtain objects out of reach. A third concentrates on imitation of vocalization and gesture. A fourth charts anticipatory behaviors for identifying the infant's comprehension of causality. A fifth follows the infant's ability to track and locate objects and, therefore, to appreciate space. A sixth evaluates the changing role of toys as extensions of the infant, as objects of curiosity, and eventually, as separate functional units.

Bayley and Užgiris and Hunt were by no means alone in their efforts to develop infant tests (Nugent, 2010). During the first part of the 20th century, many others, both in the United States (Cattell, 1940/1960; Escalona & Corman, 1969; Gesell, 1945, 1954; Shirley, 1933) and elsewhere (in England, Griffiths, 1954), worked toward the development of assessment instruments for infants. We have selected the Bayley and Užgiris-Hunt tests for special consideration here in part because of their historical primacy, in part because of the two traditions they represent, and in part because they have been used most frequently in research on infant mental development.

Traditional Infant Tests and Their Predictive Validity

When researchers want to assess the validity of an IQ measure, for example among college students, they ask how well IQ scores correlate with, say, achievement in college. (The answer is moderately well.) In other words, with adults, and even older children, the degree to which a test measures what it was designed to measure is assessed by comparing test scores with independent measures of achievement in the desired domain. In infants, however, there is no definitive or obvious concurrent external index of cognitive performance with which to compare test performance. The validity of infant tests has more typically been assessed by comparing infants' performance early in life with their performance years later as children or even adults. Logically, researchers argue, if individuals who perform well on infant tests do well on standardized IQ tests as children, then the infant tests must be telling us something about "intelligence" in infancy. This is the general approach to assessing the **predictive validity** of infant measures.

Bayley (1949) conducted a classic longitudinal study in this regard, and her results exemplify both the findings and far-reaching conclusions that characterize much of the early tradition in infant testing. Bayley followed 27 children from 3 months to 18 years of age, correlating their BSID scores in infancy and early childhood with their intelligence test scores in young adulthood. Figure 7.7 shows her results. As can be seen, she found essentially no correlation between infants' and children's test performance in the first 3 to 4 years of life with their intelligence test performance at 18 years. Only after children reached about 5 years of age did the association between child scores and eventual adult scores emerge, subsequently attaining a very high level between 11 and 18 years. The predictive validity of the Užgiris-Hunt *Ordinal Scales* is not better, except after 18 to 20 months, when a variety of scales appears to predict IQ (Užgiris, 1989).

The repeated finding that there is little or no prediction of mental development from infancy to later childhood may be a function of limitations inherent to the traditional standardized tests. The kinds of items measured in young infants in traditional infant tests such as the Bayley and Užgiris-Hunt largely tap sensory capacities, motor achievements, and affective responses such as orienting, reaching, and smiling. For an older child, very different items are used in evaluating intelligence—normally skills related to language, reasoning, and memory. Thus, the underlying constructs that are compared bear little or no

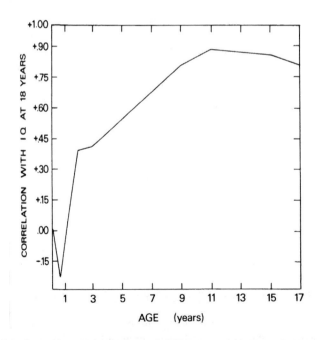

Fig. 7.7 The correlation of cognitive test performance at different ages with IQ at 18 years of age. The correlation between test performance in the first 3 or 4 years of life and IQ test performance in maturity is low; the correlation after 5 to 6 years is substantially higher. (After Bayley, 1949.)

conceptual relation to each other. In essence, children are asked such different questions across developmental periods that there is little reason to expect predictive validity between performance on traditional infant tests and performance on subsequent intelligence tests.

For these reasons, it is understandable that the predictive validity of the Bayley, the Užgiris-Hunt, and other traditional infant tests are all relatively poor for typically developing infants. This means that the low correlations between performance on the standard array of infant tests and later intelligence tests might be valid, but it would be invalid to conclude because of them that there is no predictive validity in mental development from infancy. To assess predictive validity in mental development from infancy, early measures that more appropriately evaluate cognitive functioning and performance must be employed. Newer longitudinal assessments of cognitive predictability beginning in infancy should tap information-processing skills in ways that are conceptually parallel (to the degree possible) to cognitive functions in childhood. In the next section, we review the results of validity research on various types of information-processing measures in infancy, notably habituation and novelty responsiveness. As we have seen, these measures show individual variation and possess reasonable short-term reliability. As we will see, performance on them predicts cognitive competencies in childhood, not perfectly, but better than scores on traditional infant tests.

The Information-Processing Orientation to Assessment of Cognitive Competencies in Infancy

Generally speaking, infants who process information more efficiently are thought to acquire knowledge more quickly. Thus, as we discussed earlier in this chapter, quicker decay and lower looking time in habituation are considered indices of more efficient information processing. We certainly understand the everyday meaning of "quick" and "slow" when used to connote a person's intelligence. Learning rate and reactivity are traditional parts of defining intelligence (Durkin, 1966), and there is an established relation between reaction time and intelligence test performance (Deary & Der, 2005).

A key question for any infant evaluation is whether it predicts scores on intelligence tests administered later in life. Measures of both decrement and recovery of attention in infancy have moderate validity in this regard. Young infants who show efficient visual information processing perform better on traditional assessments of cognitive competence in childhood and adolescence (Fagan, 2011; Kavsek, 2004; Rose et al., 2011). Importantly, this validity is found in different laboratories, with different populations of both healthy and at-risk infants, for different measures in infancy across visual and auditory senses. Although it is far from perfect, the prediction between information-processing measures in infancy and cognitive performance in childhood is also notably higher than that between traditional infant tests and childhood IQ tests (see also Box 1.1).

Some important points need to be considered concerning this predictive relation. First, this finding may be robust because decrement and recovery of attention are related to central cognitive capacities in infants, and prediction is not limited to one modality or to one population. Second, as we elaborate below, habituation in infancy predicts cognitive status in childhood independent of family influences (including maternal behaviors) that one might expect also affect infant performance. This finding points to a direct tie between habituation performance in infants and their cognitive skills as children. In short, validity appears to be in the individual. Third, habituation could covary with some other factor(s), and it might be that those factors are responsible for the predictive association between habituation performance in infancy and later intelligence. For example, an infant presumably needs to be developed perceptually, to possess a vigilant or persistent cognitive style, and to have an attentive temperament to succeed first at habituation and later in an intelligence test. Alternatively, it could be that babies who process information efficiently also expose themselves to more appropriate amounts, kinds, or patterns of environmental stimulation (Barbaro et al., 2011).

Taken together, these results substantiate an important view of mental development, one that supports the notion that there is some predictive validity in individual cognitive performance from infancy. Measures of attention in the first year of life show moderate predictive validity for selected measures of cognitive competence perhaps through adolescence. Although these predictive data in mental development are telling, they are modest and certainly do not mean that intelligence is innate or fixed in early life. They do, however, overturn the view that cognition in infancy is not meaningfully associated with later development. In the final section of this chapter we take up the important consideration of how the social and physical environments in which the infants grow, and the capacities they bring to these settings, jointly contribute to the child's future cognitive development.

COGNITIVE DEVELOPMENT IN ITS SOCIAL CONTEXT

How does the mind bring itself into close coordination with physical and social reality? In the strong form of the maturationist argument, mental life in infancy is given genetically and unfolds biologically, wholly within the child. There is undeniably some validity to this position. Modern behavior geneticists argue that individual differences among infants reflect inheritance to some degree, and reliable familial similarities with respect to IQ support their conclusion (Brant et al., 2009; Horn & Loehlin, 2010). The performance and developmental pattern of infants on traditional tests (like the Bayley) have been linked to heredity as well. Wilson (1983, 1984) found that identical twins are more alike in their scores on the Bayley Scales and later tests than are fraternal twins or mere siblings.

Genetics could very well contribute to mental development, but all other prominent theories put experience in the world either as the principal source of individual cognitive growth or as a major contributing component (Chapter 1). In this final section of the chapter, we make explicit some specific views on how infant cognitive development is assisted and guided by others—the social context of mental development in infancy.

Parental Interaction and Teaching

Many theories of development hold that the environment exerts a strong influence. Behaviorism propounded this view as a "main effect" (Chapter 1), and social scientists have argued that aggregate-level variables, such as social status or cultural practice, constitute chief influences on mental development in children (Bornstein, 2010; Bornstein & Bradley, 2003). For example, the NICHD study on child care described in Chapter 2 documented the relation between socioeconomic status and intellectual development in children (NICHD, 2005).

However, individual modes of caregiving presumably mediate between global influences on the one hand and variation in mental functioning and cognitive growth in infants on the other. McLoyd et al. (2006), for example, cited punitive, harsh parental discipline as an important mediator of relations between poverty and intellectual deficits or socioemotional difficulties in childhood. Extensive studies comparing mental growth in children from adoptive versus non-adoptive families confirm the view that aspects of the mother–infant relationship also predict later developmental status in the child, free from genetic confounds (Horn & Loehlin, 2010). This conclusion calls for more intense empirical focus on everyday activities in the family. As a consequence, we take a closer look at behaviors thought to affect cognitive development from infancy. Echoing the orientation laid out in Chapter 2, one of our principal reference points in making sense of this literature is the **specificity principle**, namely that specific experiences at specific times in early life affect specific aspects of the infant's growth and development in specific ways (Bornstein, 2002). Whereas the overall level of parental stimulation was once believed to affect the child's overall level of development, evidence increasingly suggests that specific environmental events and parental activities relate concurrently and predictively to specific aspects of child performance and that parent and infant alike influence infant mental development (Bornstein, Hahn, & Wolke, 2013).

Perhaps the most influential early proponent of a **transactional perspective** was Lev Vygotsky (1978), who emphasized the crucial importance of interaction with others for cognitive development. As you may recall from Chapter 1, the transactional view states that both child and parent bring distinctive characteristics to every interaction and are believed to change as a result. Vygotsky contended that the more advanced or expert partner (e.g., the mother) raises the level of performance of the less skilled partner (the infant) through social interaction. The difference between children's spontaneous performance on a task without guidance and that observed with guidance represents a central cognitive concept in Vygotskian theory known as the **zone of proximal development** (ZPD). Vygotsky's (1978, p. 86) idea of the ZPD centers on "problem solving under adult guidance," even in infancy.

Before children are old enough to enter formal social-learning situations like school, or even informal ones like play groups, the vast majority of their experiences stem directly from interactions within the family. Adult caregiving figures are responsible for determining most, if not all, of the infants' early experiences. What, then, are prominent caregiving strategies that relate to cognitive functioning in infancy? Parents take principal responsibility for structuring teaching exchanges with infants: They engage infants in early games as well as in turn-taking exchanges in play (Bornstein, 2002). Wood, Bruner, and Ross (1976) identified the informal teaching roles adults adopt in interactions with infants under the rubric of **scaffolding**. As engineers do in constructing a building, parents sometimes use temporary aids to help their child advance. Later, the scaffold may be replaced or taken away entirely. Some scaffolding strategies may be more effective than others, depending on the nature and age of the child, and parents can be expected to vary in the scaffolds they favor. **Joint attention** appears to be one kind of support that facilitates opportunities for learning (Figure 7.8). In joint attention, both the infant and adult jointly inspect an object or event, and joint attention in infancy has been linked to infants' and children's later cognitive and communicative competence (Kristen et al., 2011; Strid, Tjus, Smith, Meltzoff, & Heimann, 2006). Parental responsiveness appears to be another (Bornstein, 2002). Sensitive parents tailor their scaffolding behaviors to match their infants' developmental progress, such as providing less scaffolding as infant competency increases (Conner & Cross, 2003). Moreover, actions and/or responses do not have to be verbalized (Pearson et al., 2011). The environmental provisions (e.g., toys and books) that parents make available to their infants constitute a third type of support (Bradley, 2010). Finally, in terms of individual variation, some parents demonstrate more, whereas others guide more (Shannon, Tamis-LeMonda, & Margolin, 2005).

In a series of studies designed to evaluate different kinds of caregiving effects on infant development, Bornstein and his colleagues found that mothers show individual differences in teaching activities, that parenting has short-term reliability, and that different parenting activities relate to different forms of early mental growth, such as visual and tactual exploration in 2- and 5-month-olds, perceptual-cognitive competence in 3-month-olds, language and play in 13-month-olds, and intellectual ability in preschoolers (Bornstein, 2006a).

The Joint Contribution of Parent and Infant

Rogoff and her colleagues have formally studied maternal teaching in infancy from the perspective of Vygotsky's ZPD, and they have discussed adult-assisted learning in children, pointing out that learning and socialization are actually interactive processes that require joint problem solving (Rogoff, 2003). This group looked at variations in role relations of infants and toddlers with their families in cultural communities as far flung as Turkey, Guatemala, India, and the United States. They documented how children

Fig. 7.8 A father and his infant are engaged in joint attention. Activities such as these support learning in infancy. Note also the use of pointing by the father and the point hand shape by the baby (pointing will be discussed in more detail in Chapter 9). (Copyright: Igor Stepovik, courtesy of Shutterstock, Inc.)

experience multiple settings, multiple caregivers, and widely contrasting outcomes in growing up. In all of these interactions, however, children participate actively in culturally organized activities, and in this way gain an understanding of the world they live in. Rogoff likened young children to "apprentices": Infants and toddlers must learn to think, act, and interact with all of the central characters in their culture in order to grow up and adapt successfully.

In this connection, the concept of **intent participation**, when keen observation is motivated by the expectation that at a later time the observer will be responsible for the action in question, is relevant (Rogoff, Paradise, Arauz, Correa-Chavez, & Angelillo, 2003). Intent participation might involve more experienced participants facilitating a learner's participation and participating along with the learner, or it could involve direct verbal instruction (Maynard, 2002). Intent participation is a special form of learning by observation and contributes to ongoing activities that have cultural roots. It places a heavy role on observation compared to verbal instruction, which is prominent in formal schooling.

Many factors in early life contribute to the eventual performance of the individual. Bornstein, Hahn, and Wolke (2013; Box 1.1) conducted a large-scale 14-year longitudinal study that showed that information-processing efficiency in infancy (4 months), general mental development in toddlerhood (18 months), behavior difficulties in early childhood (36 months), psychometric intelligence in middle childhood (8 years), and maternal education directly and/or indirectly contribute to academic achievement in adolescence (14 years).

What motivates infants' parents to behave in the ways they do? In Chapter 11, we discuss parental belief systems and prominent factors that determine how parents interact with their infants. Whatever the reasons, parents bring more to interactions with their infants than simple learning; they promote their infants' mental development through the structures they create and the meanings placed on those structures. By the same token, infants bring an active mental life to their everyday interactions with adults, and they carry more away from their interactions than simply the specific contents of individual lessons, as we have illustrated in Box 7.1.

SUMMARY

In this chapter, we described the fundamental premises and objectives of two major schools of thought about mental life in infancy. In his theory of sensorimotor intelligence, Piaget differs from empiricist and nativist theorists by emphasizing the importance of constructivism and motor activity in the development of knowledge. Post-Piagetian researchers have since elaborated on, and in some cases refuted, some of Piaget's basic tenets regarding sensorimotor development. Learning and information-processing theorists have advanced an alternative view of infant mental life, noting that even newborns can be operantly and classically conditioned, imitate, and habituate and show novelty responsiveness. These competing schools work toward different scientific goals. The quantitative approach attempts to define antecedents of cognition and learning and focuses on individual differences—the ABCs of how children learn, acquire, and process information about the environment. By contrast, Piaget defined a qualitative series of invariant and universal stages in development. Both traditions teach us about cognitive status and development from infancy, and so at some level (or, so many theorists believe) they complement one another and should converge.

In recent years, two revolutions have taken place in the study of infant cognitive development. Whereas earlier infant assessments did not predict later cognitive stature in the child, contemporary studies using new techniques have unearthed significant levels of cognitive prediction from infancy. And, whereas investigators suspected that early experiences ought to influence intellectual growth but could not find predictive relations, researchers have more recently developed specific measures that are predictively telling. The social environment of the infant also promotes cognitive development. Together these diverse points of view meet the design criteria for mental development we listed at the start of this chapter and show that both endogenous (internal of biological) and exogenous (external or experiential) forces work together to help to bring the infant's mind in line with the external physical and social reality.

KEY TERMS

A-not-B error	Deferred imitation
Accommodation	Décalage
Adaptation	Egocentrism
Assimilated	Equilibration
Assimilation	Equilibrium
Classical conditioning	Face validity
Conditioned response	Fluctuate
Conditioned stimulus	Habituation

Imitation
Increases then decreases
Individual variation
Intent participation
Invisible displacements
Joint attention
Linear or exponential decrease
Mental representation
Mirror neurons
Novelty responsiveness
Observational learning
Operant conditioning
Reinforced
Predictive validity
Primary circular reactions
Punished

Qualitative
Quantitative
Scaffolding
Schemas
Scheme
Secondary circular reactions
Sensorimotor period
Short-term reliability
Tertiary circular reactions
Transactional perspective
Unconditioned response
Unconditioned stimulus
Validity
Violation of Expectation
Zone of proximal development

Chapter 8
Representation in Infancy

- *What is mental representation?*
- *Do babies categorize? How do we know?*
- *How does categorization change across infancy?*
- *How have behavioral and electrophysiological techniques been used to study infant memory development?*
- *How does memory develop in infancy?*
- *What factors affect how well infants remember?*
- *How is play related to memory and categorization?*
- *How does play change developmentally across infancy?*
- *How do interactions with adults and other children shape infant play?*

Using sophisticated ways to question infants, researchers have acquired a good understanding of many basic capabilities of infants. We described our understanding of infant perceptual sensitivities and cognitive competencies in the preceding chapters. Developmentalists now do much more than ask whether or not the senses function in infancy, or even whether infants think, in seeking to identify more sophisticated infant mental and social capacities. One of the most significant of these is mental representation, first discussed in Chapter 7 and explored in more detail here.

As we indicated in Chapter 7, Piaget proposed that the first two years of life culminate in the development of **representational thinking**—the ability to think about people and objects even in their absence. The Russian developmental psychologist Lev Vygotsky (1967) also focused on this transition. He theorized that a critical change in infancy consisted of **interiorization**, making the external world accessible to the internal. With development, he argued, infants increasingly represent the external world in their internal thoughts. Vygotsky hypothesized that thinking increasingly involves internalized speech. Although the capacity for some kind of representation appears to exist from birth (Chapter 7), many theorists consider representational capacities to be crucial aspects of early mental growth. In their classic study of symbol formation, Werner and Kaplan (1963) asserted that the development of symbolic and representational capacities were characteristic of early childhood, as demonstrated in important changes in memory, categorization, imitation, play, and verbal competence.

For Piaget (1962), Werner and Kaplan (1963), and Vygotsky (1967), representational ability is integrally related to the issue of object independence. In essence, these theorists argued that the child does not truly understand the role of symbols until there is clear movement beyond **prerepresentational** thinking (dependence on immediate perceptual and contextual support) to representational thinking (mental manipulation in the absence of feedback from concrete objects). This development is sometimes called **decontextualization**. (We shall meet this concept again in Chapter 9, when we note that real naming may only occur when the child can refer verbally to something even when it is not present.)

Using different investigative techniques, researchers have further refined our understanding of representation. For example, in the Piagetian view, newborns cannot integrate incoming sensory information. Thus, the construction of an integrated, solid, three-dimensional world from "disconnected sights, sounds, and touches" is only accomplished over a considerable amount of time. Piaget even characterized children's first words as imitative schemas not yet invested with representation. However, the perceptual world is coherent and differentiated much earlier in life than Piaget supposed. For example, multimodal perception (discussed in Chapter 6) implies that information arriving at different senses is related across modalities in the first year of life.

When Piaget studied acquisition of the object concept in his own children, he relied on their manual search for a hidden object. In an elementary sense, this mode of testing underestimates the child's competence because children might know something about the properties of a hidden object yet be constrained by their motor control, their understanding of how to search, or even their motivation to search. This point is persuasively demonstrated by the experimental work we discussed in Chapter 7 showing that the capacity to represent things mentally is present at birth or very shortly thereafter, many months before infants develop manual search skills. However, it is important to note that representation hardly begins or ends with the child's attainment of the object concept. The term representation applies to a broad range of mental phenomena, such as categorization, memory, and pretense play. Furthermore, the essence of cognitive growth in infancy and beyond may involve the emergence and development over time of different representational capacities and skills. DeLoache (2011), for example, documented young children's confusion regarding symbolic relations. Very young infants appear to confuse pictures with their real objects and slightly older infants have difficulty equating pictures, particularly line drawings, with real world objects. Even later still, around 2½ years of age, children have difficulty understanding the equivalence between scale models and real spaces. In one of DeLoache's tasks, a miniature toy was hidden in a scale model of a room while a young child watched. Then the child was brought into the actual room and asked to find the toy. Three-year-olds knew precisely where to search for the hidden toy, but children only 6 months younger did not. The younger children did not fail to find the toy because their memory of the hiding event was faulty. Most could readily find the miniature toy in the scale model. Instead, the 2½-year-olds appeared unable to use the hiding event to symbolize the hidden location of the real toy in the actual room.

It is important, therefore, to keep in mind that the study of early representation tells us not only about the *nature* of the young child's mind, but also about the ability to *use* his or her mind. In DeLoache's task, the child must understand that the model represents the room. A moment's reflection reveals that the appreciation of books and television calls on similar abilities. When and to what degree do children believe that what they see and hear actually represent reality?

In this chapter, we address three topics that, in one way or another, illustrate mental representation. More specifically, we describe and review categorization and conceptual understanding in infants, the development of memory in infancy, and the growth of pretend play at the end of infancy. Each of these capacities reflects the infant's increasing sophistication and cognitive flexibility. Infancy is the period of life without much spoken language; yet, each one of these abilities also articulates with or is presumptive of language. Many theorists have argued that, as linguistic comprehension begins during the first year, even young infants must possess a representational system that enables language learning. On this account, we also refer from time to time in this chapter to emerging relations of categories and concepts, memory, and play on the one hand, with the dawning of language capacities in infants on the other. The origins of language take center stage in Chapter 9.

CATEGORIES AND CONCEPTS

Our world consists of an infinite number of objects, events, and people, and without conscious thought, we group them into categories. According to Rakison and Oakes (2003, p. 4), "categories are collections of things in the world and concepts are the internal mental depiction of those collections." Categories can vary (is it a category of "red things," "kitchen utensils," or "things that are human-made"?), and the same object or event can be categorized along different dimensions (e.g., a dog is both an animal and a living object). Concepts are thought to be the mental representation of the criteria for a category.

Conceptual abilities were once believed to begin when infants first demonstrated object permanence, as described by Piaget. From this perspective, knowledge of an object implied that the infant knew that the object existed by virtue of mental representation because there was no immediate perceptual feedback. There are, however, very different ways to think about conceptual abilities. Exactly when infants start forming concepts about the world, and what specifically defines concepts in infancy, are topics that have been debated extensively. We begin this section with a discussion of categorization and its study in infancy. We address different perspectives on category formation and ask whether and when categories in infancy can be considered conceptual.

Categorization

Categorization involves the grouping of separate items into a set according to some type of precept or rule. Members of a category may be classified together because they share a common attribute, element, or relation. Categories have breadth (the variety of items which are included), **prototypes** (best examples), and **boundaries** (regions or instances where inclusion is marginal). Consider the category of birds. Although all birds have feathers and beaks, there is variation in color, size, manner of locomotion, and preferred habitat (e.g., trees, ground, water). Thus, a category for birds must include this variation but, at the same time there is a need for boundaries. Penguins do not fly, but they lay eggs like other birds. Reptiles also lay eggs and do not fly, but they are not birds. Penguins have other characteristics in common with birds that reptiles do not, thus allowing their inclusion in the category of bird. The best examples of a category are called prototypes. These examples possess many (or perhaps all) of the distinguishing features of the category, and it is often what we think of when someone names the category. For many, robin, duck, and pigeon are prototypical birds. Ostrichs, penguins, and road runners are not. The demonstration of categorization requires that otherwise discriminable properties, objects, or events are grouped together. We encountered examples of categorization in Chapter 6 when discussing categorical perception. As you may recall, infants treated different shades of the same color (e.g., blue) similarly despite their being of different shades, and infants treated them differently from green.

Categorization reflects mental activity in three distinct spheres (Bornstein, 1984). First, categorization structures and clarifies perception. The environment into which infants are born is complex and constantly changing, with many opportunities to encounter new objects and events. Categorization helps organize the environment and facilitates learning. Consider infants' perception of animals. If infants have a category of animals, when seeing a new animal, they do not have to start anew in order to figure out how the animal might move or behave. Using the information contained in a general category for animal, they can rely on what they already know about animals. Thus, in addition to helping with a new encounter, infants might be able to use the knowledge of this category to make inferences. For example, if shown a turtle and told it is an animal, the infant may infer that it might eat, move, and breathe like other animals. Relatedly, categorization also facilitates the storage and retrieval of information. It supplies a principle of organization by which new information can be stored efficiently in memory. For example, all information pertaining to animal can be stored together and accessed when presented with familiar or novel animals.

Methods of Studying Categorization in Infancy

Older children easily discriminate and categorize when asked, but evidence of categorization in infancy involves detailed observations of infant looking in habituation studies and infant object manipulation. In habituation procedures, infants are first familiarized with several items from the same category and are then presented with a novel item from the same category and a novel item from a different category. Categorization is inferred if infants pay more attention to the novel out-of-category item than to the novel in-category item. For example, in a study of infants' categorization of the facial expression of smiling, infants were habituated to four different intensities of smiles (Figure 8.1; Bornstein & Arterberry, 2003). Following habituation, infants looked significantly longer at a new facial expression (fear) than at a new intensity of smile even on the same face, suggesting that they categorized the facial expression of smiling. Habituation paradigms have been widely used to document infants' ability to categorize geometric forms and patterns (e.g., triangles and squares), animals (cats, dogs, birds, and horses), phonemes, colors, gender of human voices, furniture, vehicles, and spatial relations (Jusczyk, 2003; Quinn, 2011; Rakison & Oakes, 2003).

For older infants who have developed more advanced motor skills (Chapter 5), inferences about categorization can be made based on patterns of object exploration. One technique, called object examining, is similar to a habituation technique in that infants are given one object at a time and the amount of time they engage in active exploration of the object is measured (Oakes, Madole, & Cohen, 1991; Figure 8.2). During a familiarization phase, infants are given the chance to explore exemplars from the same category (such as animals). During the test phase, infants are given trials with a new exemplar from the familiar category (such as another animal) and an exemplar from a new category (a vehicle). Welder and Graham (2006) used this procedure to explore the role of perceptual features in 14- to 15-month-olds' categorization. They found that infants formed categories of objects that had obvious or easily visible features but not with objects that had less obvious (e.g., accessible by lifting a flap) features.

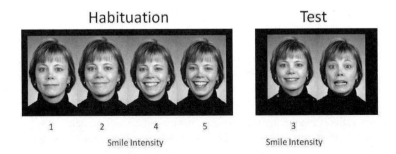

Fig. 8.1 Stimuli used to test 5-month-old infants' categorization of the facial expression of smiling. Note that in the test display the smile exemplar was not presented earlier in the habituation phase and that it represents a midpoint along the smile intensity continuum (1 is a slight smile and 5 is a broad toothy grin). (From Bornstein & Arterberry, 2003; reproduced with permission.)

Fig. 8.2 Twelve-month-old infant exploring a toy dolphin in an object examining task. (Courtesy of M. Arterberry.)

Categorization is also studied using the sequential touching task (Mandler, Fivush, & Resnick, 1987). Typically, infants are shown four small three-dimensional models belonging to two categories (such as animals and vehicles). All eight stimuli are presented randomly on a table in front of the infant, and the experimenter encourages the infant to play with them (Figure 8.3). Categorization is inferred if the infant sequentially manipulates objects within a category more frequently (i.e., at greater than chance levels) than objects across categories. Using this procedure, Bornstein and Arterberry (2010) assessed categorization at different levels of inclusiveness for animals, vehicles, fruit, and furniture between 12 and 30 months of age (more on this study below).

Fig. 8.3 An 18-month-old's categorization abilities being assessed using the sequential touching procedure. In this procedure, children are presented with eight objects, four from one category and four from another category. Depicted here are the categories of telephones and hairbrushes used by Arterberry and Bornstein (2012). (Courtesy of M. Arterberry.)

Issues in the Study of Categorization

A number of questions and controversies surround the nature and development of categorization in infancy. One is the order in which infants acquire categories; another is the basis on which infants categorize; a third is when categories become concepts.

Order of Acquisition of Categories   A central feature of category structure is **hierarchical inclusiveness**, the organization of more encompassing categories subsuming less encompassing ones (Murphy, 2002). For a simple example, a collie is a type of dog, which is a type of animal. When people spontaneously categorize objects in a neutral setting, they typically categorize into hierarchically organized taxonomies that have nested categories connected by some sort of relation. Hierarchical networks allow for set inclusion (sometimes called the "IS-A Relation") between category levels (Murphy, 2002). A collie is a type of dog is an example of an IS-A Relation. The taxonomic system for organizing species is a prime example and, importantly, it is found widely across human cultures (Atran, 1990; Berlin, Breedlove, & Raven, 1973). Many domains around us are organized hierarchically with different levels of inclusiveness, normally on the basis of instrumental and/or perceptual attributes.

At high levels of category inclusiveness (commonly referred to as the **superordinate** or **global level**), category members are grouped functionally and share some perceptual attributes; thus, within-category functional similarity tends to be high, and perceptual similarity middle to high, whereas between-category functional and perceptual similarity tend to be low. For example, dogs, horses, rabbits, and fish are all subsumed under the more inclusive category of animal because animals share many properties, but different animals do not (necessarily) look alike. Moreover, the animal domain differs from other category domains, such as vehicles, in instrumental and perceptual properties.

At middle levels of inclusiveness (often called the **basic level**), entities share instrumental and usually (although not always) perceptual properties; thus, within-category functional and perceptual similarity tend to be high, whereas between-category functional and perceptual similarity tend to be middle to low. For example, dogs of different species share many characteristics as well as a number of perceptual properties, but dogs are easily distinguished from fish, a different basic level category in the same domain of animals.

At low levels of category inclusiveness (the **subordinate level**), members of a category share both instrumental and perceptual similarity, which tend to be high; however, between-category instrumental and perceptual similarity (for categories nested within the same basic level) also tend to be high. For example, collies, shepherds, and retrievers represent subordinate categories of dogs, and members in each category are discriminable from one another, yet they are also similar to one another.

A long-standing question is at what level do infants first categorize. Do they begin with overarching superordinate or global categories that allow for greater inclusiveness even though the individual members may not share a high amount of perceptual similarity, or do they begin with more constrained categories, such as at the basic or subordinate levels, that have considerable similarity among members? Charting the development of the order of acquisition of object categories has been difficult because there is no one method that can be used across 0 to 2 years of age. Older infants do not tolerate habituation/novelty techniques as well as younger infants, and younger infants lack motor skills that are needed for object examining or sequential touching. Unfortunately, different methods have revealed different developmental time tables for categorization, and even with infants of the same age (5 months), different methods may reveal different patterns of results (Mash & Bornstein, 2012). Generally, habituation/novelty-responsiveness tasks show earlier and more advanced categorization than object examining or sequential touching tasks. For example, Quinn, Doran, Reiss, and Hoffman (2010) showed that 6- to 7-month-olds categorized different breeds of dogs in a looking-time task, but with a sequential touching task Bornstein and Arterberry

(2010) found no evidence of categorization at the subordinate level among apples, chairs, sharks, or sports cars as late as 30 months of age.

Methodological complications aside, it has been difficult to address the larger question of the order of emergence of categorization level because few studies tested the same aged infants with the same categorization levels using the same procedure. One exception is the study by Bornstein and Arterberry (2010) mentioned earlier. They used the sequential touching task with infants aged 12, 18, 24, and 30 months, and they tested each age group with seven object sets representing superordinate, basic, and subordinate levels within the same domain (animals-vehicles or fruit-furniture; Figure 8.4). They found that from 12 to 30 months of age infants categorized at more inclusive levels (e.g., superordinate: animals or vehicles) before less inclusive levels (e.g., basic: types of animals or vehicles) before even less inclusive levels (e.g., subordinate: specific animals or vehicles). As a group, even the youngest children categorized at the superordinate level, and the oldest children did not categorize at the subordinate level. Moreover, superordinate categorization and basic level categorization were present in the youngest children, as long as the between-category exemplars were of high contrast (for example, frogs and cows as opposed to horses and dogs). This finding suggests that superordinate and basic level categorization might develop in parallel, rather than one before the other, but subordinate categorization is clearly the last to emerge. That subordinate categorization may lag behind categorization at the superordinate or basic level is also reflected in research conducted with younger children using looking-time tasks. A number of researchers have demonstrated superordinate or basic level categorization at 3 to 4 months of age, whereas subordinate categorization is not present before 6 to 7 months of age (Arterberry & Bornstein, 2001; Quinn, 2004, 2011).

Flexibility in Categorization   The objects, events, and people that we encounter every day are not each bound into a single category, but can be situated into different categories. Adults flexibly categorize the same entities in different ways in response to changing instructions, contexts, and task demands (Schyns & Rodet, 1997). For example, telephones and walkie-talkies can be categorized as communication devices, but they could also be grouped with hammers and hair brushes under the larger category of tools or based on color—red, blue, yellow, and silver objects. Whether children form a category that includes or excludes certain exemplars depends on the distribution of exemplars they are

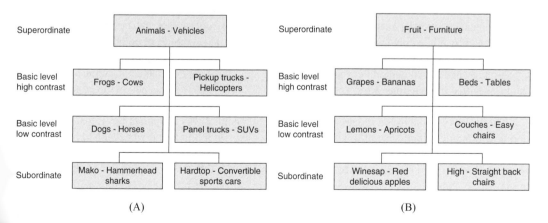

(A)   (B)

Fig. 8.4 Hierarchical organization of stimuli used by Bornstein and Arterberry (2010) to test the development of categorization in 12-, 18-, 24-, and 30-month-old infants. Infants received seven sets from one of the two domains, (A) Animals-Vehicles or (B) Fruit-Furniture. High contrast sets include objects that have a greater amount of perceptual dissimilarity across categories. Low contrast sets are perceptually similar across categories.

exposed to, and children can shift from categorizing a set of stimuli using one dimension to categorizing the same stimuli using another dimension (Ellis & Oakes, 2006; Horst et al., 2009; Kovack-Lesh & Oakes, 2007). Even in the same testing session, infants can change criteria. Ellis and Oakes (2006), for example, presented 14-month-old infants with a set of objects that could be categorized either by shape (balls vs. blocks) or by material (soft vs. hard). After an initial 2-minute session with the objects (in which infants who categorized did so based on shape), the compressibility of the objects was demonstrated to them. After the demonstration, infants were allowed to interact with the objects again for 2 minutes. Some infants categorized the objects the second time based on whether the objects were hard or soft rather than on their shape.

Learning about a new object property during the course of an experiment is one type of learning. However, infants have many opportunities to learn about objects in their everyday experiences, and recent evidence points to their ability to use these experiences to guide their categorization. In one study testing categorization of dogs and cats, 4-month-old infants who had pets at home showed more visual comparison of stimuli during the habituation phase, suggesting that their experience with animals provided them with a more advanced strategy for learning the category (Kovack-Lesh, Horst, & Oakes, 2008). Similarly, Bornstein and Mash (2010) found that experience with novel objects in the home for two months facilitated categorization in a laboratory visit.

Perceptual vs. Conceptual Categorization and Development of Concepts   On what basis do infants categorize? A possible answer to this question might come from the distinction between perceptual and conceptual categorization. Mandler (2000) suggested that infants categorize at either a perceptual or conceptual level. **Perceptual categorization** is based on knowing what objects look like and relies heavily on the physical appearance of objects. **Conceptual categorization** is based on knowing what objects are and relies on what they do or the roles they play in events.

Viewing categorization as a process that can occur at different levels based on the type of information infants use suggests an important role for specific stimulus variables in some types of categorization (e.g., perceptual categorization) but not for others (e.g., conceptual categorization). For example, an adult will recognize a full color photograph of an animal as representing an object from the same domain as a line drawing of the animal, a three-dimensional replica of the animal, and video footage of the animal. On the surface level, these displays look very different; however, despite their being specified by different stimulus information, their resulting representations are common—it is an animal. Infants who categorize at a perceptual level need to match objects based on their physical appearance, and how the object is specified (whether by a line drawing, a full color moving video, or a 3-D replica of an object) may influence the infants' categorization process. Infants who categorize at a conceptual level need to be able to access object representations to determine what the objects are and what they do. Object meaning and function can be specified in numerous ways, and categorizers (whatever their age) sometimes need to overcome specific stimulus variables when categorizing.

The majority of the infant research on categorization is likely documenting perceptual categorization. For example, infants attend to key parts (such as legs on animals and wheels on vehicles), they notice correlations among attributes (like long necks go together with short tails), and they are likely to group objects based on more easily observable properties rather than less easily observable properties (Rakison, 2003; Welder & Graham, 2006; Younger, 2003). Despite the possibility that infants rely heavily on perceptual information when categorizing, infants are also capable of conceptual categorization. In one test of conceptual categorization, Arterberry and Bornstein (2002) changed the perceptual information from habituation to test such that infants could not rely on perceptual features. In their experiment, 6- and 9-month-olds were habituated to black-and-white random-dot displays that specified either moving animals or vehicles (Figure 8.5). Following habituation, infants viewed static full

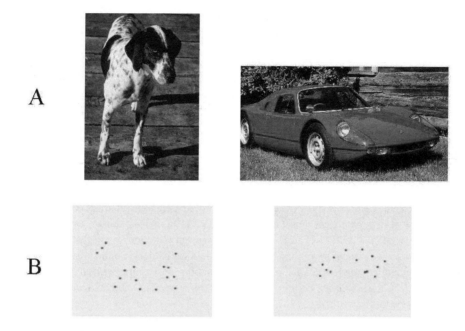

A

B

Fig. 8.5 Static (A) and dynamic (B) images of animals and vehicles used to assess infants' conceptual categorization. (From Arterberry & Bornstein, 2002; reproduced with permission from Elsevier.)

color images of animals and vehicles. If infants extracted the category of animals or vehicles from the motion patterns they saw during the habituation phase, they were expected to show generalization (not increase their looking) to the within-category exemplar and show a novelty response to the out-of-category exemplar during the test phase. Nine-month-olds showed this pattern of results, but not 6-month-olds, a finding that suggests that conceptual categorization may emerge between 6 and 9 months of age. Other work addressing infants' understanding of animacy, a concept that is based on both perceptual properties (self-propulsion) and conceptual understanding (it is alive) suggests continued development in the interplay between children's perceptual and conceptual categorization (Poulin-Dubois, Frenkiel-Fishman, Nayer, & Johnson, 2006).

Some investigators argue that concepts are theories or abstract role systems, whereas others propose that concepts are ideas about kinds of things that depend on perceptual associations (Mandler, 2004). For example, horses, dogs, and cats are different kinds of animals, and an animal is a different kind of thing from a vehicle. From the first perspective, to have a concept of animals, the infant must understand that animals share features that go beyond perceptual similarities (not just that animals, unlike children, have four legs, a tail and so forth, but that they can self-propel, reproduce, and so forth). Mandler (2004) argued that concepts such as these begin to develop very early in life and become more sophisticated as infants mature and gain experience. She cited evidence for the superordinate-basic-subordinate trend in the development of infant categorization as an indication that infants first possess holistic, undifferentiated concepts about the world (e.g., animals versus vehicles) before fine-tuning those broad concepts into smaller, fine-grained conceptual categories (e.g., dogs versus cats). However, others believe that early categorization may simply depend on perceptual similarities among stimuli (Mareschal & French, 2000; Quinn, Johnson, Mareschal, Rakison, & Younger, 2000; Rakison, 2000).

It is easier to distinguish animals from vehicles perceptually than it is to distinguish dogs from cats, and this ease might explain why infants can make superordinate distinctions earlier in development than basic or subordinate ones.

In summary, the study of infant categorization has contributed greatly to our understanding of early cognitive development, particularly regarding the manner in which infants begin to make sense of the world around them. Categorization represents a many-to-one reduction process that functions adaptively across many different domains of thinking. Indeed, it would be difficult to overstate the significance of categorization for cognition and its development. Categorization is pervasive and essential for perceiving, thinking, remembering, and communicating. Haith and Benson (1998, p. 229) illustrate this point succinctly:

> Imagine an infant who must learn anew its parents' face for each perspective rotation, each expression, and each change of hair style. Or, consider the task of an infant who must acquire a new knowledge base for each separate cat that it encounters—that each meows, drinks, eats, and so on. And, one can appreciate the utility of categorization. By incorporating individual percepts of the mom's face into a mom-face category and individual cats into a cat category, infants gain enormous leverage in accumulating knowledge. Each piece of information one acquires with an individual exemplar can generalize to the whole set, permitting appropriate expectations and behavior in encounters with completely new instances.

MEMORY

It is obviously important that infants attend to properties, objects, and events in their environment to gain information about them, but it is also crucial that they be able to store, retrieve, and use that information later. Memory representations underlie the infant's awareness, experience, knowledge, and interpretation of the world. Developmental scientists are interested in all dimensions of infant memory—in what infants can remember, in the nature of their memory representations, in the ways in which infants remember, and in how good infant memory is. In this section of the chapter, we describe the tools researchers have exploited to study infant memory, and with those tools, what has been learned about early memory development, including the roles of age, study time, duration of memory, and the problems of forgetting and interference.

Memory plays a key role in the general model of mental functioning. This model is traditionally believed to involve (at least) three stages:

1   The **sensory register** temporarily stores all incoming sensory information.
2   **Short-term/working memory** has limited and momentary access to information, and it is where conscious cognition takes place.
3   **Long-term memory** represents a limitless, permanent storehouse of knowledge, but one that depends on processes that are generally unavailable to infants or even very young children. Failure to remember is more likely to result from an inability to retrieve information from long-term store rather than actual loss of information. As a consequence, **strategies** to remember play a key role in long-term memory.

Many physiological and behavioral components of memory change during childhood (Johnson, 2011b; Nelson & Lucianna, 2008), and so infants' memory systems and memories differ in many ways from adults' and older children's. Neuropsychological sites of memory (e.g., the hippocampus, thalamus, rhinal cortex, basal forebrain, and orbital prefrontal cortex) are still forming during the first year (Bauer,

2009; Johnson, 2011b). Adults also process information much more rapidly than infants. Adults have had many more experiences, and hence they have many more memories to associate with new to-be-remembered material, thereby facilitating their memory processes (although past experiences can interfere with memory retrieval and accuracy as well).

Interest in the dynamics of memory development in infancy has developed alongside the increase in popularity of the information-processing approach to cognitive development (Chapter 7). With infants, information-processing theorists seek, first, to identify component skills involved in remembering certain types of information and, then, by assessing development of each of these component skills, to determine whether their immaturity slows the attainment of more competent memory skills. This approach holds the promise to yield much information about the nature of representation in memory and about the ways in which memory and representations develop.

Cognitive scientists who study memory typically distinguish between two major pairs of processes. One pair involves encoding and retrieval. **Encoding** specifies the transformation(s) of incoming information into memory. **Retrieval** specifies the search-and-find process(es) used to get information out of memory. The second pair of processes further differentiates retrieval into recognition and recall. To retrieve via **recognition** requires only that we remember having previously experienced whatever is to be remembered, and contextual cues are provided to help with memory. To retrieve via **recall** requires that we remember a prior experience without the advantage of any cues.

Cognitive scientists also distinguish between two different kinds of memory—declarative and procedural. **Declarative**, or explicit memory, includes memory for names, events, places, and so forth. Subsumed within declarative memory are **episodic** memory (memory of events that have been experienced) and **semantic** memory (memory of facts about the world). Four basic features characterize declarative memory: (1) It is conscious (memories are accessed by conscious effort); (2) it is fast (memories can be formed in an instant); (3) it is fallible (memories can fade or can fail to be retrieved); and (4) it is flexible (memories tend not to be context dependent). By contrast, **procedural** memory refers to habits and skills that are shaped by experience (e.g., riding a bike). These memories are: (1) largely unconscious; (2) slow to develop; (3) relatively infallible (not prone to forgetting); and (4) inflexible (dependent on context). The vast majority of experiments on infant memory involve declarative memories, although, as we note in Chapter 11, procedural memories may be particularly important for understanding social relationships (Crittenden, Lang, Claussen, & Partridge, 2000).

For years, scientists believed that infants could not remember much of anything because adults and older children typically have great difficulty remembering events that took place before they were 3 to 4 years of age (Peterson, Warren, & Short, 2011). Indeed, Freud (1916–1917/1966) coined the term **infantile amnesia** to describe this phenomenon, which he attributed to the repression of memories of traumatic events. Piaget (1954) theorized that recall would not be possible during the first year because it demands the capacity to encode representationally, an ability he thought only emerged at about 2 years of age. Some evidence supports this timetable for recall of early memories (Cleveland & Reese, 2008; Box 8.1). For example, children 6 to 7 years of age had difficulty recalling an emergency room visit that happened at 1 year of age; however, those who visited the emergency room at age 2 were able to recall a great deal (Peterson & Parsons, 2005). Also, children whose mothers engage in elaborative reminiscing, in which they provided a rich amount of information when questioning their children about events, show longer retention of memory across the 2- to 3-year age span, suggesting the need for external support for long-term recall (Reese & Newcomb, 2007).

Infants, however, are not only capable of recognizing previously experienced events but also of recalling them. We begin with a discussion of methods employed to study infant memory and then move to discussions of factors that influence memory formation and developmental changes in infant memory.

Box 8.1   Set For Life? Charting the Onset of Infantile Amnesia

Despite the fact that memory abilities have been documented from early in infancy, an intriguing phenomenon is that adults and even older children do not remember much of their infancy. In fact, almost no events before 3½ years of age are remembered. This lack of memory is called infantile amnesia. To better understand infantile amnesia, Cleveland and Reese (2008) investigated the accuracy of children's memories and their language abilities in 19- to 65-month-olds. For the memory assessment, children were asked to recall personal events, and the story was cross-referenced with a parent to see if the retelling was accurate. Cleveland and Reese found a qualitative difference in recall for memories before 2 years versus after 2 years of age. Children were 75% accurate in recalling memories for events that occurred after the age of 2 years, but only 50% accurate for memories before this age. Accuracy of memory was correlated with language development for memories formed before 40 months of age, suggesting a role for language in facilitating encoding of events.

Techniques Used to Study Infant Memory

Researchers of memory in infancy have used at least five different techniques. Two are habituation and novelty-responsiveness procedures that we know from other domains of infant study (Chapters 3 and 7); specifically, they tap recognition memory. Look back to Figure 3.9. When an infant looks at a repeated stimulus less on its fifth showing (indicted –1 on the graph) than on its first (indicated –5 on the graph), the infant's loss of interest strongly suggests that the infant is coming to recognize the stimulus. Presumably, the infant is comparing each new stimulus presentation with a developing memory, or mental representation, of the stimulus based on previous exposures. And, thus, there is no need to look as long at each subsequent exposure of the stimulus (or trial). Figure 3.9 shows this decrement in looking.

Once habituation is complete, the familiar stimulus and a new (novel) stimulus are presented. If the infant looks more at the novel than at the familiar stimulus, researchers infer that the infant has recognized the familiar stimulus and so remembers something about it. That is, a low level of looking at the familiar stimulus on retest is usually interpreted as recognition, whereas recovery of looking at the familiar stimulus is interpreted as forgetting. If, however, the baby regards the novel and familiar stimuli equally, researchers cannot assume that the infant failed to remember. Instead, the infant might simply find the novel stimulus as interesting as the familiar stimulus. Because "interestingness" is determined by many factors other than novelty, the absence of recovery is always difficult to interpret.

Habituation and novelty responsiveness involve mental representation and memory, and researchers of infancy have transformed the two paradigms into versatile and powerful tools with which to investigate the development of memory. Using habituation, for example, it is possible to track the rate at which a stimulus is encoded. Presumably, faster habituation is an index of quicker encoding. By habituating infants and testing them immediately afterward with the same stimulus, it is possible to study short-term recognition memory, just as it is possible to impose a delay between the end of habituation and a later test to assess long-term recognition memory. Similarly, comparing the rate of habituation to a stimulus at one time with the rate of habituation to the same stimulus at a later time can be used to assess short- or long-term retention of a stimulus. If the second course of habituation is quicker than the first course, it must indicate that the infant remembered the stimulus.

A third approach designed to tap recognition memory involves **operant conditioning techniques**, also discussed in Chapters 3 and 7. The most commonly used technique with 3- to 6-month-olds involves foot kicking to move a mobile (Rovee-Collier, 2011). Using a mobile as a stimulus, a baseline reading is taken of how often an infant kicks. A ribbon is then tied from the infant's ankle to a mobile hanging over the crib. Infants quickly learn that foot kicking moves the mobile. When attached to the mobile in this way, the infant kicks at two to three times the baseline rate. Testing involves disconnecting the ribbon and again monitoring infants' foot kicks (Figure 3.8). If the rate of kicking remains high, this indicates that the infant remembers something about the mobile. Primarily under the initiative of Rovee-Collier and her colleagues, we have learned a tremendous amount about memory in very young infants using this technique (Rovee-Collier, 2011, Rovee-Collier & Cuevas, 2009a).

Another operant conditioning paradigm, the train paradigm, has been used to study memory in infants older than 6 months of age (Barr, Rovee-Collier, & Learmonth, 2011). In this procedure, the infant learns to press a lever to move a miniature electric train around a track (Figure 8.6). Like the mobile conjugate reinforcement paradigm, infants learn the association between their response (the lever press) and its consequence (movement of the train car). Infants are then tested after a delay. Retention of the event is assumed if the infant presses the lever at a rate that equals or exceeds the rate observed at the end of training.

Other research techniques designed specifically to assess infant recall involve more advanced manual actions. In the **search** paradigm, for example, the experimenter hides an object of interest to the infant and then observes whether the infant seeks it and, if so, whether the search is appropriate and successful (recall the **A-not-B task** described in Chapter 7; Shinskey & Munakata, 2003). In **deferred imitation tasks**, the infant's imitation of a modeled sequence of events after a time delay gives evidence of infant recall. For

Fig. 8.6 The train operant conditioning memory task, used with 6- through 18-month-olds. Each lever press moves the train around the track for two seconds. (From Rovee-Collier & Gehardstein, 1997; reproduced with permission.)

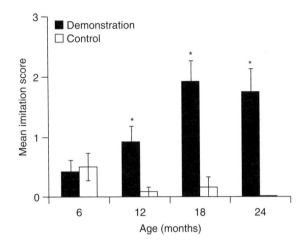

Fig. 8.7 Mean imitation scores of 6-, 12-, 18-, and 24-month-old infants tested after a 24-hour delay in the puppet-mitten task as a function of experimental group (Demonstration, Control). An asterisk indicates that the mean imitation score of the demonstration group (solid bars) was significantly above the mean imitation score of their age-matched control group (open bars). Units on the *y*-axis are the mean number of the three modeled events that were correctly imitated. (From Barr & Hayne, 2000; reproduced with permission.)

example, Barr and Hayne (2000) modeled a three-step event sequence of (1) removing a mitten from a puppet's hand, (2) shaking the mitten (which rang a bell inside the mitten), and (3) putting the mitten back on the puppet's hand. After a 24-hour delay (or longer), infants were given the puppet with the mitten, and the researchers observed which of the steps infants reproduced. As can be seen in Figure 8.7, 6-month-olds did not remember any of the steps 24 hours later, however, 12-, 18-, and 24-month-olds did.

The five techniques we have outlined to this point all rely on behavioral responses. Other useful measures of memory involve neuroscience techniques, and the one most commonly used with infants is **event-related potentials** (ERPs). As described in Chapter 3, ERP techniques measure activation in the brain, and they may be especially useful in documenting not only when learning in infancy takes place, but also which neural substrates might support it (Johnson, 2011b). Carver, Bauer, and Nelson (2000) used ERPs to demonstrate the recall of ordered events. Infants who demonstrated recall of an ordered event sequence via deferred imitation showed a different ERP from specific brain regions than did infants who did not recall the ordered sequence.

In summary, we have reviewed five behavioral and one electrophysiological technique that have been used to study memory in infancy. Each has advantages and limitations with regard to the ages and types of memory to which it can be applied. No one technique alone is sufficient to study the dimensions and limitations of infant memory, but the several techniques complement one another, and in a short time they have yielded a surprisingly detailed picture of the basic dimensions of memory in infancy.

Influences on Infant Memory

Infant age clearly affects memory, and several key questions flow from this observation: How early in life do infants begin to remember? Does age affect memory processing? Does age influence forgetting? Perhaps the fact that so few of us remember anything about our own infancy provokes this intense interest, although reports of habituation and novelty responsiveness in newborns strongly imply memory functions even from birth (Chapter 7). Indeed, the ability to remember may even go back to the prenatal period: One classic prenatal conditioning study reported that fetuses can retain a learned association for 18 days (Spelt, 1948).

The influence of age on the ability to remember is more complicated than simply older infants remembering more than younger infants. Some argue that there are two memory systems, one primitive (implicit), operating at younger ages, and one adult-like (explicit), beginning to operate at the end of the first year of life (Carver & Bauer, 2001). Factors that influence memory, such as study time and repetition, have interactive effects with age. For example, in an associative learning experiment involving imitation of a puppet, 6-, 9-, and 18-month-olds remembered an association between two puppets and the target actions, but 12- and 15-month-olds did not (Rovee-Collier & Giles, 2010). Rovee-Collier and Giles (2010, p. 198) suggest that the earliest months of infancy are a time of "exuberant learning" and what changes across age is attention, not the memory system.

Study time and repetition also affect infant memory. Habituation–novelty-responsiveness experiments show that babies do not require extremely long exposures to to-be-remembered information to develop mental representations that allow them to recognize study stimuli (or, at least, prefer a novel stimulus by comparison). As we reviewed earlier, a characteristic feature of declarative memory is that it can be formed quickly. At the same time, practice or repeated experience with an event facilitates memory. For example, Barr and Hayne (2000) enlisted two groups of 18-month-olds in the puppet-mitten task described earlier. A practice group was given three opportunities to imitate the sequence of actions performed by the experimenter. The other no-practice group was shown the action sequence six times by the experimenter but was given no opportunity to perform the actions. Six weeks later, half of the infants in both groups were given a reminder session, which involved a brief exposure to the same puppet and experimenter, but the experimenter did not model the action sequence. All infants were then tested for retention. Retention of the action sequence was significantly better among infants in the practice group which was given the reminder, indicating that prior practice with the event and a reminder facilitated memory.

Timing of the repeated experience is important. There appears to be a time window after experiencing an event during which the memory of the event is accessible (Hsu, 2010). If the event is re-experienced toward the end of this time window, it is likely to be remembered longer than if it is experienced at the beginning of the time window. Galluccio and Rovee-Collier (2006) tested the boundaries of this time window. In a mobile task, 3-month-olds were trained with the mobile for 2 days. Infants were then given a session to reinstate memory—another training session with the mobile 1 day, 3 days, or 5 days later. Without reinstatement, infants remember the mobile for 5 five but not 6 days. Memory for the mobile was affected by the timing of the reinstatement. When reinstatement was 1 day after training, infants remembered the mobile for 6 days, when reinstatement was 3 days after training, infants remembered the mobile for 10 days, but when reinstatement was 5 days after training, infants remembered the mobile for 21 days. As infants age, the time windows become longer, yet reinstatement toward the end of the time window continues to be most effective for maintaining memories (Hsu, 2010).

Repeated exposure to an event also affects later recall. To assess the effects of repeated presentation, Campanella and Rovee-Collier (2005) showed 3-month-old infants two puppets (A and B) paired together across 7 days. On Day 8, infants saw a novel action with one of the puppets (B). Over the next 3 months, the infants saw puppet B (but not the modeled action) for approximately 30 seconds five more times. At 6 months of age, the infants were allowed to interact with puppet A, and they imitated the action they saw demonstrated with puppet B. This finding suggests that infants remembered the action done with puppet B, that seeing puppet B in the intervening months reminded infants of the novel action, and that infants associated the two puppets such that what was done with B could be done with A. Moreover, infants retained this information over three months!

Infants' long-term memory is not limited to only events involving inanimate objects. Infants remember people, and apparently they can do so for a very long time. Bornstein, Arterberry, and Mash (2004) took advantage of a still-face procedure to test infants' long-term memory for people. In the still-face procedure, an adult interacts with the baby in a normal animated interactive style for 1 minute. Then the adult assumes a neutral facial expression and does not interact with the baby for 2 minutes. Infants differ in their response to this change in demeanor, but typically it is not a very pleasant experience for them. The session ends with 1 more minute of normal interaction (Gusella, Muir, & Tronick, 1988). In this memory study, the investigators gave infants the still-face experience at 5 months and tested infants for their memory of the person 15 months later, when the infants were 20 months of age. When the infants were 20 months of age, they were given the opportunity to view three videotaped sequences of different females engaging with the infant in animated friendly manner. One of the females ("familiar") was the same person from the still-face procedure 15 months earlier; the other two were unfamiliar ("novel"). There was also a control group of infants tested at 20 months who did not experience the still-face procedure at 5 months. Infants who previously experienced the still-face procedure looked significantly less to the familiar person than infants who did not experience the still-face procedure. These findings suggest that personal memories are possible early in life and the memories for unique or emotional experiences or faces associated with them can be retained across long periods of time.

Despite the preceding examples of impressive memory skills in young infants, we should not forget that infants forget more rapidly than adults. One factor that influences memory, or contributes to forgetting, is context. Context refers to aspects of the internal and external environments that are present during object information processing (Spear, 1978). External context defines characteristics of the setting in which the object or event is processed and encoded. Some attributes of context may be integral to object or event processing; others may be incidental. Nonetheless, both are important and influence how we sense, think, and remember objects. For example, Rovee-Collier and colleagues (2009a) trained 3-month-olds to move a mobile by kicking. During learning, the infants' cribs were lined with a colorful bumper (the context). Changes in the bumper did not affect retention of the contingency 1 day later when the memory was easily retrieved. However, after delays of 3, 5, and 7 days, when the same mobile was present at training and retention, retrieval was evident only when the bumper surrounding the crib during the retention test matched the bumper present during training. With age, infants are better able to tolerate context changes (different patterned cloths in their cribs or different rooms of their home), a development that coincides with self-produced locomotion (DeFrancisco & Rovee-Collier, 2008).

Rovee-Collier and Giles (2010) suggested that "rapid forgetting is not a memory deficit but is an evolutionarily selected survival-related strategy" (p. 203). In their view, forgetting allows the young infant to adapt to rapidly changing surroundings by forgetting unnecessary information and quickly learning new things. People and events that are frequently encountered (and thus are unchanging aspects of the infants' environment) are remembered due to the processes we discussed above, such as study time, repetition, and context.

In summary, infants have sophisticated memory capacities. Even newborns can remember. Investigators now ask *how* infants remember; that is, what skills or strategies infants use and what the dimensions of memory in infancy are. Encoding skills and short-term memory improve rapidly over the first year, whereas retrieval skills and long-term memory improve later and gradually. Even in the first weeks of life, babies give good evidence that they recognize (for example, their mothers' face, voice, and scent), and their memories seem to last. As infants age, they demonstrate an ability to hold events in memory for longer time spans, and they require fewer cues and shorter periods of familiarization to recall past events. Babies appear to save some specific memories, and they can retrieve seemingly forgotten information if they are given a reminder. These memory abilities may be especially true for patterned, repeated events, such as those that occur in the context of parent–child interactions. Although the capacity for ordered recall early in development is quite developed, its rapid growth allows memory to guide infants' continuing behavior with objects and people. The implications for learning are many, including what types of stimulation contribute to learning and memory (Box 8.2).

PLAY

It might seem odd to include a discussion of play in a chapter on mental representation. Isn't infant play

---

Box 8.2   Science in Translation: What do Babies Remember from Baby-Targeted Media?

We have learned that infants are active perceivers of their environment, active partners in inter-actions with others, and can remember what they have experienced under the right circum-stances. These fascinating discoveries have led to questions not only about the importance of early experience but whether parents should be doing more to foster the development of their babies. In the last 10 years or so, there has been a growth in products designed specifically for babies, and one popular product are videos or DVDs (perhaps the most popular is the *Baby Einstein* series). Moreover, there is a special satellite TV channel with programming designed just for babies called *BabyTV*. Baby-targeted media typically combine visual and auditory stimuli (e.g., 3-D objects floating in space along with music), and some have words (spoken, written, and sometimes signed with American Sign Language) paired with objects.

The exposure of screen media to young babies raises a number of questions, but the one germane to a chapter on representation is whether babies understand and remember the infor-mation presented in the videos. Certainly the videos are attention-getting. For example, 12- to 18-month-olds attend to 65% of a *Baby Mozart* video (Barr, Zack, Garcia, & Muentner, 2008), and parents believe that their children learn from them (Rideout & Hamel, 2006). But do babies learn and remember?

DeLoache and her colleagues addressed this question (DeLoache et al., 2010). They asked a group of parents to expose their 12- to 18-month-olds to a popular DVD several times a week for 4 weeks. The DVD had a variety of scenes of a house and a yard and a voice labeled com-mon objects, and after the 4 weeks infants were tested for memory of the words. Half of the par-ents were asked to also interact with their infant while watching the DVD, and the other half were asked to allow their infant to watch the DVD without interacting with their child. Two more groups of parents and infants who did not watch the video also participated in this study. One group of parents was asked to try to teach their child a list of 25 words (the same words presented in the DVD), and the last group was a control condition in which only the infants' vocabulary was assessed. DeLoache et al. found that children learned the most words when their parent tried to teach them the words and that fewer words were learned by infants in the DVD conditions (with and without interaction). Notably, the performance by the DVD infants was not different from the control group.

Thus, exposing infants to baby-targeted media does not appear to facilitate learning. Con-sistent with other research, it appears that direct interaction with people and objects is the best context for promoting infants' learning about and remembering the world around them.

---

social? Of course, it is. But imagine for a moment what play looks like in its earliest stages. Play is cer-tainly fun and interactive, but play also involves studying a doll, manipulating a busy-box, building with a set of blocks, or entertaining at a make-believe tea party. Play frequently imitates life, and it is quite common to observe toddlers reenacting in play specific events that they observe or participate in routinely ("driving" a toy car). Such play indicates that infants explore and represent events mentally, reproducing them in play. The advent of symbolic or pretend play (as well as language) during the second year of life reflects an underlying developmental progression in the capacity for representation (Bornstein, 2006c).

Play shows us the infant's level of competence in physical, motor, linguistic, and socioemotional domains of development. The quality of infant play relates to adaptive and fine-motor skills in 12-month-olds and predicts linguistic development around 24 months (Eisert & Lamorey, 1996; Smith & Jones, 2011; Sung & Hsu, 2009). Infant play also holds special significance for professionals with a wide range of interests, including those working with children with disabilities (Bornstein, Scrimin et al., 2012; Cress, Arens, & Zajicek, 2007; Schaefer, Kelly-Zion, McCormick, & Ohnogi, 2008).

In this section, we first describe the early development of play which, in bold outline, begins as inspection and manipulation and moves gradually to symbolism and pretense. Then, we examine the ways in which play becomes embedded in interaction. Play brings the child into contact with many physical and social features of the environment and, in many ways, is a critical kind of self-initiated learning.

The Development of Play

Piaget (1954, 1962) was among the first theorists to study infant play seriously. Because Piaget was primarily concerned with the philosophical problems of epistemology (Chapter 1), most of his research on infant cognitive development focused on children's beliefs about space, objects, and causation; in other words children's understanding of physical laws that govern actions and objects. However, Piaget also motivated researchers to examine related mental processes in infants, and Piaget himself saw infant play as a platform for integrating different cognitive abilities. He studied play for the light it promised to throw on cognitive development in infancy generally. After all, play is exploration, and how exploration proceeds reveals much about mental growth.

For Piaget, infants' activities with a single object were the most primitive. The very youngest infant manipulates one object at a time, relying on sensorimotor behaviors (for example, pushing, pulling, squishing, and so forth). Older infants move on to more advanced operations, manipulating the parts of objects or several objects together to look at relations among them (putting a spoon into a cup). The use children make of objects in play appears to reflect developmental changes in cognition. Many researchers have therefore studied play to learn what it tells us about children's cognitive development, what knowledge children possess, how they acquire new knowledge, and the factors affecting the acquisition and use of knowledge.

Piaget examined his own children's play closely and articulated four major principles about child play:

1   Play follows an ordinal developmental sequence.
2   Action is the basis of knowledge, as exemplified in the slow but steady decreasing egocentrism of child play.
3   Representational (pretend) play, involving the use of one object to stand for another or pretending to engage in an action, has a late onset and slow development.
4   Pretend play shifts from play that involves only the self (pretending to sleep), through pretense involving self–object relations (pretending to drink from a cup), to pretense involving objects exclusively (having a doll pretend to drink).

Piaget's successors have confirmed many of his observations, but they have also found need for considerable refinement in the ways that play is assessed (Bornstein, 2006c; Tamis-LeMonda, Užgiris, & Bornstein, 2002). Assessments vary depending on whether they study children's naturalistic, unstructured free play, children's modeling, or parents' prompting play. Some have also integrated play assessment into interventions for infants at risk for special needs (Ravn et al., 2011). These approaches to assessment, based on careful, systematic observations of infants' interactions with toys, reveal that the earliest forms of infant play involve the repetition of actions. Objects in the environment do not have an important role in the child's play during the first 2 or 3 months of life. Three-month-olds, for instance, may coo repeatedly or kick their legs while lying awake in their cribs, or they might arch their backs and drop their bodies onto the mattress over and over again. These actions are recognizable as Piaget's primary circular reactions—activities apparently repeated for their own sake (Chapter 7). Even after infants develop more sophisticated manipulative skills, they appear to be primarily interested in the actions they can perform rather than in the objects being manipulated. Thus, the youngest babies might look at a toy in their field of vision (Figure 8.8A), but rarely do they scan systematically or study the objects they are playing with. Instead, they might put them into their mouths (Figure 8.8B). Even when two objects appear related to one another—a cup and a spoon—the older infant often still focuses on actions—banging the spoon in the cup—rather than objects. Remove the spoon, and the action is likely to continue.

At around 9 months of age, a major change in the complexity and quality of infant play occurs. Infants begin to engage in what are called functional, relational, and functional-relational play. **Functional play** involves playing with an object in the way the object was intended to be played with (e.g., rolling a toy car on its wheels across the floor). In **relational play**, the infant brings together two unrelated objects (e.g., a spoon and a block) with no indication of pretense (Figure 8.9A). **Functional-relational play** brings together two objects but now in a meaningful and appropriate way. For example, the child may take a spoon and stir it inside a cup or place blocks inside a container of some sort (Figure 8.9B).

For the next several months, clear-cut pretense or symbolism is seldom evident. According to Piaget, pretense requires bringing to mind a physically absent object, and hence involves representational skills

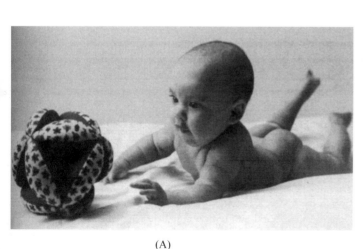
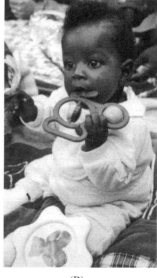

(A)   (B)

Fig. 8.8 An infant in the earliest stage of play looks at the toy (A) but quickly develops the ability to interact with the toy manually and orally (B).

(A)   (B)

Fig. 8.9 An infant in a later stage of play may bring two objects into juxtaposition (A) and then as a toddler use two objects together functionally (B).

(that you will recall, he claimed were not attained until the second year of life). Consistent with this notion, pretend play does not occur with any regularity until the second year of life, although some infants show this capacity as early as 13 months of age.

Symbolic play can be clearly identified in the second year by the emergence of object substitution. When the young child builds a tower out of blocks, the tower seems to mean more to the child than the characteristics of the blocks per se. There can, therefore, be two kinds of representation reflected in object substitutions (Leslie, 1988a, 1988b). First, **primary representations** reflect perceptual features of the objects. Blocks have substance, shape, and color, and so different blocks may be used for different purposes. Second are **meta-representations** of the objects. These are representations of objects apart from their normal meaning; assembled, a set of blocks is now a tower. The object substitutions of younger toddlers tend to be restricted by physical resemblance—different colors of blocks—whereas older toddlers are not as dependent on physical characteristics, so blocks may stand for people. In the second year, toddlers also use objects to represent other objects to which the objects bear no physical resemblance.

Even when the child is operating at the level of pretense, play initially centers on the child's own body and actions. In self-directed pretense play, children might pretend that they are going to sleep, or they might pretend to drink from a cup or talk on a telephone (Figure 8.10). Later, children involve objects other than the self in their pretense. Children first pretend to sleep themselves by lying down on a pillow and only later make a doll lie down and sleep. Even after this movement away from the self has taken place, significant developmental changes lie ahead. Play becomes more complex with age through the

Fig. 8.10 A toddler in a still later stage of play can pretend to use a telephone.

incorporation of combinations and sequences of pretend actions. Older children also make more elaborate plans for future play, as when they play "kitchen" and appear to prepare a whole meal.

We can broadly summarize the development of play. In the first year, play is predominantly characterized by sensorimotor manipulation; infant play appears designed to extract information about objects, what objects do, what perceivable qualities they have, and what immediate effects they can produce. This form of play is commonly referred to as **exploratory** or **non-symbolic play** because children's play activities are tied to the tangible properties of objects rather than being representational. In the second year, children's play actions take on more of a non-literal quality: The goal of play now appears to be **symbolic** or **representational**. Play is increasingly generative, as children enact activities performed by self, others, and objects in simple pretense scenarios, pretending to drink from empty teacups, talking on toy telephones, and the like (Bornstein, 2006c).

Table 8.1 shows a single comprehensive scheme of play for infants. Eight basic play levels are defined, and the table shows predominant play acts for each level that infants of 13 and 20 months might exhibit, along with an index of the relative frequency of those examples. The eight play levels are: (1) Unitary functional activity, (2) Inappropriate combinatorial activity, (3) Appropriate combinatorial activity, (4) Transitional play, (5) Self-directed pretense, (6) Other-directed pretense, (7) Sequential pretense, and (8) Substitution pretense. Levels 1 to 4 constitute exploratory play, and levels 5 to 8 constitute symbolic play. More sophisticated forms of play became increasingly common with age among infants in a variety of cultures, including France, Italy, Korea as well among different cultural groups in the United States

(Bornstein, Venuti, & Hahn, 2002; Cote & Bornstein, 2009; Kwak, Putnick, & Bornstein, 2008; Suizzo & Bornstein, 2006).

Table 8.1 Infant play levels

			Predominant Examples	
Play Level	Label	Definition	13 Months	20 Months
1	Unitary functional activity	Production of an effect that is unique to a single object	Throw or squeeze foam ball (25%)[a]	Dial telephone (21%)
2	Inappropriate combinatorial activity	Inappropriate juxtaposition of two or more objects	Put ball in vehicle[b]	Put ball in vehicle
3	Appropriate combinatorial activity	Appropriate juxtaposition of two or more objects	Put lid on teapot (44%)	Nest blocks (27%)
4	Transitional play	Approximate of pretense but without confirmatory evidence	Put telephone receiver to ear (without vocalization, 44%)	Put telephone receiver to ear (without vocalization, 57%)
5	Self-directed pretense	Clear pretense activity directed toward self	Eat from spoon or cup (39%)	Eat from spoon or cup (36%)
6	Other-directed pretense	Clear pretense activity directed toward other	Kiss or hug doll (41%)	Pretend vehicle makes sound (48%)
7	Sequential pretense	Link of two or more pretense actions	Dial telephone and speak into receiver (45%)	Dial telephone and speak into receiver (30%)
8	Substitution pretense	Pretend activity involving one or more object substitutions	Pretend block is telephone and talk into it[b]	Pretend block is telephone and talk into it[b]

a Percentages in parentheses reflect the frequency of the associated example over the total frequency of play acts at that level.
b Because any inappropriate combination for Level 2 or any object substitution for Level 8 exemplifies that play level, none dominated.

We have introduced the distinction between exploratory and symbolic play as a guide to general changes that take place in representation in infancy, but there are also individual differences in the rates at which individual children achieve representation, and there may be individual differences in children's levels of achievement. The sequence we describe represents an idealized developmental progression: Most children progress this way, but children of a given age vary greatly among themselves with respect to, say, their symbolic play. For example, Tamis-LeMonda and Bornstein (1990) found that 15% of 13-month-olds' total play was symbolic, but some individual 13-month-olds never exhibited symbolic play, whereas for others as much as 51% of play was symbolic. At 20 months, 31% of infants' total play was symbolic, but some individual 20-month-olds showed as little as 2% symbolic play, whereas for others 83% of play was symbolic. Furthermore, 13-month symbolic-play levels predicted 20-month symbolic-play levels—infants who showed more representational play at 13 months also showed more representational play at 20 months—but this stability depended on the support of mothers.

In summary, much as Piaget proposed, infants transit from exploratory play not specific to the object manipulated, through functional-relational play tailored to specific objects, to pretend play with objects, to freedom from specific objects altogether. Infants do not play in isolation, and in the next section we explore the role that significant adults, such as parents, play in facilitating the development of infants' play.

Play Development and Social Interaction

"Play is something contented children do when adults are not bothering them to do other things; and play is something adults tell demanding children to do to get them out of the way" (Fein, 1991, p. 144). As this statement illustrates, many early researchers looked at play as a solitary child activity. In contrast, Vygotsky (1978) proposed that social interaction actually fosters symbolic functioning in people. Indeed, Vygotsky motivated a major conceptual shift in the study of play, regarding it not as a solitary activity reflecting underlying cognitive schema that the child already possessed, but as a formative activity shaped by the child's interactions with parents.

The achievement of symbolic play is now seen as a reflection of children's individual growth in the context of their interpersonal interactions and sociocultural setting (Bornstein, 2006c). It is quite normal to think of play in the context of social interaction. Play emerges in the child, but adults influence its development by outfitting the play environment, engaging children actively, and responding to children's play overtures. Two questions we will focus on are (1) how does interaction affect play and (2) how does play affect interaction?

Bornstein and his colleagues have addressed these questions in a series of studies examining infant play, change, and growth in the context of mother–infant interaction. Bornstein, Haynes, O'Reilly, and Painter (1996) found that the play of 20-month-olds with their mothers was more sophisticated, complex, and varied than the infants' play when they were alone. Importantly, what the mothers did with their infants during play appeared to affect the quality of the infants' play. Mothers of 20-month-olds who initiated symbolic play more frequently had infants who engaged in symbolic play more frequently, whether initiated by the mother or the child. Mothers and infants appear to be attuned to each other during play, with the play level of one partner being closely geared to the play level of the other. In addition, individual differences in symbolic play in mothers and infants appear to be stable at least over the short term (Bornstein, Haynes, Legler, O'Reilly, & Painter, 1997).

What mothers know about play and how it develops predicts the degree to which mothers can facilitate the sophistication of their infants' play (Tamis-LeMonda, Damast, & Bornstein, 1994). Generally speaking, mothers of 21-month-olds recognize that exploratory play (mouthing and nonfunctional manipulation) is less sophisticated than functional play, and that functional play is less sophisticated than symbolic, pretend play. However, mothers' ratings are highly variable; some mothers have more accurate knowledge of play than others. These accuracy differences, in turn, predict the degree to which mothers successfully support or **scaffold** (Chapter 7) their children's play. That is, mothers who know more about play tend to prompt their children to play at more sophisticated levels than do mothers with less accurate knowledge. Thus, the more parents know about play and how it develops, the more they may foster their infants' play in daily interactions with them.

Evidence of social-interactional determinants of play in infancy comes from many quarters. For example, mothers' ability to time and attune their own emotional displays relative to their infants' emotional states during face-to-face exchanges in the first year of life predicts children's symbolic play at 24 months of age, suggesting that successful emotional signaling and responsiveness in the first year helps to lay the foundation for later symbolic development (Feldman & Greenbaum, 1997). Noll and Harding (2003) found that when mothers responded to their 12- to 47-month-olds' object play in an "options-promoting" manner (encouraging, affirming, and/or expanding on the child's activities), their children engaged in significantly higher levels of symbolic play than did children whose mothers responded in an "options-limiting" manner (disapproving of or obstructing the child's play). Moreover, certain personality dimensions in mothers contribute to more symbolic play in children. Mothers scoring high on openness and extraversion show more symbolic demonstrations when playing with their infants (Bornstein, Hahn, & Haynes, 2011). Fathers, too, facilitate play in ways uniquely different from mothers (Malmberg et al., 2007; Roggman, Boyce, Cook, Christiansen, & Jones, 2004). For example, fathers show more exploratory play and solitary play, and fathers who spend more time with their infants (as primary care givers) help to create a more positive emotional tone during play sessions than fathers who are not engaged in primary care activities (DeFalco, Esposito, Venuti, & Bornstein, 2010; Lewis et al., 2008). Clearly, both holistic characteristics of parenting (quality of emotional attunement) as well as parents' specific behaviors during play (exploratory, symbolic) affect infants' play competence.

Play Partners and Functions

All theories of play focus on the functions of children's play with peers in addition to the importance of adults (Piaget, 1952; Vygotsky, 1962). Play facilitates growth in five major domains of development: psychological, mastery, cognitive, social, and cultural. Infants' play partners' characteristics and style support these different functions. Psychologically, children can regulate arousal, express a range of emotions, and resolve conflicts and traumas in play. For example, play partners who respond appropriately to children's needs for stimulation contribute to children's self-regulatory capacities (Chapter 10). Play expands the range of emotions that children express by enabling them to experience positive emotions (fun, excitement, and pleasure) as well as negative emotions, (anger, sadness, and fear). The mastery function of play helps children achieve a sense of **self-efficacy**, a belief in one's abilities. Sophistication in play is associated with improved cognition in respect to greater attention span and persistence on problem solving tasks (Tamis-LeMonda & Bornstein, 1996). In addition, during and as the result of play, children acquire information and skills, engage in creative and divergent thinking, and attain more sophisticated representational abilities (Onishi, Baillargeon, & Leslie, 2007). Socially, play fosters children's understanding of others' feelings, intentions, and perspectives, and thereby enhances their social interactions and relationships. Play also supports children's development of **reciprocity** (social exchanges such as turn taking) and **inter-subjectivity** (shared meaning), which provide a foundation for mature forms of social understanding. Finally, play is a vehicle for the transmission of social roles and cultural values. In role-play, children practice behaviors they will need as adults in their society, and role-play helps children to understand and acquire societal standards and beliefs. During social play, children learn traditional ways of thinking and behaving (Clearfield & Nelson, 2006).

Adult caregivers, siblings, and peers all support the psychological, mastery, cognitive, social, and cultural functions of play. Adult caregivers are most important during infancy. Mothers are more effective than siblings and peers at all ages in regulating children's emotions by adjusting levels of stimulation and containing emotions in play. After the first year, however, play with peers and siblings becomes prominent and is often intense and emotionally charged. The cognitive skills that parents emphasize are different from those common in sibling and peer play: Parents convey information about the real world and encourage conventional object use and convergent thinking, whereas siblings and peers are motivated by play itself. Who plays with infants varies across cultures and communicates information about cultural norms and about the role of adults and peers as well as the role of the child in the society (Rogoff, 2003). In societies in which adults frequently engage in play, social roles and cultural values are transmitted to children from the beginning of infancy. During infancy, peers are less likely to transmit specific social roles or values through role-play, both because they lack competence in coordinating social pretense and because of a lack of knowledge of social and cultural values. By 2 to 3 years of age, however, peers' and siblings' contributions to play begin to outweigh those of adults. Thus, different play partners have unique characteristics and styles that support different play functions at different developmental periods.

Sibling play has some characteristics that are similar to adult–child play and others that are similar to peer–child play. Like adults, older siblings possess more expertise than their younger siblings and can model higher levels of play. Unlike caregivers or older siblings, peers are playmates who share a similar developmental level and relate to each other without an established hierarchy. More than with adults, play with peers sustains attention, pleasure, and excitement. Thus, different social partners contribute in unique and often complementary ways to infants' psychological, mastery, cognitive, social, and cultural advances in play (Bornstein & O'Reilly, 1993).

Culture, Social Context, and Play

Research on developmental milestones, individual variation, and parental correlates of infant play has almost exclusively involved Western families. This mono-cultural emphasis restricts our understanding of early development because those characteristics that are universal cannot be distinguished from those that are culturally specific. In Mayan and tribal Indian cultures, play is considered as predominantly a child's activity, whereas in middle-income U.S. culture the parent has an important role as a play partner (Rogoff, 2003). Cultures also differ in how they value play. Some cultures believe that play provides important development-promoting experiences; others see play primarily to amuse (Bornstein, 2006c). Presumably, cultural beliefs about play affect the nature and frequency of infants' play with parents, siblings, and peers.

Bornstein and his colleagues have conducted a series of cross-cultural studies of mother–infant play in the United States, Argentina, France, Italy, Japan, and Korea (Bornstein, 2006c). Japan represents a provocative comparison with the United States in this respect because these two countries maintain reasonably similar levels of modernity and living standards, and both are child centered, but at the same time the two differ dramatically in terms of history, culture, beliefs, and childrearing goals. Also, the activities mothers in each country emphasize in interactions with their infants differ. In general, U.S. mothers promote autonomy and organize social interactions with their infants to foster physical and verbal assertiveness in children as well as interest in the external environment, whereas Japanese mothers organize social interactions so as to consolidate and strengthen mutual dependence within the dyad (Bornstein et al., in press).

Generally speaking, Japanese infants and mothers engage in more symbolic play and U.S. infants and mothers engage in more exploratory play. The difference in Japanese mothers' symbolic play is especially reflected in increased levels of other-directed pretense ("feed the dolly"). Thus, in line with their cultural preferences, Japanese mothers organize infant pretend play in ways that encourage their infants to incorporate partners into their play, whereas U.S. mothers encourage self-exploration at functional and combinatorial play levels ("push the bus"). Childrearing practices in Japan emphasize closeness and interdependency between dyad members, whereas U.S. practices encourage interest in the environment and interpersonal independence supplemented by information-oriented verbal interactions. For U.S. mothers and infants, play and the toys used during play are more frequently the topic or object of communication; by contrast, among Japanese the play setting and the toys appear to mediate dyadic communication and interaction (Chapter 2).

In summary, play changes dramatically during infancy, developing from exploration and functional manipulation toward more sophisticated acts of pretense. Play follows a species-typical development that in turn reflects broader cultural themes and values. Solitary play with objects provides a window on cognition, with play proceeding in the first year of life from simple manipulation and mouthing to functional activities that exploit the unique properties of objects. In the second year of life, infants increasingly engage in symbolic pretense that, along with the growth of language, reflects the further development, refinement, and elaboration of their representational capacities. Play also has social, emotional, attentional, and mastery components and does not develop in isolation. Indeed, it can be fostered during social interactions with parents especially when parents are sensitively attuned to their infant's emotional cues and developmental level.

SUMMARY

In this chapter, we have reviewed what is known about three prominent forms of mental representation in infancy. Infancy represents a period in which central mental abilities, such as categorization and concept formation, memory, and pretend play emerge and develop. Representation stands for the information that is stored in the head. How that information is stored, the nature of that information, its availability, and its use are the central concerns of this chapter. Our understanding of infant cognition in all its forms depends on our understanding of the nature of mental representations. Studies of representational abilities tell us about the infants' developing capacity to acquire, share, and use information about the environment. To understand the foundations and mechanisms that underpin mental growth in childhood, we must first understand representation in its several forms, including categorization and concept formation, memory, and play. Each entails important (and perhaps related) mental processes, although each is also complex and has many features.

We have treated categorization and concept formation, memory, and play separately and have discussed them largely independent of language. However, these are artificial distinctions because all of these processes are integrally interrelated. Clearly, the infant has a rich mental life, and the study of the mental life of the infant is still at a frontier. The transition from sensorimotor behavior to linguistic intelligence is awe-inspiring. This process is well ordered and universal, and the achievement is impressive, building as it does on representations in the forms of categorization and concept formation, memory, and play.

KEY TERMS

A-not-B task	Long-term memory
Basic level	Meta-representations
Boundaries	Non-exploratory play
Conceptual organization	Operant conditioning techniques
Categorization	Perceptual organization
Declarative memory	Prerepresentational thinking
Decontextualization	Pretend play
Deferred imitation tasks	Primary representations
Encoding	Procedural memory
Episodic memory	Prototypes
Event-related potentials	Recall
Exploratory play	Recognition
Functional play	Relational play
Functional-relational play	Representational play
Hierarchical inclusiveness	Representational thinking
Interiorization	Retrieval
Inter-subjectivity	Search paradigm

Self-efficacy
Semantic memory
Sensory register
Short-term/working memory
Study time

Subordinate level
Superordinate or global level
Symbolic play

Chapter 9

Language Development in Infancy

- *What are the four broad domains of language?*
- *Distinguish between production and comprehension of language.*
- *What are the major individual differences in language development?*
- *What methods are used to study language acquisition?*
- *What supports do infants have for learning language?*
- *What is "child-directed speech" and what are its main characteristics?*
- *What are infants earliest utterances like?*
- *How do infants learn new words?*
- *What is the significance of the context-restricted to context-flexible shift in semantic development?*
- *How do children put words together?*
- *What characterizes nativist and nonnativist accounts of infant word and grammar learning?*
- *How are infants neurologically prepared for language learning?*

The terms infant and baby both have their origins in language-related concepts. The word infant derives from the Latin *in + fans*, translated literally as "non-speaker," and the word baby shares a Middle English root with **babble**. In the estimation of many, children only leave infancy when they begin to communicate verbally with those around them. However, as we see in this chapter, conversations with babies begin well before words come into consideration.

Language lies at the center of impressive accomplishments in the physical, perceptual, cognitive, and social spheres of development. Human language is also a very complicated matter to study, for it simultaneously involves several overlapping broad domains. **Phonology** describes sounds that are linguistically meaningful in the language. **Semantics**, the lexicon, involves the meaning of words and phrases. **Syntax**, or grammar, defines the ways in which words and phrases are arranged. Finally, **pragmatics** is the social rules that dictate our everyday usage of language.

Consider an infant's task in understanding mother's meaning when she says simply, "*Yourteddyis-lyingonthecouchsweetie.*" The infant must segregate the sounds into individual word forms, map each word onto its meaning, and analyze the grammatical structure linking the word forms to understand the whole. To complicate matters further, these three types of decoding must take place as the utterance unfolds. Very young children rapidly become very good in both understanding and speaking, despite the abstractness and complexity of language.

Some theorists have argued that language learning proceeds strictly on the basis of the child's experiences. St. Augustine (398/1961) wrote that children learn language by imitating their elders, and B. F. Skinner (1957) asserted that children learn language just as they do any system of behavioral contingencies—through reinforcement. In contrast, other theorists have maintained that language acquisition could only develop if facilitated by innate predispositions (Chomsky, 1965; Pinker, 2007). However, language is too rich, unique, and complex a system for infants simply to learn passively, just as it is too rich, unique, and complex a system for newborns simply to know.

In this chapter, we describe how infants develop from nonverbal individualists into interactive conversationalists, ready and able to articulate their cares, needs, desires, and dreams to others. We start with a brief consideration of norms and individual variation, along with some important principles related to the mechanics of studying early language acquisition. We then discuss the social supports, such as parent speech to children and activities that teach turn taking, that facilitate infants' language development and their learning pragmatics. Next, we take up production and comprehension in three formal domains of language: producing and perceiving sounds (phonology), acquiring a vocabulary (semantics), and grammar (syntax). As we see, infants are surprisingly prepared in each of these realms, possessing both the motivation and the competencies to ensure that they quickly become full participants in language. The acquisition of language reflects the dynamic interaction between the child's developing competencies and the larger context of adult–infant social communication.

NORMS, INDIVIDUAL DIFFERENCES, AND METHODS OF STUDY

Language acquisition is one of the most fundamental human traits, and it takes place alongside dramatic changes in the brain. Speech in infants develops from babbling at around 6 to 8 months of age to the one-word stage at 10 to 12 months and then to the two-word stage at around 2 years. Figure 9.1 depicts

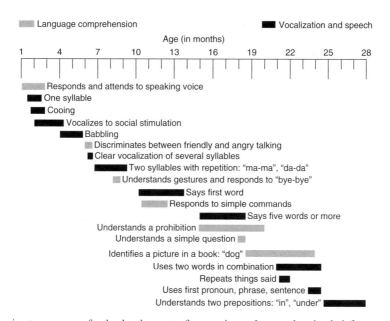

Fig. 9.1 Approximate age norms for the development of expression and comprehension in infants over the first 2½ years of life.

in a simplified format some "milestones" of language development in infancy. In the first month of life, infants coo and babble. By 24 months, toddlers generate grammatically correct sentences. In the first month, infants respond to the human voice. By 24 months, toddlers comprehend the meaning of prepositions. The very existence of a chart like this reflects the strong normative tradition in the field of **developmental psycholinguistics**, the popularity of description, and the fundamental distinction between production and comprehension. However, it also masks the central everyday consideration of individual differences.

Comprehension and Production

When examining language, it is first necessary to distinguish between comprehension and production. If you play with a 1-year-old, you might notice that the infant can follow your instructions well, but cannot tell you anything about the simple game he or she is playing. **Receptive language**, or comprehension, nearly always developmentally precedes **expressive language**, or production (Darwin, 1877; Box 3.1). For example, Benedict (1979) listed the first 50 words comprehended and produced by infants. Infants first understood words at 9 months but did not say any words until 12 months, on average. Later, children reached a 50-word milestone in comprehension at around 13 months, whereas they reached 50 words in production at 18 months.

In the latter half of the second year, many infants exhibit rapid increases in both production and comprehension. The source and nature of this **vocabulary burst** have been the focus of considerable debate. Productive and receptive vocabularies increase together: Infants and older children who comprehend more words are also likely to produce more words (Bornstein & Putnick, 2012; Fernald, Perfors, & Marchman, 2006). The association between productive and receptive vocabularies indicates that acceleration in word learning rates is not simply a consequence of improvement in motor articulation; some aspect of understanding also is involved. Perhaps vocabularies take off as soon as infants realize that things have names. On occasion, this epiphany (called **nominal insight**) is witnessed by parents, as their infants suddenly begin labeling objects and learning words rapidly.

However, the expansion in vocabulary does not always have a sudden character. For most infants, the rate at which words are learned increases a great deal in the second year, but this increase does not necessarily begin with a sudden leap. Instead, infants seem to gradually get better and better at word learning. Most likely, this reflects a range of cognitive changes, including improvements in interpreting continuous speech, development of categorization skills, and greater appreciation of the pragmatics of language use (Colombo, McCardle, & Freund, 2009). On this view, infants' conscious notion of what language is for is just one of the many developments that result in better and faster language learning.

Individual Variation

Children of the same age vary dramatically on nearly every index of language development, and individual differences in children's language, as well as the sources of variation, occupy a central position in the study of language acquisition (Bornstein & Putnick, 2012). The classic illustration of individual differences in early language production was provided by Brown (1973), who traced speech development in three children—Adam, Eve, and Sarah. Across several years, Brown indexed their verbal growth in terms of changing mean length of utterance (discussed later). Figure 9.2 shows that all three children achieved common goals and that growth rates were nearly equivalent among them. However, Eve began considerably earlier than did Adam or Sarah, and Eve made the same progress from 19 to 27 months that Adam and Sarah made from 26 to 42 months. For example, Eve used an average of three utterances at about 2 years of age, whereas Adam and Sarah did not do so until approximately 3 years of age—one-third of their lifetimes later.

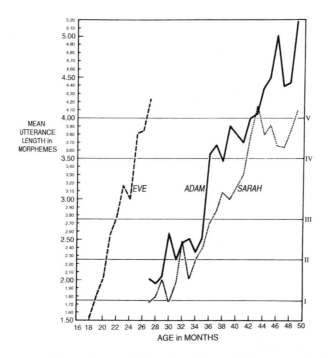

Fig. 9.2 Mean utterance length by age in three children. (From Brown, 1973; reproduced with permission.)

Tamis-LeMonda and Bornstein (1990, 1991) studied comprehension and production of children's first words longitudinally between 13 and 20 months, looking at those words infants could use or understand without environmental cues (so-called **context-flexible** words). At 13 months, some infants comprehended ten words, others 75; some produced 0 words, others 27. At 20 months, individual children had productive vocabularies ranging from 8 to 434 words. This study also looked at a variety of other verbal abilities at 20 months. The average length of children's longest utterances in **morphemes** (or meaningful units referred to as **MLU** for mean length utterance), such as "*jump*" and "*ing*" in "*jumping*," was 2.6. Some infants, however, only expressed single-morpheme utterances (e.g., saying "*jump*" to mean "*he jumped*"), whereas others linked over five morphemes (e.g., saying "He is going to jump"). Over the second year, there is also a fair amount of consistency within individual infants: 13-month productive vocabulary size predicted 20-month productive vocabulary size. That is, those infants who had high scores on language measures at 13 months also had high scores at 20 months, and those with lower scores at the younger age continued to have lower scores when they were older. Similar stability within children was found by Bornstein and Putnick (2012) from 20 to 48 months.

This work exemplifies a quantitative approach to studying individual differences in infants' language acquisition. Other investigators have focused on qualitative variation in infants' speech. Following Halliday (1975), several investigators have hypothesized that infants follow different styles of language production in the second year of life. One kind is **referential** children; their early vocabularies have a high proportion of object labels and their speech provides much concrete information. Another kind is **expressive** children; their early vocabularies have more pronouns and action words, and their speech uses social formulae and routines to communicate feelings and desires. Goldfield (1985/1986) described two children who represent these lexical extremes. She videotaped them at play with their mothers at home at 12, 15, and 18 months of age. As an example, consider Johanna, a referential child. Of Johanna's first 50 words, 49 were names for things. In play, approximately one-half of her attempts to engage her mother involved her giving or showing a toy and, reciprocally, Johanna's mother consistently labeled toys for her. Talk about toys was the most frequent category of maternal speech, and naming was a frequent strategy. In contrast, consider Caitlin, an expressive child. Nearly two-thirds of Caitlin's first 50 words consisted of social expressions, many of them in phrases. She included a toy in fewer than one-fifth of her bids to her mother, preferring instead to engage in routines of social play (e.g., peek-a-boo). These two styles of communicating appear to function differently for children. For referential youngsters the purpose of language is to label, describe, and exchange information, whereas for expressive youngsters language denotes or confirms interactive activity.

Clearly, Caitlin and Johanna are extremes. Most children exhibit a more balanced picture of referential and expressive speech. In fact, a given child may sometimes look referential and other times expressive, depending on the context or demands of the situation. For example, book reading might call for a more referential style, whereas social games call for an expressive style. First-borns are more likely to have a referential style and later borns an expressive style, due in part to the different linguistic experiences first-borns have compared to later born children (Hoff, 2006). Specifically, sole access to an adult communication partner, such as the mother, is common for first-borns, and mothers are likely to engage their infants in activities that promote referential language, at least in Western cultures.

Individual variation in language ability probably has several sources. For one, the maturational status and physical growth of the infant likely play a part. Over the first five years of life, high-risk preterm children yield a consistent (if slight) lag in the achievement of most major milestones of language relative to those children at term (Foster-Cohen, Edgin, Champion, & Woodward, 2007; Sansavini et al., 2011). Other developmental psycholinguists think that different children may have different cognitive organizations that underpin individual differences, such as the referential–expressive distinction. For example, children might differ in their conceptualization about what language is for—to categorize objects or to talk about events in the day. Different understandings of this kind, in turn, have their roots in how parents and infants interact, rather than innate biases that differ among children. For example, as early as 3 months of age, differences can be seen in interactions between infants and their German and Camaroonian Nso parents, with German parents spending more time directly talking to their infants than Nso parents (Keller, Otto, Lamm, Yovsi, & Kartner, 2008). Also, infants differ in their efficiency of speech processing, and this difference has implications for later vocabulary development (Fernald & Marchman, 2012). As we see later in the chapter, variation in many aspects of communication between parents and children has been associated with the size and composition of children's vocabularies.

Methods of Language Study

To understand how language learning proceeds, it would seem very easy—and ultimately valid—to simply observe, record, and analyze what infants appear to understand and say as they grow up. Brown's (1973) work with Adam, Eve, and Sarah (Figure 9.2) is a good example of this approach. Indeed, until relatively recently virtually all research in developmental psycholinguistics relied on such naturalistic observations. In adopting the observational strategy, of course, researchers had to decide how long and how frequently to listen to the child to be satisfied that the child's language skills have been sampled adequately. However, the pictures of a child's verbal abilities can differ depending on the social and physical contexts of the observation (Bornstein & Putnick, 2012; Colombo et al., 2009). Nearly every infant has failed to say something for a grandparent that the same infant has repeatedly said when with the parents. Furthermore, free play with parents will elicit some linguistic skills from infants, whereas language while eating or learning can be expected to be quite different. One study compared naturalistic samples of three features of language in 2-year-olds—total utterances, word roots, and utterance length—in the home in three contrasting situations: the infant observed playing by her/himself with mother nearby, the infant and mother observed in interactive play, and the infant and mother unobserved (the mother had an audio recorder) at a time the mother judged would provide a sample of the infant's optimal language, such as in the bath or before going to bed

(Bornstein, Painter, & Park, 2002). Infants produced more utterances and different word roots and expressed themselves in longer utterances when in interaction than when playing alone, but infants' utterances, word roots, and utterance lengths were greatest in optimal language production situations.

Another strategy used to assess language in infants employs parents as reporters, and much of the classic information about child language development has been obtained from parental diaries (Dromi, 1987; Leopold, 1949; Weir, 1962). As sources of information, diaries can be quite detailed, informative, and thought provoking, although they might also be biased and describe unrepresentative infants (see our discussion of baby biographies in Chapter 3). Instead of having parents report their own spontaneous and sometimes idiosyncratic impressions, researchers sometimes conduct interviews (Bornstein & Putnick, 2012). An interviewer might ask parents if the infant understands or produces specific words. A modern variant of this method is the structured parental report or checklist. The most widely used instrument of this kind is the *MacArthur Communicative Development Inventories* (CDI; Fenson et al., 1994). Language checklists offer advantages over traditional diary methods in the same way that recognition memory is better than recall; however, concern remains regarding whether parents may over-estimate their infant's language competency. There is tremendous variability in productive vocabulary size among infants in the early stages of language learning. For example, Bornstein, Cote, et al. (2004) reported that 20-month-olds around the world range from as few as one spoken word to as many as 487! Whether this wide range is due to actual differences among infants or parental under- or over-estimation cannot be fully determined.

Researchers also assess children's language abilities using standardized techniques to complement transcripts of children's spontaneous speech and parental reports. The general idea is to set up a situation that increases the likelihood that children will use a given word or sentence construction, either by directly asking children to say something or by providing toys or other aids that tend to elicit the desired kinds of comments. An example of such an assessment is the Reynell Developmental Language Scales (Reynell & Gruber, 1990). Using structured tasks, infants are asked to demonstrate comprehension of increasingly more difficult verbal expressions ranging from labeled objects to higher order concepts. Production measures include spontaneous expressions from vocalizations other than crying to the use of complex sentences, and picture prompts to help children show their level of productive vocabulary. Another example is *The Comprehension Book*, composed of 42 picture pairs organized in a picture book format (Ring & Fenson, 2000). The items represented by the pictures in the book constitute a subset of items drawn from the CDI, and infants are asked to point to the object named by the experimenter. *The Comprehension Book* has also been modified for administration via touch screen, which allows infants to receive feedback when they select the correct item (Friend & Keplinger, 2003). Use of touch screen technology makes the experience more rewarding for infants and results in more reliable assessments of their language skills.

Elicited production techniques are particularly useful when the language constructions tested might be rare or absent in diary data, but still in children's productive ability. Also, tested constructions can use words invented by the experimenter to be certain that the child is not simply imitating something he or she heard before. For example, Brooks and Tomasello (1998) taught 24-month-olds invented verbs in transitive sentences (those with a direct object), such as "*The ball is dacking the car*," and in intransitive sentences (those with no direct object), such as "*The ball is dacking*." Children were later asked "What is the ball doing?" to see if they would use the verb transitively in new sentences ("Dacking the house"). Children who had been taught the verb in intransitive sentences almost never used it transitively, suggesting that 24-month-olds are conservative in using verbs in novel constructions. Ferenz and Prasada (2002) also used an elicited production task to study the rules children use to form plurals of nouns. They found that between 24 months to 5 years of age children become more aware of the differences between singular and plural noun uses, such as "*the dogs*" versus "*one of the dogs*".

How well do measures of child language derived from different sources agree? Bornstein and Putnick (2012) obtained data from a large sample of 20-month-olds and their mothers using observation, parental report, and standardized assessment to address this question. Strong relations among all measures were evident. Those infants who used more words and longer utterances in everyday speech with their mothers had mothers who independently reported that their infants knew and spoke in more sophisticated ways. The same infants were also independently assessed by experimenters as comprehending and being able to produce more vocabulary.

The fact that infants generally understand more than they can say means that much of language development occurs covertly: Infants' language progress is not automatically reflected in what they say to us. This has important methodological consequences. If an infant says, "*bap*," for "*bottle*," is it because the infant does not know how "*bottle*" sounds, or because the infant cannot perfectly produce the word? In recent years investigators have used a number of methods to help uncover some of infants' abilities. Some of these methods are variants of ones we have encountered previously, particularly those that rely on attention or conditioning such as the **conditioned head-turn procedure** (Chapters 3 and 6).

Preference methods in infant speech research make the presentation of sounds contingent on infants' looking. In the **auditory preference procedure**, when infants look in a particular direction, they hear something; when they look away, the sound stops. In this way, infants can control how long they listen to a sound (just as infants can control how long they look at visual displays). Various questions can be asked using this method. One question pertains to preference itself. For example, 2- to 6-month-olds prefer to listen to speech more than complex nonspeech sounds (Vouloumanos & Werker, 2004). Another preference method is referred to as **preferential looking**. This task is used to evaluate infants' understanding of words and other linguistic structures. The idea is simple: Infants see two pictures or videos side by side (such as a ball and a car). Then the experimenter (or a recording) says something about one of the pictures (such as "Where's the ball?"). Even 12-month-olds look more at the named picture than the distracter picture (Hollich et al., 2000). This technique is useful for studying the process of word learning (Hollich, 2010). First a word is taught for a novel object, and then recognition of this word is tested using preferential looking. It is also possible to determine how quickly infants can recognize words by carefully measuring how much time elapses between the beginning of the spoken word and the beginning of the infant's eye movement toward the named picture.

Early language can also be studied by making high-quality recordings of infants' speech and then analyzing the recordings. This strategy showed that infants' early speech production is more sophisticated than it sounds. For example, when infants first start saying words, they often fail to make certain distinctions clear. An infant might be heard to pronounce the /p/ and /b/ at the beginnings of words in exactly the same way. This suggests that infants might fail to notice the distinction when they hear *p* and *b* words. However, analyses of recordings of infants' attempts at /p/ and /b/ sounds (and related contrasts such as /t/ vs. /d/ and /k/ vs. /g/) have revealed a developmental period in which some infants make the sounds differently, but not differently enough for adults to hear the distinction clearly (Macken & Barton, 1980). A theoretical message of this study is that learning these distinctions cannot be attributed to adult reinforcement because adults hardly hear infants' initial improvements. A methodological message is that our naked ears sometimes underestimate infants. This echoes a theme that has arisen again and again in the study of language development. The roots of complex behaviors may be discovered long before those behaviors are clear and overt, and many capacities that seem to bloom overnight have in fact been emerging for months.

One of the disadvantages of some experimental methods, including the preference and head-turning procedures, is that relatively little information is learned about each infant—typically just one bit of information, perhaps representing the difference between his or her listening times to one type of speech and another type of speech. As a result, these methods are not well suited to the study of individual differences. In most research, groups of infants are evaluated, and conclusions can be drawn about norms (for example, 6-month-olds may behave one way, 8-month-olds another). Thus, auditory preference tasks tell us about the earliest stages of language learning, but not about differences among infants at a given age.

In summary, a wide range of methods is available for the study of infant language development. The choice of methods depends on the questions to be answered and (to some extent) the ages of the infants to be tested. With infants younger than 12 months, who have not begun to talk, experimental designs are available for characterizing trends in learning over groups of infants. A wider variety of options is available for research on infants who have begun to talk, such as intensive analyses of infants' spontaneous speech, elicited production tasks, standardized assessments, and parental interviews. The most reliable information comes when several measurement techniques are used together (Bornstein & Putnick, 2012). One general conclusion about infant language learning that may be drawn is that, although there are milestones of language development that nearly all children pass, there are vast individual differences among children in when those milestones are reached and, to some extent, in the paths that children follow in reaching them.

SUPPORTS FOR LANGUAGE DEVELOPMENT

Infants quickly develop the complex, dynamic, and symbolic system that is language. In accomplishing this task, the infant is neither ill-equipped nor alone. In this section, we examine some of the sophisticated elements of language that infants and their caregivers bring to the acquisition process. Here we focus on child-directed speech, turn taking, joint attention and gesture, and parents' labeling.

Child-Directed Speech

As we learned in Chapter 6, infants have some innate perceptual preferences and capacities that aid language learning. Moreover, even in the womb fetuses hear and process more than mere bits of sound. For their part, parents repackage the language aimed at infants to match infant capacities. This adjustment is thought to facilitate language acquisition. Specifically, mothers, fathers, caregivers, and even adults who are not parents adopt a special dialect, variously called baby talk, motherese, parentese, or more neutrally **child-directed speech**, when addressing infants. The special characteristics of child-directed speech include: prosodic features (higher pitch, greater range of frequencies, more varied and exaggerated intonation); simplicity features (shorter utterances, slower tempo, longer pauses between phrases, fewer embedded clauses, fewer auxiliaries); redundancy features (more repetition over shorter amounts of time, more immediate repetition); lexical features (special forms like "*mama*"); and content features (restriction of topics to the infant's world). Notably, this speech is similar to the way people speak to their pets (Burnham, Kitamura, & Vollmer-Conna, 2002).

Child-directed speech may be intuitive and non-conscious, and cross-cultural developmental research has confirmed that child-directed speech is almost universal (Kitamura, Thanavishuth, Burnham, & Luvsaneeyanawin, 2002). When communicating with their infants, even deaf mothers modify their sign language in very much the way hearing mothers use child-directed speech (Erting, Thumann-Prezioso, & Benedict, 2000). Children as young as 4 years of age also engage in the same systematic language adjustments when speaking to an infant (Weppelman, Bostow, Schiffer, Elbert-Perez, & Newman, 2003). Within the first few months of life, infants neurologically process child-directed speech differently from other auditory stimuli (Naoi et al., 2012). EEG activity resulting from hearing child-directed speech is greatest in the temporal regions, and it is equally represented in the left and right hemispheres, in contrast to left-hemisphere adult-directed speech.

One of the most frequently investigated features of child-directed speech is the alteration in pitch, and we can use it as an illustration. Fernald (2001) analyzed the fundamental frequency as well as utterance duration and pause duration of French, Italian, German, Japanese, British English, and American English mothers' and fathers' naturalistic speech to preverbal infants. Figure 9.3 shows cross-language

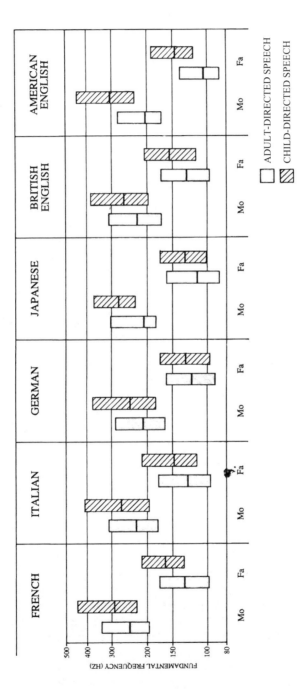

Fig. 9.3 Cross-language comparisons of fundamental frequency (F_0) characteristics of mothers' (Mo) and fathers' (Fa) speech to adults and to infants. (For each bar, the bottom line represents the mean F_0-minimum, the top line represents the mean F_0-maximum, and the intersecting line indicates the mean-F_0 per utterance. The extent of the bar corresponds to F_0 range. Open box, adult-directed speech; hatch box, child-directed speech.) Note that mothers increase their peak fundamental frequency relatively more than fathers when speaking to their infants, and American English speakers tend to use more exaggerated prosody when interacting with an infant than do the speakers of most other languages.

consistency in patterns of prosodic modification used by parents: Mothers and fathers alike used higher mean, minimum, and maximum pitch (fundamental frequency) and a greater variability in pitch. They also used shorter utterances and longer pauses in child-directed speech than in adult-directed speech. Such data provide valuable information about features of the infant's linguistic environment that are culturally widespread.

Why do people use baby talk? It has been proposed that the characteristic prosodic patterns of child-directed speech might elicit attention, modulate arousal and communicate affect, and facilitate language comprehension (Fernald, 2001; Soderstrom, Blossom, Foygel, & Morgan, 2008). First, with regard to eliciting attention, infants respond more to their own mother's voice when she is speaking child-directed speech. Infants also prefer to listen to child-directed speech than to adult-directed speech even when spoken by strangers (Fernald, 2001).

Second, the sound and rhythm of child-directed speech might regulate infant state of arousal and communicate affect to the infant. Darwin (1877; Box 3.1) reported that Doddy "understood intonation and gestures" before he was 1 year old. Papoušek and Papoušek (2002a) documented the coordination of intonation in parents' speech to pre-linguistic infants on the one hand and their communicative intent in specific parenting contexts on the other. Certain similar intonation contours in mothers' speech recur with regularity in particular interactions among American English, German, and Mandarin Chinese speakers. As Figure 9.4 shows, mothers use rising pitch contours to engage infant attention and elicit a response from an infant, falling contours to soothe a distressed infant, and bell-shaped contours to maintain infant attention. The prosodic patterns of child-directed speech may provide infants with supportive cues about the intentions of the speaker. Thus, there could be something to Darwin's observation of Doddy's first understanding the meaningfulness of speech through prosody and intonation rather than through words.

Finally, the prosodic modifications of child-directed speech facilitate the infant's speech processing and language comprehension. Exaggerated prosody helps infants segment the speech stream and provides acoustic cues to the grammatical structure of linguistic messages (Soderstrom, 2007; Soderstrom et al., 2008). For example, infants discriminate speech sounds embedded in multisyllabic sequences better in streams of child-directed speech than adult-directed speech, and children who show delayed onset of speech had mothers who did not use exaggerated pitch in their speech (D'Odorico & Jacobs, 2006).

On the direct question of whether and how child-directed speech affects language development, opinions vary. Adults engage with infants in a number of verbal and nonverbal ways that help support language acquisition, and many of these activities co-occur (Meltzoff & Brooks, 2009). Thus, it is difficult to isolate the role of child-directed speech from other behaviors, such as labeling and gesturing. Nevertheless, infants prefer to attend to child-directed speech, and infants who show greater attention skills, more generally, show advanced language development and communication skills, suggesting a facilitative effect of child-directed speech (Arterberry, Midgett, Putnick, & Bornstein, 2007; Colombo et al., 2009).

Turn Taking

An important feature of adult–infant interaction that serves as a basis of language learning is **turn taking**. Adults conversing with one another regularly match timing factors in their speech. Turn taking is fundamental to the structure of adult dialogue: It is impolite to interrupt so instead we wait for our turn to speak. Turn taking in adult–infant exchange has deep roots in infancy. For example, a nonverbal turn-taking dialogue quickly develops between mothers feeding their newborns. When the infant pauses sucking, the mother "jiggles" the nipple. When the mother stops jiggling, the infant sucks again. From an extremely early age, infants produce different sounds, and their caregivers respond differently to different infant vocalizations depending on how they interpret them (Hu & Fogel, 2003; Markova & Legerstee, 2006; Papoušek, 2007).

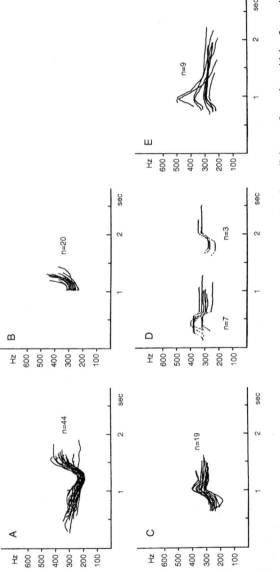

Fig. 9.4 Prototypical adjustments of repetitive melodic contour types during a 3-minute dialogue of a mother with her 2-month-old infant. Superimposed computer-generated F_0 contours of five repetitive melodies used for encouraging a vocal turn (A and B), for encouraging visual attention (C and D), and for contingent rewarding (E). (Courtesy of H. Papoušek.)

Turn taking is also apparent in games parents play with their infants. Consider peek-a-boo. In a typical scenario, the baby's face is covered with a blanket, the parent says "where is [baby's name]?" and then waits for the infant to remove the cloth. Once the cloth is removed, there is a period of shared joy (perhaps accompanied by the parent saying "Oh ... there you are!"). Repetition of this game builds up an expectation of taking turns. When infants start to vocalize, often mothers engage in alternating vocalizations with their infant, inserting pauses between her vocalizations which allow the infant the chance to respond. For infants, this is an important first lesson in pragmatics (do not talk when someone else is talking). Other lessons will be learned well into the school years (e.g., proper way to address an adult, saying "*please*" and "*thank you*").

Thus, mothers act in verbal exchanges with their preverbal infants like sophisticated conversationalists. Mothers promote turn taking: They typically vocalize rapidly after an infant vocalization, and they often prolong pauses after their own vocalizations to increase the likelihood that infant vocalizations will become part of a conversational chain. Perhaps mothers behave in this way because it is their normal way of interacting. Alternatively, turn taking may be a socializing aspect of maternal conversation with infants.

Gesture and Joint Attention

Mothers and infants provide one another with a range of nonverbal supports to communication and language learning. **Gesture** is one such mutually shared prop (Goldin-Meadow, 2006, 2009). For example, a mother might point and at the same time ask the question "*What is that?*" or "*Is that a ball?*" or "*Look! A ball.*" For their part, infants are not only active in comprehending and speaking when they acquire language, they also participate in making use of nonverbal supports such as gestures. Long before the end of their first year, infants communicate about objects by pointing, giving, and showing (Figure 9.5). Perhaps the prototypical gesture for language-learning infants in this age range is pointing. Infants begin pointing between 9 and 12 months of age, and there is a positive relation between pointing and language development (Colonnesi, Stams, Koster, & Noom, 2010; Lock & Zukow-Goldring, 2010).

Pointing by either mother or infant is likely to result in **joint attention**, a concept we introduced in Chapter 7. Generally, joint attention occurs when two people are attending to the same object or event. Joint attention in the absence of pointing can be initiated by one partner looking to the object or event and the other partner following their gaze. Brooks and Meltzoff (2008) showed that infant gaze following and pointing predicted accelerated vocabulary growth, as seen in Figure 9.6, and others have shown joint attention skills predicting toddlers' use of mental state language (such as *think*; Kirsten, Sodian, Thoermer, & Perst, 2011).

Gesture and joint attention, however, are only a support to language acquisition. Language labeling increases infants' attention to objects beyond the time that the labeling itself actually occurs, and language

Fig. 9.5 A child pointing during a categorization task. (Courtesy of M. Arterberry.)

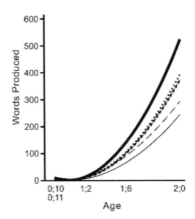

Fig. 9.6 Growth curve model of language development using infant age, gaze following, and pointing with control for maternal education. The thick, solid line represents the trajectory for infants who show prolonged visual inspection of the target looked at by the adult (long lookers) and who also point. The dotted line represents short lookers (−1 *SD*) who also point. The triangle line represents long lookers who do not point. The thin, solid line represents short lookers who do not point. The dashed line is the 50th percentile of the CDI. (From Brooks & Meltzoff, 2008; reproduced with permission of Cambridge University Press.)

maintains infant attention to objects over and above pointing. This relation may be due in part to mothers labeling in response to infants' pointing more than to infants' reaching for objects.

Labeling

Mothers often verbally refer to objects, activities, or events in the environment by describing, labeling, or asking about the unique qualities of the referent ("*That's a spoon.*" and "*What color is the spoon?*"). This form of referential language is reputedly associated with vocabulary expansion during early language development. When mothers teach infants a name for a novel toy, they also have a strong tendency to move the toy in synchrony with their verbal label, which may help infants make the association (Gogate, Bahrick, & Watson, 2000).

In addition, mothers modify their speech to infants in such a way that it may enhance their labeling. For example, Messer (1981) measured the relative loudness of labels and non-labels in the speech of mothers while they showed toys to their 1-year-old. Labels had nearly a .50 probability of being the loudest word in the sentence. From this observation, Messer supposed that the relative loudness of labels could cue infants to map new words onto referent objects. Others have pointed to links between the prosody of maternal speech and the infant's object focus. For example, mothers' speech to infants consistently positions words at points of perceptual prominence in the speech stream—notably on exaggerated fundamental frequency peaks in utterance-initial or -final position—whereas in speech to adults the use of a prosodic emphasis is more variable (Golinkoff & Alioto, 1995; Seidl & Johnson, 2006). (We learned about the importance of such intonation contours in child-directed speech earlier.)

In summary, there are a number of supports in the infant's linguistic environment that help in language learning. Adults speak to infants in such a way to help them attend to and parse speech. Moreover, infants learn turn-taking skills, gestures, and the labels for objects through their interactions with others. One important feature of these interactions is a shared focus on objects and events, often accompanied by verbal commentary. The result, in the course of typical language development, is an infant who by about 1 year of age has some comprehension of language. And it is about this time when infants begin producing speech. We explore infants' understanding and production of speech in the next section.

UNDERSTANDING AND PRODUCING SPEECH

The auditory signal that specifies speech involves a complex interplay of frequencies and intensities of sound waves arrayed over time. A **speech spectrograph**, like the one shown in Figure 9.7, makes visible such a pattern; specifically, it depicts the sound waves when we say, *Development in Infancy*. The dark bands are sounds above threshold intensity at different frequencies.

To hear and understand speech, the infant must decode the complex vibratory pattern that sound projects through changes in the air onto the auditory apparatus and reconstruct it into a psychologically meaningful signal. To speak, the infant must determine what will go into the array and then articulate it in the throat and mouth. How do babies accomplish these tasks? In this section of the chapter, we focus on infant speech perception and production. In the two sections that follow, we then discuss what we know about the infant's rudimentary understanding and use of first word forms (semantics) and grammar (syntax).

Sound Perception

We learned in Chapters 5 and 6 that the auditory system is well developed before birth. Even newborns are equipped to hear, orient to, and distinguish sounds, and babies seem primed to perceive and appreciate the sounds of human speech. Consider, however, the seemingly impossible task of segmenting the speech stream—knowing where one word ends and the next begins—before knowing any words or even what a word is. Moreover, infants have to do this for different speakers speaking in different contexts with different accents and so forth. The following sets of experiments illustrate some competencies that infants possess to recognize speech.

For years theorists had argued that because sounds vary so much from one language to another, meaningful distinctions among sounds must be shaped by experience. This implies that early in development speech would be perceived as a random mishmash of sounds. Cross-language research confirms that, although many sounds are possible (**phonetics**), each language uses only a relatively small number of distinct sounds in speech (**phonemics**). Some Polynesian languages use as few as 15 phonemes, for example, whereas some European and Asian languages use as many as 75. English uses 45. But as we learned in Chapter 6, some phonemes are distinguished universally, and these are the ones that tend to be represented in the early perceptual capacities of young babies. Infants naturally partition sounds into smaller (and presumably more manageable) categories, a process we explained in Chapter 6 and termed

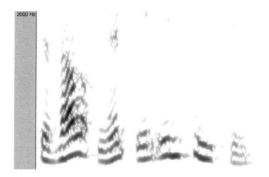

Fig. 9.7 A speech spectrograph for the utterance *Development in Infancy*. The dark areas show patterns of energy focused at different frequencies, called formants. Also indicated are different specific sound patterns, such as voicing. (Courtesy of G. McRoberts.)

categorical perception. Moreover, as infants have more experience with the language(s) around them, their categories adjust (Kuhl, 2009; Saffran et al., 2006). Some distinctions will disappear, as the /l/ and /r/ contrast among the Japanese-learning infants (Yoshida et al., 2010; see Box 9.1).

Box 9.1 Science in Translation: It's all Greek (English? Chinese?) to Them!

It is not often in the study of infancy that with development we see a decline in performance. Perception of non-native speech provides an example. Before 6 to 9 months of age, infants are able to discriminate sound contrasts that do not exist in their linguistic environment. For example, Japanese babies can hear the difference between /l/ and /r/, whereas adult Japanese cannot hear this difference. As infants grow older, they lose the ability to differentiate among sounds that are not relevant to the language (or languages, in the case of children in bilingual contexts) they are regularly exposed to and are in the course of learning. Thus, babies begin life with finely tuned perceptual abilities that disappear with age. We refer to this disappearance as an attunement or specialization for the sounds that are part of the language they will soon be speaking, and it appears to be accompanied by neurological changes (Kuhl, 2009).

The inability to recognize differences among foreign sounds obviously impedes later language acquisition and helps explain why non-native language speakers often sound different even when speaking later-acquired languages. Because it is clearly advantageous, in this age of globalization, for individuals to have multilingual skills, educators, linguists, and psychologists have wondered just how much and what types of exposure to non-native languages are necessary for infants to maintain the ability to distinguish among sounds. Patricia Kuhl, Feng-Ming Tsao, and Huei-Mei Liu (2003) tried to find out in a pair of experiments.

In the first, 16 9-month-old US infants who were otherwise only exposed to English spent about 5 hours, spread over 12 sessions, interacting with a Mandarin speaker who read to them and played with them, all the while speaking only Mandarin. Infants in a comparison group had exactly the same experiences, except that their partners read and spoke only in English. Whereas the ability to distinguish among foreign (in this case, Mandarin) sounds typically declines between 6 and 12 months of age, the decline was reversed among the Mandarin exposed infants, but it continued unchecked among infants in the control group. This study thus firmly established that even a small amount of exposure is sufficient to avert the normal decline in this important type of speech perception.

In the second experiment, groups of infants were exposed to the same amount of Mandarin as those in the first experiment, but exposure was provided by either watching and listening, or only listening, to a DVD depicting storybook reading and toy play by and with the same speakers who had participated in the first experiment. Neither simply listening nor both watching and listening to Mandarin speakers reversed the normative decline in the infants' ability to differentiate among Mandarin speech sounds. Comparison with the performance of the infants in the first experiment established that exposure had to be conveyed by social interaction to be influential. Thus, if parents want to make it easier for their children to learn additional languages, they cannot rely solely on foreign language videos or soundtracks. They need to have their infants interact with native speakers on a regular basis, especially during the critical period in the second half of the first year of life when these speech perception abilities are being honed.

During their first year, infants learn a tremendous amount about how their language sounds. In addition, infants learn a great deal about what words are like in their language. One example of this is **phonotactic learning**, or more generally, **statistical learning**. **Phonotactics** refers to constraints on combinations of speech sounds in words. In English, the sounds "*n*" and "*k*" can occur together in a syllable, but only at the end (*sink*) and only in that order ("*sikn*," "*nkis*," and "*knis*" are not possible words in English). Although there are similarities in these rules across languages, there are also clear differences. For example, in Dutch, "*kn*" is a possible word onset—the Dutch word for "*knee*" (*knie*) is pronounced like the English, except that the Dutch pronounce the initial *k*. Using the auditory preference procedure, Jusczyk et al. (1993) showed that 9-month-old infants already know some of these regularities. They played American and Dutch babies lists of words that were allowable in Dutch but not English (such as *knoest*) or allowable in English but not Dutch (such as *stewed*, whose final "*d*" is not permitted in Dutch). Infants preferred to listen to lists consistent with their own language's phonotactics.

What might this phonological knowledge be good for? One problem that infants must solve to understand language is to discover which elements of the continuous speech stream are words. This is called the **segmentation problem**. Analyses of speech sounds show that, when we talk, we tend to run words together without pausing between words or otherwise indicating word boundaries. This is true even when we talk to infants. Remember the "*Yourteddyislyingonthecouchsweetie*" example. The number of ways to divide or segment this sentence into possible words is very large, presenting a problem for word finding. But if you know that "*rt*" cannot start a word, this gives you a head start because you can rule out "*You rteddy* …". Of course, phonotactics is not a complete solution—there is nothing un-English about a possible word like "*teddyis*"—but they help. Another potentially helpful regularity in English is that stressed syllables tend to be the first syllable in a word. Knowing this, it makes more sense to guess that "*teddy*" and "*lying*" are words than guessing that "*yourte*" or "*thecouch*" are words. Indeed, infants growing up in English-language environments seem to divide speech sequences in just this way.

If infants spontaneously group together syllables that have this kind of statistical consistency, it could help them find words and, thus, facilitate their word learning (Estes, 2009; Lany & Saffran, 2011). Evidence of this phenomenon was provided by Aslin, Saffran, and Newport (Aslin & Newport, 2009; Saffran, 2009). In one study, infants first heard a series of invented words, strung together in a continuous sequence (a bit like hearing "… *bermudacolossusmandiblecolossusbermuda* …" but with made-up words like "*daropi*" and without any syllables stressed). Then infants heard lists containing isolated versions of the words ("*Bermuda*"… "*bermuda*"…) or bits of words ("*dacolos*"… "*dacolos*"…). Eight-month-olds reliably preferred the bits of words. The fact that infants could distinguish the two kinds of lists shows that they were able to detect the statistical structure of the syllables: "*da*" always followed "*mu*," which always followed "*ber*." This statistical ability is robust, helping children not only detect neighboring sounds in their primary language(s), but also words in foreign languages and even the breaking points in a continuous stream of visual events (Roseberry, Richie, Hirsh-Pasek, Golinkoff, & Shipley, 2011). Infants were learning very quickly the regularities of the language and using this newly acquired information to segment the speech into units.

Sound Production

Infants follow three broad stages in early verbal development: a pre-linguistic, a one-word, and a multi-word stage, with transitions in between. In this section, we discuss two early types of infant pre-linguistic vocalizations—crying and babbling. In the next section, we turn to semantic development.

Cry   The infant's cry is a very revealing kind of vocalization. The perception and interpretation of cries are important, because cries and their distinguishing features play significant roles in many aspects of normal and atypical infant development. Preterm babies usually have shriller and higher pitched cries, and adults perceive them as more negative than the cries of healthy term babies (Out, Pieper, Bakermans-Kranenburg, Zeskind, & van IJzendoorn, 2010). In addition to being diagnostic, cries are also communicative. Different infant physiological states (hunger and sleepiness) are associated with different spectrographic patterns of crying (Wasz-Hockert, Michelsson, & Lind, 1985), and female adults show different neural responses to cries versus an emotionally neutral sound (Purhonen, Pääkkönen, Yppärilä, Lehtonen, & Karhu, 2001). Moreover, few adults can deny or disregard a baby's cry. Cries compel us to respond, and the nearly universal response is to be nurturing in some way (Soltis, 2004).

Babbling   Although babies' cries inform parents about their state, babbling is the infant's first significant non-distress communication. Babbling typically accompanies excitation and motor activity in the first half of the first year of life, and alternates with attentive listening in the second half of the first year of life. Babbling is significant because it comprises infants' first structured vocalizations, because it sounds like fun, and because it fills the eerie void between silence and crying so common in early infancy and before the first intelligible words.

The production of speech has been called the most complex of human action patterns, and the origins of regularity in early speech production constitute one of several active topics of investigation in language development. For this reason we examine some of its significant features in detail. Sound production in newborns is constrained by the anatomy of the oral cavity and by respiratory patterns. The vocal tracts of adults and infants differ, and these differences have profound effects on articulation. Although anatomical constraints do not force all infants to babble in the same way, they do appear to promote a particular developmental scheme in speech sound production.

The linguistic theorist Jakobson (1968) proposed the romantic view that infants produce all of the sounds of the world's languages. When they first begin to speak, infants limit their articulations to a restricted set of contrasts, and infants' initial sound productions follow a universal pattern. It appears that he was partially right. Infants produce a range of sounds even in their first months, but these sounds are not truly phonemes and can be difficult to assign to standard phoneme categories. Furthermore, there is not much variety in early sounds (Oller, 2000). However, it is true that infants' first vocalizations do not depend on the language infants hear and thus are universal.

The difficulty of interpreting the sounds of babbling is not surprising given the immaturity of infants' control over the oral articulators. Infants must coordinate the movements of their mouth, tongue, and lips with the flow of air. Some sounds are produced primarily at the lips, and these are called **labials** (/p/and /b/). Some sounds, called **dentals**, are produced by positioning the tongue against the teeth (/t/and /d/), and **velars** (/k/and /g/sounded further back at the roof of the mouth). Other sounds, called **alveolars** (/n/ and /l/) are sounded at the ridge just behind the teeth. Vowel sounds (/o/, /e/, and /a/) are articulated at roughly parallel points from the front to the back of the mouth. Jakobson argued that articulation follows a general developmental progression among consonants from labials and dentals to velars and among vowels from back vowels like /u/ to front vowels like /i/. This means that infants' earliest combinations ought to be front (labial) or dental (or nasal) consonants with back (velar) vowels: that is, /p/ or /b/or /d/ or /m/ with /a/. MacNeilage and Davis (2000) pointed out that infants commonly produce syllables sounding like /ba/ and /di/ but are relatively less likely to produce /bi/, probably because making a /b/ results in a tongue position well suited to following with /a/ but not /i/.

It did not long escape notice that the highest probability syllabic combinations in infant speech, based on Jakobson's theory, tend to be those that connote important meanings very early in life. Cross-cultural linguistic research showed that the most likely first sound combinations are /pa/, /ba/, /da/, and /ma/, and further, that /pa/-like, /da/-like, and /ma/-like sounds are used as parental kin terms in an unusually large proportion of language communities. Of the four logically possible combinations, the front consonant with back vowel pairs were used in 57% of 1,072 languages studied, where only 25% would be expected by chance (Murdock, 1959). Recall, too, that Doddy's first sound, according to his father, was /da/. The implication seems to be that parents (or languages) have directly adopted generic labels for themselves based on infants' earliest, anatomically determined vocal productions.

Development of pre-speech vocalizations emerges through a series of stages, with each stage adding a new set of vocalizations to the infants' repertoire of sounds. The first stage (0 to 2 months), **phonation**, is characterized mainly by fussing, crying, sneezing, and burping, which bear little resemblance to adult speech. The second stage (2 to 3 months), **cooing**, begins when back vowels and nasals appear together with velar consonants (e.g., /gu/, /ku/). Cooing differs in its acoustic characteristics from adult vocalizations and is recorded mainly during interactions with caregivers. In the third stage (4 to 6 months), **vocal play** or **expansion**, syllable-like productions with long vowels appear. Squeals, growls, yells, trills, and friction noises demonstrate infants' playful exploration of their vocal tract capabilities during this stage. In the extremely important **canonical babbling** stage (7 to 10 months), two types of productions emerge: **reduplicated babbling**—identical, repetitive sequences of CV (consonant-vowel) syllables (e.g, /ma/ma/, /da/da/); and **variegated babbling**—sequences of different consonants and vowels (e.g., CV, V, VC, VCV = /ga/e/im/ada/). Oller (2000) defined canonical babbling as the first units of infant speech to exhibit the timing characteristics of adult consonant and vowel production. Such productions are not true words because they lack meaning. However, canonical babbling is syllabic, containing mainly frontal stops, nasals, and glides—coupled with vowels (e.g., /a/, /e/, /o/). The emergence and continuance of canonical babbling is highly important. For example, hearing-impaired infants begin vocal play at the same time as hearing infants, but in hearing-impaired infants the appearance and growth in babbling slows or stops altogether (Iver & Oller, 2008). In the fifth stage (12 to 13 months), **jargon** or **intonated babble**, infants produce long strings of syllables that have varied stress and intonation patterns. Jargon sounds like whole sentences conveying the contents of statements or questions, and often co-occurs with real words. Yet, it still lacks linguistic content or grammatical structure.

Is babbling related to infants' first speech? It was once thought that the two sorts of vocalization were distinct and separate periods of vocal production, the earlier random and passing, and the later structured and enduring (Jakobson, 1968). Continuity between babble and early words is now recognized. Infants' babble and first words rest on the same innately programmed articulatory mechanisms; they share the same fundamental speech sounds; babbling production continues to coexist with first words for several months; and infants frequently draw their early lexicon from the repertoire established in the course of babbling (Oller, 2000). Fine-grained analyses of babbling show that the sounds produced while infants are in the babbling stage change and their first words incorporate the more frequently produced babbling sounds. For example, Majorano and D'Odorico (2011) studied the utterances (both babbling and words) in Italian infants between the ages of 10 months to 2 years. They found that babbling sounds were not the most frequent sounds found in Italian initially, nor did the infants accent the sounds in a way consistent with the accent conventions in Italian. Toward the end of the first year, around 11 months, babbling sounds shifted such that they mirrored the frequency and accent characteristics of Italian. When infants began to speak their first words, almost 49% of the first words contained labial, 36% alveolar (sounds produced from just behind the teeth), and 15% velar consonants, a pattern that matched the frequency of these sounds in the infants' early stages of babbling. In a study with infants in an English-speaking environment, Fagan (2009) also found consistency between sounds produced in babbling and in first words. Thus, through babbling infants practice making the sounds that will be present in their first real words.

There is evidence that babbling is the product of an amodal (sensory independent) language capacity that is under maturational control. Manual babbling occurs in deaf infants exposed to sign languages from birth. On the basis of a comparison with babbling in hearing infants, Petitto and Marentette (1991) concluded that experience with speech is not critical per se to the onset or nature of babbling, but rather that the similarities in manual and vocal babbling indicate that babbling is an abstract and generalized language capacity of human beings related to expressive capacity. In fact, Petitto and her colleagues subsequently demonstrated differences in the manual gestures of hearing infants exposed to sign language and hearing infants exposed to speech (Petitto, Holowaka, Sergio, Levy, & Ostry, 2004). The infants exposed to sign language made an additional range of slow-moving gestures, positioned directly in front of their bodies, apparently mimicking the gestures of their signing parents. This gestural babble shows that deaf infants' hand and arm movements are a consequence of exposure to sign language and not a consequence of deafness.

If the earliest manifestations of vocal babbling emerge naturally and refer to the anatomy of the baby, different kinds of linguistic experience should not differentially influence babbling, nor should the development of babbling depend on any particular experience. There is some support for this proposition. Spanish-, Japanese-, and English-learning babies show no great differences in their basic sound production repertoires, suggesting that distinctive linguistic experiences do not shape the elements of first vocal babbling very much (Oller, 2000). However, some early experience clearly does matter.

Every child uses two sources of perceptual information when beginning to speak: the speech she or he hears and the feedback from his or her own speech. Babies who do not hear speech at all or not very well, such as hearing-impaired infants, babble as much as 5 to 19 months later than hearing infants (Oller, 2000). Deaf infants almost never learn to speak normally (although, of course, their language production in sign may be perfectly fluent; Dehqan & Scherer, 2011). Thus, auditory input is necessary for the normal and timely development of adult-like syllables.

In addition, some components of early babbling are positively influenced by local auditory input. As we saw earlier, the babbling of Italian babies comes to match the CV frequency and accent characteristic of Italian (Majorano & D'Ordorico, 2011). Moreover, vocalizations in babies can be operantly conditioned by providing contingent social reinforcement. Goldstein and Schwade (2008) studied the role of feedback from mothers on their 9½-month-old infants' vocalizations. Half of the mothers were instructed to provide contingent responses to their infants' babbling. They were instructed to provide *social* feedback (smiling, moving closer to the infant, touching) contingent on the child's speech production. The other half gave non-contingent responses. That is, they responded whenever the experimenter told them to. Infants receiving contingent responses increased in their number of speech sounds, and they restructured their babbling, incorporating the patterns from their mothers' speech.

Many studies confirm the subtle and not so subtle effects that the environment exerts over the development of infant vocalization. In several different cultures, middle-income mothers speak to their infants more frequently and with more varied sounds than do lower-income mothers, although mothers in the two groups may behave similarly with respect to physical contact and nurturance (Hoff, 2002). In turn, middle-income babies produce more sounds in the first months of life than do babies of lower-income parents. Similarly, German middle-class mothers interact more with their 3-month-old infants than Cameroonian Nso mothers, and in turn German infants vocalize more than Nso infants (Keller et al., 2008). And mothers from lower-income groups gesture less when interacting with their infants than mothers of higher income groups (Rowe & Goldin-Meadow, 2009). The amount of language input has important implications for the detection of sounds and words as well as for language processing speed and vocabulary development. Hurtado, Marchman, and Fernald (2008) demonstrated that the amount of language input a child receives affects language processing speed and trajectories of vocabulary learning in both English and Spanish children. They found that the amount of language input children received at 18 months influenced word recognition and vocabulary size at 24 months, such that those who received relatively more input at 18 months were faster in word recognition and knew more words at 24 months.

In sum, infants begin communicating with others through crying and other non-distress vocalizations, such as cooing. Additional combinations of sounds, such as the consonant-vowel pairings seen with babbling, appear to allow infants to practice the sounds they will need to form words. Infants' earliest sensitivities to sound and their earliest vocal expressions give evidence of strong biological influences. The earliest sounds that infants produce are not specific to their linguistic environment. Very soon, however, both perception and production of sound become subject to the linguistic environments provided by parent, home, and culture. For example, infants become less able to discriminate among sounds that do not exist in the language they hear. Moreover, their own vocalizations come to mirror the sounds of the language they hear. Perception and production of language are not dependent on spoken language, as deaf babies also "babble," but with their hands. Thus, language exposure—whether through audition or vision—promotes the development of language. We now turn to consider a second system of language development—semantics—and the ways by which infants' initial vocalizations transform into meaningful speech.

SEMANTICS

Infants cry, babble, and even gesture to communicate effectively before they acquire and use words. But these methods of communication have severe limitations. For example, it is impossible for an infant to use gestures to share a memory, and all parents attest to their frustration at the ambiguity of infants' cries and babbles. The next step is for infants to start learning the connections between sounds and meanings that are characteristic of all human languages but unique to their specific language. In other words, infants need to learn that specific sounds have specific shared meanings, a concept called **semantics**.

Reference and First Words

A major obstacle confronting the language-learning infant is the problem of **reference**, the link between sounds and their meaning. Recall once again "*Yourteddyislyingonthecouchsweetie*" and consider that, to understand this simple statement, even after parsing the signal into separate units correctly, the infant ("*Sweetie*") must determine which unit refers to the infant, which to objects ("*teddy*," "*couch*") in the environment, which to an action ("*is lying*"), and so forth. After all, connections between word sounds and word meanings are essentially arbitrary, which makes the decoding task challenging. Much philosophical, psychological, and linguistic energy has been spent on this issue, but just how semantic development transpires remains something of a mystery. In this section, we discuss some major questions about semantic development. How is reference defined, when does it begin, and what are its origins? Later in this chapter, we take up the equally formidable question of how the infant figures out the rule system for interrelating words.

Let us begin with an appreciation of even the most basic aspect of the problem, namely, defining what an infant's first word is. Even this, as it turns out, is somewhat problematic because what a word is for a newly talking infant is itself open to dispute. Is "*baba*" (for bottle), even if used consistently to refer to bottle and nothing else but bottle, a real word? Some would argue yes. Others would say that the infant has to say "*bottle*" for it to count as a word. Regardless of the disagreement over what a word is, there is agreement that producing a word reflects **nominal insight**—an understanding that everything has a name.

First words appear around the infant's first birthday. By 9 months, many soon-to-be English-speaking infants use single sounds in regular or stereotyped ways: "*mama*" as request, "*dat*" to show, "*bam*" for things falling. So, the infant might not have pronunciations and word meanings that are aligned with those of English, but he or she has taken the important step of using particular sounds to mean things, even if this usage only occurs in a specific and limited context. For example, an infant might use "*bam*" to refer to falling, but only falling from a high chair, or "*car*" to refer only to cars when seen from inside the house. But perhaps such **context-restricted words** do not give evidence of true nominal insight because they are not applied to classes of people, properties, objects, or events. More conservatively, infants might attain reference only when they use sounds that clearly name people, properties, objects, or events. By the time they are 12 or 13 months of age, infants use "*mama*" to mean mother in a variety of settings and situations, and not exclusively when their mother is in a particular place or performing a specific activity. More conservatively still, crediting infants with nominal insight might have to wait until around 16 to 18 months when infants use single words to convey a full sentence's worth of meaning. This strictest attribution of word knowledge involves the infant's understanding or using labels even when the referent is not present, for example, a child saying "*dog*" to ask when the family dog will be back from the kennel. In both comprehension and production, this development gives evidence of a true shift from **context-restricted** to **context-flexible** usage, signifying a distinct, mature level of understanding of what names mean.

To what do infants' first words refer? One might expect that infants' first words would be those that they hear most often and that the part of speech (noun, verb, adjective, etc.) of first words would be proportional to the number of words infants hear in each class. But this is not true—or at least the story is not this simple. The two most frequent English words in speech to infants are "*you*" and "*the*," which are rarely, if ever, in the top 50 of infants' first-produced words. Thus, word frequency is not the sole key to early vocabularies. Again, it is not always clear what infants mean when they use a word. If an infant says "*bye-bye*," the infant might be referring to waving (a verb), the waving gesture (a noun), a social routine, or any of several other possibilities. Most studies of English and other languages have found that a large number of early words are nouns, at least if the words are identified in terms of their adult part of speech (Bornstein, Cote, et al., 2004). As language development progresses, infants' lexicon expands to include adjectives, verbs, articles, and pronouns, and by 2½ to 3 years of age children have the capacity to distinguish among and use a variety of linguistic forms (Waxman & Leddon, 2011).

A number of explanations for the noun advantage in early vocabularies have been proposed. One or all of them may be true to some degree. The standard view is that the key factor is the ability of infants to learn the concept to which a word refers. Nouns often refer to concrete objects, and verbs often refer to relations between things. Because notions like "*dog*" are easier to grasp than notions like "*give*," infants learn more nouns (Gentner, 1982). A second view is that nouns are learned more readily because it is easier for infants to figure out which aspects of a scene grown-ups are talking about when they use nouns than when they use verbs. That is, it is not the concepts themselves that are hard to grasp, it is identifying which concept an adult is using a word for (Gleitman & Gleitman, 1992). A third view is that the noun advantage arises because many nouns tend to be used the same way, and refer to things—once you learn a few nouns, learning more nouns is easy because they refer to similar kinds of categories (e.g., baby, book, or dog; Sandhofer, Smith, & Luo, 2000). Verbs, on the other hand, are more heterogeneous, referring to movement ("*go*"), desires ("*want*," "*like*"), manipulation of objects ("*put*," "*get*"), and so forth and infants need to understand these concepts before understanding the verb referring to them (Golinkoff & Hirsh-Pasek, 2008; Pruden, Goksun, Rosenberry, Hirsh-Pasek, & Golinkoff, 2012). A fourth view is that input factors play a role. Adult speech consists of more nouns than verbs, and so infants first speak more nouns than verbs. A fifth argument is that nouns are much more likely to appear at the end o utterances. Perceptual studies have shown that it is easier for infants to recognize familiar words at the ends of sentences, suggesting that this structural feature of languages might influence rates of word learning as well (Fernald, McRoberts, & Swingley, 2001).

The Problem of Word Learning

Word learning is an example of **induction**, using a limited set of examples to draw conclusions that permit inferences about new cases. Suppose an infant sees a cup referred to as *cup*. For the infant to recognize that the same word also refers to other cups requires an inductive inference: going beyond the taught example to other examples. This is not as simple as it sounds. First, there is the **immediate reference problem**: What does the speaker mean when he or she says "*cup*"? Sometimes the speaker will be pointing to an object when labeling it, but even in these seemingly clear cases there are many possibilities to what the word might refer. It might mean "*cup*," but it could mean "*handle*," "*hot liquid*," "*drinking*," "*not appropriate for babies your age*," or any of an infinite number of other conceivable meanings. How do infants get it right? The second facet of word learning is the **extension problem**: Once the infant has guessed which particular entity is referred to, he or she should then be willing to extend this word to other entities belonging to the same category—unless the word is a proper name. But what makes a cup a "*cup*"? Its shape? Color? Function? We cannot simply say, "*things that are similar to the original cup*," because without a definition of similarity, we are right back where we started.

One straightforward hypothesis is that infants are not biased in any way. On hearing a word, they store in memory every percept in their senses: what they are seeing, feeling, tasting, and so on. Over multiple exposures to the word, only a few percepts will be present every time the word is heard, and over time the referent of the word will be isolated. Some context-restricted uses of words seem to arise from this kind of process. If an infant only uses "*car*" for a specific vehicle, or only while sitting in a particular location, it suggests that the meaning of the word is not distinct from a wide range of sensory associations. However, this account cannot be the general solution to how infants learn word meanings. First, words are sometimes used when their referents are absent. If father says "*I'm gonna go get your cup*," on this account the language learner should rule out the hypothesis that *cup* refers to a drinking vessel (because it is not there) and start considering things like the floor (which has been there every time). Second, chance co-occurrences would result in implausible word meanings. Suppose a parent happens to use "*cup*" several times when the cup is full but not when it is empty, and in the morning but not the evening. In this case the meaning of cup would be something like "*full drinking container in the morning*," but infants do not seem to come up with these odd definitions. Third, and most importantly, infants have been shown to learn words too quickly for a purely associative account in which meanings must be narrowed down over multiple exposures in different contexts. This **fast mapping** has been shown in many studies. Adults name an object a few times, and infants seem to pick up the name of that object quickly (Hollich, 2010).

Thus, infants must be constrained in their guesses about word meaning. Three of these constraints were proposed by Markman (1999). One is the **whole object assumption**. Under this argument, it is assumed that, when an adult points to an object and labels it, the infant first perceives the novel label as referring to the whole object, and not to its parts, substance, or other properties. A second constraint is that infants appear to be biased in interpreting nouns they hear as category labels, a bias that Markman termed the **taxonomic constraint**. On this assumption, infants are said to interpret new words as referring not only to the object that they first see labeled with a word, but also to other objects that are the same kind of thing. That is, infants try to solve the extension problem (rather than assuming all words are proper names, like Paris or Cicero), and their first guesses will be based on what the object is rather than what the object might be associated to. A third constraint is **mutual exclusivity**, a claim that infants assume that any given object should have only one name (Markman, Wasow, & Hansen, 2003). For the most part, the operation of these biases in word learning has been demonstrated in experiments in which infants are shown two objects and then hear a novel word apparently intended to refer to one of the objects, and infants as young as 15 months resist novel words being applied to an object already having a name they know (Markman et al., 2003).

The reliance on constraints to explain word learning, however, misses important facts about the process. No one denies the robustness and reliability of the effects shown in the numerous studies testing constraints; rather, the relevance of these constraints to the bigger picture of word learning has been questioned. For example, word learning constraints describe infants' behavior but do not explain it (Deák, 2000). We also need more general theories of word learning that are not limited to object labels. After all, many of the infant's first words are not names for things.

Verbs are a good example. The Western tradition of picture book reading and pointing out objects ("That's a truck. See the truck.") is not a good model for learning verbs. Verbs refer to visible actions (like "*jump*") and to non-observable processes (like "*thinking*"). They also can refer to actions that are about to happen, actions that are going on during the sentence, and actions that have already happened (Golinkoff & Hirsh-Pasek, 2008).

Infants are also sensitive to **communicative intent** (Tomasello, 2011). In other words, infants recognize that language is about people's ideas and intentions. Simple co-occurrence of a word and infants' attention to an object are not sufficient for word learning if social aspects of the situation do not support linking the word and object. In one study, infants who were focused on exploring a novel toy heard an adult say, "*A toma! It's a toma.*" For some infants, the speaker was in view and was clearly talking to the infant. For other infants, the speaker was hidden behind a screen and had previously been seen talking on the telephone. Infants in the former condition learned that the object was a "*toma.*" By contrast, infants in the latter condition did not learn the word (Baldwin, Markman, Bill, Desjardins, & Irwin, 1996). This result is striking because based on a simple associative view of word learning, one would imagine that hearing a new word and attending to a new toy would be sufficient for word learning, but this is not the case.

Experiments like these show infants' flexibility in determining what thing in the world (be it an object or an action) is referred to by a novel word. But this still leaves the question of extension: Which additional cases also qualify for the label? Markman's taxonomic constraint says that infants will try to find another thing of the same kind, but what defines a *kind*? Work on this issue has shown that there is no simple answer to this question. In a typical study such as the one conducted by Booth and Waxman (2009), infants were taught a novel label for a novel object, in this case a purple horse, and they heard "*This is a blicket.*" Then they were presented with a contrasting object, an orange carrot, and they heard "*This is not a blicket.*" At test, infants viewed two objects, a green horse and a purple chair, and were asked to "*Find the blicket.*" Infants as young as 14 months looked to the green horse, showing their willingness to extend the word "*blicket*" to the object category (horses) rather than to color (purple). When the study was conducted with adjectives ("*the blickish one*"), infants did not extend the novel word.

This study is only one example of a considerable number of experiments trying to sort out the basis of infants' extensions of word meanings (Waxman & Leddon, 2011). Relatedly, researchers are also curious about infants' naming errors. Errors are likely to occur in one of two contexts: (a) infants use an incorrect label for a known object or event (calling a "*dog*" a "*cat*") or (b) they assign a known word to a novel object (calling an RV a "car"). It appears that naming errors are most likely to occur when children have a vocabulary size between 50 and 150 words, and these errors are attributed to activation and retrieval of words from infants' rapidly changing lexicon (Gershkoff-Stowe, 2000).

Individual Differences in Vocabulary Learning

Various attempts have been made to account for widespread individual differences in infants' early vocabularies. Many accounts focus on differences in infants' experience, primarily in the speech infants hear from their parents. The types of speech parents use varies systematically with socioeconomic status (SES; which is correlated with parental education), ethnicity, multilingualism, and age of the parent (Hoff, 2006). For example, parents differ in how much they talk to their infants, with parents lower in SES talking substantially less than more affluent parents. Across the early years, the number of words children hear per hour differs dramatically across SES: 616 in group compared to 1,251 in a public assistance working-class group and 2,153 in a professional group (Hart & Risley, 1995). Moreover, their use of language differs. Higher SES mothers elicit conversations with their infants, whereas lower SES mothers direct their infants' behavior. And, infants of higher SES mothers have larger vocabularies and reach linguistic milestones earlier than infants of low SES (Hoff, 2006). Furthermore, infants exposed to more than one language acquire vocabulary in each language at levels that match the ratio of exposure to one language versus another. In other words, an infant whose linguistic environment is predominantly Spanish with some English will speak more Spanish words than English words (Song, Tamis-LeMonda, Yoshikawa, Kahana-Kalman, & Wu, 2012; Figure 9.8). Similarly, teen parents and older siblings caring for younger siblings talk less to infants than adult parents do, and these infants show slower vocabulary acquisition and other delays in language development (Hoff, 2006).

Generally speaking, input matters (Box 9.2). Not only does it affect vocabulary development, input affects language processing speed (Hurtado, Marchman, & Fernald, 2008). Moreover, there are longer term consequences: The amount of input, gesturing, and type of input (unusual words) at an early stage of development predicts language usage at a later stage (Bornstein et al., 2012; Hurtado et al., 2008; Rowe & Goldin-Meadow, 2009; Weizman & Snow, 2001). Of course, interpretation of the direction of influence is always uncertain in correlational studies. It could be that maternal speech influences infant speech *or* that infants who use nouns earlier promote the use of nouns by their mothers. However, it appears that infants with verbally responsive mothers achieve the vocabulary spurt and combine words into simple sentences sooner in development than do infants with less verbally responsive mothers (Tamis-LeMonda & Bornstein, 2002).

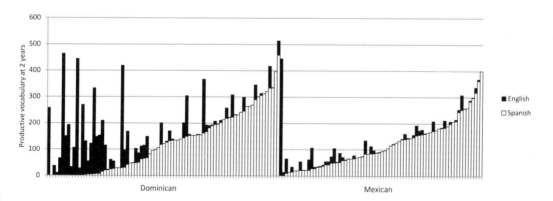

Fig. 9.8 Productive vocabulary in English and Spanish of 2-year-olds of Mexican and Dominican heritage. Each bar shows an individual child. There is variability in the proportion of English versus Spanish words each child produces, an effect attributed to the frequency of each language the infant hears in the home. (From Song et al., 2012; Copyright © 2012 by the American Psychological Association. Reproduced with permission. The use of APA information does not imply endorsement by APA.)

Box 9.2 Set For Life? Language and Thought

There is a long-standing debate about the role that language may play in shaping cognition. Pruden, Levine, and Huttenlocher (2011) were interested in how parents' use of spatial language, as when they discuss object shapes and other properties, might impact their children's later spatial abilities. Fifty-two children and their caregivers were observed every four months from 19 months to 46 months of age while engaging in common daily activities. During these observations, the researchers noted the parents' and children's use of spatial language. At 54 months of age, children were assessed for their spatial understanding in three tasks. Pruden et al. found wide variation in the extent to which parents use spatial language (range = 5 to 525 words) and similar variation in children's use of spatial language (range = 9 to 191 words). Moreover, parents who used a lot of spatial language had children who used a lot of spatial language. Parental spatial language use also predicted children's performance on tasks involving spatial transformation (e.g., select a shape that could be created from several pieces that are presented) and spatial analogies (e.g., select an abstract figure that preserves the spatial arrangement of a realistic picture). Thus, what parents say affects children's cognition.

The discussion thus far has focused on parental influences on infants' language development, but as we noted in Chapter 2, the majority of infants in the United States spend considerable amounts of time in non-parental care. Generally speaking, infants who spend some time in daycare centers do not differ much in their language achievements from infants who are cared for exclusively in the home (NICHD Early Child Care Research Network, 2005). In fact, all other factors being equal, childcare in centers appears to have a small advantage over home-based daycare or exclusive maternal care, perhaps because infants in daycare centers are exposed to a wider variety of language-based interactions. It is important to note, though, that the quality of the care arrangement is as important as what sort of care it offers. Language development is facilitated by environments in which caregivers talk to infants, and not all daycare centers provide language stimulation equally. Thus, the measured quality of the childcare situation has a modest but consistent effect on infants' language performance.

Once infants attain about 50 words, word learning appears to proceed rapidly. If lexical size estimates are at all accurate, the average 3-year-old possesses a vocabulary of 3,000 words. Therefore, between approximately 12 and 36 months, children acquire four new words per day on average. In so doing, children demonstrate not only perceptual attentiveness, but mental absorptiveness: Babies are keen and adventurous sponges.

In summary, the appearance of first words is a significant milestone, likely representing a cognitive revolution in infants' understanding of what language is and what it is used for. How infants learn words is still under debate, but it is likely that they use principles or constraints to help with this process. In addition to amassing a vocabulary, children are learning how to put words together into meaningful phrases and sentences. We address this topic in the next section.

SYNTAX

Syntax means grammar, or the rules for combining words into meaningful communications that others can interpret. Examples of early combinations of words across several languages can be seen in Table 9.1. Syntactic competence in children is a wonder to behold. First, children have the ability to detect syntactic rules and regularities even though the rules vary enormously across languages. In English, for

Table 9.1 The early expression of common meaning relations

Relations	English	Russian	German	Samoan
Agent-action	teddy fall	mama prua (Mama walk)	Puppe kommt (doll comes)	pa'u pepe (fall doll)
Action-object	hit ball	day chasy (give watch)	tur aufmachen (door open)	tapale' oe (hit you)
Entity-location	there car	Tosya tam (Tosya there)	buch da (book there)	Keith lea (Keith there)
Possessor-possession	mama dress	pup moya (navel my)	mein ball (my ball)	lol a'u (candy my)
Entity-attribute	big truck	papa bol'shoy (papa big)	milch heiss (milk hot)	fa'ali'i pepe (headstrong baby)
Rejection-action	no wash	vody net (water no)	nicht blasen (not blow)	le 'ai (not eat)

example, subjects usually precede verbs, which usually precede objects. Thus, when you hear "*The father kissed the daughter*," you know the daughter was kissed by the father. As English speakers, we are so accustomed to this word order regularity that it seems natural and perhaps even logical (Figure 9.9). But a great many languages do not work this way. For example, in Welsh the verb usually comes first, and in Turkish and Japanese, although many sentences place the verb last, subjects and objects do not have a fixed order. To tell who is who, these languages attach a suffix to objects, and word order is used instead for focus (emphasizing what is new and important in the conversation). Given that these rules vary across languages, they must be learned, and some structures are more challenging than others. For example, the English passive is learned late, and even French adults need to look up some irregular French verb forms. Generally speaking, however, the rate at which children learn, and the fact that children make far fewer errors than one might imagine based on their learning of nonlinguistic regularities, suggests that children come to the task of language learning prepared to view language in certain ways.

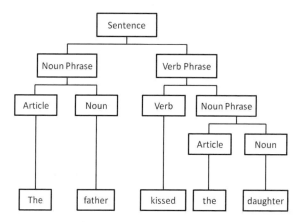

Fig. 9.9 The basic structure of an English sentence, "The father kissed the daughter," and its grammatical decomposition.

Across languages, words may be inflected not only for tense, but also gender, shape, animacy (living/nonliving), social status, aspect (whether an action is ongoing or completed), number, and many other properties. And, as we shall see, parents cannot be counted on to explicitly explain the rules: No mother tells her 19-month-old, "Listen carefully: in our language, *d* at the end of a verb means something that already happened, except in some verbs like *run*." Children sort these things out for themselves, and they are good at it.

Most researchers agree that there must be innate constraints on children's hypotheses when learning how combinations of words align with meanings. But what are these constraints? Here we find one of the great debates in psychology and language. One early view, offered by Bloomfield (1933), was that children learn grammatical rules by imitation and reinforcement. A similar view was later offered by Skinner (1957). On this account, grammar can be characterized as an associative chain of words linked by transitions of different probabilities. According to this behaviorist view, children learn **transitional probabilities** among words. Acquiring grammar is therefore simply a matter of learning that in English, "*The dog ate*" is allowable ("*dog*" can follow "*the*," and "*ate*" can follow "*dog*"), but that "*dog the ate*" is not. Word-specific order is learned by imitation and reinforcement. From this view, adults produce grammatical statements for children to model, and they also systematically reward children's grammatically correct statements.

In what must still be the best-known book review in psychology or linguistics, Chomsky (1958) argued that Skinner's account of syntax development was fatally oversimplified. Some of Chomsky's main criticisms were these. First, grammar involves more than elementary transitional probabilities among units of language that otherwise have no intrinsic order. The grammatically correct use and meaning of an initial word in a sentence just as often depends on the end of the sentence (that is, on an overall sentence plan) as it does on the next word, as is implied in a transitional probability approach. For example, the sentence "*Colorless green ideas sleep furiously*" is perfectly grammatical, although the actual transitional probabilities between the words are low. Thus, transitional probabilities from one word to the next do not provide a reasonable account of grammar, and therefore cannot serve as the guiding principle of language learning. Second, Skinner's notion of reinforcement required parents to selectively reward infants for producing correct grammatical utterances. Yet, parents do not do this reliably enough to account for language acquisition (Tomasello, 2006). In fact, parents are much more likely to correct infants' factual errors than their grammar. If an infant says, "*Me eat banana*," parents are more prone to saying, "*No, that was an apple*" than "*No, say 'I ate a banana'*." Thus, parents do not directly teach grammar the way school-teachers do. Instead, infants informally learn grammar from daily conversational interactions. Two other facts argue against a teacher–pupil view of grammar acquisition. One is that even expert linguists disagree about how to characterize many grammatical rules—certainly this knowledge is not available to every parent. The other is that infants seem extremely resistant to explicit correction of grammar; an infant saying "*Me eat banana*" will not generally switch to "*I ate a banana*" on being corrected.

Chomsky's attack went beyond mere criticism. He also argued constructively that accounting for grammar requires sets of rules that operate over phrases rather than words. These phrases each have a chief element or head that is drawn from a limited set of formal categories such as noun and verb (thus, a noun phrase has a noun as its head, a verb phrase has a verb, and so on; Figure 9.9). Grammatical rules determine how these categories can be arranged into **syntactic structures**. For example, possible noun phrases include "*Ernie*," "*the socks*," "*twelve hungry ducks*," or "*the burritos left over from lunch*." These noun phrases could all fit in the part of a sentence calling for a noun phrase. Thus, "*Ernie arrived*," "*The socks arrived*," and so on are all grammatically correct (although they might not make much sense). You could also say, "*Did you know that Ernie/the socks/twelve ducks ... arrived?*" One of Chomsky's crucial contributions was to introduce into psychology the idea that any adequate description of language has to refer to structures like these and not just words. This idea is called **structure dependence**: Grammatical rules are defined not only over words, but also over syntactic phrases such as noun phrases. Structure dependence explains why the "*colorless green ideas*" sentence is grammatical even though it is improbable. "*Colorless green ideas*" is a noun phrase and is allowed the full syntactic rights of noun phrases. Structure dependence is a critical constraint on the possible rules of grammar. One of the boldest of Chomsky's claims was that structure dependence, and a number of other aspects of syntax, are innate and are built into every infant in what he called **Universal Grammar** (UG). UG is said to account for the fact that, although infants' language environments differ enormously, infants' syntactic outputs are strikingly similar. Whereas variation in the vocabularies of language-learning infants can be traced to environmental factors such as amount of parent speech, variation in grammar hardly seems to exist among infants learning a given language. Chomsky compared language learning to the growth of an organ such as the liver. As long as certain very basic preconditions are met, both develop in all children. The claim is not that language itself is innate; that would imply that an English infant reared in a Cantonese family would speak English instead of Cantonese. Rather, the claim is that infants are innately biased to interpret language in certain ways. Some of these biases, such as structure dependence, are widely agreed on. Other innate knowledge, such as specific constraints on what a pronoun can refer to, or the existence of categories like noun and verb, are still the focus of intense debate.

A current version of Chomsky's theory is referred to as the **Principles and Parameters Approach**, which holds that in some basic respects all languages share a set of basic rules (called principles) and that grammars vary in only a restricted number of ways (called parameters). As infants gain experience with language, they discover the values of the parameters. For example, in some languages it is grammatical to leave off the subject of a sentence, whereas in other languages it is ungrammatical. Thus, in Spanish, one may say, "*Yo canto*" (*I sing*) or just "*Canto*" (which also means "*I sing*," but the "*I*" is implied by the *o* ending of the verb). But in French, like English, one must say, "*Je chante*." to mean "*I sing*"; leaving off the *je* changes the meaning of the sentence. Whether or not it is grammatical to omit the subject of a sentence in these constructions is argued to be a parameter that all languages have. Infants must learn whether their language is a "subject-drop-okay" language or a "subject-drop-not-okay" language. An interesting feature of the Principles and Parameters Approach is that some parameter values are held to be innate default settings. A candidate default was the "subject-drop-okay" value. Because infants often omit subjects of sentences, the theory proposed that infants at first behave as if they were learning languages like Spanish. Infants who really are learning these languages stick with the default parameter setting, whereas infants who are not (such as English learners) must switch.

A crucial feature of UG is that the innately specified knowledge is particular to language. In other words, UG applies to no other domain. For example, the notion that languages either require subjects of sentences or do not is not a kind of innate knowledge that could be shared with other cognitive processes such as visual perception or memory. For those who do not share the Chomskyan perspective, the innate specification of linguistic structure is a key sticking point (Mehler, Nespor, & Pena, 2008). For these researchers there might be innate biases that concern children's ways of interpreting the world, including the interpretation of speech, but these biases are not special to language. For example, proponents of the standard Chomskyan approach argue that there are innate rules to tell children that in sentences like "*Julien brought him a ladder.*" it is impossible for *Julien* and *him* to refer to the same person (in contrast with "*When he came, Julien brought a ladder,*" which allows *he* and *Julien* to be the same). Some psycholinguists consider this level of detail in innate specification unlikely.

If language is like an organ, as Chomsky proposed, is it an organ that can be identified as a biological structure in the brain? At present it is not possible to give a complete answer to this question, but it is certain that there is no special piece of brain tissue that can be said to wholly contain language processes. However, neuroscientific studies of adult linguistic performance show that certain structures in the brain are involved in particular aspects of language processing (Figure 9.10). For example, injury to **Broca's area** (in the left frontal lobe) tends to cause problems in producing fluent speech, whereas injury to **Wernicke's area** (in the left temporal lobe) tends to cause poor comprehension generally as well as fluent but relatively meaningless speech. It is not clear the extent to which these areas are specialized for language processing in infants, but *neural interplay between production & comp.*

there are a few studies that show adults and infants process words in much the same way. For example, Travis et al. (2011) combined MEG and fMRI techniques to look at the neural dynamics of word understanding in 12- to 18-month-olds. They found activation localized to the left frontal temporal areas, occurring about 400 milliseconds (termed the N400) after word onset. This finding is similar to what is found with adults in word comprehension tasks, both in terms of cortical activation and in the timing (the relatively later timing reflects cognitive process rather than lower level perceptual processes). Recall from earlier in this chapter that infants this age typically have a small productive vocabulary, although there is tremendous variation in the number of words spoken by infants. Infants with larger productive vocabularies show a stronger N400 response in studies measuring event-related potentials than infants with smaller vocabularies (Friedrich & Friederici, 2010). This finding suggests a neural interplay between production and comprehension.

One implication of Travis et al.'s work is that the specialization of the left temporal areas for language processing starts earlier than 1 year of age (Dehaene-Lambertz, Hertz-Pannier, Dubois, & Dehaene, 2008). There are several pieces of intriguing evidence suggesting that neural specialization may start early, and this specialization facilitates language learning. For example, newborns respond differently to repetitive syllabic sequences (like /gamama/) compared to non-repetitive stimuli (like /gamada/) suggesting a preparedness to respond differently to sounds with higher probabilities of occurring. Moreover, the left temporal and frontal areas appear to govern this response (Gervain, Macagno, Cogoi, Peña, & Mehler, 2008). In another example, diminished perception of non-native speech contrasts is accompanied by changes in neural activity. Kuhl (2009) found that infants who showed less neural activity to non-native contrasts at 7½ months had larger vocabularies at 24 months, suggesting that the infants who were more attuned to the sounds in their language were better at learning words.

The question of whether children possess a natural language has been asked with surprising frequency in history—and by a surprising group of individuals, from pharaohs to phoneticians. James I of England (1566–1625), for example, posed the question and thought of how to address it. Long interested in the Bible—his is the *King James* version—James sought to identify the original language of Adam and

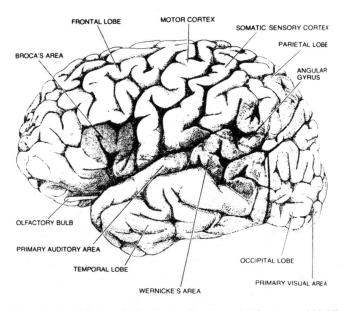

Fig. 9.10 A view of the left side of the human brain indicating the major features and highlighting two areas of speech, Broca's area and Wernike's area, concerned with producing and comprehending language, respectively.

Eve, and to do so he conceived of a unique experiment. He proposed to place two infants on an otherwise uninhabited island in the care of a deaf-mute nurse. James reasoned that, if the two spontaneously developed speech, theirs would be the natural language of humankind. Although probably within his power, King James never (to our knowledge) conducted his study. To determine natural language, and whether or not linguistic structures develop spontaneously and reflect worldly experience, would constitute a telling experiment, but a wholly unethical one.

However, experiments of opportunity that approximate King James's conditions tend to confirm that children develop functional language categories in the absence of formal linguistic experience. Goldin-Meadow (2006), for example, studied language development in deaf infants who were of normal intelligence but whose parents (for various reasons) prohibited them from learning manual sign language. As a consequence, these infants have essentially no experience with any formal language, although their other life experiences are normal. Goldin-Meadow categorized infants' communicative gestures into units (analogous to words) and connected multi-sign units (analogous to phrases). By the middle of the second year, deaf infants gave good evidence that they developed signs to refer to objects, people, and actions, and they combined signs into phrases to express relations among words in ordered ways. Their communication systems were not only structured, they incorporated many properties found in different languages. Clearly, in the absence of formal training and imitation, infants develop comprehensible syntactic rules: They sign actors before actions, and acts before objects acted on.

Further analysis of mothers' interactions with their infants shows that the infants (rather than their mothers) originated such sign systems. Even under these challenging circumstances, infants reveal a natural inclination to develop a grammatically structured communication system. Furthermore, the timing of infants' invention of communication systems is roughly the same as that of hearing infants learning spoken languages—their first "words" appear at around 12 months, and their first combinations of words appear several months later.

Infants appear to be driven to produce language, or at least communication systems, with some kind of structure. Intriguing evidence in support of this notion has emerged from other studies of deaf children in Nicaragua where, until relatively recently, no sign language existed. Deaf children from around the country were collected in a special school in Managua, where teachers (unsuccessfully) tried to teach them to lipread Spanish. However, the children began using a gesture system to communicate with each other, and over time this system acquired complex features that are found in true sign languages (Senghas & Coppola, 2001). Later-arriving children learned the language from children already at the school, and these children improved on the language in ways that were similar in complexity and grammar to mature languages.

In sum, it is not well understood how children learn syntax. Infants are exposed to a language that has a set of rules for putting words together, but they are not directly taught the rules. Instead, every infant must figure the rules out. It is likely that the processes underlying the learning of grammar reflect both innate and learned components. The infant may come prepared for the task of extracting the rules and exposure to a specific language helps shape the rules. Moreover, neural circuitry appears to be ready for this process early in development.

SUMMARY

Infancy literally means "incapable of speech," yet is paradoxically the point of departure for understanding language development and the time of some of the greatest achievements in language learning. Because the adult end point of language acquisition is so complex and variable, many have argued that specific sounds, semantics, and syntax, indeed the act of communicating, must all be learned. On the same grounds, however, others have argued that the intricate and multifaceted edifice of language must be constructed on inborn propensities and abilities. In the space of about two years, infants master language without explicit instruction. By that time, babies comprehend others and express themselves using the complex symbol system we know as language. Children everywhere travel the same road to achieve basic linguistic proficiency at more or less the same rate, largely (although not wholly) independent of their general intelligence, the language community in which they are reared, and the amount of instruction they receive. Language lies at the intersection of perceptual, cognitive, and social competencies.

However, all manifestations of the language system are constructed or transformed by specific experiences. Infants learn only the particular language (and even the idiosyncratic dialect) to which they are exposed, and individual experiences seem to be associated with individual differences in language competencies. Happily, parents readily adjust the language they direct to their infants in ways that appear to ease their infants' task. Thus, language acquisition must be both rigid and flexible. It must assure desired outcomes even in the face of environmental instability, while at the same time encouraging flexibility in response to environmental diversity.

KEY TERMS

Auditory preference procedure
Aveolars
Babble
Broca's area
Canonical babbling
Categorical speech perception
Child-directed speech
Communicative intent
Conditioned head-turn procedure
Context-flexible words
Context-restricted words
Cooing
Dentals
Developmental psycholinguistics
Expansion
Expressive language
Extension problem
Fast mapping
Gesture
Immediate reference problem
Induction
Intonated babble
Jargon
Joint attention
Labials
Morphemes
Mutual exclusivity
Nominal insight
Phonation
Phonemics

Phonetics
Phonology
Phonotactics
Phonotactic learning
Pragmatics
Preference methods
Preferential looking
Principles and Parameters Approach
Receptive language
Reduplicated babbling
Reference
Referential
Segmentation problem
Semantics
Speech spectrograph
Statistical learning
Structure dependence
Syntactic structures
Syntax
Taxonomic constraint
Transitional probabilities
Turn taking
Universal Grammar
Variegated babbling
Velars
Vocabulary burst
Vocal play
Wernicke's area
Whole object assumption

Chapter 10

Emotions and Temperament in Infancy

- *What are emotions?*
- *What are the relative strengths and weaknesses of learning, psychoanalytic, cognitive, and ethological theories of emotional development?*
- *How are infants' emotional expressions studied, and how do they change developmentally?*
- *How emotionally expressive are babies, and how sensitive are they to others' emotional signals?*
- *What is temperament in infancy? What determines temperament?*
- *What are the principal dimensions of infant temperament?*
- *How does temperament affect early development?*
- *How is infant temperament measured, and how accurate are the measurements?*
- *Does temperament differ across gender and cultures?*

Emotional development has long fascinated infancy researchers because emotions help shape children's encounters with the social and inanimate world. Emotional reactions organize infants' responses to events, and parents pay careful attention to these reactions in order to manage, pacify, accentuate, or redirect them effectively. During the first two years of life, changes in infants' emotional reactions mark important and meaningful developmental transitions including the first elicited smiles, the earliest indications of stranger wariness, and initial signs of embarrassment. These emotional reactions are also significant because parents view them as indicators of emerging personality—cues to what children's behavioral styles are like now and what they may be like in future years. Along with variations in activity level, individual differences in predominant mood, soothability, and emotional intensity are characteristics by which infants become behaviorally organized early in life, and by which parents increasingly characterize their children. These individual differences are what we mean by the term temperament. Rothbart (2011) defined temperament partly in terms of individual differences in emotional reactivity, which she viewed as genetically or biologically based stable patterns over time. Thus, studies of emotions and temperament are linked, not only because they involve similar aspects of behavioral individuality, but also because both significantly affect immediate and enduring reactions to other people and experiences.

In this two-part chapter, we discuss central features of early emotions and the development of temperament. In the first part, we consider how emotions have been defined and measured in infancy. Then, we turn to questions concerning the development of emotional responses and sensitivity to the emotional cues of others before considering the various ways in which researchers have tried to explain these developmental changes. In the second part, we discuss definitions and measurement of temperament. In addition, we ask how differences in temperament affect infants' behavioral functioning, and the factors that contribute to the stability of temperament over time. As we see, researchers have repeatedly shown how infants affect their interactions and future development by virtue of their emotional behavior because of their individually distinctive and stable temperaments.

EMOTIONS IN INFANCY

Toward a Definition of Emotions

The study of emotional development poses fundamental questions for the measurement and interpretation of infant behavior. How should emotion be defined? Do facial expressions reliably reflect underlying emotions? Does the capacity to tell the difference among others' facial expressions reflect an understanding of emotions? In this section, we begin to consider these questions, starting with the definition of **emotion**.

It is more difficult to define an emotion than you might think, and as a result philosophers have long disagreed about the nature of emotions. Plato and Socrates believed that emotions got in the way of good judgment and thus should be kept under control so that they could serve reason. **Structural theories** define emotions in terms of their component processes and focus on identifying the range of emotions that developing individuals can experience at different ages depending on underlying physiological, cognitive, and experiential processes. Lewis (2000), for example, proposed that emotions have five defining characteristics. First, there are **emotion elicitors**, internal and external events that trigger biological changes, which are the basis for emotion. Second, there are **emotion receptors** in the brain that make it easier to register and encode emotion-relevant events. Third, there are **emotion states** that involve changes in psychophysiological activity when emotional receptors are activated. Fourth, there are **emotional expressions**, including facial, gestural, and other behaviors. Finally, there is **emotional experience**, which is the interpretation and evaluation of perceived emotional states and expressions. Like most researchers, Lewis believes that emotional development depends, in part, on underlying changes in physiological arousal and cognitive experience (especially social experience).

Structural theorists have also attempted to identify the basic or **primary emotions**. Not surprisingly, researchers disagree about what are the primary emotions. Izard (2002), for example, identified 11 primary emotions: interest, joy, surprise, sadness, anger, disgust, contempt, fear, shame, guilt, and shyness. Other theorists do not consider emotions like shame to be primary, but do include different ones, such as affection. In general, most structural theorists believe that primary emotions must be so deeply rooted in human biology that they are either innate or develop very early. In this way, primary emotions are distinct from **secondary emotions**, which depend on more advanced developmental capacities, including milestones in cognitive development. Lewis (2011a) proposed that the secondary emotions of embarrassment, pride, guilt, shame, and envy could only emerge during the second and third years of life after the capacities for self-referent thought and appraisal developed.

In general, structuralist views have advanced our understanding of emotional development by describing some of the constituent processes involved in emotional experience. By identifying cognitive influences underlying emotional reactions, structural theorists have helped us understand how events are evaluated and interpreted in different ways by infants of various ages, as well as how infants' appraisals affect their emotionality. Similarly, by intensively studying the facial expressions that usually accompany emotional experiences, researchers have developed useful methodologies for studying emotions in very young infants. However, this line of thinking has led some critics to argue that structuralists sometimes mistakenly portray emotions as nothing more than the by-product of the perceptual or cognitive processes. They fear that if emotions are portrayed as the outcomes of other developmental achievements, researchers might overlook the ways in which emotional development influences perception, cognition, and sociability. Thus, emphasizing constituent processes can yield useful insights, but could mislead students of infant development to underestimate the reciprocal influence of emotions on other aspects of development.

From an alternative perspective, theorists have emphasized the role of emotions in everyday experience. Emotions provide potent and informative internal cues that can, for example, cause people to reevaluate their current circumstances and make new plans. Emotions also provide significant cues to others about an individual's current state that might lead them to respond differently. These perspectives comprise the **functionalist theory** of emotions, which emphasizes the purpose and role of emotion in ongoing transactions between individuals and their environments (Saarni et al., 2006). Functionalist definitions of emotion derive, in part, from ethological theories that emphasize the adaptive purpose of emotion in human evolution. (We will consider ethological theories later in this chapter.) Campos, Campos, and Barrett (1989, p. 395) provided a good example of the functionalist approach when they wrote that emotions are "processes of establishing, maintaining, or disrupting the relations between the person and the internal or external environment, when such relations are significant to the individual." Events can become personally significant in various ways. First, events may be directly relevant to an individual's goals or objectives, and emotional reactions vary depending on whether or not these goals are achieved. Second, some events (such as sudden loud noises or noxious odors) are inherent elicitors of emotion because they trigger innate emotive processes. Third, events may induce affective resonance—with individuals taking on others' emotional experiences—that can lead to emotional arousal. Infants experience emotions in all of these ways.

From a functionalist perspective, emotions can be further defined in terms of what they do (Saarni et al., 2006). For example, emotions can regulate other internal psychological processes: They influence perception, cognition, and motivation and in doing so cause people to reevaluate their current conditions and adjust their actions accordingly. Emotions influence how people appraise and interpret events and how they organize their experiences conceptually. Emotions can also regulate interpersonal behavior because individuals respond socially to the emotions they "read" in others and regulate their emotional expressions to achieve their social goals. The approach of someone who is visibly angry (with clenched fists, a flushed face, and an angry facial expression) arouses different emotions and reactions than the approach of someone who looks joyful or fearful. Finally, emotions organize and motivate reactions to environmental events that may be biologically and/or psychologically adaptive. Compare, for example, the goals, appreciation, action tendencies, and adaptive functions of the four emotions (joy, anger, sadness, and fear) presented in Table 10.1. Joy is expressed when individuals conclude that significant objectives or goals have been attained, and these emotional experiences energize them, reinforcing the activity, encouraging others to maintain the pleasurable interaction, and stimulating them to attempt new challenges. Anger, by contrast, occurs when individuals perceive obstacles that prevent them from attaining their goals. Anger motivates efforts to restore progress toward achieving the goal, changing the behavior of others, and/or striving for revenge or retaliation.

Functionalist views of emotion avoid many of the weaknesses of structuralist views. By regarding emotions as central organizing features of human experience, for example, functionalist theorists recognize that emotions are influenced by perception and cognition but are never merely the by-product of those internal processes. Emphasis on the functions and purposes of emotions, rather

Table 10.1 Generalized schema for predicting elicitation of some basic emotions

Emotion	Goal	Appreciation	Action tendency	Adaptive function
Joy	Any significant objective	Goal is perceived or predicted to be attained	Approach Energizing	Reinforcement of successful strategy Facilitation of rehearsal of new challenges Social message to initiate or continue interaction
Anger	Any significant objective	Perception of or anticipation of an obstacle to attainment of goal; perception of obstacle as not easily removable	Elimination (not just removal) of properties of an object that make it an obstacle	Restoration of progress toward a goal Effecting a change in behavior of a social other In later development: revenge, retaliation
Sadness	Securing or maintaining an engagement with either an animate or inanimate object	Perception of the goal as unattainable	Disengagement	Conservation of energy Eventual redirection of resources to other pursuits perceived to be more attainable Encourages nurturance from others
Fear	Maintenance of integrity of the self, including self-survival and, later, self-esteem	Perception that the goal is not likely to be attained, unless protective action is taken	Flight, withdrawal	Survival Avoidance of pain Maintenance of self-esteem Alert others to avoid the situation or help

Adapted from Campos, Barrett, Lamb, Goldsmith, & Stenberg, 1983.

than their structural constituents, has heightened interest in the notion that emotional development can catalyze other developmental processes. Functionalists argue that, by focusing on the roles of emotion in human behavior, we come closer to understanding their adaptive and maladaptive influences. Functionalist perspectives have been criticized, however, for not making clear precisely how emotions are related to other aspects of human motivation. By defining emotions in relation to individuals' goals, and by relating emotional arousal to broadly defined adaptive functions, furthermore, functionalist definitions of emotion seem imprecise. Functionalism may appear to be unduly expansive, encompassing most of human motivation including drives related to hunger, thirst, and sexuality. Functionalist views also tend to identify the purposes of emotion better than they explain why these functions emerge when they do.

Theorizing about Emotions in Infancy

In some respects, the differences between structuralist and functionalist views of emotion can be viewed as differences in emphasis rather than substance. The two often explain identical emotional processes in complementary ways, as we illustrate below by describing specific theories from each of these perspectives in more detail. First, we will consider two theories from the structuralist perspective: learning theory and cognitive theory. Then, we will consider psychodynamic and ethological theories as representatives to varying degrees of the functionalist perspective.

Learning Theories   One of the first theorists to try to explain the early course of emotional development was John B. Watson, who believed that there are three basic emotions—fear, rage, and love—elicited by a set of unconditioned stimuli (e.g., sudden noises in dark settings) that have the inherent capacity to evoke emotion. Watson also believed that most emotional reactions are the result of learned associations between unconditioned stimuli (e.g., warmth, food) and neutral events (e.g., a mother's voice or face) so that these neutral events come to elicit emotional responses through classical conditioning (Chapters 3 and 7). Operant conditioning and observational learning may also account for how much and what kinds of emotions are produced by infants (Bandura, 1969; Gewirtz & Peláez-Nogueras, 2000). The range and quality of a baby's early facial expressions of emotion are doubtlessly influenced by patterns of reinforcing responses from caregivers and by opportunities to observe and imitate adult expressions. However, learning theorists cannot satisfactorily explain why emotional reactions occur in the first place. Why, for example, do babies start smiling at about 6 weeks of age? It is not a direct result of feeding, holding, or stroking, nor does it occur by imitation because blind babies begin to smile at the same age as sighted infants (Fraiberg, 1977). As a result, many developmentalists have turned to alternative theoretical views.

Cognitive Theories   The most influential cognitive explanation of emotional development was initially proposed by Hebb (1946) to account for the unlearned, spontaneous expressions of fear by chimpanzees. Hebb postulated that perceptual experiences establish a set of memory traces in the form of neurological circuits that he called **phase sequences**. Whenever a new perceptual experience is sufficiently similar to previous ones to activate a phase sequence, yet not similar enough to maintain the continued smooth functioning of this neural circuit, the brain is disrupted in a way that produces the subjective experience of fear. By extrapolation from Hebb's theory, fear of strangers in infancy occurs because infants have established memory traces of familiar individuals that are activated, but disrupted, when unfamiliar persons are encountered. Similarly, masks, jacks-in-the-box, and the like elicit fear in infants because of discrepancies between perceptual experience and the memory traces they evoke.

One important problem with this explanation is that infants can usually discriminate visually between mothers and strangers within minutes of birth, yet they do not show wariness of strangers until 6 or 7 months of age. Consequently, Kagan amended Hebb's theory by arguing that until 6 months of age discrepancy between perceptual experience and memory traces yields interest rather than fear (Kagan, 2010). After this age, however, infants can spontaneously generate hypotheses to explain discrepancies. When interesting discrepant events cannot be explained by their hypotheses, fear or distress ensues. If the child knew what happened to the mother or could predict what the stranger would do, no negative reactions would result.

In another modification of Hebb's theory, Sroufe (1979) argued that discrepancy can account for the intensity of emotional reactions to stimulus events, but not for the positive or negative quality of the reaction. Whether an emotional reaction is positive or negative depends, among other things, on the context in which a stimulus event is encountered. Infants respond more positively to strangers in familiar circumstances (such as at home) than in unfamiliar contexts (such as a laboratory). Friendliness toward strangers is also more apparent when strangers approach slowly and gradually rather than suddenly and abruptly, and when the mother or another trusted adult reacts positively to the stranger. Thus the strangeness (or discrepancy) of the unfamiliar adult does not, in itself, determine the baby's emotional reaction; rather, the context in which the stranger is encountered influences whether the baby is scared or sociable.

Critics have sometimes viewed cognitive theories for casting emotion as a derivative of cognitive processes, without also considering how emotion might influence cognition. In addition, cognitive theorists make reference to difficult-to-measure processes such as "discrepancy from memory traces" and "hypotheses to explain discrepancy" which make the theories difficult to test. These theories offer interesting after-the-fact explanations for emotional reactions in infants, but it is difficult to specify in advance how discrepant stimulus events will be from a baby's cognitive expectations. Consequently, cognitive theories have not stimulated the amount of research that their intriguing explanations might otherwise warrant.

Psychoanalytic Theories   An alternative is psychoanalytic theory. Many psychoanalytic theorists believe that emotional development is partly a result of ego development in the context of parent–infant interaction. Spitz (1965), for example, argued that parent–infant interaction is related to emotional development in two ways. First, the parent gratifies the baby's physical needs (e.g., hunger), thereby directly influencing emotions while lending the caregiver special significance. Second, the parent must often frustrate the child—and thus elicit negative emotions—to instill self-control (e.g., restrict the child from crawling/falling down the stairs). The emotions that result from need gratification were believed by Spitz to help organize the ego processes of perception, cognition, and memory in early infancy, and they did so by heightening the salience to the baby of those environmental stimuli that coincide with need and need reduction. When parent–infant interaction is associated with need reduction, stimuli associated with the parent—especially the parent's facial features—are likely to be especially meaningful and significant to the baby. In particular, according to Spitz, the configuration of facial features involving the forehead, eyes, and nose becomes a **social releaser** that can elicit the baby's smile. Psychoanalytic and learning theorists thus interpret the onset of early smiling very differently. To learning theorists, the face becomes a **conditioned elicitor** of smiling through learning. To psychoanalysts, the face is an **automatic elicitor** of smiling. Spitz used the term **sign gestalt** to refer to the facial features that elicit social smiles from young infants. It is a gestalt because only specific facial configurations successfully elicit the smile, and it is a sign because it signals impending need reduction.

Spitz (1965) used the older infant's developing ability to represent the parent in memory to explain the onset of stranger anxiety around 7 to 9 months of age. He argued that stranger anxiety occurs when the child compares the stranger to an internal representation of the parent. If the parent is absent, the baby anticipates that the parent will not be available to satisfy needs, and distress results. Spitz was not the only psychoanalyst to discuss early development. For example, Mahler, Pine, and Bergman (1975) suggested that important transitions in early emotional development occur as the child becomes psychologically differentiated from the parent and ambivalent about becoming alone (autonomous). However, only Spitz emphasized the effects of parent–infant interaction on the emerging range and quality of emotional responsiveness and proposed that the emotional climate (e.g., warm vs. cold relations) of the home influenced emotional development directly and indirectly.

Psychoanalytic theories, however, have difficulty explaining some aspects of emotional development. For example, infants respond emotionally not just to stimuli associated with the parent but also to a variety of other stimulus events. Young infants (1½- to 3-month-olds) smile not only at faces but also at bull's-eye patterns and bells; 6- to 9-month-olds show fear not only to strangers but also to heights, masks, jacks-in-the-box, and other such events. These emotional reactions are not well explained by psychoanalytic theory. Moreover, the specific ways that parent–infant interaction supposedly affects emotional development are rather unspecified by psychoanalytic theorists, and researchers have identified a number of other factors—such as social referencing and emotional contagion—not addressed by psychoanalysts. Finally, as discussed in Chapter 1, psychoanalytic theory also involves a number of implicit assumptions about the nature of human development and the critical role of early experiences that have not been supported.

Ethological Theories   Still other theories of emotion emphasize the biological or maturational determinants of emotional development and are associated with two lines of research. Ethology is the scientific study of animal behavior. Ethological theories of emotional development involve studies of rhesus monkeys raised in isolation that nevertheless respond with fear or aversion to pictures of other monkeys in threatening postures. Because these monkeys were denied opportunities for social learning or conditioning of emotional behavior, this literature suggests that certain emotional reactions may have innate, biological bases (Snowdon, 2003). Other studies indicate that many emotional responses, including early social smiling and separation reactions, emerge early in life as if following a strict maturational timetable, independent of social determinants (Izard & Ackerman, 2000).

The impressiveness of these findings has increased the popularity of ethological theories emphasizing that emotions are associated with behavioral processes that have fostered species survival and reproductive success throughout our evolutionary history. In this view, emotions are important because they provide significant signals to social partners and are associated with autonomic behavioral reactions that facilitate adaptive responses to threat, danger, or stress (Saarni et al., 2006). Because some of the expressive patterns associated with emotion are culturally universal, and because human and primate expressive patterns are quite similar, ethologists view emotional reactions as biologically adaptive response patterns that probably evolved to foster species survival (Snowdon, 2003).

Consider, for example, the emotion of fear. Virtually from birth, infants startle in response to sudden, intense events, and they later exhibit fear or wariness in response to unfamiliar people and strange objects. When these events occur, infants typically exhibit components of a classic "fear face," emit loud, distinctive distress vocalizations, and retreat seeking a trusted attachment figure. This constellation of responses has been described by some researchers as a "fear/wariness behavioral system" (Chapter 11). It is easy to see how such reactions can be viewed as adaptive. In our evolutionary context, such as savannah settings, infants were likely to encounter strange objects, people, or events that might prove dangerous or threatening. The behaviors associated with the arousal of fear involve withdrawal from those stimuli and requests for caregiver protection. Other emotions can similarly be viewed as the consequence of adaptation.

Ethological formulations provide valuable perspectives on emotional development because they address important questions concerning the evolutionary meaning of emotional expressions and the significance of the child's understanding of others' emotional expressions. Only ethological theories attempt to explain why infants' emotional signals have such compelling effects on adult caregivers and, conversely, why others' expressions elicit interest and responses from young infants. For these reasons, ethological views provide an important foundation for the functionalist approach (Table 10.1).

Methodological Issues in the Study of Emotions in Infancy

It is extremely difficult to understand emotional development in pre-linguistic infants because infants cannot describe their subjective experiences like adults can. As a result, research on emotional sensitivity and the development of emotional expressions has proceeded in tandem. It is difficult to study one without studying the other, even though expressions might not always reflect underlying emotion very well (Lewis, 2011a).

Darwin (1872/1975) anticipated the current reliance of researchers on facial expressions of emotion when he noted that certain expressions are remarkably consistent across age and culture. In Figure 10.1, we reproduce Darwin's pictures of emotional distress in children, illustrating his belief in the universality of emotional expressions (see, too, his comments on Doddy's emotions in Box 3.1).

Because the face has many muscles and can convey a broad range of expressions, and because we commonly use the face as our primary means of evaluating emotional experience, researchers have made extensive efforts to measure facial expressions of emotion in infants. Highly detailed, anatomically based

Fig. 10.1 Expressions of distress in infants suffering slight pain, moderate hunger, or discomfort. (From Darwin, 1872/1975.)

measurement systems for coding specific muscle movements in the face have been developed. For example, Ekman's Facial Action Coding System (FACS; Ekman & Friesen, 1976, 1978) illustrates how a broad range of specific and complex muscular movements in adults' faces can be discretely coded in a detailed but time-consuming procedure. Oster (2005) modified this system for infants (called Baby FACS), taking into account the unique facial configurations of young babies. Similarly, Izard (1979; Izard & Dougherty, 1982) developed a detailed system, called the Maximally Discriminative Facial Movements Code (MAX), so that users could identify in infants 27 distinct components or patterns that may be organized to project particular emotions. A simplified version of MAX (called AFFEX) has also been developed.

If we are confident that facial expressions reliably reflect underlying emotional arousal in infants, then these detailed coding schemes allow researchers to specify precisely and unambiguously when particular emotions are being experienced, and to delineate the fluctuations between emotions and developmental changes in their expression. This technique is especially useful when researchers are studying emotional reactions to social events—such as the approach of an unfamiliar adult—in which short-term changes in facial expressions might reveal significant changes in the infant's appraisal of the stranger.

Because these detailed, anatomically based systems typically require that video-records be coded at very slow speeds (a fraction of the rate at which they occur in real time), they provide a level of detail and sophistication that on-line systems of analysis cannot provide. For example, Messinger and his colleagues (2008) described four types of smiles (Figure 10.2): (1) smiling alone involving neither cheek raising nor mouth opening (simple smiling), (2) cheek-raise smiling without mouth opening (Duchenne smiling), (3) open-mouth smiling without cheek raising (play smiling), and (4) open-mouth cheek-raise smiling (duplay smiling).

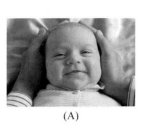   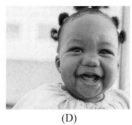

(A)   (B)   (C)   (D)

Fig. 10.2 Examples of four different types of smiles: (A) simple smile, in which there is no cheek raising nor mouth opening by dropping the jaw; (B) Duchenne smile, in which there is cheek raising but the mouth is still not opened by dropping the jaw; (C) play smile, in which the mouth is opened by dropping the jaw but there is no cheek raising; and (D) duplay smile, in which both jaw dropping to open the mouth and cheek raising are present. (Images courtesy of Shutterstock.com. Copyrights (A) Fajno; (B) qingqing; (C) Jiri Vaclavek; (D) Monkey Business Images.)

An important, yet unanswered question is how well facial expressions index underlying emotional experience in infants. Because we rely on facial expressions in our everyday estimates of others' emotional experiences, these measures have considerable face validity (Chapter 3). Facial expressions can be coded in detail using MAX, AFFEX, or Baby FACS, and it is, for the most part, clear whether fear, joy, anger, and other discrete emotions are being expressed. But the facial expressions of young infants may not necessarily or always reflect their underlying emotional experiences. For example, an open mouth, raised eyebrows facial expression (identified by facial coding schemes as "surprise") might not always denote surprise in infants. Raised eyebrows and open mouths are typical of 5- to 7-month-olds engaged in routine object exploration. Specifically, raised eyebrows occur after infants begin mouthing the toy (Camras, 2011). Additionally, infants do not consistently show the same facial expressions in the same context (Camras et al., 2007). These findings have led some theorists to argue that the associations between facial expressions of emotion and underlying emotional experiences are not innate (as some theorists believe), but develop over time through nervous system maturation, social experience, and a growing emotional repertoire (Saarni et al., 2006).

As an alternative or convergent measure, some researchers have turned to vocal or gestural expressions. Johnstone, Van Reekum, and Scherer (2001) showed that there are a number of reliable vocal indicators of emotional state in adults. Happiness, for example, is expressed by high vocal pitch, pitch variability, fast tempo, and high intensity, whereas sadness is specified by low pitch, low intensity, slow tempo, and diminished pitch variability. Infants have distinct cries for hunger and pain, and most caregivers interpret the cries as such and respond appropriately (LaGasse, Neal, & Lester, 2005). Adults rate certain cries as more distressed and aversive than others. Infants, who cry at a high pitch, with great intensity, and for a long time tend to elicit faster responses than do infants who cry briefly or minimally, because adults accurately believe that they are more distressed (Barr, Hopkins, & Green, 2000). The acoustic features of cries change as infants mature, in part due to changes in the vocal tract over the first two years of life, and the frequency of crying varies across age (LaGasse et al., 2005). For example, between 2 and 4 months of age, infants cry a lot, on average about 3 hours per day, and it is not always clear what they need (LaGasse et al., 2005). Older infants on average may cry less than younger infants, and the reason for crying might differ. For example, older infants understand language before they produce it, as we saw in Chapter 9, and they may become frustrated by their unsuccessful attempts at communication (LaGasse et al., 2005). As a result, cries may mean somewhat different things when uttered by newborns and 1-year-olds.

We know even less about gestures, movements, and behaviors other than facial expression and crying that might indicate emotional arousal in infants. Darwin observed that Doddy regularly used gestures "to explain his wishes" (Box 3.1), but Papoušek and Papoušek (2002b) were among the few researchers to study the interpretation of infants' gestures. Infants become very still when they are interested in events, turn away from stimuli that evoke fear, slump in posture when sad, look intently (often with a double take) at stimuli that surprise them, and try to repeat or duplicate experiences that elicit joy. Others have noted that infants make differential bodily movements when experiencing events that violate these expectations, more so than making a surprise expression (Camras et al., 2002; Scherer, Zentner, & Stern, 2004). Although such behaviors are certainly not associated with different emotions in a one-to-one fashion, they provide useful information when connected to facial and/or vocal measures of infants' emotions.

Instead of using highly detailed direct observations to determine whether or not emotions are present, researchers have also asked untrained observers, such as mothers, nurses, or students, to identify the emotions displayed in photographs of infants. Whether the emotions are depicted in still photographs or in video-records, identifications by untrained observers tend to be accurate (Hiltunen, Moilanen, Szajnberg, & Gardner, 1999), especially when expressions of joy, interest, surprise, and distress are involved. Expressions of fear, anger, sadness, and disgust are identified less accurately (Oster, 2005). Researchers have also asked infant caregivers to describe the range of emotions they naturally perceive in their babies. By the time their infants reached 1 month of age, 99% of mothers believed that their babies express interest, 95% joy, 84% anger, 75% surprise, 58% fear, and 34% sadness (Johnson, Emde, Pannabecker, Stenberg, & Davis, 1982). Moreover, babies make a variety of recognizable facial expressions even when they have birth defects resulting in craniofacial abnormalities (Figure 10.3; Oster, 2003). Mothers base their judgments on vocal and facial expressions, along with gestures and arm movements (Klinnert, Sorce, Emde, Stenberg, & Gaensbauer, 1984), and we do not know whether these judgments only reflect the infants' expressive capacities or also the mothers' subjective inferences based on contextual cues. Because mothers often respond differently to different perceived emotions, they have many opportunities to refine their inferences depending on their babies' responses (Riddell, Stevens, Cohen, Flora, & Greenberg, 2007). Thus, maternal judgments may be quite accurate. Interestingly, computer programs are accurate too! Messinger and his colleagues (2008) have developed an automated program to identify different types of smiling, and found that the program was as accurate as parents.

Emotion has physiological components, and thus researchers have tried to index emotion by monitoring changes in infant physiological state. Heart rate has not been a very reliable predictor of emotional state, especially in young infants. For example, when infants are presented with a stimulus thought to elicit fear, some infants show a decrease in heart rate, suggesting interest (Camras, 2011). Changes in skin temperature may provide information regarding emotional experience. Nakanishi and Imai-Matsumura (2008) measured changes in skin temperature when infants laughed. They found that after 4 months of age, laughing was accompanied by a decrease in temperature, particularly in the nose region (Figure 10.4).

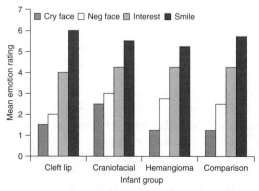

Fig. 10.3 Mean ratings made by untrained observers of infant facial expressions. The comparison group consisted of healthy infants. The other groups had birth defects that affected their facial morphology and appearance. (From Oster, 2003; reproduced with permission.)

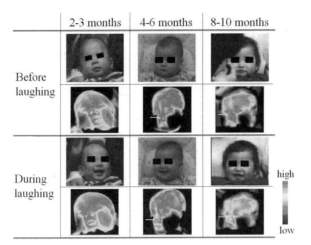

Fig. 10.4 Facial temperature differences before and after laughing. (From Nakanishi & Imai-Matsumura, 2008; reproduced with permission from Elsevier.)

Reliance on any single index of emotional arousal in infants—whether facial, vocal, or gestural—risks erroneous conclusions, and thus it is important to use multiple convergent measures when studying early emotional development. Unfortunately, this strategy is so time consuming and technically challenging that few researchers have adopted multi-method approaches.

Development of Emotional Expressions

Because emotional reactions are associated with biologically and psychologically adaptive action tendencies, it is not surprising that newborns express emotions, often in response to survival-related experiences. As discussed in Chapter 4, neonates respond to sweet tastes with positive facial expressions and to other tastes with negative expressions of disgust or distaste. Although newborns are capable of a more limited range of discrete emotional expressions than older infants, they may experience some basic emotions (Dondi et al., 2007).

Distress is also one of the primary emotions infants express from birth (Lewis, 2000). With maturation and experience, this emotion differentiates into sadness, disgust, fear, and anger by 6 months of age. Lemerise and Dodge (2000) observed expressions of anger in infants as young as 3 to 4 months of age, and anger, rather than generalized distress, becomes increasingly typical in response to events that are unpleasant or restricting. Distress predominates the emotional responses of 2-month-olds to painful inoculations, but it is replaced by anger by 19 months. Bear, Manning, and Izard (2003) concluded that very young infants are capable only of immediate emergency reactions to physical pain, but that, with increasing age, they can inhibit such reactions enough to mobilize more sophisticated attempts to alleviate their pain. Such reactions might reflect the older infant's cognitive maturation (e.g., the growth of means-end understanding) as well as the growth of neurophysiological inhibitory processes.

Sadness is another early emerging emotional expression. Tronick (2007) observed that, when mothers play with their 3-month-old infants and then suddenly become unresponsive (the still-face procedure described in Chapter 8), their babies show signs of withdrawal, wariness, and sadness in their facial and postural expressions. Additionally, more sadness is shown by infants with depressed mothers than infants with well mothers (Field, 2002).

Whether fear is present early in life is unclear. Whereas infants as young as 6 weeks of age make defensive responses to stimuli that might lead to a fearful response in adults, such as the fast approach of an object (see optical expansion discussion in Chapter 6), infants respond with a reflexive eye blink and not by a fearful expression (Náñez & Yonas, 1994). Also, infants on the visual cliff often do not display fear at the apparent drop off. Instead, they are as likely to show interest, whether by looking into the deep side of the cliff or by a deceleration of heart rate. Furthermore, Camras and her colleagues (2007) noted that anger and fear are often interchangeable in certain contexts. Also, they found that the exhibition of the facial expressions of fear and anger in challenging contexts, such as an inoculation, do not always match the level of physiological stress infants experience. Thus, fear might not be present reliably until about 7 months of age (Izard, 2002).

The capacity to express positive emotions also emerges in early infancy. Neonates make smiling movements with their faces, most often during REM (rapid eye movement) sleep (Dondi et al., 2007). The earliest elicited smiles to another person (either a voice or a face) begin to appear toward the end of the first month of life (Messinger & Fogel, 2007). Clear expressions of joy can be observed by 2½ months when infants are playing with their mothers, and by 3 to 4 months of age infants begin laughing in response to stimulation (especially social stimulation) that is more arousing and intense. Joy also occurs in nonsocial situations: Alessandri, Sullivan, and Lewis (1990) found that more joy and interest were expressed when infants as young as 2 months of age were learning a contingent game.

Thus, infants are capable of expressing a range of different emotions, including distress, disgust (or "distaste"), anger, sadness, surprise, and joy in a range of naturalistic and laboratory situations in the first few months of life. The fact that so many primary emotions are present so early in life and that they appear in survival-related situations (after tasting noxious substances, experiencing pain, or confronting a looming stimulus) strengthens the functionalist proposal that emotional arousal motivates and directs biologically adaptive action tendencies, even very early in infancy. They also support the structuralist belief that early emotional expressions may be organized around these kinds of discrete emotional experiences.

As infants grow older, they become capable of a wider range of emotional expressions and become responsive to a growing variety of eliciting conditions. Changes in neurophysiological organization help inhibit primitive distress reactions and make it easier to express more complex emotions such as anger. Other neurophysiological changes later in the first year may also make possible inhibition and self-regulation, especially of negative emotions (Leppanen, 2011). Cognitive changes further contribute to emotional growth by enabling infants to evaluate more complex situations. For example, toward the end of the first year, reactions to strangers not only involve evaluation of the adults' unfamiliarity, but also of the context (e.g., mother's presence or absence), the setting (e.g., a comfortable and familiar environment or an unfamiliar one), the stranger's appearance (e.g., male or female, child or adult), and behavior (e.g., approaching fast or slow, looming overhead or looking at eye level). Such observations indicate that the growth of information-processing skills and reasoning processes (such as the capacity to anticipate events or to link means and ends) facilitate the complex appraisals that underlie emotional reactions later in the first year. In other words, as infants become more sophisticated thinkers, their emotional responses also become more sophisticated. Moreover, growing language skills make possible alternative forms of emotional expression—through words rather than cries or clenched fists—and alter emotionality as well.

Social experiences significantly shape emotional expression in infants (Saarni et al., 2006). Malatesta and Haviland (1982, 1986) reported that mothers changed their facial expressions an average of seven to nine times per minute during periods of face-to-face play with their infants. Roughly 25% of the time, mothers responded promptly to their infants' expressions, typically by imitating or responding positively to positive expressions, especially those of younger infants, and by ignoring negative expressions. Contingent emotional responding of this sort could reinforce the expression of positive emotions and mute the expression of negative emotions. Similarly, as described in Box 10.1, infants' fearfulness and reactions to stress may also be learned from caregivers.

Box 10.1   Science in Translation: Can Infants Learn to Be Less Fearful and Less Easily Stressed?

Parents who have two or more children often joke that they began believing that personality differences were innate the minute their second child was born! Whereas one baby was calm, cuddly, and friendly from the start, they note, the other may be anxious, stiff, and fearful from birth. As we show in this chapter, many individual differences in infants appear to be innate—they describe commonly accepted dimensions of temperament. But are differences in fearfulness and reactivity to stress always innate? Can anything be done about these dispositions? The results of recent research suggest that some of these features are learned and that they might be amenable to intervention.

Hane and Fox (2006) suspected that individual differences in infants' reactions might be learned from studies showing that rat pups whose mothers groomed and licked them less grew up to be more fearful adults (Francis, Diorio, Liu, & Meaney, 1999). Reasoning that differences in maternal responsiveness might affect human infants similarly, they observed nearly 200 mothers and their 8- to 9-month-old babies to identify groups of mothers who were either extremely sensitive or extremely insensitive and intrusive. The fearfulness of the infants was assessed by observing their reactions in a battery of tasks designed to elicit fearful behavior. The positive affect infants shared with their mothers while observing interesting toys was also recorded. Last, the asymmetry between the levels of electroencephalographic (EEG) activation in the frontal and parietal regions of the right frontal cortex was measured while the infants watched a spinning bingo wheel because earlier research had shown that the degree of asymmetry in brain response is associated with levels of stress reactivity.

The infants whose mothers behaved sensitively and non-intrusively were less fearful, shared more positive affect with their mothers, and had less frontal lobe asymmetry than did the infants whose mothers were less sensitive and more intrusive. These findings suggest that individual differences in fearfulness and reactivity to stress result from early experiences. Importantly, they also suggest that it might be possible to reduce hyper-reactivity and fearfulness in children by increasing maternal sensitivity. This might not be as far-fetched an idea as it sounds: van den Boom (1994) showed that it was possible to affect the security of infant–mother attachment by training mothers to be more sensitively responsive. There is no reason to think that the same techniques could not be used to affect infant stress reactivity, too.

As their infants grow to around 7½ months, mothers become increasingly responsive to expressions of interest and decreasingly responsive to expressions of pain (Malatesta, Grigoryev, Lamb, Albin, & Culver, 1986). Not surprisingly, infants also change their expressive patterns over this period, showing more positive and fewer negative emotions, partly in response to maternal behavior. The expressive behavior of mothers and infants tends to be consistent over time, with substantial similarities between mothers and infants, suggesting that mothers may socialize their infants' expressive styles from the early months of life (Field, 2002). Harkness and Super (2002) described several ways in which adults from different cultures socialize the emotional displays of their infants by responding in accordance with culture-specific interpretations of the infants' expressions and emotions. Of course, it is also possible that familial similarities reflect shared genetics, and we consider this possibility later in the chapter.

In more extreme circumstances, parents can foster affective disturbances through similar socialization processes (Field, 2000; Box 10.2). For example, infants of depressed mothers showed depressed social behavior (withdrawn, immobile, and non-responsive) not only when interacting with their mothers but also when interacting with strangers. It is likely that these infants have acquired such socioemotional styles by having fewer opportunities to develop social skills at home, imitating their mothers' behavior, through genetic similarity, and/or through the psychological effects of the mothers' depression on their babies (e.g., the baby's learned helplessness, coping activities, and so forth; Field, 2010). It is well established that infants of depressed mothers display more negative affect, and it is important for researchers to disentangle these diverse and overlapping influences so that they can design effective intervention and remediation programs (Hatzinikolaou & Murray, 2010).

Box 10.2   Set For Life? The Effects of Experience on Perception of Emotions

Infants are able to recognize different facial expressions that characterize a range of emotions. Pollak, Messner, Kistler, and Cohn (2009) discovered that over-exposure to certain emotions affects how children perceive these certain emotions but not others. Pollak studied abused children who likely experience more anger emotions than well-treated children. Nine-year-olds viewed five emotional expressions that ranged in intensity and were posed by different models. Children were asked to determine if the model looked happy, afraid, angry, surprised, or showed no emotion. Children who had been abused recognized anger earlier than children who had not experienced abuse. In other words, abused children correctly identified less intense angry expressions as angry compared to well-treated children. When identifying happiness, surprise, and fear, the abused and well-treated children performed the same. The researchers attributed these results to the fact that children who are abused experience anger expressions more often than well-treated children, and thus may be more sensitive to the early displays of anger. The results suggest that when over-exposed, the child is able to detect early signs of this specific emotion. The emotions that infants experience seem to impact how they perceive emotions when they

---

Emotional development can also be socialized through the baby's emotionally resonant or empathic response to the parent's emotional state. Darwin wrote that, when only 6 months old, Doddy may have expressed sympathy when his nurse pretended to cry (Box 3.1). Pre-empathic capacities are evident very early in a form of **emotional contagion** whereby the baby spontaneously resonates with another's salient emotional expressions, most often observed in response to another's distress (Geangu, Benga, Stahl, & Striano, 2010, 2011). Such responses later become more genuinely empathic with the emergence of self–other differentiation and growth in the understanding of others' emotional expressions (Hutman & Dapretto, 2009; Thompson, 2006).

Later in infancy, emotional growth is prompted by the development of self-awareness that, for the first time, permits a variety of **self-conscious** or **secondary emotions** such as embarrassment, shame, and later guilt and pride (Lewis, 2011a; Saarni et al., 2006). For example, infants 15 to 24 months of age who recognized themselves in a mirror also looked embarrassed when they were effusively praised by an adult: They smiled and looked away, covered their faces with their hands, and showed related behaviors. Infants who did not recognize themselves did not respond in this way to adult praise. The emergence of self-awareness also fosters interpersonal understanding and better understanding of others' emotions (Dunn, 2003), as we note in the next section.

In summary, current findings convincingly show that newborns and young infants express a variety of emotions that are predictably related to specific eliciting conditions. These findings support structuralist and functionalist portrayals of emotional development. With subsequent growth in a variety of developmental domains, the infants' emotional repertoire continues to broaden. Infants become responsive to a greater range of eliciting conditions, they are increasingly capable of coping with or regulating emotional experiences, and as a result, more complex emotions and emotional interrelations emerge. Emotional development not only involves these internal changes, but also changes in the behavior of adult partners.

Development of Sensitivity to Emotional Signals

Emotional competence involves reading as well as sending emotional signals, and many researchers have studied infants' capacity to read the facial expressions of emotion in others. However, discriminating different facial expressions is not the same as understanding their meaning, and thus "reading" emotions requires important interpretive as well as perceptual capacities. As we saw in Chapter 6, visual acuity in early infancy is limited, possibly making it hard for newborns to distinguish among different facial features and expressive patterns. At around 1½ to 2 months of age, infants discriminate among different facial expressions of emotion, at 3 months they generalize emotional expressions among familiar faces (namely their parents), and by 5 months they can even distinguish among and categorize variations in the intensity of some emotional expressions (Bornstein & Arterberry, 2003; Walker-Andrews, Krogh-Jesperen, Mayhew, & Coffield, 2011). Again, this does not mean that young infants understand the emotional meaning of these expressions. Infants may respond differently to different facial configurations (e.g., eyebrow position or mouth open or closed) without assigning specific emotional meanings to them.

Between 4 and 9 months of age, infants become more emotionally responsive to the expressions they observe (Striano & Vaish, 2006). As noted earlier, infants of this age range can match their expressions to the emotional expressions of adults, and they may also acquire more enduring socioemotional dispositions when, for example, their caregivers are depressed (Bridgett et al., 2009). In fact, infants of depressed mothers might process facial expressions differently from those of non-depressed mothers (Bornstein, Arterberry, Mash, & Manian, 2011). In one study comparing infants' discrimination between a smiling and a neutral expression, infants of depressed mothers did not show any evidence that they made this distinction. This pattern of results was found despite the fact that both groups (infants of depressed and non-depressed mothers) habituated to the repeated presentation of the stimulus in the same way, suggesting that results were not due to some general difference in information processing. Thus, the experience of having a depressed mother could affect infants' perceptual development and subsequent responsiveness to facial expressions.

The first year of life may be a sensitive period for developing sensitivity to different emotional displays. Camras and her colleagues (2006) explored this possibility by taking advantage of a natural experiment: In many Chinese and Eastern European orphanages, children experience emotional and social deprivation. Thus, Camras et al. conducted an experiment comparing the perception of emotions among Chinese and Eastern European 4- to 5-year-old children who had been adopted. The Eastern European children experienced on average 16.6 months of institutionalized care, whereas, the Chinese children experienced only 8.0 months of institutionalized care. The children were tested in two tasks. One task involved hearing stories about an emotional situation, and the children were asked to identify the appropriate emotion. The second task was an emotion-labeling task: Children were asked to select from four facial expressions the one that matched an emotional label, such as "happy." The Eastern European children performed worse on both tasks compared to the Chinese children. Camras et al. attribute this difference to the length of time spent in institutionalized care in the first years of life.

There are several other related developments in this time period. Infants begin to respond differently to different vocal correlates of emotional expression and begin to coordinate vocal and facial features of emotional expressions (Walker-Andrews, 2008). Also, infants show enhanced neural processing (as measured by EEG) to negative emotional expressions, particularly when the face is looking toward an object (Hoehl & Striano, 2010). Moreover, infants' scanning of threat-related facial expressions, such as fear and anger, develops over this time period, with increased avoidance of the eye region (Hunnius, de Wit, Vrins, & von Hofsten, 2011). In short, as infants grow older, they begin to take others' expressions into account more comprehensively, an ability that appears to develop in concert with other advances in face perception and categorization (Quinn et al., 2011).

Starting around 8 to 9 months of age, infants show that they begin to appreciate that others' emotional messages pertain to specific objects or events (Saarni et al., 2006). They can use others' emotional expressions to guide their own reactions, and **social referencing**, the deliberate search for information to help clarify uncertain events, begins. Social referencing involves using others' emotional expressions to understand situations, particularly those that could be ambiguous (Kim & Kwak, 2011). For example, Hornik, Risenhoover, and Gunnar (1987) found that infants stop playing with unusual toys when their mothers show disgust as opposed to pleasure, and they continue to behave in this way even after their mothers stop posing distinct emotional expressions and are instead silent and neutral. Mumme and Fernald (2003) found that infants also reference emotional information presented by televised models, and Hertenstein and Campos (2004) showed that 14-month-olds retain information gained in social referencing contexts for 24 hours. Peers are also recognized as sources of information, but not until around 24 months of age (Nichols, Svetlova, & Brownell, 2010).

Taken together, research on social referencing, like research on infants' developing sensitivity to emotional signals, indicates that facial and vocal expressions of emotion assume great significance once babies can perceive them clearly. This development is hardly surprising. Emotional expressions are among the most important social signals, and thus we should expect that babies become attuned to them from early in life. As infants proceed through their second year, their social competence and sensitivity are fostered, in part, by their enhanced sophistication at reading the emotions of others. Unfortunately, although sensitivity to others' emotions sometimes leads to pro-social behavior (i.e., sharing toys), it can also facilitate conflict with siblings and other family members when it is manifested in teasing, testing the limits of parental demands, and arguments (Dunn, 2003).

Summary

If our current understanding of emotional development is rather disappointing, it is because theorists have had difficulty explaining such extraordinarily complex phenomena. Indeed, the existing shortcomings of each theory are balanced by the contributions each makes to explaining emotional development—in terms of learning influences, the emotional climate of parent–infant interaction, cognitive development, or the biological heritage of the human species. Our earlier review of research in this area indicates that each theory helps to explain small but important parts of emotional development in infancy.

Recently, a third perspective has been proposed that attempts to incorporate aspects of both the structuralist and functionalist perspectives. Named the **differentiation and dynamical integration perspective**, it is based on dynamical systems theory (Camras, 2011). Systems theory, as you might recall from Chapter 1, appreciates the interconnectedness of abilities and how change impacts the whole organism during the course of development. As one subsystem emerges, that change brings with it a host of new experiences that influence and are influenced by changes in related component systems. Thus, development in one system influences and is influenced by development in another system. Applying systems theory to emotional development, Camras proposed that facial expressions should be viewed as a dynamical system that is itself embedded in a larger system of emotion. The emphasis of the interplay between felt emotion and the importance of communication of emotion may eventually move our understanding of emotional development in infancy forward.

TEMPERAMENT IN INFANCY

Although theorists have portrayed the dimensions and origins of temperament in many different ways, most today regard **temperament** as the biologically based source of individual differences in behavioral functioning that tend to be stable over time (Rothbart & Bates, 2006). Temperament emerges early in life and expresses itself behaviorally in various ways, but temperament itself is the underlying construct inferred from observable behaviors. In other words, a temperamentally sociable child is likely to manifest high sociability in different ways at different ages: in smiles and reaches as an infant, in approaching and exploring other people as a toddler, in animated conversation as a preschooler, and in the development of a range of more complex social skills in adolescence.

The fact that features of temperament are biologically based does not necessarily mean that these features are genetically fixed or that experience has little impact on temperament. Researchers agree that an adequate portrayal of temperament must acknowledge the reciprocal influences that exist between temperament and the environment (Rothbart, 2011). Researchers also tend to agree on the kinds of individual differences that are likely to describe temperament in quality. In particular, the temporal and intensive features of individual behavior have been of special interest. **Temporal** features include the speed with which behaviors begin after stimulation (latency), how rapidly they escalate (rise time), how long they last (duration), and how slowly they go away (decay or recovery). **Intensive** features include how strongly behaviors express themselves (amplitude) and how sensitive they are to stimulation (threshold). Most conceptualizations of temperament also emphasize three attributes: variations in activity level, sociability, and emotionality. As an example, consider a procedure used to study crying in newborns developed by LaGasse and her colleagues (2005). To record the cries of newborn babies, a rubber band is snapped against their foot. Temporal features of the crying response would be how quickly the infant cries after the snap and how long they cry after each snap. Intensive features pertain to acoustic features of the cry or properties of the snap, such as how loud or how hard the snap has to be in order to elicit a cry.

Emotional expressions are one important way that infants influence those around them. Individuality of temperament is another. Emotionality and temperament share some common features. Features of temperament—such as variations in predominant mood, difficulty, and proneness to fear or to smiling and laughter—often have an emotional quality, although they also include variations in activity level, predictability, sociability, and other aspects of individuality. Parents and other caregivers devote considerable energy to identifying, adapting to, and channeling the temperaments of their offspring, just as they try to interpret, respond to, and manage their infants' emotional states. In this respect, emotion and temperament have similar implications for adults.

In other respects, however, the two are quite different. Whereas a baby's emotional states are often fleeting or reactive, we commonly think of attributes of temperament as more enduring. Infants might show momentary periods of fussiness owing to changes in routine or unfamiliar people nearby, but when fussiness is part of the baby's more persistent style we usually view it as an attribute of the child (rather than as attributable to immediate circumstances) and thus as an aspect of temperament. This example illustrates another way that the study of emotional development and temperament differ. Short-term fluctuations in a child's emotional state are seldom thought to have long-term implications, but attributes of temperament are considered meaningful precisely because they are considered prognostic, with temperament viewed as an early foundation for personality. Personality includes temperament, but it also includes the effects of social experience, self-referent belief systems, knowledge structures, values, and goals.

Many of these processes, however, have not yet developed or become consolidated in infancy. Socializing influences are only beginning, and thus the hereditary and/or constitutional bases for the individuality of temperament are likely to be most apparent. To the extent that we can see the person-to-be in the baby, we see the personality-to-be in temperament.

Researchers have expended considerable efforts to identify the dimensions along which infants differ in temperament. Many researchers have also explored the factors that can account for consistency and change over time. The study of temperament is interesting for an additional reason. It raises questions about how infants' enduring individuality influences their own development. By studying the effects of temperament on social interaction, cognition, behavioral problems, and other domains, researchers are acquiring an understanding of the developmentally complex roles played by temperament.

Researchers have long believed that whether a child's long-term adjustment is favorable or unfavorable depends on the interaction of the child's temperament and the demands of the environment. More specifically, what is important is the **goodness-of-fit**, or match, between the child and the developmental context (Lerner et al., 2011). A child with a low activity level, positive mood, and poor adaptability fits well in a home or school setting that makes few demands and provides many opportunities for self-direction. But such an environment is a poorer fit for a child with a high activity level, high distractibility, and unhappy mood. A child's successful adjustment thus depends on an interaction between his or her temperament and the demands of the setting. In this light, it is clear that a temperamentally difficult child will not inevitably experience later problems if, say, parents understand and are tolerant of the child's behavioral style and can provide activities in which the child's characteristics can be channeled and valued. Conversely, even a temperamentally easy child will experience problems if parents impose excessive demands or ignore reasonable needs. As a consequence, the sensitivity and adaptability of parents to their child's temperamental profile is an important predictor of long-term child adjustment.

Behavior genetics perspectives inject even more complexity into how temperament influences development. Scarr (1993), for example, suggested that children evoke certain responses from others based on their attributes of temperament and that these responses, in turn, affect their development. Highly sociable infants tend to elicit interest and play from adults, and this social stimulation has many benefits. Moreover, as children grow older, their temperament might lead them to prefer certain environments over others, especially those settings that best suit their behavioral style. A highly active child might choose to become involved in sports, whereas a low-activity child might select settings that foster sedentary activities, such as reading or conversation. Admittedly, this kind of **niche picking** is harder for infants to accomplish, but similar preferences might be expressed by selective interest in certain activities (e.g., highly active soccer with father versus more low-key interactions with mother) which in turn have different developmental implications.

Wachs (2006) argued that individuals do not necessarily shape their environments, but simply experience them differently depending on their temperament. Unexpected encounters with friendly but unfamiliar adults will be experienced very differently by children who are sociable and positive in mood than by those who are low in adaptability and high in fear. Primary caregivers play a large role in shaping the context within which temperament develops. For example, mothers, in their daily interactions with their babies, can influence their infants' attentional styles and expressions of negativity (Bridgett et al., 2009, 2011). Such results have given researchers rich insight into the ways individual characteristics in temperament interact with environmental demands to shape and guide developmental outcomes. Contrary to simpler views that good features of temperament lead to optimal developmental outcomes and bad features predict later behavioral problems, it appears that the effects of particular temperamental profiles depend in part on the demands of the environments in which the children live, the sensitivity and adaptability of their social partners, and the ways in which temperament itself guides children's choice of activities and interpretation of their experiences. Predictions of later outcomes are complex, and temperament is an important but certainly not an exclusive determinant of development (Gagne & Goldsmith, 2011).

Conceptualizing Infant Temperament

Scientific interest in infant temperament has a fairly long history. Thomas, Chess, and their colleagues began the New York Longitudinal Study (NYLS) in the 1950s and stimulated interest in infant temperament (Klein, 2011). This interest intensified in the 1990s as new conceptualizations of temperament emerged and several programmatic research efforts were inaugurated (Putnam & Stifter, 2008).

The New York Longitudinal Study   Thomas and Chess (1977) began their longitudinal studies by interviewing mothers extensively about their 2- to 3-month-old infants. From these interviews, babies were rated on several dimensions, listed in Table 10.2. In devising these dimensions, including activity level, rhythmicity, attention span, and quality of mood, Thomas and Chess sought to delineate the stylistic features of infants' emerging individuality (rather than what infants did or why they did so). In distinguishing temperament from motivations, abilities, or personality, Thomas and Chess viewed temperament as early emerging, constitutionally based behavioral tendencies that influence the effect of the environment on the child. The nine dimensions were selected because they could be evaluated in all children, and they appeared to be important dimensions of individuality that should affect development.

From nine dimensions, Thomas and Chess created a four-way typology of broader temperamental profiles. **Easy babies** were positive in mood, regular in body functions, and adaptable; these babies approached new situations positively and reacted with low or moderate intensity. Approximately 40% of the babies in the NYLS were deemed easy. **Difficult babies**, by contrast, were negative in mood, irregular, and slow to adapt; they withdrew from new situations and reacted with high intensity. Difficult children accounted for about 10% of the NYLS sample. **Slow-to-warm-up babies** were negative in mood and slow to adapt; they withdrew from new situations, reacted with low to moderate intensity, and were low in activity. They constituted about 15% of the sample. The remaining babies (about 35%) constituted **average babies** and did not fit into the other profiles.

Thomas and Chess followed these children at regular intervals from infancy to young adulthood to try to understand the temperamental origins of later behavioral disorders. Their findings suggest that early individuality of temperament can have long-term consequences, but does not always determine later development. Some behavioral features, of course, have a strong influence on later development. For example, Lerner, Hertzog, Hooker, Hassibi, and Thomas (1988) found, in a re-analysis of the NYLS data, that high levels of childhood aggression predicted adjustment problems in adolescence, but early

Table 10.2 Dimensions of temperament portrayed by major theorists

Thomas and Chess	Buss and Plomin	Rothbart and Bates
1. Activity level	1. Activity level	1. Broad factors (and narrow dimensions)
2. Approach—withdrawal	2. Negative	Negative emotionality
3. Adaptability	emotionality	(Fear, sadness, frustration/irritability, falling reactivity)
4. Quality of mood	3. Sociability	2. Surgency/extraversion
5. Attention span and persistence		(Approach, smiling/laughter, vocal reactivity, activity
6. Distractibility		level, high intensity pleasure, perceptual sensitivity)
7. Rhythmicity (regularity)		3. Orienting/regulation
8. Intensity of reaction		(Low intensity pleasure, cuddliness, duration of
9. Threshold of responsiveness		orienting, soothability)

individuality of temperament was not always predictive, in part because (as we reviewed earlier) temperament and the environment jointly determine goodness-of-fit. It is difficult to predict long-term outcomes for children based on temperament alone because the fit with the environment at any one time might be good or bad, and the fit might also change with development.

In addition, temperament itself might change as the result of environmental challenges and personality development. Whereas environmental experiences reinforce certain attributes of temperament, they may modify or help to change others. Furthermore, children might acquire strategies for controlling certain attributes of temperament (like activity level) that are poorly suited for certain settings (such as school). As a consequence, developmental outcomes are influenced not only by the fit between temperament and environment, but also by how attributes of temperament themselves evolve through the transactions between settings and emerging personality.

Like many pioneering studies, the NYLS has been criticized on various grounds. Some researchers questioned the reliance on parent interviews and worried that the interviewers' familiarity with the families they studied could have biased their evaluations. To avoid these problems, Carey (1970) developed the Infant Temperament Questionnaire (ITQ), which was later revised into the Early Infancy Temperament Questionnaire (EITQ; Medoff-Cooper, Carey, & McDevitt, 1993) for use with infants about 4 months old and younger. The ITQ and EITQ are standardized parent-report questionnaires that allow infants to be rated along each of the nine temperament dimensions. Other critics question whether the nine dimensions of temperament best characterize behavioral individuality, and they have proposed different, and fewer, dimensions, as we will see.

Behavior Genetics Perspective Whereas Thomas and Chess's orientation was clinical, Buss and Plomin (1984) approached the study of temperament from a behavioral genetics perspective. They viewed temperament as a set of inherited personality traits that appear early in life, and their conceptualization of temperament differs from Thomas and Chess's in at least four ways. First, they did not seek to distinguish temperament from personality, but instead regarded temperament as an early core of personality. As a result, temperament included motivation and other characteristics that Thomas and Chess excluded from their definition. Second, they viewed temperament as having exclusively genetic rather than constitutional origins; this is important because hereditary influences on behavioral style are presumed to be more stable than are constitutional factors (such as consequences of prenatal experience). Third, Buss and Plomin emphasized that attributes of temperament remain highly stable throughout life and thus have enduring effects on personality development. Fourth, Buss and Plomin identified different dimensions of temperament (Table 10.2). Rather than nine, they identified only three (activity level, negative emotionality, and sociability), which are also the same dimensions that Thomas and Chess, and other researchers, used to identify difficult temperaments. These three dimensions were identified by Buss and Plomin because they appear very early in life, are strongly inherited, and are sufficiently distinct to be characterized as independent of one another.

Although Buss and Plomin underscored the genetic and stable attributes of temperament, they did not ignore the importance of environmental influences. A child's adjustment is affected, they noted, by the match between attributes of temperament and environmental demands (similar to the goodness-of-fit concept), and individuals may choose environmental settings that match their inherited behavioral characteristics (earlier referred to as niche picking). Buss and Plomin proposed, however, that the environment had a limited effect on temperament and that attributes of temperament may influence contextual events as much as the reverse, especially when individuals have strong features of temperament. Sociable people tend to make their environments more interactive; active people tend naturally to quicken the tempo of a setting. Moreover, they noted that individuals can modify the nature of their environments even when setting demands are fixed. For example, a child with a high activity level who is restricted to his or her room may, nevertheless, manage to expend a great amount of energy in that setting, perhaps to the dismay of parents.

Biological and Psychological Factors   Rothbart's (2011) view of individuality of temperament integrates developmental perspectives with work from the cognitive sciences, psychobiology, adult personality, and Pavlovian research in the Soviet tradition. Rothbart defined temperament in terms of relatively stable, primarily biologically based individual differences in reactivity and self-regulation. **Reactivity** refers to the excitability or arousability of the individual's response systems and is measured in terms of the response parameters (time and intensity) we defined earlier. **Self-regulation** refers to the processes that modulate reactivity through approach or avoidance, inhibition, or attention. Rothbart argued that individual differences in these tendencies have genetic and/or constitutional origins, and they are based in specifiable neurophysiological, endocrinological, and/or behavioral processes.

Rothbart and her colleagues focused on three broad factors consisting of numerous narrow dimensions (Rothbart & Bates, 2006). As can be seen in Table 10.2, these dimensions overlap in some ways with those of Thomas and Chess and Buss and Plomin, but there are some independent features as well. For example, Rothbart included individual differences in frustration and fear that resemble Buss and Plomin's emotionality dimension, but she also included positive emotionality, such as smiling and laughter. Like many other theorists, Rothbart viewed personality as a much broader construct than temperament, with temperament perhaps as the biological foundation.

Rothbart's conceptualization of temperament also emphasized development. Temperament is modified over time not only because of the various environmental influences discussed above, but also because its constituent biological response systems grow and mature. With neuro-cortical maturation, such as development of connections among brain regions, infants gradually develop self-control over activity and emotion in ways that affect the self-regulatory features of their temperament (Gao et al., 2009). The growth of emotional responsiveness discussed earlier also has implications for emotion-based dimensions of temperament like distress to limitations, smiling and laughter, and fear. Partly for these reasons, Rothbart concluded that, although dimensions of temperament are more likely to be stable over time than are other aspects of behavioral individuality, stability is more likely within, rather than between, periods of rapid developmental change. In other words, stability of temperament is a highly contingent, rather than an absolute, feature of temperament depending not only on environmental demands but also on intrinsic maturational processes.

It is clear from this discussion (and from inspection of Table 10.2) that theorists conceptualize and study temperament in very different ways, but it is unclear whether this diversity of approaches is desirable or not. On the one hand, different conceptualizations of temperament have led researchers to ask varied questions of different behavioral processes, often concerning individuals at markedly different periods of development. This complicates the integration of findings from different research groups. On the other hand, research on temperament is not well advanced, and the proliferation of viewpoints is not only a common but also a desirable feature of research in initial stages. Indeed, the willingness of most theorists to revise their theories, and the current generation of new research findings that may contribute to such revisions, make us optimistic that a diversity of research efforts will yield useful findings that converge on common issues. If, in the end, the value of these theories is measured by their usefulness in explaining individuality of temperament, theorists might be approaching a common definition. In the meantime, we next review studies about the measurement of infant temperament and its development.

Issues in the Measurement of Infant Temperament

Caregivers are likely to provide insightful reports of attributes of temperament based on their long-term and intimate experiences with their children. However, reliance on caregiver-report measures invites bias attributable to the rater's subjective viewpoint, personality, or unique experiences. Indeed, parents' expectations for how their infants will be precede the appearance of the characteristic. For example, parents were asked to rate their infants on several domains, including positive emotionality, negative emotionality, and fear (Pauli-Pott, Mertesacker, Bade, Haverkock, & Beckmann, 2003). In this longitudinal study, parents made ratings when their infants were 4-, 8-, and 12-months of age, and infant temperament was independently observed. Pauli-Pott and her colleagues found that parents' perception of the positive emotionality at 4 months was followed by high levels of positive emotionality at 8 months. A similar pattern was found for negative emotionality between 8-month parent report and observation at 12 months. Parents' ratings of fear at 4 and 8 months were predictive of fearful behavior at 8 and 12 months. Thus, parent ratings might reflect concurrent temperamental characteristics in their infants, and also forecast characteristics that are to come later.

Efforts to measure temperament more objectively through direct observations by unacquainted researchers inevitably involve limited sampling, observer effects (reactions of infants to a stranger), context effects (as in the difference between laboratory and home observations), and other potential biases (Gartstein & Marmion, 2008). Thus, some researchers have opted to use a multi-method approach. Some investigators combine home observation and matching parent-report procedure to assess infants' spontaneous activity as well as their responsiveness in both free-play and structured situations (Bornstein, Gaughran, & Seguí, 1991), whereas others compare laboratory-based assessments with home observations (Gagne, Van Hulle, Aksan, Essex, & Goldsmith, 2011).

Researchers confront other challenges in their efforts to develop useful measures of temperament. If parent-report measures (usually questionnaires or interviews) are used, considerable effort must be made to select items representing the desired range of attributes of temperament in a broad variety of situations and that translate across cultural groups. If observational measures (whether at home or in the laboratory) are used, they must be based on a broad sampling of infant behavior in different situations that reveal the range of attributes of temperament to be studied. In either case, reliability and validity are key concerns.

Reliability   As we discussed in Chapter 3, reliability involves the consistency with which measures yield the same information about the same child. **Test-retest reliability** asks whether the measure provides the same score on one day that it does on another day (assuming temperament remains stable). Not surprisingly, test-retest reliability is greater over short periods than over longer intervals, and for temperament it tends to be moderate or high. For example, Putnam, Gartstein, and Rothbart (2006) reported high long-term stability for three factors (Surgency, Effortful Control, and Negative Affect) from 6 to 12 months and moderate stability from 18 to 36 months. Obviously, if features of temperament in infancy can be altered by developmental and experiential influences, stability over long periods of time is affected by potential changes in temperament itself, rather than the actual reliability of the measure.

Inter-rater reliability asks whether the measure provides the same score when used by different observers or raters. If the child's features of temperament are clear and the measure is objective, correlations between the scores assigned by different observers should be high. Unfortunately, when parents and non-related observers rate a child's temperament, reported convergence is only fair (Saudino, 2003, 2005). This low reliability could be attributable, in part, to the fact that different observers note different features of the child's behavior because they have had different experiences with the child.

Internal reliability or consistency asks whether individuals receive the same scores on different items that tap the same dimension of temperament. Most temperament measures include a number of items that are intended to assess the same dimension of temperament (activity level, emotionality, and so forth). If the measure is well designed, and if each item relates to the same dimension of temperament, individual scores on each of the items in a dimension should agree. Internal consistency estimates for dimensions of many infant temperament measures are variable (Rothbart & Bates, 2006) so that some temperamental scales are consistent and coherent in themselves and others less so. This is an area ripe for more research.

Validity   As you might recall also from Chapter 3, validity refers to whether a measure actually measures what it intends to measure. This is obviously a crucial measurement issue because the conclusions researchers derive about temperament depend on the validity of the measures they employ. **Discriminant validity** asks whether a measure assesses dimensions of temperament that are independent and non-overlapping. To the extent that temperament dimensions are genuinely independent of each other, the scores on each dimension should be uncorrelated with each other. Unfortunately, most researchers provide little information about discriminant validity, perhaps because some degree of mutual overlap in dimensions of temperament (e.g., between emotionality and sociability) might be theoretically expected. **Predictive validity** asks whether a measure provides scores that enable us to predict later behavior in the child. Does a child rated high in activity level behave actively in everyday settings? Predictive validity is important because of concerns, discussed earlier, that parental perceptions of temperament could be biased by characteristics of the parent. Indeed, there is some evidence that maternal personality characteristics are associated with mothers' ratings of their infants (Mangelsdorf, McHale, Diener, Goldstein, & Lehn, 2000). These findings suggest that parents are not necessarily accurate reporters of their children's temperaments, although their objectivity can be enhanced by asking them to provide very specific behavioral ratings based on observations of their infants over specific periods of time, rather than general conclusions about their children's general temperament (Bornstein et al., 1991; Goldsmith & Hewitt, 2003).

The validity of observational measures is not necessarily better than that of parental reports, and the strengths and limitations of both approaches still need to be explored more thoroughly (Rothbart & Bates, 2006). In the end, the most useful studies of temperament entail convergent multi-method approaches in which contributions associated with parent and observer ratings can be studied and compared (Gagne & Goldsmith, 2011 for an example).

Origins and Consequences of Individuality of Temperament

Because most theorists have described underlying differences in biological processes (e.g., heredity and constitutional factors), research on the psychobiological factors and their links to temperament are important. Two sets of studies have been conducted: one concerning the neural correlates of inhibited and reactive children, and the other concerning the heritability of differences in temperament.

In a longitudinal study conducted by Kagan and his colleagues, 4-month-old infants were classified as either high (showing high levels of motor activity and distress in response to a battery of auditory, olfactory, and visual stimuli) or low (showing low-level reactions to the same stimuli) in reactivity and were then examined throughout childhood and into adolescence (Kagan, 2010). Reactivity in temperament was fairly stable over time. Children classified as highly reactive in infancy were significantly more likely to react fearfully to novel stimuli at 14 and 21 months than were children classified as non-reactive. By 4½ years, highly reactive children showed less spontaneity and sociability with adults than non-reactive children did, but highly reactive children were not as likely to appear fearful in response to novelty than they were at younger ages. By 7 years, highly reactive children were more likely to behave anxiously than were non-reactive children. Highly reactive 7-year-olds were also more likely to have a higher diastolic blood pressure than were non-reactive children, and by adolescence, inhibited children were more likely to have generalized social anxiety disorders (Box 10.3).

Box 10.3 Set for Life? Behavioral Inhibition Links to Social Anxiety Disorder in Adolescence

Social Anxiety Disorder (SAD) causes someone to experience intense fear and distress in a social situation. Chronis-Tuscano and her colleagues (2009) investigated whether behavioral inhibition, a temperamental disposition to withdraw from unfamiliar social interactions, might be an early sign of SAD. The researchers measured temperament at ages 4 months, 24 months, 4 years, and 7 years using both maternal reports and laboratory assessments. When the children were between the ages of 14 and 16 years, they were assessed for SAD using a questionnaire or a psychiatric interview. The age of onset for SAD was after 7 years for all but one participant. Temperament remained relatively stable from infancy to adolescence. Children who showed early stable and high maternal-reported behavioral inhibition were most likely to show SAD by 14 to 16 years of age. These findings have implications for early diagnosis of, and intervention for, anxiety disorders in children.

Kagan and his colleagues speculated that inhibited children have a lower threshold of reactivity in limbic structures (such as the hypothalamus and amygdala) that mediate fear and defense, whereas uninhibited children have higher reactivity thresholds. Because of these differences in sympathetic arousal tendencies, inhibited children show more fearful, wary, and shy behavior, whereas uninhibited children are generally more outgoing and emotionally flexible (Kagan, 2010). As predicted, fMRI examinations showed that, at 21 years of age, previously inhibited individuals showed more activity in the amygdala than did previously uninhibited individuals when shown novel, as opposed to familiar, faces (Schwartz, Wright, Shin, Kagan, & Rauch, 2003).

These studies indicate that indexes of autonomic reactivity are related in a predictable manner to stable behavioral measures of reactivity and inhibition/self-regulation. According to Kagan (2007), however, these characteristics sometimes change when parents make concerted efforts to modify their children's attributes. We still need to learn whether these nervous system differences anticipate or follow the development of behavioral indicators of inhibition or reactivity and how they are related to other attributes of temperament.

Insights into the heritability of temperament come from twin studies and genetic analyses. As discussed in Chapter 3, researchers often study infant twins to determine whether behaviors have identifiable genetic contributions. Monozygotic (MZ) twins share 100% of their genes, whereas dizygotic (DZ) twins share only 50% on average (as do siblings). If a behavior has a significant genetic component, therefore, MZ twins ought to behave more similarly than DZ twins, because MZ twins share more genetic material than DZ twins. In general, twin studies indicate that individual differences in emotionality (especially distress and fearfulness), activity level, and sociability (or shyness) are heritable (Gagne & Goldsmith, 2011). Whereas correlations between MZ twins ranged from .50 to .80, correlations between DZ twins were .50 or less. These findings are consistent with the behavior genetics approach. In this view, people are inclined by their unique genetic endowments to act and respond to events in particular ways. Their genetic endowments also guide their selection of environmental settings and partners within those settings that are consistent with their heritable behavioral style (niche picking), and affect the environment because they evoke reactions that are consistent with their genotypic characteristics. Also, MZ twins are treated more equally than DZ twins by those around them. Advances in genetic analyses have revealed correlates between certain allele profiles and temperament (Gagne & Goldsmith, 2011; Kochanska, Philibert, & Barry, 2009). For example, Sheese and his colleagues (Sheese, Voelker, Posner, & Rothbart, 2009) found evidence that emotional reactivity and its regulation were governed by different genes. Specifically, different genes that directly or indirectly regulate dopamine, a neurotransmitter that is involved in regulating cognitive and affective processes, were associated with different temperamental dimensions. COMT was related to positive affect, SNAP25 was related to negative affect, and CHNA4 was related to effortful control.

Because we too readily tend to equate early genetic influence with immutable and unchanging consequences, it is wise to remember why behavioral geneticists themselves do not do so (Goldsmith & Lemery, 2000; Plomin, 2000). First, heritability estimates are specific to the population being studied, and the heritability of certain dispositional attributes may change with groups. Second, gene action may vary over time, with genetic influences accounting for developmental accelerations and lags rather than smooth underlying growth functions. Moreover, some children may be genetically inconsistent, with heredity programming changing over time. Third, experience can alter temperament by modifying the physiological systems through which genes affect behavior. Thus, although certain attributes of temperament are associated with differences in underlying genetic or biological functions, these attributes are not necessarily stable and unchanging.

Culture and Temperament

When cultural groups are compared, culture and gene pool are naturally confounded, so it is difficult to determine whether observed differences in temperament are due to differences in social customs and socialization practices or to genetic differences. This is one reason why researchers have focused on cultural differences in neonates or very young infants (Bornstein, Putnick, Suwalsky, et al., 2012). For example, cross-cultural studies have found that Chinese American and Japanese American newborns are less perturbable, better able to soothe themselves, and experience less variation in arousal than their European American counterparts (Camras et al., 2007). Other studies have compared temperament in cultures varying across the collectivist/ individualist dimension (Chapter 2). For example, when comparing infants between 3 and 12 months in the United States, Poland, Russia, and Japan, Gartstein, Slobodskaya, Zylicz, Gosztyla, and Nakagawa (2010) found differing rates of positive and negative behaviors (Figure 10.5). Polish infants received the highest scores for positive affectivity dimensions such as smiling and laughter, high intensity pleasure, and vocal reactivity. Japanese and Russian infants showed the highest levels of fearfulness. The researchers attribute some of these differences in temperament to differences in cultural ideology which, in turn, affect parenting practices. In particular, they note that Japan and Russia may be more collectively focused than Poland or the US. Infants in collectivist cultures spend little time away from their mothers, and as a result may show more fear under these unusual circumstances than infants from individualist cultures (see also Chapter 11).

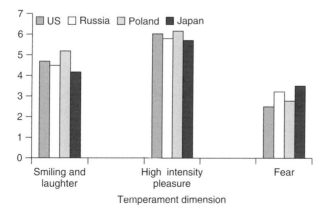

Fig. 10.5 Levels of smiling and laughter, high intensity pleasure, and fear found in infants across four cultural groups. (Created using data from Gartstein et al., 2010.)

Gender Differences

Studies of gender differences in temperament also illustrate how difficult it is to disentangle the experiential and genetic bases of temperament. There appear to be a few consistent gender differences in temperament (Else-Quest, Hyde, Goldsmith, & Van Hulle, 2006). Assessing the results of numerous studies involving children aged 3 months to 13 years, Else-Quest and her colleagues found that girls are rated higher in effortful control and boys are rated higher in surgency. There was no difference between boys and girls on negative affectivity. Others have found girls to show higher levels of fear among several cultural groups (Gartstein et al., 2006, 2010; Montirosso, Cozzi, Putnam, Gartstein, & Borgatti, 2011). Moreover, levels of testosterone appear to differentially affect boys and girls, with boys who have high levels of testosterone showing greater levels of negative affectivity (Alexander & Saenz, 2011).

How should we interpret such gender differences? A nativist explanation would propose that such differences are genetically based. Moreover, as we will discover in the next chapter, parents and other caregivers treat male and female infants differently, from birth, in ways that are consistent with cultural stereotypes and beliefs about the higher activity level of boys.

Temperament and Cognition

Among the more intriguing effects of temperament on behavioral functioning is the possibility that individuality of temperament affects cognitive processing. Studies have documented links between infants' information processing and effortful control (Vonderlin, Pahnke, & Pauen, 2008). For example, infants scoring high in focused attention (a dimension of temperament related to orienting; Table 10.2) were slower to habituate at 5 months of age and had larger vocabularies at 20 months of age (Dixon & Smith, 2008).

What can account for these findings? On the one hand, certain attributes of temperament could facilitate cognitive performance. Infants who are emotionally positive and persistent are likely to approach cognitive tasks more constructively than infants with more negative or distractible dispositions. These features of temperament might also facilitate cognitive functioning indirectly by evoking certain responses from others. If parents and other caregivers are likely to interact more positively with infants who have positive, persistent, and sociable temperaments, these characteristics could indirectly foster infants' cognitive performance because the social responses they promote are development enhancing. In addition, infants with these characteristics of temperament may receive better scores on cognitive performance measures because they respond better to unfamiliar examiners, adapt better to unfamiliar testing procedures, and/or are perceived more positively by testers. Rothbart, Sheese, Rueda, and Posner (2011) suggested that very early in life, parents assist in the development of self-regulation by engaging their infant's attention. By showing the baby new objects, encouraging exploration of new people, environments, and objects, and/or reading to babies, parents are engaging executive systems that underlie attentional and regulatory processes.

In summary, popular notions that temperament involves early emerging, rigidly stable attributes that resist modification and have consistent long-term influences on the individual are inaccurate. Although attributes of temperament tend to be stable over time, the expression of individuality of temperament—and the nature of one's underlying temperamental profile—might change due to development and maturation, experiential influences, the contexts in which temperament is expressed, and the integration of features of temperament into emerging personalities. Similarly, the consequences of temperament for later behavioral functioning are complex and hard to predict.

Researchers have learned that temperament is only one of many factors affecting development. Perhaps for these reasons, the temporal stability of features of temperament varies depending on the particular dimension of temperament studied, the period of time over which stability is assessed, the measures of temperament that are employed, the age of the infants studied, the consistency of environmental settings in which children live, and a variety of other influences (Rothbart, 2011). In short, the stability of temperament is contingent, never absolute.

SUMMARY

As we have noted throughout this chapter, emotional expressions and individuality of temperament share many features. Most theorists regard variability in emotionality (especially negative emotion) as important, and a baby's emotional expressions influence the caregiving environment in ways that are similar to the effects of activity level, sociability, and other dimensions of temperament. In focusing on emotional development and temperament, researchers increasingly acknowledge that infants make significant contributions to their social interactions. This conclusion is not new, of course, but research shows both the sophistication of the baby's emotional world and the complexity of its influence on social relationships. As a result, earlier portrayals of the infant's diffuse emotional reactivity guided by underlying, unchanging dispositional attributes have been replaced by portrayals that acknowledge the multidimensionality of the baby's emotional life and its diverse influences on temperament. At the same time, perspectives of the caregiving context are being modified to reflect caregiving influences that accommodate, interpret, and channel the child's socioemotional characteristics. Because of the transactional influences underlying these portrayals of infant and context, the study of infant emotional development and temperament contributes to a much richer, and more provocative, understanding of infant development.

KEY TERMS

Automatic elicitor
Average babies
Conditioned elicitor
Differentiation and dynamical integration perspective
Difficult babies
Discriminant validity
Easy babies
Emotions
Emotion elicitors
Emotion receptors
Emotion states
Emotional contagion
Emotional experience
Emotional expressions
Functionalist theory
Goodness-of-fit
Intensive features

Internal reliability
Inter-rater reliability
Niche picking
Phase sequences
Primary emotions
Reactivity
Secondary emotions
Self-conscious or secondary emotions
Self-regulation
Sign gestalt
Slow-to-warm-up babies
Social referencing
Social releaser
Structural theories
Temperament
Temporal features
Test-retest reliability

Chapter 11

Infant Social Development in the Family

- *Describe the phases of infant–parent attachment.*
- *How do infant attachments form?*
- *What is the attachment behavior system, and how does it work?*
- *What is security of attachment, how is it determined, and how is it typically measured?*
- *How stable and valid are individual differences in infant attachment security?*
- *What factors affect the quality of parental behavior?*
- *What are the principal domains of parent–infant interaction?*
- *How stable are individual differences in characteristics of parent–infant interaction?*
- *Do girls and boys have different social experiences as infants?*

To many theorists, the development of relationships with other people (mainly parents) constitutes one of the most important aspects of social development in infancy. In this chapter, we describe stages in the development of the infant's first social relationships, commonly referred to as **attachments**. After considering what appear to be universal developmental stages, we review ideas about the origins of individual differences in attachments—differences that may be consequences of very early interactions between infants and parents or other caregivers. As we then show, there are different types of attachments infants form with their parents, and these differences appear to affect children's later cognitive, social, and personality development. The quality of infant–parent attachments is itself influenced by a variety of factors. Following a consideration of attachments, we discuss infant–parent interaction. In particular, we describe prominent domains of infant–mother interaction, individual differences, stability and continuity of those domains, and the correspondences between infant and parent activities. The chapter concludes with a brief review of gender differences in infant social behavior and development. Here we focus exclusively on social development within the nuclear family. Of course, interactions with people other than parents and caregivers (for example, siblings, grandparents, and peers) also affect the infant's development, as we pointed out in Chapter 2.

ATTACHMENT

All the major theories of social development in infancy we discussed in Chapter 2 have addressed the development of attachments; however, no theory has been as enduring as the one provided by John Bowlby

(1969; see Roisman & Groh, 2011). Bowlby, a psychoanalyst who was much impressed by the capacity of ethological theorists to explain early emotional communications and the formation of social bonds in nonhuman species, assumed that the behavioral propensities of infants and parents are most profitably considered in the context of the environment in which our species evolved. In that environment of evolutionary adaptedness, the survival of infants would have depended on their ability to maintain proximity to protective adults to obtain nourishment, comfort, and security. Unlike the young of many other species, however, human infants are unable to move closer to or follow adults for several months after birth, and they are even incapable of clinging to adults to stay in contact. Instead, human infants have to rely on signals of various sorts to entice adults to approach and stay near them. For these signals to be effective, adults must be predisposed to respond to them. The best example of such a signal is the infant cry, which very effectively entices adults to approach, pick up, and soothe the infant (LaGasse et al., 2005; Soltis, 2004). As they grow older, infants develop a variety of other means to achieve proximity or contact, including independent locomotion, and they gradually come to focus their bids on people with whom they are most familiar, thereby forming attachments. It was first believed that infants developed attachments to the individuals responsible for their basic care and feeding. In a classic study involving rhesus monkey infants, however, Harlow and Zimmermann (1959) showed that infants formed attachments to cuddly terrycloth mother surrogates rather than the wire surrogates that fed them (Figure 11.1). This study helped pave the way for Bowlby's theory of attachment, which placed emphasis on proximity and contact seeking rather than feeding and reduction of physical needs as a basis of attachment.

Fig. 11.1 A baby monkey showing a preference for the cuddly terrycloth "mother" despite the fact that she does not provide any food. (Courtesy of S. J. Suomi.)

Basic Phases of Social Development

Bowlby (1969) described four phases in the development of infant–parent attachments: (1) the newborn phase of indiscriminate social responsiveness (months 1 to 2), (2) discriminating sociability (months 2 to 7), (3) attachments (month 7 through the second year), and (4) goal-corrected partnership (year 3 on). In this book, we concentrate on the first three phases because the fourth does not begin until after infancy.

Phase 1: Newborn Indiscriminate Social Responsiveness (1 to 2 Months of Age) This first phase in the attachment process is marked by the development of a repertoire of signals. From the time of birth, at least one very effective signal is at the baby's disposal—the cry. Crying motivates adults to soothe infants by picking them up and is the first-emerging example of a class of behaviors that Bowlby called attachment behaviors. The defining or common characteristic of these behaviors is that they all help to provide comfort and security by bringing the baby close to a protective, caregiving adult (Figure 11.2). Another potent attachment behavior enters the baby's repertoire in the second month of life—smiling. Like crying, smiling is a signal that powerfully affects adult behavior. Smiles are effective because they encourage adults to stay near the baby, whereas cries encourage adults to approach the baby.

From birth, infants are capable of affecting the social environment around them and adults respond to newborns' behaviors and signals. The defining feature of this phase, however, is that infants are indiscriminate in the use of proximity-promoting signals. They appear to be satisfied by whoever responds to their cries, smiles, and other similar signals. Adults, of course, respond selectively depending on their relative investment and responsibility (Fouts, Hewlett, & Lamb, 2005; Soltis, 2004).

The newborn baby is characterized by marked, sudden, unpredictable changes in state (levels of arousal and distress) and by poor coordination of movements (Chapters 4 and 5). Behavior becomes more organized over time as internal neural control mechanisms develop. During the first two months, caregivers have

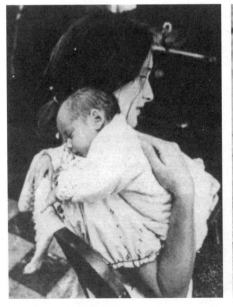

Fig. 11.2 Physical contact between young infants and their parents dominates interactions early in life.

a major impact on the baby's state of arousal. When babies are distressed, adults intervene to soothe them. Even when babies are drowsy, they become alert when held erect at the adult's shoulder. Rousing infants is important because infants learn little about their environment when they are not alert. Relatively long periods of alertness do not occur spontaneously during this early phase, and it is only through adult intervention that their value can be optimized. In practice, this means that, when infants are alert and able to learn about the environment, they are often in the arms of their caregivers. Because the caregivers who are close by can be felt, smelled, heard, and seen when infants are alert, babies come to learn a great deal about them. They also rapidly learn to associate the caregiver's presence with alertness and the relief of distress (Thompson & Virmani, 2010). This association may be one of the earliest, and certainly one of the most dramatic, associations that infants acquire. For example, Lamb and Malkin (1986) found that babies rapidly learned to expect their parents to respond when they cried, and so began to quit crying as soon as they heard or saw their mothers approaching, rather than when they were actually picked up.

Distress-relief sequences are not the only contexts in which young infants interact with their parents (Roopnarine, Fouts, Lamb, & Lewis-Elligan, 2005). Various caregiving routines, including feeding and social play, provide other contexts for social interaction (Tamis-LeMonda, Užgiris, & Bornstein, 2002). Kaye (1982) described the interactions between mothers and their very young infants during feeding. He observed a consistent tendency for mothers and infants to take turns, with the mother jiggling the nipple in the baby's mouth whenever the infant paused. This turn taking alerts the infant to the basic principle of **reciprocity**. In addition, mothers and fathers try to capture and maintain their infants' attention in the course of face-to-face play by moving their heads, exaggerating their facial expressions, and modulating the intonation of their voices. At 2 months, **dyadic** (between the parent and the child) and **extradyadic interactions** (those in which the parent encourages the child to examine some property, object, or event in the environment) are equally emphasized by parents, but over time extradyadic interactions become increasingly prominent (Bornstein, 2006a). Thus, 2-month-olds are oriented to social interactions, whereas 5-month-olds are focused more on exploration of the environment.

Frequent encounters with adults when infants are alert also facilitate infants' capacities to recognize their parents. Bowlby suggested that acquiring the ability to recognize specific people marked the transition to the second phase of attachment development. As described in Chapter 6, however, studies show that infants are able to recognize their own mothers' voice and smell within the first days of life, much earlier than Bowlby believed.

Phase 2: Discriminating Sociability (2 to 7 Months of Age) Bowlby (1969) wrote that discriminating sociability began in the second or third month of life, although this capacity may in fact emerge much earlier. Presumably because significant others (such as parents) have been associated with pleasurable experiences (e.g., feeding, cuddling, rocking, and play) and with the relief of distress, familiar people become persons with whom the baby prefers to interact. Initially, infants' preferences manifest themselves in fairly subtle ways. Certain people will be able to soothe the baby more easily, and to elicit smiles and coos more readily and regularly. Parents are enormously rewarded by this change in their baby's behavior. It indicates that they are special to the baby and that the infant appreciates the effort they put into caregiving. Prior to this phase, the baby appeared to enjoy interacting with anyone without apparent preference.

During this second phase of social development, infants are far more coordinated behaviorally than they were earlier. Their arousal level is far less variable, and infants now spend larger proportions of their time in alert states. Distress is less frequent, and interactions with adults more often involve play (Roopnarine et al., 2005). In many Western cultures, face-to-face games make their appearance in the first phase of attachment, but become most prominent when infants are between 3 and 6 months of age, following which infants seem more interested in exploration than in social play (Lamb & Lewis, 2011). In early face-to-face interactions, the adult assumes major responsibility for keeping the interaction going. Babies coo or smile or stick out their tongues, and adults respond with similar actions. However, babies are not simply passive partners in face-to-face games. Two- to 3-month-olds respond with boredom, distress, or withdrawal when their mothers adopt unresponsive "still-faces" instead of behaving in their typical interactive fashion (Tronick, 2007). They seem concerned over adults' failure to follow the rules of interaction, indicating that infants understand something of these rules, find synchronized and reciprocal interactions more enjoyable, and expect their partners to follow the rules (Chapter 9 and 10).

From repeated experiences in face-to-face play and distress-relief sequences, infants seem to learn at least three important things: The first is the rule of **reciprocity**. In social interactions, partners take turns acting and reacting to the other's behavior. The second is **effectance**. Infants learn that their behavior can affect the behavior of others in a consistent and predictable fashion. The third is **trust**. The caregiver can be counted on to respond when signaled. These attainments are major developmental milestones in the process of becoming social. Once infants realize that their cries, smiles, and coos elicit predictable responses from others, they begin to develop a coherent view of the social world and concepts of themselves as individuals who significantly affect others. The degree to which babies feel confident in their predictions regarding the behavior of others—that is, the degree to which they trust or have faith in the reliability of specific people—in turn influences the security of their attachment relationships. Individual differences in the amount of trust or perceived effectance infants develop probably depend on individual differences in the responsiveness of the adults with whom they interact in different contexts (play, feeding, distress-relief, and so forth).

Phase 3: Attachments (7 to 24 Months of Age)   By 6 or 7 months of age, the infant bears little resemblance to the neonate. Seven-month-olds clearly understand and respect the rule of reciprocity in their interactions, and they have preferences for interaction with certain people (called **attachment figures**). Their confidence in others reinforced, 7-month-olds enjoy their newly acquired ability to creep around and to take responsibility for getting close to their parents, instead of waiting for others to come in response to their cries or coos. Between 6 and 12 months of age, infants are increasingly likely to initiate interaction using directed social behaviors, and infants find a balance between physical proximity to the parent and exploring their environment. At this phase, the parent provides a secure base for venturing farther afield (Roisman & Groh, 2011).

In addition to assuming an increasingly active role in their relationships, infants also begin in Phase 3 to protest (by crying) when left by attachment figures. According to Bowlby, separation protest should be viewed as a signal aimed at making attachment figures return. Its emergence can be linked to the infant's attaining a primitive conception of **person permanence**, the notion that people have a permanent existence independent of the infant, similar to the concept of object permanence (Ainsworth, 1973; see Chapter 7). Similar patterns are evident when infants are placed in foster families and start to form attachments to foster parents, with younger children forming attachments more readily than those placed at older ages (Stovall-McClough & Dozier, 2004).

Major changes in social relationships occur between 7 to 8 months (the beginning of Phase 3) and at about 24 months (the end of this phase). Infants become increasingly sophisticated in their abilities to behave intentionally, communicate verbally, and respond appropriately in different contexts. As infants grow older, they initiate an increasing proportion of their interactions and are therefore respondents in a decreasing proportion. They can tolerate a growing distance from attachment figures, and they become more and more adept at interacting with peers and unfamiliar adults. Figure 11.3 shows that these developmental trends are the same across a variety of primates, including langurs, baboons, gorillas, and human beings. For humans, however, this stage is marked by the emergence of discriminating attachments, which we discuss in detail following a brief discussion of Phase 4.

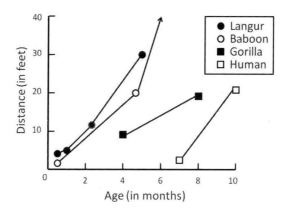

Fig. 11.3 Distances between infants and mothers of some primate species at a variety of ages; the data points represent the maximum distances observed at each age, with the curve for the baboon reaching 90 feet at the end of 10 months. (From Rheingold & Eckerman, 1970; reproduced with permission.)

Phase 4: Goal-Corrected Partnerships (Year 3 Onward)   According to Bowlby (1969), the next major social transition occurs at the beginning of the third year of life when children become able to take their parents' needs into account when interacting with them. For example, they now appear to recognize for the first time (and begrudgingly) that parents must sometimes give priority to other activities, and the child's own needs or wants must wait. Key to this stage is representation of the parent–child relationship, referred to by some as a cognitive map of the parent–child–environment interaction or an **internal working model** (Roisman & Groh, 2011). Included in this representation are expectations for how social partners interact, and these expectations are theorized to guide future social interactions (Sroufe et al., 2005).

Some Features of Attachment Bonds

The beginning of Phase 3 marks the time at which the first infant–adult attachments form. **Attachments** are specific, enduring, emotional bonds whose existence is of major importance in social and personality development. In light of this, it is necessary to ask: What are the processes by which attachments form? To whom do infants become attached?

Studying young ducklings, Konrad Lorenz (1935/1970) described what seemed to be their innate predisposition to **imprint** on an object—to attempt to remain close to whatever salient moving object is present during a **sensitive period** (Chapter 1) occurring shortly after hatching. Attachment formation takes far longer in humans than in birds, and we doubt whether imprinting in ducklings and attachment in humans should be viewed as the result of similar mechanisms (Roisman & Groh, 2011). Nevertheless, Bowlby was influenced by Lorenz's work on imprinting when he proposed a comparable predisposition in humans to form attachments (Oates, Lewis, & Lamb, 2005). According to Bowlby, the consistency of adults' presence and availability during the sensitive period—the first six postnatal months—determines to whom the baby will become attached. If there is no consistent caregiver over this period (as might occur in institutions such as orphanages), the baby would not form attachments. Bowlby and his co-theorist, Mary Ainsworth, believed that most babies develop a hierarchy of attachment figures and that their primary caregivers—usually their mothers—become primary attachment figures before any other relationships are formed. Once infants have this foundation, Ainsworth and Bowlby argued, they may (and often do) form relationships with others, for example, fathers, daycare workers, and older siblings.

The amount of time adults spend with infants and the quality of adult–infant interaction are the principal factors determining whether infant–adult attachments will form. Bowlby and Ainsworth believed that infants become attached to those persons who have been associated over time with consistent, predictable, and appropriate responses to the baby's signals and needs (Cummings & Cummings, 2002; Thompson & Virmani, 2010). The importance of the quality of interaction, over and above the quantity of interaction, is underscored by evidence we review below. Whether or not a baby becomes attached to and protests separation from someone seems to depend on the quality of their interaction, not on the amount of time, over and above some minimum, the baby spends with the person.

Before the mid-1970s, psychologists assumed that infants formed their first and most important relationships with their mothers. Researchers still agree that mothers play a central role and that the stages and processes described above apply especially to infant–mother attachment. However, this conception is too narrow because it pays too little attention to the ways in which the mother's other relationships might affect her relationship with the child and to the influences of fathers and other caregivers (Bornstein & Sawyer, 2006). Moreover, babies may become attached to both of their parents at about the same time, contrary to Ainsworth and Bowlby's hypothesis, even though they might spend much less time with their fathers than with their mothers (Lamb & Lewis, 2011). Family systems theorists are now keenly aware of the number of individuals (other than mothers) who may directly influence the child, and of the elaborate ways in which children's behavior is affected by the multiple other social relationships in which they are involved, as we discussed in Chapter 2.

There is substantial evidence that infants develop attachments to both their mothers and fathers (Lamb & Lewis, 2011). However, it was initially unclear how early in their lives infants form these attachments, because no data were available concerning the period between 6 and 9 months of age. Controversy also arose concerning the existence of preferences for mothers over fathers—some studies reported such preferences, whereas others failed to find them—and no data were available concerning father–infant interaction in the unstructured home environment rather than in the laboratory. In fact, studies of infant–mother and infant–father attachments have indicated that 7-, 8-, 12-, and 13-month-old infants show no systematic preference for one parent over the other on attachment behavior measures (infants' propensity to stay near, approach, touch, cry to, and ask to be held by specific adults; Lamb, 2002). Measures of separation protest and greeting behavior also show no preferences for either parent. Thus, most infants form attachments to both their parents at about the same time. When distressed, the display of attachment behaviors increases, and infants organize their behavior similarly around whichever parent is present. When both parents are present, distressed infants do turn to their mothers preferentially. Some boys show strong preferences for their fathers during this period; yet, they turn to their mothers preferentially when distressed, suggesting that mothers are still deemed more reliable sources of comfort and security even when fathers become more desirable partners for other types of interactions. Thus, although many infants become attached to both of their parents at the same time, they rank attachment figures in a hierarchy, preferring those who are more prominently involved in their care.

Characteristics of Mother– and Father–Infant Interaction

Fathers and mothers engage their infants in different types of interactions. When videotaped in face-to-face play with their 3-week- to 6-month-old infants, for example, fathers tend to provide staccato bursts of both physical and social stimulation, whereas mothers tend to be more rhythmic and containing (Barnard & Solchany, 2002; Parke, 2002). And, as mentioned in Chapter 2, fathers are more playful than mothers when interacting with their infants (Lamb & Lewis, 2010; Parke & Buriel, 2006). Contrary to popular conceptions, however, fathers are neither inept nor uninterested in interacting with their newborns. For example, when observed feeding their infants, both fathers and mothers respond to their infants' cues either with social bids or by adjusting the pace of the feeding (Lamb, 2000).

Fathers typically spend less time than mothers do with their infants, and this is true of families in the United States, Australia, Belgium, and Great Britain, and of families of varying ethnicity in the United States (European American, Latin American, and African American; Parke & Buriel, 2006; O'Brien, 2004; Roopnarine et al., 2005). Despite recent increases in the amount of time fathers spend with their children, most fathers continue to assume less responsibility for their infants' care and rearing than mothers do. Fathers typically see themselves (and are seen by their partners and others) as helpers rather than parents with the primary responsibility for caregiving. All parties see income generation as the primary responsibility of fathers. Fathers are sensitive interaction partners; what differs is the nature of the interactions (Lucassen et al., 2011). Most infants must have enough quality interaction with their fathers, despite the low quantity, because most infants become attached to their fathers. When fathers take a greater role in infant care, fathers' responsiveness and sensitivity increases (Lamb & Lewis, 2010).

In summary, infants generally form attachments around the middle of the first year of life to those adults with whom they have had most consistent and extended interaction. Infants generally establish significant relationships with both of their parents, even though they tend to have more interaction with their mothers than with their fathers. The types of interactions that infants have with their parents also tend to differ. When mothers assume primary responsibility for childcare within the family (as they typically do), infant–mother interactions are characterized by childcare activities, whereas infant–father interactions are dominated by play. As a result, infants' relationships with their two parents are often distinctive from a very early age. Infants also form relationships with siblings, peers, and non-familial caregivers as well as with their parents (Chapter 2). These early relationships with mothers, fathers, brothers, sisters, and others all ensure that the social world of the young infant is rich and we need to consider all the people in the child's social world when trying to understand the social context in which the infant is developing.

Behavior Systems Relevant to Infant Attachment

In this section, we examine more closely the characteristics of infant–parent attachments, particularly those that distinguish attachment from nonattachment relationships. To do so, we need to consider some additional facets of attachment theory. Attachment theorists are particularly interested in the biologically adaptive function (i.e., survival value) of infants' behavioral tendencies. Bowlby (1969) stressed the fact that attachment behaviors promote proximity between infants and adults; proximity to protective caregivers is of obvious adaptive value to dependent and helpless infants. Bowlby drew on control systems theory to derive a metaphor for the functioning of the attachment behavior system, which mediates multiple distinct behaviors (for example, directed crying and approaching) employed to achieve the same goal (proximity and protection). In addition to the attachment system, theorists have suggested that three other systems also mediate infant social behavior. Each system controls a set of behaviors that may be used to achieve an adaptive goal. In this section, we describe the four behavioral systems and the interrelations that exist among them.

Four Behavior Systems   The **attachment behavior system** controls or coordinates infant activities that are most clearly and obviously related to attaining and maintaining proximity to or contact with attachment figures. Examples of these behaviors are gestures or signals indicating a desire to be held, crying, and so forth. These attachment behaviors are frequently directed to persons with whom infants are attached, meaning that researchers can identify attachment figures by determining the people to whom babies direct these behaviors. The function of the attachment behavior system is to ensure that infants retain access to persons on whom they can rely for nurturance and protection. Such behavioral propensities would have adaptive significance (i.e., would maximize the probability of infant survival) in the environment of evolutionary adaptedness.

The second behavior system is the **fear/wariness system**. It coordinates avoidant, wary, or fearful responses to strangers. These behaviors are unlike those controlled by the attachment behavior system, although both systems are of adaptive value. For the same reason that it is important for infants to ensure access or proximity to protective adults, it is of survival value to avoid encounters with unknown and potentially dangerous persons and situations. As we described in Chapter 10, apprehension over the appearance of strange persons becomes marked in many infants around 7 to 8 months of age. This apprehension is a product of the fear/wariness system.

Although it may be adaptive to be wary when first encountering strangers, it is assuredly not adaptive for human infants to avoid all contact or interaction with nonattachment figures. People other than parents have a profound impact on psychosocial development, as most interactions in later life involve people to whom children are not attached. Consequently, it is not surprising that the wariness response diminishes rapidly over time, and infants eventually enter, if only tentatively at first, into friendly interactions with nonattachment figures. These kinds of interactions typically involve social behaviors at a distance, such as smiling and vocalizing, and are mediated by the third behavior system, the **affiliative system**. During an intermediate period when both affiliation and fear/wariness are activated, coy responses may be prominent.

Unlike attachment behaviors, affiliative behaviors do not promote physical contact with the person to whom they are directed, and consequently, affiliative behaviors (such as vocalizing) are often used in interaction with attachment figures as well as with persons to whom babies are not attached. It is not possible to investigate attachment relations by considering only behaviors such as smiling, because they can reflect either attachment or affiliation.

The existence of the affiliative behavior system speaks to the importance of infants' interactions with people to whom they are not attached. In the course of interaction with other people, babies have the opportunity to gain social competence and to learn social skills through modeling and reinforcement. Affiliating with a variety of individuals sets the occasion for infants to learn how to modulate their style of interaction in accordance with another individual's characteristic and unique interpersonal style; therefore, infants benefit from their varied social interactions in a variety of ways.

Infants also engage in interaction with their physical environment to develop competence in and mastery over it (Wachs, 2006). The **exploratory behavior system** mediates contact with the physical or nonsocial environment, whereas social encounters are mediated by the affiliative system. The exploration and manipulation of objects also facilitate the development of cognitive competencies (Bornstein, 2002).

Interdependencies among the Behavior Systems   One major claim of attachment theorists is that the four behavior systems are complementary and interrelated rather than independent of one another. Furthermore, the immediate goals of all the behavior systems usually cannot be achieved simultaneously. Consequently, the degree to which one of the systems is activated arouses or inhibits the others. The specific effects that any one system has on arousing or inhibiting the others can be predicted by considering the adaptive functions of the four systems. These predictions are generally supported by both anecdotal and scientific evidence about infant behavior. A few examples are enough to demonstrate how these behavior systems operate and interrelate.

The appearance of an unfamiliar individual should, according to attachment theory, arouse the infant's fear/wariness behavioral system. In most cases, the infant's response involves both an attempt to avoid interaction with the stranger (fear/wariness) and an attempt to move closer to the familiar attachment figure (attachment). Furthermore, activation of either (or both) of these systems is incompatible with affiliation or exploration. Consequently, affiliation and exploration are typically inhibited when either the attachment or the fear/wariness system is activated. The corollary is also true. When infants are not distressed and are in familiar (and thus not anxiety-provoking) surroundings, they might feel free to engage in interaction with less familiar persons (i.e., the affiliative system is activated) and to explore the environment actively (i.e., the exploratory system is activated) without notable concern for remaining near their attachment figures (i.e., the attachment system is either not activated or is inhibited). According to Ainsworth, the presence of attachment figures provides infants with sufficient security that they are able to explore the environment extensively and adaptively. Thus, attachment figures provide infants with the secure base from which they can confidently engage in interaction with other persons and explore the physical environment. In the next section, we discuss individual differences in attachment and the extent to which adults actually serve as secure bases for their children.

The Security of Infant–Parent Attachments

Many proponents of attachment theory are clinically oriented scholars primarily interested in the ways that early attachment relationships affect subsequent development (Main, Hesse, & Hesse, 2011). To explore this question, Ainsworth developed a procedure—the Strange Situation—for assessing what she called the security of attachment (Ainsworth, Blehar, Waters, & Wall, 1978). She also provided an elegant and persuasive account of relations among early infant–mother interaction, security of infant attachment, and subsequent child development. In this section, we first describe the Strange Situation procedure and Ainsworth's hypotheses concerning security of attachment, and then summarize research on this topic.

The **Strange Situation** is a popular technique to study attachment. It can be used only when infants are old enough to have formed attachments and are mobile, yet are not so old that brief separations and encounters with strangers are no longer noteworthy. As a result, the Strange Situation is appropriate for infants ranging in age from about 10 to 24 months. The procedure has seven episodes, which are outlined in Table 11.1. The procedure is designed to expose infants to increasing amounts of stress to observe how they organize their attachment behaviors around their parents when distressed. An unfamiliar environment, the entrance of an unfamiliar adult, and two brief separations from the parent induce stress.

Table 11.1 The Strange Situation

Episode	Persons Present	Change
1.	Parent, infant	Enter room
2.	Parent, infant, stranger	Unfamiliar adult joins the dyad
3.	Infant, stranger	Parent leaves
4.	Parent, infant	Parent returns, stranger leaves
5.	Infant	Parent leaves
6.	Infant, stranger	Stranger returns
7.	Parent, infant	Parent returns, stranger leaves

After Ainsworth and Wittig (1969).
All episodes are usually 3 minutes long, but episodes 3, 5, and 6 can be curtailed if the infant becomes too distressed, and episodes 4 and 7 are sometimes extended.

As suggested earlier, infants should be able to use attachment figures as secure bases from which to explore the novel environment. Considering the four behavior systems, the stranger's entrance should lead infants to inhibit exploration and draw a little closer to their parents, at least temporarily. The parents' departure should lead infants to attempt to bring them back by crying or searching, and to reduced exploration and affiliation. Following the parents' return, infants should seek to re-engage in interaction with the parent, and, if distressed, the infant may wish to be cuddled and comforted. The same responses should occur, with somewhat greater intensity, following the second separation and reunion. In fact, this is precisely how about 65% of the infants studied in the United States behave in the Strange Situation (Thompson & Virmani, 2010). Following the practices of Ainsworth and her colleagues, these infants (designated Type B) have a **secure attachment** because their behavior conforms to theoretical predictions about how babies should behave in relation to attachment figures.

By contrast, some infants seem unable to use their parents as secure bases from which to explore. Furthermore, although they are distressed by their parents' absence, they behave ambivalently on reunion, both seeking contact and interaction and angrily rejecting it when it is offered. These infants are conventionally labeled **insecure-resistant or ambivalent** (Type C). They typically account for about 10% to 15% of the infants in U.S. samples (Thompson & Virmani, 2010).

A third group of infants appears unconcerned by their parents' absence. Instead of greeting their parents on reunion, they actively avoid interaction and ignore their parents' bids. These infants are said to exhibit **insecure-avoidant attachments** (Type A), and they typically constitute about 20% of the infants in U.S. samples (Thompson & Virmani, 2010).

Main and Solomon (1991) have also described a fourth group of infants whose behavior is **disoriented** and/or **disorganized** (Type D). These infants (5–10% of U.S. samples) simultaneously display contradictory behavior patterns, make incomplete movements, and appear confused or apprehensive about approaching their parents.

Determinants of Strange Situation Behavior

Considerable debate has arisen about the origins of individual differences in infants' behavior in the Strange Situation. Attachment theorists have emphasized the role played by prior infant–mother interactions, whereas critics have suggested that Strange Situation behavior reflects temperament as much as attachment security.

According to attachment theorists, infants count on attachment figures to protect them and to be accessible when needed, and so use them as secure bases from which to interact with other people and explore the environment. However, as noted above, infants do not trust their attachment figures equally, and these differences in security of attachment might affect how willingly infants will use their attachment figures as bases of security in situations like the Strange Situation. Almost from birth, infants learn about people from their interactions with them. Because adults differ in their style and sensitivity, differences should be evident among infants in the extent to which infants have confidence in their own effectance (their ability to act on the environment successfully) and in the reliability of others (Ainsworth et al., 1978; Lamb, 1981).

Since Ainsworth's hypotheses were proposed, many researchers have attempted to test them in independent longitudinal studies (Grossmann, Grossmann, & Waters, 2005). There appears to be general support for the notion that **sensitive parenting**—that is, nurturant, attentive, nonrestrictive parental care—and synchronous infant–mother interactions are associated with secure (Type B) infant behavior in the Strange Situation, and this appears to be true of U.S. samples of varying ethnicities as well as samples from cultures outside the United States (Bakermans-Kranenburg, van IJzendoorn, & Kroonenberg, 2004; Huang, Lewin, Mitchell, & Zhang, 2012; Van IJzendoorn & Sagi-Schwartz, 2008). The mothers of infants who behave in either insecure-avoidant (Type A) or insecure-resistant (Type C) fashions manifest less socially desirable patterns of behavior. They may over- or under-stimulate, fail to make their behaviors contingent on infant behavior, appear cold or rejecting, and sometimes act ineptly. Because there is much variability in these results, it has been difficult to identify precisely what aspects of parental behavior are important. Some studies identify warmth but not sensitivity, some patterning of stimulation but not warmth or amount of stimulation, and so forth.

There is some consensus that insecure-avoidant attachments are associated with intrusive, over-stimulating, rejecting parenting, and insecure-resistant attachments are linked to inconsistent, unresponsive parenting. However, it also has been suggested that the different types of insecure attachments might represent different ends of the same continuum (Fraley & Spieker, 2003). Although the antecedents of disorganized (Type D) attachments are less well established, Type D attachments are more common among abused and maltreated infants and among infants exposed to other pathological caregiving environments. Moreover, disorganized attachments may be consequences of parental behaviors that infants find frightening or disturbing (Roisman & Groh, 2011). Rather than considering insecure attachments as non-optimal, a more accurate conceptualization might be to view them as adaptive responses to non-optimal caregiving environments (Weinfield, Sroufe, Egeland, & Carlson, 2008). For example, if a parent is not consistently responsive to the infant's needs, as in anxious-ambivalent attachments, it might be good strategy for the infant not to rely on the parent.

Most researchers suggest that temperament does not have a direct effect on whether or not infants are classified as Type A, B, or C (Vaughn, Bost, & van IJzendoorn, 2008). However, there may be indirect effects because temperament likely affects the quality of infant–parent interaction (Chapter 10). Distractible babies, for example, might be less affected by their parents' behavior than attentive babies are. Most researchers have relied on parent-report measures of temperament, and as we discussed in Chapter 10, these reports tell us about the parents' personality in addition to the baby's style. It is possible that temperament may affect only the degree of distress manifest in the Strange Situation. Thus, the quality of infant–parent interaction would determine whether the child will become securely or insecurely attached, but constitutionally based differences in irritability would determine whether the insecurity will be manifest in a low distress (i.e., avoidant) or high distress (i.e., resistant) fashion. It remains likely that temperament and attachment security are independent dimensions, with temperament affecting irritability and emotionality but not the security of attachment per se.

The above findings add credence to Ainsworth's (1989) notions about the origins of individual differences in Strange Situation behavior. Recall our discussion in Chapter 10 on the goodness-of-fit among child, parent, and context. This fit is of paramount importance, as it affects the quality of their interaction. From this perspective, the nature of the child's temperament is less important than the fit between that temperament and the parent's own temperament and expectations (Davis, Schoppe-Sulliva, Mangelsdorf, & Brown, 2009).

Stability of Infant Attachment

The notion that Strange Situation behavior reflects something that is not ephemeral but intrinsic to infant relationships was initially supported by findings showing that there is remarkable stability over time in these patterns of infant behavior. According to Waters (1978), 48 out of 50 infants (96%) obtained the same A, B, or C classification on two occasions. Later, Main and Cassidy (1988) reported a high degree of stability between 12-month assessments in the Strange Situation and 6-year assessments. Fraley (2002) suggests that attachment security is moderately stable across the first 19 years of life.

These impressive examples aside, test-retest reliability is not always high, and, in fact, short-term stability estimates for Strange Situation classifications show much variation (Thompson & Virmani, 2010). In some cases, instability of attachment classifications is related to changes in the infants' environment. For example, in their study of attachment stability in a low-SES sample, Sroufe et al. (2005) found that many infants changed from one classification to another between 12 and 18 months of age and that such changes were asymmetric. When the families experienced considerable social stress during the 6-month period, Type B attachments often changed to Type A or C, although when families experienced a low degree of stress, Type A or C attachments did not necessarily become Type B. Attachment theory would predict that changes in attachment over time should be associated in some way with changes in parental sensitivity. For example, a change from secure to insecure should coincide with a decrease across the same time period in parental sensitivity.

At this point, a coherent explanation of stability or instability in Strange Situation classifications remains to be provided. We propose that stability and instability of attachments in infancy may be explained by continuities and discontinuities in parental behavior, although researchers still need to study representative samples of parents and infants in several ecologically valid contexts over time to provide an adequate test of this hypothesis. It is also likely that changes in attachment security are partially independent of parenting quality and may relate to normative family life transitions experienced by children. Teti and Cole (2011) found that the birth of a second child predicted a significant decrease in attachment security among firstborn children and that this decrease was not linked to changes, from before to after birth, in mothers' sensitivity with their firstborns, mothers' levels of psychiatric symptoms, or mothers' reports of marital harmony. Indeed, the decrease in firstborn attachment security might have reflected changes in children's perceptions of their relationships with their mothers in response to the introduction of the new family members, who may have been perceived as threats (Teti, 2002).

Predictive Validity of Attachment Classifications

Attachment classifications also intrigue developmental scientists because they appear to predict aspects of the child's future behavior. Attachment theorists believe that when babies encounter people for the first time, they tend to assume that those persons will treat them in the same way that other people have treated them in the past. Thus, babies who have developed trust in their attachment figures will tend to regard the new people they encounter as trustworthy too. As babies get to know each individual, of course, they develop a set of expectations about that specific individual.

The relation between Strange Situation behavior and styles of interaction with others has been well documented (Sroufe et al., 2005; Thompson & Virmani, 2010). Babies with Type B attachments to their mothers were later more cooperatively playful when interacting with a friendly stranger than were Type A or C infants. Similarly, quality of early attachment relates to social encounters with peers both at the same and at later points in time. Strange Situation behavior may affect social relationships in contemporaneous encounters with peers. Type B infants engage in more frequent, more prosocial, and more mature forms of interaction with their siblings and peers, sharing more and showing a greater capacity to initiate and maintain interactions.

Researchers have also examined the relation between Strange Situation classifications and aspects of later achievement motivation in children (Sroufe et al., 2005). Secure infant–mother attachments at 12 or 18 months are associated with superior problem-solving abilities in a variety of stressful and challenging contexts in the preschool years, and they could have long-term implications for health (Box 11.1). In particular, children who showed Type B attachments to their mothers as infants persist longer and more enthusiastically in cognitively challenging situations than do children who had Type A or Type C attachments. Type B infants also seem to be more resilient and robust when stressed or challenged and appear more socially competent and independent when they later enter preschool. Insecure attachment in infancy, and in particular the disorganized/disoriented (Type D) classification, predicts elevated rates of antisocial behavior, depression and anxiety in later childhood (Groh, Roisman, van IJzendoorn, Bakermans-Kranenburg, & Fearon, 2012). Poor attachment histories are also associated with dropping out of school prematurely (Sroufe et al., 2005).

Box 11.1   Set For Life? Secure Attachments Decrease Likelihood of Child-hood Obesity

Anderson and Whitaker (2011) investigated a possible connection between attachment security in infancy and childhood obesity. Childhood obesity is a national epidemic, and emotional regulation could be a contributing factor. Anderson and Whitaker observed mothers and their infants playing at 24 months, and they later measured the children's growth at 4½ years. The interactions were rated on the child's level of engagement and negativity and the mother's emotional responsiveness to determine the degree of attachment security. Infants who showed signs of insecure attachments were increasingly likely to be obese at 4½ years of age: Obesity was found in 23.1% of the insecurely attached children compared to only 16.6% in the securely attached children. Secure attachments help children to regulate their emotions, which is particularly helpful when managing stress, and managing stress well could have longer-term consequences for eating behavior.

Evidence concerning the temporal stability of Strange Situation behavior and its relations to measures of earlier infant–parent interaction and later child achievement and personality suggests that the Strange Situation measures some meaningful aspect of mother–infant attachment and has important implications for understanding and predicting development. Presumably, Strange Situation behavior with fathers affects development in analogous ways, although the child's relationships with primary attachment figures, be they mothers or fathers, are likely to be more significant than other attachment relationships.

The degree of predictive validity is far from perfect. Rather, the relation between Strange Situation behavior in infancy and subsequent child behavior is found only when there is stability in caregiving arrangements and family circumstances. This observation raises the interesting question: Is the prediction over time attributable to individual differences in the quality of early infant–parent attachments? Or, is it attributable to the continuing quality of child–parent interactions over time? Researchers often assume the former, namely that Strange Situation behavior reflects a part of the child's personality. But, if the latter were true, it would imply that the quality of early relationships was predictively valuable not because of direct cause, but because it presaged later differences in the quality of the child's relationships that, in turn, support continuing differences. Such a pattern of findings would place the locus of stability in continuing parent–child interactions rather than in some aspect of the child's personality. Surprisingly, this possibility has not yet been tested directly, although it has major relevance for long-standing assumptions concerning the critical importance of early experiences and is consistent with the transactional view of development.

Although Strange Situation behavior, prior infant–parent interaction, and the child's later behavior are all interrelated, correlations obtained among them are not very strong (e.g., Sroufe et al., 2005). This finding suggests that factors other than quality of attachment, such as temperament or familiarity with strangers and brief separations, influence Strange Situation behavior. In turn, this means that researchers need to rely on multiple converging methods to assess constructs as complex and as important as the quality of infant attachments, rather than rely on a single measure like the Strange Situation in which behavior could be influenced by factors other than quality of attachment.

Cross-Cultural Research on Attachment Classifications

One of Bowlby's hypotheses regarding attachment is its universality (Roisman & Groh, 2011). Universality refers to the fact that all infants come in to the world with the skills to form attachments. A simplistic test of this hypothesis is to explore whether attachment develops in different cultures despite the wide variation in caregiving environments.

Figure 11.4 shows the distribution of infants across the A, B, and C categories in several countries. Note that most infants are Type B, securely attached. There is considerable variation, however, among countries in the percentages of infants classified as Types A and C (van IJzendoorn & Sagi-Schwartz, 2008). These results could mean that parents in the cultures concerned were either much more or less sensitive. An alternative explanation is that the results may underscore the importance of factors other than the quality of parental behavior in explaining infant behavior, including their behavior in the Strange Situation (Lamb, 2005b; Rothbaum, Pott, Azuma, Miyake, & Weisz, 2000; Thompson & Virmani, 2010). For example, Japanese and Israeli babies typically show high degrees of stress in the Strange Situation. This high level of stress may have led to increases in the proportion of infants classified as Type C (Lamb, 2005b). Japanese infants appear distressed either because they have much less experience with separations from their mothers than infants from some other cultures, such as the U.S., typically have, or because their mothers are much more stressed by the procedures and the infants are responding to their mothers' stress. In either case the situation would not be psychologically similar for Japanese and U.S. babies (Lamb, 2005b). Likewise, for infants growing up on Israeli kibbutzim, encounters with total strangers are more unusual and thus elicit distress. Again, even though the procedure was structurally the same for Japanese, Israeli, and U.S. infants, the psychological experiences or meaning for infants from each culture may have been very different (Lamb, 2005b). There is a great deal of intra-cultural variability as well, for example among infants from different ethnic and socioeconomic groups in the U.S., making it important not to reach conclusions about cross-cultural differences on the basis of small, often unrepresentative, samples from each culture (Bakermans-Kranenburg et al., 2004; Huang et al., 2012).

In summary, the picture emerging from the many studies in which Strange Situation behavior was assessed is complex. Strange Situation behavior appears to reflect individual differences in patterns of infant–parent interaction, with Type B attachments fostered (in Western cultures) by warm, sensitive, and supportive parental behavior. Infant temperament appears to affect the degree of distress infants manifest in contexts like the Strange Situation, but it does not clearly determine the degree of security that the baby will show. Other factors, such as culture-specific rearing practices, seem to be important as well.

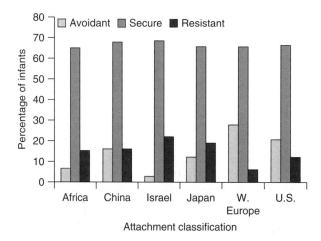

Fig. 11.4 Percentage of infants classified as avoidant (A), secure (B), and resistant (C) from 39 samples across six locations. (Created using data from Van IJzendoorn & Sagi-Schwartz, 2008.)

PARENTAL BEHAVIOR AND INTERACTION WITH INFANTS

Origins of Parenting Characteristics

The origins of individual differences in parenting are extremely complex, as we noted in Chapter 2, but most researchers consider six spheres of influence to be especially important: (1) parents' enduring personality characteristics, (2) parents' cognitions, (3) situational influences on parents' psychological state, (4) parents' attachment representations, (5) the actual or perceived characteristics of infants, and (6) critical events. In this section we discuss these factors as well as the principal domains of parent–infant interaction, including their stability, continuity, and covariation, correspondence with infant activity, and some cross-cultural variations in parental behavior.

Personality Theorists have usually assumed that parental sensitivity reflects adults' enduring personality traits and that sensitive parenting is more likely to occur when parents are psychologically healthy (Belsky & Barends, 2002; Bornstein, Hahn, & Haynes, 2011). For example, characteristics such as self-centeredness and adaptability might be especially pertinent. Parents' adaptability may be important in the infants' first few months, when infant state and activities appear unpredictable and disorganized and their cues less distinct and undifferentiated. Parent self-centeredness can lead to insensitivity when adults fail to put infants' needs ahead of their own. Other aspects of parental personality include cheerfulness, agreeableness, and depression or anxiety.

One of the strongest personality predictors of parenting is depression. Many parents—mothers and fathers—experience bouts of depression from time to time. Some reflect enduring psychological characteristics; others may be transient as a response to poor economic or social circumstances. These feelings influence parental perceptions and behaviors toward the baby. Certainly, depressed mothers fail to experience—or convey to their infants—much happiness with life. Tronick and his colleagues (2007) observed that depressed mothers are less responsive to infant signals, and therefore more often engage in inadequately coordinated interactions. In turn, depressed behaviors have short- as well as long-term consequences for infants. For example, Wright, George, Burke, Gelfand, and Teti (2000) found that clinical levels of maternal depression when children were between 3 months and 3 years of age were associated with more behavior problems (i.e., aggressive and antisocial behaviors) at 5 to 8 years of age than were observed in children whose mothers were not depressed during this early period. Some influential aspects of adult personality may be enduring, but most researchers also assume a more dynamic view of personality. A parent's personality is likely to change as a result of formative experiences, such as childbirth, marriage, prolonged hostility from a spouse, divorce, or intolerable degrees of stress.

Parental Cognitions Goodnow (2002) has discussed the developmental scripts or developmental scenarios that represent parents' informal theories of development. Most parents implicitly assume particular relations between infant age and behavior, and parents continually assess their infants' level of development when deciding how best and most productively to interact with them. Parents' scripts are constantly in flux, as they actively acquire new information about infants through observation, feedback, experimentation, and so forth. These parental cognitions play an important role in shaping parental behavior. For example, when parents see children as active participants in their own development, parents are more likely to use teaching strategies in their interactions. When parents believe that they have little or no effect on their children's intelligence or temperament, they might not assume a very active role in teaching children at all. So, the ways in which parents choose to interact with their children reflect the parents' own general cognitions.

A central parental cognition is the adult's perception of his or her **efficacy** as a parent (Hess, Teti, & Hussey-Gardner, 2004). By definition, parents who believe that they are efficacious see themselves as competent caregivers and interpret interactions between themselves and their infants as enjoyable for the infants. Parental skill, of course, is not the only relevant factor here. A parent who feels incompetent may feel rewarded by even modest levels of success, and the infant's temperament, readability, predictability, and responsiveness also influence the effectiveness of parenting. The same behavioral intervention might rapidly soothe one infant yet seem totally ineffective when another infant is involved, leading the parents of different infants to reach very different conclusions about their own competence as parents, despite similarities in their behavioral styles. Through the quality and contingency of infants' responses, infants influence the way parents perceive their own effectiveness. We return to these so-called infant effects later in this section. Perceived efficacy is likely to affect parental sensitivity because parents who feel effective are motivated to engage in further interaction, which in turn provides additional opportunities to read infants' signals, interpret them correctly, and respond appropriately. Mothers' feelings of efficacy in the parental role are a stronger predictor of parenting competence (i.e., sensitivity and warmth) in interactions with their infants as long as their knowledge of child development is also high (Hess et al., 2004). Interestingly, mothers who have low knowledge of development appear to be naively confident about their parenting skills, but they show the least amount of sensitivity when interacting with their infants.

These suppositions about cognitions raise the question of how parents develop their cognitions about parenting. Family constellation, socioeconomic status, and culture as well as factors such as spousal beliefs, childhood experiences, and the beliefs of one's own parents have all been identified as potential sources of influence (Bornstein, 2006a). Interest in parents' attitudes and actions with respect to their infants' development is increasing, so we can anticipate considerable progress in our knowledge of the factors affecting parental cognitions.

Some components of parenting are driven by individual personality characteristics and cognitions and are in this way thoughtful and conscious (i.e., **meta-parenting**; Hawk & Holden, 2006). However, Papoušek and Papoušek (2002b) developed a complementary notion of intuitive parenting. **Intuitive parenting** consists of behaviors enacted in a non-conscious fashion that are sensitive and developmentally suited to the ability and stage of a child, and thus enhance child adaptation. We reviewed an example of intuitive parenting when we discussed child-directed speech in Chapter 9. Parents (as well as others) unconsciously and habitually modulate many aspects of their communication to match infant competencies appropriately. Parents find it difficult to inhibit such intuitive behaviors, even when asked. Intuitive behaviors, in the Papoušeks' view, do not require the time and effort of conscious decision-making, and, being more rapid and efficient, they require much less attention.

Social-Situational Factors   Parents' personalities and perceptions of their roles and responsibilities clearly constitute factors that influence their behavior toward infants. Of course, other factors can also be influential. Most important among these are stress and the availability of social support (Cochran & Niego, 2002; Roopnarine et al., 2005). Financial and social stress demand attention from parents, and, as a result, reduce their attentiveness, patience, and tolerance and undermine their general well-being and psychological health (Stack et al., 2012). It is not surprising, therefore, that child maltreatment is more common when parents are subjected to high levels of economic or social stress and are socially and emotionally isolated from potential support networks (Stack et al., 2011). As we saw in Chapter 2, the larger social context also affects the intimate world of infants and their parents. The quality of parenting is influenced by the levels of stress and social support available to parents, even when the stresses are modest and the quality of parenting is clearly not abusive (Smith, Landry, & Swank, 2000). Support from fathers predicts parenting quality of mothers and can serve as a buffer against other environmental stressors (Bornstein, Putnick, & Suwalsky, 2012).

Parental Attachment Representations The manner in which parents mentally represent their own attachment relationships also predicts parental quality. These representations are believed to be rooted in the parent's own attachment-related experiences with her or his parents during childhood, although attachment theorists acknowledge that how one represents attachment relationships can undergo considerable revision as one enters into and experiences new relationships (Sroufe et al., 2005). To evaluate parent attachment representation, most researchers have used the Adult Attachment Interview (AAI; George, Kaplan, & Main, 1985), in which the parent discusses her or his relationships with her or his own mother and father, and the rater pays particular attention not to the content of the response per se (i.e., whether the relationship is described positively or negatively), but to whether the parent can provide convincing details to back up her or his descriptions. The interview yields four adult attachment groupings: **Autonomous** parents relate experiences and relationships in an open, fluid, objective, coherent manner, clearly value and appreciate attachment relationships, and view them as important influences on their lives. Importantly, adults need not recall a history of nurturant parenting to be classified as autonomous. It is not uncommon for parents who report problematic childhoods to have forgiven their parents for perceived transgressions and to see how they might have contributed to some of the difficulties they encountered. **Dismissing** parents, by contrast, view attachment relationships as having limited influence on their lives and appear to avoid detailed discussions of their early attachment experiences. Idealization of parental figures is typical, as is lack of recall for attachment-related experiences. **Preoccupied** parents are mentally entangled, conflicted, and angry about past and present attachment relationships. Their extensive preoccupation with past and present parental transgressions precludes an ability to describe these events objectively and coherently. Finally, **unresolved** parents give evidence of mental disorganization over abuse or loss, indicating that such events continue to have a major disorganizing influence on the quality of their thinking and discourse.

Parental AAI classifications are predictive of corresponding infant–parent attachment classifications (Hesse, 2008). That is, mothers classified with the AAI as autonomous (the analog of a secure attachment in infancy) are likely to have securely attached infants. Mothers classified as dismissing (analogous to insecure-avoidant infant–mother attachment) are likely to have insecure-avoidant infants. Mothers classified as preoccupied (analogous to an insecure-resistant attachment in infancy) are likely to have insecure-resistant attachments. Finally, mothers classified as unresolved (conceptually akin to insecure-disorganized attachment in infancy) are likely to have insecure-disorganized infants. In addition, autonomous mothers are more sensitive toward their infants than are non-autonomous mothers.

The AAI allows for opportunities to chart the trans-generational continuity of attachment relationships from parent to child; however, self-report measures are always open to criticism. An ideal way to study the concordance of attachment classification and parenting would be to know the attachment classification of the parent and the type of parenting experienced when he/she was an infant and then observe their parenting and their children's behavior in the Strange Situation. The Minnesota Longitudinal Study of Risk and Adaptation is in a position to make such a comparison (Sroufe et al., 2005). Families were enrolled in this study before the birth of the first child. Many of these families are still being followed today, and many of the babies are now parents. Comparing the parenting the babies received to the parenting they are showing with their own children, Sroufe and his colleagues found correlations in the .50 range among several parenting dimensions, suggesting that parents parent the way their parents did. Moreover, this finding identifies parenting as one mechanism for the transmission of attachment styles across generations. Stack et al.'s (2012) study on intergenerational families shows that the mother's emotional availability is an important component of parenting that has a significant effect on the parent–child relationship.

Infant Characteristics Most theorists believe that infants' characteristics affect parental cognitions and behaviors, but there is long-standing disagreement about the relative importance of parental and infant contributions to interaction and development. Even if very young infants can construct complex internal representations of their parents' behavior, limitations in motor and cognitive skills may reduce their capacities to alter their behavior to mesh their activities and emotions with those of their interactive partners. Parents, by contrast, presumably can generate internal models of infant behavior and alter their behavioral strategies to elicit specific responses and to meet their infants' activities and needs. With age and experience, babies begin to interpret the behaviors of others. For example, by 9 months of age, infants are able to predict others' actions (Southgate, Johnson, El Karoui, & Csibra, 2010). Moreover, infants learn about relationships via their interactions with their parents. In one study, infants were shown an animation of sensitive versus insensitive responding to a crying infant (Johnson et al., 2010). In actuality, the objects involved in the interaction were ovals of different colors and sizes (Figure 11.5). One oval was a small oval representing a child, and the other was a large oval representing a parent. The animation begins with the two ovals in close proximity. As the animation continues, the larger oval moves away from the small oval, and the small oval cries. In the sensitive condition, the adult oval moves closer in response to the crying, and in the insensitive condition, the adult oval moves away. Infants classified as securely attached looked significantly longer to the insensitive response, suggesting that they found this reaction novel. Insecurely attached infants showed the opposite pattern of results: They looked significantly longer to the sensitive response. In sum, it appears that infants bring expectations about actions and appropriate responses to their interactions with others.

Moreover, infants have in-born behavioral propensities that permit them to provide contingent feedback to their parents, and these in turn contribute to feelings of effectance in their parents. Infants' readiness to respond to social stimulation, mutual eye contact, and soothing when held indicate to parents that their behaviors are effective and enjoyable. Furthermore, under ordinary conditions, specific infant behaviors predictably elicit from parents responses that allow infants to develop notions of effectance as well. Successful dyadic interactions thus help parents and infants alike to perceive themselves as effective and their relationships as positive.

Habituation Event: Separation

Test Events:

Responsive Caregiver

Unresponsive Caregiver

Fig. 11.5 Habituation and test events used to assess infants' expectations regarding relationships. In the habituation event, a "parent" (the large oval) moves away from a "child" (the small oval) and the child cries. The two test events show a sensitive response (moving toward the child as in the responsive caregiver event) and an insensitive response (moving further away from the child as in the unresponsive caregiver event). (From Johnson et al., 2010; reproduced with permission.)

Lamb and Esterbrooks (1981) listed a number of infant characteristics that affect parental effectance. These include infants' responsiveness, readability, and predictability. **Responsiveness** refers to the extent and quality of infant reactivity to stimulation, and **readability** to the definitiveness of infant behavioral signals. An easily read infant is one who produces unambiguous cues that allow caregivers to recognize the infant's states quickly, interpret the infant's signals promptly, and thus respond contingently. **Predictability** refers to the degree to which the infant's behaviors can be anticipated reliably from the infant's own preceding behaviors or contextual events.

The health and developmental maturity of infants also affect parents and the quality of infant–parent interaction, as has been illustrated in the research on preterm infants and their parents (Goldberg & DiVitto, 2002). Studies of healthy preterm infants and mothers consistently show that these infants are more passive and reactive and that their mothers are more active and directive than are term infants of comparable age with their mothers (Figure 11.6). However, this does not necessarily mean that the mothers of preterm infants are more insensitive. Rather, the differences could arise in part because preterm infants are immature and call for more directiveness from their adult partners. Thus, the differences might actually attest to the sensitivity of these mothers. Support for this view can be found in the fact that the interaction styles of preterm infants and their mothers are similar to those involving younger term infants—infants who are of the same conceptional age but have spent a briefer period of time outside the womb. Such findings indicate that the maturity level of the child influences social interactions.

Child characteristics other than maturity influence parents as well. When newborns are unhealthy, for example, they seem to require more work from their adult partners to complement their own low energy level and sluggishness (Goldberg & DiVitto, 2002). Furthermore, the differences attributed to maturity

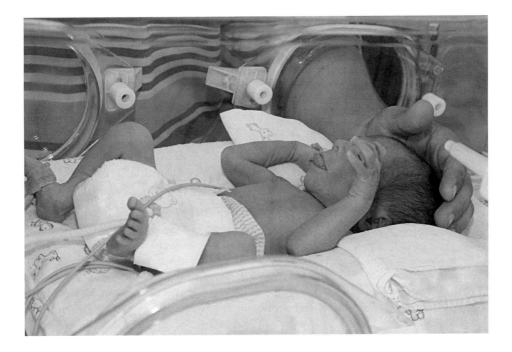

Fig. 11.6 A preterm baby in an incubator. (Image Courtesy of Shutterstock, Inc. Copyright: Reflekta.)

level appear to diminish over time, but those attributable to ill health may be more enduring. Therefore, perhaps as a result of deficiencies in both social and perceptual-cognitive arenas, very small and unhealthy preterm infants often grow up to have cognitive and educational deficits, as we discussed in Chapter 4. Also, healthy newborns may become ill in the early years of life. For example, pediatric cancer is a serious illness that has the potential to affect both parenting and infant development (Bornstein, Scrimin, et al., 2012).

One problem researchers face when trying to identify the cause of poor developmental outcomes among infants is that risk factors co-occur. Preterm births are more common in poor, ill-nourished, and socially stressed families, and it is not known how great an impact these factors have, separately or together. It is known, however, that preterms growing up in advantaged circumstances are much more likely to achieve normal cognitive and intellectual status at school age than are those reared in disadvantaged situations (Goldberg & DiVitto, 2002). Indeed, it was this observation that fostered the development of the **transactional perspective** (Chapter 1). Presumably, more affluent parents are spared many of the stresses that distract poorer parents and are able to have higher quality interactions with their children.

Critical Events There has been long-standing interest in the possibility that certain critical life experiences might affect parental behavior. One of these is early mother–neonate contact, which is believed by some to influence the process of mother–infant bonding and thus the quality of subsequent maternal behavior. A second is the mother's own experience of abuse as a child.

There is no question that childbirth is one of the most profound emotional experiences that parents have, and historical changes in obstetrical practice have been designed to maximize the opportunity for new parents to share in and to enjoy the experience. It was once argued that there exists in human mothers a sensitive period immediately after delivery, during which skin-to-skin contact is more likely to produce affectionate bonding to infants than at any other time (Kennell & Klaus, 1979). If this bonding process were interrupted, various forms of aberrant parental behavior, including child abuse and neglect, were thought more likely to occur, and suboptimal child development more probable.

Prior to about 1980, the obstetrical practices prevalent throughout the Western world (especially the United States) involved regular mother–infant separations immediately after birth. According to Kennell and Klaus's argument, this meant that many mothers and infants were at risk for parenting failure. Critique of obstetrical practices provided the support needed to convince a skeptical medical establishment to accept changes that should have been welcomed on humanitarian grounds alone. Although the reforms they spurred were long overdue, empirical evidence has not supported most claims that birth attendance affects the behavior and attitudes of fathers or mothers (Carter et al., 2005).

Most researchers agree that brief early contact with infants has little or no enduring effect on parental behavior, at least in part because early contact is only one of many factors that affect the bonding process. Moreover, if early contact were a necessary condition, adopted children would be at higher risk for not developing attachments to their adoptive parents, but this is not the case. Infants adopted from China, for example, show clear attachments to their adoptive mothers at 2 years of age (Cohen & Farnia, 2011).

A similar conclusion is appropriate when considering claims concerning the effects of a history of maltreatment on parents. It is not the case that abused children automatically become abusive parents or engage in violent behavior (Box 11.2). In a 25-year longitudinal study, Widom (2000) found that, although individuals who had been abused in childhood were more likely to be violent and antisocial in adulthood than were non-abused individuals, the percentage of abused individuals with violent histories was only 26.4% (vs. 15.6% for controls). Whether or not early abuse predicts abusive parenting behavior is believed to be a complex function of a variety of personality and social-ecological factors, all of which make it more or less likely that individuals will engage in violence and/or abuse (Cicchetti, 2010; Thompson & Virmani, 2010). Indeed, it is no longer justifiable simply to assume that abused children are likely to become abusive parents as adults. We need to determine which abused children are likely to behave in this fashion and why. The answers presumably can be found in considering the parents' personality, the characteristics of their children, and the family's economic and social circumstances.

Box 11.2   Science in Translation: Can Maltreated Children Learn to Love Again?

As explained in this chapter, the loving, attentive, responsive care that infants receive from their parents over the first months of life lead them to form trusting and loving attachment relationships. In the normal course of affairs, these relationships continue to deepen over the succeeding months, and appear to form the social and emotional foundations that shape children's characteristic reactions to people as well as the cognitive and emotional challenges in the years ahead.

When children experience maltreatment rather than responsive care at the hands of their parents, they nevertheless form attachments to the abusive parents, although these relationships are often the disorganized-insecure type even when those children have been able to develop and maintain secure attachments to other (non-abusing) parents and care providers (Lamb, Gaensbauer, Malkin, & Schultz, 1985; Ruth-Lyons, Bronfman, & Parsons, 1999). What happens when these infants are removed from their families and placed in foster homes? Can these infants form attachments to new parent figures, despite having spent the early, attachment-forming months in conditions that were so poor that social service agencies had to intervene?

Stovall-McClough and Dozier (2004) used detailed diary entries by foster parents to assess the status of the infants' behavior with them. They reported that the majority of fostered infants showed signs that they were developing attachments to their foster mothers within the first two months that they were together. Nearly 60% of the attachments also appeared to be secure, and the likelihood that these infants would develop secure rather than insecure relationships was evident from differences in their behavior in the first week or two after placement (Bernier, Ackerman, & Stovall-McClough, 2004). The younger the infants were when first placed with the foster families—some were as young as 5 months—the more likely they were to develop secure attachments to their foster mothers. Because secure attachments appear to offer many benefits to children, these findings strongly suggest that maltreated infants should be removed from inadequate parents and placed with foster or adoptive parents as soon as possible. Dozier and her colleagues (2009) have since shown that foster mothers can successfully be trained to interact more sensitively with their foster infants, and that the foster mothers' increased sensitivity in turn facilitates the infants' adaptation to their new homes.

Infant–Parent Interactions

In many ways, interactions between parents and infants model an intricate dance, not only in rhythm, but also in style. If the mother does one kind of step, the infant may follow or lead with a different step. Often it is not clear who is in the lead. More directly, parent and child alike may have idiosyncratic styles or patterns of interacting, and one may influence the short- and long-term development of the other. The **transactional perspective** on infant–parent interaction proposes that infants not only are influenced by their environment but also alter the environment as they interact with it, interpreting the environment in their own ways (Bornstein, 2009). In other words, infant and environment actively shape one another through time. What are the activities infants and parents bring to their interactions with one another? What is their nature? What are their effects?

Domains and Stability of Interaction   Despite the dynamic range and intricacy of individual activities infants naturally engage in with their parents, two major domains of infant–parent interaction have been distinguished. They are conceptually separable and developmentally significant. The two have been called animate versus inanimate, affective versus informational, person-oriented versus environment-oriented, social versus didactic, or dyadic versus extradyadic (Bornstein, 2006a). The **dyadic**, or social, domain describes those interactions that, for the infant, have their focus on mother and baby. For mother, dyadic activities encompass physical and verbal strategies used in engaging the infant interpersonally. Many published studies of the infant–mother relationship have concentrated on dyadic interactions within the first year of life. Babies and their parents, however, increasingly incorporate the outside world into their interactions. An **extradyadic** domain describes interactions that turn outward from the dyad and focus on properties, objects, and events in the environment. Importantly, dyadic and extradyadic styles appear to be largely unrelated to one another. Infants and mothers who focus more on one another are not necessarily or automatically more or less attentive to their environment, and infants and mothers who attend more to the environment are not necessarily or automatically more or less attentive to one another. As Bornstein and his colleagues in different cultures have found, this is true in U.S. as well as in Argentine, French, and Japanese dyads (Bornstein, 2006a; Cote, Bornstein, Haynes, & Bakeman, 2008). In other words, infants and their mothers appear to specialize in particular kinds of activities.

Having defined domains of infant–mother interaction, we can examine the **stability** of individual variation over time as well as the **continuity** in group behavior over time. Recall from Chapters 1 and 3 that stability in the relative ranks of individuals over time is independent of continuity in the mean level of group performance over time. Summarizing across a wide variety of samples, time intervals, and home assessments, Gottfried (1984) determined that parent-provided experiences are very consistent during the early years. It is important to note, however, that stability of parent and infant characteristics derived from observations of parents and infants also depends on the duration of the observations, the duration between observations, and whether the dyads are observed across consistent or inconsistent contexts (Holden & Miller, 1999).

Stability of individual differences does not necessarily imply group continuity. Infant investigators have long observed that around the middle of the first year, the nature of infant–mother interaction changes from dyadic to extradyadic (Bornstein, 2006a). Mothers show continuity in some activities but discontinuity in other activities.

Correspondence in Infant–Mother Interaction   Developmental scientists have long believed that the child's overall level of development reflects the overall level of parental engagement, but more recent research indicates that specific infant activities relate concurrently and predictively to specific parental activities (Bornstein, 2006a; Tamis-LeMonda, Shannon, Cabrera, & Lamb, 2004). In achieving correspondence, infants who perform a specific kind of activity more have parents who perform a corresponding activity more. Studies of infant–parent correspondence offer answers to important questions about interaction. Are infant activities linked to specific and conceptually relevant parental activities? Are these patterns of correspondence consistent in the infant's first months? Furthermore, concurrent and predictive correspondences begin to define the mutual influences that infant and parent exert on one another.

For example, Bornstein and Tamis-LeMonda (1997) found that only maternal responsiveness to infant non-distress activities (e.g., exploration and play) predicted infant attention span and level of symbolic play at 13 months. Maternal responsiveness to infant distress bore no such relations, suggesting that infant development in a specific domain can be facilitated by parental behavior that is appropriately responsive to infant functioning within that specific domain. Tamis-LeMonda et al. (1996) found that maternal responsiveness to 13-month-olds' vocalizations specifically predicted child language use, but not play competence, at 21 months, whereas maternal responsiveness to the same 13-month-olds' play predicted child play competence, but not language, at 21 months. Furthermore, mothers' verbal responses to infants at 20 months were sensitive to increases in infant vocabulary from 13 to 20 months (Bornstein et al., 1996). Similar predictive relations are evident in father–infant interactions (Tamis-LeMonda et al., 2004).

The specificity of mother–infant (and, presumably, father–infant) influences is evident across cultures too. In a study of U.S. and Argentine mothers of 20-month-olds, Bornstein, Haynes, et al. (1999) found that girls in both cultures engaged in more symbolic play than did boys, whereas boys in both cultures engaged in more exploratory play than did girls. In both cultures, mothers engaged in more symbolic play with girls and in more exploratory play with boys, which is consistent with the premise that infant functioning in a particular developmental domain is tied closely to parental input received in that domain.

In summary, parental personality, cognitions, social and economic circumstances, parents' attachment representations, infant characteristics, and critical events all play important roles in determining parenting. The complex formative interactions among these factors continue to challenge empirical researchers and applied practitioners alike, as both would like to fully understand the best ways to intervene with parents to improve the quality of infants' lives.

GENDER DIFFERENCES IN INFANT DEVELOPMENT

In Chapter 10, we discussed the roles that children's endogenous temperamental characteristics play in shaping their development. However, temperament is not the only such characteristic that children bring to their own social development. Gender is another important variable of this sort. Like temperament, the infant's gender is not only associated with differences in behavioral style and potential, but also influences the ways in which others perceive and relate to the child.

Evidence about innate gender differences in neonatal behavior always is controversial (Ruble, Martin, & Berenbaum, 2006). There is some evidence that male infants are more active than female infants and that female infants show more distress or fear to novelty than male infants (Else-Quest et al., 2006). However, these gender differences are sometimes more apparent than real, and researchers studying them must take into consideration prevailing stereotypes about girls and boys as well as differences in the early experiential histories of babies that can affect adult perceptions. For example, Hernandez-Martinez and colleagues (2011) found that mothers and fathers had equally positive perceptions of their 3-day-old infants; however, by 1 month of age mothers tended to rate their sons, and fathers tended to rate their daughters, less positively. Moreover, Teichner, Ames, and Kerig (1997) found that mothers and fathers of 4-month-old infants tended to view their daughters in more negative terms as their infants' crying increased. No such negative perceptions emerged when sons cried more. In fact, higher levels of crying by boys were associated with mothers' tendency to rate their sons as more powerful, whereas higher levels of crying in daughters were associated with mothers' tendencies to rate their daughters as less powerful.

Similar biases are evident in other maternal appraisals of infants. Mondschein, Adolph, and Tamis-LeMonda (2000) found that mothers of 11-month-old boys *over*estimated how well their babies would crawl down a sloped pathway, whereas mothers of 11-month-old girls *under*estimated how well their babies would do (subsequent tests of crawling ability on a sloped path revealed no gender differences in infant crawling). Parents constitute initial influences on the development of their children's gender.

Parents have a strong tendency to treat children differently by gender. Classic "Baby X" studies (where the gender of the infant is not known to study participants) in the United States have shown that parents (and other adults) conceive of and behave toward infants differently depending on whether they think they are interacting with a girl or a boy (Seavey, Katz, & Zalk, 1975; Sidorowicz & Lunney, 1980). Boys are described as "big" and "strong" and are bounced and handled more physically than girls who are described as "pretty" and "sweet" and are handled more gently. Even before birth, after finding out their child's gender via ultrasound, parents describe girls as "finer" and "quieter" than boys, who are described as "more coordinated" (Sweeney & Bradbard, 1988). It is important to note that such experiential influences do not imply free will and easy malleability because social forces may be significant and robust in themselves. Parents further influence gender development in their children by tending to place girls and boys in gender-distinctive contexts (e.g., rooms with certain furnishings; Pomerleau, Bolduc, Malcuit, & Cossette, 1990). Sex-differentiated behavior by parents is quite consistent. Parents have been reported to purchase gender-stereotyped toys for their children within a few months of the child's birth—prior to when children could express gender-typed toy preferences themselves (Pomerleau et al., 1990). Such findings are consistent with the premise that adult perceptions of infant competencies and characteristics tend to favor boys over girls.

Given these biases, it is likely that adults play a large role in shaping gender stereotypes in their children beginning from the first moments of life (Blakemore, Berenbaum, & Liben, 2009). Male and female infants are treated differently from birth, newborn nurseries prominently display color codes (blue for a boy and pink for a girl), and early presents to infants use similarly gender-typed color codes. Naming patterns also reflect gender biases (Blakemore et al., 2009). Parents are more likely to give boys traditional names and are more likely to name boys after a parent or relative. Girls are more likely to be given a made-up name, and when a traditional boy name becomes commonly used for girls, the name no longer is given to boys (e.g., Evelyn used to be a boy's name). In addition, from birth onward, fathers appear to interact preferentially with sons and mothers with daughters (Lamb & Lewis, 2010). The ways that mothers and fathers interact with their sons and daughters differ. Mothers are more likely to play with their girls with dolls and engage them in social pretense, whereas boys are encouraged to play with vehicles. Because social pretense elicits more complex language, questioning, and description about objects, from an early age parents could be providing their male and female infants with different cognitive experiences in addition to teaching them what types of toys are appropriate for boys and girls (Blakemore et al., 2009). Child care providers also play a role in shaping gender stereotypes by the types of activities they encourage, the toys they provide, and the comments they make, such as praising a girl for her appearance and a boy for his activity level (Chick, Heilman-Houser, & Hunter, 2002).

The gender typing of infant–parent play is perennially fascinating because girls and boys gravitate in such different directions, seemingly regardless of the parents' stated beliefs. Before infants are able to label themselves as a boy or a girl (an ability that emerges around age 2), boys show preferences for trucks and girls show preferences for dolls (Jadva, Hines, & Golombok, 2010). Even younger boy and girl infants show differences in imitation of hitting motions. In a study conducted by Benenson, Tennyson, and Wrangham (2011), infants aged 6 to 9 months were shown videos of adults cradling and hitting a balloon. When given the chance to interact with a similar balloon, boys hit the balloon significantly more than girls.

The early appearance of gender differences in play and related behaviors suggests a role for biological forces. Recall from Chapter 4 that very early in development boy and girl fetuses are exposed to different hormonal environments, and this might affect the appearance of differences in later behaviors. Indeed, girls exposed to testosterone *in utero* make masculine toy choices between 3 and 10 years of age, despite the fact that parents encouraged feminine toy choices (Pasterski et al., 2005). Additional evidence for biological basis of gender differences comes from studies with nonhuman primates. Juvenile chimpanzee often play with sticks, and female chimpanzees are more likely than males to carry the sticks like mother chimpanzees carry infants (Kahlenberg & Wrangham, 2010).

The effects of gender expectancies—formed and met—spill over to other spheres of infant development. Infants who acquire gender labels before they are nearing the end of the second year are also more gender-typed in their toy choices than late labelers (Zosuls et al., 2009). Moreover, parents' responses to infants' gender-typed play at 1½ years predict whether the infant will be early or late in acquiring the ability to label gender. Parents of infants who label early give more attention (both positive and negative) when their children play with either male- or female-gender-typed toys, regardless of the child's gender (Fagot, Rogers, & Leinbach, 2000).

SUMMARY

In this chapter, we have reviewed evidence concerning the earliest development of social relationships, emphasizing infant–parent attachments and infant–parent interactions. We began by describing major stages in the development of attachments. Initially, infants appear not to recognize specific people. Once this capacity develops, infants interact preferentially with familiar people, and attachments are gradually formed with those adults who have been consistently and reliably accessible during the first months of their lives. Most form attachments to both their mothers and fathers at the same time, although they tend to prefer their primary caregiver.

Individual differences in the security of attachment relationships seem to depend on the quality of early interactions, which is determined by the infant's actual and perceived temperament and by adults' behavioral propensities. When the interaction between infant and adult is warm and well meshed, secure attachments are likely to develop. Mismatches between infants and parents lead to insecure attachments. Instead of using their attachment figures as bases of security from which to explore, and as sources of comfort when distressed, insecure infants either avoid their attachment figures or interact angrily with them. The attachment relationship can have pervasive effects on the child's development. Long-term predictions between type of attachment and measures of later child behavior emerge only where there appears to be stability in family circumstances.

Infant behaviors with parents are divisible into different conceptual domains, and infants and parents tend to show consistency over time in certain of these domains. Most infant activities increase in frequency, whereas some aspects of parenting increase and others decrease over the course of infancy. The interactive aspects of infant and parent activities have important consequences for the post-infancy development of a child. Finally, gender differences in infant behavior are initially quite ephemeral. However, over time, adults help to shape infants' gender-stereotyped patterns of behavior.

KEY TERMS

Affiliative system
Ambivalent
Attachments
Attachment behavior system
Attachment figures
Autonomous
Continuity
Dismissing
Disorganized

Disoriented
Dyadic
Effectance
Efficacy
Exploratory behavior system
Extradyadic interactions
Fear/wariness system
Imprint
Insecure-avoidant attachments

Insecure-resistant attachment
Internal working model
Intuitive parenting
Meta-parenting
Person permanence
Predictability
Preoccupied
Readability
Reciprocity
Responsiveness

Secure attachment
Sensitive parenting
Sensitive period
Stability
Strange Situation
Transactional perspective
Trust
Unresolved

Chapter 12
Infant Social Cognition

- *What biases or abilities prepare young infants to be social partners?*
- *What is the importance of turn taking and joint attention?*
- *How do infants learn what to interact with?*
- *What role does beginning to crawl or walk play in changing infants' interactions?*
- *What assumptions govern interactions?*
- *How does a sense of self develop?*
- *What are the roots of false belief understanding?*
- *Do infants have a theory of mind?*
- *How does culture affect the development of social cognition?*

Because we have organized *Development in Infancy* topically, we have devoted separate chapters to each of the major substantive aspects of development in infancy. Organizing the material in this way, however, may obscure the coherence of development across domains. In this final chapter, therefore, we use the development of social cognition (social understanding) in infancy to illustrate relations among different aspects of development. We do so by recalling details presented earlier and integrating them with new research on social cognition to create a broader, comprehensive perspective on infancy.

Social cognition refers to the ways that young infants perceive and understand social interaction, the people with whom they interact, and the differences between others' perspectives and knowledge and the infant's own. We organize this discussion around a number of tasks infants need to accomplish to become effective social partners: (1) Whom to interact with? (2) How to interact? (3) With what to interact? and (4) What assumptions govern interactions? In this discussion, we emphasize the bidirectional nature of infants' early interactions, both in terms of the preparedness of the infant for interaction and the supports others provide so that early interactions are successful. We conclude the chapter by discussing social cognition in a cross-cultural context, followed by some closing comments.

THE SHARED MIND: FITTING THE PIECES TOGETHER

Although some claim that the neonate is prepared to be a social partner, tremendous advances in the infancy period support babies' interactions with others (Nagy, 2011). During the course of the first half year, infants come to recognize specific individuals and associate them with pleasurable events. The appreciation that people continue to exist even when they cannot be seen or heard makes possible advances toward maturity in the baby's social relationships. At last, true, enduring, affectionate relationships are possible because of the infant's new understanding of person permanence. The consolidation of such interpersonal relationships is marked by the fact that infants begin to protest separation from their parents for the first time. Because infants are now able to recognize specific individuals, they learn which particular individual (or individuals) can be counted on to respond to their signals. Recognition of the reliability and predictability of other people follows and constitutes another important step in social development. This whole process involves the integration of neurological, motor, perceptual, cognitive, language, emotional, and social processes.

With Whom to Interact?

Interactions are bidirectional, so infants must first figure out which objects in the environment respond to social bids. People are multimodally specified. In other words, there is a variety of perceptual information we can use to identify people generally. People can be distinguished from other living things by specific visual features such as faces, arms, and legs, specific sounds that they make, such as speech, specific odors, and specific patterns of movement. To recognize specific people, infants must be able to distinguish among different faces, voices, smells, and movements. We learned in earlier chapters that infants may have several predispositions to help them differentiate people from objects and to quickly recognize and remember people who are around them. Among these early predispositions is a preference for face-like stimuli, which appears to be present at birth (Farroni, Csibra, Simion, & Johnson, 2002). Moreover, eyes play a large role in infant face processing. For example, Farroni and her colleagues (2002, 2006) showed that newborn infants preferred to look at faces with direct eye gaze rather than averted eye gaze (Figure 12.1). Moreover, newborns show unique patterns of electrical activity in the occipital cortex in response to these faces. Specifically, they show higher amplitude responses to faces with direct gaze than averted gaze. These findings suggest an innate predisposition by newborns to look at faces that engage them in mutual gaze. This predisposition may facilitate the learning of faces. Guellai and Streri (2011) found that newborn infants remembered faces that previously talked to them with direct eye gaze, but they did not remember faces with averted gazes.

Attention to eyes continues well into the first year of life. Using eye-tracking methodology, Oakes and Ellis (2013) found that, when scanning faces, infants at 4½, 6½, and 8½ months spent significantly

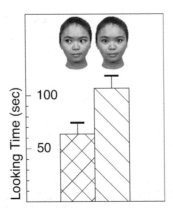

Fig. 12.1 Seconds of looking by newborn infants to faces with direct and averted eye gaze. (From Farroni et al. 2002. Copyright 2002 National Academy of Sciences, USA.)

more time looking at the eye region than other internal areas of the face. It was only by 12½ months that infants explored other regions, such as the nose and mouth, as much as the eyes. When shown inverted faces, scanning to the eye region was comparatively frequent at all ages, suggesting that, despite the inverted nature of the face, the eyes were still of greatest interest.

People are also identifiable by how they move. Three-month-old infants are sensitive to the different motion patterns that specify animate and inanimate objects, and 5-month-old infants perceive the human form with the barest of information such as presented in point-light displays (Arterberry & Bornstein, 2001; Booth, Pinto, & Bertenthal, 2002; Chapter 6). Moreover, infants appear to be neurologically prepared to make distinctions between biological and nonbiological motions. For example, Lloyd-Fox and her colleagues (2011) presented 5-month-old infants with displays of a human female moving her hand, mouth, or eyes, or to mechanical movements provided by pistons, cogs, and toys. Infants' neurological responses were measured using near-infrared spectroscopy (Chapter 3). Lloyd-Fox et al. found differential responding to human motion versus mechanical motion. Perception of the eyes and hands resulted in cortical activation in the frontal temporal areas, and perception of the mouth resulted in cortical activation in the right middle temporal area, a region where the primary motor cortex lies. This pattern of response is consistent with findings from adults, suggesting an early specialization of the human cortex for the processing of human biological motion.

Learning about people is enhanced because auditory and visual attending is coordinated: Babies look at things they hear. Not only does this propensity help form a visual concept that permits recognition of specific faces, it also helps form audiovisual concepts. Thus, coordinated information specifying a parent's face and voice might well be among the very first concepts developed in infancy. This learning process is facilitated by the fact that fetuses hear *in utero* (Chapter 4), and thus, infants come into the world with familiarity with at least one voice—their mother's (Kisilevsky et al., 2003). Moreover, familiarity with a person helps young infants interpret auditory information. For example, as we learned in Chapter 10, 3-month-old infants match emotional sounds to visual displays more successfully when the stimuli were of their mothers. Familiarity also helps when processing language. Barker and Newman (2004), for example, gave infants the opportunity to listen to their own mothers or a different woman repeating isolated words while another female voice spoke fluently in the background. Subsequently, infants heard only one voice (either their mother's or another infant's mother's) speaking passages, some of which contained the target words. Infants attended longer to the passages with the target words when their mothers spoke than to the passages with novel words or to passages with familiar words spoken by other infants' mothers. This finding suggests that familiarity with the mother's voice is special.

Infants also quickly learn how familiar people smell. As we learned in Chapter 4, breastfeeding infants recognize their mothers within a few days of birth, and infants can associate a smell, such as vanilla, with their mothers; thereafter, this smell can even help alleviate distress during certain medical procedures. Similarly, infants can quickly associate taste with specific people. Blass and Camp (2001) provided infants with the opportunity to look at an unfamiliar person while tasting a sweet solution. When the unfamiliar person engaged in direct eye contact, 9- and 12-week-old infants showed a preference for that person 3½ minutes later. Eye contact alone or the sweet solution alone did not lead to a preference for the unfamiliar person, suggesting the importance of coordination of sensory information for learning about and remembering people.

The choice of interactive partners is also affected by other peoples' responsiveness. Newborn imitation may serve this purpose. As reported in Chapter 7, newborn infants imitate facial gestures, such as tongue protrusion, mouth opening, and lip pursing. Although imitation, when tested experimentally, is initiated by an experimenter, imitation by the infant communicates a readiness to interact and allows the infant to test the social responsiveness of the partner. If the infant's response is met with another action to imitate, then the interaction can continue. Inherent in this process is the notion of turn taking, a topic we revisit below.

Thus, it appears that infants come prepared to find interactive partners. Their early bias for faces and direct gaze, their preparedness to recognize voices, and their quick multimodal learning provide a foundation for becoming social agents. Let us consider these biases and abilities in the context of the development of attachment. In the first stage of social awareness described by Bowlby (1969), the 1- to 2-month-old appears to be indiscriminately sociable. People are of interest but particular people are not preferred. This early stage gives way within short order to a stage of discriminating sociability in which the 2- to 7-month-old baby responds more positively to some people (typically parents) than to others. This transition is made possible by attentional, perceptual, and memory capacities, which not only permit infants to remember the faces of specific people (who the person is) but also the experiences they have had with specific people (the ways they typically behave). **Specific attachments** emerge around 7 months of age, a time frame not surprising in light of all that infants need to learn. It takes time to become familiar with specific people across a variety of interactions and contexts. Faces provide information in addition to identity. Faces are dynamic and are viewed from various angles. Moreover, facial expressions convey emotional information important for social interactions.

In summary, infants' first task as social partners is to find people with whom to interact. Infants are prepared at birth to be social partners, and their perceptual and motor capabilities, albeit limited, help them find interactive partners. Infants respond in specialized ways to social stimuli, such as faces and human movement patterns, and they are adept at learning which faces are associated with comfort, support, and/or entertainment. Moreover, infants engage in behaviors that facilitate ongoing interactions, such as imitation. Thus, during the first several months of life, infants are learning a tremendous amount about those around them, and they consequently come to prefer a specific few.

How to Interact?

In addition to determining likely social partners, infants need to know how to interact with them. There are a number of rules that govern social interactions, and here we consider several. One important rule is **turn taking** which promotes the synchrony of interaction. We discussed the importance of turn taking in Chapter 9 in the context of language development, but long before infants produce formal speech, "conversations" between mothers and their infants involve a variety of alternating activities (Bigelow & Rochat, 2006). For example, infants tend to produce positive vocalizations when gazing into their parents' eyes (Keller, Poortinga, & Schölmerich, 2002). When infants produce negative vocalizations, parents often respond by touching and cuddling them. Moreover, infants produce more vocalizations when parents vocalize to them, rather than merely responding with touch or gesture (Bloom, Russell, & Wassenberg, 1987). Reciprocal responding to vocalization is evident even in preterm infants as young as 32 weeks conceptional age (Caskey, Stephens, Tucker, & Vohr, 2011). Infant vocalization is more likely to occur when a parent is present, and the amount of parent–preterm infant vocalization increases between 32 and 36 weeks conceptional age, suggesting the facilitative effect of a conversational partner. A longitudinal study of naturalistic talk in older infants found a continuing increase in child speech: The number of speech acts in 10-minute segments increased from four acts at 14 months to seven acts at 20 months to 11 acts at 32 months (Snow, Pan, Imbens-Bailey, & Herman, 1996). This early and increasing propensity to engage in conversation in appropriate ways illustrates the extent to which infants are being mainstreamed into a world of continual conversational turn taking.

Infants come to expect turn taking in many, if not all, of their interactions with others. This expectation is most notable in the **still-face paradigm**. Described in Chapter 8, this paradigm intentionally disrupts the normal course of interaction by asking an adult, typically the mother, to assume a still face and not to respond to the normal social bids of the infant. This disruption often leads to sadness and upset on the part of the infant. In fact, infants typically show more distress than when the adult physically leaves the interaction altogether (Field et al., 2007; Goldstein, Schwade, & Bornstein, 2009). The salience of this disruption is evident by infants' memory for the person involved in a still-face interaction 15 months later (Bornstein, Arterberry, & Mash, 2004).

When infants move beyond face-to-face interactions to include objects, typically interactions are more successful if both partners are attending to the same object or event. **Joint attention** is another rule that guides social interaction that infants might need to discover. There are two ways for partners to engage in joint attention. One is to take the lead role by **initiating joint attention**. Such bids for joint attention can be verbal, such as saying "look!" Verbal bids can be combined with nonverbal actions, and nonverbal actions alone can also initiate attention. Pointing, as we already discussed in Chapter 9, is an effective gesture for capturing a person's attention to an object or an event, and pointing begins in an apparently communicative fashion in the latter half of the first year of life (Butterworth, 2003). Early in the second year of life, infants point and look at the face of social partners, as though checking to be sure that they are looking at the designated targets. Such checking suggests that the infant is pointing to communicate and influence the other person's attention (Tomasello, Carpenter, & Liszkowski, 2007). It also suggests that the infant realizes that the other person might not always understand or respond appropriately to the infant's gestures. Over the course of the second year, infants point in increasingly sophisticated ways, with older children pointing more when the other person did not appear to have seen or looked at the interesting target (Moore & D'Entremont, 2001). Another nonverbal strategy for initiating joint attention involves making eye contact with someone and then shifting the eyes to an object. This action may result in the other person also moving his/her eyes to the object (Figure 12.2).

Joint attention is not successful until the bid has been responded to. **Responding to joint attention** is the second way for social partners to engage in joint attention, and it involves a social partner acting in response to a verbal or nonverbal signal. Responses can be as simple as moving the eyes to where someone is pointing or looking. Given the limited repertoire of actions available to young infants, it is not surprising that responses to joint attention appear earlier than initiating joint attention (Mundy & Newell, 2007). Moreover, it appears that different brain regions underlie the two types of joint attention. Initiating joint attention appears to be governed by the left frontal cortex, whereas the earlier developing response to joint attention appears to be governed by the parietal areas (Paterson, Heim, Friedman, Choudhury, & Benasich, 2006).

Gaze following is one example of a successful response to a bid for joint attention, and one that infants can accomplish in the first few days of life (Farroni et al., 2004). Initially, gaze following can be accomplished only with near objects, but with age infants show more mature responses to others' gaze, including following the gaze of a social robot by 18 months (Meltzoff, Brooks, Shon, & Rao, 2010). Ten months appears to be an important transition point. For example, Brooks and Meltzoff (2005) showed that infants at this age will follow head turns but only when adults' eyes are open. In their task, an adult and an infant sat across from each other and on a table between them were two objects, one to their left and

Fig. 12.2 The sequence of events for a task designed to assess gaze following. In Brooks and Meltzoff's (2005) study, the experimenter: (left) first made eye contact with the infant then (middle) looked at one of two objects. (right) The infant shows successful gaze following by also looking at the object. (From Meltzoff & Brooks, 2009; reproduced with permission.)

one to their right (Figure 12.2). The adult made a head movement to look at one of the objects. On half of the trials the adult's eyes were open, and on the other half of the trials the eyes were closed. Infants at 10 months demonstrated true gaze following by following the adult's head movements when the eyes were open but not when they were closed. Younger infants of 9 months followed the head movement but they did so regardless of whether the eyes were open or closed, and they often overshot the target, indicating that they were not truly following the adult's gaze. Around 10 months, infants also understand gaze in third-party interactions (Beier & Spelke, 2012). When observing two other people interacting with either mutual or averted gaze, infants demonstrate that they expect social partners to look at each other when conversing. Thus, at 10 months infants appear to understand the role that vision plays in joint attention and the way that joint attention is used in communication. Children who do not acquire this understanding suffer from disrupted social interactions, as we see in children with autism (Box 12.1).

Box 12.1 Science in Translation: Training Autistic Children to Engage in Joint Attention

One in every 88 children in the United States is estimated to suffer from autism spectrum disorder (ASD; Baio, 2012). ASD can be diagnosed by age 2; however, many children are not diagnosed until a later age. Children with ASD exhibit deficits in social behavior. In Chapter 5, we noted that children with ASD appear to process social and nonsocial stimuli in a relatively undifferentiated manner. Moreover, from observing home movies, researchers have noted that infants later diagnosed with ASD showed deficits in eye contact, pointing, and gaze monitoring (Clifford et al., 2007).

In light of the importance of joint attention in social interaction, interventions for children with ASD focus on training them to engage in this behavior. One training program was conducted by Whalen and Schreibman (2003) with 4-year-old children diagnosed with autism and had a nonverbal mental age of 14 months or higher. A second group of typically developing children aged 2½ years served as a control group. Training consisted of three 1½-hour sessions per week until the children mastered each task, and then they were tested for retention three months later. Training focused both on response to joint attention bids and initiating joint attention. Training sessions moved through different types of joint attention activities—responding to someone touching an object, responding to someone showing an object, making eye contact with another person, following a point, and following eye gaze. Training for initiating attention based on gaze included the trainer moving the child's head so that he/she viewed an object, then the trainer, and then the object again. Training for initiating attention based on pointing involved helping the child mold his/her hand into a point and touching the index finger to an object. For the children with ASD, the training of response to joint attention took longer, 16 to 26 days across the children, than training to initiate joint attention. However, the responses were still remembered when the children were retested three months later. Initiating joint attention was acquired more quickly, in 2 to 13 days, but this behavior tended not to be remembered. This difference in training timetables and retention of the behaviors supports the belief that response and initiating joint attention are governed by different neurological pathways (Hoehl et al., 2009). A longer-term implication of this work is early intervention. Detection of difficulty engaging in joint attention could lead to programs focusing on training infants, and perhaps reduce the social deficits seen in children diagnosed with ASD later in life.

How to interpret infants' eye gaze following is the subject of ongoing debate, particularly in terms of what it says, if anything, about infants' understanding of other people (Mundy & Newell, 2007; Tomasello, Carpenter, Call, Behne, & Moll, 2005). Some investigators believe that gaze following reflects (1) infants' understanding of what it means to see and (2) infants' understanding that when someone looks at an object they desire or want it. Let us consider these two interpretations in turn. First, when we see someone looking at something, we usually want to see it too. This is a relatively straightforward interpretation of someone's head and/or eye movement. But does an infant share this interpretation? To explore this interpretation, Moll and Tomasello (2004) tested infants' gaze following in the context of barriers. In their task, an infant and an experimenter sat on the floor in a room with a variety of objects and barriers. For example, in one condition, a toy was placed in a box on the floor and the opening of the box faced the experimenter in such a way that the infant could not see the toy. When the experimenter looked toward the opening of the box, the infant's response was recorded. To see the object, infants needed to move around the box to the side with the opening. Moll and Tomasello found that both 12- and 18-month-old infants moved by crawling or walking to see objects behind barriers, and they did not do so on control trials in which the object was always in full view. This finding suggests that infants interpreted the experimenter's shift in eye gaze as a cue that an object was present. Thus, at least by 12 months, it is likely that, when infants watch someone shift their eyes and/or head, they wish to see what the other person sees.

Meltzoff and Brooks (2008) suggested that infants learn about what can and cannot be seen through their own experience with opening and closing their eyes. To show the possible role of experience, Meltzoff and Brooks (2008) provided infants with experiences with blindfolds. As shown in Figure 12.3, blindfolds were raised in front of the infants' faces, allowing them to experience how one's view is blocked. Then, infants and an adult participated in a head-eye gaze following task in which the adult either did or did not wear a blindfold. Twelve-month-olds correctly did not follow the head turn of experimenters wearing blindfolds. In contrast, a control group of 12-month-olds who did not receive experience with blindfolds followed the head turn of the blindfolded experimenters. Only until 18 months did infants resist following the head turn of blindfolded experimenters in the absence of specific training with blindfolds.

The second interpretion that the infant knows the person desires the object is more difficult to demonstrate. In fact, there are several conclusions infants may draw when viewing someone looking at an object: (1) the person and the object are connected, (2) the person likes the object, (3) the person wants to do something with the object, (4) some combination of these conclusions, or (5) some other conclusion. A number of researchers suggest that young infants understand others' intentions, such as desiring objects, from their looking at objects (Barna & Legerstee, 2005; Phillips, Wellman, & Spelke, 2002).

Evidence for this conclusion is mixed, however. On the one hand, results from habituation studies suggest that infants anticipate what actors might do or what actors might want. For example, Barna and Legerstee (2005) tested 9-month-old infants' predictions of whether people would hold objects after the individuals either smiled and said something positive about the objects or frowned and said something negative about them. They concluded that the infants were able to use the looking behavior and emotional responses to the objects to predict another person's future action. Similarly, measurement of EEG while 9-month-old infants viewed incomplete actions showed that infants neurologically respond differently to actions that do and do not predict a goal (Southgate, Johnson, Karoui, & Csibra, 2010; Woodward, 2009). Yet, research has not always documented that infants expect particular outcomes based on the way others look at objects. In an experiment conducted by Paulus (2011), 14-month-old infants first observed an experimenter looking at one of two objects. Then, the experimenter began to reach for an object by raising her hand midway between the two objects. Paulus measured infants' eye movements and noted

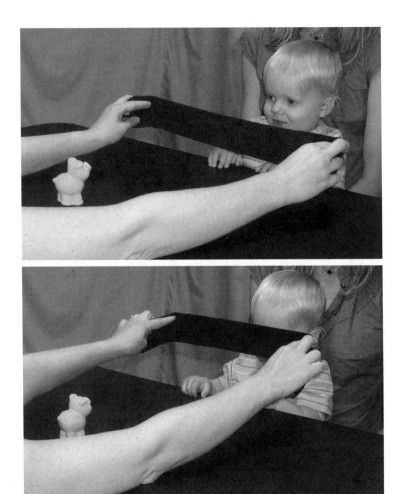

Fig. 12.3 An infant receiving experience with a blindfold in an experiment conducted by Meltzoff and Brooks (2008). (From Meltzoff, 2011; reproduced with permission.)

which object the infant looked at in anticipation of the experimenter completing the reach to one of the two objects. He found that 14-month-olds did not look at the object that the experimenter had previously inspected. Moreover, when the same task was presented with grasping rather than gazing, 14-month-olds showed anticipatory looking to the object. Paulus concluded that infants were unable to discern the experimenter's desire for the object from their gaze alone. Thus, it is not clear how infants interpret others' gaze.

The importance of engaging in joint attention for social interaction cannot be emphasized enough, and it is not surprising that mothers support their infants' behavior in a number of ways (Mendive, Bornstein, & Sebastián, 2013). Mothers normally regulate their infants' focus of attention in three main ways: (1) **introducing**, when the mother orients the focus of attention of the infant when the infant is not already involved with an object, (2) **maintaining**, when the mother follows and reinforces the infant's focus of attention, and (3) **redirecting**, when the mother changes the infant's ongoing focus of attention to a different topic. These three ways in which mothers scaffold attention result in longer bouts of **coordinated joint attention** by the infant, namely the sharing of an object or an activity with another person and actively coordinating his/her gaze between the object and the other person. In their research, Mendive et al. found that 9-month-old infants followed their mothers' attention-directing strategies, and the way mothers regulated their infants' attention had differential results. Mothers' maintaining behaviors predicted coordinated joint attention, whereas mothers' introducing and redirecting affected infant attention to objects. Mundy and Sigman (2006) suggested that engagement in joint attention allows infants to practice social attention management, which is the foundation for social interaction. In addition, they pointed out that engagement provides opportunities for social learning.

In summary, to interact successfully, infants need to know the rules of social interaction. Turn taking is one of the earliest appearing rules, and this is no surprise given its importance for early communication. Later in the first year, infants respond to joint attention bids and then start initiating joint attention. Joint attention moves the interaction beyond two people to include objects, thus increasing infants' opportunities to learn about the world.

With What to Interact?

Infants' interactions in the world are varied; they involve different people and objects, and they can be initiated by the self and others. As we discussed in Chapter 11, there are two domains of activities infants naturally engage in with the help of others, especially mothers (Bornstein, 2006a). The **dyadic**, or social, domain describes those interactions that, for the infant, have their focus on the baby and another person. **Extradyadic** interactions turn outward from the dyad and focus on properties, objects, and events in the environment. Dyadic and extradyadic styles appear to be largely unrelated to one another. Infants and mothers who focus more on one another are not necessarily or automatically more or less attentive to their environment, and infants and mothers who attend more to the environment are not necessarily or automatically more or less attentive to one another.

In traditional families, mothers play a key role in guiding what their infants interact with. We already saw one example in the study by Mendive et al. (2013), described in the previous section. Mothers introduced, maintained, and redirected their infants' attention in interactions with other people and objects. Mothers also adjust their guidance as infants develop. Cross-cultural research, for example, shows a change in mothers' speech with advances in infant cognitive and motor development. Mothers of younger infants use more affect-laden speech, but, as infants achieve more sophisticated levels of cognitive comprehension and motor exploration, mothers increasingly orient, comment, and prepare children for the world outside the dyad by providing increasing amounts of information in their speech (Bornstein et al., 2013). Over the second half of the first year of life, U.S., Argentine, and Japanese mothers use language increasingly to reference the environment—to orient, comment, and prepare infants for the world outside the dyad. That is, mothers expect that their infants need to be directed more, expect that their infants know more or will better comprehend their questions, and expect that they can and should give their infants more information about the infants themselves, their mothers, and the environment. In other words, infants and their mothers appear to focus on particular kinds of activities depending on the infants' developmental level.

Advances in motor development over the first two years influences infants' opportunities for interaction, both with people and objects (Chapter 5). We emphasized the importance of self-produced locomotion in several chapters, but it is worth reiterating here, especially in light of the opportunities locomotor development affords for engaging with people (Campos et al., 2000). Once infants can reach, they can engage with the objects that others give them, and they can explore the people around them by touching parts of their bodies (putting fingers in someone's mouth and grabbing hair and jewelry are common at

Fig. 12.4 Toddler sharing with mom. (Image Courtesy of Shutterstock, Inc. Copyright: Olga Sapegina.)

this time). From a psychodynamic perspective, the onset of locomotion has been viewed as the event that breaks the symbiosis between mother and baby (Mahler et al., 1975); however, more recent views cast the onset of locomotion as changing the way mothers and babies interact (Campos et al., 2000). Once they begin to crawl and walk, infants can take more initiative in interactions, such as maintaining proximity to familiar people or moving away from parents to interact with strangers. They also begin to share. While exploring their world, they may turn to an adult, usually a parent, and show or give an object (Figure 12.4).

As infants become more independent, adults need to become more vigilant of infants' activities to protect them from harm. In addition to "baby proofing" the home, parents cue infants emotionally regarding appropriate and inappropriate activities. Often this cueing takes the form of emotional expressions and emotional vocalizations, and infants use this information in a variety of ways. **Social referencing** is one example of emotional cueing, as we discussed in Chapter 10. Social referencing involves using others' emotional expressions to understand, often ambiguous, situations (Kim & Kwak, 2010). Social referencing first appears around 8 or 9 months of age and involves awareness that adults may have valuable knowledge that infants can access and use to help regulate their own behavior in uncertain settings. For example, an infant who is exploring an unfamiliar room might be uncertain how to react when encountering an unfamiliar insect. The insect is a novel and intriguing sight, yet there is some evidence that insects intrinsically elicit wariness. To help resolve the ambiguity, infants typically look to see how their parents (or other companions) respond. If a parent appears fearful, the infant is likely to retreat, but if the parent smiles and speaks in a friendly, supportive voice, the infant is likely to approach the insect to examine it more closely.

Perception, cognition, attachment, emotion as communication, and learning are all at play in this situation. First, the infant is unable to evaluate the situation alone and so seeks clarifying information from others. Second, the infant must have the perceptual ability to detect the affective expressions of the parent: Parents of infants with sensory deficits (such as deafness) have to be much more directive, working harder to influence their babies' behavior (Meadow-Orlans, 2002). Third, if emotions did not have social communicative significance, and if the infant had not developed a sense of trust in the parents, the infant would have no reason to appraise the parents' expressions. Fourth, to ensure that the parent's expression pertains to the stimulus in question, the infant must note whether the parent is oriented toward the ambiguous stimulus. Finally, the infant must learn how to behave toward this stimulus in future encounters when the parent is unavailable: She or he needs to associate the insect with the emotional information the parent provided.

Social referencing may be developmentally important because it facilitates learning through indirect experience. By responding to and learning from the parent's emotional cues in uncertain but potentially harmful circumstances (e.g., electric outlets, noxious chemicals, or poisonous plants), infants learn to avoid these dangers without first experiencing the unpleasant consequences of direct experience with them.

The ability to use others' emotional displays as information regarding objects or events is later manifest in sensitivity to third-party displays of emotion by 18 months. For example, Repacholi and Meltzoff (2007) provided infants with the opportunity to observe experimenters engaged in a novel action with an object. During the demonstration sequence, other experimenters entered the room and displayed either angry or neutral expressions while talking to the other adults (not to the infants). In the angry condition, they said in an angry tone: "That's aggravating! That's so annoying!" Later, when infants were allowed to interact with the object, those who saw the angry interaction imitated less than those who saw the neutral interaction. Thus, not only can infants guide their actions based on emotional communication directed toward them, they can, by the middle of the second year, use information obtained from communication between others to guide their own actions.

Social referencing has powerful effects, not only on reactions to objects, but also on social behavior, such as reactions to strangers, as well. Developmental scientists have long been interested in the fact that infants in the middle of the first year often react negatively to unfamiliar adults. This common response is known as **stranger anxiety**. Theorists have proposed a variety of explanations for it. One interpretation is based on social referencing. Strangers are somewhat uncertain and ambiguous stimuli for young infants, who turn to trusted adults for emotional information about them. Infants respond less negatively, and even positively, to strangers when parents respond positively to them (Murray et al., 2008). Thus, it is not the strangers' unfamiliarity per se that elicits fearfulness in infants, but the reactions of trusted adults who are referenced by uncertain infants. When adults are positive and sociable, infants are likely to respond with greater friendliness than fearfulness.

In summary, the general answer to the question of what to interact with is pretty straightforward: people, objects, and people and objects at the same time. Adults, especially parents, direct infants toward certain types of interactions, and they provide important information in times of ambiguity. Thus, through social interactions infants learn what to interact with and what not to interact with. Combined with their understanding of how to interact, infants are in the position to develop assumptions or implicit rules that govern interactions, a topic we turn to next.

What Assumptions Govern Interactions?

Interactions with other people rely on each partner bringing expectations or assumptions to the interaction. We have already discussed some important expectations, for example that people will take turns. Other assumptions have to do with understanding of self and others. This understanding is based on inferences, such as what someone wants, desires, or believes, based on observed actions, and this understanding can be used to interpret and predict others' behavior.

Watson (1985) once observed that, in the course of their everyday experiences, infants do much more than learn simple associations. In his view, by learning that their actions (for example, crying) are associated with observable consequences (for example, being picked up) infants come to develop a sense of **effectance**, a notion we introduced in Chapter 11 that refers to recognizing that infants have some control over their environments. This rewarding realization increases infants' motivation to learn to control the environment even more. This momentous consequence of learning should not be underestimated, for it affects children's performance in many everyday situations. Effectance can thus be seen as an especially important type of motivation. It is a motivation to try to act on and alter the environment that comes from knowing that to do so successfully is, indeed, within one's grasp.

Developing Concepts of Oneself   In addition to understanding that one can affect others, infants also come to understand that they are separate from others. The development of a **sense of self** is marked by recognition of oneself in a mirror or a photograph (Amsterdam, 1972; Gallup, 1970). The mirror task, commonly referred to as the **Rouge Test**, involves placing a mark on the infant's face, usually the nose or forehead, with a substance like rouge, and then watching the infant's reaction when looking at his/her reflection in the mirror (Lewis, 2011b). Infants who have a sense of self, between 18 and 24 months of age, typically touch the mark and/or avert their eyes from their reflection while showing embarrassment or shame. Infants who have yet to develop a sense of self do not show this reaction. Instead, they continue to look at the reflection or find something else to do. The onset of the sense of self is timed with the emergence of the self-conscious or secondary emotions such as shame, pride, and guilt, as we discussed in Chapter 10, and it represents infants' realization of how the self is perceived by others (Rochat & Zahavi, 2011).

Whereas behavior in the mirror task appears to represent a full understanding of a sense of self, there are signs that some self-understanding is possible earlier than 18 to 24 months. As we discussed in Chapter 6, Morgan and Rochat (1997) showed that 3- to 5-month-old infants differentiated video images of themselves moving their legs from another infant's moving legs. In Chapter 6, we emphasized that these results indicated infants' perception of the difference between views of their leg movements that are congruent with their own actual movements from views that are incongruent with their actual movements, which in turn suggests a coordination of visual perception and felt action. These results also point to a nascent understanding of self. Because infants differentiated videos of their own leg movements from those of another, infants had to know in some way that they were viewing themselves. Another sign of the emerging sense of self is the fact that infants differentiate themselves from other objects. Consider two examples. When newborns feel a touch to their cheek, they usually move their head toward it. This action is driven by a rooting reflex, as typically the touch means food is available. Newborns differentiate between a touch from someone else versus themselves (e.g., their own finger stroking their cheek; Rochat & Hespos, 1997): They only make the head turn when someone else touches them. (This is like trying to tickle oneself; typically it does not work as well as when someone else does it.) To differentiate these two types of touches (self versus other), infants must have some understanding of their own bodies as differentiated from others. A second example pertains to infants' reaching for objects. They adjust their body posture to reach for objects, and when objects are beyond reach, they lean forward (Yonas & Hartman, 1993). Moreover, when they attempt to grasp objects, they modify their reach and hand shape in anticipation of the properties of the object (Yonas et al., 2005). In these examples, infants must have some understanding of their bodies in relation to, but yet as separate from, other objects. Rochat (2003) claimed that these behaviors require some rudimentary understanding of the self as differentiated from other people and objects, and Meltzoff (2011) suggested that the recognition that other people are "like me" develops from self-understanding and facilitates social cognition in infants.

Developing a Theory of Mind   Complementing research on the developing concepts of self and others is research on the roots of theory of mind in 3- to 5-year-old children (Doherty, 2008). **Theory of mind** is the ability to attribute mental states—beliefs, intents, desires, pretending, knowledge—to oneself and others and to understand that others have beliefs, desires, and intentions that differ from one's own (Premack & Woodruff, 1978). It has long been recognized that young children are deeply egocentric and have difficulty recognizing that others' perspectives differ from their own. Piaget wrote at length about the gradual decentration that takes place over the first years of life (Chapter 7), and Bowlby (1969; Chapter 11) described the fourth stage of attachment development as one in which children come to understand that attachment figures have goals and needs that sometimes differ from children's own concerns. Interest in the development of theory of mind grew dramatically, when Perner and his colleagues (Perner, Leekam, & Wimmer, 1987; Wimmer & Perner, 1983) showed that children under 4½ years of age, on average, strongly believe that others' perspectives are similar to their own, and they resisted efforts to demonstrate that the two might differ. In one variant of the classic procedure designed to show how children maintain such **false beliefs**, a boy was seen hiding a bar of chocolate in a jar and then leaving the room. His mother then entered the room and moved the chocolate bar into a drawer. Then, young children in the study were asked where the boy would look for the chocolate when he came back into the room. The overwhelming majority of children 4 years and younger said that the child would look in the drawer where his mother had put it. Children around 4½ years and older realized that the boy would falsely believe that the bar was in the jar where he had originally placed it and would not know where it was now located because, unlike the participants, the boy had not seen his mother move the chocolate. Numerous studies have employed variations of this procedure, many designed to simplify the task for children, and yet the age shift in false belief understanding remains around 4½ to 5 years for children from North American and European countries (Wellman, Cross, & Watson, 2001). Similar analyses comparing North American English-speaking Caucasian children and Chinese-speaking children from mainland China and Hong Kong show a similar trend in acquiring false belief understanding but with different ages of onset in different communities. Caucasian Canadian children showed earlier understanding of false belief, mainland Chinese children and U.S. Caucasian children showed similar timing, and Hong Kong Chinese children showed the latest onset (Figure 12.5; Liu, Wellman, Tardif, & Sabbagh, 2008). We return to this finding in the section on culture and social cognition.

In North American and European countries, the developmental transition between 4 to 5 years of age appears reliable. Currently, researchers debate whether or not theory-of-mind understanding is possible in infancy, and much of the argument centers on whether infants understand others' goals, intentions, beliefs, and desires (Apperly, 2012; Baillargeon, Scott, & He, 2010; Frith & Frith, 2012; Rakoczy, 2012; Stone, Carpendale, Sugarman, & Martin, 2012). Testing theory-of-mind understanding in infancy is tricky, for reasons we explained in Chapter 3. Infants do not make verbal responses, and their attention spans are short. Thus, researchers need to infer what infants are thinking about what others might be thinking.

To test theory of mind in infants, Onishi and Baillargeon (2005) adapted the traditional false belief task to a **violation of expectation** paradigm (described in Chapter 7). They presented infants an event

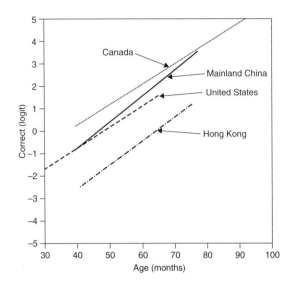

Fig. 12.5 Age of onset of false belief understanding across different Chinese and European-American communities. (From Liu et al., 2008. Copyright © 2008 by the American Psychological Association. Reproduced with permission. The use of APA information does not imply endorsement by APA.)

during the test phase that either confirmed or violated an expectation that was set up in an earlier familiarization phase. To test infants' false belief understanding, infants first saw an experimenter interact with a toy and then place it in a green box. During the experimenter's absence, the toy was moved to a yellow box. On the test trial, the experimenter returned and reached into either the yellow box (the true location of the toy) or the green box (the location where the experimenter believed the toy to be). Fifteen-month-olds looked longer when the person searched in the true location, the yellow box, rather than the false location, the green box. Onishi and Baillargeon interpreted this pattern of looking as indicating that infants understood that the experimenter still believed the object to be where she placed it, and they found it surprising when she looked in the new location. Using a similar procedure, Luo (2011) obtained similar findings with 10-month-olds.

When we consider theory of mind research across the first five years of life, we see a discontinuity. When 4-year-olds are asked where someone might search for an object that has changed location, they incorrectly report the true location of the object rather than the last location the person saw the object hidden. Yet, the findings reported by both Onishi and Baillargeon (2005) and Luo (2011) suggest that much younger infants correctly predict where someone will look for an object even though it has been moved to a new location. We are reminded here of other instances, such as searching for hidden objects (Chapter 7), in which infants appear to be smart but older children do not (Keen, 2003). One source of this discrepancy may be the use of mentalistic language in the interpretation of results from infant studies (Woodward, 2009). "Think," "know," "believe," and "desire" are terms that adults use to convey our understanding of events, but they might not be the way infants understand them. Stone and his colleagues (2012) argued that the infant may be anticipating the actions of others by associating objects, actions, and people. For example, after observing people looking at objects, infants come to expect the coupling of looking and reaching in relation to the objects without necessarily having an understanding of desire or goals.

Frith and Frith (2012) explained infant theory of mind success and 4-year-old theory of mind failure by suggesting that there are two types of mentalizing: implicit and explicit. **Implicit mentalizing**, which appears first, results from observing and interacting with others but this information is not available to conscious thought. For example, an infant who sees someone looking at an object will associate the person with the object but will not necessarily have expectations that the person *wants* the object. **Explicit mentalizing**, in contrast, is a process built on higher order understanding of thinking, both by self and other, and it is a process that involves active self-monitoring and reflection. Thus, it develops later, and it might be what is being assessed in false belief tasks presented to 3- to 5-year-old children. The two types of mentalizing suggested by Frith and Frith provide a framework for considering the discrepancies in findings between infant theory of mind competencies and the deficits seen in children just a few years older. From this perspective, it is possible that, through the development of abilities to self-monitor and reflect, infants come to understand the minds of others.

Can we be more explicit about how theory of mind might develop? A separate body of research shows that understanding of others' distinct knowledge emerges at least in part as a result of social interaction, particularly within the family. In one study of 2½-year-olds, Dunn, Brown, Slomkowski, Tesla, and Youngblade (1991) learned that children from families where there was more talk about emotions, feelings, and the psychological reasons for emotions ("I'm upset because you hurt me.") are later better able to explain others' behavior by discussing false beliefs and perspectives. These findings suggest that children might learn to respect others' perspectives because feelings and the factors affecting them are part of the ongoing discourse. Children who have siblings also understand others' perspectives better and earlier (Peterson, 2000). Furthermore, older children who have secure attachment relationships have more advanced understanding that others' beliefs might differ because they have had a greater number and variety of experiences with other people (Meins et al., 2002; Box 12.2). Presumably, securely attached infants have more interactions with adults who engage in sensitive empathic interactions that provide examples of other-oriented thinking. These experiences promote more sophisticated understanding of others' feelings and knowledge (Hobson, 2002). Therefore, social interactions with sensitive adults foster the development of social cognition. Stated differently, social interaction not only builds on earlier neurological, attentional, and perceptual tendencies but facilitates both cognitive and social development as well.

In summary, assumptions governing social interactions include understanding (1) the self as separate from other people and objects, (2) the ways the self can affect others' behavior, and (3) the way thoughts, desires, and beliefs predict behavior. Infants appear to have some rudimentary understanding in these three areas early in the first year, and experience with interacting with others fosters infants' further development.

Box 12.2 Set for Life? Understanding what Others Think

An impressive number of studies conducted over the last 40 years have shown that sensitive mothering is associated with positive outcomes for children. In this context, it is not surprising that infants who are securely attached to their mothers also develop a more mature theory of mind. Theory of mind is the ability to attribute mental states to oneself and others and to understand that others have beliefs, desires, and intentions that differ from one's own. Meins and her colleagues (2002) challenged this line of reasoning. They proposed that sensitive mothering might directly affect theory-of-mind understanding independent of its effect on security of attachment. Meins and her colleagues observed mothers interacting at home with their 6-month-old infants. Two types of sensitive behavior were rated separately—the extent to which the mothers appropriately commented on their infants' mental states (e.g., asking "Does that make you angry, sweetie?" when their infants were restrained) and the extent to which they spoke inappropriately about their infants' mental states. Security of attachment was assessed six months later, and theory-of-mind understanding was assessed at 4 years of age. Appropriate references to the infants' emotional states reflected the mothers' "mind-mindedness," and this characteristic predicted children's theory-of-mind understanding.

CULTURE AND SOCIAL COGNITION

We have seen that the development of infants' social cognition is aided by adults. Supports provided by others, such as parents, are influenced by culture (Chapter 2). Recall from Chapter 1 that there are several reasons to study development in different cultural contexts. Cross-cultural work helps to uncover universals, and it helps us to understand life forces at work in development. In other words, cross-cultural research helps us to understand the parts played by **culture-dependent** and **culture-independent** forces in development (Bornstein, 2010; Cole & Packer, 2011). We have already seen one example of cultural variation in the development of social cognition: Chinese children in Hong Kong develop theory-of-mind understanding as much as two years later than Canadian English-speaking children (Liu et al., 2008). Liu and his colleagues are not sure what accounts for this difference, but their analyses show that it is not due solely to the presence (Hong Kong) or absence (mainland China) of siblings, the presence of verb forms that cue false thinking (Chinese) or not (English), executive functioning differences among Chinese (higher) and North American (lower) children, or SES and its effect on cognitive abilities (there is no difference in vocabulary levels between Hong Kong and mainland children despite SES differences).

Additional cross-cultural work on social cognition shows that some aspects of social cognition are universal and others are not. In a study of infants in three rural cultures in Canada, Peru, and India, Callahan and her colleagues (2011) assessed a number of social cognitive skills in 9- to 24-month-olds, including gaze following behind a barrier, imitation of an intentional action, communicative pointing, and helping. The helping task involved the infant seeing the experimenter accomplish a task successfully, and then needing help reaching objects to repeat the task. If infants were responsive to the nonverbal cues, such as the experimenter looking at an out-of-reach object, and if infants understood the intentions of the experimenter, infants would reach the object and assist with the task. From 2 to 4½ years of age, children were tested for pretense, both the comprehension and production of pretend acts, and their understanding of pictorial symbols, including drawings. The inclusion of pretense and pictorial symbols was based on the researchers' belief that social cognition involves shared understanding of culturally specific symbol systems. Between 1 and 2 years of age, few differences emerged among the cultural groups in gaze following, imitation, helping, and pointing. The cultural differences that were found tended to be due to Indian infants showing slower development in imitation of an intended action and pointing between 12 and 24 months of age. By 24 months, the differences among groups had all but disappeared. At 2 and 3 years of age, children showed differences in pretense and use of pictorial symbols, with Canadian children showing earlier onset. From these findings, Callahan et al. concluded that the gaze following, imitation, pointing, and helping are foundational social cognitive skills that are universal across cultures. Unlike these foundational skills, social use of culturally specific symbol systems, such as pictorial representations and pretend play, depends more on specific cultural experiences and thus infant development across cultures differs (Bornstein, 2006c).

SUMMARY

The development of social cognition reveals the coherence of infant development and the place of infancy in human development generally. Here we have illustrated the close relations among neuroscience, perception, cognition, language, emotion, and social development in infancy. Both social and cognitive development are facilitated by perceptual strategies or predispositions characteristic of young infants. Furthermore, central aspects of personality development—the development of self-concept—and key social processes—trust in the reliability of other people, social referencing, and realization that others' perspectives and knowledge differ from ones' own—depend on the baby's cognitive understanding of relations between her or his own behavior and specific environmental consequences. Learning connections between social behaviors and social consequences can be facilitated by frequency and regularity. Awareness that others have different perspectives depends on cognitive capacity and on social interactions that prompt consideration of others' feelings and emotions. Some abilities that form the foundation for social cognition are present early in infancy and across cultures. Others take time to emerge and are more likely to depend on specific experiences.

CONCLUSIONS FOR THE READER

We have now covered a number of areas of development in the first two years of life, and we hope you have a new appreciation for what a remarkable period of life infancy is. There is tremendous growth and development from conception to 2 years of age! The newborn, who cannot communicate very well and who sleeps most of the time, changes into a toddler who appears to never stop talking or walking. This miracle of development also makes it difficult to study development because our subject matter, the growing child, is changing by month, week, or perhaps even by the day. Thus, we also hope you have an appreciation for the sophistication of the science behind the study of infant development, including the inferential nature of the work, the creative methods used to discover competencies, and the factors limiting the interpretation of findings.

In this book, we have illustrated several key themes that pervade the study and understanding of this important period in development. For example, we explored sensitive periods when discussing prenatal development and speech perception, we emphasized the interaction between nature and nurture when discussing gender socialization, language development, and visual perception, we illustrated stages of development when discussing Piaget's theory of cognitive development and attachment theory, and throughout we illustrated various aspects of stability and continuity including in information processing and temperament. Moreover, we considered the wider social contexts of development—the roles of parents, siblings, daycare workers, and culture. We also covered a number of theoretical perspectives including Piaget's theory of cognitive development, attachment, dynamic systems, and transactional theory. At this point, we encourage you to reread Chapter 1. This might seem like an odd suggestion, but we hope that reading the first chapter from your current vantage point will deepen your understanding of the important themes and theories in infancy.

We would like to leave you with a few questions stemming from our current understanding of infancy. One question, already raised in this chapter, is how to reconcile discrepancies between impressive early competencies in infancy and later poor behavior in childhood. It is undeniable that infants have many competencies, yet how do these competencies relate to behavior shown by older children, especially when older children's capacities appear more primitive than those of infants? Answers to questions of this type will involve more comprehensive longitudinal research and a clearer understanding of the phenomenon and its development. For example, what processes underlie successful search in objects, and are they the same processes that infants demonstrate in the violation of expectation paradigm and the A-not-B task? Complicating the task of understanding the phenomena and development is the fact that multiple factors can have direct or indirect effects on change. As we have seen in several areas, the infant is a dynamic being developing in an ever changing context, and many factors have the potential to impact change. Moreover, researchers need to find ways to test equivalent concepts at different ages despite the limitations in the responses that infants can make.

A second question pertains to how to foster optimal development in infancy. This question is especially important for preterm infants and atypically developing children. Better understanding of the processes of typical development will help. For example, we need to know more about the connections between neural development and behavior and how social and cultural contexts influence the ways infants are cared for and expectations parents have for their children. Moreover, we must keep in mind the interconnections between child, parent, and the environment. Bornstein (2009) illustrates this interconnection using a variant of Sameroff's (2009) transactional model (Figure 12.6). We cannot talk about fostering optimal development by focusing on only one component, such as the child or the parent. Instead we need to understand the dynamic processes amongst all three components.

These certainly are not the only questions that will guide future research on infancy. In fact, it is likely that you have already generated a list of questions of your own. It is our hope that learning about infancy has further enhanced your interest in developmental science and that you will continue to study this fascinating topic.

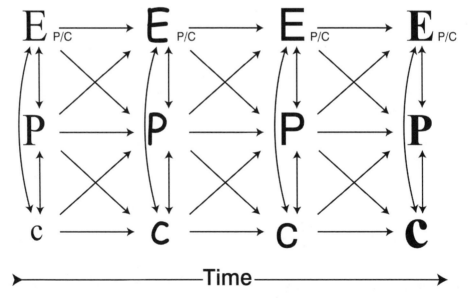

Fig. 12.6 Transactions over time involving, at the top, the changing physical and cultural environment, in the middle, the changing parent, and, at the bottom, the growing child. (From Bornstein, 2009. Copyright © 2009 by the American Psychological Association. Reproduced with permission. The use of APA information does not imply endorsement by APA.)

KEY TERMS

Culture-dependent
Culture-independent
Explicit mentalizing
False beliefs
Implicit mentalizing
Joint attention
Rouge Test

Social cognition
Specific attachments
Still-face paradigm
Stranger anxiety
Theory of mind
Violation of expectation

Glossary

Absolute threshold   The strength of a physical stimulus that is necessary to elicit a sensation of some sort.

Accommodation   The modification of an existing scheme to apply to a new situation.

Accretion-deletion of texture   When moving through the environment, closer surfaces are perceived to block more distant ones.

Action potential   The electrochemical exchange along the axon fiber.

Acuity   The ability to see fine detail.

Adaptation   The fundamental process whereby schemes are altered by experience; involves two complementary processes: assimilation and accommodation.

Adaptive responses   Actions or behaviors made by infants that promote survival. Examples include blinking, reaching, and crawling.

Affiliative system   Social behaviors at a distance, such as smiling and vocalizing.

Age-held-constant paradigm   Used to assess the influence of variables other than age on development.

Age of viability   The age at which a fetus can survive if premature birth occurs; typically within the seventh month of gestation.

Alveolars   Sounds created by placing the tongue against the ridge behind the teeth.

Amniocentesis   A procedure used to evaluate the chromosomal structure of a fetus; amniotic fluid is drawn through the abdominal wall of the mother and chemically examined.

Amodal   Perception that is not tied to a particular modality.

Amplitude   The intensity of sound waves, indicating how loud a sound is (volume).

Anal phase   A stage suggested by Freud in which activities are centered on the anus.

A-not-B error   A search task across several trials in which the object location is changed. When the object is hidden at location A, infants find it successfully. When the object is moved to a new location, B, infants search at A. Thus, infants can find the object at location A but not B.

Anoxia   Oxygen deprivation.

Apgar   A test administered to newborns to determine the need for intervention and to document normal functioning on each of five dimensions: Appearance, Pulse, Grimace, Activity, and Respiration.

Approach reflexes Concerned with intake, include breathing and rooting, sucking, and swallowing.

Arborization In reference to dendrites, the growth of spines or trees connected to neighboring cells.

Assimilated When meaning has been assigned to something according to an existing scheme.

Assimilation Processing information according to an existing scheme.

Attachments Specific, enduring, emotional bonds whose existence is of major importance in social and personality development; infant's first social relationships, often with parents.

Attachment behavior system Controls or coordinates infant activities that are most clearly and obviously related to attaining and maintaining proximity to or contact with attachment figures.

Attachment figures Preferences for interaction with certain people.

Attentional inertia The decrease in likelihood of disengagement as the duration of a look increases.

Attunement Certain experiences speed up or slow down the development of a structure or function and the final outcome is affected.

Auditory localization The utilization of sound arriving at two different times to each ear to locate its origin.

Auditory preference procedure Depending on the direction infants look, they have a choice regarding what they hear.

Auditory threshold How loud a sound has to be for a person to hear it.

Automatic elicitor An unconditioned stimulus that elicits an unconditioned response.

Autonomic In the nervous system, concerned with automatic and nonvoluntary processes.

Autonomic nervous system (ANS) An involuntary control system that operates at the level below consciousness. Responsible for heart rate, respiration, digestion, among other basic processes necessary for survival.

Autonomous attachment Adults who relate experiences and relationships in an open, fluid, objective, coherent manner, clearly value and appreciate attachment relationships, and view them as important influences on their lives.

Autonomy A stage suggested by Erikson in which the infant moves toward greater independence from the parent.

Average babies Babies that do not fit one of the other temperamental profiles (easy, difficult, or slow-to-warm-up).

Avoidance A reflex group which keep foreign substances or stimulation away from the baby.

Babble The infant's first nondistress communication.

Babinski reflex When the bottom of the baby's foot is stroked, the toes fan out.

Baby biography A psychological diary of the growth of a young child.

Basal ganglia Located at the base of the forebrain and plays a role in the control of motor behavior.

Basic level Members of a category share instrumental and usually (although not always) perceptual properties; within-category functional and perceptual similarities tend to be high, whereas between-category functional and perceptual similarities tend to be middle to low.

Bayley scales of infant development-II An age-based norm-referenced test for infant assessment.

Binocular Having two eyes.

Binocular convergence The convergence angle of the two eyes, and the disparity between the two images they yield, provides information about depth.

Binocular cues Depth cue based on the fact that our two eyes receive slightly different images of the visual world. The convergence angle of the two eyes, and the disparity between the two images they yield, provide some information about depth.

Blastocyst   The developing organism once it reaches 70–100 cells; see **zygote**.

Bottom-up approach   Focusing on the input to the senses and how the perceiver makes sense of it.

Boundaries   Regions or instances where category inclusion is marginal.

Breech   When a baby is born in an abnormal position, such as feet or buttocks first instead of head first.

Brightness   Luminance.

Broca's area   Part of the brain in the left frontal lobe that controls fluent speech.

Bronchopulmonary dysplasia   Chronic lung disease, identified by a thickening and inflammation of the walls of the lung and a reduced airway.

Canalization   Refers to the persistence of a developmental outcome despite less than optimal circumstances.

Canonical babbling   A stage in pre-speech vocalization during which infants produce repetitive sequences of vowels and consonents.

Case study   A close focus on a single individual.

Categorical perception   The propensity to treat as similar otherwise discriminable stimuli and to respond differently to another (even physically close) range of stimuli.

Categories of hue   Qualitative organization of the color spectrum (e.g., red is distinct from blue).

Categorization   The grouping of separate items into a set according to some type of property or rule.

Causal   Evidence that one event directly affects or causes another.

Cell assemblies   Units of aggregate pathways in the brain that help construct familiar perceptions.

Cell body   Component of the neuron containing the nucleus.

Central nervous system (CNS)   Consists of the brain and the spinal cord and plays a fundamental role in the control of all behavior.

Cephalocaudally   Directionality from head to tail.

Cesarean section   A surgical procedure involving cutting into the uterus to remove the baby.

Child-directed speech   Differs from and simplifies normal adult-directed speech; usually higher in pitch, exaggerated in intonation, follows a sing-song rhythm, abbreviates utterances, and repeats.

Chorionic villus sampling   A procedure for early fetal chromosomal evaluation.

Chromosomes   Contain genes that themselves are composed of chemical codes of DNA that guide development of all structure and function.

Circadian clock   An internally driven biochemical, physiological, and behavioral process that adjusts to environmental cues, such as day–night light cycles.

Classical conditioning   Relies on the existence of stimulus–response relations built into the organism (such as a loud noise causing a blink).

Cochlea   The part of the inner ear responsible for perceiving sound.

Cohort effects   When children in different age groups have experiences that render the two groups different.

Collectivist cultures   The group tends to be valued over the individual, and thus there is an emphasis on the interconnectedness of the members of the community.

Communicative intent   A purpose of language; sharing ideas and intentions.

Comorbid   Occurs simultaneously.

Compensation   The ability of some cells to substitute for others, permitting recovery of function after neuronal loss or damage.

Competence   Defines the infant's potential ability.

Conceptional age   Age or time from conception.

Conceptual organization   Organization based on knowing what objects are; relies on what they do or the roles they play in events.

Concordance Co-occurrence.

Conditioned elicitor A stimulus that has become conditioned to elicit a response.

Conditioned response A concept from classical conditioning: After repeated pairings of the unconditioned and conditioned stimulus, the conditioned stimulus begins to take on the properties of the unconditioned stimulus to elicit the same response—now called the conditioned response.

Conditioned stimulus A concept from classical conditioning: a stimulus that is initially neutral that does not elicit the unconditioned response.

Congenital Applies to structures or functions that are present at the time of birth but are not acquired by heredity.

Context-flexible words Words whose meanings are understood without environmental cues.

Context-restricted Words whose meanings are understood only in specific environments.

Continuity Consistency in average group scores on some aspect of development over time.

Converging operations The use of several different strategies to assess the same phenomenon.

Cooing The second stage of pre-speech vocalization that involves back vowels and nasals appearing together with velar consonants.

Corpus callosum A bundle of neural fibers that allows communication between the two cortical hemispheres.

Correlational An approach to evaluate developmental change and stability over time which looks for lawful relations between the growth of a structure or function and the infant's age.

Cortex Outermost layer of cortical tissue in the brain.

Cortical association areas Areas of the brain involved in higher level processes such as awareness, attention, memory, and the integration of information.

Cortical event-related potential (ERP) Measurement of electrical activity in the cortex in response to a specific event, such as a visual display or a tone.

Cortisol A substance secreted by the body at times of stress.

Co-sleeping Parent and child sleep in the same bed.

Criterion-referenced assessments Provide information about how an infant performs on a logically ordered series of items without reference to a standardization group.

Critical or sensitive period A time during which the organism is especially vulnerable to external influences that alter or modify its structures or functions, often, though not always, in irreversible fashion.

Cross-sectional designs Investigators test a group of babies at one age or compare groups of participants of different ages to determine whether and how structure and function vary depending on the age of the participants being tested.

Customary Typical of a group.

Cycle Predictable fluctuations in patterns or rhythms.

Daycare All nonparental care.

Décalage An unevenness in development across domains.

Declarative memory Memory for names, events, places, also called explicit memory.

Decontextualization Representational thinking (mental manipulation in the absence of concrete objects). See also **context-flexible words**.

Deferred imitation Infants' imitation at some delay after observing the action.

Deferred imitation tasks Tasks in which infants are asked to imitate a modeled sequence of events after a time delay.

Dendrites Part of the neuron that conducts information to the cell body.

Dendritic Pertaining to dendrites.

Dentals Sounds created by placing the tongue against the teeth.

Developmental course   Timetable for emergence and change.

Developmental psycholinguistics   Field of study focused on the development of language.

Differentiation and dynamical integration perspective   A theory proposed by Camras (2011) to explain emotional development. Specifically, she suggested that facial expressions should be viewed as a dynamical system that is itself embedded in a larger system of emotion.

Difficult babies   Babies who are negative in mood, irregular, and slow to adapt.

Directionality   A general principle of physical growth.

Directional sensitivity   Sensitivity to direction of movement.

Discriminant validity   Tests whether a measure assesses dimensions that are independent and non-overlapping.

Discrimination threshold   The amount a physical stimulus must change to yield a new sensation.

Disorganized   See **disoriented**.

Dismissing   Adults who view attachment relationships as having limited influence on their lives and appear to avoid detailed discussions of their early attachment experiences.

Disoriented   Infants simultaneously display contradictory behavior patterns, make incomplete movements, and appear confused or apprehensive about approaching their parents.

Dizygotic   Twins born from different eggs fertilized by different sperm.

Domestic diaries   Baby biographies written by mothers for their personal satisfaction.

Dose-effect relation   The function between amount of exposure to a substance, such as a medication, and the resulting effect.

Down syndrome   A disorder resulting from having an extra chromosome. See **Trisomy-21.**

Dubowitz test   Used to estimate the infant's gestational age.

Dyadic   Interactions that, for the infant, have their focus on mother and baby.

Easy babies   Babies who are positive in mood, regular in body functions, and adaptable.

Ecological validity   The extent to which an experimental situation can be generalized to natural settings and behaviors.

Ectoderm   Will form skin, sense organs, and central nervous system structures of the brain and spinal cord.

Educational diaries   Baby diaries written to explore the impact of teaching or childrearing practices on children's behavior and development.

Effectance   Behavior can affect the behavior of others or the environment in a consistent and predictable fashion.

Effectors   Nerve fibers that end in structures that allow for action, such as muscles.

Efficacy   A central parental cognition is the adult's perception of his or her abilities as a parent.

Egocentrism   Refers to infants' understanding of the world in terms of their own motor activity, and their inability to understand it from any other perspective.

Electrocardiogram   Noninvasive heart-rate monitor.

Embryo   The developing organism from approximately 2 weeks to 8 weeks prenatally.

Embryologists   Researchers of prenatal physiology.

Emotion elicitors   Internal and external events that trigger biological changes that are the basis for emotion.

Emotion receptors   Receptors in the brain that make it easier to register and encode emotion-relevant events.

Emotion states   Changes in psychophysiological activity when emotional receptors are activated.

Emotional contagion   When one spontaneously resonates with another's salient emotional expressions, most often observed in response to another's distress.

Emotional experience   The interpretation and evaluation of perceived emotional states and expressions.

Emotional expressions   Facial, gestural, and other behaviors that cue an internal feeling of affect.

Empiricists   Philosophers and scientists who believe all knowledge comes through the senses, and mental development reflects learned associations.

Encoding   Processes for the transformation of incoming information into memory.

Endoderm   Will form digestive, respiratory, and internal organs.

Endogenous   Natural to the development of the being.

Endometrium   The nutrient-rich lining of the uterus.

Epigenesis   The hypothesis that new phenomena not present in the original fertilized egg can emerge over the course of development through the interaction of preexisting elements with environmental influences.

Episodic memory   Memory of events that have been experienced.

Epistemology   Understanding where knowledge comes from and how it changes.

Equilibration   A process of adaptation to resolve contradictions between the child's comprehension of the world at any given stage and the reality in which the child lives.

Equilibrium   A state of balance between reality and a child's existing schemes.

Equipotentiality   Cells' equal potential to be sensitive to specific stimuli.

Ethologists   Researchers of animal behavior.

Event-related potential   See **cortical event-related potential**.

Expansion   See **vocal play**.

Experience-dependent processes   Involve the active formation of new synaptic connections that are a product of experience with particular individual events and thereby contribute to individuality.

Experience-expectant processes   A neural preparation for incorporating general information from the environment efficiently and satisfactorily.

Experiential age   Age since birth.

Explicit mentalizing   A meta-cognitive process that involves active self-monitoring and reflection.

Exploratory behavior system   Mediates contact with the physical or nonsocial environment.

Exploratory play   Play that appears designed to extract information about objects, what objects do, what perceivable qualities they have, and what immediate effects they can produce.

Expressive   Children with early vocabularies that consist of more pronouns and action words, and their speech uses social formulae and routines to communicate feelings and desires.

Expressive language   Production of language.

Extension problem   Generalizing the meaning of a word to other entities belonging to the same category.

External validity   Constructs investigated in one situation relate in a theoretically meaningful way to constructs assessed in another situation and perhaps at another age.

Extradyadic   Interactions in which the parent encourages the child to examine some property, object, or event in the environment.

Extrapyramidal system   Controls posture and coordination.

Eye tracking   Technological monitoring of precise eye movements.

Face validity   Measures should have an obvious, commonsense association with what they are supposed to measure.

Facilitation   Certain experiences speed up or slow down the development of a structure or function, but the final outcome is not affected.

False beliefs   Beliefs that a person believes to be true but which, in reality, are false.

Fast mapping   A process for learning words quickly by narrowing down references over multiple exposures in different contexts.

Fear/wariness system   Coordinates avoidant, wary, or fearful responses to strangers.

Fetal alcohol spectrum disorder   Broad category for birth defects due to maternal alcohol use; considered to be the leading cause of mental and growth retardation with a known etiology.

Fetal alcohol syndrome   A birth defect with patterns of malformation, growth deficiency, central nervous system dysfunction, and mental retardation.

Fetus   The developing organism from approximately 8 to 40 weeks prenatally.

Figural coherence   The perceptual grouping of elements having an invariant set of spatial relations.

Fluctuate   Type of looking pattern for infants; characterized by patterns of long and short looks across the habituation.

Frequency   The rate at which sound waves vibrate, and encodes pitch (bass to treble).

Frontal cortex   Area of the brain believed to mediate memory and cognitive skills in infants.

Functional magnetic resonance imaging (fMRI)   Identifies regions of brain activity by electronically scanning slices of the brain in different orientations and measuring subtle, ongoing changes in oxygen usage.

Functional play   Play with an object in the way the object was intended to be played with.

Functional-relational play   Play that brings together two objects in a meaningful and appropriate way (e.g., spoon and a bowl).

Functionalist theory   Emphasizes the purposes and roles of emotion in ongoing transactions between individuals and their environments.

Gametes   Reproductive cells.

Gaze following   When an infant looks in a new location based on the gaze (and sometimes head movement) of another person.

Genotype   The genetic makeup of the individual.

Gesture   A range of nonverbal supports to communication and language learning.

Goodness-of-fit   Match between the child and the developmental context.

Gyri   Protrusions in the cerebral cortex.

Habituation   The process whereby infants become bored with the stimulus, suggesting they recognize it as the same one seen previously, and their level of attention declines across repetitions. It is shown by a decline in response to a stimulus that is continuous or repeatedly presented.

Head-turning paradigm   Baby sits on a parent's lap with a loudspeaker to one side. When a sound (a tone or speech syllable) is played through the loudspeaker and the baby responds by orienting to it, the baby is rewarded by the activation of a colorful mechanical toy just above the speaker.

Hemispheric asymmetry   Differential responding across the left and right hemispheres of the cerebral cortex.

Heritable influences   Factors that distinguish one person's tendencies from another's; they are the basis of genetically rooted individual differences.

Heterotypic stability   Behavior at Time 1 is related to a different behavior at Time 2.

Hierarchical inclusiveness   The organization of more encompassing categories subsuming less encompassing ones.

Hierarchical integration   Simple skills develop separately and then become organized into more complex ones.

Homotypic stability   Behavior at Time 1 is related to the identical behavior at Time 2.

Hormones   Chemicals released by a cell or a gland in one part of the body that send out messages that affect cells in other parts of the organism.

Hue   Based on the wavelength of light; what we typically think of as color.

Ideology   Worldview of a cultural group.

Imitation   Form of learning wherein infant copies the behaviors of those around.

Immediate reference problem The problem of determining the specific referent of an utterance.

Implicit mentalizing Resulting from observing and interacting with others but this information is not available to conscious thought.

Imprint Attempt to remain close to whatever salient moving object is present.

In vitro fertilization A fertilization procedure where the egg and sperm are united outside of the mother's body and then introduced into the uterus after fertilization.

Increases then decreases Type of infant looking pattern; infant initially shows an increase in attention before a decrease.

Independence of systems Components of the human being are differentially developed at or soon after birth and grow along very different courses through the first year or two of life.

Individual differences How organisms differ from each other, resulting from their unique combination of biology and experience.

Individual variation Differences between individual infants in terms of looking time, habituation, and other developmental variables.

Individualist cultures Tend to value independence of the self more.

Induction (a) when a particular experience or set of experiences completely determines whether some aspect of development emerges; (b) using a limited set of examples to draw conclusions that permit inferences about new cases.

Infant From Latin meaning "non-speaker"; the developmental stage before a child is able to communicate verbally with those around them.

Inference Because of the lack of language, research on infants is based on deriving the meanings of their behaviors.

Initiating joint attention A form of communication in which verbal bids can be combined with nonverbal actions and nonverbal actions alone can also initiate attention.

Innate Present at birth or biologically programmed to develop at a particular time.

Insecure-ambivalent attachment Children who are unable to use their parents as secure bases from which to explore, which leads to distress by their parents' absence and ambivalent behavior on reunion.

Insecure-avoidant attachment Children who appear unconcerned by their parents' absence and actively avoid interaction when reuniting with their parents.

Insecure-resistant attachment See insecure-ambivalent.

Intensive features of temperament How strongly behaviors express themselves (amplitude) and how sensitive they are to stimulation (threshold).

Intent participation When keen observation is motivated by the expectation that at a later time the observer will be responsible for the action in question.

Interactional model Nature and nurture shape development jointly.

Interiorization Making the external world accessible to the internal.

Internal reliability Whether individuals receive the same scores on different items that tap the same dimension.

Internal validity The ability to make causal statements about whether one variable caused another to change.

Internal working model A cognitive map of the parent–child–environment interaction.

Interposition When contours of one object partially block another object from view, the first object is perceived to be closer than the second.

Interrater reliability Whether the measure provides the same score when used by different observers or raters.

Intersensory redundancy hypothesis Consists of several components, including the importance of multimodal events in capturing infant attention, which then facilitates information processing, learning, and memory of multimodal events over unimodal ones.

Intersubjectivity Shared meaning among two or more people.

Intonated babble The fifth stage of pre-speech vocalization that involves infants producing long strings of syllables having varied stress and intonation patterns.

Intraventricular hemorrhage Bleeding in the brain areas surrounding the ventricles.

Intuitive parenting Consists of behaviors enacted in a nonconscious fashion that are sensitive and developmentally suited to the ability and stage of a child.

Invisible displacements When an object that is hidden is concealed by an adult's hand during the hiding.

Israeli kibbutzim Community that practices communal childrearing.

Jargon See **intonated babble**.

Joint attention When two people, such as a child and adult, attend to an object or event at the same time.

Kinetic cues Depth information that stems from movement of the object or the observer.

Klinefelter syndrome A birth disorder in males wherein there are multiple X chromosomes (XXY as opposed to the normal XY).

Labials Sounds created by placing the two lips together.

Labor Involves involuntary uterine contractions, beginning at the top of the muscle, that literally forces the fetus out.

Limbic system A set of structures in the brain that support a variety of functions including emotions and memory.

Linear or exponential decrease Type of looking pattern for an infant; looks a lot at first and then rapidly declines.

Linear perspective Two lines that are known to be parallel in real life converge in a two-dimensional representation.

Long-term memory A function of memory that represents a seemingly limitless, permanent storehouse of knowledge.

Longitudinal designs Repeated measurement of the same infants over time and constitute a principal method of assessing development.

Looming When an object moves directly toward us on a "hit path," its image on the retina expands and we normally move to avoid the impending collision.

Magnetoencephalography (MEG) Technique used to measure cortical functioning at the scalp.

Main effects Models of development that hold that maturation or experience has obvious and direct short- and long-term consequences.

Maintenance Experience preserves an already partially or fully developed structure or function; the absence of experience will result in loss of the structure or function.

Mass-to-specific Directionality from large muscle groups to fine ones.

Material caregiving Involves the manner in which parents structure infants' physical environments (provision of toys and books and restrictions on physical freedom).

Maternal serum alphafetoprotein (MSAFP) A noninvasive measure of fetal chromosomal structure.

Maturational age Age since birth.

Meiosis Complex changes in the reproductive cells of each parent that split so as to retain half the number of chromosomes present in the original cell.

Mental representation The ability to think about objects or people, even in their absence.

Mesoderm Will form muscles, blood, and the circulatory system.

Meta-parenting Thoughtful and conscious consideration of parenting by the parent.

Metaplot Professional caregivers on kibbutzim.

Meta-representations A type of symbolic play in which representations of objects are independent of their normal meaning (e.g., when assembled, a set of blocks becomes a tower).

Mirror neurons Neurons that respond when a person observes another person making an action, typically with an object.

Modifiability In terms of cellular sensitivity, the ability for a cell to become specifically attuned to one stimulus.

Monozygotic Twins born from the same egg and fertilized by a single sperm.

Moro response The tendency to swing the arms wide and bring them together again in the midline (as if around the body of a caregiver).

Morpheme Smallest meaningful unit in language.

Motion parallax Objects that are closer to you move faster in your field of vision than objects that are farther from you.

Motor-neurological theory A theory of perceptual development stating that a few rudimentary perceptual abilities—such as the capacity to distinguish figure from ground—might be inborn.

Mullerian duct system The precursor of the internal female reproductive organs.

Mullerian inhibiting substance A hormone secreted by the testes that discourages the development of the Mullerian duct system.

Multimodal When information about objects and events is available to different sensory modalities simultaneously.

Multiple assessments The use of several different items to assess one phenomenon.

Mutual exclusivity Any given object should have only one name.

Myelin A fatty tissue that surrounds the axon of neurons and facilitates the speed of nerve conduction, rendering information transmission more efficient.

Myelinate When a neuron becomes wrapped in insulating cells called myelin.

Nativists Philosophers and scientists who believe knowledge is present at birth.

Natural experiment A study design that arises due to everyday circumstances (e.g., some children living in orphanages whereas others live with their parents).

Natural preferences Babies' individual likes and dislikes.

Near infra-red spectroscopy (NIRS) Identifies regions of brain activity by electronically scanning the brain in different orientations and measuring subtle, ongoing changes in oxygen usage.

Neonatal Behavioral Assessment Scale Evaluates the baby's neurological intactness on 18 reflex items and the baby's interactional repertoire on 27 items of information processing, motoric capacities, ability to control state, and response to stress.

Neoteny The prolongation of immaturity, especially in human beings.

Neuroendocrines Cells that are stimulated by neuronal processes to release hormones into the blood.

Neurogenesis Cell birth.

Neuron Core component of the nervous system (the brain and spinal cord). Composed of a cell body, an axon, and dendrites.

Neurotransmitters Neurochemicals that neurons use to communicate with each other.

Niche Match between an organism and its environment.

Niche picking Preferring certain environments over others, especially those settings that best suit their behavioral style.

Nominal insight Realization that things have names.

Nonshared environment   Environmental differences that act on individuals in the same situation or setting differently, such as illness.

Non-symbolic play   See exploratory play.

Normative development   Characterized by a developmental function, which reflects the changing status of infants on some aspect of development at different ages.

Norm-referenced tests   Tests that have undergone standardization on a carefully chosen, typically large reference group that represents the population of infants to be assessed by the test.

Norms   The averages for a population and their distribution.

Novelty responsiveness   The amount the infant looks at the novel stimulus relative to the familiar following habituation.

Nucleus   The region of the cell that contains the genetic material.

Nurturant caregiving   Aims at promoting infants' basic survival (providing protection, supervision, and sustenance).

Observational learning   An efficient way to learn, just by listening or watching.

Operant conditioning   Learning that involves associations between one's own action and its consequences; a naturally occurring behavior is rewarded so that it will occur more frequently.

Operant conditioning techniques   Procedures based on the principles of operant conditioning. An example is Rovee-Collier's task in which infants learn that a foot kick causes a mobile to move.

Optic flow Stimulus   Movement on the retina caused by our movement through the visual world.

Optical expansion   See **looming**.

Oral phase   A stage suggested by Freud in development in which feeding experiences and other activities are centered on the mouth.

Ovum   An unfertilized egg (female gamete).

Oxytocin   A hormone secreted by the pituitary gland which induces contractions and then labor. May also play a role in regulation of social behavior.

Palmar grasp   Babies close their fingers when something touches their palm.

Perceptual organization   Organization based on knowing what objects look like; relies heavily on the physical appearance of objects.

Performance   Concerns what infants do under certain conditions in certain contexts.

Peripheral   As part of the nervous system, includes nerves/nerve fibers.

Person permanence   The notion that people have a permanent existence independent of the infant.

Phase sequences   Perceptual experiences establish a set of memory traces in the form of neurological circuits.

Phenotype   The observed characteristics of the individual.

Phonation   The first stage of pre-speech vocalization.

Phonemes   The smallest units of sound.

Phonemics   Sounds that have linguistic meaning within specific languages.

Phonetics   All possible sounds across languages.

Phonology   Sounds that are linguistically meaningful in the language.

Phonotactic learning   See **statistical learning**.

Phonotactics   Constraints on combinations of speech sounds in words.

Physical circumstances   Environmental factors affecting how a child is reared.

Pictorial cues   See **static monocular information**.

Placenta   Connects the body of the developing organism to the body of the mother, and permits the exchange of nutrients and waste.

Plasticity   The ability to be shaped by experience, flexible or malleable.

Positron emission tomography (PET)   Measures the release of positrons that results from th decay of radioactive glucose previously injected into the bloodstream. Higher levels of positron emission take place in brain regions where higher levels of brain activity are occurring.

Postnatal The time after birth.

Postnatal age Age starting from birth.

Pragmatics The social rules that dictate our everyday usage of language.

Predictability The degree to which the infant's behaviors can be anticipated reliably from the infant's own preceding behaviors or contextual events.

Predictive validity When a measure in one domain foretells later performance in another domain.

Preference methods Methods based on infants' natural preferences; see **auditory preference procedure**.

Preferential looking Infants are given the choice of looking at two displays and their preference is recorded.

Prenatal experiences The time before birth.

Preoccupied attachment Adults who are mentally entangled, conflicted, and angry about past and present attachment relationships.

Prerepresentational thinking Thinking dependent on immediate perceptual and contextual support.

Pretend play See **representational play**.

Preterm When a baby is born before his/her due date.

Primary circular reactions Infants' tendency to repeat chance discoveries involving the coordination of two actions.

Primary emotions Emotions that are so deeply rooted in human biology that they are either innate or develop very early.

Primary representations A type of symbolic play that is based on the perceptual features of the objects.

Primitive streak The first overt stage in the development of the central nervous system.

Principles and Parameters Approach The idea that in some basic respects all languages share a set of basic rules and that grammars vary in only a restricted number of ways.

Procedural memory Memory for how to do things.

Process measures of child care contexts Measures of language-reasoning experiences, caregivers' interactional competence with the children, and the breadth and diversity of the learning curriculum.

Proprioception The sense of our body in physical space.

Prosody Rhythm.

Prototypes Best examples of a category.

Proximodistally Directionality from the center of the body outward.

Pruning The elimination of unused synapses.

Punished Negative consequence to an action; actions that are punished are less likely to be repeated.

Pyramidal system Controls precise, rapid, and skilled movements of the extremities (such as walking).

Qualitative change Change in structure or organization.

Quantitative change Changes in amount or degree.

Quasi-experiment Subjects are not randomly assigned to conditions; generally used in studies where assignment would be unethical.

Quickening Felt movement of fetus *in utero*, beginning at around 4 months gestation.

Rapid eye movements During sleep a period of dreaming referred to as REM.

Reactivity The excitability or arousability of the individual's response systems.

Readability   The definitiveness of infant behavioral signals.

Recall   A form of retrieval that requires that we remember a prior experience without the advantages of any cues.

Receptive language   Comprehension of language.

Receptors   Where sensory nerves come into contact with the external world, such as the eyes, ears, skin, nose, and taste buds.

Reciprocity   Taking turns acting and reacting to the other's behavior.

Recognition   A form of retrieval that requires only that we remember having previously experienced whatever is to be remembered, and contextual cues are provided to help with memory.

Reduplicated babbling   Identical, repetitive sequences of consonant-vowel syllables.

Reference   The link between sounds and their meaning.

Referential   Children with early vocabularies that consist of a high proportion of object labels.

Reflexes   Stimulus-dependent behaviors.

Reinforced   An event that comes after a response; behaviors that are reinforced are more likely to be repeated.

Relational play   Play that brings together two unrelated objects (e.g., a spoon and a block) with no indication of pretense.

Relative size   A pictorial cue, where two objects of known similar size are represented as different sizes; the smaller one is perceived as "farther" away.

Reliability   Consistency in measurement of the same subject.

Representational play   Play that involves the use of one object to stand for another or pretending to engage in an action.

Representational thinking   The ability to think about people and objects even in their absence.

Respiratory distress syndrome   A breathing disorder in preterm babies.

Respiratory sinus arrhythmia (RSA)   Rhythmic change in heart-rate variability.

Responding to joint attention   A form of communication in which the social partner must act in response to a verbal or nonverbal signal.

Responsiveness   Extent and quality of infant reactivity to stimulation.

Reticular formation   A subcortical structure which regulates sleep/wake patterns.

Retinopathy of prematurity   A disorder produced by excess oxygen that involves damage to the retinas, causing permanent blindness.

Retrieval   Processes used to get information out of memory.

Room sharing   Infant sleeping in her/his own bed in the parent's bedroom.

Rooting   Occurs in response to stimulation around the mouth; it involves tracking, searching, and head redirection toward the source of stimulation, and it typically concludes with sucking.

Rouge Test   A test of self-recognition that involves placing a mark on the infant's face, usually the nose or forehead, with a substance like rouge, and then watching the infant's reaction when looking at his/her reflection in the mirror.

Scaffolding   Informal teaching aids adults use in interactions with infants and children to facilitate learning.

Schemas   The signifiers or symbols that constitute mental life after the advent of representational abilities.

Scheme   A way of acting in the world; in newborns, more or less automatic motor activities.

Scientific diaries   Written to yield empirical knowledge about infant behavior and development.

Search paradigm   Techniques designed specifically to assess infant recall that involve manual actions.

Secondary circular reactions   Infants' repetition of movements that accidentally produce environmental events.

Secondary emotions   Emotions that depend on advanced developmental capacities, including milestones in cognitive development.

Secure attachment   Children who use their parents as a secure base from which they can confidently engage in interaction with other persons and explore the physical environment.

Segmentation problem   Dividing the continuous speech stream into units such as words.

Self-conscious emotions   Emotional growth that is prompted by the development of self-awareness that for the first time permits a variety of emotions such as embarrassment, shame, and later guilt and pride.

Self-efficacy   Belief in one's abilities.

Self-regulation   The processes that modulate reactivity through approach or avoidance, inhibition, or attention.

Semantic memory   Memory for facts about the world such as meanings, understandings, and concept-based information.

Semantics   The meaning of words and phrases.

Sensitive parenting   Nurturant, attentive, nonrestrictive parental care.

Sensitive period   A time during which the organism is especially vulnerable to external influences that alter or modify its structures or functions, often, though not always, in irreversible fashion.

Sensorimotor   The integration of sensory and motor processes.

Sensorimotor period   The stage which encompasses infancy in Piaget's theory during which infants learn about their world primarily through perception and action.

Sensory register   A function of memory that temporarily stores all incoming sensory information.

Sexual differentiation   The biological processes that result in the developing organism becoming a girl or a boy.

Shading   Contours of an object oriented away from a light source will appear darker than contours oriented toward the light, providing the illusion of depth.

Shape constancy   The notion that even though the image on the retina is a different shape depending on a person's distance from an object, the perceived shape of the object remains the same.

Shared environment   The environment that affects individuals similarly, such as nutrition, household, and neighborhood.

Short-term/working memory   A function of memory that has limited and momentary access to information; it is where conscious cognition takes place.

Short-term reliability   Given the same testing conditions, the same baby is likely to behave in approximately the same way on different occasions spaced reasonably close together in time.

Sign gestalt   A term used by Spitz (1963) to refer to facial features that elicit social smiles from young infants.

Size constancy   The notion that even though the image on the retina is different depending on a person's distance from an object, the perceived size of the object remains the same.

Slow-to-warm-up babies   Babies who are negative in mood, slow to adapt, and withdraw from new situations.

Somesthetic   The system which regulates temperature, tactile, and positional information.

Social caregiving   Parental efforts to involve infants in interpersonal exchanges (soothing, touching, smiling, and vocalizing).

Social cognition   The ways that young infants perceive and understand social interaction, the people with whom they interact, and the differences between others' perspectives and knowledge and the infant's own.

Social referencing   The deliberate search for information from other people to help clarify uncertain events.

Social releaser   A stimulus that elicits a social response in another person, such as configuration of facial features of a face that elicits a baby's smile.

Somatic   A division of the nervous system comprised of voluntary conscious functions.

Species-typical tendencies   Tendencies and heritable influences that are found within one species.

Specific attachments   The ability to become familiar with specific people across a variety of interactions and contexts.

Specificity principle   States that specific forms of parenting at specific times shape specific infant abilities in specific ways.

Speech spectrograph   A display that breaks up the speech signal into frequency components.

Stability   Consistency over time in the relative ranking of individuals in a group.

Static monocular information   Depth information that is available when looking at a distance or with one eye without the observer or the object moving.

Statistical learning   Learning based on extracting regularities in patterns.

Statistically normal   A distribution of scores that show a pattern like a bell-shaped curve.

Still-face paradigm   A procedure which disrupts the normal course of interaction when an adult, typically the mother, does not respond to the social bids of the infant.

Strange Situation   Popular technique to study attachment that is designed to expose infants to increasing amounts of stress to observe how they organize their attachment behaviors around their parents when distressed.

Stranger anxiety   When infants react negatively to unfamiliar adults.

Structural measures of child care contexts   Measures of group size, teacher–child ratios, and teacher training.

Structural theories   Theories that define emotions in terms of their component processes and focus on identifying the range of emotions that developing individuals can experience at different ages depending on underlying physiological, cognitive, and experiential processes.

Structure dependence   The idea that grammatical rules are defined not only over words, but also over syntactic phrases such as noun phrases.

Study time   The amount of time given to study items in a test of memory.

Subcortical structures   Phylogenetically older parts of the brain that are beneath the cortex.

Subjective contours   Perception of an edge or boundary in the absence of physical stimulation.

Subordinate level   Members of a category share both instrumental and perceptual similarity, which tend to be high; however, between-category instrumental and perceptual similarity (for categories nested within the same basic level) also tend to be high.

Sudden infant death syndrome (SIDS)   The unexpected and unexplained death of an infant younger than 1 year of age.

Sulci   Indentations in the cerebral cortex.

Superordinate or global level   Category members are grouped functionally and share some perceptual attributes; thus, within-category functional similarity tends to be high, and perceptual similarity middle to high, whereas between-category functional and perceptual similarity tend to be low.

Surfactin   A soapy substance that coats the lungs and facilitates the exchange of oxygen from the air.

Symbolic play   A form of play that takes on more of a non-literal quality (e.g., using a stick as gun).

Synapses   Connections between axons and dendrites which are necessary for communication between neurons.

Synaptogenesis   Growth of the synapses.

Syntactic structures   Grammatical components, such as noun phrases and clauses.

Syntax Grammar or the rules for combining words into meaningful communications.

Systems models A dynamic view of development in that the organization of the system as a whole changes as the infant matures and acquires new experiences.

Tabula rasa Means "blank slate"; refers to the idea that infants come into the world with no preconceived knowledge.

Taxonomic constraint Interpret new words as referring, not only to the object that they first see labeled with a word, but other objects that are the same kind of thing.

Temperament The biologically based source of individual differences in behavioral functioning that tend to be stable over time.

Temporal features of temperament The speed with which behaviors begin after stimulation (latency), how rapidly they escalate (rise time), how long they last (duration), and how slowly they go away (decay or recovery).

Teratogens Harmful factors to the fetus.

Tertiary circular reactions When an infant accidentally causes an event, and then intentionally repeats the event, systematically and deliberately varying the manner in which it was brought about.

Test-retest reliability Whether a measure provides the same score across repeated testing.

Texture gradients Signal depth when the elements of the textured surface gradually reduce in size.

Theory of mind The ability to attribute mental states—beliefs, intents, desires, pretending, knowledge—to oneself and others and to understand that others have beliefs, desires, and intentions that are different from one's own.

Time-based records Assessments based on frequency, duration, and/or contingency of certain behaviors.

Top-down approach Perceiver relies on higher cognitive processes instead of sensory input.

Transactional perspective or model Inherent characteristics are shaped by experience and vice versa, thus parent and infant alike influence development across time.

Transactional principle States that infants shape their experiences with parents just as they are shaped by those experiences.

Transitional probabilities The likelihood of combinations of sounds and words in a language.

Trisomy-21 A disorder resulting from having an extra chromosome, also known as **Down syndrome**.

Trust The idea that someone can be counted on to respond when signaled.

Trust or mistrust A stage suggested by Erikson in which parent–child relationships center on building on mutual dependability.

Turn taking The ability to alternate timing factors in conversations when speaking or interacting in some form.

Turner syndrome A female birth disorder where the female has only one X chromosome (as opposed to the normal XX).

Ultrasound imaging A noninvasive fetal assessment tool. Sounds are sent into the pregnant woman's body from a probe applied to the abdominal skin. A computer analyzes pulses that are reflected back and uses them to map structures within the body.

Umbilical cord Contains channels which allow the exchange of nutrients and waste between the fetus and the mother.

Unconditioned response A concept from classical conditioning; automatic response to the unconditioned stimulus.

Unconditioned stimulus A concept from classical conditioning; a stimulus which elicits a response in the absence of any learning or conditioning.

Universal grammar The idea that syntax is innate.

Unresolved attachment   Parents who give evidence of mental disorganization over abuse or loss, indicating that such events continue to have a major disorganizing influence on the quality of their thinking and discourse.

Uzgiris-Hunt Ordinal Scales of Psychological Development   Criterion-based test which assesses infant performance on a variety of Piagetian-based tasks.

Vagal tone   A reflection of heart-rate changes mediated by the vagus nerve and controlled by the parasympathetic branch of the autonomic nervous system.

Validity   When an instrument measures what it was designed to measure.

Velars   Sounds created by placing the tongue against the roof of the mouth.

Variegated babbling   Sequences of different consonants and vowels.

Viewpoint invariance   The understanding that an object viewed from different viewpoints is still the same object.

Violation of expectation   Experimental method wherein the infant shows longer looking to an event that is unusual or one that the infant was not prepared for (such as two objects occupying the same space at the same time).

Vocabulary burst   Rapid increases in both production and comprehension of words.

Vocal play   The third stage of pre-speech vocalization that involves the appearance of syllable-like productions with long vowels.

Voicing   When a speaker produces different frequencies of sound waves at slightly different times.

Visual acuity   The ability to see fine detail.

Visual cliff   Used to test infant depth perception; one side of a table only appears to drop off and the other does not.

Wernicke's area   A part of the brain in the left temporal lobe that involves comprehension.

White-matter fiber tracts   Bundles of myelinated axons.

Whole object assumption   When a label is taken to refer to a whole object, and not to its parts, substance, or other properties.

Wolffian duct system   The precursor to male internal reproductive organs.

Zone of proximal development   Problem solving alongside a more skilled partner allows the child to perform at a higher level than he/she would have if working alone. The difference between children's spontaneous performance on a task without guidance and that observed with guidance is the zone of proximal development.

Zygote   The developing organism from approximately conception to 2 weeks prenatally.

References

Abramovitch, R., Corter, C., & Lando, B. (1979). Sibling interaction in the home. *Child Development, 50*, 997–1003.

Adams, J., Sibbritt, D., & Lui, C. (2011). The use of complementary and alternative medicine during pregnancy: A longitudinal study of Australian women. *Birth, 38*, 200–206.

Adams, R. J., Courage, M. L., & Mercer, M. E. (1994). Systematic measurement of human neonatal color vision. *Vision Research, 34*, 1691–1701.

Adolph, K. E., & Berger, S. E. (2011). Physical and motor development. In M. H. Bornstein & M. E. Lamb (Eds.), *Developmental science: An advanced textbook* (6th ed., pp. 241–302). New York, NY: Psychology Press.

Adolph, K. E., Joh, A. S., & Eppler, M. A. (2010). Infants' perception of affordances of slopes under high- and low-friction conditions. *Journal of Experimental Psychology: Human Perception and Performance, 36*, 797–811.

Aguiar, A., & Baillargeon, R. (2002). Developments in young infants' reasoning about occluded objects. *Cognitive Psychology, 45*, 267–336.

Ahnert, L., Gunnar, M., Lamb, M. E., & Barthel, M. (2004). Transition to child care: Associations of infant-mother attachment, infant negative emotion and cortisol elevations. *Child Development, 75*, 639–650.

Ahnert, L., & Lamb, M. E. (2000). Infant-care provider attachments in contrasting German child care settings II: Individual-oriented care after German reunification. *Infant Behavior and Development, 23*, 211–222.

Ahnert, L., Pinquart, M., & Lamb, M. E. (2006). Security of children's relationships with non-parental care providers: A meta-analysis. *Child Development, 74*, 664–679.

Ahnert, L., Rickert, H., Lamb, M. E. (2000). Shared caregiving: Comparisons between home and child care settings. *Developmental Psychology, 36*, 339–351.

Ainsworth, M. (1967). *Infancy in Uganda.* Baltimore, MD: The Johns Hopkins University Press.

Ainsworth, M. D. S. (1973). The development of infant-mother attachment. In B. M. Caldwell & H. N. Ricciuti (Eds.), *Review of child development research* (Vol. 3). Chicago, IL: University of Chicago Press.

Ainsworth, M. D. S. (1989). Attachments beyond infancy. *American Psychologist, 44*, 709–716.

Ainsworth, M. D. S., Blehar, M. C., Waters, E., & Wall, S. (1978). *Patterns of attachment: A psychological study of the Strange Situation.* Hillsdale, NJ: Erlbaum.

Ainsworth, M. D. S., & Wittig, B. A. (1969). Attachment and exploratory behavior of one-year-olds in a strange situation. In B. M. Foss (Ed.), *Determinants of infant behavior* (Vol. 4, pp. 111–136). London: Routledge Methuen.

Alessandri, S. M., Sullivan, M. W., & Lewis, M. (1990). Violation of expectancy and frustration in early infancy. *Developmental Psychology, 26*, 738–744.

Alexander, G. M., & Saenz, J. (2011). Postnatal testosterone levels and temperament in early infancy. *Archive of Sexual Behavior, 40*, 1287–1292.

Alexander, G. R., & Slay, M. (2002). Prematurity at birth: Trends, racial disparities, and epidemiology. *Mental Retardation and Developmental Disabilities Research Reviews, 8*, 215–220.

Alkon, A., Boyce, W. T., Davis, N. V., & Eskenazi, B. (2011). Developmental changes in autonomic nervous system resting and reactivity measures in Latino children from 6 to 60 months of age. *Journal of Developmental and Behavioral Pediatrics, 32*, 668–677.

Allam, M. D., Marlier, L., & Schaal, B. (2006). Learning at the breast: Preference formation for an artificial scent and its attraction against the odor of maternal milk. *Infant Behavior and Development, 29*, 308–321.

American Academy of Pediatrics Committee on Public Education. (2001). Children, adolescents, and television. *Pediatrics, 107*, 423–426.

American Dietetic Association (2002). Position of the American Dietetic Association: Nutrition and lifestyle for a healthy pregnancy outcome. *Journal of the American Dietetic Association, 102*, 1479–1490.

Amsterdam, B. (1972). Mirror self-image reactions before age two. *Developmental Psychobiology, 5*, 297–305.

Anastasi, A. (1958). Heredity, environment, and the question, "how?" *Psychological Review, 65*, 197–208.

Anderson, S. E., & Whitaker, R. C. (2011). Attachment security and obesity in US preschool-aged children. *Archives of Pediatrics & Adolescent Medicine, 165*, 235–242.

Anzures, G., Pascalis, O., Quinn, P. C., Slater, A. M., & Lee, K. (2011). Minimizing skin color differences does not eliminate the own-race recognition advantage in infants. *Infancy, 16*, 640–654.

Apgar, V. A. (1953). Proposal for a new method of evaluation of the newborn infant. *Anesthesia and Analgesia, Current Researches, 22*, 260.

Apperly, I. A. (2012). What is "theory of mind?" Concepts, cognitive processes and individual differences. *Quarterly Journal of Experimental Psychology, 65*, 825–839.

Archer, J. (2006). Testosterone and human aggression: An evaluation of the challenge hypothesis. *Neuroscience and Biobehavioral Review, 30*, 219–345.

Arnon, S., Anat, S., Forman, L., Regev, R., Bauer, S., et al. (2006). Live music is beneficial to preterm infants in the neonatal intensive care unit environment. *Birth: Issues in Perinatal Care, 33*, 131–136.

Arterberry, M. E. (2001). Perceptual unit formation in infancy. In T. F. Shipley & P. J. Kellman (Eds.), *From fragments to objects: Segmentation and grouping in vision* (pp. 37–69). Amsterdam, Netherlands: Elsevier North Holland.

Arterberry, M. E. (2008). Infants' sensitivity to the depth cue of height-in-the-picture-plane. *Infancy, 13*, 544–555.

Arterberry, M. E., & Bornstein, M. H. (2001). Three-month-old infants' categorization of animals and vehicles based on static and dynamic attributes. *Journal of Experimental Child Psychology, 80*, 333–346.

Arterberry, M. E., & Bornstein, M. H. (2002). Variability and its sources in infant categorization. *Infant Behavior and Development, 25*, 515–528.

Arterberry, M. E., & Bornstein, M. H. (2012). Categorization of real and replica objects by 14- and 18-month-old infants. *Infant Behavior and Development, 35*, 606–612.

Arterberry, M. E., Midgett, C., Putnick, D. L., & Bornstein, M. H. (2007). Early attention and literacy experience predict adaptive communication. *First Language, 27*, 175–189.

Arterberry, M. E., & Yonas, A. (2000). Perception of structure from motion by 8-week-old infants. *Perception and Psychophysics, 62*, 550–556.

Aslin, R. N. (1981). Experiential influences and sensitive periods in perceptual development: A unified model. In R. N. Aslin, J. R. Alberts, & M. R. Peterson (Eds.), *Development of perception: Psychobiological perspectives: The visual system* (Vol. 2). New York, NY: Academic Press.

Aslin, R. N. (2012). Infant eyes: A window on cognitive development. *Infancy, 17*, 126–140.

Aslin, R. N., & Newport, E. L. (2009). What statistical learning can and can't tell us about language acquisition. In J. Colombo, P. McCardle, & L. Freund (Eds.), *Infant pathways to language* (pp. 15–29). New York, NY: Psychology Press.

Atran, S. (1990). *Cognitive foundations of natural history: Towards an anthropology of science.* New York, NY: Cambridge University Press.

Aydin, M., Kabakus, N., Balci, T., & Ayar, A. (2007). Correlative study of the cognitive impairment, regional cerebral blood flow, and electroencephalogram abnormalities in children with Down's syndrome. *International Journal of Neuroscience, 117*, 327–336.

Aylward, G. P. (2005). Neurodevelopmental outcomes of infants born prematurely. *Journal of Developmental and Behavioral Pediatrics, 26*, 427–440.

Bahrick, L. E. (2004). The development of perception in a multimodal environment. In G. Bremner & A. Slater (Eds.), *Theories of infant development* (pp. 90–120). Malden, MA: Blackwell Publishing.

Bahrick, L. E. (2006). Up versus down: The role of intersensor redundancy in the development of infants' sensitivity to the orientation of moving objects. *Infancy, 9*, 73–96.

Bahrick, L. E., & Lickliter, R. (2000). Intersensory redundancy guides attentional selectivity and perceptual learning in infancy. *Developmental Psychology, 36*, 190–201.

Bahrick, L. E., Lickliter, R., Castellanos, I., & Vaillant-Molina, M. (2010). Increasing task difficulty enhances effects of intersensory redundancy: Testing a new prediction of the intersensory redundancy hypothesis. *Developmental Science, 13*, 731–737.

Bahrick, L. E., Lickliter, R., & Flom, R. (2006). Up versus down: The role of intersensory redundancy in the development of infants' sensitivity to the orientation of moving objects. *Infancy, 9*, 73–96.

Bahrick, L. E., & Watson, J. S. (1985). Detection of intermodal proprioceptive-visual contingency as a potential basis of self-perception in infancy. *Developmental Psychology, 21*, 963–973.

Bailey, D. B., Jr., & Bruer, J. T. (Eds.) (2001). *Critical thinking about critical periods.* Baltimore, MD: Paul H. Brookes.

Baillargeon, R., Li, J., Gertner, Y., & Wu, D. (2010). How do infants reason about physical events? In U. Goswami (Ed.), *The Wiley-Blackwell Handbook of Childhood Cognitive Development* (pp. 11–48). Malden, MA: Wiley-Blackwell.

Baillargeon, R., Scott, R. M., & He, Z. (2010). False belief understanding in infants. *Trends in Cognitive Sciences, 14*, 110–118.

Baillargeon, R., Spelke, E. S., & Wasserman, S. (1985). Object permanence in 5-month-old infants. *Cognition, 20*, 191–208.

Baio, J. (2012). Prevalence of autism spectrum disorders—autism and developmental disabilities monitoring network, 14 sites, United States, 2008. *Center for Disease Control and Prevention Morbidity and Mortality Weekly Report*, http://www.cdc.gov/mmwr/preview/mmwrhtml/ss6103a1.htm?s_cid=ss6103a1_w.

Bakermans-Kranenburg, M. J., van IJzendoorn, & Kroonenberg, P. M. (2004). Differences in attachment security between African-American and white children: Ethnicity or socio-economic status? *Infant Behavior and Development, 27*, 417–433.

Balas, B., Westerlund, A., Hung, K., & Nelson, C. A. (2011). Shape, color and the other-race effect in the infant brain. *Developmental Science, 14*, 892–900.

Baldwin, D. A., Markman, E. M., Bill, B., Desjardins, R. N., & Irwin, J. M. (1996). Infants' reliance on a social criterion for establishing word-object relations. *Child Development, 67*, 3135–3153.

Baldwin, J. M. (1895). In *Mental development in the child and the race: Method and processes.* New York, NY: Macmillan Publishing.

Bandstra, E. S., Morrow, C. M., Mansoor, E., & Accornero, V. H. (2010). Prenatal drug exposure: Infant and toddler outcomes. *Journal of Addictive Diseases, 29*, 245–258.

Bandura, A. (1969). *Principles of behavior modification.* Oxford, UK: Holt, Rinehart, & Winston.

Banks, M. S., & Munsinger, H. (1974). Pupillometric measurement of difference spectra for three color receptors in an adult and a four-year-old. *Vision Research, 14*, 813–817.

Barbaro, K. D., Chiba, A., & Deák, G. O. (2011). Micro-analysis of infant looking in a naturalistic social setting: Insights from biologically based models of attention. *Developmental Science, 14*, 1150–1160.

Barker, B. A., & Newman, R. S. (2004). Listen to your mother! The role of talker familiarity in infant streaming. *Cognition, 94*, B45–B53.

Barna, J., & Legerstee, M. (2005). Nine- and twelve-month-old infants related emotions to people's actions. *Cognition and Emotion, 19*, 53–67.

Barnard, K. E., & Solchany, J. E. (2002). Mothering. In M. H. Bornstein (Ed.), *Handbook of parenting: Being and becoming a parent* (2nd ed., Vol. 3, pp. 3–25). Mahwah, NJ: Erlbaum.

Barr, R., & Hayne, H. (2000). Age-related changes in imitation: Implications for memory development. In C. Rovee-Collier, L. Lipsitt, & H. Hayne (Eds.), *Progress in infancy research* (Vol. 1, pp. 21–67). Mahwah, NJ: Erlbaum.

Barr, R. G., Hopkins, B., & Green, J. A. (Eds.). (2000). Crying as a sign, a symptom, and a signal: Clinical, emotional, and developmental aspects of infant and toddler crying. London: Mac Keith Press.

Barr, R., Rovee-Collier, C., & Learmonth, A. (2011). Potentiation in young infants: The origin of the prior knowledge effect? *Memory and Cognition, 39*, 625–636.

Barr, R., Zack, E., Garcia, A., & Muentener, P. (2008). Infants' attention and responsiveness to television increases with prior exposure and parental interaction. *Infancy, 13*, 30–56.

Barrett, T. M., Traupman, E., & Needham, A. (2008). Infants' visual anticipation of object structure in grasp planning. *Infant Behavior and Development, 31*, 1–9.

Batty, M., & Taylor, M. J. (2006). The development of emotional face processing during childhood. *Developmental Science, 9*, 207–220.

Bauer, P. J. (2009). The cognitive neuroscience of the development of memory. In M. L. Courage & N. Cowan (Eds.), *The development of memory in infancy and childhood* (pp. 115–144). New York, NY: Psychology Press.

Baxter, J. (2011). Flexible work hours and other job factors in parental time with children. *Social Indicators Research, 101*, 239–242.

Bayley, N. (1933). *Bayley scales of infant development* (2nd ed., manual). Orlando, FL: Psychological Corporation.

Bayley, N. (1949). Consistency and variability in the growth of intelligence from birth to eighteen years. *Journal of Genetic Psychology, 75*, 165–196.

Bayley, N. (1969). *Bayley scales of infant development.* New York, NY: Psychological Press.

Bayley, N. (1993). *Bayley scales of infant development* (2nd ed.). Orlando, FL: The Psychological Corporation.

Bear, G. G., Manning, M. A., & Izard, C. E. (2003). Responsible behavior: The importance of social cognition an emotion. *School Psychology Quarterly*, *18*, 140–157.

Behrens, K. Y. (2004). A multifaceted view of the concept of Amae: Reconsidering the indigenous Japanese concept of relatedness. *Human Development*, *47*, 1–27.

Behrens, K. Y. (2010). Amae through the eyes of Japanese mothers: Redefining differences and similarities between attachment and amae. In P. Erdman & K.-M. Ng (Eds.), *Attachment* (pp. 55–69). New York, NY: Taylor and Francis Group.

Behrens, K. Y., Hesse, E., & Main, M. (2007). Mothers' attachment status as determined by the adult attachment interview predicts their 6-year-olds' reunions responses: A study conducted in Japan. *Developmental Psychology*, *43*, 1553–1567.

Behrman, R. E., & Butler, A. S. (Eds.). (2006). *Preterm birth: Causes, consequences, and prevention.* Washington, DC: National Academies Press.

Beier, J. S., & Spelke, E. S. (2012). Infants developing understanding of social gaze. *Child Development*, *83*, 486–496.

Belfort, M. B., Martin, C. R., Smith, V. C., Gillman, M. W., McCormick, M. C., et al. (2010). Infant weight gain and school-age blood pressure and cognition in former preterm infants. *Pediatrics*, *125*, s1419–s1426.

Bell, M. A. (2012). A psychobiological perspective on working memory performance at 8 months of age. *Child Development*, *83*, 251–265.

Belsky, J., & Barends, N. (2002). Personality and parenting. In M. H. Bornstein (Ed.), *Handbook of parenting: Status and social ecology of parenting* (Vol. 3, pp. 415–438). Mahwah, NJ: Erlbaum.

Belsky, J., Goode, M. K., & Most, R. K. (1980). Maternal stimulation and infant exploratory competence: Cross-sectional, correlational, and experimental analyses. *Child Development*, *51*, 1168–1178.

Belsky, J., Vandell, D. L., Burchinal, M., Clarke-Stewart, K., McCartney, K., Owne, M. T., et al. (2007). Are there long-term effects of early child care? *Child Development*, *78*, 681–701.

Benasich, A. A., Choudhury, N., Friedman, J. T., Realpe-Bonilla, T., Chojnowska, C., et al. (2006). The infant as a prelinguistic model for language learning impairments: Predicting from event-related potentials to behavior. *Neuropsychologia*, 44, 396–411.

Benasich, A. A., & Tallal, P. (2002). Infant discrimination of rapid auditory cues predicts later language impairment. *Behavioural Brain Research*, *136*, 31–49.

Benedict, H. (1979). Early lexical development: Comprehension and production. *Journal of Child Language*, *6*, 183–200.

Benenson, J. F., Tennyson, R., & Wrangham, R. W. (2011). Male more than female infants imitate propulsive motion. *Cognition*, *121*, 262–267.

Berg, W. K., & Berg, K. M. (1987). Psychophysiological development in infancy: State, startle, and attention. In J. D. Osofsky (Ed.), *Handbook of infant development* (2nd, ed., pp. 238–317). New York: Wiley.

Berger, R. P., Fromkin, J. B., Stutz, H., Makoroff, K., Scribano, P. V., Feldman, K., et al. (2011). Abusive head trauma during a time of increased unemployment: A multicenter analysis. *Pediatrics*, *128*, 637–643.

Bergström, R. M. (1969). An entropy model of the developing brain. *Developmental Psychobiology*, *2*, 139–152.

Berkeley, G. (1709/1910). *Essay towards a new theory of vision.* London, UK: Dutton.

Berlin, B., Breedlove, D. E., & Raven, P. H. (1973). General principles of classification and nomenclature in folk biology. *American Anthropologist*, *75*, 214–242.

Bernier, A., Ackerman, J. P., & Stovall-McClough, K. C. (2004). Predicting the quality of attachment relationships in foster care dyads from infants' initial behaviors upon placement. *Infant Behavior and Development*, *27*, 366–381.

Bertenthal, B. I., Longo, M. R., & Kenny, S. (2007). Object permanence and the development of predictive tracking in infancy. *Child Development, 78*, 350–363.

Bertenthal, B. I., Proffit, D. R., & Cutting, J. E. (1984). Infant sensitivity to figural coherence in biomechanical motions. *Journal of Experimental Child Psychology, 37*, 213–230.

Berthier, N. E., & Carrico, R. L. (2010). Visual information and object size in infant reaching. *Infant Behavior and Development, 33*, 555–566.

Bhatt, R. S., Bertin, E., Hayden, A., & Reed, A. (2005). Face perception in infancy: Developmental changes in the use of different kinds of relational information. *Child Development, 76*, 169–181.

Bigelow, A. E., Littlejohn, M., Bergman, N., & McDonald, C. (2010). The relation between early mother-infant skin-to-skin contact and later maternal sensitivity in South African mothers of low birth weight infants. *Infant Mental Health Journal, 31*, 358–377.

Bigelow, A. E., & Rochat, P. (2006). Two-month-old infants' sensitivity to social contingency in mother-infant and stranger-infant interaction. *Infancy, 9*, 313–325.

Birtles, D., Braddick, O. J., Wattam-Bell, J., Wilkinson, A. R., & Atkinson, J. (2007). Orientation and motion-specific visual cortex responses in infants born preterm. *NeuroReport, 18*, 1975–1979.

Bischof-Koehler, D. (1991). The development of empathy in infants. In M. E. Lamb & H. Keller (Eds.), *Infant development: Perspectives from German-speaking countries* (pp. 245–273). Hillsdale, NJ: Erlbaum.

Bishop, E. G., Cherny, S. S., Corley, R., Plomin, R., DeFries, J. C., & Hewitt, J. K. (2003). Development genetic analysis of general cognitive ability from 1 to 12 years in a sample of adoptees, biological siblings, and twins. *Intelligence, 13*, 31–49.

Black, M. M., Hess, C., & Berenson-Howard, J. (2000). Toddlers from low-income families have below normal mental, motor, and behavior scores on the Revised Bayley Scales. *Journal of Applied Developmental Psychology, 21*, 655–666.

Black, M. M., & Matula, K. (2000). *Essentials of Bayley scales of infant development—Assessment.* New York, NY: John Wiley & Sons.

Blakemore, C., & Mitchell, D. E. (1973). Environmental modification of the visual cortex and the neural basis of learning and memory. *Nature, 241*, 467–468.

Blakemore, J. E., Berenbaum, S. A., & Liben, L. S. (2009). *Gender development.* New York, NY: Psychology Press.

Blasi, A., Mercure, E., Lloyd-Fox, S., Thomson, A., Brammer, M., Sauter, D., et al. (2011). Early specialization for voice and emotion processing in the infant brain. *Current Biology, 21*, 1220–1224.

Blass, E. M., & Camp, C. A. (2001). The ontogeny of face recognition: Eye contact and sweet taste induce face preference in 9- and 12-week-old human infants. *Developmental Psychology, 37*, 762–774.

Blass, E. M., Ganchrow, J. R., & Steiner, J. E. (1984). Classical conditioning in newborn humans 2–48 hours of age. *Infant Behavior and Development, 7*, 223–235.

Block, R. W., & Block, S. A. (1980). Outreach education: A possible preventer of teenage pregnancy. *Adolescence, 15*, 657–660.

Bloom, B. S. (1964). *Stability and change in human characteristics.* New York, NY: Wiley.

Bloom, K. (1979). Evaluation of infant vocal conditioning. *Journal of Experimental Child Psychology, 27*, 60–70.

Bloom, K., Russell, A., & Wassenberg, K. (1987). Turntaking affects the quality of infant vocalizations. *Journal of Child Language, 14*, 211–227.

Bloomfield, L. (1933). *Language.* Oxford, UK: Holt.

Booth, A. E., Pinto, J., & Bertenthal, B. I. (2002). Perception of the symmetric patterning of human gait by infants. *Developmental Psychology, 38*, 554–563.

Booth, A. E., & Waxman, S. R. (2009). A horse of a different color: Specifying with precision infants' mappings of novel nouns and adjectives. *Child Development, 80*, 15–22.

Booth, C. L., Clarke-Stewart, K. A., Vandell, D. L., McCartney, K., & Owen, M. T. (2002). Child-care usage and mother-infant "quality time." *Journal of Marriage and Family, 64*, 16–26.

Borkowski, J. G., Farris, J. R., Whitman, T. L., Weed, K., & Keogh, D. A. (2007). *Risk and resilience: Adolescent mothers and their children grow up*. Mahwah, NJ: Erlbaum.

Bornstein, M. H. (1981). Psychological studies of color perception in human infants: Habituation, discrimination and categorization, recognition, and conceptualization. *Advances in Infancy Research, 1*, 1–40.

Bornstein, M. H. (1984). A descriptive taxonomy of psychological categories used by infants. In C. Sophian (Ed.), *Origins of cognitive skills* (pp. 313–338). Hillsdale, NJ: Erlbaum.

Bornstein, M. H. (1989). Sensitive periods in development: Structural characteristics and causal interpretations. *Psychological Bulletin, 105*, 179–197.

Bornstein, M. H. (2001). Arnold Lucius Gesell. *Pediatrics and Related Topics/Pädiatrie und Grenzgebiete, 40*, 395–409.

Bornstein, M. H. (2002). Parenting infants. In M. H. Bornstein (Ed.), *Handbook of parenting* (2nd ed., Vol. I, pp. 3–43). Mahwah, NJ: Erlbaum.

Bornstein, M. H. (2006a). Parenting science and practice. In K. A. Renninger & I. E. Sigel (Eds.), W. Damon (Series Ed.), *Handbook of child psychology: Child psychology in practice* (6th ed., Vol. 4, pp. 893–949). Hoboken, NJ: Wiley.

Bornstein, M. H. (2006b). Hue categorization and color naming: Physics to sensation to perception. In N. J. Pitchford & C. P. Biggam (Eds.), *Progress in colour studies: Psychological aspects* (Vol. 2, pp. 35–68). Philadelphia, PA: John Benjamins.

Bornstein, M. H. (2006c). On the significance of social relationships in the development of children's earliest symbolic play: An ecological perspective. In A. Göncü & S. Gaskins (Eds.), *Play and development: Evolutionary, sociocultural, and functional perspectives* (pp. 101–129). Mahwah, NJ: Erlbaum.

Bornstein, M. H. (2007). Hue categorization and color naming: Cognition to language to culture. In R. E. MacLaury, G. V. Paramei, & D. Dedrick (Eds.), *Anthropology of color: Interdisciplinary multilevel modeling* (pp. 3–27). Philadelphia, PA: John Benjamins.

Bornstein, M. H. (2009). Toward a model of culture-parent-child transactions. In A. Sameroff (Ed.), *The transactional model of development: How children and contexts shape each other* (pp. 139–161). Washington, DC: American Psychological Association.

Bornstein, M. H. (Ed.). (2010). *The handbook of cultural developmental science. Part 1. Domains of development across cultures. Part 2. Development in different places on earth*. New York, NY: Psychology Press.

Bornstein, M. H. (2012). Cultural approaches to parenting. *Parenting: Science and Practice, 12*, 212–221.

Bornstein, M. H., & Arterberry, M. E. (2003). Recognition, categorization, and apperception of the facial expression of smiling by 5-month-old infants. *Developmental Science, 6*, 585–599.

Bornstein, M. H., & Arterberry, M. E. (2010). The development of object categorization in young children: Hierarchical inclusiveness, age, perceptual attribute and group versus individual analyses. *Developmental Psychology, 46*, 350–365.

Bornstein, M. H., Arterberry, M. E., & Mash, C. (2004). Long-term memory for an emotional interpersonal interaction occurring at 5 months of age. *Infancy, 6*, 407–416.

Bornstein, M. H., Arterberry, M. E., Mash, C., & Manian, N. (2011). Discrimination of facial expression by 5-month-old infants of nondepressed and clinically depressed mothers. *Infant Behavior and Development, 34*, 100–106.

Bornstein, M. H., & Benasich, A. A. (1986). Infant habituation: Assessments of individual differences and short-term reliability at five months. *Child Development, 57*, 87–99.

Bornstein, M. H., & Bornstein, L. (2008). Psychological stability. In W. A. Darity, Jr. (Ed.), *International encyclopedia of social sciences* (2nd ed., Vol. 8, pp. 74–75). Detroit, MI: Macmillan.

Bornstein, M. H., & Bradley, R. H. (Eds.). (2003). *Socioeconomic status, parenting, and child development*. Mahwah, NJ: Erlbaum.

Bornstein, M. H., & Colombo, J. (2012). Infant cognitive functioning and mental development. In S. Pauen (Ed.), *Early Childhood development and later achievement* (pp. 118–147). New York, NY: Cambridge University Press.

Bornstein, M. H., & Cote, L. R. (2001). Mother-infant interaction and acculturation I: Behavioral comparisons in Japanese American and South American families. *International Journal of Behavioral Development, 25*, 549–563.

Bornstein, M. H., Cote, L. R., Haynes, O. M., & Bakeman, R. (in press). Modalities of infant-mother interaction in Japanese, Japanese American immigrant, and European American dyads. *Child Development*.

Bornstein, M. H., Cote, L. R., Maital, S., Painter, K., Park, S., Pasucal, L., et al. (2004). Cross-linguistic analysis of vocabulary in toddlers: Spanish, Dutch, French, Hebrew, Italian, Korean, and English. *Child Development, 75*, 1115–1139.

Bornstein, M. H., Gaughran, J. M., & Seguí, I. (1991). Multimethod assessment of infant temperament: Mother questionnaire and mother and observer reports evaluated and compared at five months using the Infant Temperament Measure. *International Journal of Behavioral Development, 14*, 131–151.

Bornstein, M. H., Gini, M., Putnick, D. L., Haynes, O. M., Painter, K. M., & Suwalsky, J. T. D. (2006). Short-term reliability and continuity of emotional availability in mother-child dyads across contexts of observation. *Infancy, 10*, 1–16.

Bornstein, M. H., Hahn, C., & Haynes, O. M. (2011). Maternal personality, parenting cognitions, and parenting practices. *Developmental Psychology, 47*, 658–675.

Bornstein, M. H., Hahn, C., Haynes, O. M., Belsky, J., Azuma, H., Kwak, K., et al. (2007). Maternal personality and parenting cognitions in cross-cultural perspective. *International Journal of Behavioral Development, 31*, 193–209.

Bornstein, M. H., Hahn, C., & Wolke, D. (2013). Systems and cascades in cognitive development and academic achievement. *Child Development, 84*, 154–162.

Bornstein, M. H., Haynes, O. M., Legler, J. M., O'Reilly, A. W., & Painter, K. M. (1997). Symbolic play in childhood: Interpersonal and environmental context and stability. *Infant Behavior and Development, 20*, 197–207.

Bornstein, M. H., Haynes, O. M., O'Reilly, A. W., & Painter, K. (1996). Solitary and collaborative pretense play in early childhood: Sources of individual variation in the development of representational competence. *Child Development, 67*, 2910–2929.

Bornstein, M. H., Haynes, O. M., Painter, K. M., & Genevro, J. L. (2000). Child language with mother and with stranger at home and in the laboratory: A methodological study. *Journal of Child Language, 27*, 407–420.

Bornstein, M. H., Haynes, O. M., Pascual, L., Painter, K. M., & Galperin, C. (1999). Play in two societies: Pervasiveness of process, specificity of structure. *Child Development, 70*, 317–331.

Bornstein, M. H., Kessen, W., & Weiskopf, S. (1976a). The categories of hue in infancy. *Science, 191*, 201–202.

Bornstein, M. H., Kessen, W., & Weiskopf, S. (1976b). Color vision and hue categorization in young human infants. *Journal of Experimental Psychology: Human Perception and Performance, 2*, 115–129.

Bornstein, M. H., & Mash, C. (2010). Experience-based and on-line categorization of objects in early infancy. *Child Development, 81*, 884–897.

Bornstein, M. H., Mash, C., & Arterberry, M. E. (2011). Perception of object-context relations: Eye-movement analysis in infants and adults. *Developmental Psychology, 47*, 364–375.

Bornstein, M. H., Mayes, L. C., & Park, J. (1998). Language, play, emotional availability, and acceptance in cocaine-exposed and non-cocaine exposed young children and their mothers. *Revue Parole, 7/8*, 235–260.

Bornstein, M. H., & O'Reilly, A. W. (Eds.). (1993). *The role of play in the development of thought.* San Francisco, CA: Jossey-Bass.

Bornstein, M. H., Painter, K. M., & Park, J. (2002). Naturalistic language sampling in typically developing children. *Journal of Child Language, 29*, 687–699.

Bornstein, M. H., Pécheux, M. G., & Lécuyer, R. (1988). Visual habituation in human infants: Development and rearing circumstances. *Psychological Research, 50*, 130–133.

Bornstein, M. H., & Putnick, D. L. (2007). Chronological age, cognitions, and practices in European American mothers: A multivariate study of parenting. *Developmental Psychology, 43*, 850–864.

Bornstein, M. H., & Putnick, D. L. (2012). Stability of language in childhood: A multiage, multidomain, multimeasure, and multisource study. *Developmental Psychology, 48*, 477–491.

Bornstein, M. H., Putnick, D. L., & Suwalsky, J. T. D. (2012). A longitudinal process analysis of mother-child emotional relationships in a rural Appalachian European American community. *American Journal of Community Psychology, 59*, 89–100.

Bornstein, M. H., Putnick, D. L., Suwalsky, J. T. D., & Gini, M. (2006). Maternal chronological ages, prenatal and perinatal history, social support, and parenting of infants. *Child Development, 77*, 875–892.

Bornstein, M. H., Putnick, D. L., Suwalsky, J. T. D., Venuti, P., de Falco, S., Galperin, C. Z., et al. (2012). Emotional relationships in mothers and infants: Culture-common and community-specific characteristics of dyads from rural and metropolitan settings in Argentina, Italy, and the United States. *Journal of Cross-Cultural Psychology, 43*, 171–197.

Bornstein, M. H., & Sawyer, J. (2006). Family systems. In K. McCartney & D. Phillips (Eds.), *Blackwell handbook of early childhood development* (pp. 381–398). Malden, MA: Blackwell Publishing.

Bornstein, M. H., Scrimin, S., Putnick, D. L., Capello, L., Haynes, O. M., de Falco, S., et al. (2012). Neurodevelopmental functioning in very young children undergoing treatment for non-CNS cancers. *Journal of Pediatric Psychology, 37*, 660–673.

Bornstein, M. H., & Suess, P. E. (2000a). Child and mother cardiac vagal tone: Continuity, stability, and concordance across the first 5 years. *Developmental Psychology, 36*, 54–65.

Bornstein, M. H., & Suess, P. E. (2000b). Physiological self-regulation and information processing in infancy: Cardiac vagal tone and habituation. *Child Development, 71*, 273–287.

Bornstein, M. H., Suwalsky, J. T. D., Putnick, D. L., Gini, M., Venuti, P., de Falco, S., et al. (2010). Developmental continuity and stability of emotional availability in the family: Two ages and two genders in child-mother dyads from two regions in three countries. *International Journal of Behavioral Development, 34*, 385–397.

Bornstein, M. H., & Tamis-LeMonda, C. S. (1990). Activities and interactions of mothers and their firstborn infants in the first six months of life: Covariation, stability, continuity, correspondence, and prediction. *Child Development, 61*, 1206–1217.

Bornstein, M. H., & Tamis-LeMonda, C. S. (1997). Maternal responsiveness and infant mental abilities: Specific predictive relations. *Infant Behavior and Development, 20*, 283–296.

Bornstein, M. H., Venuti, P., & Hahn, C. (2002). Mother-child play in Italy: Regional variation, individual stability, and mutual dyadic influence. *Parenting: Science and Practice, 2*, 273–301.

Bower, T. G. R. (1977). *A primer of infant development.* San Francisco, CA: Freeman.

Bowlby, J. (1951). *Maternal care and mental health.* Geneva, Switzerland: World Health Organization.

Bowlby, J. (1969). *Attachment and loss: Attachment* (2nd ed., Vol. 1). New York, NY: Basic Books.

Boynton, R. M., & Gordon, J. (1965). Bezold-Brucke hue shift measured by color-naming technique. *Journal of the Optical Society of America, 55*, 78–86.

Braddick, O., Birtles, D., Wattam-Bell, J., & Atkinson, J. (2005). Motion- and orientation-specific cortical responses in infancy. *Vision Research, 45*, 3169–3179.

Bradley, R. H. (2010). *Handbook of cultural developmental science.* New York, NY: Psychology Press.

Bradley, R. H., Burchinal, M. R., & Casey, P. H. (2001). Early intervention: The moderating role of the home environment. *Applied Developmental Science, 5*, 2–8.

Bradley-Johnson, S., Johnson, C. M., Swanson, J., & Jackson, A. (2004). Exploratory behavior: A comparison of infants who are congenitally blind and infants who are sighted. *Journal of Visual Impairment and Blindness, 98*, 496–502.

Brant, A. M., Haberstick, B. C., Corley, R. P., Wadsworth, S. J., DeFries, J. C., & Hewitt, J. K. (2009). The developmental etiology of high IQ. *Behavior Genetics, 39*, 393–405.

Braun, J. M., Kalkbrenner, A. E., Calafat, A. M., Yolton, K., Ye, X., Dietrich, K. N., et al. (2011). Impact of early-life bisphenol A exposure on behavior and executive function in children. *Pediatrics, 128*, 873–882.

Brazelton, T. B., & Nugent, J. K. (1995). *Neonatal Behavioral Assessment Scale* (3rd ed.). London, UK: Cambridge University Press.

Brian, J. A., Landry, R., Szatmari, P., Niccols, A., & Bryson, S. (2003). Habituation in high-risk infants: Reliability and patterns of responding. *Infant and Child Development, 12*, 387–394.

Bribiescas, R. G. (2001). Reproductive ecology and life history of the human male. *American Journal of Physical Anthropology, 44*, 148–176.

Bridgett, D. J., Gartstein, M. A., Putnam, S. P., Lance, K. O., Iddins, E., Waits, R., et al. (2011). Emerging effortful control in toddlerhood: The role of infant orienting/regulation, maternal effortful control, and maternal time spent in caregiving activities. *Infant Behavior and Development, 34*, 189–199.

Bridgett, D. J., Gartstein, M. A., Putnam, S. P., McKay, T., Iddins, E., et al. (2009). Maternal and contextual influences and the effect of temperament development during infancy on parenting in toddlerhood. *Infant Behavior & Development, 32*, 103–116.

Bronfenbrenner, U. (1961). The changing American child. *Journal of Social Issues, 17*, 6–18.

Bronfenbrenner, U. (1979). Contexts of child rearing: Problems and prospects. *American Psychologist, 34*, 844–850.

Brooks, P., & Tomasello, M. (1998). How children avoid overgeneralization errors when acquiring transitive and intransitive verbs. In R. Brooks & M. Tomasello (Eds.), *The proceedings of the twenty-ninth annual child language research forum* (pp. 171–179). Chicago, IL: Center for the Study of Language and Information.

Brooks, R., & Meltzoff, A. N. (2005). The development of gaze following and its relation to language. *Developmental Science, 8*, 535–543.

Brooks, R., & Meltzoff, A. N. (2008). Infant gaze following and pointing predict accelerated vocabulary growth through two years of age: A longitudinal, growth curve modeling study. *Journal of Child Language, 35*, 207–220.

Brosseau-Lachine, O., Casanova, C., & Faubert, J. (2008). Infant sensitivity to radial optic flow fields during the first months of life. *Journal of Vision, 8*, 1–14.

Brown, R. (1973). *A first language: The early stages.* London, UK: George Allen.

Brubaker, C. J., Schmithorst, V. J., Haynes, E. N., Deitrick, K. N., Egelhoff, J. C., Lindquist, D. M., et al. (2009) Altered myelination and axonal integrity in adults with childhood lead exposure: A diffusion tensor imaging study. *NeuroToxicology, 30*, 867–875.

Bryant, P. E. (1974). *Perception and understanding in young children: An experimental approach.* London, UK: Methuen.

Bugental, D. (2009). Predicting and preventing child maltreatment: A biocognitive transactional approach. In A. Sameroff (Ed.), *The transactional model of development: How children and contexts shape each other* (pp. 97–115). Washington, DC: American Psychological Association.

Burchinal, M. R., Peisner-Feinberg, E., Bryant, D. M., & Clifford, R. (2000). Children's social and cognitive development and child-care quality: Testing for differential associations related to poverty, gender, or ethnicity. *Applied Developmental Science, 4*, 149–165.

Burnham, D., Kitamura, C., & Vollmer-Conna, U. (2002). What's new, pussycat? On talking to babies and animals. *Science, 296*, 1453.

Burns, T. C., Verfaillie, C. M., & Low, W. C. (2009). Stem cells for ischemic brain injury: A critical review. *The Journal of Comparative Neurology, 515*, 125–144.

Burns, T. C., Yoshida, K. A., Hill, K., & Werker, J. F. (2007). The development of phonetic representation in bilingual and monolingual infants. *Applied Psycholinguistics, 28*, 455–474.

Bushnell, I. W. (1982) Discrimination of faces by young infants. *Journal of Experimental Child Psychology, 33*, 298–308.

Bushnell, I. W., Sai, F., & Mullin, J. T. (1989). Neonatal recognition of the mother's face. *British Journal of Developmental Psychology, 7*, 3–15.

Buss, A. H., & Plomin, R. (1984). *Temperament: Early developing personality traits.* Hillsdale, NJ: Erlbaum.

Buss, D. M., Block, J. H., & Block, J. (1980). Preschool activity level: Personality correlates and developmental implications. *Child Development, 51*, 401–408.

Buswell, S. D., & Spatz, D. L. (2007). Parent-infant co-sleeping and its relation to breastfeeding. *Journal of Pediatric Health Care, 21*, 22–28.

Butterworth, G. (2003). *Pointing: Where language, culture, and cognition meet.* Mahwah, NJ: Erlbaum.

Call, J. (2001). Object permanence in orangutans (*Pongo pygmaeus*), chimpanzees (*Pan troglodytes*), and children (*Homo sapiens*). *Journal of Comparative Psychology, 115*, 159–171.

Call, J., & Tomasello, M. (1999). A nonverbal false belief task: The performance of children and great apes. *Child Development, 70*, 381–395.

Callaghan, T., Moll, H., Rakoczy, H., Warneken, F., Liszkowski, U., Behne, T., et al. (2011). Early social cognition in three cultural contexts. *Monographs of the Society for Research in Child Development, 299*, 1–142.

Campanella, J., & Rovee-Collier, C. (2005). Latent learning and deferred imitation at 3 months. *Infancy, 7*, 243–262.

Campos, J. J., Anderson, D. I., Barbu-Roth, M. A., Hubbard, W. M., Hertenstein, M. J., & Witherington, D. (2000). Travel broadens the mind. *Infancy, 1*, 149–219.

Campos J. J., Barrett, K. C., Lamb, M. E., Goldsmith, H. H., & Stenberg, C. (1983). Socioemotional development. In M. M. Haith & J. J. Campos (Eds.), P. H. Mussen (Series Ed.), *Handbook of child psychology: Vol. 2. Infancy and developmental psychobiology* (pp. 783–915). New York, NY: Wiley.

Campos, J. J., Campos, R. G., & Barrett, K. C. (1989). Emergent themes in the study of emotional development and emotion regulation. *Developmental Psychology, 25*, 394–402.

Camras, L. A. (2011). Differentiation, dynamical integration and functional emotional development. *Emotion Review, 3*, 138–146.

Camras, L. A., Meng, Z., Ujiie, T., Dharamisi, S., Miyake, K., Oster, H., et al. (2002). Observing emotion in infants: Facial expression, body behavior, and rater judgments of responses to an expectancy-violating event. *Emotion, 2*, 179–193.

Camras, L. A., Perlman, S. B., Fries, A. B. W., & Pollak, S. D. (2006). Post-institutionalized Chinese and East European children: Heterogeneity in the development of emotion understanding. *International Journal of Behavioral Development, 30*, 193–199.

Camras, L. A., Oster, H., Bakeman, R., Meng, Z., Ujiie, T., & Campos, J. J. (2007). Do infants show distinct facial expressions for fear and anger? Emotional expression in 11-month-old European American, Chinese, and Japanese infants. *Infancy, 11*, 131–155.

Capogna, G., Camorcia, M., & Stirparo, S. (2007). Expectant fathers' experience during labor with or without epidural analgesia. *International Journal of Obstetric Anesthesia, 16*, 110–115.

Carey, W. B. (1970). A simplified method for measuring infant temperament. *Journal of Pediatrics, 77*, 188–194.

Carlson, M. J., Pilkauskas, N. V., McLanahan, S. S., & Brooks-Gunn, J. (2011). Couples as partners and parents over children's early years. *Journal of Marriage and Family, 73*, 317–334.

Carlsson, J., Lagercrantz, H., Olson, L., Printz, G., & Bartocci, M. (2008). Activation of the right fronto-temporal cortex during maternal facial recognition in young infants. *Acta Paediatrica, 97*, 1221–1225.

Caron, R. F., & Caron, A. J. (1969). Degree of stimulus complexity and habituation of visual fixation in infants. *Psychonomic Science, 14*, 78–79.

Carter, S. C., Ahnert, L., Grossmann, K. E., Hrdy, S. B., Lamb, M. E., Porges, S. W., & Sachser, N. (Eds.) (2005). *Attachment and bonding: A new synthesis* (Dahlem Workshop Report 92). Boston, MA: MIT Press.

Carver, L. J., & Bauer, P. J. (2001). The dawning of the past: The emergence of long-term explicit memory in infancy. *Journal of Experimental Psychology: General, 130*, 726–745.

Carver, L. J., Bauer, P. J., & Nelson, C. A. (2000). Associations between infant brain activity and recall memory. *Developmental Science, 3*, 234–246.

Caskey, M., Stephens, B., Tucker, R., & Vohr, B. (2011). Importance of parent talk on the development of preterm infant vocalizations. *American Academy of Pediatrics, 128*, 910–916.

Cattell, P. (1940/1960). *The measure of intelligence in infants and young children.* New York, NY: Psychological Corporation.

Cernoch, J. M., & Porter, R. H. (1985). Recognition of maternal auxiliary odors by infants. *Child Development, 56*, 1593–1598.

Chacko, M. R., Anding, R., Kozinetz, C. A., Grover, J. L., & Smith, P. B. (2003). Neural tube defects: Knowledge and preconceptional prevention practices in minority young women. *Pediatrics, 112*, 536–542.

Cheffins, T., Chan, A., Haan, E. A., Ranieri, E., Ryall, R. G., Keane, R. J., et al. (2000). The impact of maternal serum screening on the birth prevalence of Down's syndrome and the use of amniocentesis and chorionic villus sampling in South Australia. *BJOG: An International Journal of Obstetrics and Gynaecology, 107*, 1453–1459.

Chen, C., Chern, S., Cheng, S., Chang, T., Yeh, L., Lee, C., et al. (2004). Second-trimester diagnosis of complete trisomy 9 associated with abnormal maternal serum screen results, open sacral *spina bifida* and congenital diaphragmatic hernia, and review of the literature. *Prenatal Diagnosis, 24*, 455–462.

Chen, Y., Keen, R., Rosander, K., & von Hofsten, C. (2010). Movement planning reflects skill level and age changes in toddlers. *Child Development, 81*, 1846–1858.

Chick, K. A., Heilman-Houser, R. A., & Hunter, M. W. (2002). The impact of child care on gender role development and gender stereotypes. *Early Childhood Education Journal, 29*, 149–154.

Chomsky, N. (1958). Review of the book *Verbal behavior* by B. F. Skinner. *Language, 35*, 26–58.

Chomsky, N. (1965). *Aspects of the theory of syntax.* Cambridge, MA: MIT Press.

Chronis-Tuscano, A., Degnan, K. A., Pine, D. S., Perez-Edgar, K., Henderson, H. A., Diaz, Y., et al. (2009). Stable early maternal report of behavioral inhibition predicts lifetime social anxiety disorder in adolescence. *American Academy of Child and Adolescent Psychiatry, 48*, 1–8.

Cicchetti, D. (2010). Developmental psychopathology. In M. E. Lamb & A. M. Freund (Eds.), *The handbook of life-span development: Social and emotional development* (Vol. 2, pp. 511–589). Hoboken, NJ: Wiley.

Clearfield, M. W., & Nelson, N. M. (2006). Sex differences in mothers' speech and play behavior with 6-, 9-, and 14-month-old infants. *Sex Roles, 54*, 127–137.

Cleveland, E. S., & Reese, E. (2008). Children remember early childhood: Long-term recall across the offset of child-hood amnesia. *Applied Cognitive Development, 22*, 127–142.

Clifford, S., Young, R., & Williamson, P. (2007). Assessing the early characteristics of autistic disorder using video analysis. *Journal of Autism and Developmental Disorders, 37*, 301–313.

Cochran, M., & Niego, S. (2002). Parenting and social networks. In M. H. Bornstein (Ed.), *Handbook of parenting: Applied parenting* (Vol 4, pp. 123–148). Mahwah, NJ: Erlbaum.

Cohen, L. B., & Cashon, C. H. (2006). Infant cognition. In D. Kuhn & R. S. Siegler (Ed.), W. Damon (Series Ed.), *Handbook of child psychology: Cognition, perception, and language* (6th ed., Vol. 2, pp. 214–251). Hoboken, NJ: Wiley.

Cohen, M. C., Chen-Yee, Y., Evans, C., Hinchliffe, R., & Zapata-Vazquez, R. E. (2010). Release of erythroblasts to the peripheral blood suggests higher exposure to hypoxia in cases of SIDS with co-sleeping compared to SIDS non-co-sleeping. *Forensic Science International, 197*, 54–58.

Cohen, N. J., & Farnia, F. (2011). Children adopted from China: Attachment security two years later. *Children and Youth Services Review, 33*, 2342–2346.

Cole, M., & Packer, M. (2011). Culture in development. In M. H. Bornstein & M. E. Lamb (Eds.), *Developmental science: An advanced textbook* (pp. 51–107). Mahwah, NJ: Erlbaum.

Cole, W. G., Lingeman, J. M., & Adolph, K. E. (2012). Go naked: Diapers affect infant walking. *Developmental Science, 15*, 783–790.

Coley, R. L., & Chase-Landsdale, P. L. (1998). Adolescent pregnancy and parenthood: Recent evidence and future directions. *American Psychologist, 53*, 152–166.

Coley, R. L., & Schindler, H. S. (2008). Biological fathers' contributions to maternal functioning. *Parenting: Science and Practice, 8*, 294–318.

Collins, W. A., Maccoby, E. E., Steinberg, L., Hetherington, E. M., & Bornstein, M. (2000). Contemporary research on parenting: The case for nature and nurture. *American Psychologist, 55*, 218–232.

Collis, R. E., & Davis, H. (2010). Analgesia in labour: Induction and maintenance. *Obstetric Anaesthesia, 11*, 266–269.

Colombo, J., McCardle, P., & Freund, L. (2009). *Infant pathways to language.* New York, NY: Psychology Press.

Colombo, J., & Mitchell, D. W. (2009). Infant visual habituation. *Neurobiology of Learning and Memory, 92*, 225–234.

Colombo, J., Shaddy, D. J., Anderson, C. J., Gibson, L. J., Blaga, O. M., & Kannas, K. N. (2010). What habituates in infant visual habituation? A psychophysical analysis. *Infancy, 15*, 107–124.

Colombo, J., Shaddy, D. J., Blaga, O. M., Anderson, C. J., Kannass, K. N., & Richman, W. A. (2009). Early attentional predictors of vocabulary from infancy. In J. Colombo, P. McCardle, & L. Freund (Eds.), *Infant pathways to language: Methods, models, and research directions* (pp. 143–168). New York, NY: Psychology Press.

Colombo, J., Shaddy, D. J., Richman, W. A., Maikranz, J. M., & Blaga, O. M. (2004). The developmental course of habituation in infancy and preschool outcome. *Infancy, 5*, 1–38.

Colonnesi, C., Stams, G. J. J. M., Koster, I., & Noom, M. J. (2010). The relation between pointing and language development: A meta-analysis. *Developmental Review, 30*, 352–366.

Conboy, B. T., & Mills, D. L. (2006). Two languages, one developing brain: Event-related potentials to words in bilingual toddlers. *Developmental Science, 9,* 12.

Conboy, B. T., Sommerville, J. A., & Kuhl, P. K. (2008). Cognitive control factors in speech perception at 11 months. *Developmental Psychology, 44,* 1505–1512.

Conel, J. L. (1939–1959). *The postnatal development of the human cerebral cortex* (Vols. 1–6). Cambridge, MA: Harvard University Press.

Conner, D. B., & Cross, D. R. (2003). Longitudinal analysis of the presence, efficacy and stability of maternal scaffolding during informal problem-solving interactions. *British Journal of Developmental Psychology, 21,* 315–334.

Conrad, R. (1998). Darwin's baby and baby's Darwin: Mutual recognition in observational research. *Human Development, 41,* 47–64.

Cooper, L. G., Leland, N. L., & Alexander, G. (1995). Effects of maternal age on birth outcomes among young adolescents. *Social Biology, 42,* 22–35.

Corbetta, D., Guan, Y., & Williams, J. L. (2012). Infant eye-tracking in the context of goal-directed actions. *Infancy, 17,* 102–125.

Cornwell, A. C., & Feigenbaum, P. (2006). Sleep biological rhythms in normal infants and those at high risk for SIDS. *Chronobiology International, 23,* 935–961.

Cote, L. R., & Bornstein, M. H. (2000). Social and didactic parenting behaviors and beliefs among Japanese American and South American mothers of infants. *Infancy, 1,* 363–374.

Cote, L. R., & Bornstein, M. H. (2001). Mother-infant interaction and acculturation: II. Behavioural coherence and correspondence in Japanese American and South American families. *International Journal of Behavioral Development, 25,* 564–576.

Cote, L. R., & Bornstein, M. H. (2003) Cultural and parenting cognitions in acculturating cultures: I. Cultural comparisons and developmental continuity and stability. *Journal of Cross-Cultural Psychology, 34,* 323–349.

Cote, L. R., & Bornstein, M. H. (2009). Child and mother play in three U.S. cultural groups: Comparisons and associations. *Journal of Family Psychology, 23,* 355–363.

Cote, L. R., Bornstein, M. H., Haynes, O. M., & Bakeman, R. (2008). Mother-infant person- and object-directed interactions in Latino immigrant families: A comparative approach, *Infancy, 13,* 338–365.

Cotter, A. L. (2004). Prenatal diagnosis of de novo X autosome translocations. *Clinical Genetics, 65,* 423–428.

Craton, L. G., & Yonas, A. (1990). The role of motion in infants' perception of occlusion. In L. G. Craton & A. Yonas (Eds.), *The development of attention: Research and theory* (pp. 21–46). Oxford, UK: North-Holland.

Cress, C. J., Arens, K. B., & Zajicek, A. K. (2007). Comparison of engagement patterns of young children with developmental disabilities between structured and free play. *Education and Training in Developmental Disabilities, 42,* 152–164.

Crittenden, P. M., Lang, C., Claussen, A. H., & Partridge, M. F. (2000). Relations among mothers' dispositional representations of parenting. In P. M. Crittenden & A. H. *Claussen (Eds.), The organization of attachment relationships: Maturation, culture, and context* (pp. 214–233). New York, NY: Cambridge University Press.

Cryer, D., Tietze, W., & Wessels, H. (2002). Parents' perceptions of their children's child care: A cross-national comparison. *Early Childhood Research Quarterly, 17,* 259–277.

Cummings, E. M., & Cummings, J. S. (2002). Parenting and attachment. In M. H. Bornstein (Ed.), *Handbook of parenting: Practical parenting* (Vol. 5, pp. 35–58). Mahwah, NJ. Erlbaum.

Dao, H., Mofenson, L. M., Ekpini, R., Gilkas, C. F, Barnhart, M., Bolu, O., et al. (2007). International recommendations on antiretroviral drugs for treatment of HIV-infected women and prevention of mother-to-child transmission in resource-limited settings: 2006 update. *American Journal of Obstetrics and Gynecology, 3,* S42–S55.

Darwin, C. R. (1872/1975). *The expression of the emotions in man and animals*. Chicago, IL: University of Chicago Press. (Original work published in 1872.)

Darwin, C. R. (1877). A biographical sketch of an infant. *Mind, 2*, 286–294.

Davis, E., Schoppe-Sullivan, S. J., Mangelsdorf, S. C., & Brown, G. L. (2009). The role of infant temperament in stability and change in coparenting behavior across the first year of life. *Parenting: Science and Practice, 9*, 143–159.

Dawson, G., Ashman, S. G., & Carver, L. J. (2000). The role of early experience in shaping behavioral and brain development and its implications for social policy. *Development and Psychopathology, 12*, 695–712.

Deák, G. O. (2000). Hunting the fox of word learning: Why "constraints" fail to capture it. *Developmental Review, 20*, 29–80.

Deák, G., Flom, R., & Pick, A. (2000). Effects of gesture and target on 12- and 18-month-olds' joint visual attention to objects in front of or behind them. *Developmental Psychology, 36*, 511–523.

Décarie, T. G. (1969). A study of the mental and emotional development of the thalidomide child. In B. M. Foss (Ed.), *Determinants of infant behavior* (Vol. 4). London, UK: Methuen.

De Falco, S., Esposito, G., Venuti, P., & Bornstein, M. H. (2010). Mothers and fathers play with their children with Down Syndrome: Influence on child exploratory and symbolic activity. *Journal of Applied Research in Intellectual Disabilities, 23*, 597–605. DeFrancisco, B. S., & Rovee-Collier, C. (2008). The specificity of priming effects over the first year of life. *Developmental Psychobiology, 50*, 486–501.

DeFries, J. C., Fulker, D. W., & LaBuda, M. C. (1987). Evidence for a genetic aetiology in reading disability of twins. *Nature, 329*, 537–539.

deHaan, M., & Carver, L. J. (2013). Development of brain networks for visual social-emotional information processing in infancy. In M. Legerstee, D. Haley, and M. H. Bornstein (Eds.), *The developing infant mind: Integrating biology and experience* (pp. 123–145). New York, NY: Guilford Press.

Dehaene-Lambertz, G., Hertz-Pannier, L., Dubois, J., & Dehaene, S. (2008). How does early brain organization promote language acquisition in humans? *European Review, 16*, 399–411.

Dehqan, A., & Scherer, R. C. (2011). Objective voice analysis of boys with profound hearing loss. *Journal of Voice, 25*, e61–e65.

Dejonghe, E. S., Bogat, G. A., Levendosky, A. A., Von Eye, A., & Davidson, W. S. (2005). Infant exposure to domestic violence predicts heightened sensitivity to adult verbal conflict. *Infant Mental Health Journal, 26*, 268–281.

Del Giudice, M., Manera, V., & Keysers, C. (2009). Programmed to learn? The ontogeny of mirror neurons. *Developmental Science, 12*, 350–363.

DeLoache, J. S. (2011). Early development of the understanding and use of symbolic artifacts. In U. Goswami (Ed.), *The Wiley-Blackwell handbook of childhood cognitive development* (pp. 312–336). Malden, MA: Wiley-Blackwell.

DeLoache, J. S., Chiong, C., Sherman, K., Islam, N., Vanderborght, M., Troseht, G. L., et al. (2010). Do babies learn from baby media? *Psychological Science, 21*, 1570–1574.

De Marco, P. D., Merello, E., Cama, A., Kibar, Z., & Capra, V. (2011). Human neural tube defects: Genetic causes and prevention. *Biofactors, 37*, 261–268.

Dennis, W., & Dennis, M. G. (1940). The effect of cradling practices upon the onset of walking in Hopi children. *Journal of Genetic Psychology, 56*, 77–86.

Descartes, R. (1825). La dioptrique (M. D. Boring, trans.). In V. Coursin (Ed.), *Oeuvres de Descartes*. Paris, FR: np. (Original work published in 1638.)

Deuber, C., & Terhaar, M. (2011). Hyperoxia in very preterm infants: A systematic review of the literature. *Journal of Perinatal and Neonatal Nursing, 25*, 268–274.

de Vries, J. I. P., Wimmers, R. H., Ververs, I. A. P., Hopkins, B., Savelsbergh, G. J. P., van Geijin, H. P. (2001). Fetal handedness and head position preference: A developmental study. *Developmental Psychobiology*, *39*, 171–178.

Diaz, A., & Bell, M. A. (2011). Information processing efficiency and regulation at five months. *Infant Behavior & Development*, *34*, 239–247.

DiPietro, J. A., Costigan, K. A., & Pressman, E. K. (2002). Fetal state concordance predicts infant state regulation. *Early Human Development*, *68*, 1–13.

DiPietro, J. A., Ghera, M. M., & Costigan, K. A. (2008). Prenatal origins of temperamental reactivity in early infancy. *Early Human Development*, *84*, 569–575.

Dixon, W. E., Lawman, H. G., Johnson, E. B. H., May, S., Patton, L. A., Lowe, A. K., et al. (2012). Effects of exogenous and endogenous distracters on immediate and long-term recall in toddlers. *Infancy*, *17*, 525–557.

Dixon, W. E., & Smith, P. H. (2008). Attentional focus moderates habituation-language relationships: Slow habituation may be a good thing. *Infant and Child Development*, *17*, 95–108.

D'Odorico, L., & Jacobs, V. (2006). Prosodical and lexical aspects of maternal linguistic input to late-talking toddlers. *International Journal of Language and Communication Disorders*, *41*, 293–311.

Doherty, M. J. (2008). *Theory of mind: How children understand others' thoughts and feelings.* New York, NY: Psychology Press.

Doi, T. (1973). *The autonomy of dependence.* (J. Bester, trans.). Tokyo: Kodansha International.

Dollard, J., & Miller, N. E. (1950). *Personality and psychotherapy: An analysis in terms of learning, thinking, and culture.* New York, NY: McGraw-Hill.

Dondi, M., Messinger, D., Colle, M., Tabasso, A., Simion, F., Barba, B. D., et al. (2007). A new perspective on neonatal smiling: Differences between the judgments of expert coders and naive observers. *Infancy*, *12*, 235–255.

Dozier, M., Lindheim, O., Lewis, E., Bick, J., Bernard, K., & Peloso, E. (2009). Effects of a foster parent training program on young children's attachment behaviors: Preliminary evidence from a randomized clinical trial. *Child and Adolescence Social Work Journal*, *26*, 321–332.

Dreary, I. J., & Der, G. (2005). Reaction time explains IQ's association with death. *Psychological Science*, *16*, 64–69.

Dromi, P. G. (1987). The social worker as leader of task groups. *Dissertation Abstracts International*, *48*, 1016.

Dubowitz, L., & Dubowitz, V. (1981). The neurological assessment of the preterm and fullterm newborn infant. *Clinics in Developmental Medicine,* No. 79. London, UK: Spastics International Medical Publications.

Dunn, J. (2003). Emotional development in early childhood: A social relationship perspective. In R. J. Davidson, K. R. Scherer, & H. H. Goldsmith (Eds.), *Handbook of affective sciences* (pp. 332–346). New York, NY: Oxford University Press.

Dunn, J. (2007). Siblings and socialization. In J. E. Grusec & P. D. Hastings (Eds.), *Handbook of socialization: Theory and research* (pp. 309–327). New York, NY: Guilford Press.

Dunn, J., Brown, J., Slomkowski, C., Tesla, C., & Youngblade, L. (1991). Young children's understanding of other people's feelings and beliefs: Individual differences and their antecedents. *Child Development*, *62*, 1352–1366.

Durkin, D. (1966). The achievement of pre-school readers: Two longitudinal studies. *Reading Research Quarterly*, *1*, 5–36.

Durston, S., & Casey, B. J. (2006). What have we learned about cognitive development from neuroimaging? *Neuropsychologia*, *44*, 2149–2157.

Early Child Care Resource Network (2005). *Child care and child development results from the NICHD Study in Early Child Care and Youth Development.* New York, NY: Guilford.

Eimas, P. D. (1975). Speech perception in early infancy. In L. B. Cohen, & P. Salapetek (Eds.), *Infant perception: From sensation to cognition* (Vol. 2). New York: Academic Press.

Eimas, P. D., Siqueland, E. R., Jusczyk, P., & Vigorito, J. (1971). Speech perception in infants. *Science, 171,* 303–306.

Eisert, D., & Lamorey, S. (1996). Play as a window on child development: The relationship between play and other developmental domains. *Early Education and Development, 7,* 221–235.

Ekman, P., & Friesen, W. V. (1976). Measuring facial movement. *Environmental Psychology & Nonverbal Behavior, 1,* 56–75.

Ekman, P., & Friesen, W. (1978). *Facial action coding system.* Palo Alto, CA: Consulting Psychologists Press.

Ellis, A. E., & Oakes, L. M. (2006). Infants flexibly use different dimensions to categorize objects. *Developmental Psychology, 42,* 1000–1011.

Else-Quest, N. M., Hyde, J. S., Goldsmith, H. H., & Van Hulle, C. A. (2006). Gender differences in temperament: A meta-analysis. *Psychological Bulletin, 132,* 33–72.

Emde, R. N., & Hewitt, J. K. (Eds.). (2001). *Infancy to early childhood: Genetic and environmental influences on developmental change.* New York, NY: Oxford University Press.

Erikson, E. H. (1950). *Childhood and society.* New York, NY: Norton.

Erting, C., Thumann-Prezioso, C., & Benedict, B. (2000). Bilingualism in a deaf family: Fingerspelling in early childhood. In C. Erting, C. Thumann-Prezioso, & B. Benedict (Eds.), *The deaf child in the family and at school: Essays in honor of Kathryn P. Meadow-Orlans* (pp. 41–54). Mahwah, NJ: Erlbaum.

Escalona, S. K., & Corman, H. (1969). *Albert Einstein scales of sensorimotor development.* New York, NY: Einstein College of Medicine of Yeshiva University.

Estes, K. G. (2009). From tracking statistics to learning words: Statistical learning and lexical acquisition. *Language and Linguistics Compass, 3/6,* 1379–1389.

Evans, M. I, & Wapner, R. J. (2005). Invasive prenatal diagnostic procedures. *Seminars in Perinatology, 29,* 215–218.

Eyler, F. D., Behnke, M., Garvan, C. W., Woods, N. S., Wobie, K., & Conlon, M. (2001). Newborn evaluations of toxicity and withdrawal related to prenatal cocaine exposure. *Neurotoxicology and Teratology, 23,* 399–411.

Fagan, J. F. (2011). Intelligence in infancy. In R. Sternberg & S. B. Kaufman (Eds.), *Cambridge handbook of intelligence* (pp. 130–143). Cambridge, UK: Cambridge University Press.

Fagan, M. K. (2009). Mean length utterance before words and grammar: Longitudinal trends and developmental implications of infant vocalizations. *Journal of Child Language, 36,* 495–527.

Fagard, J., Spelke, E., & von Hofsten, C. (2009). Reaching and grasping a moving object in 6-, 8-, and 10-month-old infants: Laterality and performance. *Infant Behavior and Development, 32,* 137–146.

Fagot, B. I., Rogers, C. S., & Leinbach, M. D. (2000). Theories of gender and socialization. In T. Eckes & H. M. Trautner (Eds.), *The developmental social psychology of gender* (pp. 65–89). Mahwah, NJ: Erlbaum.

Fantz, R. L. (1964). Visual experience in infants: Decreased attention to familiar patterns relative to novel ones. *Science, 146,* 668–670.

Fantz, R. L., Ordy, J. M., & Udelf, M. S. (1962). Maturation of pattern vision in infants during the first six months. *Journal of Comparative and Physiological Psychology, 55,* 907–917.

Faraone, S. V., Doyle, A. E., Mick, E., & Biederman, J. (2001). Meta-analysis of the association between the 7-repeat allele of the dompamine D(4) receptor gene and attention deficit hyperactivity disorder. *American Journal of Psychiatry, 158,* 1052–1057.

Farroni, T., Csibra, G., Simion, F., & Johnson, M. H. (2002). Eye contact detection in humans from birth. *Proceedings of the National Academy of Sciences, 99*, 9602–9605.

Farroni, T., Massaccesi, S., Pividori, D., & Johnson, M. H. (2004). Gaze following in newborns. *Infancy, 5*, 39–60.

Farroni, T., Menon, E., & Johnson, M. H. (2006). Factors influencing newborns' preference for faces with eye contact. *Journal of Experimental Child Psychology, 95*, 298–308.

Farzin, F., Rivera, S. M., & Whitney, D. (2011). Time crawls: The temporal resolution of infants' visual attention. *Psychological Science, 22*, 1004–1010.

Fein, G. G. (1991). The self-building potential of pretend play, or "I got a fish, all by myself." In M. Woodhead, R. Carr, & P. Light (Eds.), *Becoming a person* (pp. 328–346). Florence, KY: Taylor & Frances/Routledge.

Feldman, R., & Eidelman, A. I. (2004). Parent-infant synchrony and the social-emotional development of triplets. *Developmental Psychology, 40*, 1133–1147.

Feldman, R., & Greenbaum, C. W. (1997). Affect regulation and synchrony in mother-infant play as precursors to the development of symbolic competence. *Infant Mental Health Journal, 18*, 4–23.

Feldman, R., Weller, A., Zagoory-Sharon, O., & Levine, A. (2007). Evidence for a neuroendocrinological foundation of human affiliation: Plasma oxytocin levels across pregnancy and the postpartum period predict mother-infant bonding. *Psychological Science, 18*, 965–970.

Fenson, L., Dale, P. S., Reznick, J. S., Bates, E., Thal, D. J., & Pethick, S. J. (1994). Variability in early communicative development. *Monographs of the Society for Research in Child Development, 59*, 1–185.

Ferber, S. G., & Makhoul, I. R. (2008). Neurobehavioural assessment of skin-to-skin effects on reaction to pain in preterm infants: A randomized, controlled within-subject trial. *Acta Paediatrica, 97*, 171–176.

Ferenz, K. S., & Prasada, S. (2002). Singular or plural? Children's knowledge of the factors that determine the appropriate form of count nouns. *Journal of Child Language, 29*, 49–70.

Fernald, A. (2001). Hearing, listening, and understanding: Auditory development in infancy. In G. Bremner & A. Fogel (Eds.), *Blackwell handbook of infant development* (pp. 35–70). Malden, MA: Blackwell.

Fernald, A., & Marchman, V. A. (2012). Individual differences in lexical processing at 18 months predict vocabulary growth in typically developing and late-talking toddlers. *Child Development, 83*, 203–222.

Fernald, A., McRoberts, G., & Swingley, D. (2001). Infants' developing competence in recognizing and understanding words in fluent speech. *Developmental Science, 9*, F33–F40.

Fernald, A., Perfors, A., & Marchman, V. A. (2006). Picking up speed in understanding: Speech processing efficiency and vocabulary growth across the 2nd year. *Developmental Psychology, 42*, 98–116.

Field, T. M. (2000). Infant massage therapy. In C. H. Zeanah (Ed.), *Handbook of infant mental health* (2nd ed., pp. 494–500). New York, NY: Guilford.

Field, T. M. (2002). Early interactions between infants and their postpartum depressed mothers. *Infant Behavior and Development, 25*, 25–29.

Field, T. M. (2010). Postpartum depression effects on early interactions, parenting, and safety practices: A review. *Infant Behavior and Development, 33*, 1–6.

Field, T., Hernandez-Reif, M., Diego, M., Feijo, L., Vera, Y., Gil, K., et al. (2007). Still-face and separation effects on depressed mother-infant interactions. *Infant Mental Health Journal, 28*, 314–323.

Field, T. M., Woodson, R., Greenberg, R., & Cohen, D. (1982). Discrimination and imitation of facial expressions by neonates. *Science, 218*, 179–181.

Fifer, W. P., Byrd, D. L., Kaku, M., Eigsti, I., Isler, J. R., Grose-Fifer, J., et al. (2010). Newborn infants learn during sleep. *Proceedings of the National Academy of Sciences, 107*, 10320–10323.

Fisher, K. W., & Silvern, L. (1985). Stages and individual differences in cognitive development. *Annual Review of Psychology, 36,* 613–648.

Fleming, A. S., Corter, C., Stallings, J., & Steiner, M. (2002). Testosterone and prolactin are associated with emotional responses to infant cries in new fathers. *Hormone Behavior, 42,* 399–413.

Flom, R., & Bahrick, L. E. (2007). The development of infant discrimination of affect in multimodal and unimodal stimulation: The role of intersensory redundancy. *Developmental Psychology, 43,* 238–252.

Flom, R., & Bahrick, L. E. (2010). The effects of intersensory redundancy on attention and memory: Infants' long-term memory for orientation in audiovisual events. *Developmental Psychology, 46,* 428–436.

Flom, R., Gentile, D. A., & Pick, A. D. (2008). Infants' discrimination of happy and sad music. *Infant Behavior and Development, 31,* 716–728.

Fontenelle, S. A., Kahrs, B., Neal, S. A., Newton, A. T., & Lockman, J. J. (2007). Infant manual exploration of composite substrates. *Journal of Experimental Child Psychology, 98,* 153–167.

Forman, D. R., Aksan, N., & Kochanska, G. (2004). Toddlers' responsive imitation predicts preschool-age conscience. *Psychological Science, 15,* 699–704.

Foster-Cohen, S., Edgin, J. O., Champion, P. R., & Woodward, L. J. (2007). Early delayed language development in very preterm infants: Evidence from the MacArthur-Bates CDI. *Journal of Child Language, 34,* 655–675.

Fouts, H. N., Hewlett, B. S., & Lamb, M. E. (2005). Parent-offspring weaning conflicts among the Bofi farmers and foragers of Central Africa. *Current Anthropology, 46,* 29–50.

Fouts, H. N., Hewlett, B. S., & Lamb, M. E. (2012). A biocultural approach to breastfeeding interactions in Central Africa. *American Anthropologist, 114,* 123–136.

Fouts, H., Roopnarine, J. L., & Lamb, M. E. (2007). Social experiences and daily routines of African American infants in different socioeconomic contexts. *Journal of Family Psychology, 21,* 655–664.

Fouts, H. N., Roopnarine, J. L., Lamb, M. E., & Evans, M. (2012). Infant social interactions with multiple caregivers: The importance of ethnicity and socioeconomic status. *Journal of Cross-Cultural Psychology, 43,* 328–348.

Fraiberg, S. (1977). *Insights from the blind.* New York, NY: Basic Books.

Fraley, R. C. (2002). Attachment stability from infancy to adulthood: Meta-analysis and dynamic modeling of developmental mechanisms. *Personality and Social Psychology Review, 6,* 123–151.

Fraley, R. C., & Spieker, S. J. (2003). Are infant attachment patterns continuously or categorically distributed? A taxometric analysis of Strange Situation behavior. *Developmental Psychology, 39,* 387–404.

Franchak, J. M., & Adolph, K. E. (2012). What infants know and what they do: Perceiving possibilities for walking through openings. *Developmental Psychology, 48,* 1254–1261.

Franchak, J. M., Kretch, K. S., Soska, K. C., & Adolph, K. E. (2011). Head-mounted eye tracking: A new method to describe infant looking. *Child Development, 82,* 1738–1750.

Francis, D., Diorio, J., Liu, D., & Meaney, M. J. (1999). Nongenomic transmission across generations of maternal behavior and stress responses in the rat. *Science, 286,* 5442.

Franklin, A., Bevis, L., Ling, Y., & Hurlbert, A. (2010). Biological components of colour preference in infancy. *Developmental Science, 13,* 346–354.

Franklin, A., & Davies, I. R. L. (2004). New evidence for infant colour categories. *British Journal of Developmental Psychology, 22,* 349–377.

Frantz, R. L., Ordy, J. M., & Udelf, M. S. (1962). Maturation of pattern vision in infants during the first six months. *Journal of Comparative and Physiological Psychology, 55,* 907–917.

Freud, S. (1949). *An outline of psycho-analysis.* New York, NY: Norton.

Freud, S. (1966). *Introductory lectures on psychoanalysis* (J. Strachey, trans. & ed.). New York, NY: Norton. (Original work published 1916–1917.)

Friedman, J. A. (2008). *Emotionally healthy twins: A new philosophy for parenting two unique children*. Cambridge, MA: Da Capo Press.

Friedrich, M. (2011). Early word learning: Reflections on behavior, connectionist models, and brain mechanisms indexed by ERP components. In J. Guendouzi, F. Lonchke, & M. J. Williams (Eds.), *The handbook of psycholinguistic and cognitive processes: Perspectives in communication disorders* (pp. 145–188). New York, NY: Psychology Press.

Friedrich, M., & Friederici, A. D. (2010). Maturing brain mechanisms and developing behavioral language skills. *Brain and Language, 114*, 66–71.

Friend, M., & Keplinger, M. (2003). An infant-based assessment of early lexical acquisition. *Behavior Research Methods, Instruments, & Computers, 35*, 302–309.

Frith, C. D., & Frith, U. (2012). Mechanisms of social cognition. *Annual Review of Psychology, 63*, 287–313.

Gagne, J. R., & Goldsmith, H. H. (2011). A longitudinal analysis of anger and inhibitory control in twins from 12 to 36 months of age. *Developmental Science, 14*, 112–124.

Gagne, J. R., Van Hulle, C. A., Aksan, N., Essex, M. J., & Goldsmith, H. H. (2011). Deriving childhood temperament measures from emotion-eliciting behavioral episodes: Scale construction and initial validation. *Psychological Assessment, 23*, 337–353.

Gallese, V., & Rochat, M. (2013). The evolution of motor cognition: Its role in the development of social cognition and implications for the Autistic Spectrum Disorder. In M. Legerstee, D. W. Haley, & M. H. Bornstein (Eds.), *The infant mind: Origins of the social brain* (pp. 19–47). New York, NY: Guilford.

Galluccio, L., & Rovee-Collier, C. (2006). Nonuniform effects of reinstatement within the time window. *Learning and Motivation, 37*, 1–17.

Gallup, J. J. (1970). Chimpanzees: Self-recognition. *Science, 167*, 86–87.

Galton, F. (1876). The history of twins, as a criterion for the relative powers of nature and nurture. *Journal of the Anthropological Institute, 5*, 391–406.

Gao, W., Zhu, H., Giovanello, K. S., Smith, J. K., Shen, D., Gilmore, J. H., & Lin, W. (2009). Evidence on the emergence of the brain's default network from 2-week-old to 2-year-old healthy pediatric subjects. *Proceedings of the National Academy of Sciences USA, 106*, 6790–6795.

Gartstein, M. A., Gonzalez, C., Carranza, J. A., Ahadi, S. A., Ye, R., et al. (2006). Studying cross-cultural differences in the development of infant temperament: People's Republic of China, the United States of America, and Spain. *Child Psychiatry and Human Development, 37*, 145–161.

Gartstein, M. A., & Marmion, J. (2008). Fear and positive affectivity in infancy: Convergence/discrepancy between parent-report and laboratory-based indicators. *Infant Behavior & Development, 31*, 227–238.

Gartstein, M. A., Slobodskaya, H. R., Zylicz, P. O., Gosztyla, D., & Nakagawa, A. (2010). A cross-cultural evaluation of temperament: Japan, USA, Poland and Russia. *International Journal of Psychology and Psychological Therapy, 10*, 55–75.

Gazzaniga, M. S. (1970). *The bisected brain*. New York, NY: Appleton-Century-Crofts.

Geangu, E., Benga, O., Stahl, D., & Striano, T. (2010). Contagious crying beyond the first days of life. *Infant Behavior and Development, 33*, 279–288.

Geangu, E., Benga, O., Stahl, D., & Striano, T. (2011). Individual differences in infants' emotional resonance to a peer in distress: Self-other awareness and emotion regulation. *Social Development, 20*, 450–470.

Geber, M., & Dean, R. F. A. (1957a). Gesell tests on African children. *Pediatrics, 20*, 1055–1065.

Geber, M., & Dean, R. F. A. (1957b). The state of development of newborn African children. *Lancet, 272,* 1216–1219.

Gentner, D. (1982). Why nouns are learned before verbs: Linguistic relativity versus natural partitioning. In S. S. Koczaj II (Ed.), *Language development: Vol. 2. Language thought and culture.* Hillsdale, NJ: Erlbaum.

George, C., Kaplan, N., & Main, M. (1985). *An adult attachment interview.* Unpublished manuscript, University of California at Berkeley, Department of Psychology.

Gershkoff-Stowe, L. (2000). The course of children's naming errors in early word learning. *Journal of Cognition and Development, 2,* 131–155.

Gervain, J., Macagno, F., Cogoi, S., Peña, M., & Mehler, J. (2008). The neonate brain detects speech structure. *PNAS Proceedings of the National Academy of Sciences of the United States of America, 105,* 14222–14227.

Gesell, A. L. (1945). *The embryology of behavior.* New York, NY: Harper and Row.

Gesell, A. L. (1954). The ontogenesis of infant behavior. In L. Carmichael (Ed.), *Manual of child psychology* (2nd ed.). New York, NY: Wiley.

Gesell, A. L., & Armatruda, C. S. (1945). T*he embryology of behavior: The beginnings of the human mind.* New York, NY: Harper.

Gettler, L. T., McDade, T. W., Agustin, S. S., & Kuzawa, C. W. (2011). Short-term changes in fathers' hormones during father-child play: Impacts of paternal attitudes and experience. *Hormones and Behavior, 60,* 599–606.

Gewirtz, J. L., & Peláez-Nogueras, M. (2000). Infant emotions under the positive-reinforcer control of caregiver attention and touch. In J. C. Leslie & D. Blackman (Eds.), *Experimental and applied analysis of human behavior* (pp. 271–291). Reno, NV: Context Press.

Gibson, E. J., & Walk, R. D. (1960). The "visual cliff." *Scientific American, 202,* 64.

Gibson, J. J. (1979). *The ecological approach to visual perception.* Boston, MA: Houghton Mifflin.

Gilmore, R. O., Baker, T. J., & Grobman, K. H. (2004). Stability in young infants' discrimination of optic flow. *Developmental Psychology, 40,* 259–270.

Gleitman, L., & Gleitman, H. (1992). A picture is worth a thousand words, but that's the problem: The role of syntax in vocabulary acquisition. *Current Directions in Psychological Science, 1,* 31–35.

Gogate, L., Bahrick, L., & Watson, J. (2000). A study of multimodal Motherese: The role of temporal synchrony between verbal labels and gestures. *Child Development, 71,* 878–894.

Goldberg, A. E., & Sayer, A. (2006). Lesbian couples' relationship quality across the transition to parenthood. *Journal of Marriage and the Family, 68,* 87–100.

Goldberg, S. (1977). Infant development and mother-infant interaction in urban Zambia. In P. H. Leiderman, S. R. Tulkin, & A. Rosenfeld (Eds.), *Culture and infancy: Variations in the human experience* (pp. 211–243). New York, NY: Academic.

Goldberg, S., & DiVitto, B. (2002). Parenting children born preterm. In M. H. Bornstein (Ed.), *Handbook of parenting* (2nd ed., Vol. 1, pp. 329–354). Mahwah, NJ: Erlbaum.

Goldfield, B. A. (1985/1986). Referential and expressive language: A study of two mother-child dyads. *First Language, 6,* 119–131.

Goldin-Meadow, S. (2006). Nonverbal communication: The hand's role in talking and thinking. In W. Damon, D. Kuhn, & R. Siegler (Eds.), *The handbook of child psychology: Cognition, perception, and language* (6th ed., pp. 336–369). Hoboken, NJ: John Wiley & Sons.

Goldin-Meadow, S. (2009). Using the hands to study how children learn language. In J. Colombo, P. McCardle, & L. Freund (Eds.), *Infant pathways to language* (pp. 195–210). New York, NY: Psychology Press.

Goldman-Rakic, P. S., Bourgeois, J. P., & Rakic, P. (1997). Synaptic substrata of cognitive development: Life-span analysis of synaptogenesis in the prefrontal cortex of the nonhuman primate. In N. A. Krasnegor, G. R. Lyon, & P. S. Goldman-Rakic (Eds.), *Development of the prefrontal cortex: Evolution, neurobiology, and behavior* (pp. 27–47). Baltimore, MD: Brookes.

Goldschmidt, L., Richardson, G. A., Willford, J., & Day, N. L. (2008). Prenatal marijuana exposure and intelligence test performance at age 6. *Journal of American Academy of Child and Adolescent Psychiatry, 47,* 254–263.

Goldsmith, H. H., & Hewitt, E. C. (2003). Validity of parental report of temperament: Distinctions and needed research. *Infant Behavior and Development, 6,* 108–111.

Goldsmith, H. H., & Lemery, K. S. (2000). Linking temperamental fearfulness and anxiety symptoms: A behavior-genetic perspective. *Biological Psychiatry, 48,* 1199–1209.

Goldstein, M. H., & Schwade, J. A. (2008). Social feedback to infants' babbling facilitates rapid phonological learning. *Psychological Science, 19,* 515–523.

Goldstein, M. H., Schwade, J. A., & Bornstein, M. H. (2009). The value of vocalizing: Five-month-old infants associate their own noncry vocalizations with responses from caregivers. *Child Development, 80,* 636–644.

Golinkoff, R. M., & Alioto, A. (1995). Infant-directed speech facilitates lexical learning in adults hearing Chinese: Implications for language acquisition. *Journal of Child Language, 22,* 703–726.

Golinkoff, R. M., & Hirsh-Pasek, K. (2008). How toddlers begin to learn verbs. *Trends in Cognitive Sciences, 12,* 397–403.

Goodnow, J. J. (2002). Parents' knowledge and expectations: Using what we know. In M. H. Bornstein (Ed.), *Handbook of parenting: Status and social condition parenting* (2nd ed., Vol. 3, pp. 439–460). Mahwah, NJ: Erlbaum.

Gottfried, A. W. (Ed.). (1984). *Home environment and early cognitive development.* New York, NY: Academic Press.

Gottlieb, G. (1971). Ontogenesis of sensory function in birds and mammals. In E. Tobach, L. R. Aronson, & E. Shaw (Eds.), *Biopsychology of development* (pp. 67–128). New York: Academic Press.

Gottlieb, G., Wahlsten, D., & Lickliter, R. (2006). The significance of biology for human development: A developmental psychobiological systems view. In G. Gottlieb, D. Wahlsten, & R. Lickliter (Eds.), *Handbook of child psychology: Theoretical models of human development* (6th ed., Vol. 1, pp. 210–257). Hoboken, NJ: John Wiley & Sons Inc.

Goubet, N., Rattaz, C., Pierrat, V., Allemann, E., Bullinger, A., & Lequien, P. (2002). Olfactory familiarization and discrimination in preterm and full-term newborns. *Infancy, 3,* 53–76.

Goubet, N., Strasbaugh, K., & Chesney, J. (2007). Familiarity breeds content? Soothing effect of a familiar odor on full-term newborns. *Journal of Developmental and Behavioral Pediatrics, 28,* 189–194.

Greenfield, P. M., & Bloom, L. (1975). Developing Language in Context. *PsycCRITIQUES20, 11,* 894–895.

Greenough, W. T., Black, J. E., & Wallace, C. S. (2002). Experience and brain development. In W. T. Greenough, J. E. Black, & C. S. Wallace (Eds.), *Brain development and cognition* (pp. 186–216). Malden, MA: Blackwell Publishing.

Grewen, K. M., Davenport, R. E., & Light, K. C. (2010). An investigation of plasma and salivary oxytocin responses in breast- and formula-feeding mothers of infants. *Psychophysiology, 47,* 625–632.

Grewen, K. M., Girdler, S. S., Amico, J., & Light, K. C. (2005). Effects of partner support on resting oxytocin, cortisol, norepinephrine, and blood pressure before and after warm partner contact. *Psychosomatic Medicine, 67,* 531–538.

Griffiths, R. (1954). *The abilities of babies.* New York, NY: McGraw-Hill.

Groh, A. M., Roisman, G. I., van IJzendoorn, M. H., Bakermans-Kranenburg, M. J., & Fearon, R. P. (2012). The significance of insecure and disorganized attachment for children's internalizing symptoms: A meta-analytic study. *Child Development, 83,* 591–610.

Groome, L. J., Swiber, M. J., Holland, S. B., Bentz, L. S., Atterbury, J. L., et al. (1999). Spontaneous motor activity in the perinatal infant before and after birth: Stability in individual differences. *Developmental Psychobiology*, *35*, 15–24.

Gronqvist, H., Brodd, K. S., & von Hofsten, C. (2011). Reaching strategies of very preterm infants at 8 months corrected age. *Experimental Brain Research*, *209*, 225–233.

Grossmann, K. E., Grossmann, K., & Waters, E. (2005). *Attachment from infancy to adulthood: The major longitudinal studies*. New York, NY: Guilford.

Guastella, A. J., Mitchell, P. B., & Dadds, M. R. (2008). Oxytocin increases gaze to the eye region of human faces. *Biological Psychiatry*, *63*, 3–5.

Guedeney, A., & Tereno, S. (2010). Transition to parenthood. In S. Tyano, M. Keren, H. Herrman, & J. Cox (Eds.), *Parenthood and mental health: A bridge between infant and adult psychiatry* (pp. 171–179). Hoboken, NJ: Wiley-Blackwell.

Guellai, B., & Streri, A. (2011). Cues for early social skills: Direct gaze modulates newborns' recognition of talking faces. *Plos One*, *6*, 1–6.

Gusella, J., Muir, D., & Tronick, E. (1988). The effect of manipulating maternal behavior during an interaction with three- and six-month-olds' affect and attention. *Child Development*, *59*, 1111–1124.

Hackshaw, A., Rodeck, C., & Boniface, S. (2011). Maternal smoking in pregnancy and birth defects: A systematic review based on 173,687 malformed cases and 11.7 million controls. *Human Reproduction Update*, *17*, 589–604.

Haith, M. M. (1980). *Rules that babies look by*. Hillsdale, NJ: Erlbaum.

Haith, M. M. (1991). Gratuity, perception-action integration and future orientation in infant vision. In F. Kessel, A. Sameroff, & M. Bornstein (Eds.), *Contemporary constructions of the child: Essays in honor of William Kessen*. Hillsdale, NJ: Erlbaum.

Haith, M. M. (2004). Progress and standardization in eye movement work with human infants. *Infancy*, *6*, 257–265.

Haith, M. M., & Benson, J. B. (1998). Infant cognition. In D. Kuhn & R. S. Siegler (Eds.), W. Damon (Series Ed.), *Handbook of child psychology: Cognition, perception, and language* (5th ed., Vol. 2, pp. 199–254). New York, NY: Wiley.

Halberstadt, A. G., & Lozada, F. T. (2011). Emotion development in infancy though the lens of culture. *Emotion Review*, *3*, 158–168.

Haley, D. W., Grunau, R. E., Weinbert, J., Keidar, A., & Oberlander, T. F. (2010). Physiological correlates of memory recall in infancy: Vagal tone, cortisol, and imitation in preterm and full-term infants at 6 months. *Infant Behavior and Development*, *33*, 219–234.

Halliday, M. (1975). *Learning how to mean: Explorations in the development of language*. London, UK: Edward Arnold Publishing.

Hane, A., & Fox, N. A. (2006). Ordinary variations in maternal caregiving influence human infants' stress reactivity. *Psychological Science*, *17*, 550–556.

Hannesdottir, D. K., Doxie, J., Bell, M. A., Ollendick, T. H., & Wolfe, C. D. (2010). A longitudinal study of emotion regulation and anxiety in middle childhood: Associations with frontal EEG asymmetry in early childhood. *Developmental Psychobiology*, *52*, 197–204.

Harkness, S., & Super, C. M. (1983). The cultural construction of child development: A framework for the socialization of affect. *Ethos*, *11*, 221–231.

Harkness, S., & Super, C. M. (2002). Culture and parenting. In M. H. Bornstein (Ed.), *Handbook of parenting: Biology and ecology of parenting* (2nd ed., Vol. 2, pp. 253–280). Mahwah, NJ: Erlbaum.

Harlow, H. F. (1958). The nature of love. *American Psychologist*, *13*, 673–685.

Harlow, H. F. (1960). Primary affectional patterns in primates. *American Journal of Orthopsychiatry, 30*, 676–684.

Harlow, H. F., & Zimmermann, R. R. (1959). Affectional responses in the infant monkey. *Science, 130*, 421–432.

Harms, T., Cryer, D., & Clifford, R. M. (2003). *Infant/Toddler Environment Rating Scale* (rev. ed). New York, NY: Teachers College Press.

Harris, J. R. (2007). *No two alike: Human nature and human individuality.* New York, NY: Norton.

Hart, B., & Risley, T. R. (1995). *Meaningful differences in the everyday experience of young American children.* Baltimore, MD: Brookes.

Hartmann, D.P., Pelzel, K. E., & Abbott, C. B. (2011). Design, measurement, and analysis in developmental research. In D. Hartmann, K. Pelzel, C. Abbott. *Developmental science: An advanced textbook* (6th ed., pp. 109–197). New York, NY: Psychology Press.

Hartshorn, K., Rovee-Collier, C., Gerhardstein, P., Bhatt, R. S., Wondoloski, T. L., Klein, P. J., et al. (1998). Developmental changes in the specificity of memory over the first year of life. *Developmental Psychobiology, 33*, 61–78.

Harwood, R. L., & Feng, X. (2006). Studying acculturation among Latinos in the United States. In M. H. Bornstein & L. R. Cote (Eds.), *Acculturation and parent-child relationships: Measurement and development* (pp. 197–222). Mahwah, NJ: Erlbaum.

Hatzinikolaou, K., & Murray, L. (2010). Infant sensitivity to negative maternal emotional shifts: Effects of infant sex, maternal postnatal depression, and interactive style. *Infant Mental Health Journal, 31*, 591–610.

Hawk, C. K., & Holden, G. W. (2006). Meta-parenting: An initial investigation into a new parental social cognition construct. *Parenting: Science and Practice, 6*, 21–42.

Hebb, D. O. (1946). On the nature of fear. *Psychological Review, 53*, 259–276.

Hebb, D. O. (1949). *The organization of behavior: A neuropsychology theory.* New York, NY: Wiley.

Heckman, J. J. (2006). Skill formation and the economics of investing in disadvantaged children. *Science, 312*, 1900–1902.

Heckman, J. J. (2007). The economics, technology, and neuroscience of human capability formation. *Proceedings of the National Academy of Sciences, 104*, 13250–13255.

Heckman, J. J. (2011). The American family in black and white: A post-racial strategy for improving skills to promote equality. *IZA Discussion Paper*, #5495.

Held, R., & Hein, A. (1963). Movement-produced stimulation in the development of visually guided behavior. *Journal of Comparative and Physiological Psychology, 56*, 872–876.

Helmholtz, H. v. (1965). *Handbook of psychological optics.* In R. Herrnstein and E. G. Boring (Eds.), *A sourcebook in the history of psychology* (Vol. 3, pp. 151–163). Cambridge, MA: Harvard University Press. (Original work published in 1885.)

Hemker, L., Granrud, C. E., Yonas, A., & Kavsek, M. (2010). Infant perception of surface texture and relative height as distance information: A preferential-reaching study. *Infancy, 15*, 6–27.

Herbert, J., Gross, J., & Hayne, J. (2007). Crawling is associated with more flexible memory retrieval by 9-month-old infants. *Developmental Science, 10*, 183–189.

Hernandez-Martinez, C., Sans, J. C., & Fernandez-Ballart, J. (2011). Parents' perceptions of their neonates and their relation to infant development, *Child: Care, health and development, 37*, 484–492.

Hertenstein, M. J., & Campos, J. J. (2004). The retention effects of an adult's emotional displays on infant behavior *Child Development, 75*, 595–613.

Hespos, S. J., & Baillargeon, R. (2001). Reasoning about containment events in very young infants. *Cognition, 78* 207–245.

Hess, C. R., Teti, D. M., & Hussey-Gardner, B. (2004). Self-efficacy and parenting of high-risk infants: The moderating role of parent knowledge of infant development. *Applied Developmental Psychology*, *25*, 423–437.

Hesse, E. (2008). The adult attachment interview: Protocol, method of analysis, and empirical studies. In J. Cassidy & P. R. Shaver (Eds.), *Handbook of attachment* (2nd ed., pp. 552–598). New York, NY: Guilford.

Hewlett, B. S., & Lamb, M. E. (2005). *Hunter-gatherer childhoods: Evolutionary, developmental, and cultural perspectives.* New Brunswick, NJ: Aldine/Transaction.

Hill-Soderlund, A. L., Mills-Koonce, W. R., Propper, C., Calkins, S. D., Granger, D. A., Moore, G. A., et al. (2008). Parasympathetic and sympathetic responses to the stranger situation in infants and mothers from avoidant and securely attached dyads. *Developmental Psychobiology*, *50*, 361–376.

Hiltunen, P., Moilanen, I., Szajnberg, N., & Gardner, N. (1999). The IFEEL pictures: Transcultural aspects of importing a new method. *Nordic Journal of Psychiatry*, *53*, 231–235.

Hinde, R. A., & Stevenson-Hinde, J. (1973). *Constraints on learning: Limitations and predispositions.* Oxford, UK: Academic Press.

Hines, M. (2004). *Brain gender.* Oxford: Oxford University Press.

Hines, M. (2010). Gendered behavior across the lifespan. In R. M. Lerner, M. E. Lamb, & A. Freund (Eds.), *The handbook of lifespan development* (Vol. 2, pp. 341–378). Hoboken, NJ: Wiley.

Hobson, P. (2002). *The cradle of thought.* Basingstoke, UK: Macmillan.

Hoehl, S., Reid, V. M., Parise, E., Handl, A., Palumbo, L., & Striano, T. (2009). Looking at eye gaze processing and its neural correlates in infancy-implications for social development and autism spectrum disorder. *Child Development*, *80*, 968–985.

Hoehl, S., & Striano, T. (2010). The development of emotional face and eye gaze processing. *Developmental Science*, *13*, 813–825.

Hoff, E. (2002). The specificity of environmental influence: Socioeconomic status affects early vocabulary development via maternal speech. *Health Promotion International*, *17*, 1368–1378.

Hoff, E. (2006). How social contexts support and shape language development. *Developmental Review*, *26*, 55–88.

Hoff, E., Laursen, B., & Tardif, T. (2002). Socioeconomic status and parenting. In M. H. Bornstein (Ed.), *Handbook of parenting* (2nd ed.). Mahwah, NJ: Erlbaum.

Hoffman, H. S., Cohen, M. E., & de Vido, D. J. (1985). A comparison of classical eyelid conditioning in adults and infants. *Infant Behavior & Development*, *8*, 247–254.

Holden, G. W., & Miller, P. C. (1999). Enduring and different: A meta-analysis of the similarity in parents' child rearing. *Psychological Bulletin*, *125*, 223–254.

Holland, J. W. (2008). Reading aloud with infants: The controversy, the myth, and a case study. *Early Childhood Education Journal*, *35*, 383–385.

Hollich, G. (2010). Early language. In U. Goswami (Ed.), *Wiley-Blackwell handbook of infant development, early research* (pp. 426–449). Malden, MA: Wiley-Blackwell.

Hollich, G. J., Hirsh-Pasek, K., Golinkoff, R. M., Brand, R. J., Brown, E., Chung, H.-L., et al. (2000). Breaking the language barrier: An emergentist coalition model for the origins of word learning. *Monographs of the Society for Research in Child Development*, *65*, v-123.

Hopkins, B., & Westra, T. (1988). Maternal handling and motor development: An intracultural study. *Genetic, Social, and General Psychology*, *31*, 384–390.

Hopkins, B., & Westra, T. (1990). Motor development, maternal expectation, and the role of handling. *Infant Behavior and Development*, *13*, 117–122.

Horn, J. M., & Loehlin, J. C. (2010). *Heredity and environment in 300 adoptive families: The Texas Adoption Project.* New Brunswick, NJ: Aldine Transaction.

Hornik, R., Risenhoover, N., & Gunnar, M. (1987). The effects of maternal positive, neutral and negative affective communications on infant responses to new toys. *Child Development, 58*, 937–944.

Horst, J. S., Ellis, A. E., Samuelson, L. K., Trejo, E., Worzalla, S. L., Peltan, J. R., et al. (2009). Toddlers can adaptively change how they categorize: Same objects, same session, two different categorical distinctions. *Developmental Science, 12*, 96–105.

Houston, D. M., Santelmann, L. M., & Jusczyk, P. W. (2004). English-learning infants' segmentation of trisyllabic words from fluent speech. *Language and Cognitive Processes, 19*, 97–136.

Howe, N., Aquan-Assee, J., & Bukowski, W. M. (2001). Predicting sibling relations over time: Synchrony between maternal management styles and sibling relationship quality. *Merrill-Palmer Quarterly, 47*, 121–141.

Howes, C., & Guerra, A. G. W. (2009). Networks of attachment relationships in low-income children of Mexican heritage: Infancy through preschool. *Social Development, 18*, 896–914.

Hsu, V. C. (2010). Time windows in retention over the first year-and-a-half of life: Spacing effects. *Developmental Psychobiology, 52*, 764–774.

Hu, H., & Fogel, A. (2003). Social regulatory effects on infant nondistress vocalization on maternal behavior. *Developmental Psychology, 39*, 976–991.

Huang, Z. J., Lewin, A., Mitchell, S. J., & Zhang, J. (2012). Variations in the relationship between maternal depression, maternal sensitivity, and child attachment by race/ethnicity and nativity: Findings from a national representative cohort study. *Maternal Child Health Journal, 16*, 40–50.

Hunnius, S., de Wit, T. C. J., Vrins, S., & von Hofsten, C. (2011). Facing threat: Infants' and adults' visual scanning of faces with neutral, happy, sad, angry, and fearful emotional expressions. *Cognition and Emotion, 25*, 193–205.

Hunsley, M., & Thoman, E. B. (2002). The sleep of co-sleeping infants when they are not co-sleeping: Evidence that co-sleeping is stressful. *Psychobiology, 40*, 14–22.

Hurtado, N., Marchman, V., & Fernald, A. (2008). Does input influence uptake? Links between maternal talk, processing speed and vocabulary size in Spanish-learning children. *Developmental Science, 11*, F31–F39.

Hutman, T., & Dapretto, M. (2009). The emergence of empathy during infancy. *Cognition, Brain, Behavior, 13*, 367–390.

Huttenlocher, P. R. (1990). Morphometric study of human cerebral cortex development. *Neuropsychologia, 28*, 517–527.

Imada, T., Yang, Z., Cheour, M., Taulu, S., Ahonen, A., & Kuhl, P. K. (2006). Infant speech perception activates Broca's area: A developmental magnetoencephalography study. *Brain Imaging, 17*, 957–962.

Iyer, S. N., & Oller, D. K. (2008). Prelinguistic vocal development in infants with typical hearing and infants with severe-to-profound hearing loss. *Volta Review, 108*, 115–138.

Izard, C. E. (1979). *Emotions in personality and psychopathology.* Oxford, UK: Plenum.

Izard, C. E. (2002). Translating emotion theory and research into preventive interventions. *Psychological Bulletin, 128*, 796–824.

Izard, C. E., & Ackerman, B. P. (2000). Motivational, organizational, and regulatory functions of discrete emotions. In M. Lewis & J. M. Haviland-Jones (Eds.), *Handbook of emotions* (2nd ed., pp. 253–264). New York, NY: Guilford.

Izard, C. E., & Dougherty, L. M. (1982). Two systems for measuring facial expressions. In C. E. Izard (Ed.), *Measuring emotions in infants and children* (pp. 97–126). New York, NY: Cambridge University Press.

Jabes, A., Lavenex, P. B., Amaral, D. G., & Lavenex, P. (2010). Quantitative analysis of postnatal neurogenesis and neuron number in the macaque monkey dentate gyrus. *European Journal of Neuroscience, 31*, 273–285.

Jacobson, J. L., & Jacobson, S. W. (1994). The effects of perinatal exposure to polychlorinated biphenyls and related contaminants. In H. L. Needleman & D. Bellinger (Eds.), *Prenatal exposure to toxicants: Developmental consequences* (pp. 130–147). Baltimore, MD: The Johns Hopkins University Press.

Jacobson, S. W., Jacobson, J. L., Stanton, M. E., Meintjes, E. M., & Molteno, C. D. (2011). Biobehavioral markers of adverse effect in fetal alcohol spectrum disorders. *Neuropsychological Review, 21*, 148–166.

Jadva, V., Hines, M., & Golombok, S. (2010). Infants' preferences for toys, colors, and shapes: Sex differences and similarities. *Archives of Sexual Behavior, 39*, 1261–1273.

Jakobson, R. (1968). *Child language, aphasia, and phonological universals.* Oxford, UK: Mouton.

James, W. (1890). *The principles of psychology.* New York, NY: Henry Holt.

Jansen, P. W., Saridjan, N. S., Hofman, A., Jaddoe, V. W. V., Verhulst, F. C., & Tiemeier, H. (2011). Does disturbed sleeping precede symptoms of anxiety or depression in toddlers? The Generation R study. *Psychosomatic Medicine, 73*, 242–249.

Jensen, A. (1969). How much can we boost IQ and scholastic achievement? *Harvard Educational Review, 39*, 1–123.

Jessee, A., Mangelsdorf, S. C., Brown, G. L., Schoppe-Sullivan, S. J. Shigeto, A., & Wong, M. S. (2010). Parents' differential susceptibility to the effects of marital quality on sensitivity across the first year. *Infant Behavior and Development, 33*, 442–452.

Jirikowic, T., Kartin, D., & Olson, H. C. (2008). Children with fetal alcohol spectrum disorders: A descriptive profile of adaptive function. *Revue Canadienne D'Ergotherapie, 75*, 238–248.

Johnson, M. H. (2011a). *Developmental Cognitive Neuroscience* (3rd ed.). Malden, MA: Wiley-Blackwell.

Johnson, M. H. (2011b). Developmental neuroscience, psychophysiology and genetics. In M. H. Bornstein & M. E. Lamb (Eds.), *Developmental science: An advanced textbook* (6th ed., pp. 201–239). New York, NY: Psychology Press.

Johnson, M. H., Dziurawiec, S., Ellis, H., & Morton, J. (1991). Newborns' preferential tracking of face-like stimuli and its subsequent decline. *Cognition, 40*, 1–19.

Johnson, M. H., Griffin, R., Csibra, G., Halit, H., Farroni, T., et al. (2005). The emergence of the social brain network: Evidence from typical and atypical development. *Development and Psychopathology, 17*, 509–619.

Johnson, M. H., & Morton, J. (1993). Authors' response. *Early Development and Parenting, 2*, 248–249.

Johnson, S. C., Dweck, C. S., Chen, F. S., Stern, H. L., Ok, S., & Barth, M. (2010). At the intersection of social and cognitive development: Internal working models of attachment in infancy. *Cognitive Science, 34*, 807–825.

Johnson, S. P. (2004). Development of perceptual completion in infancy. *Psychological Science, 15*, 769–775.

Johnson, S. P., Davidow, J., Hall-Haro, C., & Frank, M. C. (2008). Development of perceptual completion originates in information acquisition. *Developmental Psychology, 44*, 1214–1224.

Johnson, W., Emde, R. N., Pannabecker, B., Stenberg, C., & Davis, M. (1982). Maternal perception of infant emotion from birth through 18 months. *Infant Behavior and Development, 5*, 313–322.

Johnstone, T., Van Reekum, C. M., & Scherer, K. R. (2001). In T. Johnstone, C. M. Van Reekum, & K. R. Scherer (Eds.), *Appraisal processes in emotion: Theory, methods, research* (pp. 271–284). New York, NY: Oxford University Press.

Jones, H. E. (2006). Drug addiction during pregnancy: Advances in maternal treatment and understanding child outcomes. *Current Directions in Psychological Science, 15*, 126–130.

Jones, K. L., & Smith, D. W. (1973). Recognition of the fetal alcohol syndrome in early infancy. *Lancet, 2*, 999–1001.

Jones, S. S. (2009). Imitation and empathy in infancy. *Cognition, Brain, Behavior, 8*, 391–413.

Jung, M., & Fouts, H. N. (2011). Multiple caregivers' touch interactions with young children among the Bofi foragers in Central Africa. *International Journal of Psychology, 46*, 24–32.

Jusczyk, P. W. (2003). Chunking language input to find patterns. In D. H. Rakison & L. M. Oakes (Eds.), *Early category and concept development: Making sense of the booming, buzzing confusion* (pp. 27–49). Oxford, UK: Oxford University Press.

Jusczyk, P., Friederici, A., Wessels, J., Svenkerud, V., Jusczyk, A., et al. (1993). Infants' sensitivity to the sound patterns of native language words. *Journal of Memory and Language, 32*, 402–420.

Kabuto, H., Amakawa, M., & Shishibori, T. (2004). Exposure to bisphenol A during embryonic/fetal life and infancy increases oxidative injury and causes underdevelopment of the brain and testis in mice. *Life Sciences, 74*, 2931–2940.

Kagan, J. (1984). *The nature of the child.* New York, NY: Basic Books.

Kagan, J. (2007). *What is emotion? History, measures, and meanings.* New Haven, CT: Yale University Press.

Kagan, J. (2008). The biological contributions to temperaments and emotions. *European Journal of Developmental Science, 2*, 38–51.

Kagan, J. (2010). Temperaments as sets of preparedness. In B. M. Lester & J. D. Sparrow (Eds.), *Nurturing children and families: Building on the legacy of T. Berry Brazelton* (pp. 164–173). Oxford, UK: Wiley-Blackwell.

Kagan, J., & Klein, R. (1973). Cross-cultural perspectives on early development. *American Psychologist, 28*, 947–961.

Kagan, J., Snidman, N., Kahn, V., & Towsley, S. (2007). The preservation of two infant temperaments into adolescence: I Introduction. *Monographs of the Society for Research in Child Development, 72*, 1–9.

Kahlenberg, S. M., & Wrangham, R. W. (2010). Sex differences in chimpanzees' use of sticks as play objects resemble those of children. *Current Biology, 20*, 1067–1068.

Kant, I. (1924). *Critique of pure reason* (F. M. Miller, trans.). New York, NY: Macmillan. (Original work published in 1781.)

Karasik, L. B., Adolph, K. E., Tamis-LeMonda, C. S., & Zuckerman, A. L. (2012). Carry on: Spontaneous object carrying in 13-month-old crawling and walking infants. *Developmental Psychology, 48*, 389–397.

Karasik, L. B., Tamis-LeMonda, C. S., & Adolph, K. E. (2011). Transition from crawling to walking and infants' actions with objects and people. *Child Development, 82*, 1199–1209.

Kavsek, M. J. (2002). The perception of static subjective contours in infancy. *Child Development, 73*, 331–334.

Kavsek, M. J. (2004). Predicting later IQ from infant visual habituation and dishabituation: A meta-analysis. *Applied Developmental Psychology, 25*, 369–393.

Kavsek, M. J. (2009). Infant perception of static two-dimensional transparency information. *European Journal of Developmental Psychology, 6*, 281–293.

Kavsek, M. J., & Bornstein, M. H. (2010). Visual habituation and dishabituation in preterm infants: A review and meta-analysis. *Research in Developmental Disabilities, 31*, 951–975.

Kavsek, M. J., Granrud, C. E., & Yonas, A. (2009). Infants' responsiveness to pictorial depth cues in preferential reaching studies: A meta-analysis. *Infant Behavior and Development, 32*, 245–253.

Kaye, K. (1982). *The mental and social life of babies: How parents create persons.* Chicago, IL: University of Chicago Press.

Keegan, J., Parva, M., Finnegan, M., Gerson, A., & Belden, M. (2010). Addiction in pregnancy. *Journal of Addictive Diseases, 29*, 175–191.

Keen, R. (2003). Representation of objects and events: Why do infants look so smart and toddlers look so dumb? Current Directions in Psychological Science, 12, 79–83.

Keen, R. (2011). The development of problem solving in young children: A critical cognitive skill. *Annual Review of Psychology, 62,* 1–21.

Keller, H., Otto, H., Lamm, B., Yovsi, R. D., & Kartner, J. (2008). The timing of verbal/vocal communications between mothers and their infants: A longitudinal cross-cultural comparison. *Infant Behavior and Development, 31,* 217–226.

Keller, H., Poortinga, Y. H., Schölmerich, A. (2002). In H. Keller, Y. Poortinga, & A. Schölmerich (Eds.), *Between culture and biology: Perspectives on ontogenetic development,* (pp. 384–402). New York, NY: Cambridge University Press.

Kellman, P. J., & Arterberry, M. E. (2000, 1998). *The cradle of knowledge: The development of perception in infancy.* Cambridge, MA: MIT Press.

Kellman, P. J., & Arterberry, M. E. (2006). Perceptual development. In W. Damon, D. Kuhn, & R. Siegler (Eds.), *The handbook of child psychology: Cognition, perception, and language* (6th ed., pp. 109–160). Hoboken, NJ: John Wiley & Sons, Inc.

Kellman, P. J., & Short, K. R. (1987). Development of three dimensional form perception. *Journal of Experimental Psychology: Human Perception and Performance, 13,* 545–557.

Kellman, P. J., & Spelke, E. S. (1983). Perception of partly occluded objects in infancy. *Cognitive Psychology, 15,* 483–524.

Kellman, P. J., Yin, C., & Shipley, T. F. (1995). A common mechanism for occluded and illusory contours: Evidence from hybrid displays. *Investigative Ophthalmology and Visual Science Supplements, 36,* S847.

Kelly, D. J., Liu, S., Lee, K., Quinn, P. C., Pascalis, O., Slater, A. M., et al. (2009). Development of the other race effect in infancy: Evidence toward universality? *Journal of Experimental Child Psychology, 104,* 105–114.

Kelly, S. J., Day, N., & Streissguth, A. P. (2000). Effects of prenatal alcohol exposure on social behavior in humans and other species. *Neurotoxicology Teratology, 22,* 143–149.

Kennell, J. H., & Klaus, M. H. (1979). Early mother-infant contact: Effects on the mother and the child. *Bulletin of the Menninger Clinic, 43,* 69–78.

Keskinoglu, P., Bilgic, N., Picakciefe, M., Giray, H., Karakus, N., & Gunay, T. (2007). Perinatal outcomes and risk factors of Turkish adolescent mothers. *Journal of Pediatric Adolescent Gynecology, 20,* 19–24.

Kessen, W., Haith, M. M., & Salapatek, P. H. (1970). Human Infancy: A bibliography and guide. In P. Mussen (Ed.), *Carmichael's manual of child psychology.* New York, NY: Wiley.

Kim, G., & Kwak, K. (2011). Uncertainty matters: Impact of stimulus ambiguity on infant social referencing. *Infant and Child Development, 20,* 449–462.

Kirsten, S., Sodian, B., Thoermer, C., & Perst, H. (2011). Infants' joint attention skills predict toddlers' emerging mental state language. *Developmental Psychology, 47,* 1207–1219.

Kisilevsky, B. S., Hains, S. M. J., Lee, K., Xie, X., Huang, H., Ye, H. H., et al. (2003). Effects of experience on fetal voice recognition. *Psychological Science, 14,* 220–224.

Kitamura, C., Thanavishuth, C., Burnham, D., & Luksaneeyanawin, S. (2002). Universality and specificity in infant-directed speech: Pitch modifications as a function of infant age and sex in a tonal and non-tonal language. *Infant Behavior & Development, 24,* 372–392.

Kitzman, J. O., Snyder, M. W., Ventura, M., Lewis, A. P., Qui, R., Simmons, L. E., et al. (2012). Noninvasive whole-genome sequencing of a human fetus. *Science Translational Medicine, 4,* 1–8.

Klein, R. G. (2011). Temperament: Half a century in the *Journal. Journal of the American Academy of Child & Adolescent Psychiatry, 50,* 1090–1092.

Kleiner, K. A. (1987). Amplitude and phase spectra as indices of infants' pattern preferences. *Infant Behavior & Development, 10*, 49–59.

Kleitman, N. (1963). *Sleep and wakefulness.* Chicago, IL: University of Chicago Press.

Klingberg, T. (2008). White matter maturation and cognitive development during childhood. In C. A. Nelson & M. Lucianna (Eds.), *Handbook of developmental cognitive neuroscience* (2nd ed., pp. 237–244). Cambridge, MA: MIT Press.

Klinnert, M., Sorce, J., Emde, R. N., Stenberg, C., & Gaensbauer, T. (1984). Continuities and change in early affective life: Maternal perceptions of surprise, fear, and anger. In R. N. Emde & R. J. Harmon (Eds.), *Continuities and discontinuities in development* (pp. 339–354). New York, NY: Plenum.

Kluger, A. N., Siegfried, Z., & Ebstein, R. P. (2002). A meta-analysis of the association between DRD4 polymorphism and novelty seeking. *Molecular Psychiatry, 7*, 712–717.

Knafo, A., & Plomin, R. (2006). Parental discipline and affection and children's social behavior: Genetic and environmental links. *Journal of Personality and Social Psychology, 90*, 147–164.

Kochanska, G., Philibert, R. A., & Barry, R. A. (2009). Interplay of genes and early mother-child relationship in the development of self-regulation from toddler to preschool age. *Journal of Child Psychology and Psychiatry, 50*, 1331–1338.

Koffka, K. (1935). *Principles of Gestalt psychology.* Oxford, UK: Harcourt, Brace.

Köhler, W. (1929). *Gestalt Psychology.* Oxford, UK: Liveright.

Kohn, M. L. (1987). Cross national research as an analytic strategy. *American Sociological Review, 52*, 713–731.

Kolb, B. (1989). Brain development, plasticity, and behavior. *American Psychologist, 44*, 1203–1212.

Kong, A., Frigge, M. L., Masson, G., Besenbacher, S., Sulem, P., Magnusson, G., et al. (2012). Rate of *de novo* mutations and the importance of father's age to disease risk. *Nature, 488*, 471–475.

Kovack-Lesh, K. A., & Oakes, L. M. (2007). Hold your horses: How exposure to different items influences infant categorization. *Journal of Experimental Child Psychology, 98*, 69–93.

Kovack-Lesh, K. A., Horst, J. S., Oakes, L. M. (2008). The cat is out of the bag: The joint influence of previous experience and looking behavior on infant categorization. *Infancy,13*, 285–307.

Kowal, A. K., Krull, J. L., & Kramer, L. (2007). Shared understanding of parental differential treatment in families. *Social Development, 15*, 276–295.

Kraebel, K. S., & Gerhardstein, P. C. (2006). Three-month-old infants' object recognition across changes in viewpoint using an operant learning procedure. *Infant Behavior and Development, 29*, 11–23.

Kretch, K. S., & Adolph, K. E. (2013). Cliff or step? Posture-specific learning at the edge of a drop-off. *Child Development, 84*, 226–240.

Kristen, S., Sodian, B., Thoermer, C., & Perst, H. (2011). Infants' joint attention skills predict toddlers' emerging mental state language. *Developmental Psychology, 47*, 1207–1219.

Kuhl, P. K. (2009). Linking infant speech perception to language acquisition. In J. Colombo, P. McCardle, & L. Freund (Eds.), *Infant pathways to language* (pp. 213–244). New York, NY: Psychology Press.

Kuhl, P. K., Tsao, F. M., Liu, H. M. (2003). Foreign-language experience in infancy: Effects of short-term exposure and social interaction on phonetic learning. *Proceedings of the National Academy of Science USA, 10*, 9096–9101.

Kutzman, J. O., Snyder, M. W., Ventura, M., Lewis, A. P., Qui, R., Simmons, L. E., et al. (2012). Noninvasive whole genome sequencing of a human fetus. *Science Translational Medicine, 4*, 1–8.

Kwak, K., Putnick, D. L., & Bornstein, M. H. (2008). Child and mother play in South Korea: A longitudinal study across the second year of life. *Psychologia, 51*, 14–27.

Ladd, G. W., & Pettit, G. D. (2002). Parents and children's peer relationships. In M. H. Bornstein (Ed.), *Handbook of parenting: Practical parenting* (2nd ed., Vol. 5, pp. 269–309). Mahwah, NJ: Erlbaum.

LaGasse, L. L., Neal, A. R., & Lester, B. M. (2005). Assessment of infant cry: Acoustic cry analysis and parental perception. *Mental Retardation and Developmental Disabilities Research Reviews, 11,* 83–93.

LaMaestra, S., Kisby, G. E., Micale, R. T., Johnson, J., Kow, Y. W., Bao, G., et al. (2011). Cigarette smoke induces DNA damage and alters base-excision repair and tau levels in the brain of neonatal mice. *Toxicological Sciences, 123,* 471–479.

Lamb, M. E. (1978a). The development of sibling relationships in infancy: A short-term longitudinal study. *Child Development, 49,* 1189–1196.

Lamb, M. E. (1978b). Interactions between 18-month-olds and their preschool-aged siblings. *Child Development, 49,* 51–59.

Lamb, M. E. (1981). Developing trust and perceived effectance in infancy. In L. P. Lipsitt (Ed.), *Advances in infancy research* (Vol. 1, pp. 101–127). Norwood, NJ: Ablex.

Lamb, M. E. (2000). The history of research on father involvement: An overview. *Marriage and Family Review, 29,* 23–42.

Lamb, M. E. (2002). The development of father-infant relationships. In C. Tamis-LeMonda & N. Cabrerra (Eds.), *Handbook of father involvement* (pp. 93–117). Mahwah, NJ: Erlbaum.

Lamb, M. E. (2005a). Développement socio-émotionnel et scolarisation précoce: Recherches expérimentale. In J.-J. Ducret (Ed.), *Constructivisme et education (II): Scolariser la petite enfance?* (Vol. 1, pp. 257–267). Geneva, Switzerland: Service de la Recherche en Education (SRED).

Lamb, M. E. (2005b). Attachments, social networks, and developmental contexts. *Human Development, 48,* 108–112.

Lamb, M. E. (2010). *The role of the father in child development.* New York, NY: Wiley.

Lamb, M. E. (2012a). Mothers, fathers, families, and circumstances: Factors affecting children's adjustment. *Applied Developmental Science, 16,* 98–111.

Lamb, M. E. (2012). Non-parental care and emotional development. In S. Pauen (Ed.), *Early childhood development and later outcome* (pp. 168–179). New York, NY: Cambridge University Press.

Lamb, M. E. (2013). The changing faces of fatherhood and father-child relationships: From fatherhood as status to father as dad. In M. A. Fine & F. D. Fincham (Eds.), *Handbook of family theories: A content-based approach* (pp. 87–102). New York, NY: Routledge.

Lamb, M. E., & Ahnert, L. (2006). Nonparental child care: Context, concepts, correlates, and consequences. In K. A. Renninger & I. E. Sigel (Eds.), *Handbook of child psychology: Child psychology in practice* (6th ed., Vol. 4, pp. 950–1016). New York, NY: Wiley.

Lamb, M. E., & Esterbrooks, M. A. (1981). Individual differences in parental sensitivity: Origins, components, and consequences. In M. E. Lamb & L. R. Sherrod, (Eds.), *Infant social cognition: Empirical and theoretical considerations.* Hillsdale, NJ: Erlbaum.

Lamb, M. E., Gaensbauer, T. J., Malkin, C. M., & Schultz, L. (1985). The effects of abuse and neglect on the security of infant-adult attachment. *Infant Behavior and Development, 8,* 35–45.

Lamb, M. E., & Lewis, C. (2010). The development and significance of father-child relationships in two-parent families. In M. E. Lamb (Ed.), *The role of the father in child development* (5th ed., pp. 94–153). Hoboken, NJ: Wiley.

Lamb, M. E., & Lewis, C. (2011). The role of parent-child relationships in child development. In M. H. Bornstein & M. E. Lamb (Eds.), *Developmental science: An advanced textbook* (6th ed., pp. 469–517). New York, NY: Psychology Press.

Lamb, M. E., & Malkin, C. M. (1986). The development of social expectations in distress-relief sequences: A longitudinal study. *International Journal of Behavioral Development, 9*, 235–249.

Lany, J., & Saffran, J. R. (2011). Interactions between statistical and semantic information in infant language development. *Developmental Science, 14*, 1207–1219.

Laplante, D. P., Barr, R. G., Brunet, A., Du Fort, G. G., Meaney, M. L., Saucier, J., et al. (2004). Stress during pregnancy affects general intellectual and language functioning in human toddlers. *Pediatric Research, 56*, 400–410.

Lashley, K. S. (1938). Factors limiting recovery after central nervous lesions. *Journal of Nervous and Mental Disease, 88*, 733–755.

Laurent, H. K., Ablow, J. C., & Measelle, J. (2011). Risky shifts: How the timing and course of mothers' depressive symptoms across the perinatal period shape their own and infant's stress response profiles. *Development and Psychopathology, 23*, 521–538.

Lavoie, C., & Desrochers, S. (2002). Visual habituation at five months: Short-term reliability of measures obtained with a new polynomial regression criterion. *Journal of Genetic Psychology, 163*, 261–271.

Lebedeva, G. C., & Kuhl, P. K. (2010). Sing that tune: Infants' perception of melody and lyrics and the facilitation of phonetic recognition in songs. *Infant Behavior and Development, 33*, 419–430.

Lebel, C., Roussotte, F., & Sowell, E. R. (2011). Imaging the impact of prenatal alcohol exposure on the structure of the developing human brain. *Neuropsychological Review, 21*, 102–118.

Lécuyer, R., Berthereau, S., Ben Taieb, A., & Tardif, N. (2004). Location of a missing object and detection of its absence by infants: Contribution of an eye-tracking system to the understanding of infants' strategies. *Infant and Child Development, 13, 287–300.*

Le Grand, R., Mondloch, C. J., Maurer, D., & Brent, H. P. (2003). Expert face processing requires visual input to the right hemisphere during infancy. *Nature Neuroscience, 6*, 1108–1112.

Leerkes, E. M., & Crockenberg, S. C. (2006). Antecedents of mothers' emotional and cognitive responses to infant distress: The role of family, mother, and infant characteristics. *Infant Mental Health Journal, 27*, 405–428.

Lemerise, E. A., & Dodge, K. A. (2000). The development of anger and hostile interactions. In M. Lewis & J. M. Haviland-Jones (Eds.), *Handbook of emotions* (2nd ed., pp. 594–606). New York, NY: Guilford.

Leopold, W. F. (1949). *Speech development of a bilingual child; a linguist's record. Vol. IV. Diary from age 2.* (Northwestern U. Stud. in Humanities, No. 19.). Evanston, IL: Northwestern University Press.

Leppanen, J. M. (2011). Neural and developmental bases of the ability to recognize social signals of emotion. *Emotion Review, 3*, 179–188.

Lerner, J. V., Hertzog, C., Hooker, K. A., Hassibi, M., & Thomas, A. (1988). A longitudinal study of negative emotional states and adjustment from early childhood through adolescence. *Child Development, 59*, 356–366.

Lerner, R. M., Lewin-Bizan, S., & Warren, A. E. A. (2011). Concepts and theories of human development. In M. H Bornstein & M. E. Lamb (Eds.), *Developmental science: An advanced textbook* (6th ed., pp. 3–49). New York NY: Psychology Press.

Leslie, A. M. (1988a). Some implications of pretense for mechanisms underlying the child's theory of mind. In J. W Astington, P. L. Harris, & D. R. Olson (Eds.), *Developing theories of mind* (pp. 19–46). New York, NY: Cambridge University Press.

Leslie, A. M. (1988b). The necessity of illusion: Perception and thought in infancy. In L. Weiskrantz (Ed.), *Though without language* (pp. 185–210). New York, NY: Clarendon Press/Oxford University Press.

Leuner, B., & Gould, E. (2010). Structural plasticity and hippocampal function. *Annual Review of Psychology, 6* 111–140.

Leve, L. D., Neiderhiser, J. M., Ge, X., Scaramella, L. V., Conger, R. D., Reid, J. B., et al. (2007). The early grow and development study: A prospective adoption design. *Twin Research and Human Genetics, 10*, 84–95.

Levi, S., & Chervenak, F. A. (Eds.). (1998). Ultrasound screening for fetal anomalies: Is it worth it? *Annals of the New York Academy of Sciences,* No. 847. New York, NY: The New York Academy of Sciences.

Levy, R., Friedman, H. R., Davachi, L., & Goldman-Rakic, P. S. (1997). Differential activation of the caudate nucleus in primates performing spatial and nonspatial working memory tasks. *The Journal of Neuroscience, 17,* 3870–3882.

Lew, A. R., Hopkins, B., Owen, L. H., & Green, M. (2007). Postural change effects on infants' AB task performance: Visual, postural, or spatial? *Journal of Experimental Child Psychology, 97,* 1–13.

Lewis, C., & Lamb, M. E. (2006). *Fatherhood: Connecting the strands of diversity across time and space.* York, UK: Joseph Rowntree Foundation.

Lewis, M. (2000). Self-conscious emotions: Embarrassment, pride, shame, and guilt. In M. Lewis & J. M. Haviland-Jones (Eds.), *Handbook of emotions* (2nd ed., pp. 623–636). New York, NY: Guilford.

Lewis, M. (2011a). Inside and outside: The relation between emotional states and expressions. *Emotion Review, 3,* 189–196.

Lewis, M. (2011b). The origins and uses of self-awareness or the mental representation of me. *Consciousness and Cognition, 20,* 120–129.

Lewis, S. N., West, A. F., Stein, A., Malmberg, L., Bethell, K., Barnes, J., et al. (2008). A comparison of father-infant interaction between primary and non-primary care giving fathers. *Child: Care, Health, and Development, 35,* 199–207.

Lewkowicz, D. J. (2004). Perception of serial order in infants. *Developmental Science, 7,* 175–184.

Libertus, K., & Needham, A. (2010). Teach to reach: The effects of active vs. passive reaching experiences on action and perception. *Vision Research, 50,* 2750–2757.

Libertus, K., & Needham, A. (2011). Reaching experience increases face preference in 3-month-old infants. *Developmental Science, 14,* 1355–1364.

Liégeois, F., Bentejac, L., & de Schonen, S. (2000). When does inter-hemispheric integration of visual events emerge in infancy? A developmental study on 19- to 28-month-old infants. *Neuropsychologia, 38,* 1382–1389.

Lipsitt, L. P. (2002). Early experience and behavior in the baby of the twenty-first century. In J. Gomes-Pedro, J. K. Nugent, J. G. Young, & T. B. Brazleton (Eds.), *Bebe XXI Conference.* New York, NY: Brunner-Routledge.

Liu, D., Wellman, H. M., Tardif, T., & Sabbagh, M. A. (2008). Theory of mind development in Chinese children: A meta-analysis of false-belief understanding across cultures and languages. *Developmental Psychology, 44,* 523–531.

Lloyd-Fox, S., Blasi, A., Everdell, N., Elwell, C. E., & Johnson, M. H. (2011). Selective cortical mapping of biological motion processing in young infants. *Journal of Cognitive Neuroscience, 23,* 2521–2532.

Lock, A., & Zukow-Goldring, P. (2010). Preverbal communication. In U. Goswami (Ed.), *Wiley-Blackwell handbook of infant development, early research* (pp. 394–425). Malden, MA: Wiley-Blackwell.

Locke, J. (1689/1959). *An essay concerning human understanding.* New York, NY: Dover.

Loeb, S., Fuller, B., Kagan, S. L., & Carroll, B. (2004). Child care in poor communities: Early learning effects of type, quality, and stability. *Child Development, 75,* 47–65.

Lorenz, K. (1970). *Studies in animal and human behavior* (R. Martin, trans.). London, UK: Methuen. (Original work published in 1935.)

Love, J. M., Harrison, L., Sagi-Schwartz, A., van Ijzendoorn, M. A., Ross, C., Ungerer, J., et al. (2003). Child-care quality matters: How conclusions may vary with context. *Child Development, 74,* 1021–1033.

Lucassen, N., Tharner, A., van IJzendoorn, M. H., Bakermans-Kranenburg, M. J., Volling, B. L., Verhulst, F. C., et al. (2011). The association between paternal sensitivity and infant-father attachment security: A meta-analysis of three decades of research. *Journal of Family Psychology, 25*, 986–992.

Luck, S. J. (2005). *An introduction to the event-related potential technique*. Cambridge, MA: MIT Press.

Luke, B., & Brown, M. B. (2007). Elevated risks of pregnancy complications and adverse outcomes with increasing maternal age. *Human Reproduction, 22*, 1264–1272.

Luo, Y. (2010). Do 10-month-old infants understand others' false beliefs? *Cognition, 121*, 289–298.

Lynn, F. A., Alderdice, F. A., Crealey, G. E., & McElnay, J. C. (2011). Associations between maternal characteristics and pregnancy-related stress among low-risk mothers: An observational cross-sectional study. *International Journal of Nursing Studies, 48*, 620–627.

Lyytinen, H., Ahonen, T., Eklund, K., Guttorm, T. K., Laakso, M.-L., et al. (2001). Developmental pathways of children with and without familial risk for dyslexia during the first years of life. *Developmental Neuropsychology, 20*, 535–554.

MacDonald, K., & MacDonald, T. M. (2010). The peptide that binds: A systematic review of oxytocin and its prosocial effects in humans. *Harvard Review of Psychiatry, 18*, 1–21.

Macken, M., & Barton, D. (1980). The acquisition of the voicing contrast in English: A study of voice onset time in word-initial stop consonants. *Journal of Child Language, 7*, 1–74.

MacNeilage, P., & Davis, B. (2000). *Evolution of speech: The relation between ontogeny and phylogeny*. Cambridge, UK: Cambridge University Press.

Magnusson, K. A., & Duncan, G. J. (2002). Parents in poverty. In M. H. Bornstein (Ed.), *Handbook of parenting* (2nd ed., pp. 95–122). Mahwah, NJ: Erlbaum.

Mahler, M., Pine, A., & Bergman, F. (1975). *The psychological birth of the human infant*. New York, NY: Basic Books.

Main, M., & Cassidy, J. (1988). Categories of response to reunion with a parent at age six: Predictable from infant attachment classifications and stable over a one-month period. *Developmental Psychology, 24*, 415–426.

Main, M., Hesse, E., & Hesse, S. (2011). Attachment theory and research: Overview with suggested applications to child custody. *Family Court Review, 49*, 426–463.

Main, M., & Solomon, J. (1991). Procedure for identifying infants as disorganized/disoriented during the Ainsworth Strange Situation. In M. Greensberg, D. Ciccetti, & E. M. Cummings (Eds.), *Attachment during the preschool years: Theory, research, and intervention*. Chicago, IL: University of Chicago Press.

Maital, S. L., & Bornstein, M. H. (2003). The ecology of collaborative child rearing: A systems approach to child care on the kibbutz. *Ethos, 31*, 274–306.

Majorano, M., & D'Odorico, L. (2012). The transition into ambient language: A longitudinal study of babbling and first word production of Italian children. *First Language, 31*, 47–66.

Malatesta, C. Z., Grigoryev, P., Lamb, C., Albin, M., & Culver, C. (1986). Emotion, socialization and expressive development in preterm and full term infants. *Child Development, 57*, 316–330.

Malatesta, C. Z., & Haviland, J. M. (1982). Learning display rules: The socialization of emotion expression in infancy *Child Development, 53*, 991–1003.

Malatesta, C. Z., & Haviland, J. M. (1986). Measuring change in infant emotional expressivity: Two approache applied in longitudinal investigation. In C. Z. Malatesta & J. M. Haviland (Eds.), *Measuring emotions in infant and children* (pp. 51–74). New York, NY: Cambridge University Press.

Malmberg, L., Stein, A., West, A., Lewis, S., Barnes, J., Leach, P., et al. (2007). Parent-infant interaction: A growt model approach. *Infant Behavior and Development, 30*, 615–630.

Mandler, J. M. (2000). Perceptual and conceptual processes in infancy. *Journal of Cognition and Development,* 3–36.

Mandler, J. M. (2004). *The foundations of the mind: Origins of conceptual thought.* New York, NY: Oxford University Press.

Mandler, J. M., Fivush, R., & Reznick, J. S. (1987). The development of contextual categories. *Cognitive Development, 2,* 339–354.

Mangelsdorf, S. C., McHale, J. L., Diener, M., Goldstein, L. H., & Lehn, L. (2000). Infant attachment: Contributions of infant temperament and maternal characteristics. *Infant Behavior & Development, 23,* 175–196.

Maratos, O. (1998). Neonatal, early and later imitation: Same order phenomena? In F. Simion & G. Butterworth (Eds.), *The development of sensory, motor and cognitive capacities in early infancy: From perception to cognition* (pp. 145–160). Hove, UK: Psychology Press.

Mareschal, D., & French, R. (2000). Mechanisms of categorization. *Infancy, 1,* 59–76.

Marin-Padilla, M. (2010). *The human brain: Prenatal development and structure.* Berlin, DE: Springer-Verlag.

Markman, E. M. (1999). Multiple approaches to the study of word learning in children. *Japanese Psychological Research, 41,* 79–81.

Markman, E. M., Wasow, J. L., & Hansen, M. B. (2003). Use of the mutual exclusivity assumption by young word learners. *Cognitive Psychology, 47,* 241–275.

Markova, G., & Legerstee, M. (2006). Contingency, imitation, and affect sharing: Foundations of infants' social awareness. *Developmental Psychology, 42,* 132–141.

Marshall, P. J., & Shipley, T. F. (2009). Event-related potentials to point-light displays of human actions in five-month-old infants. *Developmental Neuropsychology, 34,* 368–377.

Martin, J. A., Osterman, M. J. K., & Sutton, P. D. (2010). Are preterm births on the decline in the United States? Recent data from the national vital statistics system. *NCHS Data Brief, 39.*

Martin, J. L., & Ross, H. S. (2005). Sibling aggression: Sex differences and parents' reactions. *International Journal of Behavioral Development, 29,* 129–138.

Mash, C., Arterberry, M. E., & Bornstein, M. H. (2007). Mechanisms of object recognition in 5-month-old infants. *Infancy, 12,* 31–43.

Mash, C., & Bornstein, M. H. (2012). Five-month-olds' categorization of novel objects: Tasks and measure dependence. *Infancy, 17,* 179–197.

Mason, A. J. S., Braddick, O. J., & Wattam-Bell, J. (2003). Motion coherence thresholds in infants: Different tasks identify two distinct motion systems. *Vision Research, 43,* 1149–1157.

Masur, E. F. (2006). Vocal and action imitation by infants and toddlers during dyadic interactions. In S. J. Rogers & J. H. G. Williams (Eds.), *Imitation and the social mind: Autism and typical development* (pp. 27–47). New York, NY: Guilford Press.

Mattock, K., & Burnham, D. (2006). Chinese and English infants' tone perception: Evidence for perceptual reorganization. *Infancy, 10,* 241–265.

Maurer, D., Lewis, T. L., Brent, H. P., & Levin, A. V. (1999). Rapid improvement in the acuity of infants after visual input. *Science, 286,* 108–110.

Maurer, D., Lewis, T. L., & Mondloch, C. J. (2005). Missing sights: Consequences for visual cognitive development. *TRENDS in Cognitive Sciences, 9,* 144–151.

May, L. E., Glaros, A., Yeh, H., Clapp, J. F., & Gustafson, K. M. (2010). Aerobic exercise during pregnancy influences fetal cardiac autonomic control of heart rate and heart rate variability. *Early Human Development, 86,* 213–217.

Hayes, L. C., & Truman, S. D. (2002). Substance abuse and parenting. In M. H. Bornstein (Ed.), *Handbook of parenting. Vol. 4: Social conditions and applied parenting* (2nd ed., pp. 329–359). Mahwah, NJ: Erlbaum.

Maynard, A. E. (2002). Cultural teaching: The development of teaching skills in Maya sibling interactions. *Child Development, 73,* 969–982.

McCall, R. B., van IJzendoorn, M. H., Juffer, F., Groark, C. J., & Groza, V. K. (2011). Children without permanent parents: Research, practice, and policy. *Monographs of the Society for Research in Child Development, 76,* 1–318.

McEwen, F., Happe, F., Boton, P., Rijsdijk, F., Ronald, A., Dworzynski, K., et al. (2007). Origins of individual differences in imitation: Links with language, pretend play, and socially insightful behavior in two-year-old twins. *Child Development, 78,* 474–492.

McGraw, M. B. (1933). The functions of reflexes in the behavior development of infants. *The Pedagogical Seminary and Journal of Genetic Psychology, 42,* 209–216.

McGraw, M. B. (1939). Later development of children specially trained during infancy: Johnny and Jimmy at school age. *Child Development, 10,* 1–19.

McKenna, J. J., & McDade, T. (2005). Why babies should never sleep alone: A review of the co-sleeping controversy in relation to SIDS, bedsharing, and breast feeding. *Paediatric Respiratory Reviews, 6,* 134–152.

McKenna, J. J., & Volpe, L. E. (2007). Sleeping with baby: An internet-based sampling of parental experiences, choices, perceptions, and interpretations in a western industrialized context. *Infant and Child Development, 16,* 359–385.

McLoyd, V. C., Aikens, N. L., & Burton, L. M. (2006). Childhood poverty, policy, and practice. In K. A. Renninger & I. E. Sigel (Eds.), W. Damon (Series Ed.), *Handbook of child psychology: Child psychology in practice* (6th ed., Vol. 4, pp. 700–775). Hoboken, NJ: Wiley.

Mead, M., & MacGregor, F. C. (1951). *Growth and culture.* New York, NY: Putnam's Sons.

Medoff-Cooper, B., Carey, W. B., & McDevitt, S. C. (1993). The early infancy temperament questionnaire. *Journal of Developmental and Behavioral Pediatrics, 14,* 230–235.

Meadow-Orlans, K. P. (2002). Parenting with a sensory or physical disability. In M. H. Bornstein (Ed.), *Handbook of parenting. Vol. 4: Social conditions and applied parenting* (2nd ed., pp. 259–293). Mahwah, NJ: Erlbaum.

Mehler, J., Nespor, M., & Pena, M. (2008). What infants know and what they have to learn about language. *European Review, 16,* 429–444.

Meins, E., Fernyhough, C., Wainwright, R., Das Gupta, M., Fradley, E., & Tuckey, M. (2002). Maternal mind-mindedness and attachment security as predictors of theory of mind understanding. *Child Development, 73,* 1715–1726.

Meltzoff, A. N. (1988). Infant imitation after a 1-week delay: Long-term memory for novel acts and multiple stimuli. *Developmental Psychology, 24,* 470–476.

Meltzoff, A. N. (2007). "Like me": A foundation for social cognition. *Developmental Science, 10,* 126–134.

Meltzoff, A. N. (2011). Social cognition and the origins of imitation, empathy, and theory of mind. In U. Goswami (Ed.), *The Wiley-Blackwell handbook of childhood cognitive development* (2nd ed., pp. 49–75). New York, NY: Wiley-Blackwell.

Meltzoff, A. N., & Brooks, R. (2008). Self-experience as a mechanism for learning about others: A training study in social cognition. *Developmental Psychology, 44,* 1257–1265.

Meltzoff, A. N., & Brooks, R. (2009). Social cognition and language. In J. Colombo, P. McCardle, & L. Freund (Eds.), *Infant pathways to language* (pp. 169–194). New York, NY: Psychology Press.

Meltzoff, A. N., Brooks, R., Shon, A. P., & Rao, R. P. N. (2010). "Social" robots are psychological agents for infants: A test of gaze following. *Neural Networks, 23,* 966–972.

Meltzoff, A. N., & Moore, M. K. (1977). Imitation of facial and manual gestures by human neonates. *Science, 198,* 75–78.

Meltzoff, A. N., & Moore, M. K. (1992). Early imitation within a functional framework: The importance of person identity, movement, and development. *Infant Behavior and Development, 15,* 479–505.

Meltzoff, A. N., & Moore, M. K. (2001). "Discovery procedures" for people and things: The role of representation and identity. In F. Lacerda, C. von Hofsten, & M. Heimann (Eds.), *Emerging cognitive abilities in early infancy* (pp. 213–230). Mahwah, NJ: Erlbaum.

Menacker, F., & Hamilton, B. E. (2010). Recent trends in Cesarean delivery in the United States. *NCHS Data Brief*, *35*.

Menacker, S. J., & Batshaw, M. L. (1997). Vision: Our window to the world. In M. L. Batshaw (Ed.), *Children with disabilities* (4th ed., pp. 211–239). Baltimore, MD: Paul H. Brookes.

Mendive, S., Bornstein, M. H., & Sebastián, C. (2013). The role of maternal attention-directing strategies in 9-month-old infants attaining joint engagement. *Infant Behavior and Development*, *36*, 115–123.

Mennella, J. A., & Beauchamp, G. K. (1996). The early development of human flavor preferences. In E. D. Capaldi (Ed.), *Why we eat what we eat* (pp. 83–112). Washington, DC: American Psychological Association.

Mennella, J. A., & Beauchamp, G. K. (1997). The ontogeny of human flavor perception. In G. K. Beauchamp & L. Bartoshuk (Eds.), E. C. Carterette & Morton P. Friedman (Series Eds.), *Tasting and smelling: Handbook of perception and cognition* (2nd ed., pp. 199–221). San Diego, CA: Academic Press.

Messer, D. (1981). The identification of names in maternal speech to infants. *Journal of Psycholinguistic Research*, *10*, 69–77.

Messinger, D. S., Cassel, T. D., Acosta, S. I., Ambadar, Z., & Cohn, J. F. (2008). Infant smiling dynamics and perceived positive emotion. *Journal of Nonverbal Behavior*, *32*, 133–155.

Messinger, D., & Fogel, A. (2007). The interactive development of social smiling. In D. Messinger & A. Fogel (Eds.), *Advances in child development and behavior* (pp. 327–366). San Diego, CA: Elsevier Academic Press.

Mezzacappa, E., Buckner, J. C., & Earls, F. (2011). Prenatal cigarette exposure and infant learning stimulation as predictors of cognitive control in childhood. *Developmental Science*, *14*, 881–891.

Miller, G. A. (1981). *Language and speech*. San Francisco, CA: Freeman.

Mirowsky, J. (2002). Parenthood and health: The pivotal and optimal age at first birth. *Social Forces*, *81*, 315–349.

Molfese, D. L., Fonaryova-Key, A. P., Maguire, M. J., Dove, G. O., & Molfese, F. J. (2008). Event-related potentials (ERPs) in speech perception. In D. B. Pisoni & R. E. Remez (Eds.), *The handbook of speech perception* (pp. 99–121). Malden, MA: Blackwell.

Moll, H., & Tomasello, M. (2004). 12- and 18-month-old infants follow gaze to spaces behind barriers. *Developmental Science*, *7*, F1–F9.

Mondschein, E. R., Adolph, K. E., & Tamis-LeMonda, C. S. (2000). Gender bias in mothers' expectations about infant crawling. *Journal of Experimental Child Psychology*, *77*, 304–316.

Montirosso, R., Cozzi, P., Putnam, S. P., Gartstein, M. A., & Borgatti, R. (2011). Studying cross-cultural differences in temperament in the first year of life: United States and Italy. *International Journal of Behavioral Development*, *35*, 27–37.

Moore, C., & D'Entremont, B. (2001). Developmental changes in pointing as a function of attentional focus. *Journal of Cognition and Development*, *2*, 109–129.

Moore, D. G., Goodwin, J. E., George, R., Axelsson, E. L., & Braddick, F. M. B. (2007). Infants perceive human point-light displays as solid forms. *Cognition*, *104*, 377–396.

Moore, G. A. (2009). Infants' and mothers' vagal reactivity in response to anger. *Journal of Child Psychology and Psychiatry*, *50*, 1392–1400.

Morgan, R., & Rochat, P. (1997). Intermodal calibration of the body in early infancy. *Ecological Psychology*, *9*, 1–23.

Mosca, F., Colnaghi, M., & Fumagalli, M. (2011). BPD: Old and new problems. *Journal of Maternal-Fetal & Neonatal Medicine*, *24*, 80–82.

Moss, B. G., & Yeaton, W. H. (2011) Young children's weight trajectories and associated risk factors: Results from the Early Childhood Longitudinal Study—Birth Cohort. *American Journal of Health Promotion, 25*, 190–198.

Motlagh, M. G., Sukhodolsky, D. G., Landeros-Weisenberger, A., Katsovich, L., Thompson, N., Scahill, L., et al. (2011). Adverse effects of heavy prenatal maternal smoking on attentional control in children with ADHD. *Journal of Attention Disorders, 15*, 593–603.

Moulson, M. C., Fox, N. A., Zeanah, C. H., & Nelson, C. A. (2009). Early adverse experiences and the neurobiology of facial emotional processing. *Developmental Psychology, 45*, 17–30.

Moulson, M. C., Westerlund, A., Fox, N. A., Zeanah, C. H., & Nelson, C. A. (2009). The effects of early experience on face recognition: An event-related potential study of institutionalized children in Romania. *Child Development, 80*, 1039–1056.

Mumme, D. L., & Fernald, A. (2003). The infant as onlooker: Learning from emotional reactions observed in a televised scenario. *Child Development, 74*, 221–237.

Mundy, P., & Newell, L. (2007). Attention, joint attention, and social cognition. *Current Directions in Psychological Science, 16*, 269–274.

Mundy, P., & Sigman, M. (2006). Joint attention, social competence, and developmental psychopathology. In D. Cicchetti & D. J. Cohen (Eds.), *Developmental Psychopathology* (2nd ed., Vol. 1, pp. 293–332). New York, NY: Wiley.

Muraskas, J. K., Rau, B. J., Castillo, P. R., Gianopoulos, J., & Boyd, L. A. C. (2012). Long-term follow-up of 2 newborns with a combined birthweight of 540 grams. *Pediatrics, 129*, 1–5.

Murdock, B. (1959). A reply to Battig, Gibson, Runquist. *Psychological Review, 66*, 345–346.

Murphy, G. L. (2002). *The big book of concepts.* Cambridge, MA: MIT Press.

Murray, L., de Rosnay, M., Pearson, J., Bergeron, C., Schofield, E., Royal-Lawson, M., et al. (2008). Intergenerational transmission of social anxiety: The role of social referencing processes in infancy. *Child Development, 79*, 1049–1064.

Nagy, E. (2011). The newborn infant: A missing stage in developmental psychology. *Infant and Child Development, 20*, 3–19.

Nakanishi, R., & Imai-Matsumura, K. (2008). Facial skin temperature decreases in infants with joyful expression. *Infant Behavior and Development, 31*, 137–144.

Nakano, T., Watanabe, H., Homae, F., & Taga, G. (2009). Prefrontal cortex involvement in young infants' analysis of novelty. *Cerebral Cortex, 19*, 455–463.

Náñez, J. E., & Yonas, A. (1994). Effects of luminance and texture motion on infant defensive reactions to optical collision. *Infant Behavior and Development, 17*, 165–174.

Naoi, N., Minagawa-Kawai, Y., Kobayashi, A., Takeuchi, K., Nakamura, K., Yamamato, J., & Kojima, S. (2012). Cerebral responses to infant-directed speech and the effect of talker familiarity. *NeuroImage, 59*, 1735–1744.

Nawrot, E., Mayo, S. L., & Nawrot, M. (2009). The development of depth perception from motion parallax in infancy. *Attention, Perception, and Psychophysics, 71*, 194–199.

Needham, A. (2000). Improvements in object exploration skills may facilitate the development of object segregation in early infancy. *Journal of Cognition and Development, 1*, 131–156.

Needham, A. (2009). Learning in infants' object perception, object-directed action, and tool use. In A. Woodward & A. Needham (Eds.), *Learning and the infant mind* (pp. 208–226). New York, NY: Oxford.

Needham, A., Barrett, T., & Peterman, K. (2002). A pick-me-up for infants' exploratory skills: Early simulated experiences reaching for objects using "sticky mittens" enhances young infants' object exploration skills. *Infant Behavior and Development, 25*, 279–295.

Needleman, H. L., & Bellinger, D. (Eds.). (1994). *Prenatal exposure to toxicants: Developmental consequences.* Baltimore, MD: Johns Hopkins University Press.

Neil, P. A., Chee-Ruiter, C., Scheier, C., Lewkowicz, D. J., & Shimojo, S. (2006). Development of multisensory spatial integration and perception in humans. *Developmental Science, 9,* 454–464.

Nelson, C. A. (Ed.). (2000). *The effects of early adversity on neurobehavioral development.* Mahwah, NJ: Erlbaum.

Nelson, C. A., de Haan, M., & Thomas, K. M. (2006). *Neuroscience of cognitive development: The role of experience and the developing brain.* Hoboken, NJ: Wiley.

Nelson, C. A., & Lucianna, M. (Eds.). (2008). *Handbook of developmental cognitive neuroscience* (2nd ed). Cambridge, MA: MIT Press.

Newell, M. L., Coovadia, H., Cortina-Borja, M., Rollines, N., Gaillard, P., Dabis, F., et al. (2004). Mortality of infected and uninfected infants born to HIV-infected mothers in Africa: A pooled analysis. *Lancet, 364,* 1236–1243.

Newman, C. G. (1985). Teratogen update: Clinical aspects of thalidomide embryopathy: A continuing preoccupation. *Teratology, 32,* 133–144.

Newman, R. S., & Hussain, I. (2006). Changes in preference for infant-directed speech in low and moderate noise by 4.5- to 13-month-olds. *Infancy, 10,* 61–76.

NICHD Early Child Care Research Network (2005). *Child care and child development: Results from the NICHD study of early child care and youth development.* New York, NY: Guilford.

Nichols, S. R., Svetlova, M., & Brownell, C. A. (2010). Toddlers' understanding of peers' emotions. *Journal of Genetic Psychology, 171,* 35–53.

Noll, L. M., & Harding, C. G. (2003). The relationship of mother-child interaction and the child's development of symbolic play. *Infant Mental Health Journal, 24,* 557–570.

Novitski, N., Huotilainen, M., Tervaniemi, M., Näätänen, R., & Fellman, V. (2007). Neonatal frequency discrimination in 250–4000-Hz range: Electrophysiological evidence. *Clinical Neurology, 118,* 412–419.

Nugent, J. K. (2010). The development of the NBAS: A turning point in understanding the newborn. In B. M. Lester & J. D. Sparrow (Eds.), *Nurturing children and families: Building on the legacy of T. Berry Brazleton.* Hoboken, NJ: Wiley-Blackwell.

Numan, M. (2006). Hypothalamic neural circuits regulating maternal responsiveness toward infants. *Behavioral and Cognitive Neuroscience Reviews, 5,* 163–190.

Nunes, M. L., & Costa da Costa, J. (2010). Sleep and epilepsy in neonates. *Sleep Medicine, 11,* 665–673.

Oakes, L. M. (2012). Advances in eye tracking in infancy research. *Infancy, 17,* 1–8.

Oakes, L. M., & Ellis, A. E. (2013). An eye-tracking investigation of developmental changes in infants' exploration of upright and inverted human faces. *Infancy, 18,* 134–148.

Oakes, L. M., Kannass, K. N., & Shaddy, D. J. (2002). Developmental changes in endogenous control of attention: The role of target familiarity on infants' distraction latency. *Child Development, 73,* 1644–1655.

Oakes, L., M., Madole, K. L., & Cohen, L. B. (1991). Infants' object examining: Habituation and categorization. *Cognitive Development, 6,* 377–392.

Oakes, L. M., & Ribar, R. J. (2005). A comparison of infants' categorization in paired and successive presentation familiarization tasks. *Infancy, 7,* 85–98.

Oates, J., Lewis, C., & Lamb, M. E. (2005). Parenting and attachment. In J. Oates, C. Lewis, & M. E. Lamb (Eds.), *Children's personal and social development* (pp. 12–51). Malden, MA: Blackwell Publishing.

O'Brien, M. (2004). Social science and public policy perspectives on fatherhood in the European union. In M. O'Brien (Ed.), *The role of the father in child development* (4th ed., pp. 121–145). Hoboken, NJ: John Wiley & Sons Inc.

Oliver, B., Dale, P. S., & Plomin, R. (2004). Verbal and nonverbal predictors of early language problems: An analysis of twins in early childhood back to infancy. *Journal of Child Language, 31*, 609–631.

Oller, J. (2000). Language and its normal processing. *The Modern Language Journal, 84*, 302–303.

Olsho, L. W., Schoon, C., Sakai, R., Turpin, R., & Sperduto, V. (1982). Auditory frequency discrimination in infancy. *Developmental Psychology, 18*, 721–726.

Olson, S. E., & Lunkenheimer, E. S. (2009). Expanding concepts of self-regulation to social relationships: Transactional processes in the development of early behavioral adjustment. In A. Sameroff (Ed.), *The transactional model of development: How children and contexts shape each other* (pp. 55–76). Washington, DC: American Psychological Association.

Onishi, K. H., & Baillargeon, R. (2005). Do 15-month-old infants understand false belief? *Science, 308*, 255–258.

Onishi, K. H., Baillargeon, R., & Leslie, A. M. (2007). 15-month-old infants detect violations in pretend scenarios. *Acta Psychologica, 124*, 106–128.

Ornoy, A., Daka, L., Goldzweig, G., Gil, Y., Mjen, L., Levit, S., et al. (2010). Neurodevelopmental and psychological assessment of adolescents born to drug-addicted parents: Effects of SES and adoption. *Child Abuse and Neglect, 34*, 354–368.

Oster, H. (2003). Emotion in the infant's face: Insights from the study of infants with facial anomalies. *Annals of the New York Academy of Sciences, 1000*, 197–204.

Oster, H. (2005). The repertoire of infant facial expressions: An ontogenetic perspective. In J. Nadel & D. Muir (Eds.), *Emotional development: Recent research advances* (pp. 261–292). New York, NY: Oxford University Press.

Out, D., Pieper, S., Bakermans-Kranenburg, M. J., Zeskind, P. S., & van IJzendoorn, M. H. (2010). Intended sensitive and harsh caregiving responses to infant crying: The role of cry pitch and perceived urgency in an adult twin sample. *Child Abuse and Neglect, 34*, 863–873.

Palomo, R., Belinchon, M., & Ozonoff, S. (2006). Autism and family home movies: A comprehensive review. *Journal of Developmental and Behavioral Pediatrics, 27*, S59–S68.

Papoušek, H. (2007). Communication in early infancy: An area of intersubjective learning. *Infant Behavior and Development, 30*, 258–266.

Papoušek, H., & Bernstein, P. (1969). Basic cognitive functions in the pre-verbal period of infancy. *Acta Nervosa Superior, 11*, 285–286.

Papoušek, H., & Papou{s}ek, M. (2002a). Parent-infant speech patterns. In H. Papoušek & M. Papoušek (Eds.), *The infant and family in the twenty-first century* (pp. 101–108). New York, NY: Brunner-Routledge.

Papoušek, H., & Papou{s}ek, M. (2002b). Intuitive parenting. In M. H. Bornstein (Ed.), *Handbook of parenting: Biology and ecology of parenting* (Vol. 2, pp. 183–203). Mahwah, NJ: Erlbaum.

Parke, R. D. (2002). Fathers and families. In M. H. Bornstein (Ed.), *Handbook of parenting: Status and social conditions of parenting* (2nd ed., Vol. 3, pp. 27–73). Mahwah, NJ: Lawrence Erlbaum Associations.

Parke, R. D., & Buriel, R. (1998). Socialization in the family: Ethnic and ecological perspectives. In W. Damon (Editor-in-Chief) & N. Eisenberg (Vol. Ed.), *Handbook of child psychology: Social, emotional, and personality development* (Vol. 3, pp. 463–552). New York, NY: Wiley.

Parke, R. D., & Buriel, R. (2006). Socialization in the family: Ethnic and ecological perspectives. In D. Kuhn & R. S. Siegler (Ed.), W. Damon (Series Ed.), *Handbook of child psychology: Vol. 2. Cognition, perception, and language* (6th ed., pp. 429–504). Hoboken, NJ: Wiley.

Pasterski, V. L., Geffner, M. E., Brain, C., Hindmarsh, P., Brook, C., & Hines, M. (2005). Prenatal hormones and postnatal socialization by parents as determinants of male-typical toy plan in girls with congenital adrenal hyperplasia. *Child Development, 76*, 264–278.

Paterson, S. J., Heim, S., Friedman, J. T., Choudhury, N., & Benasich, A. A. (2006). Development of structure an function in the infant brain: Implications for cognition, language and social behavior. *Neuroscience and Biobehavioral Reviews, 30*, 1087–1105.

Pathak, R., Mustafa, M. D., Ahmed, T., Ahmed, R. S., Tripathi, A. K., Guleria, K., et al. (2011). Intra uterine growth retardation: Association with organochlorine pesticide residue levels and oxidative stress markers. *Reproductive Toxicology, 31*, 534–539.

Patra, J., Bakker, R., Irving, H., Jaddoe, V. W. V., Malini, S., & Rehm, J. (2011). Dose-response relationship between alcohol consumption before and during pregnancy and the risks of low birthweight, preterm birth and small for gestational age (SGA): A systematic review and meta-analysis. *BJOG: An International Journal of Obstetrics and Gynaecology, 118*, 1411–1421.

Patrick, S. W., Schumacher, R. E., Benneyworth, B. D., Krans, E. E., McAllister, J. M., & Davis, M. M. (2012). Neonatal abstinence syndrome and associated health care expenditures. *National Institutes of Health, 1*, E1–E7.

Paul, I. M., Lehman, E. B., Suliman, A. K., & Hillemeier, M. M. (2008). Perinatal disparities for black mothers and their newborns. *Maternal and Child Health Journal, 12*, 452–460.

Pauli-Pott, U., Mertesacker, B., Bade, U., Haverkock, A., Beckmann, D. (2003). Parental perceptions and infant temperament development. *Infant Behavior & Development, 26*, 27–48.

Paulus, M. (2011). How infants relate looker and object: Evidence for a perceptual learning account of gaze following in infancy. *Developmental Science, 14*, 1301–1310.

Paulus, M., Hunnius, S., Vissers, M., & Bekkering, H. (2011). Imitation in infancy: Rational or motor resonance? *Child Development, 82*, 1047–1057.

Paz, N. C., Sanchez, S. E., Huaman, L. E., Chang, G. D., Pacora, P. N., Garcia, P. J., et al. (2011). Risk of placental abruption in relation to maternal depression, anxiety, and stress symptoms. *Journal of Affective Disorders, 130*, 280–284.

Pearson, R. M., Heron, J., Melotti, R., Joinson, C., Stein, A., Ramchandani, P. G., et al. (2011). The association between observed nonverbal maternal responses at 12 months and later infant development at 18 months and IQ at 4 years: A longitudinal study. *Infant Behavior and Development, 34*, 525–533.

Peeples, D. R., & Teller, D. Y. (1975). Color vision and brightness discrimination in two-month-old human infants. *Science, 189*, 1102–1103.

Peiper, A. (1963). *Cerebral function infancy and childhood.* New York, NY: Consultants Bureau.

Peltola, M. J., Leppanen, J. M., & Hietanen, J. K. (2011). Enhanced cardiac and attentional responding to fearful faces in 7-month-old infants. *Psychophysiology, 48*, 1291–1298.

Pempek, T. A., Kirkorian, H. L., Richards, J. E., Anderson, D. R., Lund, A. F., & Stevens, M. (2010). Video comprehensibility and attention in very young children. *Developmental Psychology, 46*, 1283–1293.

Perner, J., Leekam, S. R., & Wimmer, H. (1987). Three-year-olds' difficulty with false belief: The case for a conceptual deficit. *British Journal of Developmental Psychology, 5*, 125–137.

Perone, S., Madole, K. L., Ross-Sheehy, S., Carey, M., & Oakes, L. M. (2008). The relation between infants' activity with objects and attention to object appearance. *Developmental Psychology, 44*, 1242–1248.

Perra, O., & Gattis, M. (2010). The control of social attention from 1 to 4 months. *British Journal of Developmental Psychology, 28*, 891–908.

Peterson, C. C. (2000). Influence of siblings' perspectives on theory of mind. *Cognitive Development, 15*, 435–455.

Peterson, C., & Parsons, B. (2005). Interviewing former 1- and 2-year-olds about medical emergencies 5 years later. *Law and Human Behavior, 29*, 743–754.

Peterson, C., Warren, K. L., & Short, M. M. (2011). Infantile amnesia across the years: A 2-year follow-up of children's earliest memories. *Child Development, 82*, 1092–1105.

Petitto, L. A., Holowka, S., Sergio, L. E., Levy, B., & Ostry, D. (2004). Baby hands that move to the rhythms of language: Hearing babies acquiring sign language babble silently with their hands. *Cognition, 93,* 43–73.

Petitto, L., & Marentette, P. (1991). Babbling in the manual mode: Evidence for the ontogeny of language. *Science, 251,* 1493–1496.

Petrill, S. A., Deater-Deckard, K., Schatschneider, C., & Davis, C. (2007). Environmental influences on reading-related outcomes: An adoption study. *Infant and Child Development, 16,* 171–191.

Pettersen, L., Yonas, A., & Fisch, R. O. (1980). The development of blinking in response to impending collision in preterm, full-term, and postterm infants. *Infant Behavior & Development, 3,* 155–165.

Peyvandi, F., Garagiola, I., & Mortarino, M. (2011). Prenatal diagnosis and preimplantation genetic diagnosis: Novel technologies and state of the art PDG in different regions of the world. *Haemophilia, 17,* 14–17.

Phillips, A. T., Wellman, H. M., & Spelke, E. S. (2002). Infants' ability to connect gaze and emotional expression to intentional action. *Cognition, 85,* 53–78.

Piaget, J. (1952). *The origins of intelligence in children.* New York, NY: Norton.

Piaget, J. (1954). *The construction of reality in the child.* New York, NY: Basic Books. (Original work published in 1937.)

Piaget, J. (1962). The relation of affectivity to intelligence in the mental development of the child. *Bulletin of the Menninger Clinic, 26,* 129–137.

Piaget, J., & Inhelder, B. (1967). *The child's conception of space* (F. J. Langdon & J. L. Lunzer, trans.) New York, NY: Norton. (Original work published in 1948.)

Pierce, K., Carter, C., Weinfeld, M., Desmond, J., Hazin, R., Bjork, R., et al. (2011). Detecting, studying, and treating autism early: The one-year well-baby check-up approach. *Journal of Pediatrics, 159,* 458–466.

Pinker, S. (2007). *The language instinct: How the mind creates language.* New York, NY: Harper Collins.

Pivik, R. T., Andres, A., & Badger, T. M. (2011). Diet and gender influences on processing and discrimination of speech sounds in 3- and 6-month-old infants: A developmental ERP study. *Developmental Science, 14,* 700–712.

Plomin, R. (2000). Behavioural genetics in the 21st century. *International Journal of Behavioral Development, 24,* 30–34.

Pluess, M., & Belsky, J. (2011). Prenatal programming of postnatal plasticity? *Development and Psychopathology, 23,* 29–38.

Pluess, M., & Belsky, J. (2012). Parenting effects in the context of child genetic differences. *ISSBD Bulletin, 2,* 2–5.

Pollak, S. D., Messner, M., Kistler, D. J., & Cohn, J. F. (2009). Development of perceptual expertise in emotion recognition. *Cognition, 110,* 242–247.

Pomerleau, A., Bolduc, D., Malcuit, G., & Cossette, L. (1990). Pink or blue: Environmental gender stereotypes in the first two years of life. *Sex Roles, 22,* 359–367.

Pomerleau, A., Malcuit, G., Chicoine, J., Seguin, R., Belhumeur, C., Germain, P., et al. (2005). Health status, cognitive and motor development of young children adopted from China, East Asia, and Russia across the first 6 months after adoption. *International Journal of Behavioral Development, 29,* 445–457.

Porges, S. W. (2011). *The polyvagal theory: Neurophysiological foundations of emotions, attachment, communication, and self-regulation.* New York, NY: Norton.

Porter, R. H., Bologh, R. D., & Makin, J. W. (1988). Olfactory influences on mother-infant interactions. In C. Rovee-Collier & L. P. Lipsitt (Eds.), *Advances in infancy research* (Vol. 5, pp. 39–69). Norwood, NJ: Ablex.

Porter, R. H., & Winberg, J. (1999). Unique salience of maternal breast odors for newborn infants. *Neuroscience and Biobehavioral Reviews, 23,* 439–449.

Poulin-Dubois, D., Frenkiel-Fishman, S., Nayer, S., & Johnson, S. (2006). Infants' inductive generalization of bodily, motion, and sensory properties to animals and people. *Journal of Cognition and Development, 7*, 431–453.

Poulin-Dubois, D., Sodian, B., Metz, U., Tilden, J., & Schoeppner, B. (2007). Out of sight is not out of mind: Developmental changes in infants' understanding of visual perception during the second year. *Journal of Cognition and Development, 8*, 401–425.

Premack, D., & Woodruff, G. (1978). Does the chimpanzee have a theory of mind? *Behavioral and Brain Sciences, 1*, 515–526.

Preyer, W. (1881). *Mind of the child.* (H. W. Brown, trans.) New York, NY: Appleton.

Preyer, W. (1888). *The mind of the child, Part 1: The senses and the will; Part 2: The development of the intellect.* London, UK: Routledge/Thoemmes Press.

Price, T. S., Eley, T. C., Dale, P. S., Stevenson, J., Saudino, K., & Plomin, R. (2000). Genetic and environmental covariation between verbal and nonverbal cognitive development in infancy. *Child Development, 71*, 948–959.

Pruden, S. M., Goksun, T., Roseberry, S., Hirsh-Pasek, K., & Golinkoff, R. M. (2012). Find your manners: How do infants detect the invariant manner of motion in dynamic events? *Child Development, 83*, 977–991.

Pruden, S. M., Levine, S. C., & Huttenlocher, J. (2011). Children's spatial thinking: Does talk about the spatial world matter? *Developmental Science, 14*, 1417–1430.

Purhonen, M., Pääkkönen, A., Yppärilä, H., Lehtonen, J., & Karhu, J. (2001). Dynamic behavior of the auditory N100 elicited by a baby's cry. *International Journal of Psychophysiology, 41*, 271–278.

Putnam, S. P., Gartstein, M. A., & Rothbart, M. K. (2006). Measurement of fine-grained aspects of toddler temperament: The early childhood behavior questionnaire. *Infant Behavior and Development, 29*, 386–401.

Putnam, S. P., Rothbart, M. K., & Gartstein, M. A. (2008). Homotypic and heterotypic continuity of fine-grained temperament during infancy, toddlerhood, and early childhood. *Infant and Child Development, 17*, 387–405.

Putnam, S. P., & Stifter, C. A. (2008). Reactivity and regulation: The impact of Mary Rothbart on the study of temperament. *Infant and Child Development, 17*, 311–320.

Quinn, P. C. (2004). Development of subordinate-level categorization in 3- to 7-month-old infants. *Child Development, 75*, 886–899.

Quinn, P. C. (2011). Born to categorize. In U. Goswami (Ed.), *The Wiley-Blackwell handbook of childhood cognitive development* (2nd ed., pp. 129–152). Malden, MA: Wiley-Blackwell.

Quinn, P. C., Anzures, G., Izard, C. E., Lee, K., Pascalis, O., Slater, A. M., et al. (2011). Looking across domains to understand infant representation of emotion. *Emotion Review, 3*, 197–206.

Quinn, P. C., Doran, M. M., Reiss, J. E., & Hoffman, J. E. (2010). Neural markers of subordinate-level categorization in 6- to 7-month-old infants. *Developmental Science, 13*, 499–507.

Quinn, P. C., Kelly, D. J., Lee, K., Pascalis, O., & Slater, A. M. (2008). Preference for attractive faces in human infants extends beyond conspecifics. *Developmental Science, 11*, 76–83.

Quinn, P. C., Johnson, M. H., Mareschal, D., Rakison, D. H., & Younger, B. A. (2000). Understanding early categorization: One process or two? *Infancy, 1*, 111–122.

Raby, K. L., Cicchetti, D., Carlson, E. A., Cutuli, J. J., Englund, M. M., & Egeland, B. (2012). Genetic and caregiving-based contributions to infant attachment: Unique associations with distress reactivity and attachment security. *Psychological Science, 23*, 1016–1023.

Rakison, D. H. (2000). When a rose is just a rose: The illusion of taxonomies in infant categorization. *Infancy, 1*, 77–90.

Rakison, D. H. (2003). Parts, motion, and the development of the animate-inanimate distinction in infancy. In D. H. Rakison & L. M. Oakes (Eds.), *Early category and concept development: Making sense of the blooming, buzzing confusion* (pp. 159–192). Oxford, UK: Oxford University Press.

Rakison, D. H. (2006). Make the first move: How infants learn about self-propelled objects. *Developmental Psychology*, *42*, 900–912.

Rakison, D. H., & Oakes, L. M. (Eds.). (2003). *Early category and concept development: Making sense of the blooming, buzzing confusion*. New York, NY: Oxford University Press.

Rakoczy, H. (2012). Do infants have a theory of mind? *British Journal of Development Psychology*, *30*, 59–74.

Rasmussen, S. A. (2011). Human teratogens update 2011. *Birth Defects Research Part A: Clinical and Molecular Teratology*, *91*, 306.

Rauh, H., Ziegenhain, T., Müller, B., & Wijnroks, L. (2000). Stability and change in infant-mother attachment in the second year of life: Relations to parenting quality and varying degrees of day-care experience. In P. M. Crittenden & A. H. Claussen (Eds.), *The organization of attachment relationships: Maturation, culture, and context* (pp. 251–276). New York, NY: Cambridge University Press.

Ravn, I. H., Smith, L., Lindemann, R., Smedy, N. A., Kyno, N. M., Bunch, E. H., et al. (2011). Effect of intervention on social interaction between mothers and preterm infants at 12 months of age: A randomized controlled trial. *Infant Behavior and Development*, *34*, 215–225.

Ray, E., & Heyes, C. (2011). Imitation in infancy: The wealth of the stimulus. *Developmental Science*, *14*, 92–105.

Reef, S. E., Strebel, P., Dabbagh, A., Gacic-Dobo, M., & Cochi, S. (2011). Progress toward control of rubella and prevention of congential rubella syndrome—Worldwide, 2009. *Journal of Infectious Diseases*, *204*, S24–S27.

Reese, E., & Newcombe, R. (2007). Training mothers in elaborative reminiscing enhances children's autobiographical memory and narrative. *Child Development*, *78*, 1153–1170.

Renzaho, A. M. N., & Vignjevic, S. (2011). The impact of a parenting intervention in Australia among migrants and refugees from Liberia, Sierra Leone, Congo, and Burundi: Results from the African Migrant Parenting Program. *Journal of Family Studies*, *17*, 1–79.

Repacholi, B. M., & Meltzoff, A. N. (2007). Emotional eavesdropping: Infants selectively respond to indirect emotional signals. *Child Development*, *78*, 503–521.

Reynell, J., & Gruber, C. P. (1990). *Reynell developmental language scales*. Los Angeles, CA: Western Psychological Services.

Reynolds, G. D., & Courage, M. L. (2010). Infant attention and visual preferences: Converging evidence from behavior, event-related potentials, and cortical source localization. *Developmental Psychology*, *46*, 886–904.

Reynolds, G. D., & Richards, J. E. (2005). Familiarization, attention, and recognition memory in infancy: An event-related potential and cortical course localization study. *Developmental Psychology*, *41*, 598–615.

Rheingold, H. L., & Eckerman, C. O. (1970). The infant separates himself from his mother. *Science*, *168*, 78–83.

Richards, J. E. (2010). The development of attention to simple and complex visual stimuli in infants: Behavioral and psychophysiological measures. *Developmental Review*, *30*, 203–219.

Richards, J. E., & Anderson, D. R. (2004). Attentional inertia in children's extended looking at television. *Advances in Child Development and Behavior*, *32*, 163–212.

Richards, J. E., & Casey, B. J. (1991). Heart rate variability during attention phases in young infants. *Psychophysiology*, *28*, 43–53.

Richards, J. E., & Cronise, K. (2000). Extended visual fixation in the early preschool years: Look duration, heart rate changes, and attentional inertia. *Child Development*, *71*, 602–620.

Riddell, R. R. P., Stevens, B. J., Cohen, L. L., Flora, D. B., & Greenberg, S. (2007). Predicting maternal and behavioral measures of infant pain: The relative contribution of maternal factors. *Pain*, *133*, 138–149.

Rideout, V. J., & Hamel, E. (2006). *The media family: Electronic media in the lives of infants, toddlers, preschoolers and their parents*. Menlo Park, CA: Kaiser Family Foundation.

Rimmele, U., Hediger, K., Heinrichs, M., & Klaver, P. (2009). Oxytocin makes a face in memory familiar. *The Journal of Neuroscience, 29*, 38–42.

Ring, E. D., & Fenson, L. (2000). The correspondence between parent report and child performance for receptive and expressive vocabulary beyond infancy. *First Language, 20*, 141–159.

Riviere, J., & Lecuyer, R. (2008). Effects of arm weight on C-not-B task performance: Implications for motor inhibitory deficit account of search failures. *Journal of Experimental Child Psychology, 100*, 1–16.

Riviere, V., Darcheville, J. C., & Clement, C. (2000). Rapid timing of transitions in inter-reinforcement interval duration in infants. *Behavioural Processes, 52*, 109–115.

Rivkees, S. A. (2003). Developing circadian rhythms in infants. *Pediatrics, 112*, 373–381.

Rivkees, S. A., & Hao, H. P. (2000). Developing circadian rhythmicity. *Seminars in Perinatology, 24*, 232–242.

Rivkees, S. A., Mayes, L., Jacobs, H., & Gross, I. (2004). Rest-activity patterns of premature infants are regulated by cycled lighting. *Pediatrics, 113*, 833–839.

Rivkin, M. J., Davis, P. E., Lemaster, J. L., Cabral, H. J., Warfield, S. K., Mulkern, R. V., et al. (2008). Volumetric MRI study of brain in children with intrauterine exposure to cocaine, alcohol, tobacco, and marijuana. *American Academy of Pediatrics, 121*, 741–750.

Rochat, P. (2003). Five levels of self-awareness as they unfold early in life. *Consciousness and Cognition, 12*, 717–731.

Rochat, P., & Hespos, S. J. (1997). Differential rooting response by neonates: Evidence for an early sense of self. *Early Development and Parenting, 6*, 105–112.

Rochat, P., & Zahavi, D. (2011). The uncanny mirror: A re-framing of mirror self-expression. *Consciousness and Cognition, 20*, 204–213.

Roggman, L. A., Boyce, L. K., Cook, G. A., Christiansen, K., & Jones, D. (2004). Playing with daddy: Social toy play, early head start, and developmental outcomes. *Fathering, 2*, 83–108.

Rogoff, B. (2003). *The cultural nature of human development.* New York, NY: Oxford University Press.

Rogoff, B., Paradise, R., Arauz, R. M., Correa-Chavez, M., & Angelillo, C. (2003). Firsthand learning through intent participation. *Annual Review of Psychology, 54*, 175–203.

Roisman, G. I., & Groh, A. M. (2011). Attachment theory and research in developmental psychology: An overview and appreciative critique. In M. K. Underwood & L. H. Rosen (Eds.), *Social Development: Relationships in infancy, childhood, and adolescence.* New York, NY: Guilford.

Roopnarine, J. L., Fouts, H. N., & Lamb, M. E. (2007). Social experiences and daily routines of African American infants in different socioeconomic contexts. *Journal of Family Psychology, 21*, 655–664.

Roopnarine, J. L., Fouts, H. N., Lamb, M. E., & Lewis-Elligan, T. Y. (2005). Mothers' and fathers' behaviors toward their 3- to 4-month-old infants in lower, middle, and upper socioeconomic African American families. *Developmental Psychology, 41*, 723–732.

Rose, S. A., Feldman, J. F., Jankowski, J. J., & Van Rossem, R. (2008). A cognitive cascade in infancy: Pathways from prematurity to later mental development. *Intelligence, 36*, 367–378.

Rose, S. A., Feldman, J. F., Jankowski, J. J., & Van Rossem, R. (2011). Basic information processing abilities at 11 years accounts for deficits in IQ associated with preterm birth. *Intelligence, 39*, 198–209.

Roseberry, S., Richie, R., Hirsh-Pasek, K., Golinkoff, R., & Shipley, T. (2011). Babies catch a break: 7- to 9-month-olds track statistical probabilities in continuous dynamic events. *Psychological Science, 22*, 1422–1424.

Rothbart, M. K. (2011). *Becoming who we are: Temperament and personality in development.* New York, NY: Guilford Press.

Rothbart, M. K., & Bates, J. E. (2006). Temperament. In N. Eisenberg, W. Damon, & R. M. Lerner (Eds.), *Handbook of child psychology: Social, emotional, and personality development* (6th ed., Vol. 3, pp. 99–166). Hoboken, NJ: Wiley.

Rothbart, M. K., Sheese, B. E., Rueda, M. R., & Posner, M. I. (2011). Developing mechanisms of self-regulation in early life. *Emotion Review, 3*, 207–213.

Rothbaum, F., Pott, M., Azuma, H., Miyake, K., & Weisz, J. (2000). The development of close relationships in Japan and the United States: Paths of symbiotic harmony and generative tension. *Child Development, 71*, 1121–1142.

Roth-Hanania, R., Davidov, M., & Zahn-Waxler, C. (2011). Empathy development from 8 to 16 months: Early signs of concern for others. *Infant Behavior and Development, 34*, 447–458.

Rousseau, J. J. (1781). *Confessions.* New York: Dover.

Rovee-Collier, C. (2011). Preserving infant memories. In M. A. Gernsbacher, R. W. Pew, L. M. Hough, & J. R. Pomerantz (Eds.), *Psychology and the real world: Essays illustrating fundamental contributions to society.* New York, NY: Worth.

Rovee-Collier, C., & Cuevas, K. (2009a). The development of infant memory. In M. L. Courage & N. Cowan (Eds.), *The development of memory in infancy and childhood* (2nd ed., pp. 11–41). New York, NY: Psychology Press.

Rovee-Collier, C., & Cuevas, K. (2009b). Multiple memory systems are unnecessary to account for infant memory development: An ecological model. *Developmental Psychology, 45*, 160–174.

Rovee-Collier, C., & Gehardstein, P. (1997). The development of infant memory. In C. Hulme (Series Ed.) & N. Cowan (Ed.), *The development of memory in childhood. Studies in Developmental Psychology* (pp. 5–30). Hove, UK: Psychology Press.

Rovee-Collier, C., & Giles, A. (2010). Why a neuromaturational model of memory fails: Exuberant learning in infancy. *Behavioural Processes, 83*, 197–206.

Rowe, M., & Goldin-Meadow, S. (2009). Differences in early gesture explain SES disparities in child vocabulary size at school entry. *Science, 323*, 951–953.

Rozhkov, V. P., & Soroko, S. I. (2000). Formation of the interaction between the wave components of the main EEG rhythms in children up to five years of age. *Human Physiology, 26*, 5–19.

Rubin, K., Coplan, R., Chen, X., Bowker, J., & McDonald, K. (2011). Peer relations in childhood. In M. H. Bornstein & M. E. Lamb (Eds.). *Developmental science: An advanced textbook (*6th ed., pp. 519–570). New York, NY: Psychology Press.

Ruble, D. N., Martin, C. L., & Berenbaum, S. A. (2006). In D. N. Ruble, C. L. Martin, & S. A. Berenbaum (Eds.), *Handbook of child psychology: Social, emotional, and personality development* (6th ed., Vol. 3, pp. 858–932). Hoboken, NJ: John Wiley & Sons Inc.

Ruff, H. A. (1982). Visual following of moving objects by full-term and preterm infants. *Journal of Pediatric Psychology, 7*, 375–386.

Ruff, H. A. (1985). Detection of information specifying the motion of objects by 3- and 5-month-old infants. *Developmental Psychology, 21*, 295–305.

Ruffman, T., Slade, L., & Redman, J. (2005). Young infants' expectations about hidden objects. *Cognition, 97*, B35–B43.

Ruth-Lyons, K., Bronfman, E., & Parsons, E. (1999). Maternal frightened, frightening, or atypical behavior and disorganized infant attachment patterns. *Monographs of the Society for Research in Child Development, 64*, 67–96.

Saarni, C., Campos, J. J., Camras, L. A., & Witherington, D. (2006). Emotional development: Action, communication and understanding. In N. Eisenberg (Ed.), *Handbook of child psychology: Social, emotional, and personality development* (6th ed., Vol. 3, pp. 226–299). New York, NY: Wiley.

Saffran, J. (2009). Acquiring grammatical patterns: Constraints on learning. In J. Colombo, P. McCardle, & L. Freun (Eds.), *Infant pathways to language* (pp. 31–47). New York, NY: Psychology Press.

Saffran J. R., Werker, J. F., & Werner, L. A. (2006). The infant's auditory world: Hearing, speech, and the beginnings of language. In D. Kuhn, R. S. Siegler, W. Damon, & R. M. Lerner (Eds.), *Handbook of child psychology: Cognition, perception, and language* (6th ed., Vol. 2, pp. 58–108). Hoboken, NJ: Wiley.

Salapatek, P., & Kessen, W. (1966). Visual scanning of triangles by the human newborn. *Journal of Experimental Child Psychology, 3*, 155–167.

Sales, B. D., & Folkman, S. (2000). *Ethics in Research with Human Participants.* Washington, DC: American Psychological Association.

Sameroff, A. (2009). The transactional model. In A. Sameroff (Ed.), *The transactional model of development: How children and contexts shape each other* (pp. 3–21). Washington, DC: American Psychological Association.

Sameroff, A., & Chandler, M. J. (1975). Reproductive risk and the continuum of caretaking casualty. In F. D. Horowitz (Ed.), *Review of child development research* (Vol. 4, pp. 137–244). Chicago, IL: University of Chicago Press.

Sandhofer, C., Smith, L., & Luo, J. (2000). Counting nouns and verbs in the input: Differential frequencies, different kinds of learning? *Journal of Child Language, 27*, 561–585.

Sann, C., & Streri, A. (2008). The limits of newborn's grasping to detect texture in a cross-modal transfer task. *Infant Behavior and Development, 31*, 523–531.

Sansavini, A., Guarini, A., Savini, S., Broccoli, S., Justice, L., & Alessandroni, G. F. (2011). Longitudinal trajectories of gestural and linguistic abilities in very preterm infants in the second year of life. *Neuropsychologia, 49*, 3677–3688.

Saudino, K. J. (2003). Parent ratings of infant temperament: Lessons from twin studies. *Infant Behavior and Development, 26*, 100–107.

Saudino, K. J. (2005). Behavioral genetics and child temperament. *Journal of Developmental and Behavioral Pediatrics, 26*, 214–223.

Saudino, K. J., Carter, A. S., Purper-Ouakil, D., & Gorwood, P. (2008). The etiology of behavior problems and competencies in very young twins. *Journal of Abnormal Psychology, 117*, 48–62.

Scarr, S. (1993). Biological and cultural diversity: The legacy of Darwin for development. *Child Development, 64*, 1333–1353.

Schachner, A., & Hannon, E. E. (2011). Infant-directed speech drives social preferences in 5-month-old infants. *Developmental Psychology, 47*, 19–25.

Schaefer, C. E., Kelly-Zion, S., McCormick, J., & Ohnogi, A. (Eds.). (2008). *Play therapy for very young children.* Lanham, MD: Rowman & Littlefield.

Schaller, M. J. (1975). Chromatic vision in human infants: Conditioned operant fixation to "hues" of varying intensity. *Bulletin of the Psychonomic Society, 6*, 39–42.

Scher, M. S., Ludington-Hoe, S., Kaffashi, F., Johnson, M. W., Holditch-Davis, D., & Loparo, K. A. (2009). Neurophysiologic assessment of brain maturation after an 8-week trial of skin-to-skin contact on preterm infants. *Clinical Neurophysiology, 120*, 1812–1818.

Scherer, K. R., Zentner, M. R., & Stern, D. (2004). Beyond surprise: The puzzle of infants' expressive reactions to expectancy violation. *Emotion, 4*, 389–402.

Scherling, D. (1994). Prenatal cocaine exposure and childhood psychopathology: A developmental analysis. *American Journal of Orthopsychiatry, 64*, 9–19.

Schlesinger, M., & Casey, P. (2003). Where infants look when impossible things happen: Simulating and testing a gaze-direction model. *Connection Science, 15*, 271–280.

Schmuckler, M. A., Collimore, L. M., & Dannemiller, J. L. (2007). Infants' reactions to object collision on hit and miss trajectories. *Infancy, 12*, 105–118.

Schmuckler, M. A., & Jewell, D. T. (2007). Infants' visual-proprioceptive intermodal perception with imperfect contingency information. *Developmental Psychobiology*, *49*, 387–398.

Schwartz, A. N., Campos, J. J., & Baisel, E. J. (1973). The visual cliff: Cardiac and behavioral responses on the deep and shallow sides of five and nine months of age. *Journal of Experimental Child Psychology*, *15*, 86–99.

Schwartz, C. E., Kunwar, P. S., Creve, D. N., Moran, L. R., Viner, J. C., Covino, J. M., et al. (2010). Structural differences in adult orbital and ventromedial prefrontal cortex predicted by infant temperament at 4 months of age. *Archive of General Psychiatry*, *67*, 78–84.

Schwartz, C. E., Wright, C. I., Shin, L. M., Kagan, J., & Rauch, S. (2003). Inhibited and uninhibited infants "grown up": Adult amygdala response to novelty. *Science*, *300*, 1952–1953.

Schyns, P. G., & Rodet, L. (1997). Categorization creates functional features. *Journal of Experimental Psychology: Learning, Memory, and Cognition*, *23*, 681–696.

Seavey, C. A., Katz, P. A., & Zalk, S. R. (1975). Baby X: The effect of gender labels on adult responses to infants. *Sex Roles*, *1*, 103–109.

Segal, N. L. (2010). Twins: The finest natural experiment. *Personality and Individual Differences*, *49*, 317–323.

Seidl, A., & Johnson, E. K. (2006). Infant word segmentation revisited: Edge alignment facilitates target extraction. *Developmental Science*, *9*, 565–573.

Seligman, M. E. P. (1970). On the generality of the laws of learning. *Psychological Review*, *77*, 406–418.

Senghas, A., & Coppola, M. (2001). Children creating language: How Nicaraguan sign language acquired a spatial grammar. *Psychological Science*, *12*, 323–328.

Seress, L., & Abraham, H. (2008). Pre- and postnatal morphological development of the human hippocampal formation. In C. A. Nelson & M. Lucianna (Eds.), *Handbook of developmental cognitive neuroscience* (2nd ed., pp. 187–212). Cambridge, MA: MIT Press.

Shannon, J. D., Cabrera, N. J., Tamis-LeMonda, C., & Lamb, M. E. (2009). Who stays and who leaves? Father accessibility across children's first 5 years. *Parenting: Science and Practice*, *9*, 78–100.

Shannon, J. D., Tamis-LeMonda, C. S., & Margolin, A. (2005). Father involvement in infancy: Influences of past and current relationships. *Infancy*, *8*, 21–41.

Shanok, A. F., & Miller, L. (2007). Stepping up to motherhood among inner-city teens. *Psychology of Women Quarterly*, *31*, 252–261.

Shapiro, J. R., & Mangelsdorf, S. C. (1994). The determinants of parenting competence in adolescent mothers. *Journal of Youth and Adolescence*, *23*, 621–641.

Shaw, P., Greenstein, D., Lerch, J., Clasen, L., Lenroot, R., Gogtay, N., et al. (2006). Intellectual ability and cortical development in children and adolescents. *Nature*, *440*, 676–679.

Sheese, B. E., Voelker, P., Posner, M. I., & Rothbart, M. K. (2009). Genetic variation influences on the early development of reactive emotions and their regulation by attention. *Cognitive Neuropsychiatry*, *14*, 332–355.

Shi, Y., Jin, R., Zhao, J., Tang, S., Li, H., et al. (2009). Brain positron emission tomography in preterm and term newborn infants. *Early Human Development*, *85*, 429–432.

Shinskey, J. L., & Munakata, Y. (2003). Are infants in the dark about hidden objects? *Developmental Science*, *6*, 272–282.

Shirley, M. M. (1933). *The first two years: Intellectual development* (Vol. 2). Minneapolis, MN: University Minnesota Press.

Shirley, M. (1938). Development of immature babies during their first two years. *Child Development*, *9*, 347–360.

Shonkoff, J. P., & Phillips, D. A. (2000). *From neurons to neighborhoods: The science of early childhood development.* Washington, DC: National Academy Press.

Shostak, M. (1981). *Nissa: The life and words of a !Kung woman.* Cambridge, MA: Harvard University Press.

Shrout, P. E., & Bolger, N. (2002). Mediation in experimental and nonexperimental studies: New procedures and recommendations. *Psychological Methods, 7,* 422–445.

Sidorowicz, L. S., & Lunney, G. S. (1980). Baby X revisited. *Sex Roles, 6,* 67–73.

Sireteanu, R. (1996). Development of the visual field: Results from human and animal studies. In R. Sireteanu (Ed.), *Infant vision* (pp. 17–31). New York, NY: Oxford University Press.

Sirois, S., & Jackson, I. R. (2012). Pupil dilation and object permanence in infants. *Infancy, 17,* 61–78.

Skinner, B. F. (1957). *Verbal behavior.* East Norwalk, CT: Appleton-Century-Crofts.

Slack, C., Lurix, K., Lewis, S., & Lichten, L. (2006). Prenatal genetics: The evolution and future directions of screening and diagnosis. *Journal Perinatal and Neonatal Nursing, 20,* 93–97.

Slack, K. S., Berger, L. M., DuMont, K., Yang, M.-Y., Kim, B., et al. (2011). Risk and protective factors for child neglect during early childhood: A cross-study comparison. *Children and Youth Services Review, 33,* 1354–1363.

Slater, A. M. (1993). Visual perceptual abilities at birth: Implications for face perception. In A. M. Slater (Ed.), *Developmental neurocognition: Speech and face processing in the first year of life* (pp. 125–134). New York, NY: Kluwer Academic/Plenum Publishers.

Slater, A., Bremner, G., Johnson, S. P., Sherwood, P., Hayes, R., & Brown, E. (2000). Newborn infants' preference for attractive faces: The role of internal and external facial features. *Infancy, 1,* 265–274.

Slater, A., Johnson, S. P., Brown, E., & Badenoch, M. (1996). Newborn infants' perception of partly occluded objects. *Infant Behavior and Development, 19,* 145–148.

Slater, A. M., Morison, V., & Rose, D. H. (1983). Perception of shape by the new-born baby. *British Journal of Developmental Psychology, 1,* 135–142.

Slater, A. M., Quinn, P. C., Kelly, D. J., Lee, K., Longmore, C. A., McDonald, P. R., et al. (2010). The shaping of the face space in early infancy: Becoming a native face processor. *Child Development Perspectives, 4,* 205–211.

Smith, L. B., & Jones, S. S. (2011). Symbolic play connects to language through visual object recognition. *Developmental Science, 14,* 1142–1149.

Snow, C., Pan, B. A., Imbens-Bailey, A., & Herman, J. (1996). Learning how to say what one means: A longitudinal study of children's speech act use. *Social Development, 5,* 56–84.

Snowdon, C. T. (2003). Expression of emotion in nonhuman animals. In R. J. Davidson, K. R. Scherer, & H. H. Goldsmith (Eds.), *Handbook of affective sciences* (pp. 457–480). New York, NY: Oxford University Press.

Sobelweski, J., & King, V. (2005). The importance of the coparental relationship for non-residential fathers' ties to children. *Journal of Marriage and Family, 67,* 1196–1212.

Society for Research in Child Development (2007). http://www.srcd.org/index.php?option=com_content&task=view&id=68&Itemid=499.

Soderstrom, M. (2007). Beyond babytalk: Re-evaluating the nature and content of speech input to preverbal infants. *Developmental Review, 27,* 501–532.

Soderstrom, M., Blossom, M., Foygel, R., & Morgan, J. L. (2008). Acoustical cues and grammatical units in speech to two preverbal infants. *Journal of Child Language, 35,* 869–902.

Soley, G., & Hannon, E. E. (2010). Infants prefer the musical meter of their own culture: A cross-cultural comparison. *Developmental Psychology, 46,* 286–292.

Soltis, J. (2004). The signal functions of early infant crying. *Behavioral and Brain Sciences, 27,* 443–458.

Song, L., Tamis-LeMonda, C. S., Yoshikawa, H., Kahana-Kalman, R., & Wu, I. (2012). Language experiences and vocabulary development in Dominican and Mexican infants across the first 2 years. *Developmental Psychology, 48,* 1106–1123.

Soska, K. C., & Johnson, S. P. (2008). Development of three-dimensional object completion in infancy. *Child Development*, *79*, 1230–1236.

Southgate, V., Johnson, M. H., El Karoui, I., & Csibra, G. (2010). Motor system activation reveals infants' on-line prediction of others' goals. *Psychological Science*, *21*, 355–359.

Spear, N. E. (1978). *The processing of memories: Forgetting and retention*. Hillsdale, NJ: Erlbaum.

Spelke, E. S. (2003). What makes us smart? Core knowledge and natural language. In E. S. Spelke (Ed.), *Language in mind: Advances in the study of language and thought* (pp. 277–311). Cambridge, MA: MIT Press.

Spelt, D. K. (1948). The conditioning of the human fetus in utero. *Journal of Experimental Psychology*, *38*, 375–376.

Spitz, R. A. (1965). *The first year of life*. Oxford, UK: International Universities Press.

Sroufe, L. A. (1979). The coherence of individual development: Early care, attachment, and subsequent developmental issues. *American Psychologist*, *34*, 834–841.

Sroufe, L. A., Egeland, B., Carlson, E. A., & Collins, W. A. (2005a). *The development of the person: The Minnesota study of risk and adaptation from birth to adulthood*. New York, NY: Guilford.

St. Augustine (398/1961). *Confessions*. London, UK: Penguin.

Stack, D. M., Serbin, L. A., Girouard, N., Enns, L. N., Bentley, V. M. N., Ledingham, J. E., et al. (2012). The quality of mother-child relationship in high-risk dyads: Application of the emotional availability scales in an intergenerational, longitudinal study. *Development and Psychopathology*, *24*, 93–105.

Steinberg, A. G., & Knightly, C. A. (1997). Hearing: Sounds and silences. In M. L. Batshaw (Ed.), *Children with disabilities* (4th ed., pp. 241–274). Baltimore, MD: Paul H. Brookes.

Steiner, J. E. (1977). Facial expressions of the neonate infant indicating the hedonics of food-related chemical stimuli. In J. M. Weiffenbach (Ed.), *Taste and development*. Bethesda, MD: Department of Health, Education, and Welfare.

Steiner, J. E. (1979). Human facial expressions in response to taste and smell stimulation. In H. Reese & L. Lipsitt (Eds.), *Advances in child development and behavior* (Vol. 13). New York, NY: Academic Press.

Steiner, J. E., Glaser, D., Hawilo, M. E., & Berridge, K. C. (2001). Comparative expression of hedonic impact: Affective reactions to taste by human infants and other primates. *Neuroscience and Biobehavioral Reviews*, *25*, 53–74.

Sterman, M. B., & Hoppenbrouwens, T. (1971). The development of sleep-waking and rest activity patterns from fetus to adult in man. In M. B. Sterman, D. J. McVinty, & A. M Adinolf (Eds.), *Brain development and behavior*. New York, NY: Academic Press.

Stern, D. N. (1998). The process of therapeutic change involving implicit knowledge: Some implications of developmental observations for adult psychotherapy. *Infant Mental Health Journal*, *19*, 300–308.

Stets, M., Stahl, D., & Reid, V. M. (2012). A meta-analysis investigating factors underlying attrition rates in infant ERP studies. *Developmental Neuropsychology*, *37*, 226–252.

Stiles, J. (2008). *The fundamentals of brain development: Integrating nature and nurture*. Cambridge, MA: Harvard University Press.

St. James-Roberts, I. (2007). Infant crying and sleeping: Helping parents to prevent and manage problems. *Sleep Medicine Clinics*, *2*, 363–375.

Stone, I. (1980). *The origin: A biographical novel of Charles Darwin*. New York, NY: Doubleday.

Stone, J. E., Carpendale, J. I. M., Sugarman, J., & Martin, J. (2012). A Meadian account of social understanding Taking a non-mentalist approach to infant and verbal false belief understanding. *New Ideas in Psychology*, *30* 166–178.

Stovall-McClough, K. C., & Dozier, M. (2004). Forming attachments in foster care: Infant attachment behaviors in the first 2 months of placement. *Development and Psychopathology*, *16*, 253–271.

Striano, T., & Vaish, A. (2006). Seven- to 9-month-old infants use facial expressions to interpret others' actions. *British Journal of Developmental Psychology*, *24*, 753–760.

Strid, K., Tjus, T., Smith, L., Meltzoff, A. N., & Heimann, M. (2006). Infant recall memory and communication predicts later cognitive development. *Infant Behavior and Development*, *29*, 545–553.

Suizzo, M., & Bornstein, M. H. (2006). French and European American child-mother play: Culture and gender considerations. *International Journal of Behavioral Development*, *30*, 498–508.

Sung, J., & Hsu, H. (2009). Korean mothers' attention regulation and referential speech: Associations with language and play in 1-year-olds. *International Journal of Behavioral Development*, *33*, 430–439.

Super, C. M., & Harkness, S. (1997). The cultural structuring of child development. In J. W. Berry, & P. R. Dasen (Eds.), *Handbook of cross-cultural psychology: Basic processes and human development* (2nd ed., Vol 2, pp. 1–39). Needham Heights, MA: Allyn & Bacon.

Suzigan, L., Silva, R., Guerra-Junior, G., Marini, S., & Maciel-Guerra, A. (2011). Social skills in women with Turner Syndrome. *Scandinavian Journal of Psychology*, *52*, 440–447.

Svetlova, M., Nichols, S. R., & Brownell, C. A. (2010). Toddlers' prosocial behavior: From instrumental to empathic to altruistic helping. *Child Development*, *81*, 1814–1827.

Sweeney, J., & Bradbard, M. R. (1988). Mothers' and fathers' changing perceptions of their male and female infants over the course of pregnancy. *The Journal of Genetic Psychology: Research and theory on human development*, *149*, 393–404.

Sylva, K., Stein, A., Leach, P., Barnes, J., & Malberg, L. (2011). Effects of early child care on cognition, language, and task-related behaviors at 18 months: An English study. *British Journal of Developmental Psychology*, *29*, 18–45.

Takada, A. (2005). Mother-infant interactions among the !Xun: Analysis of gymnastic and breastfeeding behaviors. In B. S. Hewlett & M. E. Lamb (Eds.), *Hunter-gatherer childhoods: Evolutionary, developmental, and cultural perspectives* (pp. 289–308). New Brunswick, NJ: Aldine Transaction Publishers.

Takahashi, K. (1986). Examining the strange situation procedure with Japanese mothers and 12-month-old infants. *Developmental Psychology*, *22*, 265–270.

Tamis-LeMonda, C. S., & Bornstein, M. H. (1990). Language, play, and attention at one year. *Infant Behavior & Development*, *13*, 85–98.

Tamis-LeMonda, C. S., & Bornstein, M. H. (1991). Individual variation, correspondence, stability, and change in mother and toddler play. *Infant Behavior & Development*, *14*, 143–162.

Tamis-LeMonda, C. S., & Bornstein, M. H. (1996). Variation in children's exploratory, nonsymbolic, and symbolic play: An explanatory multidimensional framework. In C. Rovee-Collier & L. P. Lipsitt (Eds.), *Advances in infancy research* (Vol. 10, pp. 37–78). Westport, CT: Ablex Publishing.

Tamis-LeMonda, C., & Bornstein, M. (2002). Maternal responsiveness and early language acquisition. In C. Tamis-LeMonda & M. Bornstein (Eds.), *Advances in child development and behavior*, *29*, 89–127. San Diego, CA: Academic Press.

Tamis-LeMonda, C. S., Bornstein, M. H., Baumwell, L., & Damast, A. M. (1996). Responsive parenting in the second year: Specific influences on children's language and play. *Early Development and Parenting*, *5*, 173–183.

Tamis-LeMonda, C. S., Damast, A. M., & Bornstein, M. H. (1994). What do mothers know about the developmental nature of play? *Infant Behavior & Development*, *17*, 341–345.

Tamis-LeMonda, C. S., & Kahana-Kalman, R. (2009). Mothers' views at the transition to a new baby: Variation across ethnic groups. *Parenting: Science and Practice*, *9*, 36–55.

Tamis-LeMonda, C. S., Shannon, J. D., Cabrera, N. J., & Lamb, M. E. (2004). Fathers and mothers at play with their 2- and 3-year-olds: Contributions to language and cognitive development. *Child Development*, *75*, 1806–1820.

Tamis-LeMonda, C. S., Užgiris, I. C., & Bornstein, M. H. (2002). Play in parent-child interactions. In M. H. Bornstein (Ed.), *Handbook of parenting: Practical parenting* (Vol. 5, pp. 221–241). Mahwah, NJ: Erlbaum.

Tanner, J. M. (1962). *Growth at adolescence.* Oxford, UK: Blackwell Scientific.

Tanner, J. M. (1970). Physical growth. In P. Mussen (Ed.), *Carmichael's manual of child psychology* (Vol. 1). New York, NY: Wiley.

Tasker, F. (2010). Same-sex parenting and child development: Reviewing the contribution of parental gender. *Journal of Marriage and the Family, 72,* 35–40.

Teichner, G., Ames, E. W., & Kerig, P. K. (1997). The relation of infant crying and the sex of the infant to parents' perceptions of the infant and themselves. *Psychology: A Journal of Human Behavior, 34,* 59–60.

Teinonen, T., Aslin, R. N., Alku, P., & Csibra, G. (2008). Visual speech contributes to phonetic learning in 6-month-old infants. *Cognition, 108,* 850–855.

Teller, D. Y., & Bornstein, M. H. (1987). Infant color vision and color perception. In P. Salapatek & L. B. Cohen (Eds.), *Handbook of infant perception. Volume I: From sensation to perception* (pp. 185–236). Orlando, FL: Academic Press.

Teller, D. Y., McDonald, M., Preston, K., Sebris, S. L., & Dobson, V. (1986). Assessment of visual acuity in infants and children: The acuity card procedure. *Developmental Medicine and Child Neurology, 28,* 779–789.

Teti, D. M. (2002). Sibling relationships. In J. McHale & W. Grolnick (Eds.), *Interiors: Retrospect and prospect in the psychological study of families* (pp. 193–224). Mahwah, NJ: Erlbaum.

Teti, D. M., & Cole, P. M. (2011). Parenting at risk: New perspectives, new approaches. *Journal of Family Psychology, 25,* 625–634.

Thatcher, R. W. (1994). Psychopathology of early frontal lobe damage: Dependence on cycles of development. *Development and Psychopathology, 6,* 565–596.

Thelen, E. (2000). Motor development as foundation and future of developmental psychology. *International Journal of Behavioral Development, 24,* 385–397.

Thelen, E. (2001). Dynamic mechanisms of change in early perceptual-motor development. In E. Thelen (Ed.), *Mechanisms of cognitive development: Behavioral and neural perspectives* (pp. 161–184). Mahwah, NJ: Erlbaum.

Thelen, E., Fisher, D. M., Ridley-Johnson, R. (1984). The relationship between physical growth and a newborn reflex. *Infant Behavior and Development, 7,* 479–493.

Thelen, E., & Smith, L. B. (2006). Dynamic systems theories. In R. M. Lerner (Ed.), W. Damon (Series Ed.), *Handbook of child psychology: Vol. 1. Theoretical models of human development* (6th ed., pp. 258–312). Hoboken, NJ: Wiley.

Thoman, E. B. (1990). Sleeping and waking states in infants: A functional perspective. *Neuroscience and Biobehavioral Reviews, 14,* 93–107.

Thoman, E. B., & Whitney, M. P. (1990). Behavioral states in infants: Individual differences and individual analyses. In J. Colombo & J. Fagen (Eds.), *Individual differences in infancy: Reliability, stability, and prediction* (pp. 113–136). Hillsdale, NJ: Erlbaum.

Thompson, R. A. (2006). The development of the person: Social understanding, relationships, conscience, self. In D. Kuhn & R. S. Siegler (Ed.), W. Damon (Series Ed.), *Handbook of child psychology: Cognition, Perception, and language* (6th ed., Vol. 2, pp. 24–98). Hoboken, NJ: Wiley.

Thompson, R. A., & Virmani, E. A. (2010). Self and personality. In M. H. Bornstein (Ed.), *Handbook of cultural developmental science* (pp. 195–208). New York, NY: Psychology Press.

Tinbergen, N. (1951). *The study of instinct.* Oxford, UK: Oxford University Press.

Tinbergen, N. (1963). On aims and methods of ethology. *Zeitschrif Tier Psychologie, 20,* 410–433.

Todd, R. L., & Fischer, K. W. (2009). Dynamic development: A neo-Piagetian approach. In U. Muller, J. I. M. Carpendale, & L. Smith (Eds.), *The Cambridge companion to Piaget* (pp. 400–442). New York, NY: Cambridge University Press.

Tomasello, M. (2006). Acquiring linguistic constructions. In D. Kuhn & R. S. Siegler (Ed.), W. Damon (Series Ed.), *Handbook of child psychology: Cognition, perception, and language* (6th ed., Vol. 2, pp. 255–298). Hoboken, NJ: Wiley.

Tomasello, M. (2011). Language acquisition. In U. Goswami (Ed.), *The Wiley-Blackwell handbook of childhood cognitive development* (pp. 239–257). Malden, MA: Wiley-Blackwell.

Tomasello, M., Carpenter, M., Call, J., Behne, T., & Moll, H. (2005). Understanding and sharing intentions: The origins of cultural cognition. *Behavioral and Brain Sciences, 38*, 675–691.

Tomasello, M., Carpenter, M., & Liszkowski, U. (2007). A new look at infant pointing. *Child Development, 78*, 705–722.

Torquati, J. C., Raikes, H. H., Huddleston-Casas, C. A., Bovaird, J. A., & Harris, B. A. (2011). Family income, parent education, and perceived constraints as predictors of observed program quality and parent rated program quality. *Early Childhood Research Quarterly, 26*, 453–464.

Travis, K. E., Leonard, M. K., Brown, T. T., Hagler, D. J., Curran, M., Dale, A. M., et al. (2011). Spatiotemporal neural dynamics of word understanding in 12- to 18-month-old infants. *Cerebral Cortex, 21*, 1832–1839.

Trehub, S. E. (2003). The developmental origins of musicality. *Nature Neuroscience, 6*, 669–673.

Trevarthen, C. B. (1974). Behavioral embryology. In E. C. Carterette & M. P. Friedman (Eds.), *Handbook of perception* (Vol. 3). New York, NY: Academic Press.

Trevarthen, C. B. (1988). Universal co-operative motives: How infants begin to know the language and culture of their parents. In G. Jahoda & I. M. Lewis (Eds.), *Acquiring culture: Cross cultural studies in child development* (pp. 37–90). New York, NY: Croom Helm.

Tronick, E. (2007). *The neurobehavioral and social-emotional development in infants and children.* New York, NY: Norton.

Trout, K. K., & Wetzel-Effinger, L. (2012). Flavor learning in utero and its implications for future obesity and diabetes. *Current Diabetes Reports, 12*, 60–66.

Tsang, C. D., & Conrad, N. J. (2010). Does the message matter? The effect of song type on infants' pitch preferences for lullabies and playsongs. *Infant Behavior and Development, 33*, 96–100.

Turati, C., Macchi Cassia, V., Simion, F., & Leo, I. (2006). Newborns' face recognition: Role of inner and outer facial features. *Child Development, 77*, 297–311.

Turkewitz, G., & Kenny, P. A. (1982). Limitations on input as a basis for neural organization and perceptual development: A preliminary theoretical statement. *Developmental Psychobiology, 15*, 357–368.

Tyano, S., & Keren, M. (2010). Single parenthood: Its impact on parenting the infant. In S. Tyano, M. Keren, H. Herrman, & J. Cox (Eds.), *Parenthood and mental health: A bridge between infant and adult psychiatry.* Hoboken, NJ: Wiley.

Tyson, J. E., Parikh, N. A., Langer, J., Green, C., Higgins, R. D., et al. (2008). Intensive care for extreme prematurity: Moving beyond gestational age. *New England Journal of Medicine, 358*, 1672–1681.

Uchiyama, I., Anderson, D. I., Campos, J. J., Witherington, D., Frankel, C. B., Lejuene, L., et al. (2008). Locomotor experience affects self and emotion. *Developmental Psychology, 44*, 1225–1231.

Užgiris, I. C. (1989). The social context of infant imitation. In M. Lewis & S. Feinman (Eds.), *Social influences and socialization in infancy* (pp. 215–251). New York, NY: Plenum Press.

Užgiris, I. C., & Hunt, J. (1975). *Assessment in infancy: Ordinal scales of psychological development.* Champaign, IL: University of Illinois Press.

Vaal, J., van Soest, A. J., & Hopkins, B. (2000). Spontaneous kicking behavior in infants: Age-related effects of unilateral weighting. *Developmental Psychobiology, 36*, 111–122.

Valenza, E., & Bulf, H. (2007). The role of kinetic information in newborns' perception of illusory contours. *Developmental Science, 10*, 492–501.

van den Boom, D. C. (1994). The influence of temperament and mothering on attachment and exploration: An experimental manipulation of sensitive responsiveness among lower-class mothers with irritable infants. *Child Development, 65*, 1457–1477.

van den Dries, L., Juffer, F., van IJzendoorn, M. H., Bakersman-Kranenburg, M. J. (2009). Fostering security? A meta-analysis of attachment in adopted children. *Children and Youth Services Review, 31*, 410–421.

Vanderwert, R. E., Marshall, P. J., Nelson, C. A., Zeanah, C. H., & Fox, N. A. (2010). Timing of intervention affects brain electrical activity in children exposed to severe psychosocial neglect. *PLos One, 5*, e11415.

Van IJzendoorn, M. H., & Sagi-Schwartz, A. (2008). Cross-cultural patterns of attachment: Universal and contextual dimensions. In J. Cassidy & P. R. Shaver (Eds.), *Handbook of attachment: Theory, research, and clinical applications* (2nd ed., pp. 880–905). New York, NY: Guilford Press.

Vaughn, B. E., Bost, K. K., & van IJzendoorn, M. H. (2008). Attachment and temperament: Additive and interactive influences on behavior, affect, and cognition during infancy and childhood. In J. Cassidy & P. R. Shaver (Eds.), *Handbook of attachment: Theory, research, and clinical applications* (2nd ed., pp. 192–216). New York, NY: Guilford Press.

Vaurio, L., Crocker, N., & Mattson, S. (2010). Fetal alcohol spectrum disorders. In A. Davis (Ed.), *Handbook of pediatric neuropsychology*. New York, NY: Springer Publishing.

Viholainen, H., Ahonen, T., Cantell, M., Lyytinen, P., & Lyytinen, H. (2002). Development of early motor skills and language in children at risk for familial dyslexia. *Developmental Medicine & Child Neurology, 44*, 761–769.

Viholainen, H., Ahonen, T., Lyytinen, P., Cantell, M., Tolvanen, A., & Lyytinen, H. (2006). Early motor development and later language and reading skills in children at risk of familial dyslexia. *Developmental Medicine & Child Neurology, 48*, 367–373.

Volling, B. L. (2001). Early attachment relationships as predictors of preschool children's emotion regulation with a distressed sibling. *Early Education and Development, 12*, 185–207.

Vonderlin, E., Pahnke, J., & Pauen, S. (2008). Infant temperament and information processing in a visual categorization task. *Infant Behavior and Development, 31*, 559–569.

Von Hofsten, C., Kochukhova, O., & Rosander, K. (2007). Predictive tracking over occlusions by 4-month-old infants. *Developmental Science, 10*, 625–640.

Votruba-Drzal, E., Coley, R. L., & Chase-Lansdale, P. L. (2004). Child care and low-income children's development: Direct and moderated effects. *Child Development, 75*, 296–312.

Vouloumanos, A., Hauser, M. D., Werker, J. F., & Martin, A. (2010). The tuning of human neonates' preference for speech. *Child Development, 81*, 517–527.

Vouloumanos A., & Werker, J. F. (2004). Tuned to the signal: The privileged status of speech for young infants. *Developmental Science, 7*, 270–276.

Vouloumanos, A., & Werker, J. F. (2007). Listening to language at birth: Evidence for a bias for speech in neonates. *Developmental Science, 10*, 159–171.

Vygotsky, L. S. (1962). *Thought and language.* Cambridge, MA: MIT Press.

Vygotsky, L. S. (1978). *Mind in society.* Cambridge, UK: Cambridge University Press.

Wachs, T. D. (2006). The nature, etiology, and consequences of individual differences in temperament. In L. Balter & C. Tamis-LeMonda (Eds.), *Child psychology: A handbook of contemporary issues* (pp. 27–52). New York, NY: Psychology Press.

Wachs, T. D., Posada, G., Carbonell, O. A., Creed-Kanashiro, H., & Gurkas, P. (2011). Infant nutrition and 12 and 18 months secure base behavior: An exploratory study. *Infancy*, *16*, 91–111.

Wada, K., Krejci, M., Ohira, Y., Nakade, M., Takeuchi, H., & Harada, T. (2009). Comparative study on circadian typology and sleep habits of Japanese and Czech infants aged 0–8 years. *Sleep and Biological Rhythms*, *7*, 218–221.

Waddington, C. H. (1962). *New patterns in genetics and development.* New York, NY: Columbia University Press.

Wakschlag, L. S., Chase-Lansdale, P. L., & Brooks-Gunn, J. (1996). Not just "ghosts in the nursery": Contemporaneous intergenerational relationships and parenting in young African-American families. *Child Development*, *67*, 2131–2149.

Walker-Andrews, A. S. (2008). Intermodal emotional processes in infancy. In A. S. Walker-Andrews (Ed.), *Handbook of emotions* (pp. 364–375). New York, NY: Guilford.

Walker-Andrews, A. S., Krogh-Jespersen, S., Mayhew, E. M., & Coffield, C. N. (2011). Young infants' generalization of emotional expressions: Effects of familiarity. *Emotion*, *11*, 842–851.

Wallace, D. B., Franklin, M. B., & Keegan, R. T. (1994). The observing eye: A century of baby diaries. *Human Development*, *37*, 1–29.

Wallman, J. (1979). A minimal visual restriction experiment: Preventing chicks from seeing their feet affects later responses to mealworms. *Developmental Psychobiology*, *12*, 391–397.

Wang, S., Baillargeon, R., & Paterson, S. (2005). Detecting continuity and solidity violations in infancy: A new account and new evidence from covering events. *Cognition*, *95*, 129–173.

Wasz-Hockert, O., Michelsson, K., & Lind, J. (1985). Twenty-five years of Scandinavian cry research. In B. M. Lester & C. F. Z. Boukydis (Eds.), *Infant crying: Theoretical and research perspectives* (pp. 83–104). New York, NY: Plenum.

Waters, E. (1978). The reliability and stability of individual differences in infant-mother attachment. *Child Development*, *49*, 483–494.

Watson, J. B. (1924). *Behaviorism.* New York, NY: Norton.

Watson, J. S. (1985). Contingency perception in early social development. In T. M. Field & N. A. Fox (Eds.), *Social perception in infants.* Norwood, NJ: Ablex.

Waxman, S. R., & Leddon, E. M. (2011). Early word learning and conceptual development: Everything had a name, and each name gave birth to a new thought. In U. Goswami (Ed.), *The Wiley-Blackwell handbook of childhood cognitive development* (pp. 180–208). Malden, MA: Wiley-Blackwell.

Weinfield, N. S., Sroufe, L. A., Egeland, B., & Carlson, E. (2008). Individual differences in infant-caregiver attachment: Conceptual and empirical aspects of security. In J. Cassidy & P. R. Shaver (Eds.), *Handbook of attachment: Theory, research, and clinical applications* (2nd ed., pp. 78–101). New York, NY: Guilford Press.

Weinraub, M., Horvath, D. L., & Gringlas, M. B. (2002). Single parenthood. In M. H. Bornstein (Ed.), *Handbook of parenting: Status and social conditions of parenting* (2nd ed., Vol. 3, pp. 109–140). Mahwah, NJ: Erlbaum.

Weir, C., Soule, S., Bacchus, C., Rael, J., & Schneider, J. (2000). The influence of vicarious reinforcement and habituation in contingency learning in infants. *Merrill-Palmer Quarterly*, *46*, 693–716.

Weir, M. W. (1962). Effects of age and instructions on children's probability learning. *Child Development*, *33*, 729–735.

Weizman, Z., & Snow, C. (2001). Lexical input as related to children's vocabulary acquisition: Effects of sophisticated exposure and support for meaning. *Developmental Psychology*, *37*, 265–279.

Welder, A. N., & Graham, S. A. (2006). Infants' categorization of novel objects with more or less obvious features. *Cognitive Psychology*, *52*, 57–91.

Wellman, H., Cross, D., & Watson, J. (2001). Meta-analysis of theory-of-mind development: The truth about false belief. *Child Development, 72*, 655–684.

Wendler, C. C., Busovsky-McNeal, M., Ghatpande, S., Kalinowski, A., Russell, K. S., & Rivkees, S. A. (2009). Embryonic caffeine exposure induces adverse effects in adulthood. *The FASEB Journal, 23*, 1272–1278.

Weppelman, T. L., Bostow, A., Schiffer, R., Elbert-Perez, E., & Newman, R. S. (2003). Children's use of the prosodic characteristics of infant-directed speech. *Language and Communication, 23*, 63–80.

Werker, J. F., Maurer, D. M., & Yoshida, K. A. (2010). Perception. In M. H. Bornstein (Ed.), *Handbook of cultural developmental sciences* (pp. 89–126). New York, NY: Psychology Press.

Werner, E. E. (1988). A cross-cultural perspective on infancy: Research and social issues. *Journal of Cross-Cultural Psychology, 19*, 96–113.

Werner, H., & Kaplan, B. (1963). *Symbol formation*. New York, NY: Wiley.

Wertheimer, M. (1961). Psychomotor coordination of auditory and visual space at birth. *Science, 134*, 1692.

Whalen, C., & Schreibman, L. (2003). Joint attention training for children with autism using behavior modification procedures. *Journal of Child Psychology and Psychiatry, 44*, 456–468.

Whitney, P. G., & Green, J. A. (2011). Changes in infants' affect related to the onset of independent locomotion. *Infant Behavior & Development, 34*, 459–466.

Widom, C. S. (2000). Motivation and mechanisms in the "cycle of violence." In R. A. Dienstbier (Series Ed.) & D. J. Hansen (Vol. Ed.), *Motivation and child maltreatment* (Vol. 46 of the Nebraska Symposium on Motivation, pp. 1–37). Lincoln, NE: University of Nebraska Press.

Wiesel, T. N., & Hubel, D. H. (1974). Ordered arrangement of orientation columns in monkeys lacking visual experience. *Journal of Comparative Neurology, 158*, 307–318.

Williams, S. T., Mastergeorge, A. M., & Ontai, L. L. (2010). Caregiver involvement in infant peer interactions: Scaffolding in a social context. *Early Childhood Research Quarterly, 25*, 251–266.

Williams, S. T., Ontai, L. L., & Mastergeorge, A. M. (2007). Reformulating infant and toddler social competence with peers. *Infant Behavior and Development, 30*, 353–365.

Wilson, R. S. (1983). The Louisville twin study: Development synchronies in behavior. *Child Development, 54*, 298–316.

Wilson, R. S. (1984). Twins and chronogenetics: Correlated pathways of development. *Acta Gemellogica, 33*, 149–157.

Wimmer, H., & Perner, J. (1983). Beliefs about beliefs: Representation and constraining function of wrong beliefs in young children's understanding of deception. *Cognition, 13*, 103–128.

Wolff, J. J., Gu, H. B., Gerig, G., Elison, J. T., Styner, M., Gouttard, S., et al. (2012). Differences in white matter fiber tract development present from 6 to 24 months in infants with autism. *American Journal of Psychiatry, 169*, 589–600.

Wolke, D., Schmid, G., Schreier, A., & Meyer, R. (2009). Crying and feeding problems in infancy and cognitive outcome in preschool children born at risk: A prospective population study. *Journal of Developmental & Behavioral Pediatrics, 30*, 226–238.

Wood, D., Bruner, J. S., & Ross, G. (1976). The role of tutoring in problem solving. *Journal of Child Psychology and Psychiatry, 17*, 89–100.

Woodward, A. (2009). Infants' learning about intentional action. In A. Woodward and A. Needham (Eds.), *Learning and the infant mind.* Oxford, UK: Oxford University Press.

Woodward, L. J., Edgin, J. O., Thompson, D., & Inder, T. E. (2005). Object working memory deficits predicted by early brain injury and development in the preterm infant. *Brain: A Journal of Neurology, 128*, 2578–2587.

Wright, C. A., George, T. P., Burke, R., Gelfand, D. M., & Teti, D. M. (2000). Early maternal depression and children's adjustment to school. *Child Study Journal, 30*, 153–168.

Yang, D., Sidman, J., & Bushnell, E. W. (2010). Beyond the information given: Infants' transfer of actions learned through imitation. *Journal of Experimental Child Psychology, 106*, 62–81.

Yonas, A. (1981). Infants' responses to optical information for collision. In R. N. Aslin, J. R. Alberts, & M. R. Peterson (Eds.), *Development of perception: Psychobiological perspectives* (Vol. 2). New York, NY: Academic.

Yonas, A., Arterberry, M. E., & Granrud, C. E. (1987). Four-month-old infants' sensitivity to binocular and kinetic information for three-dimensional-object shape. *Child Development, 58*, 910–917.

Yonas, A., Granrud, C. E., Chov, M. H., & Alexander, A. J. (2005). Picture perception in infants: Do 9-month-olds attempt to grasp objects depicted in photographs? *Infancy, 8*, 147–166.

Yonas, A., & Hartman, B. (1993). Perceiving the affordance of contact in four- and five-month-old infants. *Child Development, 64*, 298–308.

Yoshida, K. A., Iversen, J. R., Patel, A. D., Mazuka, R., Nito, H., Gervain, J., et al. (2010). The development of perceptual grouping biases in infancy: A Japanese-English cross-linguistic study. *Cognition, 115*, 356–361.

Youngentob, S. L., & Glendinning, J. I. (2009). Fetal ethanol exposure increases ethanol intake by making it smell and taste better. *Proceedings of the National Academy of Sciences of the United States of America, 106*, 5359–5364.

Younger, B. A. (2003). Parsing objects into categories: Infants' perception and use of correlated attributes. In D. H. Rakison & L. M. Oakes (Eds.), *Early category and concept development: Making sense of the blooming, buzzing confusion* (pp. 77–102). Oxford, UK: Oxford University Press.

Yu, J. J., & Gamble, W. C. (2008). Pathways of influence: Marital relationships and their association with parenting styles and sibling relationship quality. *Journal of Child and Family Studies, 17*, 757–778.

Zelazo, P. R., & Weiss, M. J. (2006). Infant swimming behaviors: Cognitive control and the influence of experience. *Journal of Cognition and Development, 7*, 1–25.

Zosuls, K. M., Ruble, D. N., Bornstein, M. H., Tamis-LeMonda, C. S., Shrout, P. E., & Greulich, F. K. (2009). The acquisition of gender labels in infancy: Implications for gender-typed play. *Developmental Psychology, 45*, 688–701.

Zukow-Goldring, P. (2002). Sibling caregiving. In M. H. Bornstein (Ed.), *Handbook of parenting: Status and social conditions of parenting* (2nd ed., Vol. 3, pp. 253–286). Mahwah, NJ: Erlbaum.

Author Index

Subject Index